D0004741

EDINA HIGH SCHOOL
MEDIA CENTER
6754 VALLEY VIEW ROAD
EDINA, MINNESOTA 55439

The
Greenwood Library
of
World Folktales

The Greenwood Library of World Folktales

Stories from the Great Collections

VOLUME 2

Asia

Edited by Thomas A. Green

Jack Zipes, Advisory Editor

GREENWOOD PRESS
Westport, Connecticut • London

Library of Congress Cataloging-in-Publication Data

The Greenwood library of world folktales : stories from the great collections / edited by Thomas A. Green.
    p. cm.
  Includes bibliographical references and index.
  ISBN 978–0–313–33783–3 ((set) : alk. paper) — ISBN 978–0–313–33784–0 ((v. 1) : alk. paper) — ISBN 978–0–313–33785–7 ((v. 2) : alk. paper) — ISBN 978–0–313–33786–4 ((v. 3) : alk. paper) — ISBN 978–0–313–33787–1 ((v. 4) : alk. paper)
  1. Tales. 2. Folklore. I. Green, Thomas A., 1944–
  GR74.G74 2008
  398.2—dc22   2007041323

British Library Cataloguing in Publication Data is available.

Copyright © 2008 by Thomas A. Green

All rights reserved. No portion of this book may be reproduced, by any process or technique, without the express written consent of the publisher.

Library of Congress Catalog Card Number: 2007041323
ISBN: 978–0–313–33783–3 (set)
      978–0–313–33784–0 (vol. 1)
      978–0–313–33785–7 (vol. 2)
      978–0–313–33786–4 (vol. 3)
      978–0–313–33787–1 (vol. 4)

First published in 2008

Greenwood Press, 88 Post Road West, Westport, CT 06881
An imprint of Greenwood Publishing Group, Inc.
www.greenwood.com

Printed in the United States of America

The paper used in this book complies with the Permanent Paper Standard issued by the National Information Standards Organization (Z39.48–1984).

10 9 8 7 6 5 4 3 2 1

Contents

VOLUME 2

Contents

Contents

Introduction to Volume 2

Asia for the purposes of *The Greenwood Library of World Folktales* will be divided into the subregions of East Asia, South Asia, and Southeast Asia. The two other potential subregions of Asia, Central Asia and Southwestern (or Western) Asia, are considered under other regions in this collection. The tales of Central Asia, because of the subregion's absorption into the former Union of Soviet Socialist Republics, have been incorporated into Volume 3: Europe, along with Russian tales. As explained in the Introduction to Volume 1 (page xvii), Southwestern Asia (designated in these volumes as the Middle East) has important ties to the African continent that are emphasized by including the subregion in that volume.

East Asia includes China and those areas historically associated with China—for example, Mongolia, Korea, Japan, and Tibet, as well as areas of far northeastern Asia such as Siberia. Covering one-third of the largest continent in the world, East Asia's cultural, ecological, linguistic, and religious diversity do not allow blanket statements to be made about the region. The tales included in this section are grounded in animistic worldviews (for example, the Ainu "Blessing from the Owl God," page 3) and nationalistic myths (the Japanese "A Miraculous Sword," page 64). Others are animal fables (the Tibetan "The Tiger and the Frog," page 121) and historical legends (the Japanese "The Isolated Island," page 66). Obviously, the narratives compiled in this anthology can do no more than hint at the depth and breadth of East Asian traditional repertoires.

South Asia consists of the Indian subcontinent—composed of India, Bangladesh, Pakistan, Bhutan, and Nepal—and the contiguous islands of Sri Lanka and Maldives. South Asia is the home of one of the earliest of the world's civilizations, the Harappan (3300 B.C.E.). Some of the oldest existing transcriptions of oral epics, the Ramayana and the Mahabharata have their sources in Iron Age South Asia (1000–500 B.C.E.). See, for example, the following excerpts from the *Mahabharata* "Story of Savitri" (page 133) and "Royal Rivals: The Pandavas and

Kauravas" (page 141). Invading cultures such as the Indo-Scythians left their marks later (see the Pakistani "Raja Rasalu," page 268). Trade and warfare with Macedonia, Rome, Persia, and other empires of the European and Asian classical periods are likely to account for the similarities between the South Asian narrative repertoire and the tales of the cultures with whom they came in contact. Buddhism, Hinduism, and Jainism originated in the region. These religions and later Islam made an impact on the traditional narratives of South Asia. Subsequently, the tale "The Demon with the Matted Hair" (page 156) is derived from *The Jataka* a compendium of tales of the Buddha in his previous incarnations, and "The Brahman, the Tiger, and the Six Judges" (page 153) reflects the Hindu caste system. Ultimately the influence of Buddhist and Hindu influence spread to Southeast Asia, resulting in "Indianized Kingdoms" in that neighboring region.

Southeast Asia is the subregion of Asia framed by China, India, and Australia. The subregion includes territory located on both the Asian mainland and on islands extending to within 400 miles of Australia to the southeast. In the early twenty-first century, the mainland nations comprise Cambodia, Laos, Myanmar (Burma), Thailand, and Vietnam, while the island polities are Brunei, East Timor, Indonesia, Malaysia, the Philippines, and Singapore. Most information on early Southeast Asia comes from the reports of Indian traders and dates only from ca. 300 B.C.E. From at least the first century B.C.E., India exerted a powerful presence in the area, as evidenced by the Hindu Jawa Dwipa Kingdom in Indonesia in 200 B.C.E. By 200 C.E. with the Srivijaya Empire and continuing until the Majapahit Empire (1293–ca. 1500) Indianzed Kingdoms dominated the region. China maintained strong economic and political ties to the area, and on the mainland, states began to develop at about the same time with Chinese rather than Indian influence prevailing in some areas (modern Vietnam, for example). In the 1400s, Islam came to be felt in the region and eventually came to dominate in many areas (see "The Story of Bantugan," page 398, for insights into the character of Islam on the Philippine Island of Mindanao). European explorers and merchants followed in the 1500s. The influence of the flow of trade and the cultural exchanges that followed in its wake is seen in the present collection in tales such as the Filipino versions of "Cinderella" ("Poor Little Maria," page 419) and "Ali Baba and the Forty Thieves" ("The Fifty-One Thieves," page 424). The cultural heterogeneity of Southeast Asia is further reflected in narratives such as the Malaysian Dusun myth "The Three Rajahs" (page 308). Indigenous traditions survive in the Southeast Asian love for trickster figures, both human (see the Dusun tale "Ginas and the Rajah," page 318) and especially the Malaysian *plandok* and the Indonesian *Kantjil* (mouse deer). See the Dusun "Mouse Deer the Trickster" cycle (page 328) and the Indonesian "Kantjil the Mouse Deer" cycle (page 364).

EAST ASIA

Ainu

BLESSING FROM THE OWL GOD

Tradition Bearer: Unavailable

Source: Miura, Kiyoko. "Two Songs That Were Sung and Danced by Owl God." *Yakura Epos of the Ainus: Study and Translation of Kamuy-Yukara.* http://www.harvest-fields.ca/ebook/etexts1/01/38/00.htm (July 2, 2007).

Date: Unavailable

Original Source: Ainu

National Origin: Japan

Historically, the Ainu were indigenous to the northern areas of modern Japan (Hokkaido and northern Honshu) and eastern Russia (the Kamchatka Peninsula, the Kuril Islands, and Sakhalin). While the origins of the Ainu continue to be debated, they constitute a distinct ethnic entity who displayed significant cultural and physical differences from the ethnic Japanese who gradually displaced them as they moved from south to north. Hunting, fishing, and gathering provided the primary subsistence for the Ainu. These activities were supplemented by gardens tended by the women. The Ainu paid homage through prayer and ceremony to those manifestations of the divine essence (Ainu, "kamuy") embodied in, for example, fire, water, bears, owls, various plants, boats, mountains, and lakes. By virtue of these beliefs in a supernatural presence dwelling in the surrounding world and its forces, the Ainu religion was classified as animistic. The "yukara" are the sacred songs of the Ainu, and as in the following example, they are presented as lines of poetry and in first-person voice. The following narrative is included not only for its intrinsic worth, but to illustrate the traditional manner of presentation. Other texts in this volume ("The Owl," page 13, and "The Man in the Moon," page 14) appear as prose translations in first person.

"Fall, silver tricklings, fall …
Fall, golden tricklings, fall …"
So singing I flew
Along a stream.
As flying over the hamlet, I looked
And there I saw the people—
Those who had once been poor were now rich,
Those who had once been rich were now poor.
At the seashore,
The children were playing
With their little toy bows
And with little toy arrows.
"Fall, silver tricklings, fall …
Fall, golden tricklings, fall …"
So singing I went
Gliding over the children.
Running below my eyes,
The children said each and all:
"Beautiful little bird!
Divine little bird!
Come, now, come quickly!
Whoever would shoot that little bird first,
Whoever would fetch that divine bird first
Will be our hero!
And be our leader in the true sense!"

The children of those-once-poor-but-now-rich
Notched their little golden arrows
Upon their little golden bows, and
Off they shot!
But, I let those golden arrows
Go beneath my body
And above my body.
Then,
There was a boy
Among those children,
Who had an ordinary little arrow
And an ordinary little bow.
I looked at him.
From the cloth he wore
He appeared to have come from a poor family.
But—
From the looks in his eyes

He appeared to be descended from an illustrious family.
So he stood out among all other boys
Like a bird of virtue!
And, he too
Notched his little arrow
Upon his little bow.
As he drew his bow,
The children of those-once-poor-but-now-rich
Said scornfully:
"How funny!
Such a cub of a wretched tribe!
Even our golden arrows
Can't reach
That bird—
That holy bird!
It'll be a wonder
If that bird—
That holy bird—
Would ever take
This ordinary wooden arrow—
This arrow of rotten wood—
That this son of a wretched
Would dare to shoot!"
Abusing thus,
The children gathered around the boy
Giving him kicks and cuffs.
But—
The poor boy did not hesitate and
Drew his bow at me.
Watching at him, thus,
I felt sympathy toward him.
"Fall, silver tricklings, fall …
Fall, golden tricklings, fall …"
So singing I went slowly
Gliding over in a big circle
In the sky.
The boy stood
On one foot drawn far back
And on the other stepped forward.
And, biting his lower lip,
He drew his bow at me.
Then—
Off he shot his arrow!

The tiny arrow glittered in the air
As it flew toward me;
And, as I saw it nearing me,
Soon I held out my hands
And took that little arrow.
And, while I was descending round and round,
The wind whistled by my ears.
Then—
The children all ran toward me,
Striving with one another,
And leaving sand storm behind.
As soon as I fell on the ground,
The poor boy reached
And grabbed me before anyone.
So, the boys of those-once-poor-but-now-rich
Who arrived late called him
With a score of bad names,
And pushed and beat this poor boy calling
With ten and a score of cursing names:
"Abominable cub!
Son of the wretched!
How dare you would take the lead
In what we were doing!"
But, the poor boy
Covered me again and again,
Held me under his stomach,
And escaped from the crowd of those boys
Taking as long as an age.
Then, after such hubbub
His footsteps on a run
Sounded light and rhythmic.
The boys of those-once-poor-but-now-rich
Threw stones and chips of wood
After him, but he ran
Without the least attention to them,
Leaving sand storm behind,
Until he at last arrived at a little house.
Then, the boy took me in
From the window of the honor room of the house,
And he began and told the story
Of what had happened.
From the house appeared
An old man and his wife

Shading their eyes with their hands.
They seemed, the man and his wife,
To bear an air of dignity,
In spite of their poor attire.
As they looked at me,
They were so astonished,
They doubled their bodies from the waists.
The old man then tightened his belt
And bowed at me:
"Owl, our God!
Our heavy God!
In spite of our poverty,
You have come to our house.
We thank our God a thousand times!
We had once counted ourselves among the rich,
But now we are poor and worthless as you see.
So, God of the village!
Heavy God!
We have no right to beg you to stay
At our house …; but,
As it is already after sunset,
We should offer our heavy God
The place to rest
And we shall perform a ceremony tomorrow
To send our Heavy God to where He belongs
At least with the sacred wooden symbols."
Thus saying, the old man
Bowed twenty times
And bowed thirty times.
The wife of the old man
Spread a "flower" mattress
Over the seat of honor
Below the window I entered
And put me upon it.
Then—
They went to bed and
Soon started snoring.
I sat on my empty body
Between my ears.
But, as the night advanced,
I got up:
"Fall, silver tricklings, fall …
Fall, golden tricklings, fall …"

I sang softly and went round and round
To the left and to the right
Dancing in this small house;
And, the sound I made as I danced
Was so beautiful as a rustle of gold.
When I flapped my wings,
There was about me
A mount of precious jewelry,
The God's treasures falling from heaven,
Making sound so beautiful as rustles of gold.
In a quick moment
I filled this tiny house
With those shining jewelries,
The God's treasures.
"Fall, silver tricklings, fall …
Fall, golden tricklings, fall …"
While I sang,
I made this tiny house
Into a large house,
A golden house,
In a quick moment.
In the house,
I built a magnificent altar and
Quickly wove a magnificent silk robe
And decorated the house entirely.
I decorated the now great house,
Far grander than any house of other rich people.
As I finished this job,
I sat between the ears of my body,
Just as I had been placed.
Then, to the family of this house
I sent dream to their sleep
And let them know that I saw
And took sympathy of them,
For the family-once-rich-but-now-poor,
By an ill-fortune,
Have been despised and ill-treated
By those-once-poor-but-now-rich;
And that I therefore came down
To stay at their house,
Although I was not a small god,
And thus to make them wealthy again.
In a short while

The night's black news began to thin away;
And the people of the family awoke and got up.
Rubbing their eyes still,
They looked about and instantly
They fell down on their buttocks.
The old woman
Cried in a loud voice,
The old man
Dropped big drops of tears.
But, quickly
He got up and came
Where I was, and bowed
Scores of times,
Hundreds of times;
And spoke in the meantime:
"I thought it was
But a dream I saw in sleep!
How could we imagine
To see all this in our real life!
In spite of our poverty,
In spite of our wretched life by the ill-fortune,
You have come to our humble cot.
That only gave us honor
Beyond our words of gratitude.
But, above this all,
Our God,
Our Heavy God,
You took sympathy upon us
For being misfortuned,
And bestowed a favor of us
With the heaviest of all
The heavy gifts from Heaven!"
Saying thus in tears,
The old man bowed deeply and worshipped me.
Then—
This old man cut trees,
Began to shave them to make into a bunch
Of beautiful sacred wooden decorations
With which he decorated about me.
The old lady tightened her sash
And, with a help of the little kids,
Gathered some kindlewood,
Drew water

And prepared to make Sake.
In a short while,
Six casks of Sake
Were placed at the seat of honor.
Then—
I had a pleasure
Of speaking with the "old granny of fire"
About things in Heaven.
In two days since
The aroma of Sake,
Which the Gods favor,
Began to fill the house.
Then—
The little boy who had brought me to this house
Was clothed in a ragged kimono in purpose,
And was sent to the village on an errand
Carrying invitation to the feast
Given to all those-once-poor-but-now-rich.
As I watched after him,
The little boy
Went to each house
And delivered the message;
Then, those-once-poor-but-now-rich
Laughed hard and said:
"How strange!
How dare would those poor folks invite us!
With what sort of Sake and food
They are going to entertain us!
Let's go and see,
Then, have a good laugh
Over their doings!"
So, they came
In a big crowd.
But, when they saw the house
From a good distance,
They were amazed:
Some went back
As they were so embarrassed;
But others still came to the house
Where they were taken aback.
Then—
As the lady of the house
Came out

And led them in the house
By taking their hands, one by one,
They all
Came in
Creeping
On knees and hands,
Not a single person being able to raise his face!
Then—
The master of the house
Got up
And spoke
With the voice so rich and resonant
Like a cuckoo singing,
And he told them all about
Such-and-such that had happened.
"Having been so poor,
We could not visit you folks;
But, the Heavy God
Took sympathy on us
And had mercy on us,
Since we had never had vicious thoughts in the past.
Therefore, from this time on,
I beg you, illustrious ones,
Do be friends with us
And visit with us,
As we are in one
And belong to one same family."
As the master of the house spoke,
All those-once-poor-but-now-rich
Apologized again and again for their wrongs
By rubbing their hands.
And, they swore among themselves
To become good friends with each other
From this time on.
I was, then, worshipped by them all.
And, then,
They became casual
And open-hearted
And held a grand feast with Sake.
I, myself, enjoyed a good talk
With the holy goddess "granny" of fire
And the god of the household
And the old goddess protecting the yard

Of the sacred woods standing;
And watched the men and women
Singing and dancing,
To my heart's content.
The feast went on
For two days,
For three days.
Looking at everybody
Happy and friendly,
I was relieved
And thus I bade farewell
To the old goddess "granny" of fire,
To the god of the household,
And to the old goddess of the sacred wood yard.
Then—
I returned to my own home.
Before I reached,
My house had been decorated
With full of beautiful sacred wooden symbols
And with good Sake.
Then—
I sent my messenger for to invite all
The lower gods
And the higher gods,
And held a magnificent feast.
And, I told the gods
My experiences,
Giving detailed accounts
Of the circumstances,
Of the people in the village
Where I visited,
And of the happenings in consequence.
So, the gods
Praised me.
When they were leaving,
I gave them each
Beautifully decorated sacred wooden symbol
In twos and in threes.
As I look now and then towards the village,
I can see things are now in peace;
People are keeping good friendship;
And the man I made rich is now the village chief.
That little boy

Is now
A grown-up man
And has a wife
And children,
And is taking care of his father
And his mother.
Each time he makes Sake,
He worships me
With it
And with the sacred wooden symbols,
Before having the feast of Sake.
I, too,
Sit forever
Behind
These good men and women
To protect them and
Their village.
—So told the Owl God of his experiences.

THE OWL

Tradition Bearer: Unavailable

Source: Pilsudski, Bronislas [Bronislaw]. "Ainu Folklore." *Journal of American Folklore* 25 (1912): 72.

Date: ca. 1912

Original Source: Ainu

National Origin: Japan

Horokaruru ("the back sea") is often found in Ainu traditional narratives. Apparently, the location is loosely equivalent to the concept of a far away land in European folktales.

Self-brought-up-Man, a demi-god, was according to **myth** the first Ainu and a protagonist in many of their tales. The following is a prose translation of an Ainu sung myth. Therefore, it utilizes first-person voice. Compare the style of "The Owl" to "The Man in the Moon" (page 14).

I was living happily in the Horokaruru settlement, in that part of it which is near to the big forest. But then I heard that the sister of Self-brought-up-Man was very beautiful. Therefore I wanted to see her by my side, always sitting at my knee, nearer to the door (the usual place for Ainu women to sit). So I went to Self-brought-up-Man's house and sat down. Self-brought-up-Man bade me good-morning, but he never turned to speak to me. I said, "Although I am not very powerful, nevertheless I should like to see thy younger sister in my house, at my knee. That is why I have come to see thee."

But Self-brought-up-Man answered, "Oh, thou scapegrace! thou art only a useless bird, a little man-owl, covered with bristly feathers, a small owl, and I have no idea of letting my sister marry thee." When I heard those insulting words, a mighty anger arose in my heart. I went out furious, and perched on the top of a big "inau" built at the back of the house. There I sat, full of wrath, and began to screech and to shout towards Self-brought-up-Man's house. My cries from on high fell on the women's corner. I shouted down at them from the "inau." And Self-brought-up-Man's guardian spirit, the angel (seremaki), was taken ill, and Self-brought-up-Man himself nearly saw the lower world (that is, the land of the dead).

For two days, for three days, I screeched; and at last Self-brought-up-Man said, "Little man-owl, do not be angry any more! I am no longer going to withhold my sister from thee. I shall allow thee to take my sister, and to look at her, while she shall sit at thy knee." So I kept my temper, and married the woman, and took her with me everywhere I went. Therefore I am of one blood with mankind. I am only a little man-owl, but next of kin to man.

THE MAN IN THE MOON

Tradition Bearer: Unavailable

Source: Pilsudski, Bronislas [Bronislaw]. "Ainu Folklore." *Journal of American Folklore.* 25 (1912): 73–74.

Date: ca. 1912

Original Source: Ainu

National Origin: Japan

The "Inau" is an Ainu prayer wand made from a stick with a tassel on the end. The following **myth** reveals the intimate connection between the elements of the environment that is the result of traditional Ainu animistic beliefs.

My elder sister brought me up. Every day she went out to fetch water. She hit the pail, she struck the scoop. Once she went out and I waited for her in vain. Three nights I waited, and she came not. At last I got anxious. I built an "inau" to my grandmother the Fire, and asked her about my sister, but got no answer. Then, angry, I built an "inau" to the god of the house, and asked him, but he gave no answer. So I went out, full of wrath, to the river's side, and asked the river-god, but got no news. I went also to the forest and built an "inau," and asked my grandmother the Red Fir, but she did not know; so I asked the Siberian Silver Fir, but in vain. Full of anger, I left them, and went to my grandmother the Willow-Bush Thicket, and asked her; and she said, "I am a willow-bush thicket, and fond of talking; so listen to what I shall tell thee. Thy sister went up to the moon, and got married to the Man in the Moon."

I got very angry and marched away, with evil steps, back to the house. As soon as I arrived there, I took an arrow with a black feather, and another one with a white feather, and went out. First I let fly the arrow with the black feather, then the one with the white feather, and, holding the ends of the arrows with my two hands, I rose up into the air among the clouds; and there was my elder sister, who stepped out of her house smiling, and the ends of her eyebrows drooped. She was holding the hand of a little girl. I never had seen such a girl before. From her face, beams of light were darting forth. That light spread out on all sides, and struck my head. Beautiful eyes looked at me. All my bad feelings vanished. My sister said, "Why art thou angry, my boy? Dost thou not see, that, thanks to the Man in the Moon, thou wilt be able to marry this beautiful little girl?"

From that time I was in high spirits, and my anger was gone. I entered the house, and there was my divine brother-in-law sitting on an iron stool, and smiling at me amiably. I was contented and sat down. Never had I seen a man like that before. Near the corner where the "inau" to the god of the house is set, there was a high case which reached to the roof; and at the women's corner there were likewise cases leaning on beams. In the middle, on an iron stool, sat the divine man, and he was looking at me. He looked kindly at me, as though he might have seen me before.

Then the mistress of the house gave me to eat; and the master said, "I am a god, and I wanted to have thy sister; therefore I took her who was handling the pail and the scoop to my house. There I married her, and we are living very happily. Take my child now, and marry her, though she be miserable, then wilt thou at least have somebody to fetch thy water."

Since that time I have been related to the Man in the Moon. He married my elder sister, and they had two children—a boy and a girl. We were powerful, and had no children, and grew old. And my elder sister had children and brought them up, and then grew old. This we heard from the birds.

SEAL ISLAND

Tradition Bearer: Unavailable

Source: Pilsudski, Bronislas [Bronislaw]. "Ainu Folklore." *Journal of American Folklore* 25 (1912): 76–78.

Date: ca. 1912

Original Source: Ainu

National Origin: Japan

In the following supernatural narrative, "Self-brought-up-Man" is portrayed as a personal protector of the protagonist rather than as a demi-god removed from human contact. The power displayed by this demi-god contrasts with his description as "a miserable little man," which argues against judging by superficial appearances. The tale is told in first person (like **personal experience narratives** and Ainu sacred songs), set in the historical past (like **legends**). These qualities make the following Ainu tale a good example of the difficulties inherent in cross-cultural classification of folk narratives.

My grandfather had brought me up, feeding me on the flesh of sea-animals which he brought home. Thus we lived. One year, as usual, my grandfather went out to sea to kill some animals, that I might have something to eat. When he came home, late in the afternoon, he had killed no game. Then he said to me, "I have been on the island where I go every year to get game for our living, but there was not one seal on the island. I heard their roaring, though, far out at sea—the roaring of old beasts. So I thought that the old seals had wandered away from our island to another place. It is a long time since the island that has fed us for so long has been crowded with seals. Now there is not one animal left there; so I came back without killing anything." This is what my grandfather said.

From the moment I heard his words, I kept thinking how I might reach this far-off island. The thought kept me awake nights. One night, when my grandfather was sound asleep, I went down to the seashore. There I took the boat which my grandfather used for hunting, pulled it out on the water, and steered in the direction of the other sea. Rowing with all my strength, I soon came in sight of an island far out at sea. A few more strokes of the oars brought me quite close to it, and at last I was able to land.

There were lots of seals everywhere. But from the end of the island a miserable little man appeared. He approached, and soon began to scold me. "Why did you come? Why did you come out on this island? The creatures here are much worse than elsewhere, so why did you come? It is very dangerous to stay here. Hide your boat in yonder cave in the rock, fill it with killed seals, and secret yourself among their bodies. The awful god of the island is near, so you must hide before he sees you."

The god then arrived; and I heard him ask, "What is this boat?" And Self-brought-up-Man answered, "It is my boat."

"But the little sitting-board is fastened to it with a rope which was twisted with the left hand, and it smells like the smell of a human being," said the evil god again.

"I am only half god and half man," Self-brought-up-Man answered, "so the boat may be human, and its smell is human."

"Self-brought-up-Man," said the god, "you are mighty and fearless, and so are your deeds; but today we shall measure our powers." This is what he said, and I heard it.

Then the evil god went home; and Self-brought-up-Man turned towards me, and said, "My child, go back to your village as quickly as you can; and when you are sailing near the head of the island, carve an 'inau' out of a birch tree, and one out of an ash tree, and put them into your boat. Carve out an 'inau' from the 'uita' tree, which is the tree of the evil god, and leave it on the island. Your father was a great friend of mine in my youth, therefore I warn you not to come here again, because this land is very dangerous. When you have gone, and are in the middle of the sea, you will hear the din and roar of the battle between the god and myself, and a bloody rain will fall on your boat from above. This will be a sign that I am hurt. But you will go farther still, and again a bloody rain will fall (at the rear of your boat this time), and you will look back and see me kill that evil god. As long as you are away from home, your grandfather will be uneasy about you. He is walking to and fro on the path on which you went away, to the end of it, leaning on a big stick. He knows that you are on this island, and he is praying to me to help you. His words strike the clouds, and his prayers fall on my head from above. Direct your boat under that rainbow!"

On looking up, I saw that I was near my home, and my grandfather was walking on the sand of the shore, leaning on a thick stick. He was looking so hard up at the sky, and was praying so fervently, that he never noticed me, though I landed just in front of him. I took two seals out of the boat, one in each hand, carried them to my grandfather, and threw them down in front of him. He was so frightened that he fell down on his back. Then only did he look at me, and he was very glad to see me. He patted me on the back and on the chest, and began to scold me gently. "What have you been doing? Why did you go to that island? If it had not been for my friend, the god Samaye [an alternative name for 'Self-brought-up-Man,' usually considered as an honorific] I should see your body no more."

So I went home, skinned the dead animals, cut out quantities of meat, cooked it, and gave my grandfather to eat. After a time my grandfather said to me, "I am old, and my death is near. After I am dead, do not go to the island whence you have just come, because it is dangerous for you."

SAMAYEKURU AND HIS SISTER

Tradition Bearer: Unavailable

Source: Pilsudski, Bronislas [Bronislaw]. "Ainu Folklore." *Journal of American Folklore* 25 (1912): 81–83.

Date: ca. 1912

Original Source: Ainu

National Origin: Japan

Self-brought-up-Man again defeats a god in this narrative. The god's ability to change shape into first a salmon and then a dish suggests the Ainu belief that not only animals, plants, and forces of nature can be animated by a spiritual essence, but common objects as well. The narrative told from the point of view of the god at first remains ambiguous as to whether Self-brought-up-Man is a clever **trickster** or simply lucky. The concluding episode, however, leaves no doubt as to the intent behind the sibling's triumph over the god.

I was the god of the upper heaven. There were many gods around, but, looking at the places where they lived, I nowhere could find a woman like myself. In the lower world in the Ainu land, the younger sister of Samayekuru ("Self-brought-up-Man"), though she was only an Ainu woman, had a face like mine. She seemed to be quite like myself. So I came down to the lower world. In the yard, near Samayekuru's house, fresh fish were hanging out on sticks to dry. Samayekuru himself was out hunting with his sister, and so was not at home. I entered the empty house. As Samayekuru was only a man, I thought he must be weaker than I. I went to the sticks on which the fresh fish were hanging, threw down one big salmon, and assumed its shape. Then I waited till Samayekuru and his sister brought home a big litter full of bear-meat. They pushed the litter in through an opening in the back wall, after which Samayekuru's sister went into the hut and pulled in the litter. They were both tired, so they lighted a big fire; and Samayekuru said, "I am tired of eating bear-meat all the time. Go and get some fresh fish for me to eat." His sister went out, approached the sticks with the fish, and tried to select one. At last she took me down, and carried me into the house. Samayekuru said, "The fresh fish is too cold, warm it a little at the fire." Thus he said; and she tied a thread to my tail and hung me, head down, on the hook on which the kettle usually hangs. But Samayekuru remarked, "The fire is not big enough: put on some more wood, and make it bigger." His sister then went out to get some wood, and brought in a whole pile. A huge fire blazed up, and my head became hot. It crackled aloud "putsi!" so violently that it burnt me. My soul went up to the tail, and was nearly burning. I got frightened, pushed aside the beams of the roof with much noise, and got out into the fresh air. Making a terrible ado, I returned to the upper heaven.

When I reached home, I cried, "Samayekuru was only a man born on the poor earth, and I was a mighty god!" and I thought that a man born on the poor earth would be weaker than I, but he was stronger. Angrily I went down to earth again. Samayekuru was out hunting with his sister, as before, and I entered the empty house. I hid away Samayekuru's dish, and turned into a dish myself and waited. At last I heard the steps of Samayekuru and his sister, who were coming home. Through the opening in the back wall they pushed in the litter with the bear-meat. The younger sister came in by the door, and took the litter with the meat. They were tired, and made a big fire, after which Samaye-kuru said to his sister, "Did you wash your dishes this morning before going out hunting?"

"No, I did not wash them," answered the sister.

"Then prepare some hot water and wash them now," he ordered. So she got up, took her big kettle, filled it with water, and hung it over the fire to get it hot. As soon as the water was boiling, she brought her brother's dish. I thought I should die if she should throw me into the boiling water. And she threw me in; but I jumped out of the kettle, pushed away the roof near the door with a loud rumbling noise, and flew out. Then I noisily raised myself to the upper heaven, and returned to my divine home.

When I was inside, I began to think, "Samayekuru is a man only, so he ought to be weaker than I am, but he has turned out to be stronger." Full of an-ger, I sat brooding a long time. At last I decided to go down once more, without changing my shape, in my own divine, beautiful body. So I did, and went down to the yard near Samayekuru's house, and stood there; but I did not want to enter the house as a guest. Samayekuru's sister went out in the yard, and said, "I know that you do not care to step into our house. You are walking angrily about, so I shall not lead you in; but yonder there is my little metal hut, and you will do well to go there." So I went towards this little house, and at night I stepped in and sat down.

"Samayekuru surely is angry with me," I thought. "Though I be a mighty god, and though Samayekuru be born on this poor earth, he has beaten me," I thought, and decided to tell him so. Suddenly, however, I smelled the smell of dung. I thought I had come to a little silver house. But why this nasty smell of dung? I looked around, and there I was, sitting in a very filthy place; and Samayekuru and his sister had poured out their dung on me, and soiled me from head to foot. "I am a mighty god, and Samayekuru is only a man, born on earth; but as to power, he has entirely beaten me," thought I. "Whatever I might do, I could never surpass Samayekuru in power, so I had better calm down."

From the filthy place where I was sitting, I leaped up with a terrible noise, went to the upper heaven, and returned home, quite soiled with dung from head to foot. I took off my iron armor and washed it, after having washed my head and my whole body. I was quite angry, and sat down full of wrath. My brothers, the other gods, talked with one another, and said, "As we walked around the house, in the yard, we perceived a nasty smell." I heard these words, but made no reply, and sat quite ashamed. One day, however, when I was seated, my elder brother came and began to scold me. "What is it? Samayekuru is so powerful, that he wants to beat every one, and you are stupid to have roused him." Thus they all scolded me.

THE LADY OF KUNNEPET

Tradition Bearer: Unavailable

Source: Batchelor, John. "Specimens of Ainu Folk-Lore." *Transactions of the Asiatic Society of Japan* 18 (1890): 25–39.

Date: ca. 1888

Original Source: Ainu

National Origin: Japan

The following **myth** details an epic battle between an Ainu hero and the Thunder God. Several features of the narrative have important connotations in Ainu culture, according to the collector of the myth, John Batchelor. "Slave" in the context of this narrative is likely to refer to a prisoner of war who was being trained as a household servant or even a page. The head of the fireplace is regarded as sacred space, and thus the protagonist was aided by supernatural forces in his quest. The fact that the Lady of Kunnepet cooks for the hero at their first meeting is significant, because Ainu marriage ceremony consists in the act of the bride cooking food and giving it to her betrothed. Finally, among the Ainu white symbolizes purity and goodness while black is associated with evil.

There was a person who was reared as a slave at Shinutapka. Now, once upon a time he heard it noised abroad that there was a lady residing at Kunnepet who was famous for her beauty. So, one day, after he had cooked and eaten some food, our slave buckled on his belt, stuck his trusty sword into his girdle, and fastened on his helmet; then, being taken up by the winds which arose from the head of the fireplace, he was hastily carried through the upper window; and his inspiring guardian god having rested upon him with a sound, they went before the mighty winds till he arrived at the village of Kunnepet.

So he came to the lady of Kunnepet. When he looked at her he saw that she was there weeping very exceedingly. Still shedding tears, she spake and said, "The thunder-gods who live in the heavens above are two in number, and the younger of them does nothing but make advances to me and is about to marry me. This being so, O *Poiyaumbe* [Ainu, "brave hero"] they cannot marry though you have come for me; nevertheless I will cook some food that you may eat." When she had so said she swung a pretty little pot over the fire and put some of her choice treasured-up food into it. She then dipped in her ladle and stirred up the delicious food. Next she took a pretty eating cup and set it upon a beautiful tray; then, heaping it up high, carried it to him and bowed profusely.

When he had but just commenced to eat, flashes of white lightning came through the upper window and hung upon the beams in curious forms. Upon looking up he saw a lady even more beautiful than the lady of Kunnepet, reclining in a white chariot. She had anger depicted upon her countenance; and, in her wrath said, "O Poiyaumbe listen to me for I have something to say. I am the younger sister of the wolf-god and the benefactress of the lady of Kunnepet, whilst you are watched over by my elder brother. This being so, I am here to tell you that the thunder-god is angry with you for coming to visit this lady and is going to make grievous war against you. Nay, the war is at hand. Though I am a worthless woman, I have come to assist you. Get into my white chariot"; so spake the younger sister of the wolf-god.

So he got into the chariot, which immediately went out of the upper window. Then the trappings of the chariot whistled and rattled. As they went on their way, they skirted the mountains towards the source of the river, and, proceeding along, they saw white and black lightning playing about in the clouds of the lower heavens. As he was looking at it, he saw the aforementioned thunder-god sitting in a black chariot; he was unmistakably a very little man. There too sat a little woman, who, without doubt, was his younger sister. She held a wand in her hand; with which she continually struck first one end of the chariot and then the other, as they hung and waved about over the tops of the mountains.

The thunder-god, having anger expressed upon his countenance, said, "Look here, O Poiyaumbe, listen well to me for I have something to say. You have been paying your addresses to and flirting with the lady of Kunnepet, whom I have determined to take to myself as wife. I take this as a cause for war. Be very careful, my fine fellow, for I will bring down your haughty looks." When he had so spoken, he set upon him mightily with his sword; so that his blows rattled upon the sides of the white chariot. Upon this Poiyaumbe also drew his sword and set upon the thunder-god as determinately as he was attacked by him. So they fought with might and main, but the black chariot rose and fell to meet the attack. So that the blows of the sword upon its sides and floor sent forth a clashing sound.

And now there was a tremendous roaring sound of thunder over the world, together with a mighty wind blowing; and both day and night they did nothing but fight. After the war had raged for twice ten months, the god of thunder said, "I observe that as they fight upon this land in which men dwell, they are wasting and wearing out the country, for, as you see, its foundations (back-bones) consist of rocks; they ought to be more careful of the world. Now then, come, the foundations (backbones) of the world above are made of iron, let us go up there and fight; for there they may wage war without having any regard to the spoilation of the place." So spake he.

He then withdrew into the air and the young hero followed close behind him. The younger sister of the wolf-god, having the wand in her hand, continued to strike first one end and then the other of the chariot. The thin trappings whistled and the thick trappings rattled, as the white chariot followed close upon the black one. The gates of heaven opened with a sound, and, having passed through, were shut upon us with another noise. Now, what they saw was on this wise. A splendid country lay before us and a very beautiful waterway opened up to our view. On the sides of the river were forests of magnificent oaks, and the clouds upon the horizon were floating gently along. Now, the thunder-god said, "This country is, in truth, the high heaven. Its foundations consist of iron so that if they fight here for two or three years they need have no fear of damaging it. This is indeed a place in which they can especially measure our strength."

Having so said, he set upon me mightily with his sword, and the hero too turned upon him as fiercely. Nevertheless, the edge of the black chariot clashed against the sword and warded off the blows, so there was only the sound of clashing iron. In the same way our white chariot, also rising up and guarding with its floor, sent forth a clashing sound. And now, fighting fiercely, they chased each other from one end of heaven to the other, till at length they chanced to pass over a metal house which was covered in with a lid, and, over this they stayed and fought; whilst doing so, there came forth a voice from the inside of the house which said, "Look here, O Poiyaumbe and thunder-god, I have something to say, so pay attention. It is indeed true that the foundations of Ainu-land are rocks, and it is also true that the foundations of heaven above consist of metal. But as ye continue to carry on your battles here, heaven has grown wary and waxed hot for the reason that its foundations are iron. Ye should be careful. Now then, come, underneath Ainu-land there are six countries, and beneath these again there is another, a beautiful land. The name of that country is *Chirama* [Ainu, "lotheyst"], and its foundations consist of earth. Go ye to that land and fight, for unless ye do, our country and villages will be all spoiled." So sounded forth the voice of God.

Upon this the thunder-god sheathed his sword and Poiyaumbe also sheathed his. Then, as they entered heaven, so they we went out—with a rush. They passed down through space headfirst, like snipes, and, piercing our land, they went through six countries. Having done this, they came, as they were told they should, to a truly beautiful country; without doubt this was Chirama-land, upon which they had descended.

And now they chased one another from one end of the country to the other, fighting, as before, most fiercely. Nevertheless, whenever and however they fought, the black chariot rising, falling, and swinging to and fro, kept off the hero's blows with its sides and floor, so that the result was nothing but the sound of clashing metal. In the same way the white chariot also rose up and fenced the blows with its sides and floor like a shield. However much Poiyaumbe strove, he could by no means touch the body of the thunder-god. Poiyaumbe therefore aimed at nothing but to cut the trappings by which the black chariot was suspended. And fighting hard with this intent, he was able, after a time and by the help of God, to sever them. So, too, all the trappings of our white chariot the were cut asunder. They therefore all fell down to the ground. Then the thunder-god got out of his black chariot and came to Poiyaumbe, walking by the help of his hands [that is, crawling].

Upon this the younger sister of the thunder-god shed many tears and said, "Oh my elder brother, you are a god; and if you would but marry a goddess you would have no need to carry on this fierce combat with Poiyaumbe. Why do you set your affections on this Lady of Kunnepet as though she were the only woman? Now our charmed black chariot has been quite broken up and you are as one fighting without armor. Be careful or Poiyaumbe will slay you." So spake the sister of the thunder-god through her tears.

After she had said this, the sister of the wolf-god went out and fought against her. Then the thunder-god set upon Poiyaumbe most fiercely and he returned the attack just as vehemently. Thus fighting together, Poiyaumbe managed with great difficulty to strike him now and then, so that his garments were hanging about him in rags. But he was not to be beaten; for he also in like manner cut his clothes into many pieces. Whilst things were going on so, a mighty sound as if the true gods were coming to us, issued forth from the east of Chirama-land, and all at once my Lady of Kunnepet, more beautiful than ever, and shedding many tears, alighted and came to the side of the wolf-god. And now the sister of the thunder-god fought mightily, but after two or three final struggles, she was cut down and slain. Her divine spirit roared loudly as it ascended into the skies. She went up to heaven a living goddess; and, when she had departed the roaring ceased.

After this my Lady of Kunnepet, in company with the sister of the wolf-god came to Poiyaumbe's side and they three together fought against the thunder-god. So that after a time he was, though with difficulty, cut down and slain. His spirit roared as it went up; but, as it was not possible for it to go into the western end of Chirama-land it ascended to the high heavens with a great noise. It went up a new god and then the sound died away.

When all was over, my Lady of Kunnepet and the younger sister of the wolf-god saluted one another with their swords, and then, after they had come to our country and to the village of Kunnepet, the sister of the wolf-god said, "As I am a goddess, I must take a husband from among the gods, but as you are a man, it would be well for you to marry the Lady of Kunnepet. Now, you are watched over by my elder brother the wolf-god, so henceforth do no more fighting, but when you have wine, be careful that you make some *inao* [prayer sticks] and offer libations to the wolf-god."

When she had finished speaking, she departed with a great sound. Then my Lady of Kunnepet worked away with a willing heart and great pleasure, and, having prepared food, she heaped up very full a pretty cup, and, setting it on a beautiful tray, brought it to Poiyaumbe with many bows. After eating a little of it, he pushed the remainder to her and she, lifting it up and down in thankfulness, finished it. Then, when the meal was over, my Lady of Kunnepet proceeded to get the house in order and they have lived happily ever since.

THE BRIDE RESCUES HER HUSBAND

Tradition Bearer: Unavailable

Source: Pilsudski, Bronislas [Bronislaw]. "Ainu Folklore." *Journal of American Folklore* 25 (1912): 83–86.

Date: ca. 1912

Original Source: Ainu

National Origin: Japan

The following Ainu tale builds on the familiar **motif** of a bride rescuing her betrothed or her husband from supernatural abduction. Although this is a familiar theme in the European **ordinary folktale**, it is impossible to establish any direct influence between the Ainu narrative and any Indo-European antecedent.

From childhood I was brought up by my aunt, who fed me with fine food. She fed me very well indeed, and brought me up splendidly in my father's house. On the floor there was a large pile of iron cases on which iron pots were standing, one within another; and iron pans in a row, also one within another. It was a splendid house, a fine house! In this house on the seashore I was living. My aunt gave me every day a plate of good meat and of grease, so full that I could not even hold it. I ate, and thus we lived.

At last I grew up and became a large girl. So my aunt took out different kinds of silk, and bade me sew. But I did not know how to sew. I tangled the thread, and that ended it. My aunt scolded me. "My niece does not know how to sew! Why are you such a dullard?" Thus she spoke. After trying each day, I at last learned how to sew.

My aunt said, "Far off in Otasam lives your betrothed one. He is the youngest of three brothers. A piece of silk was torn in halves for you and him [as a sign of betrothal]. He must be grown up now. He is very rich, and will not come to you; therefore you had better go to him, to the rich man." This she said; and I heard it, and thought, "Until now my aunt has brought me up well. If I leave her for one day only, I rejoice to see her again." I was grieved, and remained. My aunt, however, spoke to me again about it, and every day she repeated the same words.

So at last I gathered the most necessary of my things, made a bag in which to take them on my back, and put my clothes in properly. I prepared many different things; and when I was ready to start, my aunt said, "In Otasam, where you are going, there are three brothers, rich men. The eldest one lives in the house nearest to us; in the middle one lives the youngest, with his younger sister; and the third one lives at the end of the settlement. When you arrive, you will do well to enter the hut that is in the middle, which belongs to the youngest brother. This my aunt told me while I was taking leave.

Then I went away. Soon I saw before me a place situated high up. I stopped at the mountain Tomisa; then I walked on, and turned around and looked. There was my aunt, standing in front of her house, and she was following me with her eyes. I continued my march again, and, turning around, I still saw her looking after me. Finally I directed my steps towards the village Otasam, and set out on the way to it. I looked, and there was a big house, just as my aunt had described it to me; and behind it, as she had told me, was to be the house of my betrothed one, but, glancing around, I saw only one house in front of me. I began to think, and came to the conclusion that I was walking on the road to the house of the eldest rich brother. When I looked around, I saw another path, which I took; but soon I noticed that it led to the same house. I understood. "They are brothers," I thought, "and if I go to the eldest of them, the gods will have made me do it." So I entered the house, which was full of furniture, quite uncommon and divine. The rich man himself was living here. He met me full of joy, as if he had already seen me. He prepared food, and gave me to eat.

In the mean time it grew dark, and evening arrived. The rich man said, "You would do well if you would spend this night here." I went to sleep angry; and when I woke up, I saw the rich man sleeping with me. I got up weeping, and was just going to depart, when the rich man said, "What evil god made me do this! I had no bad intentions. You have been my younger brother's betrothed wife since childhood, and, though I did not think any evil concerning you, I did this. So when you come to your husband's house, and give him to eat, put this into his dish." Thus saying, he gave me the basket hilt of a sword. The hilt was inlaid with silver on one side, a little silver net was spread out, and a little silver man was pulling at it, and in the net were a whole lot of little silver-fishes. I was quite delighted, turned it over, and saw on the other side a little gold net spread out, and inside it a whole lot of little gold-fishes, and little gold men pulling at it.

After I had looked at it well, I put it under my shirt and went away. I walked on the path which I saw in front of me, and arrived at the house of the man who had been promised to me since childhood. Above the house two thick clouds were floating, and I entered the house. "She is as old as I am," said the rich man when he saw me. "The beautiful maiden is living." I was still at the door as he smiled at me. As soon as he saw me, I approached the fire and remained near it. When I sat down, he wanted to say something. "My little brother," he began, "has not eaten since last month, and he sleeps all the time. Therefore he has a swollen belly [suffering from dropsy]. I do not know the reason of this, and am very much astonished. Now that you have come, when he hears you are here, perhaps he will eat." This he said, and at the same time we heard footsteps near the house.

I looked up, and thought that my betrothed one was coming, but in reality it was the swollen sick man. As soon as he came in, he sat down near the fire.

The girl of the house prepared some food, put it into an iron dish, and gave me to eat; she also fed the owner of the house, my husband. As soon as we had finished eating, I gave back the rest of the food, and put on the dish the hilt which I had pulled out from the back of my shirt. Now even I looked at it with pleasure and admiration, and handed it over to my husband. He took it, and said, "My elder brother did not act according to his will when he forced you to spend a night with him. It is well for the gods to marry one another, and men and women should also marry. I am only a man; but the god of the upper heaven has a younger sister, who wants to marry me. She desires so strongly to take me up to heaven with my body, that I have not felt at all like eating since last month."

After having said these words, he seized me, ran out on the place in front of the house, and carried me towards the forest. At the back of the house there was a little iron hut, built on piles—a house which had feet. He pulled the hanging door aside, carried me into the hut, and there we lay down together. "Now we are married, therefore we sleep together for the first time. But if you are weak, the goddess will take me up, body and all. If you are strong, we shall live together a long time." This he said, and fell asleep.

When I woke up and looked around, I felt something pushing me. I looked, and saw an iron ring put around my husband's body, and an iron chain attached to it went up through the opening in the roof, and somebody was pulling at it from above. I seized the chain, naked as I was, and began to pull it down with all my strength. But the girl from heaven, being a goddess, was stronger than I. I began to weep and to scream. I called the younger sister (of my husband). She came in; but as soon as she saw me, she fled, shouting, "Oh, what is this! a naked woman!" I screamed again, and called the elder brother. He opened the door, came in, looked at me, and said, "A naked woman!" after which he ran away. At last my husband slipped out of my hands, and the goddess pulled the chain as hard as she could. She grasped it with one hand, then again with the other, and pulled my husband up quite close. Smiling, she pulled him into heaven and closed the door.

I could do no more, and began to cry. While weeping, I suddenly heard somebody coming from my native country, on the Tomisan hill. It was my aunt who had brought me up. She was carrying a sword without a scabbard. She brandished it and struck. I thought she had killed me; but suddenly I was changed into a little bird, and flew out through the hole in the roof. As I did not know where to fly, I looked down, and saw the parts of a naked woman's body lying near the house; and my aunt was sitting on them and crying, and was trembling all over.

I made a bridge out of clouds, and, walking on it, I arrived in heaven. When I came to the house of the goddess in the shape of a little bird, I fluttered my wings; and the gods said, "A maiden is walking around in heaven quite naked. We smell her body, and it makes us sick." This they said; but I entered the house through the upper hole in the roof. There was the goddess, holding the dying soul of my husband like a coral between her hands, and she was busy preparing medicine for him. I snatched my husband's soul away and returned to earth, having put it into my mouth. As we had no place to go to, I crept into the mouth of the cut-up woman, and lost all consciousness. When I recovered, I looked around, and saw my husband, who at the same time returned to life again.

This is how I resuscitated one of the three brothers of Otasan. My aunt, whose power had brought my husband back from heaven to earth again, was also alive. From that time on, we all lived happily together. I related tales about the gods, and lived with the others. This is the legend.

CHINA

IN THE BEGINNING

Tradition Bearer: Unavailable

Source: Colum, Padric. *Orpheus: Myths of the World*. New York: The Macmillan Company. 1930, 237–239.

Date: Unavailable

Original Source: Unavailable

National Origin: China

The concept of opposing but complementary forces, expressed as yang-yin in the following **myth**, is at the heart of Taoism (also Daoism) as well as other systems of Chinese philosophy and science. P'an Ku (also, Pan Gu) acts as a central figure in the dividing and ordering process that occurred to create the universe (the cosmos) out of the first state (primal chaos). The myth of a titan whose body is rent apart and whose parts give rise to various elements of the present world is found cross-culturally.

In the beginning there was *Yang-yin* which is light-darkness, heat-cold, dryness-moisture. Then that which was subtle went upward, and that which was gross tended downward; the heavens were formed from the subtle, the earth from the gross. Now there was *Yang* and *Yin*, the active and the passive, the male and the female. From the operation of *Yang* upon *Yin* came the seasons in their order, and the seasons brought into existence all the products of the earth. The warm effluence of *Yang* produced fire, and the subtlest parts of fire went to form the sun; the effluence of *Yin* produced water, and the subtlest parts of water went to form the moon. The sun operating on the moon produced the stars. The heavens became adorned with sun, moon, and stars, and the earth received rivers, rain, and dust. And *Yang* combining with *Yin*, the principle that is above combining with the principle that is below, produces all creatures, all things. The power that is *Yang*, the receptivity that is *Yin*, can never be added to, never taken away from: in these two principles is the All.

So the sages relate in their perspicuous writings. But the people say that before *Yang* and *Yin* were separated, P'an Ku, a man, came into existence. He had a chisel and a mallet. He had horns projecting from his forehead and tusks projecting from his jaws. He grew in stature every day he lived—for eighteen thousand years he grew six feet every day in stature. Nothing was in place when P'an Ku came into the universe, but with his mallet and his chisel he ordered all things; he hewed out bases for the mountains, he scooped out basins for the seas, he dug courses for the rivers, and hollowed out the valleys. In this meritorious work P'an Ku was engaged for eighteen thousand years.

He was attended by the Dragon, the Unicorn, the Tortoise, and the Phoenix—the four auspicious creatures. The Dragon is the head of all the beasts because it is the one that is most filled with the principle of *Yang*: it is bigger than big, smaller than small, higher than high, lower than low; when it breathes its breath changes to a cloud on which it can ride up to Heaven. The Dragon has five colors in its body, and it is the possessor of a pearl which is the essence of the moon and a charm against fire; it can make itself visible and invisible; in the spring it mounts up to the clouds, and in the autumn it remains supine in the waters. The Unicorn is strong of body and exceptionally virtuous of mind, and it combines in itself the principles of *Yang* and *Yin*. It eats no living vegetation and it never treads upon green grass. The Tortoise is the most propitious of all created things; it possesses the secrets of life and death, and it can, with its breath, create clouds and palaces of enchantment. The Phoenix is at the head of all birds; its color is the blending of the five colors and its call is the harmony of the five notes; it bathes in the pure water that flows down from the K'un-lun Mountains, and at night it reposes in the Cave of Tan.

But notwithstanding the fact that he was respectfully attended by the auspicious creatures, P'an Ku put the sun and moon in places that were not properly theirs. The sun and the moon went into the sea, and the world was left without luminaries. P'an Ku went out into the deep; he held out his hands to indicate where they were to go, and he repeated a powerful incantation three times. Then the sun and the moon went into the places that were properly theirs and the universe rejoiced at the ensuing harmony.

But the establishment of the universe was not completed until P'an Ku himself had perished; he died after eighteen thousand years of labor with his chisel and mallet; then his breath became the wind and clouds, and his beard became the streaming signs in the sky; his voice became the thunder, his limbs the four quarters of the earth; his head became the mountains, his flesh the soil, and his blood became the rivers of earth; his skin and hair became the herbs and trees, and his teeth, bones, and marrow became metals, rocks, and precious stones.

Even then the universe was not adequately compacted: P'an Ku had built up the world in fifty-one stories, giving thirty-three stories to the heavens and eighteen stories to the hells beneath the earth. But he had left a great cavity in the bottom of the world, and, at inauspicious times, men and women fell down through it. A woman whose name was Nu-Ku found a stone which adequately covered the cavity; rightly positioning it, she covered up the emptiness, and so completed the making of the well-ordered world.

THE WEAVER MAIDEN AND THE HERDSMAN

Tradition Bearer: Unavailable

Source: Colum, Padric. *Orpheus: Myths of the World.* New York: The Macmillan Company, 1930, 239–241.

Date: Unavailable

Original Source: Unavailable

National Origin: China

Chih Nü (also, Zhi-Nu) was the daughter of Yu-Huang (the Jade Emperor), the supreme of deity of Chinese Taoism. There are several **variants** to the **myth** given below. In one, she had descended to earth to bathe when Niu Lang the herdsman, at the instructions of his ox, stole her clothes. To retrieve her clothes, she agreed to marry Niu Lang. On returning to the heavens, she confessed her marriage, and he was made an immortal. In another version, Yu-Huang was so pleased with his daughter's diligence that he wed her to the patron deity of cowherds. All versions agree that the couple's immoderate behavior led to the conclusion described below.

Her august father, the Sun, would have the accomplished Chih Nü turn her footsteps towards his bright gardens or appear in his celestial halls. But Chih Nü would not leave her loom. All day and every day the maiden sat by the River of Heaven weaving webs that were endless.

The Sun thought in his august mind that if the maiden were wedded she would not permit herself to be a slave to the loom. He thought that if she had a husband she would depart a little from her exceptional diligence. Therefore he let it be known that he would favorably consider a proposal involving the marriage of the accomplished Chih Nü. Then one whose dwelling was at the other side of the heavenly river drew his august regard. This was Niu Lang: he herded oxen, and he was a youth who was exceedingly amiable and who had accomplishments that matched the accomplishments of Chih Nü.

They were united, the Weaver Maiden and the Herdsman Youth; they were united in the palace of the august Sun. The omens were favorable, and the heavens made themselves as beautiful as a flying pheasant for the ceremony. The guests drank of that sweet heavenly dew which makes those who drink of it more quick-witted and intelligent than they were before. The Sun, the Weaver Maiden, the Herdsman Youth, and all the guests who were present sang in mutual harmony the song that says, "The Sun and Moon are constant; the stars and other heavenly bodies have their courses; the four seasons observe their rule! How responsive are all things to the harmony that has been established in the heavens!" The august Sun expected that after this auspicious marriage his daughter would moderate her diligence and be more often at leisure.

But Chih Nü was as immoderate in her play as she was in her industry. No more did she work at her loom; no more did she attend to her inescapable duties; with her husband she played all day, and for him she danced and made music all night. The heavens went out of harmony because of this failure in right performance, and the earth was greatly troubled. Her august father came before Chih Nü and pointed out to her the dire consequences of her engaging in endless pastimes. But in spite of all he said to her the Weaver Maiden would not return to her loom.

Then the august Sun determined to make a separation between the pair whose union had such dire results. He commanded the blameless Niu Lang to go to the other bank of the River of Heaven, and to continue there his herdsman's duties. He commanded the accomplished Chih Nü to remain on her own side of the river. But the august Sun showed a spirit of kindliness to his daughter and his son-in-law. They could meet and be together for one day and one night of the year. On the seventh day of the seventh month of every year they could cross the River of Heaven and be with each other. And to make a bridge by which they might cross the river a myriad of magpies would come together, and each by catching the head-feathers of the bird next him would make a bridge with their backs and wings. And over that bridge the Weaver Maiden would cross over to where the Herdsman Youth waited for her.

All day the Weaver Maiden sat at her loom and worked with becoming diligence. Her father rejoiced that she fulfilled her duties. But no being in the heavens or on the earth was as lonely as she was, and all day the Herdsman Youth tended his oxen, but with a heart that was filled with loneliness and grief. The days and the nights went slowly by, and time when they might cross the River of Heaven and be together drew near. Then a great fear entered the hearts of the young wife and the young husband. They feared lest rain should fall; for the River of Heaven is always filled to its brim, and one drop would cause it to flood its banks. And if there was a flood the magpies could not bridge the space between the Weaver Maiden and the Herdsman Youth.

For many years after their separation no rain fell. The magpies came in their myriad. The one behind held the head-feathers of the one before, and with their backs and wings they made a bridge for the young wife to cross over to where the young husband waited for her.

With hearts that were shaken like the wings of the magpies she would cross the Bridge of Wings. They would hold each other in their arms and make over again their vows of love. Then Chih Nü would go back to her loom, and the magpies would fly away to come together in another year.

And the people of earth pray that no drop of rain may fall to flood the River of Heaven; they make such prayer when it comes near the seventh day of the seventh month. But they rejoice when no rain falls and they can see with their own eyes the magpies gathering in their myriad. Sometimes the inauspicious forces are in the ascendant; rain falls and the river is flooded. No magpies then go to form a bridge, and Chih Nü weeps beside her loom and Niu Lang laments as he drives his ox beside the flood of the River of Heaven.

THE STORY OF HOK LEE AND THE DWARFS

Tradition Bearer: Unavailable

Source: Lang, Andrew. *The Green Fairy Book.* London: Longmans, Green and Company, 1892, 229–233.

Date: Unavailable

Original Source: Unavailable

National Origin: China

The following **ordinary folktale** is a **variant** of "The Gifts of the Little People" (AT 503). A common concluding episode in the tale, a failed attempt by a companion or eavesdropper to imitate the protagonist's success, has been replaced.

There once lived in a small town in China a man named Hok Lee. He was a steady industrious man, who not only worked hard at his trade, but did all his own housework as well, for he had no wife to do it for him. "What an excellent industrious man is this Hok Lee!" said his neighbors; "how hard he works: he never leaves his house to amuse himself or to take a holiday as others do!"

But Hok Lee was by no means the virtuous person his neighbors thought him. True, he worked hard enough by day, but at night, when all respectable folk were fast asleep, he used to steal out and join a dangerous band of robbers, who broke into rich people's houses and carried off all they could lay hands on.

This state of things went on for some time, and, though a thief was caught now and then and punished, no suspicion ever fell on Hok Lee, he was such a *very* respectable, hard-working man.

Hok Lee had already amassed a good store of money as his share of the proceeds of these robberies when it happened one morning on going to market that a neighbor said to him, "Why, Hok Lee, what is the matter with your face? One side of it is all swelled up."

True enough, Hok Lee's right cheek was twice the size of his left, and it soon began to feel very uncomfortable. "I will bind up my face," said Hok Lee, "doubtless the warmth will cure the swelling." But no such thing. Next day it was worse, and day by day it grew bigger and bigger till it was nearly as large as his head and became very painful.

Hok Lee was at his wit's ends what to do. Not only was his cheek unsightly and painful, but his neighbors began to jeer and make fun of him, which hurt his feelings very much indeed.

One day, as luck would have it, a traveling doctor came to the town. He sold not only all kinds of medicine, but also dealt in many strange charms against witches and evil spirits. Hok Lee determined to consult him, and asked him into his house.

After the doctor had examined him carefully, he spoke thus, "This, O Hok Lee, is no ordinary swelled face. I strongly suspect you have been doing some wrong deed which has called down the anger of the spirits on you. None of my drugs will avail to cure you, but, if you are willing to pay me handsomely, I can tell you how you may be cured."

Then Hok Lee and the doctor began to bargain together, and it was a long time before they could come to terms. However, the doctor got the better of it in the end, for he was determined not to part with his secret under a certain price, and Hok Lee had no mind to carry his huge cheek about with him to the end of his days. So he was obliged to part with the greater portion of his ill-gotten gains.

When the Doctor had pocketed the money, he told Hok Lee to go on the first night of the full moon to a certain wood and there to watch by a particular tree. After a time he would see the dwarfs and little sprites who live underground come out to dance. When they saw him they would be sure to make him dance too. "And mind you dance your very best," added the doctor. "If you dance well and please them they will grant you a petition and you can then beg to be cured; but if you dance badly they will most likely do you some mischief out of spite." With that he took leave and departed.

Happily the first night of the full moon was near, and at the proper time Hok Lee set out for the wood. With a little trouble he found the tree the doctor had described, and, feeling nervous, he climbed up into it.

He had hardly settled himself on a branch when he saw the little dwarfs assembling in the moonlight. They came from all sides, till at length there appeared to be hundreds of them. They seemed in high glee, and danced and skipped and capered about, whilst Hok Lee grew so eager watching them that he crept further and further along his branch till at length it gave a loud crack. All the dwarfs stood still, and Hok Lee felt as if his heart stood still also.

Then one of the dwarfs called out, "Someone is up in that tree. Come down at once, whoever you are, or we must come and fetch you."

In great terror, Hok Lee proceeded to come down; but he was so nervous that he tripped near the ground and came rolling down in the most absurd manner. When he had picked himself up, he came forward with a low bow, and the dwarf who had first spoken and who appeared to be the leader, said, "Now, then, who art thou, and what brings thee here?"

So Hok Lee told him the sad story of his swelled cheek, and how he had been advised to come to the forest and beg the dwarfs to cure him.

"It is well," replied the dwarf. "We will see about that. First, however, thou must dance before us. Should thy dancing please us, perhaps we may be able to do something; but shouldst thou dance badly, we shall assuredly punish thee, so now take warning and dance away."

With that, he and all the other dwarfs sat down in a large ring, leaving Hok Lee to dance alone in the middle. He felt half frightened to death, and besides was a good deal shaken by his fall from the tree and did not feel at all inclined to dance. But the dwarfs were not to be trifled with.

"Begin!" cried their leader, and "Begin!" shouted the rest in chorus.

So in despair Hok Lee began. First he hopped on one foot and then on the other, but he was so stiff and so nervous that he made but a poor attempt, and after a time sank down on the ground and vowed he could dance no more.

The dwarfs were very angry. They crowded round Hok Lee and abused him. "Thou to come here to be cured, indeed!" they cried, "thou hast brought one big cheek with thee, but thou shalt take away two." And with that they ran off and disappeared, leaving Hok Lee to find his way home as best he might.

He hobbled away, weary and depressed, and not a little anxious on account of the dwarfs' threat.

Nor were his fears unfounded, for when he rose next morning his left cheek was swelled up as big as his right, and he could hardly see out of his eyes. Hok Lee felt in despair, and his neighbors jeered at him more than ever. The doctor, too, had disappeared, so there was nothing for it but to try the dwarfs once more.

He waited a month till the first night of the full moon came round again, and then he trudged back to the forest, and sat down under the tree from which he had fallen. He had not long to wait. Ere long the dwarfs came trooping out till all were assembled.

"I don't feel quite easy," said one; "I feel as if some horrid human being were near us."

When Hok Lee heard this he came forward and bent down to the ground before the dwarfs, who came crowding round, and laughed heartily at his comical appearance with his two big cheeks.

"What dost thou want?" they asked; and Hok Lee proceeded to tell them of his fresh misfortunes, and begged so hard to be allowed one more trial at dancing that the dwarfs consented, for there is nothing they love so much as being amused.

Now, Hok Lee knew how much depended on his dancing well, so he plucked up a good spirit and began, first quite slowly, and faster by degrees, and he danced so well and gracefully, and made such new and wonderful steps, that the dwarfs were quite delighted with him.

They clapped their tiny hands, and shouted, "Well done, Hok Lee, well done; go on, dance more, for we are pleased."

And Hok Lee danced on and on, till he really could dance no more, and was obliged to stop.

Then the leader of the dwarfs said, "We are well pleased, Hok Lee, and as a recompense for thy dancing thy face shall be cured. Farewell."

With these words he and the other dwarfs vanished, and Hok Lee, putting his hands to his face, found to his great joy that his cheeks were reduced to their natural size. The way home seemed short and easy to him, and he went to bed happy, and resolved never to go out robbing again.

Next day the whole town was full of the news of Hok's sudden cure. His neighbors questioned him, but could get nothing from him, except the fact that he had discovered a wonderful cure for all kinds of diseases.

After a time a rich neighbor, who had been ill for some years, came, and offered to give Hok Lee a large sum of money if he would tell him how he might get cured. Hok Lee consented on condition that he swore to keep the secret. He did so, and Hok Lee told him of the dwarfs and their dances.

The neighbor went off, carefully obeyed Hok Lee's directions, and was duly cured by the dwarfs. Then another and another came to Hok Lee to beg his secret, and from each he extracted a vow of secrecy and a large sum of money. This went on for some years, so that at length Hok Lee became a very wealthy man, and ended his days in peace and prosperity.

CHUKCHEE

THE YOUTH WHO RECEIVED SUPERNATURAL POWERS FROM THE KE'LET

Tradition Bearer: Rin'to

Source: Bogoras, Waldemar. "Chukchee Mythology." *The Jessup North Pacific Expedition*, ed. Franz Boas. *Memoir of the American Museum of Natural History New York*. Vol. VIII. New York: The American Museum of Natural History New York, 1910, 34–42.

Date: 1900

Original Source: Chukchee

National Origin: Siberia

The traditional home of the Chukchee was far northeastern reaches of Siberia, where temperatures average −12 degrees Celsius. Their indigenous culture was divided into two groups: nomadic reindeer herders or coastal dwellers. The Reindeer Chukchee relied on their herds for both transportation and sustenance, while the coastal dwellers exploited maritime resources, such as fish and sea mammals. As seen in the following narrative, the Chukchee world was populated by many spirits, and the shamans were invested with personal power (usually acquired from a tutelary spirit) that allowed them to divine, cure, and supernaturally attack their neighbors—abilities that led to their being both valued and feared. Death and rebirth and bizarre behavior at the onset of power are typical of shamanism cross-culturally.

Once upon a time there were only three of them. The son was suffering, so the parents (even) could not sleep. A strong gale was blowing. Notwithstanding (the noise), they heard the clattering of sledge-runners.

The man's wife looked out into the darkness and saw the visitors. They were re'kkeñ [evil supernatural beings]. She said, "Oh, they are coming down upon us! Their reindeer were breathing fire. They came and entered the house. The suffering one immediately even ceased to moan. "Oh, we come for provisions. Oh, dear! with what are you going to treat us?"

"Oh, with thong-seal meat."

"We are not used to it. Oh, with what are you going to treat us?"

"With ring-seal meat."

"We do not eat such things."

They pointed at the direction of the suffering one. "We want that one."

"Indeed, there is nothing there."

Then one of them entered the sleeping-room, caught the suffering one by the ankle and carried him out. As soon as they had caught him, they only did thus with their mouths, whp! And only his bones were left. His little mother cried. Then one of the (re'kkeñ) took off his overcoat, picked up the bones and put them into the overcoat. The ke'let [spirit] did so with the bones of that man. Then they went out and said, "We are going away, watch us." The old woman watched them when they were going to their sledges. They came to the sledges and emptied the overcoat, flinging its contents in the direction of the house. And there was that one just now eaten by them. They restored him, the suffering one, to life. He came to the house, quite naked. And he had acquired great shamanistic power. He entered the house naked.

He seemed to be out of his wits. All at once he would strike his own body with a boulder, and the boulder would crumble to a mere nothing. From every settlement in the neighborhood there came inquisitive people. They wanted to kill him, and all at once they struck him with a spear. But his body was as hard as stone. And they could not do anything.

After a while he married. His wife was very pretty. So the other people, the wrong-doers, felt a desire to have this woman. They took this shaman and carried him to the (open) country. There they strangled him, and he was killed. They took his wife and went with her to the house. Then they saw the one whom they had just killed sitting in the house, as before. "Oh, again! Oh, dear! What shall we do?" The woman was too pretty.

So they dug a cellar, filled it with insects, hairy grubs. These grubs soon became quite large in size. Then they called him.

[He said to the woman], "Oh, but now I must give up the struggle. Now they will take you for good. But you must remember to dig the ground in the cellar." They pushed him into the cellar. The grubs caught him and consumed him. Then (his enemies) took the woman.

As soon as night came, she went away quietly and followed a trail. This was the working-trail of her husband. She followed the trail, and found the duodenum of a reindeer hanging on a bush. She stopped there and made a fire. After that she departed again and felt thirsty. She saw a river quite filled with grubs, so she did not drink from that river. After a while she saw a lake. It was full of fish, but from this lake she could take a drink. At last she found her husband. He was standing outside a house, and was working at something. He said to her, "You have come?"

Meanwhile he had married also among the ke'let. The other wife said to her, "Put on my combination-suit!"

But her husband said, "Do not put it on, you will die."

His other wife said, "At least do look upon me!"

Her husband said, "Do not look upon her. She will take your soul." This was a ke'let woman: therefore, if she had looked upon her, she would have died immediately.

The other woman said again, "At least do sit on my pillow-bag!"

"Do not sit down. She will kill your child."

The human wife went out and busied herself in the outer tent. His other wife had made a cellar in the outer tent. In the darkness the human wife fell into that cellar. At last the child began to cry quite loud. Their husband said, "Oh, where is she?" He questioned his other wife. "Don't you know anything about her?"

"Oh, I do not know anything at all." Oho, the child was crying quite loud.

Their husband said, "Now, then, give me the drum!" Then he looked for his wife among the various Beings and could not find her. Then he set off (to visit) other kinds of Beings, those of the Morning Dawn, and she was not there. "Oh, oh, oh! How very extraordinary! I cannot find her." Again he struck the drum. This time he went to the Mid-Day, and searched for her there. She was not there.

He said to his ke'let wife, "It is you, who did (harm) to her." The ke'let wife answered him, "Why should I have done (harm) to my working-companion, my wife mate?"

"Now then, give me the drum again!" He searched for her among the Ground-Beings and saw her. He said to her, "Oh, what are you doing here?" She was starving.

She said, "It is your wife who made this cellar for me with the desire of murdering me."

Then her husband said, "Now let us leave her! She is bad, and so we shall be made childless."

"Oh," he said to his ke'let wife, "you are an experienced shaman! Do practice your art a little, and let us have some recreation."

"Aha, all right!" The woman practiced her art. The shaman, her husband, made a man of excrement, to give her the usual answers.

Then the woman practiced her art. The man made a fire all around the house, and flames flashed up. Meanwhile the mannikin made of excrement was giving answer, "Ġit, ġit, ġit." He proved to be quite lively. Then the ke'let woman felt quite warm, because the house was ablaze, and the fire approached the sleeping-room. The husband and his human wife went far away, taking with them their obsidian scraper.

At last the ke'let woman appeared from the sleeping-room, because she felt too hot. And the man made of excrement, who was giving answer, was downcast, because the excrement was melting. He could only call out feebly, "Ġit, ġit," because this lively answerer was melting in the heat.

Then the tip of the tongue of the ke'let woman jumped out and rushed in pursuit of the fugitives. It was quite swift, and soon drew near. The man said, "Now put down the obsidian scraper!" A big mountain originated, quite slippery. The tip of the tongue would climb up halfway, and then slide down again. Still, somehow it succeeded in crossing it, and continued the pursuit.

They stuck into the ground a piece of wood, and it turned into a dense wood. The wood had no openings, and was quite thick and dense. When passing through that wood, the tongue came to be covered with blood. Still it passed through it, and continued the pursuit. Then the man said to his wife, "Draw a line on the ground with the little finger of your left hand!" This time a river originated. As soon as the tongue left the bank, it was carried down by the current, because the river was flowing in rapids. Still it crossed the river. Then the man said to his wife, "Draw another line on the ground!"

They apply all kinds of means: it crosses again and pursues them. At last he ordered her to draw a line with soot of her lamp, using her right hand. When the tongue came to that soot river, it felt superstitious fear, and could not cross it. Then they went away and disappeared. The tongue probably turned back.

The human beings ascended to the Morning Dawn. There in the upper world they died of old age. The name of the shaman is Tai'pat. His son took his abode on the moon, and became a Sacrifice-Being. They throw up to him some thong, and in doing this they throw that thong upon every kind of game. They sacrifice also blood to the moon.

The mother was immortal. And she became the Left-Side Morning Dawn. Those probably were the people from the time of first creation.

Those that possess evil charms also dwell upon the moon in another place. Also Epilepsy was created. Of old the people were immortal. Also Coughing-of-Blood comes from there. And also a man who is visited by his enemy's anger and ceases to catch game, his misfortune is also from there. It is necessary to be on guard, else even the lucky one may feel want. Truly, the game is made scarce by supernatural means. Then it becomes hard to kill. The sacrificing-shamans also have been created from there, and every kind of "Beings" [benevolent spirits], at least part of them. The end. Let the wind cease!

RAVEN'S CREATION

Tradition Bearer: Aε'ttin·qeu

Source: Bogoras, Waldemar. "Chukchee Mythology." *The Jessup North Pacific Expedition,* ed. Franz Boas. *Memoir of the American Museum of Natural History New York.*

Vol. VIII. New York: The American Museum of Natural History New York, 1910, 151–154.

Date: 1900

Original Source: Chukchee

National Origin: Siberia

Native cultures on both sides of the Bering Strait cast the raven as creator, **trickster**, and **culture hero**. In the following Chukchee **myth**, raven (Ku'urkil, "the self-created one") brings the physical universe, trees, and animals into being. With the help of powerful female figures, his wife and spider woman, he populates the new universe with human beings.

Raven and his wife live together—the first one, not created by any one, Raven, the one self-created. The ground upon which they live is quite small, corresponding only to their wants, sufficient for their place of abode. Moreover, there are no people on it, nor is there any other living creature, nothing at all—no reindeer, no walrus, no whale, no seal, no fish, not a single living being. The woman says, "Ku'urkil [that is, Raven]."

"What?"

"But we shall feel dull, being quite alone. This is an unpleasant sort of life. Better go and try to create the earth!"

"I cannot, truly!"

"Indeed, you can!"

"I assure you, I cannot!"

"Oh, well, since you cannot create the earth, then I, at least, shall try to create a spleen-companion."

"Well, we shall see!" said Raven.

"I will go to sleep," said his wife.

"I shall not sleep," said Ku'urkil. "I shall keep watch over you. I shall look and see how you are going to be."

"All right!" She lay down and was asleep. Ku'urkil is not asleep. He keeps watch, and looks on. Nothing she is as before. His wife, of course, had the body of a raven, just like himself. He looked from the other side: the same as before. He looked from the front, and there her feet had ten human fingers, moving slowly. "Oh, my!" He stretches out his own feet—the same raven's talons. "Oh," says he, "I cannot change my body!"

Then he looks on again, and his wife's body is already white and without feathers, like ours. "Oh, my!" He tries to change his own body, but how can he do so? Although he chafes it, and pulls at the feathers, how can he do such a thing? The same raven's body and raven's feathers!

Again he looks at his wife. Her abdomen has enlarged. In her sleep she creates without any effort. He is frightened, and turns his face away. He is afraid to look any more. He says, "Let me remain thus, not looking on!" After a little while he wants to look again, and cannot abstain any longer. Then he looked again, and, lo! there are already three of them. His wife was delivered in a moment. She brought forth male twins. Then only did she awake from her sleep.

All three have bodies like ours, only Raven has the same raven's body. The children laugh at Raven, and ask the mother, "Mamma, what is that?"

"It is the father."

"Oh, the father! Indeed! Ha, ha, ha!" They come nearer, push him with their feet. He flies off, crying, "Qa, qa!" They laugh again. "What is that?"

"The father."

"Ha, ha, ha! the father!" They laugh all the time.

The mother says, "O children! You are still foolish. You must speak only when you are asked to. It is better for us, the full-grown ones, to speak here. You must laugh only when you are permitted to. You have to listen and obey." They obeyed and stopped laughing.

Raven said, "There, you have created men! Now I shall go and try to create the earth. If I do not come back, you may say, 'He has been drowned in the water, let him stay there!' I am going to make an attempt." He flew away. First he visited all the benevolent Beings and asked them for advice, but nobody gave it. He asked the Dawn—no advice. He asked Sunset, Evening, Mid-day, Zenith—no answer and no advice. At last he came to the place where sky and ground come together. There, in a hollow, where the sky and the ground join, he saw a tent. It seemed full of men. They were making a great noise. He peeped in through a hole burnt by a spark, and saw a large number of naked backs. He jumped away, frightened, ran aside, and stood there trembling. In his fear he forgot all his pride in his recent intentions.

One naked one goes out. "Oh! it seemed that we heard some one passing by, but where is he!"

"No, it is I," came an answer from one side.

"Oh, how wonderful! Who are you?"

"Indeed, I am going to become a creator. I am Ku'urkil, the self-created one."

"Oh, is that so?"

"And who are you?"

"We have been created from the dust resulting from the friction of the sky meeting the ground. We are going to multiply and to become the first seed of all the peoples upon the earth. But there is no earth. Could not somebody create the earth for us?"

"Oh, I will try!" Raven and the man who spoke flew off together. Raven flies and defecates. Every piece of excrement falls upon water, grows quickly, and becomes land. Every piece of excrement becomes land—the continent and islands, plenty of land. "Well," says Raven, "Look on, and say, is this not enough?"

"Not yet," answers his companion. "Still not sufficient. Also there is no fresh water; and the land is too even. Mountains there are none."

"Oh," says Raven, "shall I try again?" He began to pass water. Where one drop falls, it becomes a lake; where a jet falls, it becomes a river. After that he began to defecate a very hard substance. Large pieces of that excrement became mountains, smaller pieces became hills. The whole earth became as it is now.

Then he asks, "Well, how is it now?"

The other one looked. "It seems still not enough. Perhaps it would have been sufficient if there had not been so much water. Now some day the water shall increase and submerge the whole land, even the mountain-tops will not be visible."

Oh, Raven, the good fellow, flew farther on. He strains himself to the utmost, creates ground, exhausts himself, and creates water for the rivers and lakes. "Well, now, look down! Is this not enough?"

"Perhaps it is enough. If a flood comes, at least the mountain-tops will remain above water. Yes, it is enough! Still, what shall we feed upon?"

Oh, Raven, the good fellow, flew off, found some trees, many of them, of various kinds—birch, pine, poplar, aspen, willow, stone-pine, oak. He took his hatchet and began to chop. He threw the chips into the water, and they were carried off by the water to the sea. When he hewed pine, and threw the chips into the water, they became mere walrus; when he hewed oak, the chips became seals. From the stone-pine the chips became polar bears; from small creeping black birch, however, the chips became large whales. Then also the chips from all the other trees became fish, crabs, worms, every kind of beings living in the sea; then, moreover, wild reindeer, foxes, bears, and all the game of the land. He created them all, and then he said, "Now you have food! hm!" His children, moreover, became men, and they separated and went in various directions. They made houses, hunted game, procured plenty of food, became people.

Nevertheless they were all males only. Women there were none, and the people could not multiply. Raven began to think, "What is to be done?" A small Spider-Woman is descending from above on a very slender thread. "Who are you?"

"I am a Spider-Woman!"

"Oh, for what are you coming here?"

"Well, I thought, 'How will the people live, being only males, without females?' Therefore I am coming here."

"But you are too small."

"That is nothing. Look here!" Her abdomen enlarged, she became pregnant, and then gave birth to four daughters. They grew quite fast and became women. "Now, you shall see!"

A man came—that one who was flying around with Raven. He saw them, and said, "What beings are these, so like myself and at the same time quite different? Oh, I should like to have one of them for a companion! We have separated, and live singly. This is uncomfortable. I am dull, being alone. I want to take one of these for a companion."

"But perhaps it will starve!"

"Why should it starve? I have plenty of food. We are hunters, all of us. No, I will have it fed abundantly. It shall not know hunger at all."

THE SCABBY SHAMAN

Tradition Bearer: Unavailable

Source: Bogoras, Waldemar. "The Folklore of Northeastern Asia as Compared with that of Northwest America." *American Anthropologist* 4 (1902): 596–602.

Date: 1900

Original Source: Chukchee

National Origin: Siberia

The following narrative provides a thorough description of the Chukchee concept of the relative positions of and the relationships among the various worlds that make up their conception of the universe. Shamans, as seen in the tale, have the power to read thoughts, travel, and send envoys to other worlds, and raise the dead. In addition, the events reveal both the malevolent and benign sides of the Chukchee shamans.

There lived in the midland country a mighty shaman, Meemgin by name, rich in reindeer. He had eighty houses, all well filled with people, and eight large herds. His reindeer were like fallen boughs in a forest. His only son, Rintew, suddenly died. Meemgin sought for him throughout the whole earth, searched all worlds, and could not find him. In great sorrow he sat down in his sleeping-room and ceased to practice his art, not wanting to go out. His son's body lay before him on a skin. Three years it lay there. All the flesh had decayed and fallen off, because three years had passed by. The joints had become loosened, and the intestines had fallen out upon the skin and mingled with the decayed hair.

At last the father arose, called two of his working-men, and said, "Beyond the limits of the earth, where the earth meets the sky, lives the greatest of all shamans, Scabby-one. Call on him, and say to him, "Meemgin requests you to revive his son." He selected for his messengers four of his best reindeer. He hitched up, bade the men sit down, laid the reins on the reindeer, and put the

43

nooses around the men's wrists; then he charmed the heads and ears of the rein-deer, the sledges, and the harness. Then he blew on the reindeer, and they flew away high up in the air like geese.

Scabby-one has a hundred houses, which stand on the "attainable limit of the sky." He lies in his sleeping-room unable to move. His whole body is covered with scabs. His mouth and palate, hands and feet, lips and eyes, soles, and ends of his nails, are covered with scabs. His wife moves him about like a log. Before the arrival of the messengers he said to his wife, "Place me near the rear wall and give me my drum, I shall beat it for a while, I shall look around in a dream." He struck the drum, which hung on a line from the ceiling because he was unable to hold it. After awhile he said to his wife, "Have plenty of food cooked today. Guests are coming."

He had hardly finished speaking when the men came. "Oh!" said Scabby-one, "who are you, and who sent you?"

"We are Meemgin's men."

"How did you travel?"

"With reindeer."

"What are reindeer? What are they like?"

"Don't you know? What do you and your people live. on; there are so many of you? What kind of herds do you keep?"

"Herds of dogs. We live on dog meat." And indeed around the houses were walking innumerable dogs, large and fat, equal in size to reindeer. "Bring me your reindeer. I want to look at them." The men did so. The shaman looked them over and over, and said, "These reindeer are mine."

They thought, "Now, how are we going to get back?"

He guessed their thoughts immediately, and said, "Why do you doubt me? Do I need your reindeer?"

They thought again, "How can he take our reindeer? The dogs will tear them to pieces."

Well," replied Scabby-one, though nobody spoke a word, "I can so arrange that the dogs won't worry them. Bring the reindeer here." He charmed their ears, noses, and mouths; and the reindeer went to the houses, lifting their tails like dogs. "Let us go," said Scabby-one. There was a steep mountain close to the village. "Let us climb up," said he. They took him by his arms and carried him off to the top. "Now, lie down to sleep," said Scabby-one, and he made them lie down side by side. As soon as they had shut their eyes, he bade all the grass on the mountain-top to gather around his hands, and began to make a grass harness. When it was finished, he commanded it to tie itself around the necks of the sleepers. Then he took the reins and rode across the sky, alighting on the mountain near Meemgin's village. The two men did not know what had happened, but all the while remained in a deep sleep.

Scabby-one entered Meemgin's house. The father was sitting before the decayed body of his son, and did not even lift his head. "I have come at your call," said Scabby-one. "Although it may be difficult to find him who has been carried away, still an attempt may be made. And we are both equally gifted in magic. Have you sought for your son?"

"I have."

"Where have you sought?"

"Everywhere."

"Have you found anything?"

"Nothing."

"In the sky above our heads are numerous shining stars. Have you looked among them?"

"I have."

"Well?"

"Nothing."

"Oh, where can we find your son if he is not there?"

"In the sea yonder live numerous large animals, walruses, thongseals, small seals. Have you looked among them?"

"I have."

"Well?"

"Nothing."

"Oh, where can we find your son if he is not there?"

"In the depths of the sea live another set of medium-sized beings, white, red, gray fishes, naked or covered with scales. Have you sought among those?"

"I have."

"Well?"

"Nothing."

"Oh, where can we find him if not there!"

"On the bottom of the sea live a third set of small beings—shells, star-fish, worms, sea-bugs. Have you looked among those?"

"I have."

"Well?"

"Nothing."

"Oh, where shall we find him if not there?"

"On the land all kinds of animals are running around—reindeer, foxes, bears, hares, wolves. On the earth's skin creep various insects—white-capped beetles, centipedes, lady-bugs, and black beetles. Through the earth's bosom countless red worms are squeezing themselves. Have you sought among all these?"

"Yes."

"Well?"

"Nothing."

"Oh, where can we find him if he is not there?"

"On the earth's surface grow countless weeds and herbs. Have you looked among those, from one stalk to another?"

"I have."

"Have you looked over all willow-sprouts in the brush? Have you looked over all larch trees in the forest?"

"Yes, I have."

"The banks of the rivers are covered with pebbles. Have you sought among those?"

"Yes."

"Well?"

"Nothing."

"Oh, where shall we find your son if he is not there?"

"Everything visible and tangible, all that exists on the earth—have you looked over all that?"

"Yes."

"Well?"

"Nothing."

"Under this earth exists another world, belonging to the ke'let. It has skies of its own, stars, sun and moon, land and sea. Have you looked over all that exists on that earth, the stars above, the fishes in the sea, the herbs of the field, and the worms in the soil?"

"Yes."

"Well?"

"Nothing."

"Under that world there is a third world, peopled with men. It too has a sun and a moon, stars, and waters. Have you sought among the things in that world?

"Yonder, above the outer side of the sky, there is a world, belonging to the upper ke'let, with new stars, sun and moon, and sea. Have you looked among them?

"Over that world there exists one more, belonging to men, having earth and stars, with game in the forests, and fish in the water. Have you sought there?"

"Yes."

"Which world has more life, the upper or the under one?"

"They are just equal."

"Which sea has more fish, which land more game, which air more birds, the upper or the under one?"

"They are just equal."

"Have you searched the world of sunset."

"Yes."

"Have you searched the world of sunrise, and that of the last rays of the twilight, and that of the noon, and that of the midnight?"

"Yes, every one. He is nowhere."

"Highest of all there is a small world quite by itself, belonging to the female ke'let bird. Have you looked there?"

"No. I don't know it."

"He is probably there. The bird must have carried away your boy. I will go and see."

He rattled with the drum and sank into the earth. Then far away was heard the clatter of the drum. Rising out of the ground, he flew upward with his drum to the world of the ke'let bird.

Two worlds were on his road. Twice he went up, and then came down again, crossing his own tracks like a hunted fox. Then he reached the small world above, and found a large stone house. Looking down the vent-hole, he saw a sleeping-room of stone. As he looked through its walls, he saw the boy's soul pinioned with iron bands behind the large lamp, each joint tied separately. The WE-bird had carried him away for her food, and pinioned him there. Every morning she would ask, "What kind of food did you eat on earth?"

"I ate reindeer-meat, seal-blubber, walrus-fat, and whale-skin." Then she would fly away over the three worlds, and would bring back every kind of meat, which she gave him to make him fatter. Huge pieces of fat and meat were suspended from the stone walls of the house. At the time of the shaman's arrival the bird was not at home; but two re'kkeñ [evil being] dogs were tied in front of the entrance. Their ears kept turning toward every direction and noticed even the slightest noise. Scabby-one transformed himself into a mosquito and attempted to fly in, but the monsters snapped at him when they heard the buzzing of his wings. He turned into a gadfly, but to no avail. He turned into a white-capped beetle, but with no better success. "Oh, bad luck!" he cried. He turned into a carrion-fly, and in this shape flew into the house.

The re'kkeñ dogs did not hinder him, because there were many carrion-flies around the meat. He went into the sleeping-room, cut the soul's bonds and transformed it into another carrion-fly. They escaped from the house, and made their way toward their own world, crossing their tracks as before, and turning hither and thither like hunted foxes. When they had reached the lowest sky, however, the ke'let bird overtook them. She shouted, "Ko, ko, ko! Why did you carry away my little boy?"

"Stolen from the thief, restored to the owner," answered Scabby-one.

"Give him back to me, or I shall kill you!"

The beating of her wings made them flutter in the air like dry leaves. "Oh," said Scabby-one, "she really wants to kill me. Now I shall try." Pulling his right hand up his sleeve, he moved his little finger upwards. Fire fell down, singeing the ME-bird's wings. "Oh, oh!" cried she, "indeed, you want to kill me. Now it is my turn." She beat her wings again; but to no avail, for her feathers were singed.

Then Scabby-one killed the ke'let bird and burnt her to ashes. "Let us make haste," said Scabby-one. The people in Meemgin's house heard a distant clatter. It descended, sank into the earth, and after a while rose in the middle of the sleeping-room. "I have brought the boy. Let us make haste!" said Scabby-one. He called his ke'let and gave them the boy's soul to hold, and then looked hard at the decayed heap and gulped it down, spattering the putrid fluid about. Then

47

he shouted, "Bring a new white skin!" He vomited, and spat out the boy's body. All the bones were in their right places, and the flesh stuck to the bones again. Then he swallowed the body a second time and spat it out again. It was covered with new skin, all sores were smoothed down. He swallowed it a third time and spat it out again: blood mounted in the cheeks, and the lips almost wanted to speak. Scabby-one shouted, "Give me the soul!" He swallowed it and spat it down on the body. The soul passed through the body and stuck in the wall of the house. "The body is too cold," said Scabby-one; "it will not hold together." He swallowed the body a fourth time, warmed it in his stomach, and spat it out again on the skin. Then he flung the soul at it. "Oh, oh, oh!" sighed the boy, and then sat down on the skin.

Then Scabby-one was paid with a herd of reindeer. He said, "I am going now. Let all people enter the house and not come out again, because I shall take with me everything that is outside. You must take good care of the boy. Since he has come back from the dead, he will be a great shaman, even greater than I; but his heart and mind will incline to the bad. Still do not thwart him, for, if you do, he will over-power you." He beat his drum, began an incantation, and moved around the house. Presently the sound of the song, the rattling of the drum, and the clattering of the reindeer-hoofs were heard ascending higher and higher, first to the level of the vent-hole, then over it; then it gradually vanished upward.

As soon as Scabby-one had left, Rintew began to maltreat the people. He ran about in the night outraging every woman, even the oldest, and beating every man. The people were powerless against him. If they tried to work evil charms against him, he caught the charms, gathered the secret words of the would-be sorcerers in a mitten, and in the morning distributed them among their owners, saying, "This is your word, and this is yours, and this is yours."

His father began to repent of his restoration to life, for the people were coming every day with fresh complaints. Finally he said, "We will remove him to another world." He went towards sunset to find a ke'let witch.

The witch immediately complied with his request and went to Meemgin's house, carrying her long staff with blood-stained point. She posted herself in ambush before the entrance, but Rintew guessed her purpose, turned into a white goose, and flew away through the vent-hole. The witch gave chase, but he escaped to the land of darkness. Then he lost his way in the dark, wandered around, and suddenly stumbled over a screech-owl, which said, "Oh, oh! Don't kick me!"

"Why, are you a man too?"

"Yes, we are residents of this country, and have a house here in the darkness."

"If you are residents here, give me shelter; I am weary, and want to sleep."

"Come in," said the owl; and he put him under his wing. He continued, "When you want to pass water, ask for a tub."

The next day he went on, and had a similar adventure with an eagle. In the morning he bade him farewell. "There is your way," said the eagle, pointing straight ahead, where a small bright spot was visible, not larger than the hole made in the reindeer-skin by a reindeer fly's larva. "That light comes from the bright world. You must know, however, that the old woman has placed her staff across the entrance the whole length of the earth. She has transformed it into a high ridge of iron mountains. She has split herself in two, and each half keeps guard at one end of the staff. Do not try to go around the ridge, but climb across it, no matter how steep it may be. Go straight ahead to the place where you see a red line glowing, like red rust on iron. It is the blood with which the point of her staff is smeared. If you try to go around the ridge you will be killed. Even if you were the greatest of all shamans you would be killed."

In due time Rintew reached the mountains. They were quite vertical. Still he began to climb, clinging to the iron rocks with his nails and teeth. After a few steps he lost his foothold and tumbled down, but to his amazement he found himself on the other side of the mountains. Thus Rintew came back home and immediately resumed his old tricks. His father made a second attempt to put him out of the way, and summoned a little old woman of the Kerek tribe [a branch of the Siberian Koryak with a great reputation for sorcery], who suc-ceeded in depriving Rintew of his senses, and then sent him outdoors to fetch some small thing. Meanwhile she transformed the sleeping-room into one world, and the house into another. Thus when leaving the house he really went out of two worlds. He recovered his senses on a high cliff, astride of a piece of rock overhanging the sea, and in such a position that the slightest motion would have made him lose his hold. He sat there for five days, when at last he saw a raven flying by. "O, Rintew! man of many tricks, how did you get there?"

"I don't know."

"Get down!"

"I cannot."

"Will not any of your tricks make you free?"

"You had better come and help me."

"What are you ready to pay?"

"Anything you want."

"When you come home, kill every living thing for my food."

"All right."

"Then hold your breath and listen. One day and one night will pass away, then you will see a drift-log carried by on the waves. When it is close by, leap down from your seat; don't think whether you will break your neck or not. When you have alighted on the log, you will pass into the open sea. Shut your eyes, then you will reach the shore. When you hear the rattle of the pebbles, go ahead to firm ground. With eyes shut, take a handful of pebbles and pour them from one hand into the other. They will become softer and softer. When at last you feel that they are as soft as cloudberries, throw them behind you over your head. Then you will be lifted and carried across another sea. Shut your eyes and take a handful of pebbles, and pour them from hand to hand. Again you will be carried across the sea. On that shore you will find a small camping-site. Search it attentively; you will find a needle. Then on another camping-site you will find a round bead as red as a cloudberry. When you reach home, make a small drum, skin a black beetle to cover it, then perform the thanksgiving rites for the needle and the bead."

In another version the mountain-ridge, though it appears very high from afar, assumes its real size—that of the woman's staff—when he reaches it. After that he meets a large sea, which, when he reaches it, is seen to be a flat drum.

Thus Rintew came home and sent word to all his neighbors, saying he would perform a great ceremony. Meanwhile he began to construct a large wooden house, and finished it before all the people had assembled. They went into the building and entirely filled it. The Kerek witch came too, and he made a round mound for her seat, because she was so small. Then he started with his incantations. "Needle, come down!" he sang. It came down on a slender shining thread. He asked, "To whom shall I give it?"

"Me, me!" exclaimed all the women around. But the needle went up again, and vanished through the vent-hole.

Rintew beat his beetle-skin drum and chanted on. "When I wandered, lost among the unknown worlds, I held in my hand pebbles, which softened like cloudberries. Here is my cloudberry as hard as a pebble." The cloudberry bead came down on the shining metal thread. "Who will take this pendant?"

"I will!" cried all the women around, and tried to lay hold of it.

Again Rintew beat his beetle-skin drum, and chanted on, "When I sat on the stone pillar overhanging the sea, I promised some trifle to the black raven. You cackling one, take now your booty! You little Kerek witch, do you feel gratified? Your charms will fall down on your own wicked body." With a single leap he sprang out through the vent-hole. The beetle-skin drum followed, and, suddenly expanding, stuck in the opening. All doors and exits vanished. Of its own accord the drumstick began to beat the drum from beneath. The bead commenced to enlarge; at first it grew to the size of the upper piece of a drill, then to that of an infant's head; then it became as large as a reindeer's paunch, then as a blubber-bag, then as the carcass of a fat walrus, larger and larger, filling the house, and squeezing the people to the beams. The drumstick rattled on, the bead grew, blood oozed through the beams, the house burst and fell down. A bloody stream flowed to the sea from Rintew's building.

Thus he exterminated all his people, and became the ancestor of a new tribe.

THE AI'WAN SHAMANS

Tradition Bearer: Rike'wġi

Source: Bogoras, Waldemar. "Chukchee Mythology." *The Jessup North Pacific Expedition*, ed. Franz Boas. *Memoir of the American Museum of Natural History New York*. Vol. VIII. New York: The American Museum of Natural History New York, 1910, 7–25.

Date: 1900
Original Source: Chukchee
National Origin: Siberia

The following narrative begins as a history of the enmity between two Chukchee bands. By its conclusion, the narrative has changed focus to the nature and acquisition of shamanic powers and the rituals used to treat the spirits that provide power to the practitioners.

Once in olden times, the Ai'wan and the people of St. Lawrence Island were at war. One man from this shore met with misfortune through the wind. While on the ice fields he was carried away and spent two months on the ice fields. One day there was a fog, and no land was to be seen. Then he heard the roaring of walrus. Still he remained with head drawn back into his coat. Then he was visited by another man, by a shaman, who found him sleeping on [the surface of] the ice and awakened him, "Oh, how wonderful, you are here?" The other one looked up and, indeed, he wept aloud. The shaman said, "Do not weep! A settlement, though of St. Lawrence people, is quite near."

Then, suddenly, they saw it. They came ashore. A number of houses were there. The people were clad in bird-skin clothes. Those of St. Lawrence Island are also Ai'wan, their language being the same. They took hold of the strangers, they took captive those two men. They bound the shaman, the other one they killed with a drill, having perforated his head at the crown. After that they set free the shaman, intending to keep him as a slave.

He passed there only one night. When they were about to go to sleep, he went out and shouted toward the sea, calling the walrus spirit. Immediately from afar came the walrus. Oh, oh, the walrus came. Indeed, they were (as numerous) as sand. He walked along over their heads and went away. Then also the walrus which he had passed would come up in front. An old male walrus said, "Oh, now we are nearing the land. Your people are eager to pursue us. Oh, therefore some of us are going away. It seems that your people are bad." Oh, he said to two walrus, two year old ones, "Let us carry away our guest." By one of them he was made to sit on its body, and it dashed on, plunging along. The old walrus, the one that was most clever, followed it (like a leader). When one walrus got tired, he was made to sit on the other one.

When night came, they found a floe of sea-ice. The old walrus said, "Oh, all the people are tired. Let the people go to sleep." They put the man on [the surface of] the sea-ice. The old walrus said to the man, "Oh, you may sleep on [the surface of] the sea-ice. We will sleep by your side on the water." They inflated the crops on their throats and floated on the water like bladders. In due time the old walrus awoke. "Now let the people go along. Oh, my! you must be hungry."

"Oh yes!" said the man. It was still dark. The old walrus dived to the bottom of the sea and saw something like the [motionless star] Polar Star. He bent over it and it proved to be a shellfish. The little man was fed with those shellfish. They were quite warm and even hot. Probably the walrus cook them secretly, therefore they may have been hot.

They set off and moved on till midnight. The old walrus said, "It seems we are nearing land." They moved on, and before the land was near, the dawn came. "Oh, you must be hungry again."

"Oh yes!" The walrus again plunged down. This time he brought some shellfish of oblong shape. He ate again. "Now we are going to leave you. As soon as we shall see a floe of sea-ice, though a small one, we shall leave you on it." Then they saw one. "Well, your people will be here this [dawn] morning. We are beginning to feel afraid." They put him on the ice. "Oh, what are you doing, you are leaving me alone."

"It is quite certain, that they will come."

Then he was told by the walrus, "When you are overtaken by sleep, roar like a walrus, when you are going to sleep." Then the walrus dashed on, plunging on the way. They went away, very far to the open sea. Soon after that he began to be overtaken by sleep. So he roared like a walrus and immediately turned into one.

When the dawn of the day came, some people approached in a boat and began to move along towards him. Before they were too near, he awoke. Just when the bowman was going to throw the harpoon, he said, "Oh, what are you going to do unto me?"

"Oh, dear! Is it not wonderful? You have become a walrus, and we came near killing you. Oh, whence did you come back?"

"Truly, it is bad. We come from a settlement of men. My companion, however, is not with me. Those people are wrong-doers. They drilled through his head and killed him." He entered the house. "Oh, what news?"

"Truly, it is pitiful. Evil-doers are those people."

The summer came. They went to war, the men of Uñi'sak, and probably from every neighboring settlement a number of boats assembled. Then a large company of boats set off. All boats were overloaded (with warriors). Before they were too near, they saw a cluster of houses of the St. Lawrence people standing on the seashore. In the rear of the houses was a bay of St. Lawrence Island; there actually a large part of the boatsmen went ashore. They walked along in the fog from the rear, just out of sight of the islanders. Then an old man, one of the crew said, "Oh, howl like wolves!" They had not been seen by the St. Lawrence people and they were not expected by them. Now, when they uttered their howls, another old man, one from St. Lawrence Island, said, "Oh, now they are coming." The young men said, "But we are on an island."

"Give answer to them!" So they roared like walrus. Then the old man, one of the boat's crew, said again, "Oh, where are you? Now they have become our quarry."

The larger part, those who had landed in the rear (of the houses), were still unknown to the St. Lawrence people. Those from St. Lawrence island hid by the seashore. But those from the boats attacked them from the rear and a slaughter ensued. The St. Lawrence women were already strangling themselves from mere fright. The others, at the same time, were mincing a large quantity of walrus blubber with their kitchen-knives, (preparing a meal for the victors). It was a great slaughter. Many St. Lawrence women were put on board the boats and brought over here.

Some years passed. The fourth year, the St. Lawrence people went to war. They landed in the night-time and found the people sleeping. So they started to murder them, thrusting their spears from outside under the outer tent-cover, all around the sleeping-room, and stabbing the sleepers. A small orphan child hid himself somewhere near the house, while they were still killing some of the sleepers, and before they had time to go to another house. He awakened all the neighbors. They rushed out. Then those from St. Lawrence Island fled to the open sea. Two men stayed behind on the ice-floe.

They lived on the ice-floe. Before the strong winds of autumn begin to blow, they came to steal some meat and so were taken captive. "Oh, we will not kill you." They, however, struggled on, not heeding these words. The next night, they stole some warm clothes and departed again. They went away together over the sea-ice, they walked along over the newly frozen sea. The ice was salt and yielded under every step.

Then they came to the shore. A St. Lawrence old man asked them, "Well, what kind of men are the land-people?"

"Oh, they are deucedly good."

"Oh, Oh," said the St. Lawrence old man, "Now let the (two) people become friendly to each other."

Summer came again. "Oh well, now let the people set off." Then the people of St. Lawrence Island came over here. They brought a quantity of wooden vessels, walrus hides, everything they had. They landed and the people became friends. So they distributed their vessels among our people. An old man from this side said, "Indeed, what will you give as return presents?" The visitors were clothed in bird skins. "What kind of skins are these?"

"Reindeer-skins."

"And what is a reindeer?" Then they showed them the reindeer-muzzles. They examined them. They said, "Oh, thus they are; like the holes in a boat cover, (namely in the walrus-hide cover, all along the border). Now then, eat some of the meat!" They cooked fat meat. "Oh, just like blubber!" They ate of it. "Oh, oh, quite exquisite!"

After that they went away. One man was left. He was a shaman, and he was treated just like the former one (that is, he was bound). When winter came, they set him free. The shaman had a sledge. So he departed in the night-time. He was hauling the sledge loaded with walrus-blubber. He moved on until he felt tired. It was full moon. At that time he was overtaken by another shaman, one from the western country. That shaman also was hauling a sledge. The former heard only a noise above; that western shaman was flying along. On both sides he had long knives, which he used as wings. The other shaman who was hauling the sledge was startled and fled. When he was approached by the other one, just on his arrival, he also fled up with his sledge. Still, the other one was about to overtake him. Before he could catch up with him, (the other one) dived under ground, only the sledge remained there on the ground. Oh, the other one was unable to pursue him, the western shaman.

Then he sat down. "Oh, oh, oh; indeed; indeed! Not without reason was he talked about. Really I am much interested in seeing you." It seems that shaman was called Ke'mneku. "No shaman from any country whatsoever can vanquish me." Then Ke'mneku spoke to the ground downward. "Nevertheless you have frightened me. I thought you were a ke'let. Now come here." He appeared. "Give me your necklace. Let me give you this knife in exchange."

"No, I do not want to give it to you."

"Then I shall not be believed. Please, do give it to me."

"No, I won't."

"Then I will give you this big knife. Please, give me your necklace."

Then they exchanged their (assistant) spirits. And the other one gave him the necklace. He gave him the knife. The western shaman said to the other one, "Now then, move about with the knives." All at once the other one moved upwards in this manner. Then Ke'mneku said, after they had exchanged even their bodies, "Well, now put on the necklace; go away and fly up, just as I did. You will fly up, then sink down to the ground and plunge in." The other one flew up. Then, slowly moving he fell down, plunged into the ground, but (when he was in as far as) the middle of his body, he stuck fast. "Oh, I have been unable to do it. Give me your wrist-bands!"

"I will not give them to you."

"Then I will give you the tassel from my back. It is my tail, my guide in motion."

Then he consented. The western shaman said to him, after the tassel had been given [then he said to him], "Well now, fly up just as I did." He [himself] flew up and just went up clattering. The shaman from St. Lawrence Island said to the other one, "Well, now it is your turn." He gave him the wrist-bands. "You will fly up, then you will fall down again and plunge into the ground." Then the western shaman flew up. Slowly moving he fell down. Then he plunged into the ground and was submerged as in water. After a while he reappeared. He said, "Oh, oh, indeed; Ke'mneku is talked about. How is it now? I am unable (to pursue him). Still before this in my own mind I thought I could hardly be pursued by anyone. Oh, oh, truly; Ke'mneku has been talked about. How is it now? You have vanquished me. Oh, let us go away!" Then the western shaman flew up. They were traveling at night. In one night they traveled flying through every land. Ke'mneku said. "I am going away."

The western shaman came home. He said to his companions, "I saw a shaman from St. Lawrence Island. I was unable to follow him."

"You lie."

"Indeed, it is true."

"Well then, what kind (of a shaman) was he?" He showed the necklace. "This is his necklace."

"You lie. You have stolen it somewhere."

"Indeed, no!"

"Well then, what kind (of a shaman) was he?" Then he flew up with easy motion, then fell back to the ground and plunged in, as though it had been water. "Oh, really, you have acquired new shamanistic powers."

His father said to him, "Well now, let us see, whether he has really acquired new shamanistic powers. Go on, look for Children's-Death." He flew away night after night and traveled among all kinds of beings. Nothing. He came back to the house. By his father he was told, "What is the matter with you? You cause delay. Oh, surely he lied (to the people)." He departed again. This time he went underground. Then he came back and said, "I have been unable to do it." By his father he was told, "Oh, what is the matter with you?" By his son, the western shaman, (the father) was told, "Oh, but I could not find him among any kind of beings."

After that he went to the Being-of-Darkness. Then at last he saw a man; a mere mouth. This was Children's-Death. By the Darkness he was questioned, "What do you want?"

"By my father I have been sent. I was told, 'Go and look for Children's-Death'."

"Oh, oh, and for what purpose?"

"Only to show him to the people."

"Well, surely, he is in my neighbor's house."

He went there. There was an old man who dwelled in those regions, a mere mouth, smeared all around with dried blood. The shaman entered. "Oh, at last I see you." The other one questioned him.

[He replied], "By my father you are bidden to come."

"And for what purpose?"

"He said thus, 'I want to see the old woman yonder'." She refused to go.

"For what purpose?"

"They only want to see you. My father said, 'Go and look for Children's-Death'."

"Oh, but I refuse."

"Please come! It seems they will not believe me."

Then she consented. She said to him, "Sit down on my body." Then she flew up with him. A great noise spread around. It was very loud. And the whole world clattered and resounded. His father said, "Oh, what is the matter again? The world is full of noise. It appears that really he has acquired new shamanistic powers." In coming he let her plunge underground, and after that appear in the outer tent. "What luck?"

"It seems that this time I brought Children's-Death."

"Now bring her here. I want to see her." She was as large as a tree. Still she decreased in size very quickly; and he put her on the palm of his hand before he showed her to them, so small had she come to be. Before she dwindled away, he spat on her, and she grew again. Then, on becoming thus, she decreased again in size. He made her plunge underground, then he made her appear. Then he took her in the other hand, and she became as large as before.

"Oh, that is you! You are the source of sorrow among every kind of beings, to those that have children. To whomsoever a child is born, it dies suddenly, and you are the cause of it. You are Children's-Death. Now we will bind you." They tied her with thongs, but she broke them all. Then they tied her with a grass-blade. She was struggling the whole night, but the grass-blade proved to be tough, (it could) not be broken by her. The whole night through there was clamor and weeping. Then they said to her, "Will you do evil the same as before?"

"Oh, no! Not now; not from now on. I will cease doing so."

"Oh, but it seems to us, you will do evil again. You are bad, you are the source of trouble. You kill new-born children."

"Oh, no! I have been made to obey by the angry ones (evil-minded conjurers). From now on, I shall not obey them. I repent having done so (heretofore). Oh, indeed! Set me free."

"But it seems you will do evil again. Well, we will set you free."

"From now on, I will turn to the Life-Giving-Being. Now the new-born child shall grow up, it shall die only in its old age." Then they set her free.

She departed. Darkness asked her, "Well, how were you treated by the human beings?"

"Oh, I have been cruelly treated by them. Now I repent. Whatsoever I may be ordered to do by the angry ones, from now on I shall not obey them." Darkness said, "That is your way. Though you say now, 'I shall not obey the angry ones,' still you lie. It seems, when you will be hungry again, you will comply again with their requests." Nevertheless, when the angry ones spoke again, she paid no attention to them. Oh, but are the children dying only owing to the angry ones?

Again the (shaman's) father sent him, "Go and look for Death, by whom people are killed." Then again he sought among all kinds of beings, but could not find him. "What luck?"

"Oh, nothing."

"Oh, I thought you were a shaman!" He departed again, this time underground. Again he could not find Death, and came back. "What luck?"

"Oh, I could not find him."

"Oh, but what is the matter with you?" That was a wonderful father. Then he traveled along the crevices in the ground, and saw Iu'metun. Iu'metun was black like coal, and had only three fingers on each hand. "Oh, that is you. You are the source of death." Iu'metun said, "What do you want?"

"I have come to visit you."

"Oh, now you are meddling again with my affairs. No live being has ever been able to see me, and now you have seen me. I was not, however, to be seen by anybody."

"My father bids you come."

"Where to and for what purpose?"

"They only want to see you." They departed. "What luck?"

"Yes, now I have brought him."

"Well, bring him here."

Then he showed him to them. He was no larger than a reindeer-fly. "Ah, here you are! You are Iu'metun. You kill everybody without illness. We say, 'How wonderful, what has killed him?' And it is you."

"No, I am not the one."

"Indeed, you are the one. If you are not the one, then, indeed, I cannot become black. But if you are really Iu'metun, I shall become black from you."

"No, truly, I am not the one. Set me free." Indeed, he renounced his own body. "Now we will bind you." Meanwhile he was induced to touch the man's skin. All at once the place where he had been touched reddened, and then became black. "What now, then? Indeed, you are Iu'metun."

"Oh, truly I am not he."

"Yes, you are. You are evil, you are a source of trouble. Why do you meddle with the affairs of man?"

"Oh, the Ground-Beings (evil spirits) tell me to do so."

"Also, when a man is alone in the open country, you meddle with him. Oh, we will tie you up."

"Oh, set me free! From now on treat the clefts of the ground with offerings. And when a shaman accuses me as the cause of suffering of a man, that shaman shall be able to cure him. Every source of illness of man shall be seen by the shamans, and even by merely breathing on the skin, they shall set (the sick) right. Also when a ransom is paid to the spirits, a single bead shall be used by the shaman as a sufficient payment. But when in a serious illness a reindeer is presented as ransom, let it be a buck, well broken, because if it struggles, it is not good for the suffering body. Also by incantations suffering shall be alleviated."

Then the old man said to him, "You lie."

"No, I do not. I was not a murderer of my own free will; the Ground-Beings told me so. Set me free. Now, even when an orphan-child wanders alone in the open country, I shall not meddle with him. Indeed, also an orphan-child shall be able to sleep safely in the open country."

"But surely, you deceive us."

"No, indeed! Set me free. Now I shall turn to the Merciful-Being, and I will help every orphan-child. I have been induced to do wrong by the Ground-Beings.

From now on, let the Ground-Beings be placated by offerings. Let a dog be killed, let it be stabbed (with an iron knife). Also let blood be sprinkled on the ground. Sausages let also be [stabbed] offered. The Sea-Beings also must be made friendly, When the people are unable to find game, something small may be used, a small root of *Polygonum viviparum*. It must be thrown into the sea. Then sea-game shall appear again, and all kinds of sea-game shall be taken. Also a man who has trouble with his young children may call as a shaman a little old beggar-woman. Then the child's clothes must be pinned in some unusual manner. Let them be quite friendly to the conjurer. And when the conjurer comes, let them give her some small presents. She may take home some sausage. A part of it has to be thrown to the Incantation-Beings. Then the child shall cease to suffer. Oh, set me free! They set him free. Unfortunately he proved a liar. The end.

JAPAN

THE SUN GODDESS AND THE STORM GOD

Tradition Bearer: Unavailable

Source: Colum, Padric. *Orpheus: Myths of the World*. New York: The Macmillan Company, 1930, 245–248.

Date: Unavailable

Original Source: Unavailable

National Origin: Japan

Shinto the indigenous religion of Japan focuses on the veneration of both ancestors and nature spirits. Ama-terasu is the primary deity in the Shinto pantheon, and the Japanese imperial family claimed descent from her. Uzume is the Shinto goddess of joy and happiness; her name means "whirling." Her dances that provoked Ama-terasu to leave her cave continue to be formed in traditional rites. The sword Kusanagi-no-Tsurugi ("grass-cutting sword") is enfranchised in this **myth** as a treasure that links the Japanese imperial family to the god. See "A Miraculous Sword" (page 64) for another traditional narrative concerning this weapon.

That lady, the resplendent Sun Goddess, was born out of the left eye of the august Father creator, and her brother, the powerful Storm God, was born out of his nostrils. To her was given the Plain of High Heaven for dwelling with the Earth for dominion, and to him the Sea was given for dwelling and dominion.

But between Ama-terasu, the Sun Goddess, and Susa-no-wo, the Storm God, there was strife. The resplendent Goddess was beneficently careful of things that grew upon the earth; she strove against the evil spirits that were abroad on the earth, and she was especially careful of the temples that men built for their celebrations of the harvest rites. Her powerful brother had no care for these things. He would leave his own realm and go clamorously upon the earth. He would strip off branches and level trees, and tear out of the ground the crops that his beneficent sister had cared for. He would break down all that guarded men from the evil spirits that were abroad upon the earth. He would make turmoil in the temples and prevent the harvest rites from being celebrated. All the work whose beginnings on earth were helped by Ama-terasu, that shining and beneficent lady, were destroyed by Susa-no-wo, the bearded and impetuous Storm God.

Once he ascended into High Heaven. He came before the Heavenly River, the Yasu. The Goddess cried out, "You who would destroy all I have given growth to upon earth, have you come to darken and lay waste the Plain of High Heaven?" The Storm God declared that he had come to establish peace and trust between himself and his resplendent sister.

Then on the bank of the Heavenly River, the Yasu, the powerful Storm God and the resplendent Sun Goddess exchanged tokens of their trust in one another. To the Storm God the Sun Goddess gave her jewels; to the Sun Goddess the Storm God gave his sword. Then, from the spring whence rose the Heavenly River, the Yasu, Ama-terasu, the Sun Goddess, and Susa-no-wo, the Storm God, drank. They put into their mouths the tokens they had received from each other: from the sword that the Goddess put into hers was born a beautiful and courageous boy; from the jewels that the Storm God put into his, were born shining Gods of growth and power.

Thereafter the cocks, the long-singing birds of the Eternal Land, crowed everywhere upon the earth, prophesying the flourishing of all growing things and the checking of all the evil spirits that went abroad upon the earth. Men gathered full crops in and celebrated the harvest rites in temples that were blown upon no more. The beneficent lady, Ama-terasu, had her way upon earth, and the powerful God, Susa-no-wo, stayed in his own realm, the sea.

Out of the sea he went once more. He went clamorously upon the earth, destroying growing things, and breaking down the guards put up against the evil spirits that went abroad upon the earth. He threw down the temples and scattered the people who had come to celebrate the harvest rites. Then Ama-terasu would look no more upon the earth that her brother had wasted. She went within a cavern and would not come forth. Confusion came upon the eight million Gods, and the spirits of evil wrought havoc through the whole of creation.

She came forth again. The Gods seized upon Susa-no-wo, cut off his great beard, and took from him all his possessions. Then he went wandering upon the earth, but he was no longer able to work havoc upon it. He came to the mountains by the side of the ocean; he planted the mountains with the hairs of his beard, and the hairs became the Forest of Kii. The forest was his dominion; men gave homage to him as Lord of the Forest. It was he who slew the dragon of that land. Once, with its eight heads rearing up, the dragon stood in his way. Susa-no-wo slew it and cut it to pieces. In the dragon's tail there was a sword-a sword that would be ever victorious—and that sword Susa-no-wo sent to Ama-terasu as his tribute to her and to her descendants.

Many were the dragons that were in the land that Susa-no-wo had come to. Once when he was on his way from his forest to the sea he came upon an old man and woman who were weeping upon the bank of a river. They told him the reason of their grief. Every year a maiden was given to the dragon of the place, and this time their daughter was being given him. The fury of the Storm God was aroused when he heard this: he went to where the dragon waited by the river, and he destroyed him, cutting him to pieces. Susa-no-wo then took the maiden for his wife. They lived in that land of Izumo, and they and their children after them had the lordship of that place.

Another God came to woo his daughter. He came within his house when Susa-no-wo was lying in slumber on his mat. The tied the hairs of his head to the beams of the roof, and he took in his hands the things that were Susa-no-wo's most cherished possessions-his sword, his bow and arrows, and his harp. He lifted the maiden up and carried her off with the treasures. But the harp cried out as it was taken in the hand of the younger God. Susa-no-wo awakened. He could not even move his head since his hair was tied to the beams of the roof, and he had to loosen each strand of hair before he could go in pursuit of the one who had carried off his daughter and his treasures. At last he freed himself; led by the sound of the harp that still played of itself he followed that one. But when he came to where Oh-kuni-nushi was with the maiden whom he had carried off, Susa-no-wo said, "You have great craft, and because you have I will give you this maiden and all my possessions; I will take you for my son-in-law."

Together Susa-no-wo and Oh-kuni-nushi ruled the Izumo, and, through his daughter, the descendants of Susa-no-wo peopled that land. But Susa-no-wo knew, and Oh-kuni-nushi knew, that their children would have to give place to the children of the resplendent Sun Goddess who were destined to be the rulers of the Eight Islands.

When Ama-terasu, on account of the destructiveness which her brother had wrought, had hidden herself in the cavern, the Gods had come together and had consulted as to how Ama-terasu's beneficence might be brought into the world once more. They had brought the cocks, the long-singing birds of the Eternal Land, and had placed them outside the cavern; they had lighted fires that made such a brightness before the cavern that the cocks crowed perpetually. They had the Goddess Uzume dance for all their company. On an upturned tub she had danced, and her dancing and her laughter had made all the Gods laugh loudly. Their laughter and merriment and the sound of the cocks crowing had filled the air and had made the earth shake. Ama-terasu, within the cavern, had heard the merry din. She had wondered what merriment could be in the world while she was within the cavern. She had put a finger out and had made a little hole in the rock that closed her in. She had looked out at the crowd of the Gods, and she had seen the dancing and laughing Goddess. Then Ama-terasu had laughed. One of the strong-armed Gods had put his hand where the hole was in the rock and had made a wider opening. Then a long-armed God had put his hands within and had drawn the resplendent Goddess to the wide opening. Light immediately had filled the world. The cocks had crowed louder, and the evil spirits had drawn away. The Gods were made joyful, and the din of their merriment had filled all creation.

So the resplendent Sun Goddess had come back to the world. Then it was that the Storm God, banished, had gone forth and founded a new realm for himself. And the realm he had founded, he knew, was to pass to the descendants of the resplendent Goddess.

After the coming-forth of the Goddess from her cavern the growing plants flourished upon the earth, and the evil spirits were kept away. The cocks' crew. The harvests were brought in, and the harvest rites celebrated. The temples stood unshaken and unbroken. The banished Storm God went back to his own realm, and his descendants bore rule in the Eight Islands. Then the resplendent Goddess willed to have her grandson take possession of the Islands. He came; he faced the rulers of the land armed with the sword that must always be victorious. They gave him the land and they gave him power over all that was visible. But they kept for themselves the hidden world and all the powers of divination and sorcery. And since that time the children of the Sun Goddess bear rule in our land.

THE FIRST PEOPLE

Tradition Bearer: Unavailable

Source: Colum, Padric. *Orpheus: Myths of the World*. New York: The Macmillan Company, 1930, 248–250.

Date: Unavailable

Original Source: Unavailable

National Origin: Japan

In the Shinto pantheon, Izanagi is the primal sky deity who is the personification of light and the heavens. Izanami, his wife and sister, is his complementary opposite, the personification of the earth and darkness. Together they created Onogoro, the first island of the Japanese archipelago, the island where the first gods and humans were born. The **myth** of their creation of the next stage of the universe incorporates familiar **motifs** such as the obstacle flight, the descent to the underworld, and the imposition of death on humans.

There were clouds and mists; there were divine generations who came and who passed away, leaving only him who was The-Lord-in-the-center-of-the-Heavens and the august God and Goddess who stood each side of him. And then were produced Izana-gi and Izana-mi, the man and the woman. They went across the rainbow bridge. The man held his spear downwards and drops flowed from it; the drops hardened and held themselves together and they formed a place on which the Primeval Couple, Izana-gi, the man, and Izana-mi, the woman, could stay. But the mists were still all around them.

They had children there: Wind-child and Forest-child, Waterfall-child and Mountain-child, Stream-child and Field-child, Sea-child and Islands-children. They had children who became the ancestors of men and women. When Wind-child grew up he swept away the mists; the spaces became clear. Then Izana-mi bore the Fire-children. After their birth she sickened; then she was seen no more above the ground.

Izana-gi went down into Meido, Place of Gloom, to find her. He went down through a cave; he went into depths following her voice. She told him not to come farther; she told him not to look where she was. But Izana-gi disobeyed her command. He lighted a torch and looked towards where he heard her voice.

For a little while there was a light in the pale-grey land of Meido. Izana-gi saw Izana-mi. Her eyes were hollow, and her lips were fleshless, and her forehead was a bone. The torch went out, and Izana-mi cursed her husband for having looked on her in the Place of Gloom. She said she would not let him go back to the world of their children, and that she would make him remain a dweller in Meido.

Izana-gi ran back; but Izana-mi pursued him and she called upon the dread dwellers of the Place of Gloom to catch him and hold him. Izana-gi, as he ran, took the shoots of bamboo and the wild grapes that grew upon the comb that was in his hair and flung them to the dwellers in the Place of Gloom. They stopped to eat the shoots and the grapes. Then he ran on. He came to the cave through which he had entered the Place of Gloom. And here Izana-mi, angry still, nearly caught him. He ran through the cave, and he laid hold of a rock that was outside and closed the cave up. Still Izana-mi was angry; she said that on account of his looking upon her in the Place of Gloom she would draw down into Meido a thousand people every day. "Then I shall bring to birth a thousand and a half a thousand people every day," Izana-gi said.

He went out of the cave and he bathed in a stream that flowed by it. He washed off the pollution that came from what he had touched in the Place of Gloom. What he washed off became stains on the water. And these stains became beings who brought a thousand people every day down to Meido. Therefore was Izana-gi, through his folk, under the necessity of bringing into birth a thousand and a half a thousand people every day. And because, through the willfulness of Izana-gi and the anger of Izana-mi, the Primeval Pair became separated, there has been ever since death and separation in the world.

A MIRACULOUS SWORD

Tradition Bearer: Unavailable

Source: Smith, Richard Gordon. *Ancient Tales and Folklore of Japan*. London: A. and C. Black, 1908, 56–60.

Date: Unavailable

Original Source: Japan

National Origin: Japan

In spite of the approximate dates and the names of historical individuals provided in the following narrative, the tale walks a fine line between **myth** and **legend**. At least as important as the exploits of Yamato-dake no Mikoto is the confirmation of the sacred status of the "grass-cutting sword," a weapon that received its name in recognition of its powers to thwart the assassination attempt on the protagonist in Suruga Province.

About the year 110 B.C. there lived a brave prince known in Japanese history as Yamato-dake no Mikoto. He was a great warrior, as was his son, who is said to have been a husband to the Empress Jingo—I presume a second one, for it could not have been the Emperor who was assassinated before the Empress's conquest of Korea. However, that does not very much matter to my story, which is merely the legend attached to the miraculous sword known as the Kusanagi no Tsurugi (the grass-cutting sword), which is held as one of the three sacred treasures, and is handed down from father to son in the Imperial Family. The sword is kept at the Atsuta Shrine, in Owari Province.

At the date given by my interpreter, 110 B.C. (I should add "or thereabouts," allowing large margins), Yamato-dake no Mikoto had been successful at all events in suppressing the revolutionists known as the Kumaso in Kyushu. Being a man of energy, and possessing a strong force of trained men, he resolved that he would suppress the revolutionists up on the north-eastern coasts.

Before starting, Yamato-dake no Mikoto thought he should go to Ise to worship in the temples, to pray for divine aid, and to call on an aunt who lived near. Yamato-dake spent five or six days with his aunt, Princess Yamato Hime, to whom he announced his intention of subduing the rebels. She presented him with her greatest treasure—the miraculous sword—and also with a tinder-and-flint-box.

Before parting with her nephew Yamato Hime no Mikoto said, "This sword is the most precious thing which I could give you, and will guard you safely through all dangers. Value it accordingly, for it will be one of the sacred treasures."

(Legend says that in the age of the gods Susanoo-no Mikoto once found an old man and a woman weeping bitterly because a mammoth eight-headed snake had devoured seven of their daughters, and there remained only one more, whom, they felt sure, the eighth serpent's head would take. Susanoo-no Mikoto asked if they would give him the daughter if he killed the snake to which they gladly assented. Susanoo filled eight buckets with sake-wine, and put them where the serpent was likely to come, and, hiding himself in the vicinity, awaited events. The monster came, and the eight heads drank the eight buckets full of sake, and became, naturally, dead-drunk. Susanoo then dashed in and cut the beast to bits. In the tail he found a sword—the celebrated and miraculous sword "Kusanagi no Tsurugi," the grass-cutting sword of our story.)

After bidding farewell to Yamato Hime no Mikoto, the Prince took his departure, setting out for the province of Suruga, on the eastern coast, to find what he could hear, it being in a turbulent state; and it was there that he ran into his first danger, and that his enemies laid a trap for him, through their knowledge that he was fond of hunting.

There were some immense rush plains in Suruga Province where now stands the village of Yaitsu Mura ("Yaita" means "burning fields"). It was resolved by the rebels that one of them should go and invite Yamato-dake to come out and hunt, while they were to scatter and hide themselves in the long grass, until the guide should lead him into their midst, when they would jump up and kill him. Accordingly, they sent to Yamato-dake a plausible and clever man, who told him that there were many deer on the grass plains. Would he come and hunt them? The man volunteered to act as guide. The invitation was tempting; and, as he had found the country less rebellious than he had expected, the Prince accepted.

When the morning arrived the Prince, in addition to carrying his hunting-bow, carried the sword given him by his aunt, the Princess Yamato. The day was windy, and it was thought by the rebels that as the rushes were so dry it would be more sure, and less dangerous to themselves, to fire the grass, for it was certain that the guide would make the Prince hunt upwind, and if they fired the grass properly the flames would rush with lightning speed towards him and be absolutely safe for themselves.

Yamato-dake did just as they had expected. He came quietly on, suspecting nothing. Suddenly the rushes took fire in front and at the sides of him. The Prince realized that he had been betrayed. The treacherous guide had disappeared. The Prince stood in danger of suffocation and death. The smoke, dense and choking, rushed along with rapidity and great roaring.

Yamato-dake tried to run for the only gap, but was too late. Then he began cutting the grass with his sword, to prevent the fire from reaching him. He found that whichever direction he cut in with his sword, the wind changed to that direction. If to the north he cut, the wind changed to the south and prevented the fire from advancing farther; if to the south, the wind changed to the north; and so on. Taking advantage of this, Yamato-dake retaliated upon his enemies. He got fire from his aunt's tinder-box, and where there was no fire in the rushes he lit them, cutting through the grass at the same time in the direction in which he wished the fire to go. Rushing thus from point to point, he was successful in the endeavor to turn the tables on his enemies, and destroyed them all. It is important to note that there is in existence a sword, said to be this sword, in the Atsuta Shrine, Owari Province; a great festival in honor of it is held on June 21 every year.

From that place Yamato-dake no Mikoto went on to Sagami Province. Finding things quiet there, he took a ship to cross to Kazusa Province, accompanied by a lady he deeply loved, who was given the title of Hime (Princess) because of Yamato-dake's rank. Her name was Tachibana. They had not got more than ten miles from shore when a terrible storm arose. The ship threatened to go down.

"This," said Tachibana Hime, "is the doing of one of the sea-goddesses who thirst for men's lives. I will give her mine, my lord; perhaps that may appease her until you have safely crossed the wicked sea."

Without further warning, Tachibana Hime cast herself into the sea; the waves closed over her head, to the consternation and grief of all, and to the breaking of Yamato-dake's heart.

As Tachibana Hime had expected, the sea-goddess was appeased. The wind went down, the water calmed, and the ship reached Kazusa Province in safety. Yamato-dake went as far as Yezo, putting down small rebellions on the way.

Several years afterwards, accompanied by many of his old officers, he found himself back on the side of a hill in Sagami Province overlooking the place where poor Tachibana Hime had given up her life for him by throwing herself into the sea. The Prince gazed sadly at the sea, and thrice exclaimed, with tears flowing down his cheeks—brave though he was—"Azuma waya!" (Alas, my dearest wife!); and Eastern Japan, about the middle, has since then been called "Azuma."

THE ISOLATED ISLAND

Tradition Bearer: Unavailable

Source: Smith, Richard Gordon. *Ancient Tales and Folklore of Japan*. London: A. and C. Black, 1908, 120–125.

Date: Unavailable

Original Source: Japan

National Origin: Japan

The **motif** of the uncharted, lost island appears not only in literature and film, but in oral tradition as well. The following **legend** provides evidence for this assertion. Legends commonly educate the groups in which they circulate. They address dangers in the environment, explain unusual phenomena, and provide models for imitation or avoidance, for example. One set of messages in the "The Isolated Island" focuses on the dangers and rewards of seafaring—matters of crucial importance to the island empire of Japan. Another message embedded in the legend focuses on the social and kinship hierarchies in feudal Japan. The narrative includes verifiable historical details. For example, Toyotomi Hidetsugu (1568–July 15, 1595) was a nephew, retainer, and successor of Toyotomi Hideyoshi (ca. 1536–1598), who served as regent and brought an end to the "Warring States Period" (ca. the mid-fifteenth to the early seventeenth centuries) in Japanese history. In 1595, Hidetsugu was accused of plotting a coup and ordered to commit suicide at Mount Koya. These facts function as **validating devices**; they encourage the acceptance of the nonverifiable portion of the tale.

Many years ago the Lord of Kishu, head of one of the three families of the Tokugawas, ordered his people to hold a hunting-party on Tomagashima (Toma Island). In those days such hunting-parties were often ordered, more for the purpose of improving drill and organization than for sport. It brought men together, and taught others to handle them both on land and at sea. It made men recognize their commanders and superiors, and it disclosed what men were worthy of being made such. Hunting-parties of this kind were considered as military maneuvers.

On this particular hunt or maneuver, the Lord of Kishu was to make a kind of descent by water on the island of Toma, and kill all the game that his landing-party could beat up.

Boats and junks were armed as if for war, and so were the men—except that they wore no armor.

The day for the entertainment was fine. Some sixty boats put to sea, and landed successfully about eight hundred men on Toma Island; and busy indeed were they chasing boar and deer the whole morning.

Towards afternoon, however, a storm of great violence came on and completely stopped the sport. The men were ordered to return to the shore and regain their boats before these should be smashed on the beach.

On embarking they put out to sea with the intention of gaining the mainland. On shore trees were being uprooted, columns of sand flew high in the air, and the gale was indeed terrific; if on shore it was as bad as this, it must be much worse at sea. The Lord of Kishu's boats and junks were tossed about as if they were floating leaves.

One of the party was a notably brave man, Makino Heinei, who had been nicknamed "Ino shishi" (Wild Boar) on account of his reckless bravery. Seeing that neither junks nor boats were making headway against the storm, he pushed the small boat off the junk, jumped into it alone, took the oars, laughed at every one, and cried, "See here! You all seem to be too frightened to make headway.

Look at what I do and follow me. I am not afraid of the waves, and none of you should be if you are to serve our Lord of Kishu faithfully."

With that Makino Heinei shot out into the wild sea, and by extraordinary exertion managed to get some three hundred yards ahead of the rest of the fleet. Then the gale increased to such violence that he was incapable of doing anything. For fear of being blown out of the boat, he was obliged to hold tight to the mast and otherwise abandon his fate to good fortune. At times even the heart of the Wild Boar quailed. Often his boat was lifted clean out of the water by the wind; waves towered over him; he closed his eyes and awaited his fate.

Finally, one squall more powerful than the rest blew his boat out of the water, and it was seen from the other boats (which lay at anchor) to disappear into the horizon. Heinei clung to the boat tightly. When the mast blew away he held on to the ribs. He prayed hard and earnestly. Some eight hours after the storm began, Heinei found the boat in comparatively smooth water. She was flooded, and she was a wreck; but still she floated, and that was all he cared for at the moment. Moreover, Heinei felt encouraged, because between two dark clouds he could see an opening and some stars, though at present it was absolutely dark and the driving rain had not ceased.

Suddenly, when Heinei was wondering how far he had been blown from shore or from his friends, crack!—he felt his boat plump into a rock. The shock was so violent (for the boat was still being driven fast by the gale) that our hero lost his balance and was thrown fully ten feet away. Falling on soft stuff, Heinei thought he was in the sea; but his hands suddenly realized that it was soft wet sand. Delighted at this discovery, he looked at the clouds and the sky, and came to the conclusion that in another hour it would be daylight. In the meantime he thanked the gods for his deliverance, and prayed for his friends and for his lord and master.

As morning broke Heinei arose stiff, weary, and hungry. Before the sun appeared he realized that he was on an island. No other land was in sight, and it puzzled him sorely to guess where he could be, for from all the Kishu islands the mainland could be easily seen.

"Oh, here is a new tree! I have never seen that in Kishu," said he. "And this flower—that also is new—while here is a butterfly more brilliant than any I know." So saying and thinking, Heinei began looking about for food, and, being a Japanese, easily satisfied his appetite with the shellfish which were abundantly strewn everywhere after the storm.

The island on which Heinei had been cast was fair in size—some two miles across and ten in circumference. There was one small hill in the middle, which Heinei resolved to ascend, to see if he could discover Kishu from the top of it. Accordingly he started. The undergrowth of bush was so great that Heinei made a detour to another bay. The trees were quite different from any he had ever seen before, and there were many kinds of palms. At last he found to his delight a well-worn path leading up the mountain. He took it; but when he came to a damp place in the way he was in no whit reassured, for there he saw footmarks which could have been made by no one who was not a giant—they were fully eighteen inches in length. A warrior belonging to Kishu must fear nothing, thought Heinei, and, arming himself with a stout stick, he proceeded. Near the top he found the opening to a somewhat large cave, and, nothing daunted, began to enter, prepared to meet anything. What was his surprise when an enormous man, fully eight feet in height, appeared before him, not more than ten feet from the entrance! He was a hideous, wild-looking creature, nearly black, with long unkempt hair, flashing angry eyes, and a mouth that stretched from ear to ear, showing two glittering rows of teeth; and he wore no clothes except the skin of a wild-cat tied round his loins.

As soon as he saw Heinei he came to a standstill, and said, in Japanese, "Who are you? How have you got here? And what have you come for?"

Makino Heinei answered these questions as fully as he thought necessary by telling his name and adding, "I am a retainer of the Lord of Kishu, and was blown away by the storm after we had been hunting and holding maneuvers on Toma Island."

"And where are these places you speak of? Remember that this island is unknown to the world and has been for thousands of years. I am its sole occupant, and wish to remain so. No matter how I came. I am here. My name is Tomaru, and my father was Yamaguchi Shoun, who died, with his master Toyotomi Hidetsugu, on Koyasan Mountain in 1563. Both died by their own hands; and I got here, no matter how, and here I intend to remain undisturbed. I heard of your Lord of Kishu and of the Tokugawa family before I left Japan, and for that reason I will help you by giving you my old boat, in which I arrived. Come to the beach. I will send you off in the right direction, and if you continue sailing north-west you shall in time reach Kishu. But it is a long way off—a very long way."

With that they walked down to the beach.

"See," said Tomaru, "the boat is well-nigh rotten, for it is many years since she was put here; but with luck you may reach Kishu. Stay—you must have some provision. I can give only dry fish and fruits; but to these you are welcome. And I must give you a present for your master, the Lord of Kishu. It is a kind of seaweed. You shall have some for yourself also. It is my great discovery on this island. No matter how bad a sword-cut you may get, it will stop the blood flowing and cure at once. Now, jump into the boat and row away. I like to be alone. You may speak of your adventure; but you are not to mention my name. Farewell!"

Heinei could only do as he was bid. Consequently, he made off. Rowing night and day and aided by favorable currents, he found himself off the coast of Kishu on the third day after leaving the island. The people were much astonished to see him alive, and the Lord of Kishu rejoiced, especially at the sword-cut-healing seaweed, which he had planted in the sea at a part of the coast which he renamed and called Nagusa-gori (District of the Famous Seaweed).

Later Makino Heinei sailed again by permission of his Lord to get more seaweed. The island was found; but the giant had disappeared.

GHOST OF THE VIOLET WELL

Tradition Bearer: Shofukutei Fukuga

Source: Smith, Richard Gordon. *Ancient Tales and Folklore of Japan.* London: A. and C. Black, 1908, 19–26.

Date: Unavailable

Original Source: Japan

National Origin: Japan

Yoshino Yama (Mount Yoshino), the site of this supernatural **legend** is located in Nara Prefecture, Japan. Shingé was of the samurai class, the highest in feudal Japan. Moreover, her father was a daimyo, a local feudal lord whose status placed him on the level immediately below the shogun generalissimo of Japan. Doctor Yoshisawa, in contrast, was an outcaste "eta," a group that was excluded from the class system, which included samurai (military), farmers, craftspersons, and traders. As outcastes, the eta were forced to live in their own communities and were avoided by other members of Japanese society. They low status resulted from their holding occupations associated with death, for example, disposing of animal carcasses and tanning animal hides. Lists of eta families persist to modern times, and conservative Japanese used the "eta lists" to prevent a child's marriage to a spouse of eta descent. Under samurai codes, suicide was hemmed in with social considerations such as to pursue acceptable motives, to preserve one's honor, or to criticize a superior without seeming to do so. Although some people were allowed to commit suicide, women could do so only with permission, and commoners were not restricted as to the means for death.

In the wild province of Yamato, or very near to its borders, is a beautiful mountain known as Yoshino yama. It is not only known for its abundance of cherry blossoms in the spring, but it is also celebrated in relation to more than one bloody battle. In fact, Yoshino might be called the staging-place of historical battles. Many say, when in Yoshino, "We are walking on history, because Yoshino itself is history." Near Yoshino mountain lay another, known as Tsubosaka; and between them is the Valley of Shimizutani, in which is the Violet Well.

At the approach of spring in this tani [hollow] the grass assumes a perfect emerald green, while moss grows luxuriantly over rocks and boulders. Towards the end of April great patches of deep-purple wild violets show up in the lower parts of the valley, while up the sides pink and scarlet azaleas grow in a manner which beggars description.

Some thirty years ago a beautiful girl of the age of seventeen, named Shingé, was wending her way up Shimizutani, accompanied by four servants. All were out for a picnic, and all, of course, were in search of wildflowers. O Shingé San was the daughter of a Daimio who lived in the neighborhood. Every year she was in the habit of having this picnic, and coming to Shimizutani at the end of April to hunt for her favorite flower, the purple violet (sumire).

The five girls, carrying bamboo baskets, were eagerly collecting flowers, enjoying the occupation as only Japanese girls can. They raced in their rivalry to have the prettiest basketful. There not being so many purple violets as were wanted, O Shingé San said, "Let us go to the northern end of the valley, where the Violet Well is."

Naturally the girls assented, and off they all ran, each eager to be there first, laughing as they went.

O Shingé outran the rest, and arrived before any of them; and, espying a huge bunch of her favorite flowers, of the deepest purple and very sweet in smell, she flung herself down, anxious to pick them before the others came. As she stretched out her delicate hand to grasp them—oh, horror!—a great mountain snake raised his head from beneath his shady retreat. So frightened was O Shingé San, she fainted away on the spot.

In the meanwhile the other girls had given up the race, thinking it would please their mistress to arrive first. They picked what they most fancied, chased butterflies, and arrived fully fifteen minutes after O Shingé San had fainted.

On seeing her thus laid out on the grass, a great fear filled them that she was dead, and their alarm increased when they saw a large green snake coiled near her head.

They screamed, as do most girls amid such circumstances; but one of them, Matsu, who did not lose her head so much as the others, threw her basket of flowers at the snake, which, not liking the bombardment, uncoiled himself and slid away, hoping to find a quieter place. Then all four girls bent over their mistress. They rubbed her hands and threw water on her face, but without effect. O Shingé's beautiful complexion became paler and paler, while her red lips assumed the purplish hue that is a sign of approaching death. The girls were heartbroken. Tears coursed down their faces. They did not know what to do, for they could not carry her. What a terrible state of affairs!

Just at that moment they heard a man's voice close behind them, "Do not be so sad! I can restore the young lady to consciousness if you will allow me."

They turned, and saw a remarkably handsome youth standing on the grass not ten feet away. He appeared as an angel from Heaven.

Without saying more, the young man approached the prostrate figure of O Shingé, and, taking her hand in his, felt her pulse. None of the servants liked to interfere in this breach of etiquette. He had not asked permission; but his manner was so gentle and sympathetic that they could say nothing.

The stranger examined O Shingé carefully, keeping silence. Having finished, he took out of his pocket a little case of medicine, and, putting some white powder from this into a paper, said, "I am a doctor from a neighboring village, and I have just been to see a patient at the end of the valley. By good fortune I returned this way, and am able to help you and save your mistress's life. Give her this medicine, while I hunt for and kill the snake."

O Matsu San forced the medicine, along with a little water, into her mistress's mouth, and in a few minutes she began to recover.

Shortly after this the doctor returned, carrying the dead snake on a stick. "Is this the snake you saw lying by your young mistress?" he asked.

"Yes, yes," they cried, "that is the horrible thing."

"Then," said the doctor, "it is lucky I came, for it is very poisonous, and I fear your mistress would soon have died had I not arrived and been able to give her the medicine. Ah! I see that it is already doing the beautiful young lady good."

On hearing the young man's voice O Shingé San sat up. "Pray, sir, may I ask to whom I am indebted for bringing me thus back to life?" she asked.

The doctor did not answer, but in a proud and manly way contented himself by smiling, and bowing low and respectfully after the Japanese fashion; and departed as quietly and unassumingly as he had arrived, disappearing in the sleepy mist which always appears in the afternoons of spring time in the Shimizu Valley.

The four girls helped their mistress home; but indeed she wanted little assistance, for the medicine had done her much good, and she felt quite recovered. O Shingé's father and mother were very grateful for their daughter's recovery; but the name of the handsome young doctor remained a secret to all except the servant girl Matsu.

For four days O Shingé remained quite well; but on the fifth day, for some cause or another, she took to her bed, saying she was sick. She did not sleep, and did not wish to talk, but only to think, and think, and think. Neither father nor mother could make out what her illness was. There was no fever.

Doctors were sent for, one after another; but none of them could say what was the matter. All they saw was that she daily became weaker. Asano Zembei, Shingé's father, was heartbroken, and so was his wife. They had tried everything and failed to do the slightest good to poor O Shingé.

One day O Matsu San craved an interview with Asano Zembei—who, by the by, was the head of all his family, a Daimio and great grandee. Zembei was not accustomed to listen to servants' opinions; but, knowing that O Matsu was faithful to his daughter and loved her very nearly as much as he did himself, he consented to hear her, and O Matsu was ushered into his presence.

"Oh, master," said the servant, "if you will let me find a doctor for my young mistress, I can promise to find one who will cure her."

"Where on earth will you find such a doctor? Have we not had all the best doctors in the province and some even from the capital? Where do you propose to look for one?"

O Matsu answered, "Ah, master, my mistress is not suffering from an illness which can be cured by medicines—not even if they be given by the quart. Nor are doctors of much use. There is, however, one that I know of who could cure her. My mistress's illness is of the heart. The doctor I know of can cure her. It is for love of him that her heart suffers; it has suffered so from the day when he saved her life from the snake-bite."

Then O Matsu told particulars of the adventure at the picnic which had not been told before—for O Shingé had asked her servants to say as little as possible, fearing they would not be allowed to go to the Valley of the Violet Well again.

"What is the name of this doctor?" asked Asano Zembei, "and who is he?"

"Sir," answered O Matsu, "he is Doctor Yoshisawa, a very handsome young man, of most courtly manners; but he is of low birth, being only of the eta. Please think, master, of my young mistress's burning heart, full of love for the man who saved her life—and no wonder, for he is very handsome and has the manners of a proud samurai. The only cure for your daughter, sir, is to be allowed to marry her lover."

O Shingé's mother felt very sad when she heard this. She knew well (perhaps by experience) of the illnesses caused by love. She wept, and said to Zembei, "I am quite with you in sorrow, my lord, at the terrible trouble that has come to us; but I cannot see my daughter die thus. Let us tell her we will make inquiries about the man she loves, and see if we can make him our son-in-law. In any case, it is the custom to make full inquiries, which will extend over some days; and in this time our daughter may recover somewhat and get strong enough to hear the news that we cannot accept her lover as our son-in-law."

Zembei agreed to this, and O Matsu promised to say nothing to her mistress of the interview.

O Shingé San was told by her mother that her father, though he had not consented to the engagement, had promised to make inquiries about Yoshisawa.

O Shingé took food and regained much strength on this news; and when she was strong enough, some ten days later, she was called into her father's presence, accompanied by her mother.

"My sweet daughter," said Zembei, "I have made careful inquiries about Dr. Yoshisawa, your lover. Deeply as it grieves me to say so, it is impossible that I, your father, the head of our whole family, can consent to your marriage with one of so low a family as Yoshisawa, who, in spite of his own goodness, has sprung from the eta. I must hear no more of it. Such a contract would be impossible for the Asano family."

No one ventured to say a word to this. In Japan the head of a family's decision is final.

Poor O Shingé bowed to her father, and went to her own room, where she wept bitterly; O Matsu, the faithful servant, doing her best to console her.

Next morning, to the astonishment of the household, O Shingé San could nowhere be found. Search was made everywhere; even Dr. Yoshisawa joined in the search.

On the third day after the disappearance one of the searchers looked down the Violet Well, and saw poor O Shingé's floating body.

Two days later she was buried, and on that day Yoshisawa threw himself into the well.

The people say that even now, on wet, stormy nights, they see the ghost of O Shingé San floating over the well, while some declare that they hear the sound of a young man weeping in the Valley of Shimizutani.

THE STORY OF MIMI-NASHI-HOICHI

Tradition Bearer: Unavailable

Source: Hearn, Lafcadio. *Kwaidan: Stories and Studies of Strange Things.* Boston: Houghton, Mifflin and Co., 1904, 3–20.

Date: ca. 1904

Original Source: Japan

National Origin: Japan

The story of the battle at Dan-no-ura, alluded to in the following supernatural **legend**, originally existed as one of the episodes of the great military epic *Heike monogatari* (*The Tale of the Heike*). The *Heike monogatari* was compiled from oral tradition transmitted by the class of blind bards of which Hoichi was a member.

More than seven hundred years ago, at Dan-no-ura, in the Straits of Shimonoseki, was fought the last battle of the long contest between the Heike, or Taira clan, and the Genji, or Minamoto clan. There the Heike perished utterly, with their women and children, and their infant emperor likewise—now remembered as Antoku Tenno. And that sea and shore have been haunted for seven hundred years. Elsewhere I told you about the strange crabs found there, called Heike crabs, which have human faces on their backs, and are said to be the spirits of the Heike warriors. But there are many strange things to be seen and heard along that coast. On dark nights thousands of ghostly fires hover about the beach, or flit above the waves—pale lights which the fishermen call Oni-bi, or demon-fires; and, whenever the winds are up, a sound of great shouting comes from that sea, like a clamor of battle. In former years the Heike were much more restless than they now are. They would rise about ships passing in the night, and try to sink them; and at all times they would watch for swimmers, to pull them down. It was in order to appease those dead that the Buddhist temple, Amidaji, was built at Akamagaseki. A cemetery also was made close by, near the beach; and within it were set up monuments inscribed with the names of the drowned emperor and of his great vassals; and Buddhist services were regularly performed there, on behalf of the spirits of them. After the temple had been built, and the tombs erected, the Heike gave less trouble than before; but they continued to do queer things at intervals— proving that they had not found the perfect peace.

Some centuries ago there lived at Akamagaseki a blind man named Hoichi, who was famed for his skill in recitation and in playing upon the biwa [lute]. From childhood he had been trained to recite and to play; and while yet a lad he had surpassed his teachers. As a professional biwa-hoshi he became famous chiefly by his recitations of the history of the Heike and the Genji; and it is said that when he sang the song of the battle of Dan-no-ura "even the goblins [kijin] could not refrain from tears."

At the outset of his career, Hoichi was very poor; but he found a good friend to help him. The priest of the Amidaji was fond of poetry and music; and he often invited Hoichi to the temple, to play and recite. Afterwards, being much impressed by the wonderful skill of the lad, the priest proposed that Hoichi should make the temple his home; and this offer was gratefully accepted. Hoichi was given a room in the temple-building; and, in return for food and lodging, he was required only to gratify the priest with a musical performance on certain evenings, when otherwise disengaged.

One summer night the priest was called away, to perform a Buddhist service at the house of a dead parishioner; and he went there with his acolyte, leaving Hoichi alone in the temple. It was a hot night; and the blind man sought to cool himself on the verandah before his sleeping-room. The verandah over-looked a small garden in the rear of the Amidaji. There Hoichi waited for the priest's return, and tried to relieve his solitude by practicing upon his biwa. Mid-night passed; and the priest did not appear. But the atmosphere was still too warm for comfort within doors; and Hoichi remained outside. At last he heard steps approaching from the back gate. Somebody crossed the garden, advanced to the verandah, and halted directly in front of him—but it was not the priest. A deep voice called the blind man's name—abruptly and unceremoniously, in the manner of a samurai summoning an inferior.

"Hoichi!"

"Hai!" ["Yes!"] answered the blind man, frightened by the menace in the voice, "I am blind! I cannot know who calls!"

"There is nothing to fear," the stranger exclaimed, speaking more gently. "I am stopping near this temple, and have been sent to you with a message. My present lord, a person of exceedingly high rank, is now staying in Akamagaseki, with many noble attendants. He wished to view the scene of the battle of Dan-no-ura; and today he visited that place. Having heard of your skill in reciting the story of the battle, he now desires to hear your performance: so you will take your biwa and come with me at once to the house where the august assembly is waiting."

In those times, the order of a samurai was not to be lightly disobeyed. Hoichi donned his sandals, took his biwa, and went away with the stranger, who guided him deftly, but obliged him to walk very fast. The hand that guided was iron; and the clank of the warrior's stride proved him fully armed—probably some palace-guard on duty. Hoichi's first alarm was over; he began to imagine himself in good luck—for, remembering the retainer's assurance about a "person of exceedingly high rank," he thought that the lord who wished to hear the recitation could not be less than a daimyo of the first class. Presently the samurai halted; and Hoichi became aware that they had arrived at a large gateway—and he wondered, for he could not remember any large gate in that part of the town, except the main gate of the Amidaji.

"Kaimon!" [respectful request to open the gate] the samurai called, and there was a sound of unbarring; and the twain passed on. They traversed a space of garden, and halted again before some entrance; and the retainer cried in a loud voice, "Within there! I have brought Hoichi." Then came sounds of feet hurrying, and screens sliding, and rain-doors opening, and voices of women in converse. By the language of the women Hoichi knew them to be domestics in some noble household; but he could not imagine to what place he had been conducted. Little time was allowed him for conjecture. After he had been helped to mount several stone steps, upon the last of which he was told to leave his sandals, a woman's hand guided him along interminable reaches of polished planking, and round pillared angles too many to remember, and over widths amazing of matted floor, into the middle of some vast apartment. There he thought that many great people were assembled: the sound of the rustling of silk was like the sound of leaves in a forest. He heard also a great humming of voices—talking in undertones; and the speech was the speech of courts.

Hoichi was told to put himself at ease, and he found a kneeling-cushion ready for him. After having taken his place upon it, and tuned his instrument, the voice of a woman—whom he divined to be the Rojo, or matron in charge of the female service, addressed him, saying,

"It is now required that the history of the Heike be recited, to the accompaniment of the biwa."

Now the entire recital would have required a time of many nights: therefore Hoichi ventured a question, "As the whole of the story is not soon told, what portion is it augustly desired that I now recite?"

The woman's voice made answer, "Recite the story of the battle at Dan-no-ura—for the pity of it is the most deep."

Then Hoichi lifted up his voice, and chanted the chant of the fight on the bitter sea, wonderfully making his biwa to sound like the straining of oars and the rushing of ships, the whirr and the hissing of arrows, the shouting and trampling of men, the crashing of steel upon helmets, the plunging of slain in the flood. And to left and right of him, in the pauses of his playing, he could hear voices murmuring praise, "How marvelous an artist!"

"Never in our own province was playing heard like this!"

"Not in all the empire is there another singer like Hoichi!" Then fresh courage came to him, and he played and sang yet better than before; and a hush of wonder deepened about him. But when at last he came to tell the fate of the fair and helpless—the piteous perishing of the women and children—and the death-leap of Nii-no-Ama, with the imperial infant in her arms—then all the listeners uttered together one long, long shuddering cry of anguish; and thereafter they wept and wailed so loudly and so wildly that the blind man was frightened by the violence and grief that he had made. For much time the sobbing and the wailing continued. But gradually the sounds of lamentation died away; and again, in the great stillness that followed, Hoichi heard the voice of the woman whom he supposed to be the Rojo.

She said, "Although we had been assured that you were a very skillful player upon the biwa, and without an equal in recitative, we did not know that any one could be so skillful as you have proved yourself tonight. Our lord has been pleased to say that he intends to bestow upon you a fitting reward. But he desires that you shall perform before him once every night for the next six nights—after which time he will probably make his august return-journey. Tomorrow night, therefore, you are to come here at the same hour. The retainer who tonight conducted you will be sent for you…. There is another matter about which I have been ordered to inform you. It is required that you shall speak to no one of your visits here, during the time of our lord's august sojourn at Akamagaseki. As he is traveling incognito, he commands that no mention of these things be made…. You are now free to go back to your temple."

After Hoichi had duly expressed his thanks, a woman's hand conducted him to the entrance of the house, where the same retainer, who had before guided him, was waiting to take him home. The retainer led him to the verandah at the rear of the temple, and there bade him farewell.

It was almost dawn when Hoichi returned; but his absence from the temple had not been observed, as the priest, coming back at a very late hour, had supposed him asleep. During the day Hoichi was able to take some rest; and he said nothing about his strange adventure. In the middle of the following night the samurai again came for him, and led him to the august assembly, where he gave another recitation with the same success that had attended his previous performance. But during this second visit his absence from the temple was accidentally discovered; and after his return in the morning he was summoned to the presence of the priest, who said to him, in a tone of kindly reproach, "We have been very anxious about you, friend Hoichi. To go out, blind and alone, at so late an hour, is dangerous. Why did you go without telling us? I could have ordered a servant to accompany you. And where have you been?"

Hoichi answered, evasively, "Pardon me kind friend! I had to attend to some private business; and I could not arrange the matter at any other hour."

The priest was surprised, rather than pained, by Hoichi's reticence: he felt it to be unnatural, and suspected something wrong. He feared that the blind lad had been bewitched or deluded by some evil spirits. He did not ask any more questions; but he privately instructed the men-servants of the temple to keep watch upon Hoichi's movements, and to follow him in case that he should again leave the temple after dark. On the very next night, Hoichi was seen to leave the temple; and the servants immediately lighted their lanterns, and followed after him. But it was a rainy night, and very dark; and before the temple-folks could get to the roadway, Hoichi had disappeared. Evidently he had walked very fast, a strange thing, considering his blindness; for the road was in a bad condition. The men hurried through the streets, making inquiries at every house which Hoichi was accustomed to visit; but nobody could give them any news of him. At last, as they were returning to the temple by way of the shore, they were startled by the sound of a biwa, furiously played, in the cemetery of the Amidaji. Except for some ghostly fires—such as usually flitted there on dark nights—all was blackness in that direction. But the men at once hastened to the cemetery; and there, by the help of their lanterns, they discovered Hoichi, sitting alone in the rain before the memorial tomb of Antoku Tenno, making his biwa resound, and loudly chanting the chant of the battle of Dan-no-ura. And behind him, and about him, and everywhere above the tombs, the fires of the dead were burning, like candles. Never before had so great a host of Oni-bi appeared in the sight of mortal man....

"Hoichi San!—Hoichi San!" the servants cried, "you are bewitched! ... Hoichi San!"

But the blind man did not seem to hear. Strenuously he made his biwa to rattle and ring and clang—more and more wildly he chanted the chant of the battle of Dan-no-ura. They caught hold of him; they shouted into his ear, "Hoichi San!—Hoichi San!—come home with us at once!"

Reprovingly he spoke to them, "To interrupt me in such a manner, before this august assembly, will not be tolerated."

Whereat, in spite of the weirdness of the thing, the servants could not help laughing. Sure that he had been bewitched, they now seized him, and pulled him up on his feet, and by main force hurried him back to the temple—where he was immediately relieved of his wet clothes, by order of the priest. Then the priest insisted upon a full explanation of his friend's astonishing behavior.

Hoichi long hesitated to speak. But at last, finding that his conduct had really alarmed and angered the good priest, he decided to abandon his reserve; and he related everything that had happened from the time of first visit of the samurai.

The priest said, "Hoichi, my poor friend, you are now in great danger! How unfortunate that you did not tell me all this before! Your wonderful skill in music has indeed brought you into strange trouble. By this time you must be aware that you have not been visiting any house whatever, but have been passing your nights in the cemetery, among the tombs of the Heike—and it was before the memorial-tomb of Antoku Tenno that our people tonight found you, sitting in the rain. All that you have been imagining was illusion—except the calling of the dead. By once obeying them, you have put yourself in their power. If you obey them again, after what has already occurred, they will tear you in pieces. But they would have destroyed you, sooner or later, in any event.... Now I shall not be able to remain with you tonight: I am called away to perform another service. But, before I go, it will be necessary to protect your body by writing holy texts upon it."

Before sundown the priest and his acolyte stripped Hoichi: then, with their writing brushes, they traced upon his breast and back, head and face and neck, limbs and hands and feet—even upon the soles of his feet, and upon all parts of his body—the text of the holy sutra called Hannya-Shin-Kyo. When this had been done, the priest instructed Hoichi, saying, "Tonight, as soon as I go away, you must seat yourself on the verandah, and wait. You will be called. But, whatever may happen, do not answer, and do not move. Say nothing and sit still as if meditating. If you stir, or make any noise, you will be torn asunder. Do not get frightened; and do not think of calling for help—because no help could save you. If you do exactly as I tell you, the danger will pass, and you will have nothing more to fear."

After dark the priest and the acolyte went away; and Hoichi seated himself on the verandah, according to the instructions given him. He laid his biwa on the planking beside him, and, assuming the attitude of meditation, remained quite still—taking care not to cough, or to breathe audibly. For hours he stayed thus.

Then, from the roadway, he heard the steps coming. They passed the gate, crossed the garden, approached the verandah, stopped—directly in front of him.

"Hoichi!" the deep voice called. But the blind man held his breath, and sat motionless.

"Hoichi!" grimly called the voice a second time. Then a third time, savagely, "Hoichi!"

Hoichi remained as still as a stone, and the voice grumbled, "No answer!— that won't do! ... Must see where the fellow is."

There was a noise of heavy feet mounting upon the verandah. The feet approached deliberately, halted beside him. Then, for long minutes—during which Hoichi felt his whole body shake to the beating of his heart—there was dead silence.

At last the gruff voice muttered close to him, "Here is the biwa; but of the biwa-player I see—only two ears! ... So that explains why he did not answer: he had no mouth to answer with—there is nothing left of him but his ears ... Now to my lord those ears I will take—in proof that the august commands have been obeyed, so far as was possible."

At that instant Hoichi felt his ears gripped by fingers of iron, and torn off! Great as the pain was, he gave no cry. The heavy footfalls receded along the verandah—descended into the garden—passed out to the roadway—ceased. From either side of his head, the blind man felt a thick warm trickling; but he dared not lift his hands....

Before sunrise the priest came back. He hastened at once to the verandah in the rear, stepped and slipped upon something clammy, and uttered a cry of horror; for he saw, by the light of his lantern, that the clamminess was blood. But he perceived Hoichi sitting there, in the attitude of meditation—with the blood still oozing from his wounds.

"My poor Hoichi!" cried the startled priest, "What is this? You have been hurt?"

At the sound of his friend's voice, the blind man felt safe. He burst out sobbing, and tearfully told his adventure of the night.

"Poor, poor Hoichi!" the priest exclaimed, "all my fault!—my very grievous fault! ... Everywhere upon your body the holy texts had been written—except upon your ears! I trusted my acolyte to do that part of the work; and it was very, very wrong of me not to have made sure that he had done it! ... Well, the matter cannot now be helped; we can only try to heal your hurts as soon as possible.... Cheer up, friend!—the danger is now well over. You will never again be troubled by those visitors."

With the aid of a good doctor, Hoichi soon recovered from his injuries. The story of his strange adventure spread far and wide, and soon made him famous. Many noble persons went to Akamagaseki to hear him recite; and large presents of money were given to him—so that he became a wealthy man.... But from the time of his adventure, he was known only by the appellation of Mimi-nashi-Hoichi: "Hoichi-the-Earless."

THE MONKEY AND THE JELLYFISH

Tradition Bearer: Unavailable

Source: Lang, Andrew. *The Violet Fairy Book*. London: Longmans, Green and Company, 1901, 275–280.

Date: Unavailable

Original Source: Brauns, David. *Japanische Märchen und Sagen*. Leipzig: Verlag von Wilhelm Friedrich, 1885.

National Origin: Japan

Otohime, whose name means "Luminous Jewel," was the daughter of the divine dragon king of the sea Ryujin. The sea king's messengers in **myth** are turtles. In this explanatory narrative, monkey uses his guile to escape in a **variant** of "Monkey Who Left His Heart at Home" (AT 91).

Children must often have wondered why jellyfishes have no shells, like so many of the creatures that are washed up every day on the beach. In old times this was not so; the jellyfish had as hard a shell as any of them, but he lost it through his own fault, as may be seen in this story.

The sea-queen Otohime grew suddenly very ill. The swiftest messengers were sent hurrying to fetch the best doctors from every country under the sea, but it was all of no use; the queen grew rapidly worse instead of better. Everyone had almost given up hope, when one day a doctor arrived who was cleverer than the rest, and said that the only thing that would cure her was the liver of an ape.

Now apes do not dwell under the sea, so a council of the wisest heads in the nation was called to consider the question how a liver could be obtained. At length it was decided that the turtle, whose prudence was well known, should swim to land and contrive to catch a living ape and bring him safely to the ocean kingdom.

It was easy enough for the council to entrust this mission to the turtle, but not at all so easy for him to fulfill it. However, he swam to a part of the coast that was covered with tall trees, where he thought the apes were likely to be; for he was old, and had seen many things. It was some time before he caught sight of any monkeys, and he often grew tired with watching for them, so that one hot day he fell fast asleep, in spite of all his efforts to keep awake.

By and by some apes, who had been peeping at him from the tops of the trees, where they had been carefully hidden from the turtle's eyes, stole noiselessly down, and stood round staring at him, for they had never seen a turtle before, and did not know what to make of it. At last one young monkey, bolder than the rest, stooped down and stroked the shining shell that the strange new creature wore on its back. The movement, gentle though it was, woke the turtle. With one sweep he seized the monkey's hand in his mouth, and held it tight, in spite of every effort to pull it away. The other apes, seeing that the turtle was not to be trifled with, ran off, leaving their young brother to his fate.

Then the turtle said to the monkey, "If you will be quiet, and do what I tell you, I won't hurt you. But you must get on my back and come with me."

The monkey, seeing there was no help for it, did as he was bid; indeed he could not have resisted, as his hand was still in the turtle's mouth.

Delighted at having secured his prize, the turtle hastened back to the shore and plunged quickly into the water. He swam faster than he had ever done before, and soon reached the royal palace. Shouts of joy broke forth from the attendants when he was seen approaching, and some of them ran to tell the queen that the monkey was there, and that before long she would be as well as ever she was. In fact, so great was their relief that they gave the monkey such a kind welcome, and were so anxious to make him happy and comfortable, that he soon forgot all the fears that had beset him as to his fate, and was generally quite at his ease, though every now and then a fit of homesickness would come over him, and he would hide himself in some dark corner till it had passed away.

It was during one of these attacks of sadness that a jellyfish happened to swim by. At that time jellyfishes had shells. At the sight of the gay and lively monkey crouching under a tall rock, with his eyes closed and his head bent, the jellyfish was filled with pity, and stopped, saying, "Ah, poor fellow, no wonder you weep; a few days more, and they will come and kill you and give your liver to the queen to eat."

The monkey shrank back horrified at these words and asked the jellyfish what crime he had committed that deserved death.

"Oh, none at all," replied the jellyfish, "but your liver is the only thing that will cure our queen, and how can we get at it without killing you? You had better submit to your fate, and make no noise about it, for though I pity you from my heart there is no way of helping you." Then he went away, leaving the ape cold with horror.

At first he felt as if his liver was already being taken from his body, but soon he began to wonder if there was no means of escaping this terrible death, and at length he invented a plan which he thought would do. For a few days he pretended to be gay and happy as before, but when the sun went in, and rain fell in torrents, he wept and howled from dawn to dark, till the turtle, who was his head keeper, heard him, and came to see what was the matter. Then the monkey told him that before he left home he had hung his liver out on a bush to dry, and if it was always going to rain like this it would become quite useless. And the rogue made such a fuss and moaning that he would have melted a heart of stone, and nothing would content him but that somebody should carry him back to land and let him fetch his liver again.

The queen's councilors were not the wisest of people, and they decided between them that the turtle should take the monkey back to his native land and allow him to get his liver off the bush, but desired the turtle not to lose sight of his charge for a single moment. The monkey knew this, but trusted to his power of beguiling the turtle when the time came, and mounted on his back with feelings of joy, which he was, however, careful to conceal.

They set out, and in a few hours were wandering about the forest where the ape had first been caught, and when the monkey saw his family peering out from the tree tops, he swung himself up by the nearest branch, just managing to save his hind leg from being seized by the turtle. He told them all the dreadful things that had happened to him, and gave a war cry which brought the rest of the tribe from the neighboring hills. At a word from him they rushed in a body to the unfortunate turtle, threw him on his back, and tore off the shield that covered his body. Then with mocking words they hunted him to the shore, and into the sea, which he was only too thankful to reach alive.

Faint and exhausted he entered the queen's palace, for the cold of the water struck upon his naked body, and made him feel ill and miserable. But wretched though he was, he had to appear before the queen's advisers and tell them all that had befallen him, and how he had suffered the monkey to escape. But, as sometimes happens, the turtle was allowed to go scot-free, and had his shell given back to him, and all the punishment fell on the poor jellyfish, who was condemned by the queen to go shieldless for ever after.

JIKININKI

Tradition Bearer: Unavailable

Source: Hearn, Lafcadio. *Kwaidan: Stories and Studies of Strange Things*. Boston: Houghton, Mifflin and Co., 1904, 65–73.

Date: ca. 1904

Original Source: Japan

National Origin: Japan

In Japanese Buddhism, the jikininki is a ghost that, because of its craving for human flesh, seeks corpses, thus making it the equivalent of the ghul (Anglicized as "ghoul") of Arabic folklore. As the jikininki makes clear in his confession to the priest Muso Kokushi, these spirits are repelled by their own behavior, but they are compelled to their actions as punishment for sins of greed and impiety during life.

Once, when Muso Kokushi, a priest of the Zen sect, was journeying alone through the province of Mino, he lost his way in a mountain-district where there was nobody to direct him. For a long time he wandered about helplessly; and he was beginning to despair of finding shelter for the night, when he perceived, on the top of a hill lighted by the last rays of the sun, one of those little hermitages, called anjitsu, which are built for solitary priests. It seemed to be in ruinous condition; but he hastened to it eagerly, and found that it was inhabited by an aged priest, from whom he begged the favor of a night's lodging. This the old man harshly refused; but he directed Muso to a certain hamlet, in the valley adjoining where lodging and food could be obtained.

Muso found his way to the hamlet, which consisted of less than a dozen farm-cottages; and he was kindly received at the dwelling of the headman. Forty or fifty persons were assembled in the principal apartment, at the moment of Muso's arrival; but he was shown into a small separate room, where he was promptly supplied with food and bedding. Being very tired, he lay down to rest at an early hour; but a little before midnight he was roused from sleep by a sound of loud weeping in the next apartment. Presently the sliding-screens were gently pushed apart; and a young man, carrying a lighted lantern, entered the room, respectfully saluted him, and said, "Reverend Sir, it is my painful duty to tell you that I am now the responsible head of this house. Yesterday I was only the eldest son. But when you came here, tired as you were, we did not wish that you should feel embarrassed in any way: therefore we did not tell you that father had died only a few hours before. The people whom you saw in the next room are the inhabitants of this village: they all assembled here to pay their last respects to the dead; and now they are going to another village, about three miles off—for by our custom, no one of us may remain in this village during the night after a death has taken place. We make the proper offerings and prayers—then we go away, leaving the corpse alone. Strange things always happen in the house where a corpse has thus been left: so we think that it will be better for you to come away with us. We can find you good lodging in the other village. But perhaps, as you are a priest, you have no fear of demons or evil spirits; and, if you are not afraid of being left alone with the body, you will be very welcome to the use of this poor house. However, I must tell you that nobody, except a priest, would dare to remain here tonight."

Muso made answer, "For your kind intention and your generous hospitality and am deeply grateful. But I am sorry that you did not tell me of your father's death when I came; for, though I was a little tired, I certainly was not so tired that I should have found difficulty in doing my duty as a priest. Had you told me, I could have performed the service before your departure. As it is, I shall perform the service after you have gone away; and I shall stay by the body until morning. I do not know what you mean by your words about the danger of stay-ing here alone; but I am not afraid of ghosts or demons: therefore please to feel no anxiety on my account."

The young man appeared to be rejoiced by these assurances, and expressed his gratitude in fitting words. Then the other members of the family, and the folk assembled in the adjoining room, having been told of the priest's kind promises, came to thank him—after which the master of the house said, "Now, reverend Sir, much as we regret to leave you alone, we must bid you farewell. By the rule of our village, none of us can stay here after midnight. We beg, kind Sir, that you will take every care of your honorable body, while we are unable to attend upon you. And if you happen to hear or see anything strange during our absence, please tell us of the matter when we return in the morning."

All then left the house, except the priest, who went to the room where the dead body was lying. The usual offerings had been set before the corpse; and a small Buddhist lamp—tomyo—was burning. The priest recited the service, and performed the funeral ceremonies—after which he entered into meditation. So meditating he remained through several silent hours; and there was no sound in the deserted village. But, when the hush of the night was at its deepest, there noiselessly entered a Shape, vague and vast; and in the same moment Muso found himself without power to move or speak. He saw that Shape lift the corpse, as with hands, devour it, more quickly than a cat devours a rat—beginning at the head, and eating everything: the hair and the bones and even the shroud. And the monstrous Thing, having thus consumed the body, turned to the offerings, and ate them also. Then it went away, as mysteriously as it had come.

When the villagers returned next morning, they found the priest awaiting them at the door of the headman's dwelling. All in turn saluted him; and when they had entered, and looked about the room, no one expressed any surprise at the disappearance of the dead body and the offerings. But the master of the house said to Muso, "Reverent Sir, you have probably seen unpleasant things during the night: all of us were anxious about you. But now we are very happy to find you alive and unharmed. Gladly we would have stayed with you, if it had been possible. But the law of our village, as I told you last evening, obliges us to quit our houses after a death has taken place, and to leave the corpse alone. Whenever this law has been broken, heretofore, some great misfortune has followed. Whenever it is obeyed, we find that the corpse and the offerings disappear during our absence. Perhaps you have seen the cause."

Then Muso told of the dim and awful Shape that had entered the death-chamber to devour the body and the offerings. No person seemed to be surprised by his narration; and the master of the house observed, "What you have told us, reverend Sir, agrees with what has been said about this matter from ancient time."

Muso then inquired, "Does not the priest on the hill sometimes perform the funeral service for your dead?"

"What priest?" the young man asked.

"The priest who yesterday evening directed me to this village," answered Muso. "I called at his anjitsu on the hill yonder. He refused me lodging, but told me the way here."

The listeners looked at each other, as in astonishment; and, after a moment of silence, the master of the house said, "Reverend Sir, there is no priest and there is no anjitsu on the hill. For the time of many generations there has not been any resident-priest in this neighborhood."

Muso said nothing more on the subject; for it was evident that his kind hosts supposed him to have been deluded by some goblin. But after having bidden them farewell, and obtained all necessary information as to his road, he determined to look again for the hermitage on the hill, and so to ascertain whether he had really been deceived. He found the anjitsu without any difficulty; and, this time, its aged occupant invited him to enter. When he had done so, the hermit humbly bowed down before him, exclaiming, "Ah! I am ashamed!—I am very much ashamed!—I am exceedingly ashamed!"

"You need not be ashamed for having refused me shelter," said Muso. "You directed me to the village yonder, where I was very kindly treated; and I thank you for that favor."

"I can give no man shelter," the recluse made answer; and it is not for the refusal that I am ashamed. I am ashamed only that you should have seen me in my real shape—for it was I who devoured the corpse and the offerings last night before your eyes.... Know, reverend Sir, that I am a jikininki—an eater of human flesh. Have pity upon me, and suffer me to confess the secret fault by which I became reduced to this condition.

"A long, long time ago, I was a priest in this desolate region. There was no other priest for many leagues around. So, in that time, the bodies of the mountain-folk who died used to be brought here—sometimes from great distances—in order that I might repeat over them the holy service. But I repeated the service and performed the rites only as a matter of business; I thought only of the food and the clothes that my sacred profession enabled me to gain. And because of this selfish impiety I was reborn, immediately after my death, into the state of a jikininki. Since then I have been obliged to feed upon the corpses of the people who die in this district: every one of them I must devour in the way that you saw last night.... Now, reverend Sir, let me beseech you to perform a Segaki-service for me: help me by your prayers, I entreat you, so that I may be soon able to escape from this horrible state of existence."

No sooner had the hermit uttered this petition than he disappeared; and the hermitage also disappeared at the same instant. And Muso Kokushi found himself kneeling alone in the high grass, beside an ancient and moss-grown tomb of the form called go-rin-ishi, which seemed to be the tomb of a priest.

THE GOLDEN HAIRPIN

Tradition Bearer: Unavailable

Source: Smith, Richard Gordon. *Ancient Tales and Folklore of Japan.* London: A. and C. Black, 1908, 1–9.

Date: Unavailable

Original Source: Japan

National Origin: Japan

"The Golden Hairpin" is best classified as a supernatural **legend**. The **validating devices** of localization and citing specific names are hallmarks of the **genre**. The **motif** of the ghost or revenant who must return to fulfill an obligation or desire not satisfied in life is cross-culturally distributed. The appropriation of the living by the dead to accomplish this goal is a far less common theme.

Up in the northern city of Sendai, whence come the best of Japanese soldiers, there lived a samurai named Hasunuma.

Hasunuma was rich and hospitable, and consequently much thought of and well liked. Some thirty-five years ago his wife presented him with a beautiful daughter, their first child, whom they called "Ko," which means "Small" when applied to a child, much as we say "Little Mary or Little Jane." Her full name was really "Hasu-ko," which means "Little Lily"; but here we will call her "Ko" for short.

Exactly on the same date, "Saito," one of Hasunuma's friends and also a samurai, had the good fortune to have a son. The fathers decided that, being such old friends, they would wed their children to each other when old enough to marry; they were very happy over the idea, and so were their wives. To make the engagement of the babies more binding, Saito handed to Hasunuma a golden hairpin which had long been in his family, and said, "Here, my old friend, take this pin. It shall be a token of betrothal from my son, whose name shall be Kōnojō, to your little daughter Ko, both of whom are now aged two weeks only. May they live long and happy lives together."

Hasunuma took the pin, and handed it to his wife to keep; then they drank saké to the health of each other, and to the bride and bridegroom of some twenty years thence.

A few months after this Saito, in some way, caused displeasure to his feudal lord, and, being dismissed from service, left Sendai with his family—whither no one knew.

Seventeen years later O Ko San was, with one exception, the most beautiful girl in all Sendai; the exception was her sister, O Kei, just a year younger, and as beautiful as herself.

Many were the suitors for O Ko's hand; but she would have none of them, being faithful to the engagement made for her by her father when she was a baby. True, she had never seen her betrothed, and (which seemed more curious) neither she nor her family had ever once heard of the Saito family since they had left Sendai, over sixteen years before; but that was no reason why she, a Japanese girl, should break the word of her father, and therefore O Ko San remained faithful to her unknown lover, though she sorrowed greatly at his non-appearance; in fact, she secretly suffered so much thereby that she sickened, and three months later died, to the grief of all who knew her and to her family's serious distress.

On the day of O Ko San's funeral her mother was seeing to the last attentions paid to corpses, and smoothing her hair with the golden pin given to Ko San or O Ko by Saito in behalf of his son Kōnojō. When the body had been placed in its coffin, the mother thrust the pin into the girl's hair, saying, "Dearest daughter, this is the pin given as a memento to you by your betrothed, Kōnojō. Let it be a pledge to bind your spirits in death, as it would have been in life; and may you enjoy endless happiness, I pray."

In thus praying, no doubt, O Ko's mother thought that Kōnojō also must be dead, and that their spirits would meet; but it was not so, for two months after these events Kōnojō himself, now eighteen years of age, turned up at Sendai, calling first on his father's old friend Hasunuma.

"Oh, the bitterness and misfortune of it all!" said the latter. "Only two months ago my daughter Ko died. Had you but come before then she would have been alive now. But you never even sent a message; we never heard a word of your father or of your mother. Where did you all go when you left here? Tell me the whole story."

"Sir," answered the grief-stricken Kōnojō, "what you tell me of the death of your daughter, whom I had hoped to marry, sickens my heart, for I, like herself, had been faithful, and I hoped to marry her, and thought daily of her. When my father took my family away from Sendai, he took us to Yedo; and afterwards we went north to Yezo Island, where my father lost his money and became poor. He died in poverty. My poor mother did not long survive him. I have been working hard to try and earn enough to marry your daughter Ko; but I have not made more than enough to pay my journey down to Sendai. I felt it my duty to come and tell you of my family's misfortune and my own."

The old samurai was much touched by this story. He saw that the most unfortunate of all had been Kōnojō.

"Kōnojō," he said, "often have I thought and wondered to myself, Were you honest or were you not? Now I find that you have been truly faithful, and honest to your father's pledge. But you should have written—you should have written! Because you did not do so, sometimes we thought, my wife and I, that you must be dead; but we kept this thought to ourselves, and never told Ko San. Go to our Butsudan [family shrine]; open the doors of it, and burn a joss stick to Ko San's mortuary tablet. It will please her spirit. She longed and longed for your return, and died of that sane longing—for love of you. Her spirit will rejoice to know that you have come back for her."

Kōnojō did as he was bid. Bowing reverently three times before the mortuary tablet of O Ko San, he muttered a few words of prayer in her behalf, and then lit the incense-stick and placed it before the tablet.

After this exhibition of sincerity Hasunuma told the young fellow that he should consider him as an adopted son, and that he must live with them. He could have the small house in the garden. In any case, whatever his plans for the future might be, he must remain with them for the present.

This was a generous offer, worthy of a samurai. Kōnojō gratefully accepted it, and became one of the family. About a fortnight afterwards he settled himself in the little house at the end of the garden. Hasunuma, his wife, and their second daughter, O Kei, had gone, by command of the Daimio, to the Higan, a religious ceremony held in March; Hasunuma also always worshipped at his ancestral tombs at this time. Towards the dusk of evening they were returning in their palanquins. Kōnojō stood at the gate to see them pass, as was proper and respectful. The old samurai passed first, and was followed by his wife's palanquin, and then by that of O Kei. As this last passed the gate Kōnojō thought he heard something fall, causing a metallic sound. After the palanquin had passed he picked it up without any particular attention.

It was the golden hairpin; but of course, though Kōnojō's father had told him of the pin, Kōnojō had no idea that this was it, and therefore he thought nothing more than that it must be O Kei San's. He went back to his little house, closed it for the night, and was about to retire when he heard a knock at the door. "Who is there?" he shouted. "What do you want?" There came no answer, and Kōnojō lay down on his bed, thinking himself to have been mistaken. But there came another knock, louder than the first; and Kōnojō jumped out of bed, and lit the ando [lamp]. "If not a fox or a badger," thought he, "it must be some evil spirit come to disturb me."

On opening the door, with the ando in one hand, and a stick in the other, Kōnojō looked out into the dark, and there, to his astonishment, he beheld a vision of female beauty the likes of which he had never seen before. "Who are you, and what do you want?" quoth he.

"I am O Kei San, O Ko's younger sister," answered the vision. "Though you have not seen me, I have several times seen you, and I have fallen so madly in love with you that I can think of nothing else but you. When you picked up my golden pin tonight on our return, I had dropped it to serve as an excuse to come to you and knock. You must love me in return; for otherwise I must die!"

This heated and outrageous declaration scandalized poor Kōnojō. Moreover, he felt that it would be doing his kind host Hasunuma a great injustice to be receiving his younger daughter at this hour of the night and make love to her. He expressed himself forcibly in these terms.

"If you will not love me as I love you, then I shall take my revenge," said O Kei, "by telling my father that you got me to come here by making love to me, and that you then insulted me."

Poor Kōnojō! He was in a nice mess. What he feared most of all was that the girl would do as she said, that the samurai would believe her, and that he would be a disgraced and villainous person. He gave way, therefore, to the girl's request. Night after night she visited him, until nearly a month had passed. During this time Kōnojō had learned to love dearly the beautiful O Kei. Talking to her one evening, he said, "My dearest O Kei, I do not like this secret love of ours. Is it not better that we go away? If I asked your father to give you to me in marriage he would refuse, because I was betrothed to your sister."

"Yes," answered O Kei, "that is what I also have been wishing. Let us leave this very night, and go to Ishinomaki, the place where (you have told me) lives a faithful servant of your late father's, called Kinzo."

"Yes: Kinzo is his name, and Ishinomaki is the place. Let us start as soon as possible.'

Having thrust a few clothes into a bag, they started secretly and late that night, and duly arrived at their destination. Kinzo was delighted to receive them, and pleased to show how hospitable he could be to his late master's son and the beautiful lady.

They lived very happily for a year. Then one day O Kei said, "I think we ought to return, to my parents now. If they were angry with us at first they will have got over the worst of it. We have never written. They must be getting anxious as to my fate as they grow older. Yes, we ought to go."

Kōnojō agreed. Long had he felt the injustice he was doing Hasunuma.

Next day they found themselves back in Sendai, and Kōnojō could not help feeling a little nervous as he approached the samurai's house. They stopped at the outer gate, and O Kei said to Kōnojō, "I think it will be better for you to go in and see my father and mother first. If they get very angry show them this golden pin."

Kōnojō stepped boldly up to the door, and asked for an interview with the samurai.

Before the servant had time to return, Kōnojō heard the old man shout, "Kōnojō San! Why, of course! Bring the boy in at once," and he himself came out to welcome him.

"My dear boy," said the samurai, "right glad am I to see you back again. I am sorry you did not find your life with us good enough. You might have said you were going. But there—I suppose you take after your father in these matters, and prefer to disappear mysteriously. You are welcome back, at all events."

Kōnojō was astonished at this speech, and answered,

"But, sir, I have come to beg pardon for my sin."

"What sin have you committed?" queried the samurai in great surprise, and drawing himself up, in a dignified manner.

Kōnojō then gave a full account of his love affair with O Kei. From beginning to end he told it all, and as he proceeded the samurai showed signs of impatience.

"Do not joke, sir! My daughter O Kei San is not a subject for jokes and untruths. She has been as one dead for over a year—so ill that we have with difficulty forced gruel into her mouth. Moreover, she has spoken no word and shown no sign of life."

"I am neither stating what is untrue nor joking," said Kōnojō. "If you but send outside, you will find O Kei in the palanquin, in which I left her."

A servant was immediately sent to see, and returned, stating that there was neither palanquin nor any one at the gate.

Kōnojō, seeing that the samurai was now beginning to look perplexed and angry, drew the golden pin from his clothes, saying, "See! if you doubt me and think I am lying, here is the pin which O Kei told me to give you!"

"Bik-ku-ri-shi-ta-!" exclaimed O Kei's mother. "How came this pin into your hands? I myself put it into Ko San's coffin just before it was closed."

The samurai and Kōnojō stared at each other, and the mother at both. Neither knew what to think, or what to say or do. Imagine the general surprise when the sick O Kei walked into the room, having risen from her bed as if she had never been ill for a moment. She was the picture of health and beauty.

"How is this?" asked the samurai, almost shouting. "How is it, O Kei, that you have come from your sickbed dressed and with your hair done and looking as if you had never known a moment of illness?"

"I am not O Kei, but the spirit of O Ko," was the answer. "I was most unfortunate in dying before the return of Kōnojō San, for had I lived until then I should have become quite well and been married to him. As it was, my spirit was unhappy. It took the form of my dear sister O Kei, and for a year has lived happily in her body with Kōnojō. It is appeased now, and about to take its real rest."

"There is one condition, however, Kōnojō, which I must make," said the girl, turning to him. "You must marry my sister O Kei. If you do this my spirit will rest truly in peace, and then O Kei will become well and strong. Will you promise to marry O Kei?"

The old samurai, his wife, and Kōnojō were all amazed at this. The appearance of the girl was that of O Kei; but the voice and manners were those of O Ko. Then, there was the golden hairpin as further proof. The mother knew it well. She had placed it in Ko's hair just before the tub coffin was closed. Nobody could undeceive her on that point.

"But," said the samurai at last, "O Ko has been dead and buried for more than a year now. That you should appear to us puzzles us all. Why should you trouble us so?"

"I have explained already," resumed the girl. "My spirit could not rest until it had lived with Kōnojō, whom it knew to be faithful. It has done this now, and is prepared to rest. My only desire is to see Kōnojō marry my sister."

Hasunuma, his wife, and Kōnojō held a consultation. They were quite prepared that O Kei should marry, and Kōnojō did not object.

All things being settled, the ghost-girl held out her hand to Kōnojō saying,

"This is the last time you will touch the hand of O Ko. Farewell, my dear parents! Farewell to you all! I am about to pass away."

Then she fainted away, and seemed dead, and remained thus for half an hour; while the others, overcome with the strange and weird things which they had seen and heard, sat round her, hardly uttering a word.

At the end of half an hour the body came to life, and standing up, said. "Dear parents, have no more fear for me. I am perfectly well again; but I have no idea how I got down from my sick-room in this costume, or how it is that I feel so well."

Several questions were put to her; but it was quite evident that O Kei knew nothing of what had happened—nothing of the spirit of O Ko San, or of the golden hairpin!

A week later she and Kōnojō were married, and the golden hairpin was given to a shrine at Shiogama, to which, until quite recently, crowds used to go and worship.

STORY OF A TENGU

Tradition Bearer: Unavailable

Source: Hearn, Lafcadio. *Kwaidan: Stories and Studies of Strange Things.* Boston: Houghton, Mifflin and Co., 1904, 215–224.

Date: ca. 1904

Original Source: Japan

National Origin: Japan

In Japanese tradition, the Tengu are commonly represented either as winged men with the heads of birds, as birds of prey, or as men with unnaturally elongated noses. In folklore and popular culture, there is an association between the Tengu and the yamabushi (mountain-dwelling ascetics who practice Shugendo Buddhism). The protagonist of the following tale is obviously one of the latter.

In the days of the Emperor Go-Reizen, there was a holy priest living in the Temple of Seito, on the mountain called Hiyei-Zan, near Kyôto. One summer day this good priest, after a visit to the city, was returning to his temple by way of Kita-no-Ôji, when he saw some boys ill-treating a kite. They had caught the bird in a snare, and were beating it with sticks. "Oh, the poor creature!" compassionately exclaimed the priest, "Why do you torment it so, children?"

One of the boys made answer, "We want to kill it to get the feathers." Moved by pity, the priest persuaded the boys to let him have the kite in exchange for a fan that he was carrying; and he set the bird free. It had not been seriously hurt, and was able to fly away.

Happy at having performed this Buddhist act of merit, the priest then resumed his walk. He had not proceeded very far when he saw a strange monk come out of a bamboo-grove by the roadside and hasten towards him.

The monk respectfully saluted him, and said, "Sir, through your compassionate kindness my life has been saved; and I now desire to express my gratitude in a fitting manner."

Astonished at hearing himself thus addressed, the priest replied, "Really, I cannot remember to have ever seen you before: please tell me who you are."

"It is not wonderful that you cannot recognize me in this form," returned the monk, "I am the kite that those cruel boys were tormenting at Kita-no-Ôji. You saved my life; and there is nothing in this world more precious than life. So I now wish to return your kindness in some way or other. If there be anything that you would like to have, or to know, or to see—anything that I can do for you, in short—please to tell me; for as I happen to possess, in a small degree, the Six Supernatural Powers, I am able to gratify almost any wish that you can express."

On hearing these words, the priest knew that he was speaking with a Tengu; and he frankly made answer, "My friend, I have long ceased to care for the things of this world: I am now seventy years of age; neither fame nor pleasure has any attraction for me. I feel anxious only about my future birth; but as that is a matter in which no one can help me, it were useless to ask about it. Really, I can think of but one thing worth wishing for. It has been my life-long regret that I was not in India in the time of the Lord Buddha, and could not attend the great assembly on the holy mountain Gridhrakûta. Never a day passes in which this regret does not come to me, in the hour of morning or of evening prayer. Ah, my friend! If it were possible to conquer Time and Space, like the Bodhisattvas, so that I could look upon that marvelous assembly, how happy should I be!"

"Why," the Tengu exclaimed, "that pious wish of yours can easily be satisfied. I perfectly well remember the assembly on the Vulture Peak; and I can cause everything that happened there to reappear before you, exactly as it occurred. It is our greatest delight to represent such holy matters.... Come this way with me!"

And the priest suffered himself to be led to a place among pines, on the slope of a hill. "Now," said the Tengu, "you have only to wait here for awhile, with your eyes shut. Do not open them until you hear the voice of the Buddha preaching the Law. Then you can look. But when you see the appearance of the Buddha, you must not allow your devout feelings to influence you in any way; you must not bow down, nor pray, nor utter any such exclamation as, 'Even so, Lord!' or 'O thou Blessed One!' You must not speak at all. Should you make even the least sign of reverence, something very unfortunate might happen to me." The priest gladly promised to follow these injunctions; and the Tengu hurried away as if to prepare the spectacle.

The day waned and passed, and the darkness came; but the old priest waited patiently beneath a tree, keeping his eyes closed. At last a voice suddenly resounded above him—a wonderful voice, deep and clear like the pealing of a mighty bell—the voice of the Buddha Sâkyamuni proclaiming the Perfect Way. Then the priest, opening his eyes in a great radiance, perceived that all things had been changed: the place was indeed the Vulture Peak—the holy Indian mountain Gridhrakûta; and the time was the time of the Sûtra of the Lotus of the Good Law. Now there were no pines about him, but strange shining trees made of the Seven Precious Substances, with foliage and fruit of gems; and the ground was covered with Mandârava and Manjûshaka flowers showered from heaven; and the night was filled with fragrance and splendor and the sweetness of the great Voice. And in mid-air, shining as a moon above the world, the priest beheld the Blessed One seated upon the Lion-throne, with Samantabhadra at his right hand, and Mañjusrî at his left—and before them assembled—immeasurably spreading into

Space, like a flood of stars—the hosts of the Mahâsattvas and the Bodhisattvas with their countless following, "gods, demons, Nâgas, goblins, men, and beings not human." Sâriputra he saw, and Kâsyapa, and Ananda, with all the disciples of the Tathâgata—and the Kings of the Devas—and the Kings of the Four Directions, like pillars of fire—and the great Dragon-Kings—and the Gandharvas and Garudas—and the Gods of the Sun and the Moon and the Wind—and the shining myriads of Brahma's heaven. And incomparably further than even the measureless circling of the glory of these, he saw—made visible by a single ray of light that shot from the forehead of the Blessed One to pierce beyond uttermost Time—the eighteen hundred thousand Buddha-fields of the Eastern Quarter with all their habitants—and the beings in each of the Six States of Existence—and even the shapes of the Buddhas extinct, that had entered into Nirvâna. These, and all the gods, and all the demons, he saw bow down before the Lion-throne; and he heard that multitude incalculable of beings praising the Sûtra of the Lotos of the Good Law—like the roar of a sea before the Lord.

Then forgetting utterly his pledge—foolishly dreaming that he stood in the very presence of the very Buddha—he cast himself down in worship with tears of love and thanksgiving; crying out with a loud voice, "O thou Blessed One!"

Instantly with a shock as of earthquake the stupendous spectacle disappeared; and the priest found himself alone in the dark, kneeling upon the grass of the mountain-side. Then a sadness unspeakable fell upon him, because of the loss of the vision, and because of the thoughtlessness that had caused him to break his word. As he sorrowfully turned his steps homeward, the goblin-monk once more appeared before him, and said to him in tones of reproach and pain, "Because you did not keep the promise which you made to me, and heedlessly allowed your feelings to overcome you, the Gohôtendo, who is the Guardian of the Doctrine, swooped down suddenly from heaven upon us, and smote us in great anger, crying out, 'How do ye dare thus to deceive a pious person?' Then the other monks, whom I had assembled, all fled in fear. As for myself, one of my wings has been broken—so that now I cannot fly." And with these words the Tengu vanished forever.

HOW THE WICKED TANUKI WAS PUNISHED

Tradition Bearer: Unavailable

Source: Lang, Andrew. *The Crimson Fairy Book.* London: Longmans, Green and Company, 1903, 190–191.

Date: Unavailable

Original Source: Brauns, David. *Japanische Märchen und Sagen.* Leipzig: Verlag von Wilhelm Friedrich, 1885.

National Origin: Japan

The Tanuki, the Japanese raccoon-faced dog, is a real Japanese forest-dwelling canine species. According to Japanese folk belief, the tanuki is also a goblin and magician who possesses supernormal strength and can change shapes at will. Similarly, foxes are shape-shifters with magical abilities. Both creatures are popular subjects of Japanese folklore and both are portrayed as intelligent though greedy **tricksters**.

The hunters had hunted the wood for so many years that no wild animal was any more to be found in it. You might walk from one end to the other without ever seeing a hare, or a deer, or a boar, or hearing the cooing of the doves in their nest. If they were not dead, they had flown elsewhere. Only three creatures remained alive, and they had hidden themselves in the thickest part of the forest, high up the mountain. These were a grey-furred, long-tailed tanuki, his wife the fox, who was one of his own family, and their little son.

The fox and the tanuki were very clever, prudent beasts, and they also were skilled in magic, and by this means had escaped the fate of their unfortunate friends. If they heard the twang of an arrow or saw the glitter of a spear, ever so far off, they lay very still, and were not to be tempted from their hiding-place, if their hunger was ever so great, or the game ever so delicious. "We are not so foolish as to risk our lives," they said to each other proudly. But at length there came a day when, in spite of their prudence, they seemed likely to die of starvation, for no more food was to be had. Something had to be done, but they did not know what.

Suddenly a bright thought struck the tanuki. "I have got a plan," he cried joyfully to his wife. "I will pretend to be dead, and you must change yourself into a man, and take me to the village for sale. It will be easy to find a buyer, tanukis' skins are always wanted; then buy some food with the money and come home again. I will manage to escape somehow, so do not worry about me."

The fox laughed with delight, and rubbed her paws together with satisfaction. "Well, next time I will go," she said, "and you can sell me." And then she changed herself into a man, and picking up the stiff body of the tanuki, set off towards the village. She found him rather heavy, but it would never have done to let him walk through the wood and risk his being seen by somebody.

As the tanuki had foretold, buyers were many, and the fox handed him over to the person who offered the largest price, and hurried to get some food with the money. The buyer took the tanuki back to his house, and throwing him into a corner went out. Directly the tanuki found he was alone, he crept cautiously through a chink of the window, thinking, as he did so, how lucky it was that he was not a fox, and was able to climb. Once outside, he hid himself in a ditch till it grew dusk, and then galloped away into the forest.

95

While the food lasted they were all three as happy as kings; but there soon arrived a day when the larder was as empty as ever. "It is my turn now to pretend to be dead," cried the fox. So the tanuki changed himself into a peasant, and started for the village, with his wife's body hanging over his shoulder. A buyer was not long in coming forward, and while they were making the bargain a wicked thought darted into the tanuki's head, that if he got rid of the fox there would be more food for him and his son. So as he put the money in his pocket he whispered softly to the buyer that the fox was not really dead, and that if he did not take care she might run away from him. The man did not need twice telling. He gave the poor fox a blow on the head, which put an end to her, and the wicked tanuki went smiling to the nearest shop.

In former times he had been very fond of his little son; but since he had betrayed his wife he seemed to have changed all in a moment, for he would not give him as much as a bite, and the poor little fellow would have starved had he not found some nuts and berries to eat, and he waited on, always hoping that his mother would come back.

At length some notion of the truth began to dawn on him; but he was careful to let the old tanuki see nothing, though in his own mind he turned over plans from morning till night, wondering how best he might avenge his mother.

One morning, as the little tanuki was sitting with his father, he remembered, with a start, that his mother had taught him all she knew of magic, and that he could work spells as well as his father, or perhaps better. "I am as good a wizard as you," he said suddenly, and a cold chill ran through the tanuki as he heard him, though he laughed, and pretended to think it a joke. But the little tanuki stuck to his point, and at last the father proposed they should have a wager.

"Change yourself into any shape you like," said he, "and I will undertake to know you. I will go and wait on the bridge which leads over the river to the village, and you shall transform yourself into anything you please, but I will know you through any disguise." The little tanuki agreed, and went down the road which his father had pointed out. But instead of transforming himself into a different shape, he just hid himself in a corner of the bridge, where he could see without being seen.

He had not been there long when his father arrived and took up his place near the middle of the bridge, and soon after the king came by, followed by a troop of guards and all his court.

"Ah! He thinks that now he has changed himself into a king I shall not know him," thought the old tanuki, and as the king passed in his splendid carriage, borne by his servants, he jumped upon it crying, "I have won my wager; you cannot deceive me." But in reality it was he who had deceived himself. The soldiers, conceiving that their king was being attacked, seized the tanuki by the legs and flung him over into the river, and the water closed over him.

And the little tanuki saw it all, and rejoiced that his mother's death had been avenged. Then he went back to the forest, and if he has not found it too lonely, he is probably living there still.

THE SLAYING OF THE TANUKI

Tradition Bearer: Unavailable

Source: Lang, Andrew. *The Pink Fairy Book.* London: Longmans, Green and Company, 1897, 33–39.

Date: Unavailable

Original Source: Brauns, David. *Japanische Märchen und Sagen.* Leipzig: Verlag von Wilhelm Friedrich, 1885.

National Origin: Japan

The hare is a prominent animal in Japanese folklore. The hare is one of the twelve animals of the Chinese cycle of years. Rather than the "man in the moon," the Japanese see a "hare in the moon," pounding rice with a mortar and pestle. The Japanese hare is not the common **trickster** figure that it is in other traditions; that role is generally played by the kitsune (fox), the tanuki, or the badger. In the following narrative of the tanuki's malice, these roles are reversed.

Near a big river, and between two high mountains, a man and his wife lived in a cottage a long, long time ago. A dense forest lay all round the cottage, and there was hardly a path or a tree in the whole wood that was not familiar to the peasant from his boyhood. In one of his wanderings he had made friends with a hare, and many an hour the two passed together, when the man was resting by the roadside, eating his dinner.

Now this strange friendship was observed by the Tanuki, a wicked, quarrelsome beast, who hated the peasant, and was never tired of doing him an ill turn. Again and again he had crept to the hut, and finding some choice morsel put away for the little hare, had either eaten it if he thought it nice, or trampled it to pieces so that no one else should get it, and at last the peasant lost patience, and made up his mind he would have the Tanuki's blood.

So for many days the man lay hidden, waiting for the Tanuki to come by, and when one morning he marched up the road thinking of nothing but the dinner he was going to steal, the peasant threw himself upon him and bound his four legs tightly, so that he could not move. Then he dragged his enemy joyfully to the house, feeling that at length he had got the better of the mischievous beast which had done him so many ill turns. "He shall pay for them with his skin," he said to his wife. "We will first kill him, and then cook him." So saying, he hanged the Tanuki, head downwards, to a beam, and went out to gather wood for a fire.

Meanwhile the old woman was standing at the mortar pounding the rice that was to serve them for the week with a pestle that made her arms ache with its weight. Suddenly she heard something whining and weeping in the corner, and, stopping her work, she looked round to see what it was. That was all that the rascal wanted, and he put on directly his most humble air, and begged the woman in his softest voice to loosen his bonds, which her hurting him sorely. She was filled with pity for him, but did not dare to set him free, as she knew that her husband would be very angry. The Tanuki, however, did not despair, and seeing that her heart was softened, began his prayers anew. "He only asked to have his bonds taken from him," he said. "He would give his word not to attempt to escape, and if he was once set free he could soon pound her rice for her."

"Then you can have a little rest," he went on, "for rice pounding is very tiring work, and not at all fit for weak women." These last words melted the good woman completely, and she unfastened the bonds that held him. Poor foolish creature! In one moment the Tanuki had seized her, stripped off all her clothes, and popped her in the mortar. In a few minutes more she was pounded as fine as the rice; and not content with that, the Tanuki placed a pot on the hearth and made ready to cook the peasant a dinner from the flesh of his own wife!

When everything was complete he looked out of the door, and saw the old man coming from the forest carrying a large bundle of wood. Quick as lightning the Tanuki not only put on the woman's clothes, but, as he was a magician, assumed her form as well. Then he took the wood, kindled the fire, and very soon set a large dinner before the old man, who was very hungry, and had forgotten for the moment all about his enemy. But when the Tanuki saw that he had eaten his fill and would be thinking about his prisoner, he hastily shook off the clothes behind a door and took his own shape. Then he said to the peasant, "You are a nice sort of person to seize animals and to talk of killing them! You are caught in your own net. It is your own wife that you have eaten, and if you want to find her bones you have only to look under the floor." With these words he turned and made for the forest.

The old peasant grew cold with horror as he listened, and seemed frozen to the place where he stood. When he had recovered himself a little, he collected the bones of his dead wife, buried them in the garden, and swore over the grave to be avenged on the Tanuki. After everything was done he sat himself down in his lonely cottage and wept bitterly, and the bitterest thought of all was that he would never be able to forget that he had eaten his own wife.

While he was thus weeping and wailing his friend the hare passed by, and, hearing the noise, pricked up his ears and soon recognized the old man's voice. He wondered what had happened, and put his head in at the door and asked if anything was the matter. With tears and groans the peasant told him the whole dreadful story, and the hare, filled with anger and compassion, comforted him as best he could, and promised to help him in his revenge. "The false knave shall not go unpunished," said he.

So the first thing he did was to search the house for materials to make an ointment, which he sprinkled plentifully with pepper and then put in his pocket.

Next he took a hatchet, bade farewell to the old man, and departed to the forest. He bent his steps to the dwelling of the Tanuki and knocked at the door. The Tanuki, who had no cause to suspect the hare, was greatly pleased to see him, for he noticed the hatchet at once, and began to lay plots how to get hold of it.

To do this he thought he had better offer to accompany the hare, which was exactly what the hare wished and expected, for he knew all the Tanuki's cunning, and understood his little ways. So he accepted the rascal's company with joy, and made himself very pleasant as they strolled along. When they were wandering in this manner through the forest the hare carelessly raised his hatchet in passing, and cut down some thick boughs that were hanging over the path, but at length, after cutting down a good big tree, which cost him many hard blows, he declared that it was too heavy for him to carry home, and he must just leave it where it was. This delighted the greedy Tanuki, who said that they would be no weight for him, so they collected the large branches, which the hare bound tightly on his back. Then he trotted gaily to the house, the hare following after with his lighter bundle.

By this time the hare had decided what he would do, and as soon as they arrived, he quietly set on fire the wood on the back of the Tanuki. The Tanuki, who was busy with something else, observed nothing, and only called out to ask what was the meaning of the crackling that he heard. "It is just the rattle of the stones which are rolling down the side of the mountain," the hare said; and the Tanuki was content, and made no further remarks, never noticing that the noise really sprang from the burning boughs on his back, until his fur was in flames, and it was almost too late to put it out. Shrieking with pain, he let fall the burning wood from his back, and stamped and howled with agony. But the hare comforted him, and told him that he always carried with him an excellent plaster in case of need, which would bring him instant relief, and taking out his ointment he spread it on a leaf of bamboo, and laid it on the wound. No sooner did it touch him than the Tanuki leapt yelling into the air, and the hare laughed, and ran to tell his friend the peasant what a trick he had played on their enemy.

But the old man shook his head sadly, for he knew that the villain was only crushed for the moment, and that he would shortly be revenging himself upon them. No, the only way every to get any peace and quiet was to render the Tanuki harmless for ever. Long did the old man and the hare puzzle together how this was to be done, and at last they decided that they would make two boats, a small one of wood and a large one of clay. Then they fell to work at once, and when the boats were ready and properly painted, the hare went to the Tanuki, who was still very ill, and invited him to a great fish-catching.

The Tanuki was still feeling angry with the hare about the trick he had played him, but he was weak and very hungry, so he gladly accepted the proposal, and accompanied the hare to the bank of the river, where the two boats were moored, rocked by the waves. They both looked exactly alike, and the Tanuki only saw that one was bigger than the other, and would hold more fish, so he sprang into the large one, while the hare climbed into the one which was made of wood. They loosened their moorings, and made for the middle of the stream, and when they were at some distance from the bank, the hare took his oar, and struck such a heavy blow at the other boat, that it broke in two. The Tanuki fell straight into the water, and was held there by the hare till he was quite dead. Then he put the body in his boat and rowed to land, and told the old man that his enemy was dead at last. And the old man rejoiced that his wife was avenged, and he took the hare into his house, and they lived together all their days in peace and quietness upon the mountain.

THE CAT'S ELOPEMENT

Tradition Bearer: Unavailable

Source: Lang, Andrew. *The Pink Fairy Book*. London: Longmans, Green and Company, 1897, 1–5.

Date: Unavailable

Original Source: Brauns, David. *Japanische Märchen und Sagen*. Leipzig: Verlag von Wilhelm Friedrich, 1885.

National Origin: Japan

In a plot of true love and separation that is usually enacted by human characters, the heroic cat, Gon, gives up a life of luxury for true love. The ultimate success of the protagonist arises from Gon's rescue of a princess from a serpent (who ironically risked its life for love).

Once upon a time there lived a cat of marvelous beauty, with a skin as soft and shining as silk, and wise green eyes, that could see even in the dark. His name was Gon, and he belonged to a music teacher, who was so fond and proud of him that he would not have parted with him for anything in the world.

Now not far from the music master's house there dwelt a lady who possessed a most lovely little pussy cat called Koma. She was such a little dear altogether, and blinked her eyes so daintily, and ate her supper so tidily, and when she had finished she licked her pink nose so delicately with her little tongue, that her mistress was never tired of saying, "Koma, Koma, what should I do without you?"

Well, it happened one day that these two, when out for an evening stroll, met under a cherry tree, and in one moment fell madly in love with each other. Gon had long felt that it was time for him to find a wife, for all the ladies in the neighborhood paid him so much attention that it made him quite shy; but he was not easy to please, and did not care about any of them. Now, before he had time to think, Cupid had entangled him in his net, and he was filled with love towards Koma. She fully returned his passion, but, like a woman, she saw the difficulties in the way, and consulted sadly with Gon as to the means of overcoming them. Gon entreated his master to set matters right by buying Koma, but her mistress would not part from her. Then the music master was asked to sell Gon to the lady, but he declined to listen to any such suggestion, so everything remained as before.

At length the love of the couple grew to such a pitch that they determined to please themselves, and to seek their fortunes together. So one moonlight night they stole away, and ventured out into an unknown world. All day long they marched bravely on through the sunshine, till they had left their homes far behind them, and towards evening they found themselves in a large park. The wanderers by this time were very hot and tired, and the grass looked very soft and inviting, and the trees cast cool deep shadows, when suddenly an ogre appeared in this Paradise, in the shape of a big, big dog! He came springing towards them showing all his teeth, and Koma shrieked, and rushed up a cherry tree. Gon, however, stood his ground boldly, and prepared to give battle, for he felt that Koma's eyes were upon him, and that he must not run away. But, alas! His courage would have availed him nothing had his enemy once touched him, for he was large and powerful, and very fierce. From her perch in the tree Koma saw it all, and screamed with all her might, hoping that some one would hear, and come to help. Luckily a servant of the princess to whom the park belonged was walking by, and he drove off the dog, and picking up the trembling Gon in his arms, carried him to his mistress.

So poor little Koma was left alone, while Gon was borne away full of trouble, not in the least knowing what to do. Even the attention paid him by the princess, who was delighted with his beauty and pretty ways, did not console him, but there was no use in fighting against fate, and he could only wait and see what would turn up.

The princess, Gon's new mistress, was so good and kind that everybody loved her, and she would have led a happy life, had it not been for a serpent who had fallen in love with her, and was constantly annoying her by his presence. Her servants had orders to drive him away as often as he appeared; but as they were careless, and the serpent very sly, it sometimes happened that he was able to slip past them, and to frighten the princess by appearing before her. One day she was seated in her room, playing on her favorite musical instrument, when she felt something gliding up her sash, and saw her enemy making his way to kiss her cheek. She shrieked and threw herself backwards, and Gon, who had been curled up on a stool at her feet, understood her terror, and with one bound seized the snake by his neck. He gave him one bite and one shake, and flung him on the ground, where he lay, never to worry the princess any more. Then she took Gon in her arms, and praised and caressed him, and saw that he had the nicest bits to eat, and the softest mats to lie on; and he would have had nothing in the world to wish for if only he could have seen Koma again.

Time passed on, and one morning Gon lay before the house door, basking in the sun. He looked lazily at the world stretched out before him, and saw in the distance a big ruffian of a cat teasing and ill-treating quite a little one. He jumped up, full of rage, and chased away the big cat, and then he turned to comfort the little one, when his heart nearly burst with joy to find that it was Koma. At first Koma did not know him again, he had grown so large and stately; but when it dawned upon her who it was, her happiness knew no bounds. And they rubbed their heads and their noses again and again, while their purring might have been heard a mile off.

Paw in paw they appeared before the princess, and told her the story of their life and its sorrows. The princess wept for sympathy, and promised that they should never more be parted, but should live with her to the end of their days. By-and-by the princess herself got married, and brought a prince to dwell in the palace in the park. And she told him all about her two cats, and how brave Gon had been, and how he had delivered her from her enemy the serpent.

And when the prince heard, he swore they should never leave them, but should go with the princess wherever she went. So it all fell out as the princess wished; and Gon and Koma had many children, and so had the princess, and they all played together, and were friends to the end of their lives.

THE STONECUTTER

Tradition Bearer: Unavailable

Source: Lang, Andrew. *The Crimson Fairy Book*. London: Longmans, Green and Company, 1903, 112–113.

Date: Unavailable

Original Source: Brauns, David. *Japanische Märchen und Sagen*. Leipzig: Verlag von Wilhelm Friedrich, 1885.

National Origin: Japan

At the outset of this **fable**, a humble man is afflicted with envy when he sees a rich man's lifestyle. Its beginning is similar to "The Fisher and His Wife" (AT 555) because of the narrative's plot of a spirit granting a human increasingly outrageous wishes. The concluding episode, however, in which the protagonist returns full circle to his humble beginnings is reminiscent of "Stronger and Strongest" (AT 2031).

Once upon a time there lived a stonecutter, who went every day to a great rock in the side of a big mountain and cut out slabs for gravestones or for houses. He understood very well the kinds of stones wanted for the different purposes, and as he was a careful workman he had plenty of customers. For a long time he was quite happy and contented, and asked for nothing better than what he had.

Now in the mountain dwelt a spirit which now and then appeared to men, and helped them in many ways to become rich and prosperous. The stonecutter, however, had never seen this spirit, and only shook his head, with an unbelieving air, when anyone spoke of it. But a time was coming when he learned to change his opinion.

One day the stonecutter carried a gravestone to the house of a rich man, and saw there all sorts of beautiful things, of which he had never even dreamed. Suddenly his daily work seemed to grow harder and heavier, and he said to himself, "Oh, if only I were a rich man, and could sleep in a bed with silken curtains and golden tassels, how happy I should be!"

And a voice answered him, "Your wish is heard; a rich man you shall be!"

At the sound of the voice the stonecutter looked around, but could see nobody. He thought it was all his fancy, and picked up his tools and went home, for he did not feel inclined to do any more work that day. But when he reached the little house where he lived, he stood still with amazement, for instead of his wooden hut was a stately palace filled with splendid furniture, and most splendid of all was the bed, in every respect like the one he had envied. He was nearly beside himself with joy, and in his new life the old one was soon forgotten.

It was now the beginning of summer, and each day the sun blazed more fiercely. One morning the heat was so great that the stonecutter could scarcely breathe, and he determined he would stop at home till the evening. He was rather dull, for he had never learned how to amuse himself, and was peeping through the closed blinds to see what was going on in the street, when a little carriage passed by, drawn by servants dressed in blue and silver. In the carriage sat a prince, and over his head a golden umbrella was held, to protect him from the sun's rays.

"Oh, if I were only a prince!" said the stonecutter to himself, as the carriage vanished around the corner. "Oh, if I were only a prince, and could go in such a carriage and have a golden umbrella held over me, how happy I should be!"

And a prince he was. Before his carriage rode one company of men and another behind it; servants dressed in scarlet and gold bore him along, the coveted umbrella was held over his head, everything his heart could desire was his. But yet it was not enough. He looked around still for something to wish for, and when he saw that in spite of the water he poured on the grass the rays of the sun scorched it, and that in spite of the umbrella held over his head each day his face grew browner and browner, he cried in his anger, "The sun is mightier than I; oh, if I were only the sun!"

And the mountain spirit answered, "Your wish is heard; the sun you shall be."

And the sun he was, and felt himself proud in his power. He shot his beams above and below, on earth and in heaven; he burnt up the grass in the fields and scorched the faces of princes as well as of poorer folk. But in a short time he began to grow tired of his might, for there seemed nothing left for him to do. Discontent once more filled his soul, and when a cloud covered his face, and hid the earth from him, he cried in his anger, "Does the cloud hold captive my rays, and is it mightier than I? Oh, that I were a cloud, and mightier than any!"

And the mountain spirit answered, "Your wish is heard; a cloud you shall be!"

And a cloud he was, and lay between the sun and the earth. He caught the sun's beams and held them, and to his joy the earth grew green again and flowers blossomed. But that was not enough for him, and for days and week he poured forth rain till the rivers overflowed their banks, and the crops of rice stood in water. Towns and villages were destroyed by the power of the rain, only the great rock on the mountainside remained unmoved. The cloud was amazed at the sight, and cried in wonder, "Is the rock, then, mightier than I? Oh, if I were only the rock!"

And the mountain spirit answered, "Your wish is heard; the rock you shall be!"

And the rock he was, and gloried in his power. Proudly he stood, and neither the heat of the sun nor the force of the rain could move him. "This is better than all!" he said to himself. But one day he heard a strange noise at his feet, and when he looked down to see what it could be, he saw a stonecutter driving tools into his surface. Even while he looked a trembling feeling ran all through him, and a great block broke off and fell upon the ground. Then he cried in his wrath, "Is a mere child of earth mightier than a rock? Oh, if I were only a man!"

And the mountain spirit answered, "Your wish is heard. A man once more you shall be!"

And a man he was, and in the sweat of his brow he toiled again at his trade of stone cutting. His bed was hard and his food scanty, but he had learned to be satisfied with it, and did not long to be something or somebody else. And as he never asked for things he did not have, or desired to be greater and mightier than other people, he was happy at last, and never again heard the voice of the mountain spirit.

KORYAK

HOW A SMALL KAMAK WAS TRANSFORMED INTO A HARPOON LINE

Tradition Bearer: Anne

Source: Bogoras, Waldemar. *Koryak Texts, Publications of the American Ethnological Society V.* Leyden: E. J. Brill, Ltd., 1917, 35–40.

Date: ca. 1900

Original Source: Koryak

National Origin: Siberia

Evil spirits are called kamak by the Koryak. These are the same beings that the Koryak's Chukchee neighbors call "ke'let" (see "The Youth Who Received Supernatural Powers from the Ke'let," page 36, for information on the Koryak environment and the ke'let). As in this Koryak **myth**, the kamaks live much like their human neighbors, but they are capable of changing their shapes and enjoy dining on human flesh. Big Raven is the supreme supernatural and **trickster** of Koryak myth. Miti' is Big Raven's wife. Eme'mqut is his son.

A small kamak said to his mother, "I am hungry."

She said to him, "Go and eat something in the storeroom behind the sleeping-room!"

He said, "I do not want to. I want to, go to Big-Raven's house."

The mother said, "Do not do it! You will die. You will be caught in a snare." She said, "Go to the upper storeroom (in the porch) and eat something!"

He said, "What for? Those provisions taste of the upper storeroom."

She said, "Go to the cache and eat something!" He said, "What for? Those provisions taste of the cache."

Big-Raven spread a snare close to his elevated storehouse (raised on supports). The small kamak ran there, and was caught in a snare. He began to whimper, "Oh, oh, I am caught, I am caught!"

Big-Raven said, "It came to my mind to go and to look at this snare." He came to it, and wanted to enter the storehouse, but stumbled over something lying in the way. "What now, what is it?"

"It is I. I am caught." The small kamak was crying, and brushing away his tears with his small fist.

"Stop blubbering! I will take you to Miti'." He brought the small kamak to his house, and said, "O, Miti'! Dance in honor of (our) catch!"

She began to dance, "We have a small kamak, we have a small kamak!"

Big-Raven said, "You dance in a wrong way. Ġa'na, step forth and dance in honor of (our) catch!"

She came out and began to dance, "We have a small ma'kak, we have a small ma'kak!"

Big-Raven said, "Really this is right."

They took him into the house. The house-master said, "What shall we make out of you, a cover for the roof-hole?"

"Not this. If I am made into a cover for the roof-hole, I shall feel smoky, I shall feel cold."

The house-master said, "What shall we make out of you, a plug for the vent-hole?"

"Not this. If I am made into a plug for the vent-hole, I shall be afraid of evil spirits passing by."

The house-master said, "What, then, do you wish us to make of you? Perhaps a work-bag for Miti'."

He said, "Not this. I shall feel smothered." The house-master said, "We shall make you into a thong."

The small kamak began to laugh and said, "Yes!"

They made him into a thong, they cut him duly, then they carried the line out and began to stretch it (tightly). Thus stretched, they (left it there). Big-Raven's people went to sleep. Frost-Man and his people said, "Big-Raven has caught a small kamak. They made him into a thong. Let us go and steal it!" They found it, and began to untie it.

Then it cried aloud, "Quick, get up! Already they are untying me!"

Big-Raven said, "What is the matter with our small line? It wants to awaken us. Quick, let us get up!" They woke up, and said to the small kamak, "What is the matter with you? Why were you crying so loudly?"

The small kamak said, "Frost-Man's people wanted to carry me away."

The people living down the coast heard (about the thing)—how Big-Raven caught a small kamak; and how they made him into a thong; and how no one succeeded in carrying it away, it was so watchful. Those people began to say, "We will go and carry it away."

They said, "Surely we will carry it away." Big-Raven's people went to sleep. The people living down the coast came and took the line.

It wanted to awaken the other people, but it was unable to awaken them. "Oh, they are untying me already, they are carrying me away!" Indeed, they untied it and carried it away; they stole the line.

The others woke up, but there was no line whatever. It had been taken away. Big-Raven said, "People living down the coast have committed this theft. Indeed, they took it, nobody else."

Eme'mqut said, "A very good line was taken away, still we will bring it back." Eme'mqut made a wooden whale and entered it. He went away and came to the people living down the coast.

Those people were walking around. They were saying, "This is the first time that such a whale has come near to us. It is a very good whale."

They attacked the whale, came near to it, and threw at it a harpoon with a new line. The small kamak lustily bit into the whale. Eme'mqut said to him under his breath, "Why are you biting me? I have come to fetch you home." Eme'mqut threw into the boat of the whale-hunters some berries of *Rubus Arcticus*, and they began to eat them. Meanwhile Eme'mqut fled in all haste to his house. He carried away the new line, and took it home. They ceased carrying the line out of the house. They kept it always in the inner room, so the others could not steal it. That is all.

LITTLE-BIRD-MAN AND RAVEN-MAN

Tradition Bearer: Pa'qa

Source: Borgas, Waldemar. *Koryak Texts, Publications of the American Ethnological Society* V. Leyden: E. J. Brill, Ltd., 1917, 12–23.

Date: ca. 1900

Original Source: Koryak

National Origin: Siberia

Although the following **myth** appears unusual to the outsider, this narrative is consistent with indigenous Koryak conventions. Raven-Man is exposed as a **trickster**, liar and thief. Yini'a-ñaẇġut rescues the sun from Raven-Man's mouth, and Little-Bird-Man is transformed externally into the heroic figure that he is beneath his surface appearance.

Raven-Man and Little-Bird-Man wooed (the daughter) of Big-Raven. Big-Raven preferred Little-Bird-Man. He said, "I will give my daughter to Little-Bird-Man." Miti' said, "I will give my daughter to Raven-Man." After that Raven-Man would go out secretly. He would eat excrement and dog-carrion. (In the morning) they would wake up, and several wolverine-skins and wolf-skins would be there. They would ask both of the suitors, "Who killed those?" and Raven-Man would answer, "I killed them."

Then a snow-storm broke out, and continued for a long time with unabated violence. Big-Raven said to the suitors, "Go and try to calm this storm! To the one who calms it, to that one will I give my daughter to wife." Raven-Man said, "I will calm the storm." He said, "Prepare some provisions for me." They prepared several pairs of boots. He went out, and staid near by under a cliff, eating. Little-Bird-Man went out, and there he stood eating of the provisions. Raven-Man gave to Little-Bird-Man a wicked look. Little-Bird-Man entered again, and did not say anything.

Raven-Man staid at the same place. The snow-storm continued with the same vigor, without abating. Oh, at last Raven-Man entered. His boots were all covered with ice, for he would make water in his boots. That is the reason why the boots had ice.

He said, "It is impossible! There is a crack in the heavens."

After a while they said to Little-Bird-Man, "Now, then, calm this storm!"

He said, "It is impossible. Shall I also go out and make water in my boots, like Raven-Man?"

Then Big-Raven said to both suitors, "Go away! None of you shall marry her."

Then Little-Bird-Man said, "All right! I will try." He took a round stopper, a shovel, and some fat, and went up to heaven. He flew up, and came to the crack in the heavens. He stopped it with a stopper, and threw the fat on the heavens all around it. For a while it grew calmer.

He came home, and the snow-storm broke out again. Even the stopper was thrust back into the house. It was too small. He said, "It is impossible. The heavens have a crack." Big-Raven made another stopper, a larger one, and gave it to Little-Bird-Man. He also gave him a larger piece of fat. Little-Bird-Man flew up to the same place and put this stopper into the crack. It fitted well. He drove it in with a mallet. He spread the fat around over the heavens, shoveled the snow around the hole, and covered it. Then it grew quite calm.

He came back, and then Raven-Man grew hateful to all of them. He took a place close to Miti'; and she said to him, "How is it that you smell of excrement?"

"Why! It is because I have had no bread [a delicacy among the Koryak] for a long time.

She said to him, "Enough, go away! You have done nothing to quiet this storm." He went away. Little-Bird-Man married Yini'a-ñawġut.

Summer came. It was raining hard. Then Raven-Man put the sun into his mouth; so it grew quite dark.

After that they said to Čan'ai', "Čan'ai', go and fetch water!"

"How shall I fetch water? (It is too dark)."

After a while they said to her, "Why, we are quite thirsty, We are going to die."

She went groping in the dark, then she stopped and began to sing. She sang, "Both small rivers are stingy (with their water)." Then a small river came to that place, bubbling. She filled her pail bought from the Russians (that is, an iron pail), and carried it on her back. (Suddenly) a man came to her. She could not carry the pail.

He said, "I will carry the pail (for you)." She came home in the dark. The man followed. It was River-Man. They said to her, "Who is this man?"

He said, "I am River-Man. I took pity on that singer." They scolded their daughter. Nevertheless River-Man married her.

After that they remained still in complete darkness. They said to River-Man, "Why are we living in darkness?"

He said, "Why, indeed?" He put on a headband of ringed-seal thong. He went out (and practiced magic). Then at least a little light appeared. The day dawned.

They spoke among themselves, "How shall we do it?"

Then Yini'a-ñawġut prepared for a journey. She went to Raven-Man and asked, "Halloo! Is Raven-Man at home?"

Raven-Woman said, "He is."

She said to Raven-Man, "Since you went away, I have been feeling dull all the time." She found Raven-Man, and said to him, "Did not you feel dull (since that time)? Will you stay so?" He turned his back to her, but she wanted to turn him (so that he should look with) his face to her. But he turned his back to her. Then she tickled him under the arms. She put her hands under his armpits.

His sister said to him, "What is the matter with you? Stop it! This is good girl."

After that he began to a make sounds in her direction, "Ġm, ġm, ġm!" She turned him around, and at last he laughed out, "Ha, ha, ha!" The sun jumped out and fastened itself to the sky. It grew daylight.

After that they slept together. She said to him, "Have you a tent?"

"No!"

"Have you a fork?"

"No!"

"Have you a plate?"

"No!"

She said, "Then let us go home! I have all those things at home." They moved on to Big-Raven's house. She said to Raven-Man, "Oh, you are a good man!" and he felt flattered.

Afterwards she killed him.

Yini'a-ñawġut put Raven-Man's (head) on above. She said, "That spotted palate of yours, let it grow to be a fine cloudless sky!" [This is to serve as an incantation against bad weather].

She came home. And they said to her, "What have you been doing?"

She said, "I killed Raven-Man. He had the sun in his mouth."

From that time on it was quite calm.

Raven-Woman said, "Well, now, does my brother remember me? (Probably) he has plenty to eat."

She said, "Let me visit him." She visited him, and he was dead. Then she cried (and said), "He caused annoyance to the other people. (Therefore he is dead.)" She left him there. There was nothing else to do.

Then those people said to Little-Bird-Man, "Go home, both of you!"

They said to them, "Go away with a caravan of pack-sledges!"

He replied, "We will go on foot." They went away on foot, and came to a river. Little-Bird-Man said to the woman, "Let me carry you (across)!"

The woman said to him, "Do not do it!"

He said, "It is all right." He carried her, and in doing so he died.

Yini'a-ñawġut slept a night among stone-pines and was almost frozen to death. On the following morning it dawned, and close to that place a reindeer-herd was walking. All the reindeer had iron antlers. A man was walking there too. He said, "Oh, come here!"

She said, "I will not come. My husband has died."

He said to her, "I am he, I am your husband."

He took out his gloves. "These you made for me. I am your husband. I am Little-Bird-Man."

A house was there, also reindeer (for driving). He said to her, "Let us go to Big-Raven! Now let them say again that you have a bad husband!" They went with a caravan of pack-sledges, and they arrived.

The people said to Big-Raven, "Oh, your daughter has come with a caravan." Big-Raven said, "Our daughter went away on foot." She said, "Here I am, I have been brought home by Little-Bird-Man." Little-Bird-Man made numerous driving-sledges, all of silver. They lived there all together, and traveled about in all directions with a caravan of pack-sledges. They lived in joy. They stayed there.

MITI' AND MAGPIE MAN

Tradition Bearer: Anne

Source: Borgas, Waldemar. *Koryak Texts, Publications of the American Ethnological Society V.* Leyden: E. J. Brill, Ltd., 1917, 35–40.

Date: ca. 1900

Original Source: Koryak

National Origin: Siberia

This Koryak **myth** reflects both the major issues of human life and creation, but minor ones such as infidelity and "spousal revenge" can be seen in the following narrative.

Big-Raven lived with his family. Oh, Big-Raven said, "I will (go and) fetch some willow-bark." Oh, Miti' went to feed the little puppies. Magpie-Man came to eat there. He pecked at Miti''s face (to indicate his love), and her whole nose was covered with scratches.

Oh, that one (Big-Raven) comes home! He said to Miti', "What has happened to you? Your nose is scratched all over."

She said, "By hitting with my nose against the sharp ends of the door-shed corner I was scratched thus." Oh, Big-Raven cut away all the ends of the dog-shed corners. Then again he went for willow-bark. Miti' went out, perched on the top of the dog-shed, and began to sing, "I am walking along the cross beam!"

Then Magpie-Man came, and said, "Let us enter the sleeping-room! Big-Raven will not come back soon. He will not catch us."

She took him into (the house). Just as soon as they entered the sleeping-room and began to make love there, then Big-Raven came back, and called out, "Miti', take this load of willow!" Miti' said, "Let the I'kla [a magical effigy of a human being] bring it down! I am busy trampling a half-scraped skin with lily feet."

"Nay," said Big-Raven, "I want you to take it down."

Oh, Miti' took it, and with a violent pull drew it into the house.

Then Big-Raven entered the house and made a smoldering fire. He also stopped up the entrance-hole and the smoke-hole, so that the sleeping-room was full of smoke. Then a Magpie's voice was heard from the sleeping-room. That Magpie came out. He escaped through a narrow crack.

"(See) what (this) Magpie has done to me!" The Magpie, however, went home. Miti' was with child. After some time she brought forth two small eggs. (The two children) grew rapidly, and Big-Raven had a great love for them.

Big-Raven's people were storing their catch of fish. Those two said, "Mamma, we are hungry."

She said, "Go out and say to daddy, 'We are hungry'." They went out, and were given two whole dried salmon. They entered, and nibbled up (the fish).

Then they said again, "We are hungry." Miti' said to them, "Go out and ask daddy (for more)."

They went out. "Daddy, we are hungry!"

"No wonder! Two thievish magpies!"

Those two sons began to weep. "Oh, he is reproaching us!"

Miti' said to them, "Go out and tell him, 'Our real daddy is herding reindeer (with the wealthy reindeer-breeders)'." (After that) they entered again, and Miti' put them into a grass bag, (placing) each in one of the (lower) corners. She went away, and came to Magpie-Man and flung (her bag right in).

Big-Raven said, "I feel lonely. I will go to Miti'." He went and came there.

(The people said,) "Miti', come out! Your old man has come to you."

Miti' said, "Has he no legs? Let him enter of his own accord!" He entered, and she gave him food. He began to eat, and was choking. Then he ran out of the house.

Miti' called to him. She said, "Big-Raven!"

"Oi!"

Then he could not help himself, and shouted, "Oi!" The piece that choked him flew out (of his mouth, and fell down) at a great distance. Then Big-Raven went home. That is all.

TIBET

THE STORY OF THE TWO DEVILS

Tradition Bearer: Unavailable

Source: Shelton, A. L. *Tibetan Folktales*. St. Louis, MO: United Christian Missionary Society, 1925, 70–75.

Date: Unavailable

Original Source: Tibet

National Origin: China (Tibet)

Preceding the Buddhist philosophy and practices that most of the world associates with Tibet was an indigenous Himalayan belief system called Bön. This religious tradition was built on animism, and shamanistic practices were at the heart of the divination that determined the most important activities in daily life, including healing, as the following tale demonstrates. The shaman (who might be male or female) typically entered a trance state to receive the advice of the supernaturals. The sham diviner in "The Story of the Two Devils" plays the role well enough to convince the two shape-shifting devils of his abilities.

"The golden eagle flying high you are not able to bind, and great water running swiftly you are not able to dam."

—Tibetan Proverb

A long time ago in a country so high that it would make most boys and girls tired if they tried to run and play, was a great flat table-land entirely surrounded by a forest. On this table-land was located one large city and several smaller ones, all ruled over by a king who had seven sons.

The sons went out in the forest to play one day and found a beautiful girl, who was herding a yak. She told them she was the daughter of the King of the west, that her yak had wandered away and she had come to hunt it. The seven sons thought that she was very pretty to look at, so they proposed to her that she become the wife of the seven, which was the custom of the country.

Now, in reality, the girl was a she-devil and the yak was her husband. They could change their form whenever they chose. She didn't tell the men that the yak was her husband, but drove it away and consented to become the wife of the brothers and went home with them.

Every year one of the sons died, beginning with the eldest, until all were dead except the youngest, and he became very ill and was about to die. The head-men of the villages got together and wondered and wondered what could be done, shaking their heads and muttering that this was a very queer affair, that these six sons, whom they had cared for and to whom they had given all the medicine they knew of, had all died. They thought the matter over and decided to send for a man who they knew could tell fortunes, and see if he could discover what was the matter. Four men were chosen to go and see him.

They traveled until they found him, told him all about the death of the six brothers, and asked him to cast lots and see what was the matter. He told them that he would lie down and sleep and receive a vision on the affair and tomorrow would relate it. Actually he didn't know what in the world to do nor what to say, for he was not a really-truly fortune teller at all, but only a quack.

That night he went to ask his wife what to do, and she said, "You've told a lot of lies about things before this, so it won't hurt you to lie some more. You came out fairly well the other times, so I think that you can fix up a plan for this affair."

The next morning when the four men came, he said, "My vision was fine, I will get out my black clothes and black hat and read prayers for you. We will all go back together and these charms that I read will make everything all right in the palace."

So he took a big rosary in one hand and the skull of a hog in the other and traveled along with them.

When they arrived the woman didn't know exactly what to think, and wondered if this fellow really did know her and her husband and what they had done. The fortune teller made a tsamba torma [ritual offering made from parched barley flour] and placed it at the head of the sick man, along with the hog's skull, and covered them both with a cloth. When the she-devil left the room the sick man got a little better and went to sleep.

This scared the fortune teller so badly he didn't know what to do. He thought the man was dying. Really the man's soul had been about half eaten up before the woman left, and when she went away it grew stronger. The fortune teller was badly scared and called out two or three times for help and began to think he had better step out and take his things and run off, but the door was locked and he couldn't get it open. He wondered if he could hide some place until he had a chance to slip away, so he sneaked upstairs to the top of the roof and fell through the opening in the dark, astride the yak's horns, and the yak went bucking and tearing away with him on its head.

The she-devil was down there too, because she was afraid. The yak called out, "This man knows us all right, for he lit right on top of my head and knows I am the he-devil, for his charm is in his hand and he is beating me to death with it. What shall I do?"

His wife replied, "He knows me and I dare not come over and help you; and just as sure as can be in the morning he will call all the people together, and they will be planning some scheme to get rid of us."

They thought in their hearts that perhaps he would call all the women to carry wood and burn them in the fire, or kill them in some other dreadful way.

"Truly," she said, "to try and find out if we are real they will hit us with rocks to see if it will hurt, and cut us open to see what is inside of us and put us in the fire to see if it will burn us."

The man in the meantime had rolled off the yak and heard all this, so he knew now what to do. Slipping back upstairs he set up his tsamba torma and hog's skull and began to read prayers again.

The King's son was awake by this time and the fortune teller asked him if he wasn't better and he said, "Yes."

"Well then," the man said, "in the morning you must call your head-men together, have them tell all the people to bring their guns and swords and some of the women to bring wood."

The next morning they were all there with the wood piled around the center as if for an offering to an idol, as the fortune teller had commanded them. He asked that his saddle be put on the yak. He donned his black clothes and rode the yak all over the city until he came to the pile of wood. He now grabbed his hog's head and hit the yak three times saying, "I want to see the real body of this yak," and the yak turned at once into a he-devil with a hideous face, two of his upper teeth hanging down to his breast and two lower ones extending up to his forehead. The men standing around killed him with their swords and guns.

Then the fortune teller called for the woman to come. She came screaming, and he struck her with the hog's skull and she turned into a terrible thing, with a most ugly face, claw-like hands, a great long tongue and teeth like her husband's. The people killed her with rocks and knives and burned them both in the fire; then hastened to do great honor to the fortune teller, who had gone back to the sick man.

The King's son got well right away and was so pleased he said to the fortune teller, "Whatever you wish, ask, and I will give you."

"Well," said the fortune teller, "I would like some of those wooden rings that are used to lead the yak around by their noses." (The reason he wanted them was because his wife always said he couldn't make them properly.) So the son gave him one hundred rings and enough goods to make seven yak loads and he returned to his home.

115

His wife saw him coming, took some wine and went to meet him. That night she asked him all about his adventures and he told her about the death of the two devils and the recovery of the King's son.

"And is this all you have, some dried cheese and meat and a few rings for the yak?" she said, and scolded him soundly. "Tomorrow I will go and see the King's son." But she wrote a letter instead which said, "You have given my husband this little bit of stuff and the nose rings which can have but one meaning, which is, that perhaps your disease may return."

When the King's son received the letter he said, "That is all true. I gave him all he asked for, but perhaps I should have given him more." So the next day he went to visit the fortune teller and said to him, "You have saved my life and done so much for me, now I will make you ruler of half my kingdom." So he made him as powerful as himself.

THE STORY OF THE PRINCE'S FRIEND

Tradition Bearer: Unavailable

Source: Shelton, A. L. *Tibetan Folktales*. St. Louis, MO: United Christian Missionary Society, 1925, 94–102.

Date: Unavailable

Original Source: Tibet

National Origin: China (Tibet)

Tibetans consider frogs to belong to the class of beings called "nagas," along with dragons, snakes, and other reptiles. The Lukhang ("Dragon House") is a temple that was built almost five centuries ago to pay homage to the nagas on a manmade island in a pond that, tradition claims, was once home to thousands of frogs. Centuries ago lamas made annual offerings to the naga kings to ensure prosperity. The following tale begins with a remembrance of the unique place frogs held as nagas for Tibetans. Other elements of the narrative are not exclusively Tibetan, however, for example, "Unjust Umpire Misappropriates Disputed Goods" (AT 518) provides the plot structure for the episodes in which the prince and his friend acquire magical objects.

 "**A** man without jewels in the mountain has no need to fear the robbers."

—Tibetan Proverb

Away, away up in the mountains was a village, and in the village lived a very wise king and his only son. Near by flowed a river; up above was a big pond from which came the water that irrigated their fields, and above the pond, in a crevice from which flowed the water, lived two big frogs, who belonged to the lower regions. To these frogs, every year, some person had to be sacrificed or the supply of water was cut off by them as they sat in the crevice, through which the supply came. Each family in turn had paid its tax of a child, until now it was the turn of the king to furnish the yearly sacrifice. So the old king began to think and wonder which had better go—he or his son—each one thinking he should be the one. The father said, "I'm an old man, and if I go and get eaten up it doesn't matter, for I wouldn't live much longer anyway. So, my son, when I'm gone you must be a good ruler and govern the people wisely."

The prince said to his father, "This will never do; you are a good king to these people and you can get another wife and have more sons, so don't say any more about it, for I'm going."

One morning he started for the place. All the people went with him a little way and felt very bad to see him leave them and his father. After a while all of them returned home except one friend of his childhood, who still went on with him, crying and grieving.

The prince now turned to him and said, "You must go back and be a good son to your father and care for him when he is old."

But his friend replied, "When I was a child and poor you cared for me, fed me and clothed me, now you must not go and let those frogs eat you up. I'll go in your place."

The prince would hear of no such plan, however, and as his friend refused to return, they both went on together and arrived at the mouth of the gorge where they saw one green frog and one yellow frog sitting together talking. The yellow one said to the green one, "Here comes the prince and his friend, and if they are wise they would take a clod and kill us, then they would have all the water they needed, and whenever they wished they could vomit gold and jewels. But they don't understand frog talk, so they don't know what we are saying."

But the king's son did understand, for in those days all kings and their sons understood what the animals said. So he told his friend and they each got a club, killed and ate the frogs, and plenty of water came through the crevices.

"Well," the friend said, "now these frogs are eaten and out of the way, let's go home."

But the prince said, "No, it would be better if we go to a far country, as the people think we are eaten by those frogs, and if we return now, they will think we are ghosts and fear us exceedingly."

So they crossed the mountain and went down on the other side, where they came to a wine shop kept by a woman and her daughter, and went in.

"Bring out your wine," they said, "we wish to buy some. How much do you ask for it?" When brought they vomited a few jewels which they gave as pay for it.

The two women, when they saw how they got their money for the wine, said, "Drink some more, drink some more," thinking that if they got them real

117

drunk they would throw up a lot of gold. They were soon very sick sure enough and threw up gold and jewels all over the room, and the woman and the girl got more than enough to make them wealthy.

When they began to sober up, they feared they had thrown up a lot of jewels, but were a bit ashamed to ask about it, as they weren't sure what they had done.

So they went on, coming to a big plain where a lot of children were playing. They were quarreling over something, each claiming it to be his. The travelers asked what they were quarreling about and the children replied, "We found a hat and whoever puts it on can't be seen, for he turns into a ghost, and we all want it."

The prince's friend said, "You needn't quarrel over that; you children all go down there and race up here to me; the one who gets to me first may have the hat. I will hold it."

Soon they came racing back, but the man put the hat on his head and when they arrived they could not find him or the hat, though they searched everywhere and finally had to go home without it. When they were gone the man removed the hat and put it in his bosom. He and the prince then went on and came to a place where a lot of monkeys were quarreling, and when they asked what they were fussing about, they answered, "We found a pair of boots, and whoever puts them on has only to wish where he wants to go and he will be there at once, so we all want them."

The prince's friend said, "Well, don't quarrel; give them to me and you all go and run a race, and the one who wins can have them. In the meantime, I'll hold the boots."

As soon as they were gone he jerked the hat out of his gown, put it on his head, and when they got back he wasn't to be seen. They hunted every place, but could not find him, and finally went away without their boots.

Then the prince and his friend put on a boot each, and the prince wished to find a place where the king was dead, where they wanted a new ruler; and they both went to sleep. Next morning they awakened to find themselves in the midst of a great hollow tree, and around it was a crowd of men who that day were to choose a new king.

While they stood there they prayed that the god of the sky would throw down a tsamba torma [offering cake made from parched barley] from the clouds and hit whoever was to be the king. So down it came, but instead of hitting any of them it hit the big tree. "This won't do at all," they said, "We haven't any such custom as having a tree for a king."

But an old man was there who said, "Let's see if some one isn't in the tree." They looked and found the prince and his friend inside. But the people were not at all pleased.

"This will not do at all," they said, "we don't know these men, we don't know their fathers and mothers and they are probably bad men. We won't have them now, but tomorrow we will have another test and whoever can vomit the most valuable things, he shall be king."

The next day one drank a lot of milk and threw up white every place he went, another ate something green and threw up green, and others different things.

The prince vomited gold and said, "You see, I am to be king."

The friend of the prince vomited jewels, and said, "You see, I am to be the prime minister." So they were made king and prime minister of the country.

The prince found a beautiful girl, whom he took to be his queen. Now the prince had two houses, one very high on the mountains and another in the city, and every day the queen went up to this high house for a little while, but he did not know she went there.

However, his friend did, and wondered and wondered why she went up to that house every day. "Somebody or something must be in there that she wants to see," he thought. So he put on his magic hat and went along behind her when she started for the mountain.

She went in through an open door, up a flight of stairs, through another door, and up another flight, and so on for five stories, until she reached the top of the house, which was beautifully fixed with rugs and hangings. She took off her everyday clothes and bathed and perfumed and gowned herself in silks and satins and lit incense. The prince's friend was sitting by, invisible of course! After two or three hours a beautiful bird flew down from heaven. The queen lighted a piece of incense and went before the bird with it, as it had perched itself on a rock near her on the top of the house. It really was the son of a god, disguised as a bird, with only feathers or bird's clothing on the outside. She fixed food for him, and he stepped out of his bird gown, and as he held her hands he said to her, "Your husband was chosen by the gods to be the king; is he a good or a bad ruler?"

The queen answered, "I'm very young, and whether he is good or bad I'm unable to say."

Then they said good-bye and she asked him to come again tomorrow morning. So he flew away in his bird gown and she donned her everyday clothes and went back to the palace.

Next morning it was the same thing, the minister of the king accompanying her, invisible again.

The god said to her, "I'm coming tomorrow in the king's palace as a bird and see for myself whether the king is good and wise and whether or not he is handsome."

Next day, before the queen came, the prime minister told the king all about his lady, that she went to this high house on the mountain every day to meet the son of a god, and that he had put on his invisible hat and gone along and had seen them, while they could not see him, and he knew all about it.

"So tomorrow," he said, "you make a big fire of charcoal on a 'hopan' and take a sword and kill him."

They were all sitting around a big fire next morning, the king, the prime minister and the court, when the bird came hopping up the stairs into the midst of them. The minister had on his hat and couldn't be seen; he grabbed the bird by the tail, threw some fire on him and the king took his big sword to kill him, when the queen caught his arm and would not allow him to do it. The fire burned the bird on the back and wings a bit and he flew very quietly into heaven again.

The next day the queen went again to the high castle, and dressed once more in her beautiful clothes, and again the minister went. She waited a long time and felt dreadfully sad about the whole affair, but that day the bird did not come. One day after this he came flying down very slowly, for he was covered with burns and felt very ill. The queen took his hand and cried over him.

"You need not cry," he said, "the king is a very good and handsome man, but it is very queer he should throw fire all over me. I am very sick these days with all these burns and cannot fly very well, and will only come once a month to see you, not every day." And he flew slowly away.

The queen went back to her king and began to love him better, because the son of the god came only once a month to see her.

The prime minister one day put on his magic hat and his boots and wished himself back where he had drunk wine in the inn with the woman and her daughter. On the way he passed the door of a small lamasery and slipped up and looked in, where he saw two old men, caretakers of the place, drawing a donkey on a piece of paper; as they turned the paper over one of the men turned into a donkey, got up and rolled over and ran all over the lamasery, braying in a dreadful manner. It seemed that the drawing turned one way, changed the man into a donkey, and turned over, changed him back into a man. When the old man was tired of his queer piece of paper and the tricks it did, he rolled it up and put it behind the big idol.

The prince's friend, who had his magic hat on so that the old priest could not see him, slipped in and stole the paper, then went on to the wine shop and said, "I want to pay you for the wine you gave us; here is five tenths of an ounce of silver, and I will give you a paper, which, if you turn it over, it will bring you plenty of gold."

They said they would be very glad to have it if they could get hold of wealth that easily. So he gave them the paper, and as soon as they turned it over, they both turned into donkeys. Then he led them to the king who used them to carry wood and dirt to fix his houses, and they were half starved and were very bad off indeed. After working and carrying for three years they were very ill and their backs were terribly sore.

One day the king saw them with the tears rolling down their faces, and he asked, "What is the matter with these donkeys; why are they crying? Turn them out and don't make them work so hard"; but the minister had the paper and turned them back by turning the paper over and they returned to their homes. Then he told the king he had punished them for the way they had been treated so long ago.

THE TIGER AND THE FROG

Tradition Bearer: Unavailable

Source: Shelton, A. L. *Tibetan Folktales*. St. Louis, MO: United Christian Missionary Society, 1925, 21–25.

Date: Unavailable

Original Source: Tibet

National Origin: China (Tibet)

Relying on his wits in the absence of strength, the frog plays the role of **trickster**. Among the traditional **motifs** in the frog's repertoire is "Weak animal makes large believe that he has killed and eaten many of the large one's companions" (K1715). The tale concludes with a **variant** of "Animal Allows Himself to be Tied to Another for Safety" (AT 78). The casting of the frog in the trickster role is not common cross-culturally. Frogs hold a special place in Tibetan tradition, however. See the introductory notes to "The Story of the Prince's Friend" (page 116).

"The tall strong pine is a great help, for with its support the weak vine may climb as high."

—Tibetan Proverb

Once upon a time, in the days when the world was young and all animals understood each other's languages, an old, old tiger named Tsuden went out hunting for some food. As he was creeping quietly along the banks of a stream a frog saw him and was badly scared. He thought, "This tiger is coming to eat me up." He climbed up on a little bunch of sod and when the tiger came near, called out, "Hello, where are you going?"

The tiger answered, "I am going up into the forest to hunt something to eat. I haven't had any food for two or three days and I am very weak and hungry. I guess I'll eat you up. You're awfully small, but I can't find anything else. Who are you, anyway?"

The frog replied, swelling up as big as he could, "I am the king of the frogs. I can jump any distance and can do anything. Here's a river, let's see who can jump across."

The tiger answered, "All right," and as he crouched ready to jump, the frog slipped up and got hold of the end of his tail with his mouth, and when the tiger jumped he was thrown away up the bank across the river. After Tsuden got across he turned around and looked and looked into the river for the frog. But as the tiger turned, the frog let loose of his tail and said, "What are you looking for, old tiger, down there?"

The tiger whirled quickly, very much surprised to see the frog away up the bank behind him.

Said the frog, "Now I beat you in that test, let's try another. Suppose we both vomit." The tiger being empty could only throw up a little water, but the frog spit up some tiger hair.

The tiger much astonished asked, "How do you happen to be able to do that?"

The frog replied, "Oh, yesterday I killed a tiger and ate him, and these are just a few of the hairs that aren't yet digested."

The tiger began to think to himself, "He must be very strong. Yesterday he killed and ate a tiger, and now he has jumped farther than I did over the river. Guess I'd better slip away before he eats me." Then he sidled away a little piece, quickly turned and began to run away as fast as he could, up the mountain.

He met a fox coming down who asked, "What's the matter, why are you running away so fast?"

"Say," the old tiger said, "I met the king of all the frogs, who is very strong. Why, he has been eating tigers and he jumped across the river and landed farther up the bank than I did."

The fox laughed at him and said, "What, are you running away from that little frog? He is nothing at all. I am only a little fox, but I could put my foot on him and kill him."

The tiger answered, "I know what this frog can do, but if you think you can kill him, I'll go back with you. I am afraid you will get frightened and run away, however, so we must tie our tails together."

So they tied their tails fast in a lot of knots and went down to see the frog, who still sat on his piece of sod, looking as important as he could. He saw them coming and called out to the fox, "You're a great fox. You haven't paid your toll to the king today nor brought any meat either. Is that a dog you've got tied to your tail and are you bringing him for my dinner?"

Then the tiger was frightened, for he thought the fox was taking him to the king to be eaten. So he turned and ran and ran as fast as he could go, dragging the poor fox with him, and if they are not dead, they are still running today.

THE WICKED STEPMOTHER

Tradition Bearer: Unavailable

Source: Shelton, A. L. *Tibetan Folktales*. St. Louis, MO: United Christian Missionary Society, 1925, 62–69.

Date: Unavailable

Original Source: Tibet

National Origin: China (Tibet)

The following tale takes up the theme of tension between the generations and the conflict between obligation and ambition. The tsamba tormas mentioned in the narrative and the sacrifice to the snake deity are holdovers from the Tibetan religion of Bön. See introductory notes to "The Story of the Two Devils," page 113, and "The Story of the Prince's Friend," page 116.

"Eating much the tiger can swallow no more, so the vulture may safely come down."

—Tibetan Proverb

Once upon a time, on the very tiptop of a big flat mountain, there was situated a country over which ruled a king named Genchog. He married a beautiful wife who gave him one son whom they named Nyema. In giving birth to him she died, but the baby lived. The king got him another wife and had another son whom they called Däwä. One day, thinking to herself, she said, "There is no chance for my son to be king, for the older son has the birthright and he is sure to be the ruler."

So she began to plan and plot and see if she could think of some way to kill the older son and let her son rule the kingdom.

One day she feigned to be very ill and rolled over on the floor groaning and crying. The king saw her and very much alarmed exclaimed, "What is the matter with you?"

And she answered, "Oh, I have had this sickness since I was a little girl, but it has never been so hard as it is this time. There is a way to cure it, but it is too hard and bitter, so I will have to die this time."

The king asked, "What is the way to heal you? I don't want you to die, for it would break my heart and I wouldn't want to be king any longer. You must tell me the remedy so I can save you."

She demurred for some time but finally said, "Well, one of your sons must be killed and I must eat his heart with butter, but you see your older son is the prince and heir to the throne and the younger son is my own flesh and blood, so I could not eat his heart even if it were to save my life."

The king was dreadfully grieved and finally said, "Well, I love one son as much as another and my heart would ache the same for each of them, but in a day or two I will kill the elder, as it would do no good to kill the younger."

After a while the younger brother found out what was to be done and went to the older brother and told him, and asked, "What shall we do about it?"

The older brother said, "Little brother, you must stay with your father and become the king. He won't kill you and I'll run away."

The younger brother felt very sorry about it and his heart was sore as he said, "If you are going away I want to go too. I don't want to stay here without you."

"Very well," answered the other, "you may go if you wish." So they arranged together to slip away that night at midnight and tell nobody of their going. They could take no tsamba [parched barley flour] for fear some one would find out they were going. They had some tsamba bags and in them were some dried tsamba tormas [offerings made from tsamba] that the lamas had been using. Now these tormas are little cone-shaped bodies made of tsamba and are used when the lamas are reading prayers. They are supposed to be full of devils, which the lamas coaxed into them when they read their holy books.

They started about midnight on the fifteenth of the month and traveled day and night, over the mountains and through the valleys, until their dried tsamba was all gone and they were very hungry and thirsty. They finally came to a village, but there was no water. The younger was getting weak now as they had had but little food and no water for some time.

So Nyema said to him, "Wait and rest here in this little village, and I will go and see if I can find some water." He kept on going until he had gone entirely around the mountain in his search for water, but found none. Going back to the place where he had left his younger brother, he saw that he was dead. He was very much grieved and built a tomb for him of prayer stones and prayed that in his next incarnation he would have a happy life and not have to have so much sorrow as he had had this time.

Nyema then left and, crossing two mountain ranges, came to a cliff in which was a big door through which he entered, and there found an old hermit lama in the cave.

When the old man saw him he said, "You are a good man, I know by looking at you. How did you happen to come here?"

Then Nyema told all that had happened to him and why he had run away from home, so the old man said, "You can stay here and be my son and I will pray to the gods to bring your younger brother to life again." In a few days the younger brother did come to life, and following his older brother's tracks came to the old hermit's house, and the two stayed there as the old lama's sons.

Below this cave, which was high up on the mountain, was a city where dwelt a very good king, and near the city was a big lake by which all the people watered their fields. Every year an offering had to be made to the snake god who dwelt in the lake, so that he wouldn't be angry and keep the water away. For this offering the people must sacrifice a human being who had been born in the tiger year. But the time came when all the people born in this year were dead and gone, and none was left to offer. One day the children, seeing the king, said to him, "Every day when we go up on the mountain to herd the cattle, we see a lama who lives up there. This lama has two sons, and the older one was born in the tiger year." So the king sent three men to see if it was true. The men went up to the cave and knocked on the door.

The lama opened it and asked, "What do you want?"

"The king has heard you have two sons and that one was born in the tiger year," answered the men, "and we need him for the offering to the god of the lake."

The lama answered, "I am a lama. How could I have two sons?" Then he shut the door in their faces and hid the boys in a big water cask. This treatment angered the men so they took some rocks and beat the door down. They looked everywhere for the boys, but they were so carefully hidden they couldn't be found, so in their disappointment they took some rocks and beat the old man.

The boys couldn't stand this, so they came out of their hiding-place and called, "Here we are, don't beat him any more." Then the men tied the older son and took him with them to the king. The lama and the younger brother felt very sad after he was gone. The men led Nyema to the king's palace, and since it wasn't quite time for the offering to be made, he was allowed his freedom in the courtyard of the palace. The king had a daughter, who fell violently in love with Nyema when she saw how handsome he was, and watched him wherever he went.

The day finally came and they took Nyema to the lake to throw him in. The king's daughter followed, saying pleadingly, "Please don't throw him into the lake, but if you must, throw me in too."

It made the king angry to see his daughter act in that manner, and he called out, "Throw her in too." So they threw them both in.

Nyema felt very sad and he thought, "It doesn't matter if I am thrown in, as I was born in the tiger year and the people will all starve if the snake god is angry, but it seems useless that the princess should die on my account."

The girl thought to herself, "I am only a girl and it doesn't matter if they do throw me in, but it is too bad to kill this handsome young man."

The god that ruled the lake thought it would be a pity that since they loved each other so much either should die, so when they were thrown into the water he carried them to the shore and neither of them was drowned. Then the god told the people it wasn't necessary to sacrifice any more, that he would see that there was plenty of water without it.

Nyema said to the princess, "You go to your father and tell him what the snake god says. I want to go see the lama and my brother for a little while. In a few days I will return and we will be married."

The princess went back to the palace and Nyema to the cave. When he knocked on the door a faint voice answered, and when he opened the door the old lama said weakly, "I had two sons, but the king took one away from me to sacrifice to the snake god and now myself and my other son are about to die."

Nyema said, "This is your son returned." Then he washed and fed them and they were soon better and very happy to have him with them again.

When the princess returned to the palace every one was glad to see her and rejoiced. Her father asked her if Nyema was dead and she answered, "No, and it is because of his goodness that I live. The snake god doesn't want any more human sacrifices of the tiger year nor any other year, and the water will always come and will never be stopped."

The king and his head-men thought it miraculous that they had been saved and that the god of the lake had been so kind. The king then ordered Nyema to be brought before him. So they sent messengers and this time invited the three to come down the mountain, and when they arrived the king set them on high benches to give them honor.

Then he said to Nyema, "You are a worker of wonders, are you really a son of this old hermit?"

Nyema answered, "No, I am the son of King Genchog. My brother and I ran away from the kingdom and from my father's wife, who was not my real mother, to save our lives." So the king, knowing him to be the son of a king, was much pleased to give him his daughter in marriage. Not only his daughter did he give him, but his scepter as well, and let him rule in his stead, for he was growing old.

Then Nyema made a feast for all the people and gave them a happy time for a period of seven days. When he had mounted the throne one day he said to Däwä, "Little brother, you must go back home and see your father and mother, as it has been a long time since we left them."

The new king gave his brother jewels and gold and silver, and then decided they would all go. They took yak loads of goods, many presents, all their servants and the two sons with the princess, started on their way. About half way over the big mountains they wrote a letter and sent it on ahead by a runner, telling their father they were coming. When the father heard his two sons were still alive he was very happy and sent out people to meet them. When he had welcomed them and found his older son had a kingdom, he turned his crown over to the younger son, which was just what the mother wanted. After a visit the older son took his princess and went back to his kingdom, where the two ruled long and well and lived happily ever afterwards.

HOW A FOX FELL VICTIM TO HIS OWN DECEIT

Tradition Bearer: Unavailable

Source: Shelton, A. L. *Tibetan Folktales*. St. Louis, MO: United Christian Missionary Society, 1925, 36–38.

Date: Unavailable

Original Source: Tibet

National Origin: China (Tibet)

"How a Fox Fell Victim to His Own Deceit" provides a classic example of the **animal tale** functioning as a **fable** in the Tibetan corpus of folktales.

"Between the official and his people is confidence if the head-man is skillful."

—Tibetan Proverb

Once upon a time, away up in the corner of the mountains, in a little cave, lived a tiger and her baby cub. She had brought for this baby, one day when she was out hunting, a little fox to be his playmate. The fox had a happy time and an easy one, for he didn't have to work or hunt, but played all day and the mother tiger kept them all supplied with food.

One day she went out to hunt and found a little calf, which she took home to be another playmate for her son. But the fox was much displeased and became very jealous of the calf because he thought they all loved the calf better than he and that only the food that was left over was given to him. As a matter of fact, they treated him just the same as ever, but his heart was wrong and he began to plan how he might be revenged on the calf.

After a while, the mother tiger became very ill, and as she was about to die she called the calf and her son to her side and said, "Although you are not of the same father and mother, yet you are brothers. I don't want you to ever quarrel, but to live happily here together, and if any one should tell you lies don't pay any attention to them, but always be friends." So saying, she died.

Now the fox saw his opportunity. Every morning the calf was in the habit of running and playing and jumping and shaking his horns in fun, bellowing and taking exercise, while the tiger preferred to lie and rest.

So one morning while the calf was skipping around, the fox slipped up to the tiger and said, "Although the calf says he is your friend, have you any idea what he is thinking about, when he runs and jumps and shakes his horns in that manner? In his heart he hates you, and in that manner is gaining strength in order that he may be able to kill you."

This, of course, made the tiger suspicious and very angry. So daily he watched the calf very closely and became sour and surly.

Then the fox went to the calf and said, "You know your mother told you and the tiger that you were to be brothers, but see, he is growing larger and stronger every day and his heart has changed and he is preparing to kill and eat you."

The tiger and the calf were now enemies and watched each other with a great deal of suspicion and were very unhappy. Finally one day the calf said to the tiger, "Why do you want to kill me and eat me? I have done you no harm and love you just as your mother said I should."

The tiger replied, "I love you just the same and never thought of doing such a thing until the fox said you were preparing to kill me."

Then they realized that the fox had been trying to make them enemies, and they decided on a plan to get even with the fox. The tiger said, "I'll tell you what we'll do. We'll have a sham fight saying we hate each other and we're going to fight it out and see who wins. Ask him to be present and while we're in the midst of it, I'll attack him."

The day came and they began their fight. They maneuvered round and round and seemed to be fighting very fiercely until they came very near the fox, when the tiger made a jump, landed on him and killed him and sat down and had a feast of the carcass.

This shows what happens to those who try to make trouble between friends.

THE CAT AND THE MICE

Tradition Bearer: Unavailable

Source: O'Connor, W. F. *Folk Tales from Tibet.* London: Hurst and Blackett, Ltd., 1906, 26–29.

Date: ca. 1904

Original Source: Tibet

National Origin: China

The hungry cat as **trickster** and the clever mouse (or mice) are **stock characters** in traditional narratives. The following **animal tale** provides a classic example of this **tale type** (see "The Cat as Sham Holy Man," AT 113B). Other **variants** cast different predators and prey in the central roles, however, for example, the coyote and his intended victims in Native American traditions. In the related tale type, "The Fox Persuades the Cock to Crow with Closed Eyes" (AT 61), the subterfuge used by the fox to prevent the cock from detecting his attack is similar to the cat's use of a religious posture to hide his movements from the mice.

Once upon a time there was a cat who lived in a large farmhouse in which there was a great number of mice. For many years the cat found no difficulty in catching as many mice as she wanted to eat, and she lived a very peaceful and pleasant life. But as time passed on she found that she was growing old and infirm, and that it was becoming more and more difficult for her to catch the same number of mice as before; so after thinking very carefully what was the best thing to do, she one day called all the mice together, and after promising not to touch them, she addressed them as follows, "Oh! mice," said she, "I have called you together in order to say something to you. The fact is that I have led a very wicked life, and now, in my old age, I repent of having caused you all so much inconvenience and annoyance. So I am going for the future to turn over a new leaf. It is my intention now to give myself up entirely to religious contemplation and no longer to molest you, so henceforth you are at liberty to run about as freely as you will without fear of me. All I ask of you is that twice every day you should all file past me in procession and each one make an obeisance as you pass me by, as a token of your gratitude to me for my kindness."

When the mice heard this they were greatly pleased, for they thought that now, at last, they would be free from all danger from their former enemy, the cat. So they very thankfully promised to fulfill the cat's conditions, and agreed that they would file past her and make a *salaam* [a deep bow] twice every day.

So when evening came the cat took her seat on a cushion at one end of the room, and the mice all went by in single file, each one making a profound salaam as it passed.

Now the cunning old cat had arranged this little plan very carefully with an object of her own; for, as soon as the procession had all passed by with the exception of one little mouse, she suddenly seized the last mouse in her claws without anybody else noticing what had happened, and devoured it at her leisure. And so twice every day, she seized the last mouse of the series, and for a long time lived very comfortably without any trouble at all in catching her mice, and without any of the mice realizing what was happening.

Now it happened that amongst these mice there were two friends, whose names were Rambé and Ambé, who were very much attached to one another. Now these two were much cleverer and more cunning than most of the others, and after a few days they noticed that the number of mice in the house seemed to be decreasing very much, in spite of the fact that the cat had promised not to kill any more. So they laid their heads together and arranged a little plan for future processions. They agreed that Rambé was always to walk at the very front of the procession of the mice, and the Ambé was to bring up the rear, and that all the time the procession was passing, Rambé was to call to Ambé, and Ambé to answer Rambé at frequent intervals. So next evening, when the procession started as usual, Rambé marched along in front, and Ambé took up his position last of all.

As soon as Rambé had passed the cushion where the cat was seated and had made his salaam, he called out in a shrill voice, "Where are you, Brother Ambé?"

"Here I am, Brother Rambé," squeaked the other from the rear of the procession.

And so they went on calling out and answering one another until they had all filed past the cat, who had not dared to touch Ambé as long as his brother kept calling to him.

The cat was naturally very much annoyed at having to go hungry that evening, and felt very cross all night. But she thought it was only an accident which had brought the two friends, one in front and one in rear of the procession, and she hoped to make up for her enforced abstinence by finding a particularly fat mouse at the end of the procession next morning. What, then, was her amazement and disgust when she found that on the following morning the very same arrangement had been made, and that Rambé called to Ambé, and Ambé answered Rambé until all the mice had passed her by, and so, for the second time, she was foiled of her meal. However, she disguised her feelings of anger and decided to give the mice one more trial; so in the evening she took her seat as usual on the cushion and waited for the mice to appear.

Meanwhile, Rambé and Ambé had warned the other mice to be on the lookout, and to be ready to take flight the moment the cat showed any appearance of anger.

At the appointed time the procession started as usual, and as soon as Rambé had passed the cat he squeaked out, "Where are you, Brother Ambé?"

"Here I am, Brother Rambé," came the shrill voice from the rear.

This was more than the cat could stand. She made a fierce leap right into the middle of the mice, who, however, were thoroughly prepared for her, and in an instant they scuttled off in every direction to their holes. And before the cat had time to catch a single one, the room was empty and not a sign of a mouse was to be seen anywhere.

After this the mice were very careful not to put any further trust in the treacherous cat, who soon after died of starvation owing to her being unable to procure any of her customary food. But Rambé and Ambé lived for many years, and were held in high honor and esteem by all the other mice in the community.

SOUTH ASIA

INDIA

STORY OF SAVITRI

Tradition Bearer: Unavailable

Source: Mackenzie, Donald A. *Indian Myth and Legend*. London: The Gresham Publishing Company Limited, 1913, 44–59.

Date: ca. 500 B.C.E.

Original Source: India

National Origin: India

The following **myth** is drawn from the Hindu scriptures entitled *The Mahabharata*. According to Hindu theology, Brahma is God in his aspect of creator, and Yama is the Lord of Death and Justice. In her appeal to save her husband's life, Savitri's attempts to outwit Yama are cloaked in a series of appeals to statements of the law, a force to which even Yama was subservient. See also "Royal Rivals: The Pandavas and Kauravas" (page 141) for additional background on this lineage.

There was once a fair princess in the country of Madra, and her name was Savitri. Be it told how she obtained the exalted merit of chaste women by winning a great boon from Yama.

Savitri was the gift of the goddess Gayatri, wife of Brahma, the self-created, who had heard the prayers and received the offerings of Aswapati, the childless king of Madra, when he practiced austere penances so that he might have issue. The maiden grew to be beautiful and shapely like to a Celestial; her eyes had burning splendor, and were fair as lotus leaves; she resembled a golden image; she had exceeding sweetness and grace.

It came to pass that Savitri looked with eyes of love upon a youth named Satyavan "the Truthful." Although Satyavan dwelt in a hermitage, he was of royal birth. His father was a virtuous king, named Dyumatsena, who became blind, and was then deprived of his kingdom by an old enemy dwelling nigh to him. The dethroned monarch retired to the forest with his faithful wife and his only son, who in time grew up to be a comely youth.

When Savitri confessed her love to her sire, the great sage Narada, who sat beside him, spoke and said, "Alas! The princess hath done wrong in choosing for her husband this royal youth Satyavan. He is comely and courageous, he is truthful and magnanimous and forgiving, he is modest and patient and without malice; honor is seated upon his forehead; he is possessed of every virtue. But he hath one defect, and no other. He is endued with short life; within a year from this day he must die, for so hath it been decreed; within a year Yama, god of the dead, will come for him."

Said the king unto his daughter, "O Savitri, thou hast heard the words of Narada. Go forth, therefore, and choose for thyself another lord, for the days of Satyavan are numbered."

The beautiful maiden made answer unto her father the king, saying, "The die is cast; it can fall but once; once only can a daughter be given away by her sire; once only can a woman say, '*I am thine.*' I have chosen my lord; once have I chosen, nor can I make choice a second time. Let his life be brief or be long, I must now wed Satyavan."

Said Narada, "O king, the heart of thy daughter will not waver; she will not be turned aside from the path she hath selected. I therefore approve of the bestowal of Savitri upon Satyavan."

The king said, "As thou dost advise, so must I do ever, O Narada, because that thou art my preceptor. Thee I cannot disobey."

Then said Narada, "Peace be with Savitri! I must now depart. May blessings attend upon all of you!"

Thereafter Aswapati, the royal sire of Savitri, went to visit Dyumatsena, the blind sire of Satyavan, in the forest, and his daughter went with him.

Said Dyumatsena, "Why hast thou come hither?" Aswapati said, "O royal sage, this is my beautiful daughter Savitri. Take thou her for thy daughter-in-law."

Said Dyumatsena, "I have lost my kingdom, and with my wife and my son dwell here in the woods. We live as ascetics and perform great penances. How will thy daughter endure the hardships of a forest life?"

Aswapati said, "My daughter knoweth well that joy and sorrow come and go and that nowhere is bliss assured. Accept her therefore from me."

Then Dyumatsena consented that his son should wed Savitri, whereat Satyavan was made glad because he was given a wife who had every accomplishment. Savitri rejoiced also because she obtained a husband after her own heart, and she put off her royal garments and ornaments and clad herself in bark and red cloth.

So Savitri became a hermit woman. She honored Satyavan's father and mother, and she gave great joy to her husband with her sweet speeches, her skill at work, her subdued and even temper, and especially her love. She lived the life of the ascetics and practiced every austerity. But she never forgot the dread prophecy of Narada the sage; his sorrowful words were always present in her secret heart, and she counted the days as they went past.

At length the time drew nigh when Satyavan must cast off his mortal body. When he had but four days to live, Savitri took the *Tritatra* vow of three nights of sleepless penance and fast.

Said the blind Dyumatsena, "My heart is grieved for thee, O my daughter, because the vow is exceedingly hard."

Savitri said, "Be not sorrowful, saintly father, I must observe my vow without fail."

Said Dyumatsena, "It is not meet that one like me should say, 'Break thy vow,' rather should I counsel, 'Observe thy vow'."

Then Savitri began to fast, and she grew pale and was much wasted by reason of her rigid penance. Three days passed away, and then, believing that her husband would die on the morrow, Savitri spent a night of bitter anguish through all the dark and lonely hours.

The sun rose at length on the fateful morning, and she said to herself, *"Today is the day."* Her face was bloodless but brave; she prayed in silence and with fervor and offered oblations at the morning fire; then she stood before her father-in-law and her mother-in-law in reverent silence with joined hands, concentrating her senses. All the hermits of the forest blessed her and said, "Mayest thou never suffer widowhood."

Said Savitri in her secret heart, "So be it." Dyumatsena spoke to her then, saying, "Now that thy vow hath been completed thou mayest eat the morning meal."

Said Savitri, "I will eat when the sun goes down."

Hearing her words Satyavan rose, and taking his axe upon his shoulder, turned towards the distant jungle to procure fruits and herbs for his wife, whom he loved. He was strong and self-possessed and of noble seeming.

Savitri spoke to him sweetly and said, "Thou must not go forth alone, my husband. It is my heart's desire to go with thee. I cannot endure today to be parted from thee."

Said Satyavan, "It is not for thee to enter the dark-some jungle; the way is long and difficult, and thou art weak on account of thy severe penance. How canst thou walk so far on foot?"

Savitri laid her head upon his bosom and said, "I have not been made weary by my fast. Indeed I am now stronger than before. I will not feel tired when thou art by my side. I have resolved to go with thee: do not therefore seek to thwart my wish—the wish and the longing of a faithful wife to be with her lord."

Said Satyavan, "If it is thy desire to accompany me I cannot but gratify it. But thou must ask permission of my parents lest they find fault with me for taking thee through the trackless jungle."

Then Savitri spoke to the blind sage and her husband's mother and said, "Satyavan is going towards the deep jungle to procure fruits and herbs for me, and also fuel for the sacrificial fires. It is my heart's wish to go also, for today I cannot endure to be parted from him. Fain, too, would I behold the blossoming woods."

Said Dyumatsena, "Since thou hast come to dwell with us in our hermitage thou hast not before asked anything of us. Have thy desire therefore in this matter, but do not delay thy husband in his duties."

Having thus received permission to depart from the hermitage, Savitri turned towards the jungle with Satyavan, her beloved lord. Smiles covered her face, but her heart was torn with secret sorrow.

Peacocks fluttered in the green woodland through which they walked together, and the sun shone in all its splendor in the blue heaven.

Said Satyavan with sweet voice, "How beautiful are the bright streams and the blossoming trees!"

The heart of Savitri was divided into two parts: with one she held converse with her husband while she watched his face and followed his moods; with the other she awaited the dread coming of Yama, but she never uttered her fears.

Birds sang sweetly in the forest, but sweeter to Savitri was the voice of her beloved. It was very dear to her to walk on in silence, listening to his words.

Satyavan gathered fruits and stored them in his basket. At length he began to cut down the branches of trees. The sun was hot and he perspired. Suddenly he felt weary and he said, "My head aches; my senses are confused, my limbs have grown weak, and my heart is afflicted sorely. O silent one, a sickness hath seized me. My body seems to be pierced by a hundred darts. I would fain lie down and rest, my beloved; I would fain sleep even now."

Speechless and terror-stricken, the gentle Savitri wound her arms about her husband's body; she sat upon the ground and she pillowed his head upon her lap. Remembering the words of Narada, she knew that the dread hour had come; the very moment of death was at hand. Gently she held her husband's head with caressing hands; she kissed his panting lips; her heart was beating fast and loud. Darker grew the forest and it was lonesome indeed.

Suddenly an awful Shape emerged from the shadows. He was of great stature and sable hue; his raiment was blood-red; on his head he wore a gleaming diadem; he had red eyes and was fearsome to look upon; he carried a noose.... The Shape was Yama, god of death. He stood in silence, and gazed upon slumbering Satyavan.

Savitri looked up, and when she perceived that a Celestial had come nigh, her heart trembled with sorrow and with fear. She laid her husband's head upon the green sward and rose up quickly: then she spake, saying, "Who art thou, O divine One, and what is thy mission to me?"

Said Yama, "Thou dost love thy husband; thou art endued also with ascetic merit. I will therefore hold converse with thee. Know thou that I am the Monarch of Death. The days of this man, thy husband, are now spent, and I have come to bind him and take him away."

Savitri said, "Wise sages have told me that thy messengers carry mortals away. Why, then, O mighty King, hast thou thyself come hither?"

Said Yama, "This prince is of spotless heart; his virtues are without number; he is, indeed, an ocean of accomplishments. It would not be fitting to send messengers for him, so I myself have come hither."

The face of Satyavan had grown ashen pale. Yama cast his noose and tore out from the prince's body the soul-form, which was no larger than a man's thumb; it was tightly bound and subdued.

So Satyavan lost his life; he ceased to breathe; his body became unsightly; it was robbed of its luster and deprived of power to move.

Yama fettered the soul with tightness, and turned abruptly towards the south; silently and speedily he went upon his way....

Savitri followed him.... Her heart was drowned in grief. She could not desert her beloved lord.... She followed Yama, the Monarch of Death.

Said Yama, "Turn back, O Savitri. Do not follow me. Perform the funeral rites of thy lord.... Thine allegiance to Satyavan hath now come to an end: thou art free from all wifely duties. Dare not to proceed farther on this path."

Savitri said, "I must follow my husband whither he is carried or whither he goeth of his own will. I have undergone great penance. I have observed my vow, and I cannot be turned back.... I have already walked with thee seven paces, and the sages have declared that one who walketh seven paces with another becometh a companion. Being thus made thy friend, I must hold converse with thee, I must speak and thou must listen.... I have attained the perfect life upon earth by performing my vows and by reason of my devotion unto my lord. It is not meet that thou shouldest part me from my husband now, and prevent me from attaining bliss by saying that my allegiance to him hath ended and another mode of life is opened to me."

Said Yama, "Turn back now.... Thy words are wise and pleasing indeed; therefore, ere thou goest, thou canst ask a boon of me and I will grant it. Except the soul of Satyavan, I will give thee whatsoever thou dost desire."

Savitri said, "Because my husband's sire became blind, he was deprived of his kingdom. Restore his eyesight, O mighty One."

Said Yama, "The boon is granted. I will restore the vision of thy father-in-law.... But thou hast now grown faint on this toilsome journey. Turn back, therefore, and thy weariness will pass away."

Savitri said, "How can I be weary when I am with my husband? The fate of my husband will be my fate also; I will follow him even unto the place whither thou dost carry him.... Hear me, O mighty One, whose friendship I cherish! It is a blessed thing to behold a Celestial; still more blessed is it to hold converse with one; the friendship of a god must bear great fruit."

Said Yama, "Thy wisdom delighteth my heart. Therefore thou canst ask of me a second boon, except the life of thy husband, and it will be granted thee."

Savitri said, "May my wise and saintly father-in-law regain the kingdom he hath lost. May he become once again the protector of his people."

Said Yama, "The boon is granted. The king will return to his people and be their wise protector.... Turn back now, O princess; thy desire is fulfilled."

Savitri said, "All people must obey thy decrees; thou dost take away life in accordance with divine ordinances and not of thine own will. Therefore thou art called Yama—he that ruleth by decrees. Hear my words, O divine One. It is the duty of Celestials to love all creatures and to award them according to their merit. The wicked are without holiness and devotion, but the saintly protect all creatures and show mercy even unto their enemies."

Said Yama, "Thy wise words are like water to a thirsty soul. Ask of me therefore a third boon, except thy husband's life, and it will be granted unto thee."

Savitri said, "My sire, King Aswapati, hath no son. O grant that a hundred sons may be born unto him."

Said Yama, "A hundred sons will be born unto thy royal sire. Thy boon is granted.... Turn back, therefore, O princess; thou canst not come farther. Long is the path thou hast already traveled."

Savitri said, "I have followed my husband and the way hath not seemed long. Indeed, my heart desireth to go on much farther. Hear my words, O Yama, as thou dost proceed on thy journey. Thou art great and wise and powerful; thou dost deal equally with all human creatures; thou art the lord of justice.... One cannot trust oneself as one can trust a Celestial; therefore, one seeketh to win the friendship of a Celestial. It is meet that one who seeketh the friendship of a Celestial should make answer to his words."

Said Yama, "No mortal hath ever spoken unto me as thou hast spoken. Thy words are indeed pleasing, O princess. I will grant thee even a fourth boon, except thy husband's life, ere thou dost depart."

Savitri said, "May a century of sons be born unto my husband and me so that our race may endure. O grant me this, the fourth boon, thou Mighty One."

Said Yama, "I grant unto thee a century of sons, O princess; they will be wise and powerful and thy race will endure.... Be without weariness now, O lady, and turn back; thou hast come too far already."

Savitri said, "Those who are pious must practice eternal morality, O Yama. The pious uphold the universe. The pious hold communion with the pious only, and are never weary; the pious do good unto others nor ever expect any reward. A good deed done unto the righteous is never thrown away; such an act doth not entail loss of dignity nor is any interest impaired. Indeed, the doing of good is the chief office of the righteous, and the righteous therefore are the true protectors of all."

Said Yama, "The more thou dost speak, the more I respect thee, O princess. O thou who art so deeply devoted unto thy husband, thou canst now ask of me some incomparable boon."

Savitri said, "O mighty One, thou bestower of boons, thou hast already promised what cannot be fulfilled unless my husband is restored unto me; thou hast promised me a century of sons. Therefore, I ask thee, O Yama, to give me back Satyavan, my beloved, my lord. Without him, I am as one who is dead; without him, I have no desire for happiness; without him I have no longing even for Heaven; I will have no desire to prosper if my lord is snatched off; I cannot live without Satyavan. Thou hast promised me sons, O Yama, yet thou dost take away my husband from mine arms. Hear me and grant this boon: Let Satyavan be restored to life so that thy decree may be fulfilled."

Said Yama, "So be it. With cheerful heart I now unbind thy husband. He is free.... Disease cannot afflict him again and he will prosper. Together you will both have long life; you will live four hundred years; you will have a century of sons and they will be kings, and their sons will be kings also."

Having spoken thus, Yama, the lord of death, departed unto his own place. And Savitri returned to the forest where her husband's body lay cold and ashen-pale; she sat upon the ground and pillowed his head upon her lap. Then Satyavan was given back his life.... He looked upon Savitri with eyes of love; he was like to one who had returned from a long journey in a strange land.

Said Satyavan, "Long was my sleep; why didst thou not awaken me, my beloved? ... Where is that dark One who dragged me away?"

Savitri said, "Yama hath come and gone, and thou hast slept long, resting thy head upon my lap, and art now refreshed, O blessed one. Sleep hath forsaken thee, O son of a king. If thou canst rise up, let us now depart hence for the night is already dark."

Satyavan rose up refreshed and strong. He looked round about and perceived that he was in the midst of the forest. Then he said, "O fair one, I came hither to gather fruit for thee, and while I cut down branches from the trees a pain afflicted me. I grew faint, I sank upon the ground, I laid my head upon thy lap and fell into a deep slumber even whilst thou didst embrace me. Then it seemed to me that I was enveloped in darkness, and that I beheld a sable One amidst great effulgence.... Was this a vision or a reality, O fairest and dearest?"

Savitri said, "The darkness deepens.... I will tell thee all on the morrow.... Let us now find our parents, O prince. The beasts of the night come forth; I hear their awesome voices; they tread the forest in glee; the howl of the jackal maketh my heart afraid."

Said Satyavan, "Darkness hath covered the forest with fear; we cannot discover the path by which to return home."

Savitri said, "A withered tree burneth yonder. I will gather sticks and make a fire and we will wait here until day."

Said Satyavan, "My sickness hath departed and I would fain behold my parents again. Never before have I spent a night away from the hermitage. My mother is old and my father also, and I am their crutch. They will now be afflicted with sorrow because that I have not returned."

Satyavan lifted up his arms and lamented aloud, but Savitri dried his tears and said, "I have performed penances, I have given away in charity, I have offered up sacrifices, I have never uttered a falsehood. May thy parents be protected by virtue of the power which I have obtained, and may thou, O my husband, be protected also.

Said Satyavan, "O beautiful one, let us now return to the hermitage."

Savitri raised up her despairing husband. She then placed his left arm upon her left shoulder and wound her right arm about his body, and they walked on together.... At length the fair moon came out and shone upon their path.

Meanwhile Dyumatsena, the sire of Satyavan, had regained his sight, and he went with his wife to search for his lost son, but had to return to the hermitage sorrowing and in despair. The sages comforted the weeping parents and said, "Savitri hath practiced great austerities, and there can be no doubt that Satyavan is still alive."

In time Satyavan and Savitri reached the hermitage, and their own hearts and the hearts of their parents were freed from sorrow.

Then Savitri related all that had taken place, and the sages said, "O chaste and illustrious lady, thou hast rescued the race of Dyumatsena, the foremost of kings, from the ocean of darkness and calamity."

On the morning that followed messengers came to Dyumatsena and told that the monarch who had deprived him of his kingdom was dead, having fallen by the hand of his chief minister. All the people clamored for their legitimate ruler. Said the messengers, "Chariots await thee, O king. Return, therefore, unto thy kingdom."

Great was their wonder to find that Dyumatsena was no longer blind.

So the king was restored to his kingdom, in accordance with the boon which Savitri had obtained from Yama. And sons were in time born unto her father. Thus did the gentle Savitri, by reason of her great piety, raise from misery to high fortune the family of her husband and her own father also. She was the rescuer of all; the bringer of happiness and prosperity.... He who heareth the story of Savitri will never endure misery again....

The beauties of Yama's heaven are sung by the sage Narada in the great epic poem *Mahabharata*. "Listen to me," he says. "In that fair domain it is neither too hot nor too cold. Life there is devoid of sorrow; age does not bring frailties, and none ever hunger or thirst; it is without wretchedness, or fatigue, or evil feelings. Everything, whether celestial or human, that the heart seeks after is found there. Sweet are the juicy fruits, delicious the fragrance of flowers and tree blossoms, and waters are there, both cold and hot, to give refreshment and comfort. Nymphs dance and sing to the piping of celestial elves, and merry laughter ever blends with the strains of alluring music.

"The Assembly House of Yama, which was made by Twashtri, hath splendor equal to the sun; it shines like burnished gold. There the servants of the Lord of Justice measure out the allotted days of mortals. Great rishis and ancestors await upon Yama, King of the Pitris (fathers), and adore him. Sanctified by holiness, their shining bodies are clad in swan-white garments, and decked with many-colored bracelets and golden ear-rings. Sweet sounds, alluring perfumes, and brilliant flower garlands make that building ever pleasant and supremely blest. Hundreds of thousands of saintly beings worship the illustrious King of the Pitris.

"The heaven of Indra was constructed by the great artisan-god himself. Like a chariot it can be moved anywhere at will. The Assembly House has many rooms and seats, and is adorned by celestial trees. Indra sits there with his beautiful queen, wearing his crown, with gleaming bracelets on his upper arms; he is decked with flowers, and attired in white garments. He is waited upon by brilliant Maruts, and all the gods and the rishis and saints, whose sins have been washed off their pure souls, which are resplendent as fire. There is no sorrow, or fear, or suffering in Indra's abode, which is inhabited by the spirits of wind and thunder, fire and water, plants and clouds, and planets and stars, and the spirits also of Prosperity, Religion, Joy, Faith, and Intelligence. Fairies and elves (Apsaras and Gandharvas) dance and sing there to sweet music; feats of skill are performed by celestial battle heroes, auspicious rites are also practiced. Divine messengers come and go in celestial chariots, looking bright as Soma himself.

The heaven of Varuna was constructed by Vishwakarman (Twashtri) within the sea. Its walls and arches are of pure white, and they are surrounded by celestial trees, made of sparkling jewels, which always blossom and always bear fruit. In the many-colored bowers beautiful and variegated birds sing delightful melodies. In the Assembly House, which is also of pure white, there are many rooms and many seats. Varuna, richly decked with jewels and golden ornaments and flowers, is throned there with his queen. Adityas wait upon the lord of the waters, as also do hooded snakes (Nagas) with human heads and arms, and Daityas and Danavas (giants and demons) who have taken vows and have been rewarded with immortality. All the holy spirits of rivers and oceans are there, and the holy spirits of lakes and springs and pools, and the personified forms of the points of the heavens, the ends of the earth, and the great mountains. Music and dances provide entertainment, while sacred hymns are sung in praise of Varuna."

ROYAL RIVALS: THE PANDAVAS AND KAURAVAS

Tradition Bearer: Unavailable

Source: Mackenzie, Donald A. *Indian Myth and Legend*. London: The Gresham Publishing Company Limited, 1913, 173–194.

Date: ca. 500 B.C.E.

Original Source: India

National Origin: India

The following narrative is excerpted from *The Mahabharata* (*The Story of the Bharata*), an epic that is eight times the length of the *Iliad* and the *Odyssey* combined. The heart of the work is devoted to the bitter rivalry and ultimately the war between two sets of cousins, the Pandavas and the Kauravas, over the kingdom of Bharata. In addition to this core narrative, *The Mahabharata* includes ethical, genealogical, and theological material that forms the core of Hindu religion. The following selection details the early history of the warring factions and culminates in the preliminary confrontation between the opposing champions Arjuna and Karna.

King Pandu became a mighty monarch, and was renowned as a warrior and a just ruler of his kingdom. He married two wives: Pritha, who was chief rani, and Madri, whom he loved best.

Now Pritha was of celestial origin, for her mother was a nymph; her father was a holy Brahman, and her brother, Vasudeva, was the father of Krishna. When but a babe she had been adopted by the Rajah of Shurasena, whose kingdom was among the Vindhya mountains. She was of pious heart, and ever showed reverence towards holy men. Once there came to the palace the great Rishi Durvasas, and she ministered unto him faithfully by serving food at any hour he desired, and by kindling the sacred fire in the sacrificial chamber. After his stay, which was in length a full year, Durvasas, in reward for her services, imparted to Pritha a powerful charm, by virtue of which she could compel the love of a celestial being. One day she had a vision of Surya, god of the sun; she muttered the charm, and received him when he drew nigh in the attire of a rajah, wearing the celestial ear-rings. In secret she became in time the mother of his son, Karna, who was equipped at birth with celestial ear-rings and an invulnerable coat of mail, which had power to grow as the wearer increased in stature. The child had the eyes of a lion and the shoulders of a bull.

In her maidenly shame Pritha resolved to conceal her new-born babe. So she wrapped him in soft sheets and, laying under his head a costly pillow, placed him in a basket of wicker-work which she had smeared over with wax. Then, weeping bitterly, she set the basket afloat on the river, saying, "O my babe, be thou protected by all who are on land, and in the water, and in the sky, and in the celestial regions! May all who see thee love thee! May Varuna, god of the waters, shield thee from harm! May thy father, the sun, give thee warmth! ... I shall know thee in days to come, wherever thou mayst be, by thy coat of golden mail.... She who will find thee and adopt thee will be surely blessed.... O my son, she who will cherish thee will behold thee in youthful prime like to a maned lion in Himalayan forests."

The basket drifted down the River Aswa until it was no longer seen by that lotus-eyed damsel, and at length it reached the Jumna; the Jumna gave it to the

Ganges, and by that great and holy river it was borne unto the country of Anga.... The child, lying in soft slumber, was kept alive by reason of the virtues possessed by the celestial armor and the ear-rings.

Now there was a woman of Anga who was named Radha, and she had peerless beauty. Her husband was Shatananda, the charioteer. Both husband and wife had for long sorrowed greatly because that they could not obtain a son. One day, however, their wish was gratified. It chanced that Radha went down to the river bank, and she beheld the basket drifting on the waves. She caused it to be brought ashore; and when it was uncovered, she gazed with wonder upon a sleeping babe who was as fair as the morning sun. Her heart was immediately filled with great gladness, and she cried out, "The gods have heard me at length, and they have sent unto me a son." So she adopted the babe and cherished him. And the years went past, and Karna grew up and became a powerful youth and a mighty bowman.

Pritha, who was comely to behold, chose King Pandu at her swayamvara. Trembling with love, she placed the flower garland upon his shoulders.

Madri came from the country of Madra, and was black-eyed and dusky-complexioned. She had been purchased by Bhishma for the king with much gold, many jewels and elephants and horses, as was the marriage custom among her people.

The glories of King Bharata's reign were revived by Pandu, who achieved great conquests and extended his territory. He loved well to go a-hunting, and at length he retired to the Himalaya mountains with his two wives to pursue and slay deer. There, as fate had decreed, he met with dire misfortune. One day he shot arrows at two deer which he beheld sporting together; but they were, as he discovered to his sorrow, a holy Brahman and his wife in animal guise. The sage was wounded mortally, and ere he died he assumed his wonted form, and foretold that Pandu, whom he cursed, would die in the arms of one of his wives.

The king was stricken with fear; he immediately took vows of celibacy, and gave all his possessions to Brahmans; then he went away to live in a solitary place with his two wives.

Some have told that Pandu never had children of his own, and that the gods were the fathers of his wives' great sons. Pritha was mother of Yudhishthira, son of Dharma, god of justice, and of Bhima, son of Vayu, the wind god, and also of Arjuna, son of mighty Indra, monarch of heaven. Madri received from Pritha the charm which Durvasas had given her, and she became the mother of Nakula and Sahadeva, whose sires were the twin Aswins, sons of Surya, the sun god. These five princes were known as the Pandava brothers.

King Pandu was followed by his doom. One day, as it chanced, he met with Madri, his favorite wife; they wandered together in a forest, and when he clasped her in his arms he immediately fell dead as the Brahman had foretold.

His sons, the Pandava brothers, built his funeral pyre, so that his soul might pass to heaven. Both Pritha and Madri desired to be burned with him, and they debated together which of them should follow her lord to the region of the dead.

Said Pritha, "I must go hence with my lord. I was his first wife and chief rani. O Madri, yield me his body and rear our children together. O let me achieve what must be achieved."

Madri said, "Speak not so, for I should be the chosen one. I was King Pandu's favorite wife, and he died because that he loved me. O sister, if I survived thee I should not be able to rear our children as thou canst rear them. Do not refuse thy sanction to this which is dear unto my heart."

So they held dispute, nor could agree; but the Brahmans, who heard them, said that Madri must be burned with King Pandu, having been his favorite wife. And so it came to pass that Madri laid herself on the pyre, and she passed in flames with her beloved lord, that bull among men.

Meanwhile King Pandu's blind brother, Dhritarashtra, had ascended the throne to reign over the kingdom of Bharatavarsha, with Bhishma as his regent, until the elder of the young princes should come of age.

Dhritarashtra had taken for wife fair Gándhári, daughter of the Rajah of Gándhârá. When she was betrothed she went unto the king with eyes blindfolded, and ever after-wards she so appeared in his presence. She became the mother of a hundred sons, the eldest of whom was Duryodhana. These were the princes who were named the Kauravas, after the country of Kuru-jangala.

The widowed Pritha returned to Hastinapur with her three sons and the two sons of Madri also. When she told unto Dhritarashtra that Pandu his brother had died, he wept and mourned greatly; then he bathed in holy waters and poured forth the funeral oblation. The blind King gave his protection to the five princes who were Pandu's heirs.

So the Pandavas and Kauravas were reared together in the royal palace at Hastinapur. Nor was favor shown to one cousin more than another. The young princes were trained to throw the stone and to cast the noose, and they engaged lustily in wrestling bouts and practiced boxing. As they grew up they shared work with the king's men; they marked the young calves, and every three years they counted and branded the cattle. Yet, despite all that could be done, the two families lived at enmity. Of all the young men Bhima, of the Pandavas, was the most powerful, and Duryodhana, the leader of the Kauravas, was jealous of him. Bhima was ever the victor in sports and contests. The Kauravas could ill endure his triumphs, and at length they plotted among themselves to accomplish his death.

It chanced that the young men had gone to dwell in a royal palace on the banks of the Ganges. One day, when they feasted together in the manner of warriors, Duryodhana put poison in the food of Bhima, who soon afterwards fell into a deep swoon and seemed to be dead. Then Duryodhana bound him hand and foot and cast him into the Ganges; his body was swallowed by the waters.

But it was not fated that Bhima should thus perish. As his body sank down, the fierce snakes, which are called Nagas, attacked him; but their poison counter-acted the poison he had already swallowed, so that he regained consciousness. Then, bursting his bonds, he scattered the reptiles before him, and they fled in terror.

Bhima found that he had sunk down to the city of serpents, which is in the underworld. Vasuki, king of the Nagas, having heard of his prowess, hastened towards the young warrior, whom he desired greatly to behold.

Bhima was welcomed by Aryaka, the great grandsire of Pritha, who was a dweller in the underworld. He was loved by Vasuki, who, for Aryaka's sake, offered great gifts to fearless Bhima. But Aryaka chose rather that the lad should be given a draught of strength which contained the virtues of a thousand Nagas. By the king of serpents was this great boon granted, and Bhima was permitted to drain the bowl eight times. He immediately fell into a deep slumber, which continued for the space of eight days. Then he awoke, and the Nagas feasted him ere he returned again unto his mother and his brethren, who were mourning for him the while. Thus it fell that Bhima triumphed over Duryodhana, for ever afterwards he possessed the strength of a mighty giant. He related unto his brothers all that had befallen him, but they counseled him not to reveal his secret unto the Kauravas, his cousins.

About this time the prudent Bhishma deemed that the young men should be trained to bear arms; so he searched far and wide for a preceptor who was at once a warrior and a scholar, a pious and lofty-minded man, and a lover of truth. Such was Drona, the brave and god-adoring son of Bharadwaja. He was well pleased to have care of the princes, and to give them instruction worthy of their rank and martial origin.

Drona had no mother: his miraculous birth was accomplished by a beautiful nymph, and his sire was Bharadwaja, a most pious Brahman. Of similar origin was Drupada, son of a rajah named Prishata. Drona and Drupada were reared together like brothers by the wise Bharadwaja, and it was the hope of both sires that their sons would repeat their own lifelong friendship. But when, after happy youth, they grew into manhood, fate parted them. The rajah retired from the throne, and Drupada ruled the kingdom of Panchala. Bharadwaja died soon afterwards, and Drona married a wife named Kripa, who became the mother of his son Ashwatthama. The child was so named because at birth he uttered a cry like to the neighing of a horse. Drona devoted himself to rearing his son, while he accumulated the wisdom of the sages and performed sacred rites with pious mind like to his holy sire.

When the sage Jamadagni, son of Bhrigu, closed his career, he bestowed his great wealth on the sons of Brahmans. Drona received heavenly weapons and power to wield them. Then he bethought him to visit Drupada, the friend of his youth, and share his inheritance with him. Drona stood before the rajah and exclaimed, "Behold thy friend."

But Drupada frowned; his eyes reddened with anger, and for a while he sat in silence. At length he spoke haughtily and said:

"Brahman, it is nor wise nor fitting that thou shouldst call me friend. What friendship can there be between a luckless beggar and a mighty rajah? ... I grant that in youth such a bond united us, one to another, but it has wasted away with the years. Do not think that the friendship of youth endures for ever in human hearts; it is weakened by time, and pride plucks it from one's bosom. Friendship can exist only between equals as we two once were, but no longer chance to be. Hear and know! Rich and poor, wise and ignorant, warriors and cowards, can never be friends; it is for those who are of equal station to exercise mutual esteem.... Say, can a Brahman respect one who is ignorant of the Vedas? Can a warrior do other than despise one who cannot go forth to battle in his rumbling chariot? Say, can a monarch condescend to one who is far beneath him? ... Be gone, then, thou dreamer! Forget the days and the thoughts of the past.... I know thee not."

Drona heard the harsh words of his old friend with mute amaze. For a moment he paused. Then abruptly he turned away, nor spake he in reply. His heart burned with indignation as he hastened out of the city.

In time he reached the city of Hastinapur, and Bhishma bade him welcome. When Drona undertook the training of the princes he said, "I will do as is thy desire, O Bhishma, but on condition that when the young men are become complete warriors they will help me to fight against mine enemy, Drupada, the Rajah of Panchala."

Bhishma gave willing consent to this condition. Thereafter Drona abode with his wife in the royal palace, and his son Ashwatthama was trained with the Pandavas and Kauravas. He became the family priest as well as the instructor of the princes. And ere long the young men were accomplished warriors, and deeply learned in wisdom and in goodness.

Drona took most delight in the Pandavas. Yudhishthira was trained as a spearman, but he was more renowned as a scholar than for feats of arms. Arjuna surpassed all others in warrior skill; he was of noble bearing, and none like him could ride the steed, guide the elephant, or drive the rattling chariot, nor could any other prince withstand his battle charge or oppose him in single combat. He was unequaled with javelin or dart, with battleaxe or mace, and he became the most famous archer of his day. Strong Bhima learned to wield the club, Nakula acquired the secret of taming steeds, and Sahadeva became a mighty swordsman, and acquired great knowledge of astronomy.

Drona trained the Kauravas with diligence also, as well as his own son, who was wise and brave; but among all his pupils he loved Arjuna best, for he was the most modest and the most perfect, the most fearless, and yet the most obedient to his preceptor.

Duryodhana of the Kauravas was jealous of all the Pandavas, and especially of Arjuna.

The fame of Drona as a preceptor was spread far and wide, and the sons of many rajahs and warriors hastened to Hastinapur to be instructed by him. All were welcomed save one, and he was the son of the rajah of the robber Bhils. This young man pleaded that he might be trained as an archer, but without avail. Drona said, "Are not the Bhils highwaymen and cattle-lifters? It would be a sin, indeed, to impart unto one of them great knowledge in the use of weapons."

When he heard these words, the rajah's son was stricken with grief, and he turned homeward. But he resolved to become an accomplished warrior. So he fashioned a clay image of Drona and worshipped it, and wielded the bow before it until his fame as an archer was noised abroad.

One day Drona went forth with the princes to hunt in the Bhil kingdom. Their dog ran through the woods, and it beheld the dark son of the rajah of the Bhils and barked at him. Desiring to display his skill, the young man shot seven arrows into the dog's mouth ere it could be closed, and, moaning and bleeding, the animal returned thus to the princes.

Wondering greatly, the princes searched for the greatly-skilled archer, and found him busy with his bow. They spoke, saying, "Who art thou?" And the Bhil made answer, "I am a pupil of Drona."

When Drona was brought to the place, the young man kissed his feet.

Said the wise preceptor, "If thou art my pupil, I must receive my reward."

The young man made answer, "Command me, and I will give thee whatsoever thou dost desire."

Said Drona, "I should like to have the thumb of thy right hand."

The faithful prince of the Bhils did not hesitate to obey his preceptor; with a cheerful face he severed his thumb from his right hand and gave it to Drona.

After his wound had healed, the young man began to draw his bow with his middle fingers, but found that he had lost his surpassing skill, whereat Arjuna was made happy.

All the other Bhil warriors who trained in archery followed the prince's example and drew the bow with their middle fingers, and this custom prevailed ever afterwards amongst the tribe.

Now when all the Hastinapur princes had become expert warriors, Drona addressed the blind king, as he sat among his counselors, and said, "O mighty rajah, thy sons and the sons of thy brother Pandu have now attained surpassing skill in arms, and they are fit to enter the battlefield."

Said the king, who was well pleased, "So thy task is finished, O noble son of Bharadwaja? Let now a place be made ready, in accordance with thy desire, so that the princes may display their martial skill in the presence of their peers and the common people."

Then Drona, accompanied by Vidura, the king's brother, made choice of a wide and level plain on which the Pandavas and Kauravas might perform their mighty feats.

So be it next told of the great tournament on the plain, and of the coming of illustrious Karna.

On the day of the great tournament, vast multitudes of people from all parts of the kingdom assembled round the harriers on the wide plain. A scene of great splendor was unfolded to their eyes. At dawn many flags and garlands of flowers had been distributed round the enclosure; they adorned the stately royal pavilion, which was agleam with gold and jewels and hung with trophies of war; they fluttered above the side galleries for the lords and the ladies, and even among the clustering trees. White tents for the warriors occupied a broad green space. A great altar had been erected by Drona beside a cool, transparent stream, on which to offer up sacrifices to the gods.

From early morn the murmurous throng awaited the coming of king and counselors, and royal ladies, and especially the mighty princes who were to display their feats of arms and engage in mimic warfare. The bright sun shone in beauty on that festal day.

The clarion notes of the instruments of war proclaimed the coming of the king. Then entered the royal procession, and blind Dhritarashtra was led towards his throne in the gleaming pavilion. With him came the fair queen Gandhari, mother of the Kauravas, and stately Pritha, widow of King Pandu, the mother of the Pandavas. There followed in their train many high-born dames and numerous sweet maidens renowned for their beauty. When all these ladies, attired in many-colored robes and glittering with jewels and bright flowers, were mounting the decorated galleries, they seemed like to goddesses and heavenly nymphs ascending to the golden summit of the mountain of Meru.... The trumpets were sounding loud, and the clamor which arose from the surging multitude of people of every caste and every age and every tribe was like the voice of heaving ocean in sublime tempest.

Next came venerable and white-haired Drona, robed in white, with white sacrificial cord; his sandals were white, and the garlands he wore were white also. His valiant son, Aswatthama, followed him as the red planet Mars follows the white moon in cloudless heaven. The saintly preceptor advanced to the altar where the priestly choir gathered, and offered up sacrifices to the gods and chanted holy texts.

Then heralds sounded their trumpets as the youthful princes entered in bright array, bejeweled and lightly girded for exercise, their left arms bound with leather. They were wearing breastplates; their quivers were slung from their shoulders, and they carried stately bows and gleaming swords. The princes filed in according to their years, and Yudhishthira came first of all. Each saluted Drona in turn and awaited his commands.

One by one the youthful warriors displayed their skill at arms, while the vast crowd shouted their plaudits. The regent Bhishma, sitting on the right side of the throne, looked down with delight, and Vidura, sitting on the left side, informed the sightless king of all that took place.

The princes shot arrows at targets, first on foot and then mounted on rapid steeds, displaying great skill; they also rode on elephants and in chariots, and their arrows ever flew with unerring aim.

Next they engaged in mimic warfare, charging with chariots and on elephants: swords clamored on shields, ponderous maces were wielded, and falchions shimmered like to the flashes of lightning. The movements of the princes, mounted and on foot, were rapid and graceful; they were fearless in action and firm-footed, and greatly skilled in thrust and parry.

But ere long the conflict was waged with more than mimic fury. Proud Duryodhana and powerful Bhima had sought one another and were drawn apart from their peers. They towered on the plain with uplifted maces, and they seemed like two rival elephants about to fight for a mate. Then they charged with whirling weapons, and the combat was terrible to behold.

Vidura pictured the conflict to blind Dhritarashtra, as did Pritha also to the blindfolded Queen Gandhari. Round the barriers the multitudes swayed and clamored, some favoring Duryodhana and others mighty Bhima.

The princes fought on, and their fury increased until at length it seemed that one or the other would be slain. But while yet the issue hung doubtful, Drona, whose brow was troubled, marked with concern the menacing crowd, which was suspended with hope and fear, and seemed like an ocean shaken by fitful gusts of changing wind. Then he interposed, bidding his son to separate the angry combatants so that the turmoil might have end. The princes heard and obeyed, and they retired slowly like ocean billows, tempest-swollen, falling apart.

To allay excitement, trumpet and drum were sounded aloud. Then white-haired Drona stepped forward, and in a voice like thunder summoned brave Arjuna to come forth.

First of all the valiant hero performed a sacred rite. Thereafter he came before the multitude in all his splendor, clad in golden armor, like to a glorious evening cloud. Modestly he strode, while trumpets blared and the drums bellowed, and he seemed a very god. He was girdled with jewels, and he carried a mighty bow. As the people applauded and shouted his praises, Pritha, his mother, looked down, and tears dropped from her eyes. The blind king spake to Vidura, saying, "Why are the multitudes shouting now like to the tumultuous sea?"

Said Vidura, "The valiant son of Pritha hath come forth in golden armor, and the people hail him with joy.

The blind monarch said, "I am well pleased. The sons of Pritha sanctify the kingdom like to sacrificial fires."

Silence fell upon the people, and Drona bade his favorite pupil to display his skill. Arjuna performed wonders with magic arms; he created fire by the *Agneya* weapon, water by the *Varuna* weapon, wind by the *Vayavya* weapon, clouds by the *Paryanya* weapon, land by the *Bhanma* weapon, and he caused mountains to appear by the *Parvatya* weapon. Then by the *Antardhyana* weapon he caused all these to vanish.

Arjuna then set up for his target an iron image of a great boar, and at one bending of the bow he shot five arrows into its gaping jaws. Wondrous was his skill. Next he suspended a cow horn, which swayed constantly in the wind, and discharged into its hollow with unerring aim twenty rapid arrows. Heaven and earth resounded with the plaudits of the people when he leapt into his chariot and discharged clouds of arrows as he was driven speedily round the grounds. Having thus displayed his accomplishments as an archer, he drew his sword, which he wielded so rapidly round and about that the people thought they beheld lightning and heard thunder. Ere he left the field he cast the noose with exceeding great skill, capturing horses and cows and scampering deer at a single throw. Then Drona embraced him, and the people shouted his praises.

Great was the joy of the Pandavas as they rested around Drona like to the stars that gather about the white moon in heaven. The Kauravas were grouped around Aswatthama as the gods gather beside Indra when the giant Daityas threaten to assail high heaven. Duryodhana's heart burned with jealous anger because of the triumph achieved by Arjuna.

Evening came on, and it seemed that the tournament was ended; the crowds began to melt away. Then, of a sudden, a mighty tumult of plaudits broke forth, and the loud din of weapons and clank of armor was heard all over the place. Every eye immediately turned towards the gate, and the warriors and the people beheld approaching an unknown warrior, who shook his weapons so that they rattled loudly.

So came mighty Karna, son of Surya, the sun god, and of Pritha, the mother of the three Pandavas—Arjuna, Bhima, and wise Yudhishthira. He was comely as a shining god, clad in golden armor, and wearing celestial earrings. In his right hand he carried a great many-colored bow; his gleaming falchion was on his thigh. Tall as a cliff he strode forward; he was an elephant in his fury, a lion in his wrath; stately as a palm tree was that tamer of foemen, so fearless and so proud, so dauntless and so self-possessed.

He paused in the center of the plain and surveyed the people with pride. Stiffly he paid homage to Drona and Kripa. Then he, the eldest son of Pritha, spake to Pritha's youngest son, Arjuna, the brothers being unknown one to another, and he said, "Whatever feats thou hast performed this day with vain boast, Arjuna, these will I accomplish and surpass, if Drona will permit me."

His voice was like to thunder in heaven, and the multitude of people sprang up and uttered cries of wonder. Duryodhana and the other sons of Kuru heard the challenge with glad hearts, but Arjuna remained silent, while his eyes flashed fire.

Then Drona gave the warrior permission to display his skill. Karna was well pleased, and he performed every feat which had given Arjuna fame on that great day.

Duryodhana proclaimed his joy with beaming countenance, and he embraced Karna, whom he hailed as "'brother," saying, "I bid thee welcome, thou mighty warrior. Thou hast won the honors of the field. Demand from me whatsoever thou dost desire in this kingdom, and it will be given unto thee."

Said Karna, "Thy word is thy bond, O prince. All I seek is to combat against Arjuna, whom I have equaled so far. Fain would I win the victor's renown."

Duryodhana said, "Thou dost ask for a worthy boon indeed. Be our ally, and let the enemy fear thee."

Arjuna was moved to great wrath, and cried out, "Uninvited chief! Boasting thus, thou wouldst fain be regarded as mine equal, but I will so deal with thee that thou wilt die the death of a braggart who cometh here an unbidden guest, speaking boastfully ere thou art spoken to."

Said Karna, answering proudly and calm, "Waste not words, Arjuna, nor taunt me with coming hither uninvited. The field of combat is free to all warriors; they enter by their valor, and do not await until thou dost call them; they win their places by strength and skill, and their warrant is the sword. Wrathful speech is the weapon of a coward. Do not boast of thy pastimes or be vain of thy bloodless feats. Speak with thine arrows, O Arjuna, until, in Drona's presence, mine will cause all men to wonder, flying towards thee."

Drona was stirred to wrath, and spake to Arjuna, saying, "Canst thou hear him boast in this manner? I give thee leave to fight him here and now."

Arjuna at once strode forward, fully armed, and he was supported by Drona and Bhishma. Duryodhana and his band stood by Karna. Then the two warriors prepared for single combat, but not in mimic warfare.

Thick clouds gathered in the sky; lightning flashed and thunder pealed; the mighty Indra guarded his son Arjuna, who stood in shadow. Surya, the sun god, cast a shaft of light athwart the darkening plain, and Karna's golden armor gleamed bright and fair.

The noble dames looked on, and some praised Arjuna and others praised Karna. Pritha, the mother of both heroes, was alone divided in her love. She knew her firstborn by his voice and noble bearing and by his armor, and her heart was torn with grief to behold the two brothers ready to slay each other. A cloud blinded her eyes, and, uttering a low cry, she swooned where she sat. Vidura sprinkled water on her face, and she was revived. Then she wept bitterly because that she could not reveal the secret of Karna's birth.

Kripa, the foster-brother of Bhishma, performed the duties of herald, and as Arjuna strode forth to combat he proclaimed, "Behold! This is mighty Arjuna, of Bharata's great line, son of Pandu and of Pritha, a prince of valor and worth who will not shrink from battle. Unknown and long-armed chief," he said unto Karna, "declare now thy name and lineage, the royal house thou dost adorn, and the names of thy sire and thy mother. Know thou that by the rules of single combat the sons of kings cannot contend against low-born or nameless rivals."

Karna heard, but was silent. He hung his head like the dew-laden lotus bloom; he could claim nor lineage or high rank, as he believed, for he regarded the charioteer of Anga as his sire.

Duryodhana, perceiving his discomfiture, cried out to Kripa, saying, "Valor is not reckoned by birth but by deeds. Karna hath already shown himself to be the peer of princes. I now proclaim him the Rajah of Anga."

Having spoken thus, the elder of the Kauravas led Karna by the hand and placed him upon a throne, and the red umbrella was held above his head. Brahmans chanted the texts for the ceremony and anointed Karna as a king. Then the fan was waved and the royal umbrella raised on high, while the Kauravas shouted, "The rajah is crowned; blessings on the rajah; honor to the valorous warrior!"

Robed in royal attire, Karna then spake to Duryodhana and said, "With generous heart thou hast conferred upon me a kingdom. O prince, speak and say what service thou wouldst have me to render unto thee."

Said Duryodhana, "But one boon do I ask of thee, O king. Be my comrade and, O valiant warrior, be my helper also."

Karna said, "As thou desirest, so be it."

Then Duryodhana and Karna embraced one another to confirm their loyal friendship.

Lo! Now a charioteer drew nigh; he was a scantily-clad and wearied old man, and he stooped, leaning heavily upon his staff. He was the aged sire of Karna, and rejoiced in his heart to see his son so highly honored among princes. Karna cast aside his weapons, knelt down, and kissed the old man's feet. The happy sire embraced the crowned head of the warrior and wept tears of love.

The Pandava brothers gazed upon father and son, amused and scornful.... Bhima spake to Karna, saying, "So thou, with such a sire, hast presumed to seek combat with a Pandava! ... Son of a charioteer, what hast thou to do with weapons of war? Better were it that thou shouldst find thee a goad and drive a bullock-cart behind thy sire."

Karna grew pale with wrath; his lips quivered, but he answered not a word. He heaved a deep sigh and looked towards the sun.

Then Duryodhana arose like a proud elephant and spake to Bhima, saying, "Seek not with insults to give sorrow unto a mighty hero. Taunts come ill from thee, thou tiger-like chief. The proudest warrior may contend against the most humble: a hero is known by his deeds. Of Karna's birth we care naught. Hath Drona other than humble lineage? 'Tis, said, too, that thou and thy brethren are not sons of Pandu, but of certain amorous deities.... Look upon Karna, adorned with jewels and in golden armor! Do hinds bring forth tigers? ... Karna was born to he a king; he hath come to rule by reason of his valor and his worth. If any prince or warrior among you will deny my words, hear and know, now, that I will meet him in deadly combat."

The assembled multitude heard these mighty words with joy and shouted loud applause.

But darkness came on, and lamps were lit upon the plain.... Drona and the sons of Pandu made offerings at the altar, and the king and his counselors, the noble dames and the high-born maids, departed in silence to their homes.... Then all the people deserted the harriers, some shouting, "Arjuna hath triumphed"; others, "Karna is victor"; and some also, "Duryodhana hath won."

Pritha had rejoiced in her heart to behold her noble son crowned king....

Duryodhana walked by Karna's side and took him away to his own palace, glad of heart, for he no longer feared Arjuna's valor and skill at arms.

Even Yudhishthira doubted Arjuna's worth; he feared that Karna was the greatest hero in the world of men.

THE BRAHMAN, THE TIGER, AND THE SIX JUDGES

Tradition Bearer: Unavailable

Source: Frere, Mary. *Old Deccan Days*. London: J. Murray, 1868, 135–138.

Date: ca. 1866

Original Source: India

National Origin: India

The **formulaic** question-and-answer pattern upon which the following **animal tale** is structured is typical of "The Ungrateful Serpent [Animal] Returned to Captivity" (AT 155). The opinions of the various judges cite real human transgressions. Traditionally, in India, four primary caste divisions have been recognized: Brahmans (priests), Kshatriyas (kings and warriors), Vaisyas (traders and similar occupations), and Sudras (aborigines). The jackal is a common **trickster** figure in India—as elsewhere.

Once upon a time a Brahman [member of the Hindu priestly caste], who was walking along the road, came upon an iron cage, in which a great tiger had been shut up by the villagers who caught him.

As the Brahman passed by, the tiger called out and said to him, "Brother Brahman, brother Brahman, have pity on me, and let me out of this cage for one minute only, to drink a little water, for I am dying of thirst."

The Brahman answered, "No, I will not; for if I let you out of the cage you will eat me."

"O father of mercy," answered the tiger, "in truth that will not. I will never be so ungrateful. Only let me out, that I may drink some water and return."

Then the Brahman took pity on him, and opened the cage door; but no sooner had he done so than the tiger, jumping out, said, "Now, I will eat you first, and drink the water afterwards."

But the Brahman said, "Only do not kill me hastily. Let us first ask the opinion of six, and if all of them say it is just and fair that you should put me to death, then I am willing to die."

"Very well," answered the tiger, "it shall be as you say. We will first ask the opinion of six."

So the Brahman and the tiger walked on till they came to a banyan tree; and the Brahman said to it, "Banyan tree, banyan tree, hear and give judgment."

"On what must I give judgment?" asked the banyan tree.

"This tiger," said the Brahman," begged me to let him out of his cage to drink a little water, and he promised not to hurt me if I did so. But now that I have let him out he wishes to eat me. Is it just that he should do so, or no?"

The banyan tree answered, "Men often come to take refuge in the cool shade under my boughs from the scorching rays of the sun; but when they have rested, they cut and break my pretty branches, and wantonly scatter the leaves that sheltered them. Let the tiger eat the man, for men are an ungrateful race."

At these words the tiger would have instantly killed the Brahman; but the Brahman said, "Tiger, tiger, you must not kill me yet, for you promised that we should first hear the judgment of six."

"Very well," said the tiger, and they went on their way. After a little while they met a camel.

"Sir camel, sir camel," cried the Brahman, "hear and give judgment."

"On what shall I give judgment?" asked the camel.

And the Brahman related how the tiger had begged him to open the cage door, and promised not to eat him if he did so; and how he had afterwards determined to break his word, and asked if that were just or not.

The camel replied, "When I was young and strong, and could do much work, my master took care of me and gave me good food; but now that I am old, and have lost all my strength in his service, he overloads me, and starves me, and beats me without mercy. Let the tiger eat the man, for men are an unjust and cruel race."

The tiger would then have killed the Brahman, but the latter said, "Stop, tiger, for we must first hear the judgment of six."

So they both went again on their way. At a little distance they found a bullock lying by the roadside.

The Brahman said to him, "Brother bullock, brother bullock, hear and give judgment."

"On what must I give judgment?" asked the bullock.

The Brahman answered, "I found this tiger in a cage, and he prayed me to open the door and let him out to drink a little water, and promised not to kill me if I did so; but when I had let him out he resolved to put me to death. Is it fair he should do so or not?"

The bullock said, "When I was able to work, my master fed me well and tended me carefully, but now I am old he has forgotten all I did for him, and left me by the roadside to die. Let the tiger eat the man, for men have no pity."

Three out of the six had given judgment against the Brahman, but still he did not lose all hope, and determined to ask the other three.

They next met an eagle flying through the air, to whom the Brahman cried, "O eagle, great eagle, hear and give judgment."

"On what must I give judgment?" asked the eagle.

The Brahman stated the case, but the eagle answered, "Whenever men see me they try to shoot me; they climb the rocks and steal away my little ones. Let the tiger eat the man, for men are the persecutors of the earth."

Then the tiger began to roar, and said, "The judgment of all is against you, O Brahman!"

But the Brahman answered, "Stay yet a little longer, for two others must first be asked."

After this they saw an alligator, and the Brahman related the matter to him, hoping for a more favorable verdict.

But the alligator said, "Whenever I put my nose out of the water, men torment me, and try to kill me. Let the tiger eat the man, for as long as men live we shall have no rest."

The Brahman gave himself up as lost; but once more he prayed the tiger to have patience, and to let him ask the opinion of the sixth judge. Now the sixth was a jackal.

The Brahman again told his story, and said to him, "Mama jackal, mama jackal, say what is your judgment?"

The jackal answered, "It is impossible for me to decide who is in the right and who in the wrong, unless I see the exact position in which you were when the dispute began. Show me the place."

So the Brahman and the tiger returned to the place where they first met, and the jackal went with them.

When they got there, the jackal said, "Now, Brahman, show me exactly where you stood."

"Here," said the Brahman, standing by the iron tiger cage.

"Exactly there, was it?" asked the jackal.

"Exactly here," replied the Brahman.

"Where was the tiger then?" asked the jackal.

"In the cage," answered the tiger.

"How do you mean?" said the jackal.

"How were you within the cage? Which way were you looking?"

"Why, I stood so," said the tiger, jumping into the cage, "and my head was on this side."

"Very good," said the jackal. "But I cannot judge without understanding the whole matter exactly. Was the cage door open or shut?"

"Shut, and bolted," said the Brahman.

"Then shut and bolt it," said the jackal.

When the Brahman had done this, the jackal said, "Oh, you wicked and ungrateful tiger, when the good Brahman opened your cage door, is to eat him the only return you would make? Stay there, then, for the rest of your days, for no one will ever let you out again. Proceed on your journey, friend Brahman. Your road lies that way, and mine this."

So saying, the jackal ran off in one direction, and the Brahman went rejoicing on his way in the other.

THE DEMON WITH THE MATTED HAIR

Tradition Bearer: Unavailable

Source: Jacobs, Joseph. *Indian Fairy Tales*. London: David Nutt, 1912, 40–45.

Date: 1912

Original Source: India

National Origin: India

This tale of the prince of the five weapons is derived from the voluminous *Jataka*, a compendium of tales of the Buddha in his previous incarnations. Jamudipa was one of the four islands believed to comprise the inhabited world. Jamudipa included South Asia. The demon, Aṅgulimāla, was a bandit who wore a necklace of his victims' fingers and was converted by the Buddha and became an Arahat, one of the enlightened. Interesting comparisons can be made between this tale and "The Tarbaby and the Rabbit" (AT 175). (See, for example, the Caribbean tale "Brother Rabbit an' Brother Tar-Baby," Volume 4, page 414).

This story the Teacher told in Jetavana about a Brother who had ceased striving after' righteousness. Said the Teacher to him, "Is it really true that you have ceased all striving?"

"Yes, Blessed One," he replied.

Then the Teacher said, "O Brother, in former days wise men made effort in the place where effort should be made, and so attained unto royal power." And he told a story of long ago.

Once upon a time, when Brahmadatta was King of Benares, the Bodhisatta was born as son of his chief queen. On his name-day they asked eight hundred Brahmans, having satisfied them with all their desires, about his lucky marks.

The Brahmans who had skill in divining from such marks beheld the excellence of his, and made answer:

"Full of goodness, great King, is your son, and when you die he will become king; he shall be famous and renowned for his skill with the five weapons, and shall be the chief man in all India. On hearing what the Brahmans had to say, they gave him the name of the Prince of the Five Weapons, sword, spear, bow, battle-axe, and shield.

When he came to years of discretion, and had attained the measure of sixteen years, the King said to him:

"My son, go and complete your education."

"Who shall be my teacher?" the lad asked.

"Go, my son; in the kingdom of Candahar, in the city of Takkasila, is a far-famed teacher from whom I wish you to learn. Take this, and give it him for a fee." With that he gave him a thousand pieces of money, and dismissed him.

The lad departed and was educated by this teacher; he received the Five Weapons from him as a gift, bade him farewell, and leaving Takkasila, he began his journey to Benares, armed with the Five Weapons.

On his way he came to a forest inhabited by the Demon with the Matted Hair. At the entering of the forest some men saw him, and cried out:

"Hullo, young sir, keep clear of that wood! There's a Demon in it called he of the Matted Hair: he kills every man he sees!" And they tried to stop him. But the Bodhisatta, having confidence in himself, went straight on, fearless as a maned lion.

When he reached mid-forest the Demon showed himself. He made himself as tall as a palm tree; his head was the size of a pagoda, his eyes as big as saucers, and he had two tusks all over knobs and bulbs; he had the face of a hawk, a variegated belly, and blue hands and feet.

"Where are you going?" he shouted. "Stop! You'll make a meal for me!"

Said the Bodhisatta, "Demon, I came here trusting in myself. I advise you to be careful how you come near me. Here's a poisoned arrow, which I'll shoot at you and knock you down!" With this menace, he fitted to his bow an arrow dipped in deadly poison, and let fly. The arrow stuck fast in the Demon's hair. Then he shot and shot, till he had shot away fifty arrows; and they all stuck in the Demon's hair. The Demon snapped them all off short, and threw them down at his feet; then came up to the Bodhisatta, who drew his sword and struck the Demon, threatening him the while. His sword—it was three-and-thirty inches long—stuck in the Demon's hair! The Bodhisatta struck him with his spear—that stuck too! He struck him with his club—and that stuck too!

When the Bodhisatta saw that this had stuck fast, he addressed the Demon. "You, Demon!" said he, "did you never hear of me before—the Prince of the Five Weapons? When I came into the forest which you live in

I did not trust to my bow and other weapons: This day will I pound you and grind you to powder!" Thus did he declare his resolve, and with a shout he hit at the Demon with his right hand. It stuck fast in his hair! He hit him with his left hand—that stuck too!' With his right foot he kicked him—that stuck too; then with his left—and that stuck too! Then he butted at him with his head, crying, "I'll pound you to powder!" and his head stuck fast like the rest.

Thus the Bodhisatta was five times snared, caught fast in five places, hanging suspended: yet he felt no fear—was not even nervous.

Thought the Demon to himself, "Here's a lion of a man! A noble man! More than man is he! Here he is, caught by a Demon like me; yet he will not fear a bit. Since I have ravaged this road, I never saw such a man. Now, why is it that he does not fear?" He was powerless to eat the man, but asked him, "Why is it, young sir, that you are not frightened to death?"

"Why should I fear, Demon?" replied he. "In one life a man can die but once. Besides, in my belly is a thunderbolt; if you eat me, you will never be able to digest it; this will tear your inwards into little bits, and kill you: so we shall both perish. That is why I fear nothing." (By this, the Bodhisatta meant the weapon of knowledge which he had within him.)

When he heard this, the Demon thought, "This young man speaks the truth. A piece of the flesh of such a lion-man as he would be too much for me to digest, if it were no bigger than a kidney-bean. I'll let him go!" So, being frightened to death, he let go the Bodhisatta, saying:

"Young sir, you are a lion of a man! I will not eat you up. I set you free from my hands, as the moon is disgorged from the jaws of Rahu after the eclipse. Go back to the company of your friends and relations!"

And the Bodhisatta said, "Demon, I will go, as you say. You were born a Demon, cruel, blood-bibbing, devourer of the flesh and gore of others, because you did wickedly in former lives. If you still go on doing wickedly, you will go from darkness to darkness. But now that you have seen me you will find it impossible to do wickedly. Taking the life of living creatures causes birth, as an animal, in the world of Petas, or, in the body of an Asura, or, if one is reborn as a man, it makes his life short." With this and the like monition he told him the disadvantage of the five kinds of wickedness, and the profit of the five kinds of virtue, and frightened the Demon in various ways, discoursing to him until he subdued him and made him self-denying, and established him in the five kinds of virtue; he made him worship the deity to whom offerings were made in that wood; and having carefully admonished him, departed out of it.

At the entrance of the forest he told all to the people thereabout; and went on to Benares, armed with his five weapons. Afterwards he became king, and ruled righteously; and after giving alms and doing good he passed away according to his deeds.

And the Teacher, when this tale was ended, became perfectly enlightened, and repeated this verse:

> Whose mind and heart from all desire is free,
> Who seeks for peace by living virtuously,
> He in due time will sever all the bonds
> That bind him fast to life, and cease to be.

Thus the Teacher reached the summit, through sainthood and the teaching of the law, and thereupon he declared the Four Truths. At the end of the declaring of the Truths, this Brother also attained to sainthood. Then the Teacher made the connation, and gave the key to the birth-tale, saying, "At that time Angulimala was the Demon, but the, Prince of the Five Weapons was I myself."

RAMA AND LUXMAN

Tradition Bearer: Unavailable

Source: Frere, Mary. *Old Deccan Days*. London: J. Murray, 1868, 72–86.

Date: ca. 1866

Original Source: India

National Origin: India

An **ordinary folktale**, "Rama and Luxman" bears a close resemblance to "Faithful John" (AT 516), a narrative built around the theme of a faithful servant who is repeatedly misjudged and underappreciated by his master. Although Rama is son of a rajah, he is like a brother to the vizier's son Luxman. In spite of this, Luxman is saved from his sworn brother's rash judgments, and ultimately from eternal enchantment, only through the intervention of fate and his own quick wits.

Once upon a time there was a Rajah whose name was Chandra Rajah, and he had a learned Wuzeer [usually "vizier"] or Minister, named Butti. Their mutual love was so great that they were more like brothers than master and servant. Neither the Rajah nor the Wuzeer had any children, and both were equally anxious to have a son. At last, in one day and one hour~ the wile of the Rajah and the wife of the Wuzeer had each a little baby boy. They named the Rajah's son Rama, and the son of the Wuzeer was called Luxman, and there were great rejoicings at the birth of both.

The boys grew up and loved each other tenderly; they were never happy unless together; together they went to daily school, together bathed and played, and they would not eat except from off one plate. One day, when Rama Rajah was fifteen years, his mother, the Ranee, said to Chandra Rajab, "Husband, our son associates too much with low people; for instance, he is always at play with the Wuzeer's son, Luxman, which is not befitting his rank. I wish you would endeavor to put an end to their friendship, and find him better playmates."

Chandra Rajah replied, "I cannot do it; Luxman's father is a very good friend and Wuzeer, as his father's father was to my rather; let the sons be the same." This answer annoyed the Ranee, but she said no more to her husband; she sent, however, for all the wise people and seers and conjurors in the land, and inquired of them whether there existed no means of dissolving the children's affection for each other; they answered they knew of none.

At last one old Nautch [a woman who has been "married" to a temple or deity] woman came to the Ranee and said, "I can do this thing that you wish, but for it you must give me a great reward."

Then the Ranee gave the old woman an enormous bag full of gold mohurs, and said, "This I give you now, and if you succeed in the undertaking I will give you as much again.

So this wicked old woman disguised herself in a very rich dress, and went to a garden-house which Chandra Rajah had built for his son, and where Rama Rajah and Luxman, the young Wuzeer, used to spend the greater part of their playtime. Outside the house was a large well and a fine garden. When the old woman arrived, the two boys were playing cards together in the garden close to the well. She drew near, and began drawing water from it.

Rama Rajah, looking up, saw her, and said to Luxman, "Go, see who that richly dressed woman is, and bring me word." The Wuzeer's son did as he was bidden, and asked the woman what she wanted.

She answered, "Nothing, oh nothing," and nodding her head went away; then, returning to the Ranee, she said, "I have done as you wished, give me the promised reward," and the Ranee gave her the second bag of gold.

On Luxman's return, the young Rajah said to him, "What did the woman want?"

Luxman answered, "She told me she wanted nothing."

"It is not true," replied the other angrily, "I feel certain she must have told you something. Why should she come here for no purpose? It is some secret which you are concealing from me; I insist on knowing it." Luxman vainly protesting the contrary, they quarreled and then fought, and the young Rajah ran home very angry to his father.

"What is the matter, my son?" said he.

"Father," he answered, "I am angry with the Wuzeer's son. I hate that boy; kill him, and let his eyes be brought to me in proof of his death, or I will not eat my dinner." Chandra Rajah was very much grieved at this, but the young Rajah would eat no dinner, and at last his father said to the Wuzeer, "Take your son away, and hide him, for the boys have had a quarrel." Then he went out and shot a deer, and showing its eyes to Rama, said to him, "See, my son, the good Wuzeer's son has by your order been deprived of life"; and Rama Rajah was merry, and ate his dinner.

But a while after he began to miss his kind playmate; there was nobody he cared for to tell him stories and amuse him. Then for four nights running he dreamed of a beautiful Glass Palace, in which dwelt a Princess white as marble, and he sent for all the wise people in the kingdom to interpret his dream, but none could do it; and, thinking upon this fair Princess and his lost friend, he got more and more sad, and said to himself, "There is nobody to help me in this matter. Ah! If my Wuzeer's son were here now, how quickly would he interpret the dream! O my friend, my friend, my dear lost friend!" and when Chandra Rajah, his father, came in, he said to him, "Show me the grave of Luxman, son of the Wuzeer, that I also may die there."

His father replied, "What a foolish boy you are! You first begged that the Wuzeer's son might be killed, and now you want to die on his grave. What is all this about?"

Rama Rajah replied, "Oh! Why did you give the order for him to be put to death? In him I have lost my friend and all my joy in life; show me now his grave, for thereon, I swear, will I kill myself."

When the Rajah saw that his son really grieved for the loss of Luxman, he said to him, "You have to thank me for disregarding your foolish wishes; your old playmate is living, therefore be friends again, for what you thought were his eyes were but the eyes of a deer."

So the friendship of Rama and Luxman was resumed on its former footing. Then Rama said to Luxman, "Four nights ago I dreamed a strange dream. I thought that for miles and miles I wandered through a dense jungle, after which I came upon a grove of Coconut trees, passing through which I reached one composed entirely of Guava trees, then one of Supari trees, and lastly one of Copal trees. Beyond this lay a garden of flowers, of which the Malee's wife gave me a bunch; round the garden ran a large river, and on the other side of this I saw a fair palace composed of transparent glass, and in the center of it sat the most lovely Princess I ever saw, white as marble, and covered with rich jewels; at the sight of her beauty I fainted—and so awoke. This has happened now four times, and as yet I have found no one capable of throwing any light on the vision."

Luxman answered, "I can tell you. There exists a Princess exactly like her you saw in your dreams, and, if you like, you can go and marry her."

"How can I?" said Rama, "and what is your interpretation of the dream?" The Wuzeer's son replied, "Listen to me, and I will tell you. In a country very far away from this, in the center of a great Rajah's kingdom, there dwells his daughter, a most fair Princess; she lives in a glass palace. Round this palace runs a large river, and round the river is a garden of flowers. Round the garden are four thick groves of trees, one of Copal trees, one of Supari trees, one of Guava trees, and one of Cocoa-nut trees. The Princess is twenty-four years old, but she is not married, for she has determined only to marry whoever can jump this river and greet her in her crystal palace, and though many thousand kings have essayed to do so, they have all perished miserably in the attempt, having either been drowned in the river, or broken their necks by falling; thus all that you dreamed of is perfectly true."

"Can we go to this country?" asked the young Rajah.

"Oh yes," his friend replied, "this is what you must do. Go tell your father you wish to see the world. Ask him for neither elephants nor attendants, but beg him to lend you for the journey his old war-horse."

Upon this Rama went to his father, and said, "Father, I pray you give me leave to go and travel with the Wuzeer's son; I desire to see the world."

"What would you have for the journey, my son?" said Chandra Rajah, "will you have elephants, and how many?—attendants, how many?"

"Neither, father," he answered, "give me rather, I pray you, your old war-horse, that I may ride him during the journey."

"So be it, my son," he answered; and with that Rama Rajah and Luxman set forth on their travels. After going many, many thousands of miles, to their joy one day they came upon a dense grove of Coconut trees, and beyond that to a grove of Guava trees, then to one of Supari trees, and lastly to one of Copal trees; after which they entered a beautiful garden, where the Malee's wife presented them with a large bunch of flowers. Then they knew that they had nearly reached the place where the fair Princess dwelt. Now it happened that, because many kings and great people had been drowned in trying to jump over the river that ran round the Glass Palace where the Princess lived, the Rajah, her father, had made a law that, in future, no aspirants to her hand were to attempt the jump, except at stated times, and with his knowledge and permission, and that any Rajahs or Princes found wandering there, contrary to this law, were to be imprisoned. Of this the young Rajah and the Wuzeer's son knew nothing, and having reached the center of the garden they found themselves on the banks of a large river, exactly opposite the wondrous Glass Palace, and were just debating what further steps to take when they were seized by the Rajah's guard, and hurried off to prison.

"This is a hard fate," said Luxman.

"Yes," sighed Rama Rajah, "a dismal end, in truth, to all our fine schemes. Would it be possible, think you, to escape?"

"I think so," answered Luxman, "at all events I will try." With that he turned to the sentry who was guarding them, and said, "We are shut in here and can't get out; here is money for you if you will only have the goodness to call out that the Malee's cow has strayed away." The sentry thought this a very easy way of making a fortune, so he did as he was bidden, and took the money. The result answered Luxman's anticipations.

The Malee's wife hearing the sentry calling out, thought to herself, "What, sentries round the guard-room again! Then there must be prisoners: doubtless they are those two young Rajah's I met in the garden this morning; I will at least endeavor to release them." So she asked two old beggars to accompany her, and, taking with her offerings of flowers and sweetmeats, started as if to go to a little temple which was built within the quadrangle where the prisoners were kept. The sentries, thinking she was only going with two old friends to visit the temple, allowed her to pass without opposition. As soon as she got within the quadrangle she unfastened the prison-door, and told the two young men (Rama Rajah and Luxman) to change clothes with the two old beggars, which they instantly did. Then leaving the beggars in the cell, she conducted Rama and Luxman safely to her house.

When they had reached it she said to them, "Young Princes, you must know that you did very wrong in going down to the river before having made a salaam to our Rajah, and gained his consent; and so strict is the law on this subject that had I not assisted your escape, you might have remained a long time in prison; though, as I felt certain you only erred through ignorance, I was the more willing to help you; but tomorrow morning early you must go and pay your respects at Court."

Next day the guards brought their two prisoners to the Rajah, saying, "See, O King, here are two young Rajahs whom we caught last night wandering near the river contrary to your law and commandment." But when they came to look at the prisoners, lo and behold! They were only two old beggars whom everybody knew and had often seen at the palace gate.

Then the Rajah laughed and said, "You stupid fellows, you have been over vigilant for once; see here your fine young Rajahs. Don't you yet know the looks of these old beggars?" Whereupon the guards went away much ashamed of themselves.

Having learnt discretion from the advice of the Malee's wife, Rama and Luxman went betimes that morning to call at the Rajah's palace. The Rajah received them very graciously, but when he heard the object of their journey he shook his head, and said, "My pretty fellows, far be it from me to thwart your intentions, if you are really determined to win my daughter the Princess Bargaruttee, but as a friend I would counsel you to desist from the attempt—you can find a hundred Princesses elsewhere willing to marry you; why, therefore, come here, where already a thousand Princes as fair as you have lost their lives? Cease to think of my daughter, she is a headstrong girl." But Rama Rajah still declared himself anxious to try and jump the dangerous river, whereupon the Rajah unwillingly consented to his attempting to do so, and caused it to be solemnly proclaimed round the town that another Prince was going to risk his life, begging all good men and true to pray for his success. Then Rama having dressed gorgeously, and mounted his father's stout war-horse, put spurs to it and galloped to the river. Up, up in the air, like a bird, jumped the good war-horse, right across the river and into the very center courtyard of the Glass Palace of the Princess Bargaruttee: and as if ashamed of so poor an exploit, this feat he accomplished three times.

At this the heart of the Rajah was glad, and he ran and patted the brave horse, and kissed Rama Rajah, and said, "Welcome, my son-in-law!" The wedding took place amid great rejoicings, with feasts, illuminations, and much giving of presents, and there Rama Rajah and his wife, the Ranee Bargaruttee, lived happily for some time. At last, one day, Rama Rajah said to his father-in-law, "Sire, I have been very happy here, but I have a great desire to see my father, and my mother, and my own land again."

To which the Rajah replied, "My son, you are free to go; but I have no son but you, nor daughter but your wife: therefore as it grieves me to lose sight of you, come back now and then to see me and rejoice my heart. My doors are ever open to you; you will be always welcome."

Rama Rajah promised to return occasionally; and then, being given many rich gifts by the old Rajah, and supplied with all things needful for the journey, he, with his beautiful wife Bargaruttee, his friend the young Wuzeer, and a great retinue, set out to return home.

Before going Rama Rajah and Luxman richly rewarded the kind Malee's wife, who had helped them so ably.

On the first evening of their march the travelers reached the borders of the Coconut grove, on the outskirts of the jungle; here they determined to halt and rest for the night. Rama Rajah and the Ranee Bargaruttee went to their tent; but Luxman (whose tender love for them was so great, that he usually watched all night through at their door) was sitting under a large tree close by, when two little owls flew over his head, and perching on one of the highest branches, began chatting to each other.

The Wuzeer's son, who was in many ways wiser than most men, could understand their language. To his surprise he heard the little lady owl say to her husband, "I wish you would tell me a story, my dear, it is such a long time since I have heard one."

To which her husband, the other little owl, answered, "A story! what story can I tell you? Do you see these people encamped under our tree? Would you like to hear their story?"

She assented; and he began, "See first this poor Wuzeer, he is a good and faithful man, and has done much for this young Rajah, but neither has that been to his advantage heretofore, nor will it be hereafter." At this Luxman listened more attentively, and taking out his writing tablets, determined to note down all he heard. The little owl commenced with the story of the birth of Rama and Luxman, of their friendship, their quarrel, the young Rajah's dream, and their reconciliation, and then told of their subsequent adventures in search of the Princess Bargaruttee, down to that very day on which they were journeying home.

"And what more has Fate in store for this poor Wuzeer?" asked the lady owl.

"From this place," replied her husband, "he will journey on with the young Rajah and Ranee, until they get very near Chandra Rajah's dominions; there, as the whole cavalcade is about to pass under a large banyan tree, this Wuzeer Lux-man will notice some of the topmost branches swaying about in a dangerous manner; he will hurry the Rajah and Ranee away from it, and the tree (which would otherwise have inevitably killed them) will fall to the ground with a tremendous crash; but even his having thus saved the Rajah's life shall not avert his fate." (All this the Wuzeer noted down.)

"And what next?" said the wife, "what next?"

"Next," continued the wise little storyteller, "next, just as the Rajah Rama and the Ranee Bargaruttee and all their suite are passing under the palace door-way, the Wuzeer will notice that the arch is insecure, and by dragging them quickly through prevent their being crushed in its fall."

"And what will he do after that, dear husband?" she asked.

"After that," he went on, "when the Rajah and Ranee are asleep, and the Wuzeer Luxman keeping guard over them, he will perceive a large cobra slowly crawling down the wall and drawing nearer and nearer to the Ranee. He will kill it with his sword, but a drop of the cobra's blood shall fall on the Ranee's white forehead. The Wuzeer will not dare to wipe the blood off her forehead with his hand, and shall instead cover his face With a cloth that he may lick it off with his tongue, but for this the Rajah will be angry with him, and his reproaches will turn this poor Wuzeer into stone."

"Will he always remain stone?" asked the lady owl.

"Not for ever," answered her husband, "but for eight long years he will remain so."

"And what then?" demanded she.

"Then," answered the other, "when the young Rajah and Ranee have a baby, it shall come to pass that one day the child shall be playing on the floor, and to help itself along shall clasp hold of the stony figure, and at that baby's touch the Wuzeer will come to life again. But I have told you enough for one night; come, let's catch mice—twit, two, two," and away flew the owls.

Luxman had written down all he heard, and it made him heavy-hearted, but he thought, "Perhaps, after all, this may not be true." So he said nothing about it to any living soul. Next day they continued their journey, and as the owl had prophesied, so events fell out. For whilst the whole party were passing under a large banyan tree, the Wuzeer noticed that it looked unsafe. "The owl spake truly," he thought to himself, and seizing the Rajah and Ranee he hurried them from under it, just as a huge limb of the tree fell prone with a fearful crash.

A little while after, having reached Chandra Rajah's dominions, they were going under the great arch of the palace court-yard when the Wuzeer noticed some of the stones tottering. "The owl was a true prophet," thought he again, and catching hold of the hands of Rama Rajah and Bargaruttee Ranee, he pulled them rapidly through, just in time to save their lives. "Pardon me," he said to the Rajah, "that unbidden I dared thus to touch your hand and that of the Ranee, but I saw the danger imminent." So they reached home, where they were joyfully welcomed by Chandra Rajah, the Ranee, the Wuzeer (Luxman's father), and all the Court.

A few nights afterwards, when the Rajah and Ranee were asleep, and the young Wuzeer keeping guard over them as he was wont, he saw a large black cobra stealthily creeping down the wall just above the Ranee's head. "Alas!" he thought, "then such is my fate, and so it must be; nevertheless, I will do my duty"; and, taking from the folds of his dress the history of his and the young Rajah's life, from their boyhood down to that very time (as he had written it from the owl's narrative), he laid it beside the sleeping Rama, and, drawing his sword, killed the cobra. A few drops of the serpent's blood fell on the Ranee's forehead—the Wuzeer did not dare to touch it with his hand, but, that her sacred brow might not be defiled with the vile cobra's blood, he reverently covered his face and mouth with a cloth to lick the drops of blood away.

At this moment the Rajah started up, and seeing him, said, "O Wuzeer, Wuzeer, is this well done of you? O Luxman, who have been to me as a brother, who have saved me from so many difficulties, why do you treat me thus? To kiss her holy forehead. If indeed you loved her (as who could help it?), could you not have told me when we first saw her in that Glass Palace, and I would have exiled myself that she might be your wife. O my brother, my brother, why did you mock me thus?" The Rajah had buried his face in his hands; he looked up, he turned to the Wuzeer, but from him came neither answer nor reply. He had become a senseless stone. Then Rama for the first time perceived the roll of paper which Luxman had laid beside him, and when he read in it of what Luxman had been to him from boyhood, and of the end, his bitter grief broke through all bounds, and falling at the feet of the statue, he clasped its stony knees and wept aloud.

When daylight dawned Chandra Rajah and the Ranee found Rama still weeping and hugging the stone, asking its forgiveness with penitent cries and tears. Then they said to him, "What is this you have done?"

When he told them, the Rajah his father was very angry, and said, "Was it not enough that you should have once before unjustly desired the death of this good man, but that now by your rash reproaches you should have turned him into stone? Go to, you do but continually what is evil."

Now eight long years rolled by without the Wuzeer returning to his original form, although every day Rama Rajah and Bargaruttee Ranee would watch beside him, kissing his cold hands, and adjuring him by all endearing names to forgive them and return to them again. When eight years had expired, Rama and Bargaruttee had a child; and from the time it was nine months old and first began to try and crawl about, the father and mother would sit and watch beside it, placing it near the Wuzeer's statue, in hopes that the baby would some day touch it as the owl had foretold.

But for three months they watched in vain. At last, one day when the child was a year old, and was trying to walk, it chanced to be close to the statue, and tottering on its unsteady feet, stretched out its tiny hands and caught hold of the foot of the stone. The Wuzeer instantly came back to life, and stooping down seized in his arms the little baby who had rescued him, and kissed it. It is impossible to describe the delight of Rama Rajah and his wife at regaining their long-lost friend. The old Rajab and Ranee rejoiced also, with the Wuzeer (Luxman Wuzeer's father), and his mother.

Then Chandra Rajah said to the Wuzeer, "Here is my boy happy with his wife and child, while your son has neither; go fetch him a wife, and we will have a right merry wedding." So the Wuzeer fetched for his son a kind and beautiful wife, and Chandra Rajah and Rama Rajah caused the wedding of Luxman to be grander than that of any great Rajah before or since, even as if he had been a son of the royal house, and they all lived very happy ever after, as all good fathers, and mothers, and husbands, and wives, and children do.

PUNCHKIN

Tradition Bearer: Unavailable

Source: Frere, Mary. *Old Deccan Days*. London: J. Murray, 1868, 1–16.

Date: ca. 1866

Original Source: India

National Origin: India

"Punchkin" attests to the wide distribution throughout Indo-European tradition of central **tale types** and **motifs**. The cruel stepmother, the precocious youngest sibling, the abandoned children, the spouse transformed by a sorcerer's power, and the external soul (*Motif* E710), in this instance encased in a parrot, are only a few of the familiar episodes and themes contained in this extremely complex folktale.

Once upon a time there was a Rajah who had seven beautiful daughters. They were all good girls; but the youngest, named Balna, was more clever than the rest. The Rajah's wife died when they were quite little children, so these seven poor Princesses were left with no mother to take care of them.

The Rajah's daughters took it by turns to cook their father's dinner every day, whilst he was absent deliberating with his Ministers on the affairs of the nation.

About this time the Prudhan [prime minister] died, leaving a widow and one daughter; and every day, every day, when the seven Princesses were preparing their father's dinner, the Prudhan's widow and daughter would come and beg for a little fire from the hearth. Then Balna used to say to her sisters, "Send that woman away; send her away. Let her get the fire at her own house. What does she want with ours? If we allow her to come here we shall suffer for it some day." But the other sisters would answer, "Be quiet Balna; why must you always be quarreling with this poor woman? Let her take some fire if she likes." Then the Prudhan's widow used to go to the hearth and take a few sticks from it and whilst no one was looking, she would quickly throw some mud into the midst of the dishes which were being prepared for the Rajah's dinner.

Now the Rajah was very fond of his daughters. Ever since their mother's death they had cooked his dinner with their own hands, in order to avoid the danger of his being poisoned by his enemies. So, when he found the mud mixed up with his dinner, he thought it must arise from their carelessness, as it appeared improbable that any one should have put mud there on purpose; but being very kind he did not like to reprove them for it, although this spoiling of the curry was repeated many successive days.

At last, one day, he determined to hide, and watch his daughters cooking, and see how it all happened; so he went into the next room, and watched them through a hole in the wall.

There he saw his seven daughters carefully washing the rice and preparing the curry, and as each dish was completed they put it by the fire ready to be cooked. Next he noticed the Prudhan's widow come to the door, and beg for a few sticks from the fire to cook her dinner with. Balna turned to her angrily and said, "Why don't you keep fuel in your own house, and not come here every day and take ours?—Sisters, don't give this woman any more wood; let her buy it for herself."

Then the eldest sister answered, "Balna, let the poor woman take the wood and the fire; she does us no harm." But Balna replied, "If you let her come here so often, may be she will do w some harm, and make us sorry for it some day."

The Rajah then saw the Prudhan's widow go to the place where all his dinner was nicely prepared, and, as she took the wood, she threw a little mud into each of the dishes.

At this he was very angry, and sent to have the woman seized and brought before him. But when the widow came, she told him she had played this trick because she wanted to gain an audience with him; and she spoke so cleverly, and pleased him so well with her cunning words, that instead of punishing her, the Rajah married her, and made her his Ranee, and she and her daughter came to live in the palace.

Now the new Ranee hated the seven poor Princesses, and wanted to get them, if possible, out of the way, in order that her daughter might have all their riches, and live in the palace as Princess in their place; and instead of being grateful to them for their kindness to her she did all she could to make them miserable. She gave them nothing but bread to eat, and very little of that, and very little water to drink; so these seven poor little Princesses, who had been accustomed to have everything comfortable about them, and good food and good clothes all their lives long, were very miserable and unhappy; and they used to go out every day and sit by their dead mother's tomb and cry—and say—"Oh mother, mother! Cannot you see your poor children, how unhappy we are, and how we are starved by our cruel stepmother?"

One day, whilst they were thus sobbing and crying, lo and behold! a beautiful pomelo tree grew up out of the grave, covered with fresh ripe pomeloes, and the children satisfied their hunger by eating some of the fruit, and every day after this, instead of trying to eat the, bad dinner their stepmother provided for them, they used to go out to their mother's grave and eat the pomeloes which grew there on the beautiful tree.

Then the Ranee said to her daughter, "I cannot tell how it is, every day those seven girls say they don't want any dinner, and won't eat any; and yet they never grow thin nor look ill; they look better than you do. I cannot tell how it is"—and she bade her watch the seven Princesses, and see if any one gave them anything to eat.

So next day when the Princesses went to their mother's grave, and were eating the beautiful pomeloes, the Prudhan's daughter followed them, and saw them gathering the fruit.

Then Balna said to her sisters, "Do you not see that girl watching us? Let us drive her away, or hide the pomeloes, else she will go and tell her mother all about it, and that will be very bad for us."

But the other sisters said, "Oh no, do not be unkind, Balna. The girl would never be so cruel as to tell her mother. Let us rather invite her to come and have some of the fruit,"—and, calling her to them, they gave her one of the pomeloes.

No sooner had she eaten it, however, than the Prudhan's daughter went home and said to her mother, "I do not wonder the seven Princesses will not eat the dinner you prepare for them, for by their mother's grave there grows a beautiful pomelo tree, and they go there every day and eat the pomeloes. I ate one, and it was the nicest I have ever tasted."

The cruel Ranee was much vexed at hearing this, and all next day she stayed in her room, and told the Rajah that she had a very bad headache. The Rajah was deeply grieved, and said to his wife, "What can I do for you?" She answered, "There is only one thing that will make my headache well. By your dead wife's tomb there grows a fine pomelo tree; you must bring that here, and boil it, root and branch, and put a little of the water in which it has been boiled on my forehead, and that will cure my headache." So the Rajah sent his servants, and had the beautiful pomelo tree pulled up by the roots, and did as the Ranee desired; and when some of the water in which it had been boiled was put on her forehead, she said her headache was gone and she felt quite well.

Next day, when the seven Princesses went as usual to the grave of their mother, the pomelo tree had disappeared. Then they all began to cry very bitterly.

169

Now there was by the Ranee's tomb a small tank, and, as they were crying, they saw that the tank was filled with a rich cream-like substance, which quickly hardened into a thick white cake. At seeing this all the Princesses were very glad, and they ate some of the cake, and liked it; and next day the same thing happened, and so it went on for many days. Every morning the Princesses went to their mother's grave, and found the little tank filled with the nourishing cream-like cake. Then the cruel stepmother said to her daughter, "I cannot tell how it is, I have had the pomelo tree which used to grow by the Ranee's grave destroyed, and yet the Princesses grow no thinner, nor look more sad, though they never eat the dinner I give them. I cannot tell how it is!"

And her daughter said, "I will watch."

Next day while the Princesses were eating the cream cake, who should come by but their stepmother's daughter! Balna saw her first, and said, "See, sisters, there comes that girl again. Let us sit round the edge of the tank and not allow her to see it, for if we give her some of our cake, she will go and tell her mother; and that will be very unfortunate for us."

The other sisters, however, thought Balna unnecessarily suspicious, and instead of following her advice, they gave the Prudhan's daughter some of the cake, and she went home and told her mother all about it.

The Ranee, on hearing how well the Princesses fared, was exceedingly angry, and sent her servants to pull down the dead Ranee's tomb, and fill the little tank with the ruins. And not content with this, she next day pretended to be very, very ill—in fact, at the point of death—and when the Rajah was much grieved, and asked her whether it was in his power to procure her any remedy, she said to him, "Only one thing can save my life, but I know you will not do it." He replied, "Yes, whatever it is, I will do it." She then said, "To save my life, you must kill the seven daughters of your first wife, and put some of their blood on my forehead and on the palms of my hands, and their death will be my life." At these words the Rajah was very sorrowful; but because he feared to break his word, he went out with a heavy heart to find his daughters.

He found them crying by the ruins of their mother's grave.

Then, feeling he could not kill them, the Rajah spoke kindly to them, and told them to come out into the jungle with him; and there he made a fire and cooked some rice, and gave it to them. But in the afternoon, it being very hot, the seven Princesses all fell asleep, and when he saw they were fast asleep, the Rajah, their father, stole away and left them (for he feared his wife), saying to himself, "It is better my poor daughters should die here, than be killed by their stepmother."

He then shot a deer, and, returning home, put some of its blood on the forehead and hands of the Ranee, and she thought then that he had really killed the Princesses, and said she felt quite well.

Meantime the seven Princesses awoke, and when they found themselves all alone in the thick jungle they were much frightened, and began to call out as loud as they could, in hopes of making their father hear; but he was by that time far away, and would not have been able to hear them even had their voices been as loud as thunder.

It so happened that this very day the seven young Sons of a neighboring Rajah chanced to be hunting in that same jungle, and as they were returning home, after the day's sport was over, the youngest Prince said to his brothers, "Stop, I think I hear some one crying and calling out. Do you not hear voices? Let us go in the direction of the sound, and find out what it is."

So the seven Princes rode through the wood until they came to the place where the seven Princesses sat crying and wringing their hands. At the sight of them the young Princes were very much astonished, and still more so on learning their story: and they settled that each should take one of these poor forlorn ladies home with him, and marry her.

So the first and eldest Prince took the eldest Princess home with him, and married her;

And the second took the second;

And the third took the third;

And the fourth took the fourth;

And the fifth took the fifth;

And the sixth took the sixth;

And the seventh, and handsomest of all, took the beautiful Balna.

And when they got to their own land, there was great rejoicing throughout the kingdom, at the marriage of the seven young Princes to seven such beautiful Princesses.

About a year after this Balna had a little son, and his uncles and aunts were so fond of the boy that it was as if he had seven fathers and seven mothers. None of the other Princes and Princesses had any children, so the son of the seventh Prince and Balna was acknowledged their heir by all the rest.

They had thus lived very happily for some time, when one fine day the seventh Prince (Balna's husband) said he would go out hunting, and away he went; and they waited long for him, but he never came back.

Then his six brothers said they would go and see what had become of him; and they went away, but they also did not return.

And the seven Princesses grieved very much, for they feared that their kind husbands must have been killed.

One day, not long after this happened, as Balna was rocking her baby's cradle, and whilst her sisters were working in the room below, there came to the palace-door a man in a long black dress, who said that he was a Fakeer [usually spelled "fakir," a Hindu mystic capable of performing apparent miracles], and came to beg. The servants said to him, "You cannot go into the palace—the Rajah's sons have all gone away; we think they must be dead, and their widows cannot be interrupted by your begging." But he said, "I am a holy man, you must let me in." Then the stupid servants let him walk through the palace, but they did not know that this was no Fakeer, but a wicked Magician named Punchkin.

171

Punchkin Fakeer wandered through the palace, and saw many beautiful things there, till at last he reached the room where Balna sat singing beside her little boy's cradle. The Magician thought her more beautiful than all the other beautiful things he had seen, insomuch, that he asked her to go home with him and to marry him. But she said, "My husband, I fear, is dead, but my little boy is still quite young; I will stay here and teach him to grow up a clever man, and when he is grown up he shall go out into the world, and try and learn tidings of his father. Heaven forbid that I should ever leave him, or marry you!"

At these words the Magician was very angry, and turned her into a little black dog, and led her away, saying, "Since you will not come with me of your own free will, I will make you." So the poor Princess was dragged away, without any power of effecting an escape, or of letting her sisters know what had become of her. As Punchkin passed through the palace-gate the servants said to him, "Where did you get that pretty little dog?" And he answered, "One of the Princesses gave it to me as a present." At hearing which they let him go without further questioning.

Soon after this, the six elder Princesses heard the little baby, their nephew, begin to cry, and when they went upstairs they were much surprised to find him all alone, and Balna nowhere to be seen. Then they questioned the servants, and when they heard of the Fakeer and the little black dog, they guessed what had happened, and sent in every direction seeking them, but neither the Fakeer nor the dog was to be found. What could six poor women do? They gave up all hopes of ever seeing their kind husbands, and their sister, and her husband, again, and devoted themselves thenceforward to teaching and taking care of their little nephew.

Thus time went on, till Balna's son was fourteen years old. Then, one day, his aunts told him the history of the family; and no sooner did he hear it, than he was seized with a great desire to go in search of his father and mother and uncles, and if he could find them alive to bring them home again. His aunts, on learning his determination, were much alarmed, and tried to dissuade him, saying, "We have lost our husbands, and our sister, and her husband, and you are now our sole hope; if you go away, what shall we do?" But he replied, "I pray you not to be discouraged; I will return soon, and if it is possible bring my father and mother and uncles with me." So he set out on his travels; but for some months he could learn nothing to help him in his search.

At last, after he had journeyed many hundreds of weary miles, and become almost hopeless of ever hearing anything further of his parents, he one day came to a country that seemed full of stones, and rocks, and trees, and there he saw a large palace, with a high tower, hard by which was a Malee's little house.

As he was looking about, the Malee's wife saw him, and ran out of the house and said, "My dear boy, who are you that dare venture to this dangerous place?"

He answered, "I am a Rajah's son, and I come in search of my father, and my uncles, and my mother whom a wicked enchanter bewitched."

Then the Malee's wife said, "This country and this palace belong to a great enchanter; he is all-powerful, and if any one displeases him, he can turn them into stones and trees. All the rocks and trees you see here were living people once, and the Magician turned them to what they now are. Some time ago a Rajah's son came here, and shortly afterwards came his six brothers, and they were all turned into stones and trees; and these are not the only unfortunate ones, for up in that tower lives a beautiful Princess, whom the Magician has kept prisoner there for twelve years, because she hates him and will not marry him."

Then the little Prince thought, "These must be my parents and my uncles. I have found what I seek at last." So he told his story to the Malee's wife, and begged her to help him to remain in that place a while and inquire further concerning tile unhappy people she mentioned; and she promised to befriend him, and advised his disguising himself lest the Magician should see him, and turn him likewise into stone. To this the Prince agreed. So the Malee's wife dressed him up in a saree [sari], and pretended that he was her daughter.

One day, not long after this, as the Magician was walking in his garden, he saw the little girl (as he thought) playing about, and asked her who she was. She told him she was the Malee's daughter, and the Magician said, "You are a pretty little girl, and tomorrow you shall take a present of flowers from me to the beautiful lady who lives in the tower."

The young Prince was much delighted at hearing this, and went immediately to inform the Malee's wife; after consultation with whom he determined that it would be more safe for him to retain his disguise, and trust to the chance of a favorable opportunity for establishing some communication with his mother, if it were indeed she.

Now it happened that at Balna's marriage her husband had given her a small gold ring on which her name was engraved, and she had put it on her little son's finger when he was a baby, and afterwards when he was older his aunts had had it enlarged for him, so that he was still able to wear it. The Malee's wife advised him to fasten the well-known treasure to one of the bouquets he presented to his mother, and trust to her recognizing it. This was not to be done without difficulty, as such a strict watch was kept over the poor Princess (for fear of her ever establishing communication with her friends), that though the supposed Malee's daughter was permitted to take her flowers every day, the Magician or one of his slaves was always in the room at the time. At last, one day, however, opportunity favored him, and when no one was looking, the boy tied the ring to a nosegay, and threw it at Balna's feet. It fell with a clang on the floor, and Balna, looking to see what made the strange sound, found the little ring tied to the flowers. On recognizing it, she at once believed the story her son told her of his long search, and begged him to advise her as to what she had better do; at the same time entreating him on no account to endanger his life by trying to rescue her. She told him that, for twelve long years, the Magician

173

had kept her shut up in the tower because she refused to marry him, and she was so closely guarded that she saw no hope of release.

Now Balna's son was a bright, clever boy, so he said, "Do not fear, dear mother; the first thing to do is to discover how far the Magician's power extends, in order that we may be able to liberate my father and uncles, whom he has imprisoned in the form of rocks and trees. You have spoken to him angrily for twelve long years; now rather speak kindly. Tell him you have given up all hopes of again seeing the husband you have so long mourned; and say you are willing to marry him. Then endeavor to find out what his power consists in, and whether he is immortal, or can be put to death."

Balna determined to take her son's advice, and the next day sent for Punchkin, and spoke to him as had been suggested.

The Magician, greatly delighted, begged her to allow the wedding to take place as soon as possible.

But she told him that before she married him he must allow her a little more time, in which she might make his acquaintance—and that, after being enemies so long, their friendship could but strengthen by degrees. "And do tell me," she said, "are you quite immortal? Can death never touch you? And are you too great an enchanter ever to feel human suffering?"

"Why do you ask?" said he.

"Because," she replied, "if I am to be your wife, I would fain know all about you, in order, if any calamity threatens you, to overcome, or if possible to avert it."

"It is true," he said, "that I am not as others. Far, far away, hundreds of thousands of miles from this, there lies a desolate country covered with thick jungle. In the midst of the jungle grows a circle of palm trees, and in the center of the circle stand six chattees full of water, piled one above another: below the sixth chattee is a small cage which contains a little green parrot—on the life of the parrot depends my life—and if the parrot is killed I must die. It is, however," he added, "impossible that the parrot should sustain any injury, both on account of the inaccessibility of the country, and because, by my appointment, many thousand genii surround the palm trees, and kill all who approach the place."

Balna told her son what Punchkin had said; but at the same time implored him to give up all idea of getting the parrot.

The Prince, however, replied, "Mother, unless I can get hold of that parrot, you, and my father, and uncles, cannot be liberated; be not afraid, I will shortly return. Do you, meantime, keep the Magician in good humor—still putting off your marriage with him on various pretexts; and before he finds out the cause of delay, I will be here." So saying, he went away.

Many, many weary miles did he travel, till at last he came to a thick jungle; and, being very tired, sat down under a tree and fell asleep. He was awakened by a soft rustling sound; and looking about him, saw a large serpent which was making its way to an eagle's nest built in the tree under which he lay; and in the nest were two young eagles. The Prince seeing the danger of the young birds, drew his sword, and killed the serpent; at the same moment a rushing sound was heard in the air, and the two old eagles, who had been out hunting for food for their young ones, returned. They quickly saw the dead serpent and the young Prince standing over it; and the old mother eagle said to him, "Dear boy, for many years all our young ones have been devoured by that cruel serpent: you have now saved the lives of our children; whenever you are in need, therefore, send to us and we will help you; and as for these little eagles, take them, and let them be your servants."

At this the Prince was very glad, and the two eaglets crossed their wings, on which he mounted; and they carried him far, far away over the thick jungles, until he came to the place where grew the circle of palm trees: in the midst of which stood the six chattees full of water. It was the middle of the day, and the heat was very great. All round the trees were the genii, fast asleep: nevertheless, there were such countless thousands of them, that it would have been quite impossible for any one to walk through their ranks to the place; down swooped the strong-winged eaglets—down jumped the Prince: in an instant he had overthrown the six chattees full of water, and seized the little green parrot, which he rolled up in his cloak; while, as he mounted again into the air, all the genii below awoke, and finding their treasure gone, set up a wild and melancholy howl.

Away, away flew the little eagles, till they came to their home in the great tree; then the Prince said to the old eagles, "Take back your little ones; they have done me good service; if ever again I stand in need of help, I will not fail to come to you." He then continued his journey on foot till he arrived once more at the Magician's palace; where he sat down at the door and began playing with the parrot. Punchkin saw him, and came to him quickly, and said, "My boy, where did you get that parrot? Give it to me, I pray you." But the Prince answered, "Oh no, I cannot give away my parrot, it is a great pet of mine; I have had it many years." Then the Magician said, "If it is an old favorite, I can understand your not caring to give it away—but come, what will you sell it for?"

"Sir," replied the Prince, "I will not sell my parrot."

Then Punchkin got frightened, and said, "Anything, anything; name what price you will, and it shall be yours." The Prince answered, "Let the seven Rajah's sons whom you turned into rocks and trees be instantly liberated."

"It is done as you desire," said the Magician, "only give me my parrot." And with that, by a stroke of his wand, Balna's husband and his brothers resumed their natural shapes. "Now give me my parrot," repeated Punchkin.

"Not so fast, my master," rejoined the Prince, "I must first beg that you will restore to life all whom you have thus imprisoned."

The Magician immediately waved his wand again; and whilst he cried, in an imploring voice, "Give me my parrot!" the whole garden became suddenly alive: where rocks, and stones, and trees had been before, stood Rajah's, and Punts, and Sirdars, and mighty men on prancing horses, and jeweled pages, and troops of armed attendants.

"Give me my parrot!" cried Punchkin. Then the boy took hold of the parrot, and tore off one of his wings; and as he did so the Magician's right arm fell off.

Punchkin then stretched out his left arm, crying, "Give me my parrot!" The Prince pulled off the parrot's second wing, and the Magician's left arm tumbled off.

"Give me my parrot!" cried he, and fell on his knees. The Prince pulled off the parrot's right leg, the Magician's right leg fell off: the Prince pulled off the parrot's left leg, down fell the Magician's left.

Nothing remained of him save the limbless body and the head; but still he rolled his eyes, and cried, "Give me my parrot!"

"Take your parrot, then," cried the boy, and with that he wrung the bird's neck, and threw it at the Magician; and, as he did so, Punchkin's head twisted round, and, with a fearful groan, he died!

Then they let Balna out of the tower; and she, her son, and the seven Princes went to their own country, and lived very happily ever afterwards. And as to the rest of the world, every one went to his own house.

THE CHARMED RING

Tradition Bearer: Unavailable

Source: Jacobs, Joseph. *Indian Fairy Tales*. London: David Nutt, 1912, 90–99.

Date: 1912

Original Source: India

National Origin: India

The following **ordinary folktale** is categorized by the Aarne-Thompson system as a member of a large class of **tale type** plots ("The Magic Object Is Stolen from the Hero but He Forces Its Return," AT 560-568). The specific type is "The Magic Ring" (AT 560). In most **variants**, the protagonist finds the ring or is given it as a gift from a man whose son he has saved. In this case, the grateful father is Raja Indrasha, King Snake. "Animals Grateful for Rescue from Peril of Death" (*Motif* B360) figures prominently in the tale.

A merchant started his son in life with three hundred rupees, and bade him go to another country and try his luck in trade. The son took the money and departed. He had not gone far before he came across some herdsmen quarreling over a dog, that some of them wished to kill. "Please do not kill the dog," pleaded the young and tender-hearted fellow, "I will give you one hundred rupees for it." Then and there, of course, the bargain was concluded, and the foolish fellow took the dog, and continued his journey. He next met with some people fighting about a cat. Some of them wanted to kill it, but others not. "Oh! Please do not kill it," said he, "I will give you one hundred rupees for it." Of course they at once gave him the cat and took the money. He went on till he reached a village, where some folk were quarreling over a snake that had just been caught. Some of them wished to kill it, but others did not. "Please do not kill the snake," said he, "I will give you one hundred rupees." Of course the people agreed, and were highly delighted.

What a fool the fellow was! What would he do now that all his money was gone? What could he do except return to his father? Accordingly he went home.

"You fool! You scamp!" exclaimed his father when he had heard how his son had wasted all the money that had been given to him. "Go and live in the stables and repent of your folly. You shall never again enter my house."

So the young man went and lived in the stables. His bed was the grass spread for the cattle, and his companions were the dog, the cat, and the snake, which he had purchased so dearly. These creatures got very fond of him, and would follow him about during the day, and sleep by him at night; the cat used to sleep at his feet, the dog at his head, and the snake over his body, with its head hanging on one side and its tail on the other.

One day the snake in course of conversation said to its master, "I am the son of Raja Indrasha. One day, when I had come out of the ground to drink the air, some people seized me, and would have slain me had you not most opportunely arrived to my rescue. I do not know how I shall ever be able to repay you for your great kindness to me. Would that you knew my father! How glad he would be to see his son's preserver!"

"Where does he live? I should like to see him, if possible," said the young man.

"Well said!" continued the snake. "Do you see yonder mountain? At the bottom of that mountain there is a sacred spring. If you will come with me and dive into that spring, we shall both reach my father's country. Oh! How glad he will be to see you! He will wish to reward you, too. But how can he do that? However, you may be pleased to accept something at his hand. If he asks you what you would like, you would, perhaps, do well to reply, "The ring on your right hand, and the famous pot and spoon which you possess. With these in your possession, you would never need anything, for the ring is such that a man has only to speak to it, and immediately a beautiful furnished mansion will be provided for him, while the pot and the spoon will supply him with all manner of the rarest and most delicious foods."

Attended by his three companions the man walked to the well and prepared to jump in, according to the snake's directions. "O master!" exclaimed the cat and dog, when they saw what he was going to do. "What shall we do? Where shall we go?"

"Wait for me here," he replied. "I am not going far. I shall not be long away." On saying this, he dived into the water and was lost to sight.

"Now what shall we do?" said the dog to the cat.

"We must remain here," replied the cat, "as our master ordered. Do not be anxious about food. I will go to the people's houses and get plenty of food for both of us." And so the cat did, and they both lived very comfortably till their master came again and joined them.

The young man and the snake reached their destination in safety; and information of their arrival was sent to the Raja. His highness commanded his son and the stranger to appear before him. But the snake refused, saying that it could not go to its father till it was released from this stranger, who had saved it from a most terrible death, and whose slave it therefore was. Then the Raja went and embraced his son, and saluting the stranger welcomed him to his dominions. The young man stayed there a few days, during which he received the Raja's right-hand ring, and the pot and spoon, in recognition of His Highness's gratitude to him for having delivered his son. He then returned. On reaching the top of the spring he found his friends, the dog and the cat, waiting for him. They told one another all they had experienced since they had last seen each other, and were all very glad. Afterwards they walked together to the river side, where it was decided to try the powers of the charmed ring and pot and spoon.

The merchant's son spoke to the ring, and immediately a beautiful house and a lovely princess with golden hair appeared. He spoke to the pot and spoon, also, and the most delicious dishes of food were provided for them. So he married the princess, and they lived very happily for several years, until one morning the princess, while arranging her toilet, put the loose hairs into a hollow bit of reed and threw them into the river that flowed along under the window. The reed floated on the water for many miles, and was at last picked up by the prince of that country, who curiously opened it and saw the golden hair. On finding it the prince rushed off to the palace, locked himself up in his room, and would not leave it. He had fallen desperately in love with the woman whose hair be had picked up, and refused to eat, or drink, or sleep, or move, till she was brought to him. The king, his father, was in great distress about the matter, and did not know what to do. He feared lest his son should die and leave him without an heir: At last he determined to seek the counsel of his aunt, who was an ogress. The old woman consented to help him, and bade him not to be anxious, as she felt certain that she would succeed in getting the beautiful woman for his son's wife.

She assumed the shape of a bee and went along buzzing, and buzzing, and buzzing. Her keen sense of smell soon brought her to the beautiful princess, to whom she appeared as an old hag, holding in one hand a stick by way of support. She introduced herself to the beautiful princess and said, "I am your aunt, whom you have never seen before, because I left the country just after your birth." She also embraced and kissed the princess by way of adding force to her words. The beautiful princess was thoroughly deceived. She returned the ogress's embrace, and invited her to come and stay in the house as long as she could, and treated her with such honor and attention, that the ogress thought to herself, "I shall soon accomplish my errand." When she had been in the house three days, she began to talk of the charmed ring, and advised her to keep it instead of her husband, because the latter was constantly out shooting and on other such-like expeditions, and might lose it. Accordingly the beautiful princess asked her husband for the ring, and he readily gave it to her.

The ogress waited another day before she asked to see the precious thing. Doubting nothing, the beautiful princess complied, when the ogress seized the ring, and reassuming the form of a bee flew away with it to the palace, where the prince was lying nearly on the point of death. "Rise up. Be glad. Mourn no more," she said to him. "The woman for whom you yearn will appear at your summons. See, here is the charm, whereby you may bring her before you."

The prince was almost mad with joy when he heard these words, and was so desirous of seeing the beautiful princess, that he immediately spoke to the ring, and the house with its fair occupant descended in the midst of the palace garden. He at once entered the building, and telling the beautiful princess of his intense love, entreated her to be his wife. Seeing no escape from the difficulty, she consented on the condition that he would wait one month for her.

Meanwhile the merchant's son had returned from hunting and was terribly distressed not to find his house and wife. There was the place only, just as he knew it before he had tried the charmed ring, which Raja Indrasha had given him. He sat down and determined to put an end to himself. Presently the cat and dog came up. They had gone away and hidden themselves, when they saw the house and everything disappear. "O master," they said, "stay your hand. Your trial is great, but it can be remedied. Give us one month, and we will go and try to recover your wife and house."

"Go," said he, "and may the great God aid your efforts. Bring back my wife, and I shall live."

So the cat and dog started off at a run, and did not stop till they reached the place whither their mistress and the house had been taken. "We may have some difficulty here," said the cat. "Look, the king has taken our master's wife and house for himself. You stay here. I will go to the house and try to see her." So the dog sat down, and the cat climbed up to the window of the room, wherein the beautiful princess was sitting, and entered. The princess recognized the cat, and informed it of all that had happened to her since she had left them.

"But is there no way of escape from the hands of these people?" she asked.

"Yes," replied the cat, "if you can tell me where the charmed ring is."

"The ring is in the stomach of the ogress," she said.

"All right," said the cat, "I will recover it. If we once get it, everything is ours." Then the cat descended the wall of the house, and went and laid down by a rat's hole and pretended she was dead. Now at that time a great wedding chanced to be going on among the rat community of that place, and all the rats of the neighborhood were assembled in that one particular mine by which the cat had lain down. The eldest son of the king of the rats was about to be married. The cat got to know of this, and at once conceived the idea of seizing the bridegroom and making him render the necessary help. Consequently, when the procession poured forth from the hole squealing and jumping in honor of the occasion, it immediately spotted the bridegroom and pounced down on him. "Oh! let me go, let me go," cried the terrified rat. "Oh! let him go," squealed all the company. "It is his wedding day."

"No, no," replied the cat. "Not unless you do something for me. Listen. The ogress, who lives in that house with the prince and his wife, has swallowed a ring, which I very much want. If you will procure it for me, I will allow the rat to depart unharmed. If you do not, then your prince dies under my feet."

"Very well, we agree," said they all. "Nay, if we do not get the ring for you, devour us all."

This was rather a bold offer. However, they accomplished the thing. At midnight, when the ogress was sound asleep, one of the rats went to her bedside, climbed up on her face, and, inserted its tail into her throat; whereupon the ogress coughed violently, and the ring came out and rolled on to the floor. The rat immediately seized the precious thing and ran off with it to its king, who was very glad, and went at once to the cat and released its son.

As soon as the cat received the ring, she started back with the dog to go and tell their master the good tidings. All seemed safe now. They had only to give the ring to him, and he would speak to it, and the house and beautiful princess would again be with them, and everything would go on as happily as before. "How glad master will be!" they thought, and ran as fast as their legs could carry them. Now, on the way they had to cross a stream. The dog swam,, and the cat sat on its back. Now the dog was jealous of the cat, so he asked for the ring, and threatened to throw the cat into the water if it did not give it up; whereupon the cat gave up the ring. Sorry moment, for the dog at once dropped it, and a fish swallowed it.

"Oh! What shall I do? What shall I do?" said the dog. "What is done is done," replied the cat. "We must try to recover it, and if we do not succeed we had better drown ourselves in this stream. I have a plan. You go and kill a small lamb, and bring it here to me."

"All right," said the dog, and at once ran off. He soon came back with a dead lamb, and gave it to the cat. The cat got inside the lamb and lay down, telling the dog to go away a little distance and keep quiet. Not long after this a nadhar, a bird whose look can break the bones of a fish, came and hovered over the lamb, and eventually pounced down on it to carry it away. On this the cat came out and jumped on to the bird, and threatened to kill it if it did not recover the lost ring. This was most readily promised by the nadhar, who immediately flew off to the king of the fishes, and ordered it to make inquiries and to restore the ring. The king of the fishes did so, and the ring was found and carried back to the cat.

"Come along now; I have got the ring," said the cat to the dog.

"No, I will not," said the dog, unless you let me have the ring. I can carry it as well as you. Let me have it or I will kill you." So the cat was obliged to give up the ring. The careless dog very soon dropped it again. This time it was picked up and carried off by a kite.

"See, see, there it goes—away to that big tree," the cat exclaimed.

"Oh! Oh! what have I done?" cried the dog.

"You foolish thing, I knew it would be so," said the cat. "But stop your barking, or you will frighten away the bird to some place where we shall not be able to trace it."

The cat waited till it was quite dark, and then climbed the tree, killed the kite, and recovered the ring. "Come along," it said to the dog when it reached the ground. "We must make haste now. We have been delayed. Our master will die from grief and suspense. Come on."

The dog, now thoroughly ashamed of itself, begged the cat's pardon for all the trouble it had given. It was afraid to ask for the ring the third time, so they both reached their sorrowing master in safety and gave him the precious charm. In a moment his sorrow was turned into joy. He spoke to the ring, and his beautiful wife and house reappeared, and he and everybody were as happy as ever they could be.

THE MAGIC FIDDLE

Tradition Bearer: Unavailable

Source: Jacobs, Joseph. *Indian Fairy Tales*. London: David Nutt, 1912, 40–45.

Date: 1912

Original Source: India

National Origin: India

The following tale is a **variant** of "The Singing Bone" (AT 780), a plot in which the remains of a murder victim literally cry out for justice. Compare this narrative to "Under the Green Old Oak Tree" (Volume 4, page 412). According to the religion of the Santals from whom this tale was originally obtained, spirits (*bonga*) handle the daily affairs of the world and must be propitiated by prayer, rituals, and offerings. The Doma and Hadi mentioned in the tale are outcastes who practice unclean occupations, including the occupation of musician.

Once upon a time there lived seven brothers and a sister. The brothers were married, but their wives did not do the cooking for the family. It was done by their sister, who stopped at home to cook. The wives for this reason bore their sister-in-law much ill will, and at length they combined together to oust her from the office of cook and general provider, so that one of themselves might obtain it. They said, "She does not go out to the fields to work, but remains quietly at home, and yet she has not the meals ready at the proper time."

They then called upon their bonga, and vowing vows unto him they secured his goodwill and assistance; then they said to the bonga, "At midday, when our sister-in-law goes to bring water, cause it thus to happen, that on seeing her pitcher, the water shall vanish, and again slowly reappear. In this way she will be delayed. Let the water not flow into her pitcher, and you may keep the maiden as your own."

At noon when she went to bring water, it suddenly dried up before her, and she began to weep. Then after a while the water began slowly to rise. When it reached her ankles she tried to fill her pitcher, but it would not go under the water. Being frightened she began to wail and cry to her brother:

> Oh! my brother, the water reaches to my ankles,
> Still, Oh! my brother, the pitcher will not dip.
> The water continued to rise until it reached her knee, when she began to wail again:
> Oh! my brother, the water reaches to my knee,
> Still, Oh! my brother, the pitcher will not dip.
> The water continued to rise, and when it reached her waist, she cried again:
> Oh! my brother, the water reaches to my waist,
> Still, Oh! my brother, the pitcher will not dip.

The water still rose, and when it reached her neck she kept on crying:

> Oh! my brother, the water reaches to my neck,
> Still, Oh! my brother, the pitcher will not dip.
> At length the water became so deep that she felt herself drowning, then she cried aloud:
> Oh! my brother, the water measures a man's height,
> Oh! my brother, the pitcher begins to fill.

The pitcher filled with water, and along with it she sank and was drowned. The bonga then transformed her into a bonga like himself, and carried her off.

After a time she reappeared as a bamboo growing on the embankment of the tank in which she had been drowned. When the bamboo had grown to an immense size, a jogi [yogi], who was in the habit of passing that way, seeing it, said to himself, "This will make a splendid fiddle."

So one day he brought an ax to cut it down; but when he was about to begin, the bamboo called out, "Do not cut at the root, cut higher up." When he lifted his ax to cut high up the stem, the bamboo cried out, "Do not cut near the top, cut at the root." When the jogi again prepared himself to cut at the root as requested, the bamboo said, "Do not cut at the root, cut higher up"; and when he was about to cut higher up, it again called out to him, "Do not cut high up, cut at the root." The jogi by this time felt sure that a bonga was trying to frighten him, so becoming angry he cut down the bamboo at the root, and taking it away made a fiddle out of it. The instrument had a superior tone and delighted all who heard it. The jogi carried it with him when he went a begging, and through the influence of its sweet music he returned home every evening with a full wallet.

He now and then visited, when on his rounds, the house of the bonga girl's brothers, and the strains of the fiddle affected them greatly. Some of them were moved even to tears, for the fiddle seemed to wail as one in bitter anguish. The elder brother wished to purchase it, and offered to support the jogi for a whole year if he would consent to part with his wonderful instrument. The jogi, however, knew its value, and refused to sell it.

It so happened that the jogi some time after went to the house of a village chief, and after playing a tune or two on his fiddle asked for something to eat. They offered to buy his fiddle and promised a high price for it, but he refused to sell it, as his fiddle brought to him his means of livelihood. When they saw that he was not to be prevailed upon, they gave him food and a plentiful supply of liquor. Of the latter he drank so freely that he presently became intoxicated. While he was in this condition, they took away his fiddle, and substituted their own old one for it. When the jogi recovered, he missed his instrument, and suspecting that it had been stolen asked them to return it to him. They denied having taken it, so he had to depart, leaving his fiddle behind him. The chief's son, being a musician, used to play on the jogi's fiddle, and in his hands the music it gave forth delighted the ears of all who heard it.

When all the household were absent at their labors in the fields, the bonga girl used to come out of the bamboo fiddle, and prepared the family meal. Having eaten her own share, she placed that of the chief's son under his bed, and covering it up to keep off the dust, reentered the fiddle. This happening every day, the other members of the household thought that some girl friend of theirs was in this manner showing her interest in the young man, so they did not trouble themselves to find out how it came about.

The young chief, however, was determined to watch, and see which of his girl friends was so attentive to his comfort. He said in his own mind, "I will catch her today, and give her a sound beating; she is causing me to be ashamed before the others." So saying, he hid himself in a corner in a pile of firewood. In

183

a short time the girl came out of the bamboo fiddle, and began to dress her hair. Having completed her toilet, she cooked the meal of rice as usual, and having eaten some herself, she placed the young man's portion under his bed, as before, and was about to enter the fiddle again, when he, running out from his hiding-place, caught her in his arms. The bonga girl exclaimed, "Fie! Fie! You may be a dom, or you may be a hadi of some other caste with whom I cannot marry."

He said, "No. But from today, you and I are one." So they began lovingly to hold converse with each other. When the others returned home in the evening, they saw that she was both a human being and a bonga, and they rejoiced exceedingly.

Now in course of time the bonga girl's family became very poor, and her brothers on one occasion came to the chief's house on a visit. The bonga girl recognized them at once, but they did not know who she was. She brought them water on their arrival, and afterwards set cooked rice before them. Then sitting down near them, she began in wailing tones to upbraid them on account of the treatment she had been subjected to by their wives. She related all that had befallen her, and wound up by saying, "You must have known it all, and yet you did not interfere to save me." And that was all the revenge she took.

THE PRINCE'S ELOPEMENT

Tradition Bearer: Unavailable

Source: Ryder, Arthur W., trans. [author unknown, Sanskrit title *Vetalapañchavimsati*]. *Twenty-Two Goblins*. London: J.M. Dent, 1917, 1–18.

Date: Unavailable

Original Source: India

National Origin: India

The *Twenty-Two Goblins*, from which the following two tales "The Prince's Elopement" and "The Father and Son Who Married Mother and Daughter" are taken, is an anonymous **frame** tale that serves as a device for organizing a series of traditional Sanskrit narratives. A similar structure is used for the Arabian classic *One Thousand and One Nights* (see "The Fisherman and the Jinn," Volume 1, page 220 for a discussion of that work and an example of the tales included therein). The interrelated tales of *Twenty-Two Goblins* operate within a plot that is resolved at the end. To illustrate this device, one that has been used often to provide a frame for individual traditional narratives, the opening and the concluding "goblin tales" are presented below. There are obvious relationships between the individual tales and the frame story, a story that is built on a king's being duped by a corrupt monk. Given this frame, there is irony in the king's solution to the puzzle posed in "The Prince's

Elopement": "[T]he king knew the law-books very well, and he had spies to find out the facts among the people. And he knew about the doings of rascals. So he acted without thinking" (page 191). Compare this collection and its individual tales to "A Man Deceives a Woman" (page 203), "Many Wise Fools" (page 221), and "The Vampire Puzzles Raja Vikram" (page 233) drawn from *Vikram and the Vampire*.

On the bank of the Godavari River is a kingdom called the Abiding Kingdom. There lived the son of King Victory, the famous King Triple-victory, mighty as the king of the gods. As this king sat in judgment, a monk called Patience brought him every day one piece of fruit as an expression of homage. And the king took it and gave it each day to the treasurer who stood near. Thus twelve years passed.

Now one day the monk came to court, gave the king a piece of fruit as usual, and went away. But on this day the king gave the fruit to a pet baby monkey that had escaped from his keepers, and happened to wander in. And as the monkey ate the fruit, he split it open, and a priceless, magnificent gem came out. When the king saw this, he took it and asked the treasurer, "Where have you been keeping the fruits which the monk brought? I gave them to you."

When the treasurer heard this, he was frightened and said, "Your Majesty, I have thrown them all through the window. If your Majesty desires, I will look for them now." And when the king had dismissed him, he went, but returned in a moment, and said again, "Your Majesty, they were all smashed in the treasury, and in them I see heaps of dazzling gems."

When he heard this, the king was delighted, and gave the jewels to the treasurer. And when the monk came the next day, he asked him, "Monk, why do you keep honoring me in such an expensive way? Unless I know the reason, I will not take your fruit."

Then the monk took the king aside and said, "O hero, there is a business in which I need help. So I ask for your help in it, because you are a brave man." And the king promised his assistance. Then the monk was pleased, and said again, "O King, on the last night of the waning moon, you must go to the great cemetery at nightfall, and come to me under the fig tree."

Then the king said, "Certainly," and Patience, the monk, went home well pleased.

So when the night came, the mighty king remembered his promise to the monk, and at dusk he wrapped his head in a black veil, took his sword in his hand, and went to the great cemetery without being seen. When he got there, he looked about, and saw the monk standing under the fig tree and making a magic circle.

So he went up and said, "Monk, here I am. Tell me what I am to do for you."

And when the monk saw the king, he was delighted and said, "O King, if you wish to do me a favor, go south from here some distance all alone, and you will see a sissoo tree and a dead body hanging from it. Be so kind as to bring that here."

When the brave king heard this, he agreed, and, true to his promise, turned south and started. And as he walked with difficulty along the cemetery road, he came upon the sissoo tree at some distance, and saw a body hanging on it. So he climbed the tree, cut the rope, and let it fall to the ground. And as it fell, it unexpectedly cried aloud, as if alive. Then the king climbed down, and thinking it was alive, he mercifully rubbed its limbs. Then the body gave a loud laugh.

So the king knew that a goblin lived in it, and said without fear, "What are you laughing about? Come, let us be off."

But then he did not see the goblin on the ground any longer. And when he looked up, there he was, hanging in the tree as before. So the king climbed the tree again, and carefully carried the body down. A brave man's heart is harder than a diamond, and nothing makes it tremble.

Then he put the body with the goblin in it on his shoulder, and started off in silence. And as he walked along, the goblin in the body said, "O King, to amuse the journey, I will tell you a story. Listen."

First Goblin: The Prince's Elopement—Whose Fault Was the Resulting Death of His Parents-in-Law?

There is a city called Benares where Shiva lives. It is loved by pious people like the soil of Mount Kailasa. The river of heaven shines there like a pearl necklace. And in the city lived a king called Valor who burned up all his enemies by his valor, as a fire burns a forest. He had a son named Thunderbolt who broke the pride of the love-god by his beauty, and the pride of men by his bravery. This prince had a clever friend, the son of a counselor.

One day the prince was enjoying himself with his friend hunting, and went a long distance. And so he came to a great forest. There he saw a beautiful lake, and being tired, he drank from it with his friend the counselor's son, washed his hands and feet, and sat down under a tree on the bank.

And then he saw a beautiful maiden who had come there with her servants to bathe. She seemed to fill the lake with the stream of her beauty, and seemed to make lilies grow there with her eyes, and seemed to shame the lotuses with a face more lovely than the moon. She captured the prince's heart the moment that he saw her. And the prince took her eyes captive.

The girl had a strange feeling when she saw him, but was too modest to say a word. So she gave a hint of the feeling in her heart. She put a lotus on her ear, laid a lily on her head after she had made the edge look like a row of teeth, and placed her hand on her heart. But the prince did not understand her signs, only the clever counselor's son understood them all.

A moment later the girl went away, led by her servants. She went home and sat on the sofa and stayed there. But her thoughts were with the prince.

The prince went slowly back to his city, and was terribly lonely without her, and grew thinner every day. Then his friend the son of the counselor took him aside and told him that she was not hard to find. But he had lost all courage and said, "My friend, I don't know her name, nor her home, nor her family. How can I find her? Why do you vainly try to comfort me?"

Then the counselor's son said, "Did you not see all that she hinted with her signs? When she put the lotus on her ear, she meant that she lived in the kingdom of a king named Ear-lotus. And when she made the row of teeth, she meant that she was the daughter of a man named Bite there. And when she laid the lily on her head, she meant that her name was Lily. And when she placed her hand on her heart, she meant that she loved you. And there is a king named Ear-lotus in the Kalinga country. There is a very rich man there whom the king likes. His real name is Battler, but they call him Bite. He has a pearl of a girl whom he loves more than his life, and her name is Lily. This is true, because people told me. So I understood her signs about her country and the other things." When the counselor's son had said this, the prince was delighted to find him so clever, and pleased because he knew what to do.

Then he formed a plan with the counselor's son, and started for the lake again, pretending that he was going to hunt, but really to find the girl that he loved. On the way he rode like the wind away from his soldiers, and started for the Kalinga country with the counselor's son.

When they reached the city of King Ear-lotus, they looked about and found the house of the man called Bite, and they went to a house near by to live with an old woman. And the counselor's son said to the old woman, "Old woman, do you know anybody named Bite in this city?"

Then the old woman answered him respectfully, "My son, I know him well. I was his nurse. And I am a servant of his daughter Lily. But I do not go there now because my dress is stolen. My naughty son is a gambler and steals my clothes."

Then the counselor's son was pleased and satisfied her with his own cloak and other presents. And he said, "Mother, you must do very secretly what we tell you. Go to Bite's daughter Lily, and tell her that the prince whom she saw on the bank of the lake is here, and sent you with a love-message to her."

The old woman was pleased with the gifts and went to Lily at once. And when she got a chance, she said, "My child, the prince and the counselor's son have come to take you. Tell me what to do now." But the girl scolded her and struck her cheeks with both hands smeared with camphor.

The old woman was hurt by this treatment, and came home weeping, and said to the two men, "My sons, see how she left the marks of her fingers on my face."

And the prince was hopeless and sad, but the very clever counselor's son took him aside and said, "My friend, do not be sad. She was only keeping the secret when she scolded the old woman, and put ten fingers white with camphor on her face. She meant that you must wait before seeing her, for the next ten nights are bright with moonlight."

So the counselor's son comforted the prince, took a little gold ornament and sold it in the market, and bought a great dinner for the old woman. So they two took dinner with the old woman. They did this for ten days, and then the counselor's son sent her to Lily again, to find out something more.

And the old woman was eager for dainty food and drink. So to please him she went to Lily's house, and then came back and said, "My children, I went there and stayed with her for some time without speaking. But she spoke herself of my naughtiness in mentioning you, and struck me again on the chest with three fingers stained red. So I came back in disgrace."

Then the counselor's son whispered to the prince, "Don't be alarmed, my friend. When she left the marks of three red fingers on the old woman's heart, she meant to say very cleverly that there were three dangerous days coming." So the counselor's son comforted the prince.

And when three days were gone, he sent the old woman to Lily again. And this time she went and was very respectfully entertained, and treated to wine and other things the whole day. But when she was ready to go back in the evening, a terrible shouting was heard outside. They heard people running and crying, "Oh, oh! A mad elephant has escaped from his stable and is running around and stamping on people."

Then Lily said to the old woman, "Mother, you must not go through the street now where the elephant is. I will put you in a swing and let you down with ropes through this great window into the garden. Then you can climb into a tree and jump on the wall, and go home by way of another tree." So she had her servants let the old woman down from the window into the garden by a rope-swing. And the old woman went home and told the prince and the counselor's son all about it.

Then the counselor's son said to the prince, "My friend, your wishes are fulfilled. She has been clever enough to show you the road. So you must follow that same road this very evening to the room of your darling."

So the prince went to the garden with the counselor's son by the road that the old woman had shown them. And there he saw the rope-swing hanging down, and servants above keeping an eye on the road. And when he got into the swing, the servants at the window pulled at the rope and he came to his darling. And when he had gone in, the counselor's son went back to the old woman's house.

But the prince saw Lily, and her face was beautiful like the full moon, and the moonlight of her beauty shone forth, like the night when the moon shines in secret because of the dark. And when she saw him, she threw her arms around his neck and kissed him. So he married her and stayed hidden with her for some days.

One day he said to his wife, "My dear, my friend the counselor's son came with me, and he is staying all alone at the old woman's house. I must go and see him, then I will come back."

But Lily was shrewd and said, "My dear, I must ask you something. Did you understand the signs I made, or was it the counselor's son?"

And the prince said to her, "My dear, I did not understand them all, but my friend has wonderful wisdom. He understood everything and told me." Then the sweet girl thought, and said, "My dear, you did wrong not to tell me before. Your friend is a real brother to me. I ought to have sent him some nuts and other nice things at the very first."

Then she let him go, and he went to his friend by night by the same road, and told all that his wife had said. But the counselor's son said, "That is foolish," and did not think much of it. So they spent the night talking.

Then when the time for the twilight sacrifice came, a friend of Lily's came there with cooked rice and nuts in her hand. She came and asked the counselor's son about his health and gave him the present. And she cleverly tried to keep the prince from eating. "Your wife is expecting you to dinner," she said, and a moment later she went away.

Then the counselor's son said to the prince, "Look, your Majesty. I will show you something curious." So he took a little of the cooked rice and gave it to a dog that was there. And the moment he ate it, the dog died. And the prince asked the counselor's son what this strange thing could mean.

And he replied, "Your Majesty, she knew that I was clever because I understood her signs, and she wanted to kill me out of love for you. For she thought the prince would not be all her own while I was alive, but would leave her for my sake and go back to his own city. So she sent me poisoned food to eat. But you must not be angry with her. I will think up some scheme."

Then the prince praised the counselor's son, and said, "You are truly the body of wisdom." And then suddenly a great wailing of grief-stricken people was heard, "Alas! Alas! The king's little son is dead."

When he heard this, the counselor's son was delighted, and said, "Your Majesty, go tonight to Lily's house, and make her drink wine until she loses her senses and seems to be dead. Then as she lies there, make a mark on her hip with a red-hot fork, steal her jewels, and come back the old way through the window. After that I will do the right thing."

Then he made a three-pronged fork and gave it to the prince. And the prince took the crooked, cruel thing, hard as the weapon of Death, and went by night as before to Lily's house. "A king," he thought, "ought not to disregard the words of a high-minded counselor." So when he had stupefied her with wine, he branded her hip with the fork, stole her jewels, returned to his friend, and told him everything, showing him the jewels.

Then the counselor's son felt sure his scheme was successful. He went to the cemetery in the morning, and disguised himself as a hermit, and the prince as his pupil. And he said, "Take this pearl necklace from among the jewels. Go and sell it in the market-place. And if the policemen arrest you, say this: It was given to me to sell by my teacher."

So the prince went to the market-place and stood there offering the pearl necklace for sale, and he was arrested while doing it by the policemen. And as they were eager to find out about the theft of the jewels from Bite's daughter, they took the prince at once to the chief of police. And when he saw that the culprit was dressed like a hermit, he asked him very gently, "Holy sir, where did you get this pearl necklace? It belongs to Bite's daughter and was stolen." Then the prince said to them, "Gentlemen, my teacher gave it to me to sell. You had better go and ask him."

Then the chief of police went and asked him, "Holy sir, how did this pearl necklace come into your pupil's hand?"

And the shrewd counselor's son whispered to him, "Sir, as I am a hermit, I wander about all the time in this region. And as I happened to be here in this cemetery, I saw a whole company of witches who came here at night. And one of the witches split open the heart of a king's son, and offered it to her master. She was mad with wine, and screwed up her face most horribly. But when she impudently tried to snatch my rosary as I prayed, I became angry, and branded her on the hip with a three-pronged fork which I had made red-hot with a magic spell. And I took this pearl necklace from her neck. Then, as it was not a thing for a hermit, I sent it to be sold."

When he heard this, the chief of police went and told the whole story to the king. And when the king heard and saw the evidence, he sent the old woman, who was reliable, to identify the pearl necklace. And he heard from her that Lily was branded on the hip.

Then he was convinced that she was really a witch and had devoured his son. So he went himself to the counselor's son, who was disguised as a hermit, and asked how Lily should be punished. And by his advice, she was banished from the city, though her parents wept. So she was banished naked to the forest and knew that the counselor's son had done it all, but she did not die.

And at nightfall the prince and the counselor's son put off their hermit disguise, mounted on horseback, and found her weeping. They put her on a horse and took her to their own country. And when they got there, the prince lived most happily with her.

But Bite thought that his daughter was eaten by wild beasts in the wood, and he died of grief. And his wife died with him.

When he had told this story, the goblin asked the king, "O King, who was to blame for the death of the parents: the prince, or the counselor's son, or Lily? You seem like a very wise man, so resolve my doubts on this point. If you know and do not tell me the truth, then your head will surely fly into a hundred pieces. And if you give a good answer, then I will jump from your shoulder and go back to the sissoo tree."

Then King Triple-victory said to the goblin, "You are a master of magic. You surely know yourself, but I will tell you. It was not the fault of any of the three you mentioned. It was entirely the fault of King Ear-lotus."

But the goblin said, "How could it be the king's fault? The other three did it. Are the crows to blame when the geese eat up the rice?"

Then the king said, "But those three are not to blame. It was right for the counselor's son to do his master's business. So he is not to blame. And Lily and the prince were madly in love and could not stop to think. They only looked after their own affairs. They are not to blame.

"But the king knew the law-books very well, and he had spies to find out the facts among the people. And he knew about the doings of rascals. So he acted without thinking. He is to blame."

When the goblin heard this, he wanted to test the king's constancy. So he went back by magic in a moment to the sissoo tree. And the king went back fearlessly to get him.

THE FATHER AND SON WHO MARRIED MOTHER AND DAUGHTER

Tradition Bearer: Unavailable

Source: Ryder, Arthur W., trans. [author unknown, Sanskrit title *Vetalapañchavimsati*]. *Twenty-Two Goblins*. London: J.M. Dent, 1917, 209–220.

Date: Unavailable

Original Source: India

National Origin: India

Throughout the twenty-two tales of this anthology, Shiva appears here and there. In this final tale, he appears to reward the valor and integrity of King Triple-victory.

The king paid no attention to the terrible witch of night, clad in black darkness, with the funeral piles as flaming eyes. He bravely went through the dreadful cemetery to the sissoo tree, put the goblin on his shoulder, and started as before. And as he walked along, the goblin said to him, "O King, I am very tired with these comings and goings, but you do not seem to be. So I will tell you my Great Puzzle. Listen."

Long ago there was a king named Virtue in the southern country. He was the best of righteous men, and was born in a great family. His wife came from the Malwa country, and her name was Moonlight. And they had one daughter, whom they named Beauty.

When this daughter was grown up, the relatives conspired to wreck the kingdom and drive King Virtue out. But he escaped by night, took a great many jewels, and fled from his kingdom with his beautiful wife and his daughter. He started for his father-in-law's house in Malwa, and came with his wife and daughter to the Vindhya forest. There they spent a weary night.

In the morning the blessed sun arose in the east, stretching out his rays like hands to warn the king not to go into the forest where robbers lived. The king went on foot with his trembling daughter and his wife, and their feet were wounded by the thorny grass. So they came to a fortified village. It was like the city of Death; for there were no righteous people there, and it was filled with robber-men who killed and robbed other people.

As the king drew near with his fine garments and his gems, many robbers saw him from a distance, and ran out armed to rob him. When the king saw them coming, he said to his wife and daughter, "These are wild men. They must not touch you. Go into the thick woods." So the queen with her daughter Beauty fled in fear into the middle of the forest.

But the brave king took his sword and shield and killed many of the wild men as they charged down, raining arrows on him. Then their leader gave an order, and all the robbers fell on the king at once, wounded every limb in his body, and killed him; for he was all alone. So the robbers took the jewels and went away.

Now the queen had hidden in a thicket, and had seen her husband killed. Then she fled a long distance in fear and came with her daughter into another thick wood. The rays of the midday sun were so fierce that travelers had to sit in the shade. So Queen Moonlight and Princess Beauty sat down under an ashoka tree near a lotus pond in terrible weariness and fear and grief.

Now a gentleman named Fierce-lion who lived near came on horseback with his son into that wood to hunt. The son's name was Strong-lion. And the father saw the footprints of the queen and the princess, and he said to his son, "My son, these footprints are clean-cut and ladylike. Let us follow them. And if we find two women, you shall marry one of them, whichever you choose."

And the son Strong-lion said, "Father, the one who has the little feet in this line of footprints, seems to be the wife for me. The one with the bigger feet must be older. She is the wife for you."

But Fierce-lion said, "My son, what do you mean? Your mother went to heaven before your eyes. When so good a wife is gone, how could I think of another?"

But his son said, "Not so, Father. A householder's house is an empty place without a wife. Besides, you have surely heard what the poet says:

> What fool would go into a house?
> Tis a prisoner's abode,
> Unless a buxom wife is there,
> Looking down the road.

So, Father, I beg you on my life to marry the second one, whom I have chosen for you."

Then Fierce-lion said "Very well," and went on slowly with his son, following the footprints. And when he came to the pond, he saw Queen Moonlight, radiant with beauty and charm. And with his son he eagerly approached her. But when she saw him, she rose in terror, fearing that he was a robber.

But her sensible daughter said, "There is no reason to fear. These two men are not robbers. They are two well-dressed gentlemen, who probably came here to hunt." Still the queen swung in doubt.

Then Fierce-lion dismounted and stood before her. And he said, "Beautiful lady, do not be frightened. We came here to hunt. Pluck up heart and tell me without fear who you are. Why have you come into this lonely wood? For your appearance is that of ladies who wear gems and sit on pleasant balconies. And why should feet fit to saunter in a court, press this thorny ground? It is a strange sight. For the wind-blown dust settles on your faces and robs them of beauty. It hurts us to see the fierce rays of the sun fall upon such figures. Tell us your story. For our hearts are sadly grieved to see you in such a plight. And we cannot see how you could live in a forest filled with wild beasts."

Then the queen sighed, and between shame and grief she stammered out her story. And Fierce-lion saw that she had no husband to care for her. So he comforted her and soothed her with tender words, and took care of her and her daughter. His son helped the two ladies on horseback and led them to his own city, rich as the city of the god of wealth. And the queen seemed to be in another life. She was helpless and widowed and miserable. So she consented. What could she do, poor woman?

Then, because the queen had smaller feet, the son Strong-lion married Queen Moonlight. And Fierce-lion, the father, married her daughter, the princess Beauty, because of the bigness of her feet. Who would break a promise that had been made solemnly?

Thus, because of their inconsistent feet, the daughter became the wife of the father and the mother-in-law of her own mother. And the mother became the wife of the son and the daughter-in-law of her own daughter. And as time passed, sons and daughters were born to each pair.

When the goblin had told this story, he asked the king, "O King, when children were born to the father and daughter, and other children to the son and mother, what relation were those children to one another? If you know and do not tell, then remember the curse I spoke of before?"

When the king heard the goblin's question, he turned the thing this way and that, but could not say a word. So he went on in silence. And when the goblin saw that he could not answer the question, he laughed in his heart and thought, "This king cannot give an answer to my Great Puzzle. So he just walks on in silence. And he cannot deceive me because of the power of the curse.

193

Well, I am pleased with his wonderful character. So I will cheat that rogue of a monk, and give the magic power he is striving after to this king."

So the goblin said aloud, "O King, you are weary with your comings and goings in this dreadful cemetery in the black night, yet you seem happy, and never hesitate at all. I am astonished and pleased at your perseverance. So now you may take the dead body and go ahead. I will leave the body. And I will tell you something that will do you good, and you must do it. The monk for whom you are carrying this body, is a rogue. He will call upon me and worship me, and he will try to kill you as a sacrifice. He will say, 'Lie flat on the ground in an attitude of reverence.' O King, you must say to that rascal: 'I do not know this attitude of reverence. Show me first, and then I will do likewise.' Then when he lies on the ground to show you the attitude of reverence, cut off his head with your sword. Then you will get the kingship over the fairies which he is trying to get. Otherwise, the monk will kill you and get the magic power. That is why I have delayed you so long. Now go ahead, and win magic power."

So the goblin left the body on the king's shoulder and went away. And the king reflected how the monk Patience was planning to hurt him. He took the body and joyfully went to the fig tree.

So King Triple-victory came to the monk Patience with the body on his shoulder. And he saw the monk along in the dark night, sitting under the cemetery tree and looking down the road. He had made a magic circle with yellow powdered bones in a spot smeared with blood. In it he had put a jug filled with blood and lamps with magic oil. He had kindled a fire and brought together the things he needed for worship.

The monk rose to greet the king who came carrying the body, and he said, "O King, you have done me a great favor, and a hard one. This is a strange business and a strange time and place for such as you. They say truly that you are the best of kings, for you serve others without thinking of yourself. This is the very thing that makes the greatness of a great man, when he does not give a thing up, though it costs his very life."

So the monk felt sure the he was quite successful, and he took the body from the king's shoulder. He bathed it and put garlands on it, and set it in the middle of the circle. Then he smeared his own body with ashes, put on a cord made of human hair, wrapped himself in dead man's clothes, and stood a moment, deep in thought. And the goblin was attracted by his thought into the body, and the monk worshipped him.

First he offered liquor in a skull, then he gave him human teeth carefully cleaned, and human eyes and flesh. So he completed his worship, then he said to the king, "O King, fall flat on the ground before this master magician in an attitude of reverence, so that he may give you what you want."

And the king remembered the words of the goblin. He said to the monk, "Holy sir, I do not know that attitude of reverence. Do you show me first, and afterwards I will do it in the same way."

And when the monk fell on the ground to show the attitude of reverence, the king cut off his head with a sword, and cut out his heart and split it open. And he gave the head and the heart to the goblin.

Then all the little gods were delighted and cried, "Well done!" And the goblin was pleased and spoke to the king from the body he was living in, "O King, this monk was trying to become king of the fairies. But you shall be that when you have been king of the whole world."

And the king answered the goblin, "O magic creature, if you are pleased with me, I have nothing more to wish for. Yet I ask you to make me one promise, that these twenty-two different, charming puzzle-stories shall be known all over the world and be received with honor."

And the goblin answered, "O King, so be it. And I will tell you something more. Listen. When anyone tells or hears with proper respect even a part of these puzzle-stories, he shall be immediately free from sin. And wherever these stories are told, elves and giants and witches and goblins and imps shall have no power."

Then the goblin left the dead body by magic, and went where he wanted to. Then Shiva appeared there with all the little gods, and he was well pleased. When the king bowed before him, he said, "My son, you did well to kill this sham monk who tried by force to become king of the fairies. Therefore you shall establish the whole earth, and then become king of the fairies yourself. And when you have long enjoyed the delights of heaven and at last give them up of your own accord, then you shall be united with me. So receive from me this sword called Invincible. While you have it, everything you say will come true."

So Shiva gave him the magic sword, received his flowery words of worship, and vanished with the gods.

HOW THE RAJA'S SON WON THE PRINCESS LABAM

Tradition Bearer: Mániyá

Source: Jacobs, Joseph. *Indian Fairy Tales*. London: David Nutt, 1912, 40–45.

Date: 1912

Original Source: India

National Origin: India

The episodes that comprise the following folktale are internationally distributed **tale types**. Among them are "The Grateful Animals" (AT 554) and "The Judge Appropriates the Object of Dispute" (AT 926D). The success of the hero attained by the use of magical objects and the tasks required to win the bride's hand and avoid death are encountered equally as often in the world's narrative traditions.

I n a country there was a Raja who had an only son who every day went out to hunt. One day the Rani, his mother, said to him, "You can hunt wherever you like on these three sides; but you must never go to the fourth side." This she said because she knew if he went on the fourth side he would hear of the beautiful Princess Labam, and that then he would leave his father and mother and seek for the princess.

The young prince listened to his mother, and obeyed her for some time; but one day, when he was hunting on the three sides where he was allowed to go, he remembered what she had said to him about the fourth side, and he determined to go and see why she had forbidden him to hunt on that side. When be got there, he found himself in a jungle, and nothing in the jungle but a quantity of parrots, who, lived in it. The young Raja shot at some of them, and at once they all flew away up to the sky. All, that is, but one, and this was their Raja, who was called Hiraman parrot [parrot species also called Alexandrine parrot].

When Hiraman parrot found himself left alone, he called out to the other parrots, "Don't fly away and leave me alone when the Raja's son shoots. If you desert me like this, I will tell the Princess Labam."

Then the parrots all flew back to their Raja, chattering. The prince was greatly surprised, and said, "Why, these birds can talk!" Then he said to the parrots, "Who is the Princess Labam? Where does she live?" But the parrots would not tell him where she lived. "You can never get to the Princess Labam's country." That is all they would say.

The prince grew very sad when they would not tell him anything more; and he threw his gun away and went home. When he got home, he would not speak or eat, but lay on his bed for four or five days, and seemed very ill.

At last he told his father and mother that he wanted to go and see the Princess Labam. "I must go," he said, "I must see what she is like. Tell me where her country is."

"We do not know where it is," answered his father and mother.

"Then I must go and look for it," said the prince.

"No, no," they said, "you must not leave us. You are our only son. Stay with us. You will never find the Princess Labam."

"I must try and find her," said the prince. "Perhaps God will show me the way. If I live and I find her, I will come back to you; but perhaps I shall die, and then I shall never see you again. Still I must go."

So they had to let him go, though they cried very much at parting with him. His father gave him fine clothes to wear, and a fine horse. And he took his gun, and his bow and arrows, and a great many other weapons; "for," he said, "I may want them." His father too, gave him plenty of rupees.

Then he himself got his horse all ready for the journey, and he said goodbye to his father and mother; and his mother took her handkerchief and wrapped some sweetmeats in it, and gave it to her son. "My child," she said to him, "when you are hungry eat some of these sweetmeats."

He then set out on his journey, and rode on and on till he came to a jungle in which were a tank and shady trees. He bathed himself and his horse in the tank, and then sat down under a tree.

"Now," he said to himself, "I will eat some of the sweetmeats my mother gave me, and I will drink some water, and then I will continue my journey." He opened his handkerchief and took out a sweetmeat. He found an ant in it. He took out another. There was an ant in that one too. So he laid the two sweetmeats on the ground, and he took out another, and another, and another, until he had taken them all out; but in, each he found an ant. "Never mind," he said, "I won't eat the sweetmeats; the ants shall eat them." Then the Ant-Raja came and stood before him and said, "You have been good to us. If ever you are in trouble, think of me and we will come to you."

The Raja's son thanked him, mounted his horse and continued his journey. He rode on and on until he came to another jungle, and there he saw a tiger who had a thorn in his foot, and was roaring loudly from the pain.

"Why do you roar like that?" said the young Raja. "What is the matter with you?"

"I have had a thorn in my foot for twelve years," answered the tiger, "and it hurts me so; that is why I roar."

"Well," said the Raja's son, "I will take it out for you. But perhaps, as you are a tiger, when I have made you well, you will eat me?"

"Oh no," said the tiger, "I won't eat you. Do make me well."

Then the prince took a little knife from his pocket and cut the thorn out of the tiger's foot; but when he cut, the tiger roared louder than ever—so loud that his wife heard him in the next jungle, and came bounding along to see what was the matter. The tiger saw her coming, and hid the prince in the jungle, so that she should not see him.

"What man hurt you that you roared so loud?" said the wife.

"No one hurt me," answered the husband, "but a Raja's son came and took the thorn out of my foot."

"Where is he? Show him to me," said his wife.

"If you promise not to kill him, I will call him," said the tiger.

"I won't kill him; only let me see him," answered his wife.

Then the tiger called the Raja's son, and when he came the tiger and his wife made him a great many salaams [low bows]. Then they gave him a good dinner, and he stayed with them for three days. Every day he looked at the tiger's foot, and the third day it was quite healed. Then he said good-bye to the tigers, and the tiger said to him, "If ever you are in trouble, think of me, and we will come to you."

The Raja's son rode on and on till he came to a third jungle. Here he found four fakirs whose teacher and master had died, and had left four things—a bed, which carried whoever sat on it whithersoever he wished to go; a bag, that gave its owner whatever he wanted, jewels, food or clothes; a stone bowl that gave its owner as much water as he wanted, no matter how far he might be from a tank; and a stick and rope, to which its owner had only to say, if any one came to make war on him, "Stick, beat as many men and soldiers as are here," and the stick would beat them and the rope would tie them up.

The four fakirs were quarreling over these four things. One said, "I want this"; another said, "You cannot have it, for I want it"; and so on.

The Raja's son said to them, "Do not quarrel for these things. I will shoot four arrows in four different directions. Whichever of you gets to my first arrow, shall have the first thing—the bed. Whosoever gets to the second arrow, shall have the second thing—the bag. He who gets to the third arrow, shall have the third thing—the bowl. And he who gets to the fourth arrow, shall have the last things—the stick and rope." To this they agreed. And the prince shot off his first arrow. Away raced the fakirs to get it. When they brought it back to him he shot off the second, and when they had found and brought it to him he shot off his third, and when they had brought him the third he shot off the fourth.

While they were away looking for the fourth arrow the Raja's son let his horse loose in the jungle and sat on the bed, taking the bowl, the stick and rope, and the bag with him. Then he said, "Bed, I wish to go to the Princess Labam's country." The little bed instantly rose up into the air and began to fly, and it flew and flew till it came to the Princess Labam's country, where it settled on the ground. The Raja's son asked some men he saw, "Whose country is this?"

"The Princess Labam's country," they answered. Then the prince went on till he came to a house where he saw an old woman.

"Who are you?" she said. "Where do you come from?"

"I come from a far country," he said, "do let me stay with you tonight."

"No," she answered, "I cannot let you stay with me; for our king has ordered that men from other countries may not stay in his country. You cannot stay in my house."

"You are my aunty," said the prince, "let me remain with you for this one night. You see it is evening, and if I go into the jungle, then the wild beasts will eat me."

"Well," said the old woman, "you may stay here tonight; but tomorrow morning you must go away, for if the king hears you have passed the night in my house, he will have me seized and put into prison."

Then she took him into her house, and the Raja's son was very glad. The old woman began preparing dinner, but he stopped her. "Aunty," he said, "I will give you food." He put his hand into his bag, saying, "Bag, I want some dinner," and the bag gave him instantly a delicious dinner, served up on two gold plates. The old woman and the Raja's son then dined together.

When they had finished eating, the old woman said, "Now I will fetch some water."

"Don't go," said the prince. "You shall have plenty of water directly." So he took his bowl and said to it, "Bowl, I want some water," and then it filled with water. When it was full, the prince cried out, "Stop, bowl!" and the bowl stopped filling. "See, aunty," he said, "with this bowl I can always get as much water as I want."

By this time night had come. "Aunty," said the Raja's son, "why don't you light a lamp?"

"There is no need," she said. "Our king has forbidden the people in his country to light any lamps; for, as soon as it is dark, his daughter, the Princess Labam, comes and sits on her roof, and she shines so that she lights up all the country and our houses, and we can see to do our work as if it were day."

When it was quite black night the princess got up. She dressed herself in her rich clothes and jewels, and rolled up her hair, and across her head she put a band of diamonds and pearls. Then she shone like the moon and her beauty made night day. She came out of her room and sat on the roof of her palace. In the daytime she never came out of her house; she only came out at night. All the people in her father's country then went about their work and finished it.

The Raja's son watched the princess quietly, and was very happy. He said to himself, "How lovely she is!"

At midnight, when everybody had gone to bed, the princess came down from her roof and went to her room; and when she was in bed and asleep, the Raja's son got up softly and sat on his bed. "Bed," he said to it, "I want to go to the Princess Labam's bed-room." So the little bed carried him to the room where she lay fast asleep.

The young Raja took his bag and said, "I want a great deal of betel-leaf," and it at once gave him quantities of betel-leaf. This he laid near the princess's bed, and then his little bed carried him back to the old woman's house.

Next morning all the princess's servants found the betel-leaf, and began to eat it.

"Where did you get all that betel-leaf?" asked the princess.

"We found it near your bed," answered the servants. Nobody knew the prince had come in the night and put it all there.

In the morning the old woman came to the Raja's son. "Now it is morning," she said, "and you must go; for if the king finds out all I have done for you, he will seize me."

"I am ill today, dear aunty," said the prince, "do let me stay till tomorrow morning."

"Good," said the old woman. So he stayed, and they took their dinner out of the bag, and the bowl gave them water.

When night came the princess got up and sat on her roof, and at twelve o'clock, when every one was in bed, she went to her bed-room, and was soon fast asleep. Then the Raja's son sat on his bed, and it carried him to the princess. He took his bag and said, "Bag, I want a most lovely shawl"; It gave him a splendid shawl, and he spread it over the princess as she lay asleep. Then he went back to the old woman's house and slept till morning.

In the morning, when the princess saw the shawl she was delighted. "See, mother," she said, "Khuda [God] must have given me this shawl, it is so beautiful."

Her mother was very glad too. "Yes, my child," she said, "Khuda must have given you this splendid shawl."

When it was morning the old woman said to the Raja's son, "Now you must really go."

"Aunty," he answered, "I am not well enough yet. Let me stay a few days longer. I will remain hidden in your house, so that no one may see me." So the old woman let him stay.

When it was black night, the princess put on her lovely clothes and jewels and sat on her roof. At midnight she went to her room and went to sleep. Then the Raja's son sat on his bed and flew to her bed-room. There he said to his bag, "Bag, I want a very, very beautiful ring." The bag gave him a glorious ring. Then he took the Princess Labam's hand gently to put on the ring, and she started up very much frightened.

"Who are you?" she said to the prince. "Where do you come from? Why do you come to my room?"

"Do not be afraid, princess," he said, "I am no thief. I am a great Raja's son. Hiraman parrot, who lives in the jungle where I went to hunt, told me your name, and then I left my father and mother and came to see you."

"Well," said the princess, "as you are the son of such a great Raja, I will not have you killed, and I will tell my father and mother that I wish to marry you."

The prince then returned to the old woman's house; and when morning came the princess said to her mother, "The son of a great Raja has come to this country, and I wish to marry him." Her mother told this to the king.

"Good," said the king, "but if this Raja's son wishes to marry my daughter, he must first do whatever I bid him. If he fails I will kill him. I will give him eighty pounds weight of mustard seed, and out of this he must crush the oil in one day. If he cannot do this he shall die."

In the morning the Raja's son told the old woman that he intended to marry the princess. "Oh," said the old woman, "go away from this country, and do not think of marrying her. A great many Rajas and Rajas' sons have come here to marry her, and her father has had them all killed. He says who-ever wishes to marry his daughter must first do whatever he bids him. If he can, then he shall marry the princess; if he cannot, the king will have him killed. But no one can do the things the king tells him to do; so all the Rajas and Rajas' sons who have tried have been put to death. You will be killed too, if you try. Do go away." But the prince would not listen to any-thing she said.

The king sent for the prince to the old woman's house, and his servants brought the Raja's son to the king's courthouse to the king. There the king gave him eighty pounds of mustard seed, and told him to crush all the oil out of it that day, and bring it next morning to him to the courthouse. "Whoever wishes to marry my daughter." he said to the prince, "must first do all I tell him. If he cannot, then I have him killed. So if you cannot crush all the oil out of this mustard seed you will die."

The prince was very sorry when he heard this. "How can I crush the oil out of all this mustard seed in one thy?" he said to himself, "and if I do not, the king will kill me." He took the mustard seed to the old woman's house, and did not know what to do. At last he remembered the Ant-Raja, and the moment he did so, the Ant-Raja and his ants came to him. "Why do you look so sad?" said the Ant-Raja.

The prince showed him the mustard seed, and said to him, "How can I crush the oil out of all this mustard seed in one day? And if I do not take the oil to the king tomorrow morning, he will kill me."

"Be happy," said the Ant-Raja, "lie down and sleep; we will crush all the oil out for you during the day, and tomorrow morning you shall take it to the king." The Raja's son lay down and slept, and the ants crushed out the oil for him. The prince was very glad when he saw the oil.

The next morning he took it to the court-house to the king. But the king said, "You cannot yet marry my daughter. If you wish to do so, you must first fight with my two demons, and kill them." The king a long time ago had caught two demons, and then, as he did not know what to do with them, he had shut them up in a cage. He was afraid to let them loose for fear they would eat up all the people in his country; and he did not know how to kill them. So all the kings and kings' sons who wanted to marry the Princess Labam had to fight with these demons, "for," said the king to himself, "perhaps the demons may be killed, and then I shall be rid of them."

When he heard of the demons the Raja's son was very sad. "What can I do?" he said to himself. "How can I fight with these two demons?"

Then he thought of his tiger: and the tiger and his wife came to him and said, "Why are you so sad?"

The Raja's son answered, "The king has ordered me to fight with his two demons and kill them. How can I do this?"

"Do not be frightened," said the tiger. "Be happy. I and my wife will fight with them for you."

Then the Raja's son took out of his bag two splendid coats. They were all gold and silver, and covered with pearls and diamonds. These he put on the tigers to make them beautiful, and he took them to the king, and said to him, "May these tigers fight your demons for me?"

"Yes," said the king, who did not care in the least who killed his demons, provided they were killed.

"Then call your demons," said the Raja's son, "and these tigers will fight them." The king did so, and the tigers and the demons fought and fought until the tigers had killed the demons.

"That is good," said the king. "But you must do something else before I give you my daughter. Up in the sky I have a kettle-drum. You must go and beat it. If you cannot do this, I will kill you."

The Raja's son thought of his little bed; so he went to the old woman's house and sat on his bed. "Little bed!' he said, "up in the sky is the king's kettle-drum. I want to go to it." The bed flew up with him, and the Raja's son beat the drum, and the king heard him.

Still, when he came down, the king would not give him his daughter. "You have," he said to the prince, "done the three things I told you to do; but you must do one thing more."

"If I can, I will," said the Raja's son.

Then the king showed him the trunk of a tree that was lying near his court-house. It was a very, very, thick trunk. He gave the prince a wax hatchet, and said, "Tomorrow morning you must cut this trunk in two with this wax hatchet."

The Raja's son went back to the old woman's house. He was very sad, and thought that now the Raja would certainly kill him. "I had his oil crushed out by the ants," he said to himself. "I had his demons killed by the tigers. My bed helped me to beat his kettle-drum. But now what can I do? How can I cut that thick tree-trunk in two with a wax hatchet?"

At night he went on his bed to see the princess. "To morrow," he said to her, "your father will kill me."

"Why?" asked the princess.

"He has told me to cut a thick tree-trunk in two with a wax hatchet. How can I ever do that?" said the Raja's son.

"Do not be afraid," said the princess, "do as I bid you, and you will cut it in two quite easily."

Then she pulled out a hair from her head and gave it to the prince. "Tomorrow," she said, "when no one is near you, you must say to the tree-trunk, 'The Princess Labam commands you to let yourself be cut in two by this hair.' Then stretch the hair down the edge of the wax hatchet's blade."

The prince next day did exactly as the princess had told him; and the minute the hair that was stretched down the edge of the hatchet-blade touched the tree-trunk it split into two pieces.

The king said, "Now you can marry my daughter." Then the wedding took place. All the Rajas and kings of the countries round were asked to come to it, and there were great rejoicings.

After a few days the prince's son said to his wife, "Let us go to my father's country." The Princess Labam's father gave them a quantity of camels and horses and rupees and servants; and they traveled in great state to the prince's country, where they lived happily.

The prince always kept his bag, bowl, bed, and stick; only, as no one ever came to make war on him, he never needed to use the stick.

A MAN DECEIVES A WOMAN

Tradition Bearer: Bhavabhuti

Source: Burton, Richard. "The Vampire's First Story in Which a Man Deceives a Woman." *Vikram and the Vampire*, ed. Elizabeth Burton. London: Tylston and Edwards, 1893, 41–73.

Date: Unavailable

Original Source: India

National Origin: India

The following three tales "A Man Deceives a Woman," "Many Wise Fools" (page 221), and "The Vampire Puzzles Raja Vikram" (page 233) are drawn from *Vikram and the Vampire*, another Indian collection whose **framing** device closely resembles *Twenty-Two Goblins*. The framing device in both collections hinges on a sham holy man who extricates a promise from a king to enter a place of death and engage in a contest of wits with supernatural creatures. The tales in both cases are intended to teach moral lessons to those who listen carefully. For example, the first tale revolves around deceit, the crime of the yogi who has sent King Vikram, a man of high moral character, on this errand. The tales are told by the vampire Vikram has captured and carries in a bag on his back.

In Benares once reigned a mighty prince, by name Pratapamukut, to whose eighth son Vajramukut happened the strangest adventure.

One morning, the young man, accompanied by the son of his father's pradhan or prime minister, rode out hunting, and went far into the jungle. At last the twain unexpectedly came upon a beautiful "tank" [pond] of a prodigious size. It was surrounded by short thick walls of fine baked brick; and flights and ramps of cut-stone steps, half the length of each face, and adorned with turrets, pendants, and finials, led down to the water. The substantial plaster work and the masonry had fallen into disrepair, and from the crevices sprang huge trees, under whose thick shade the breeze blew freshly, and on whose balmy branches the birds sang sweetly; the grey squirrels chirruped joyously as they coursed one another up the gnarled trunks, and from the pendent llianas the longtailed monkeys were swinging sportively. The bountiful hand of Sravana had spread the earthen rampart with a carpet of the softest grass and many-hued wild flowers, in which were buzzing swarms of bees and myriads of bright winged insects; and flocks of water fowl, wild geese Brahmini ducks, bitterns, herons, and cranes, male and female, were feeding on the narrow strip of brilliant green that belted the long deep pool, amongst the broad-leaved lotuses with the lovely blossoms, splashing through the pellucid waves, and basking happily in the genial sun.

The prince and his friend wondered when they saw the beautiful tank in the midst of a wild forest, and made many vain conjectures about it. They dismounted, tethered their horses, and threw their weapons upon the ground; then, having washed their hands and faces, they entered a shrine dedicated to Mahadeva, and there began to worship the presiding deity.

Whilst they were making their offerings, a bevy of maidens, accompanied by a crowd of female slaves, descended the opposite flight of steps. They stood there for a time, talking and laughing and looking about them to see if any alligators infested the waters. When convinced that the tank was safe, they disrobed themselves in order to bathe. It was truly a splendid spectacle

"Concerning which the less said the better," interrupted Raja Vikram in an offended tone—but did not last long. The Raja's daughter—for the principal maiden was a princess—soon left her companions, who were scooping up water with their palms and dashing it over one another's heads, and proceeded to perform the rites of purification, meditation, and worship. Then she began strolling with a friend under the shade of a small mango grove.

The prince also left his companion sitting in prayer, and walked forth into the forest. Suddenly the eyes of the Raja's son and the Raja's daughter met. She started back with a little scream. He was fascinated by her beauty, and began to say to himself, "O thou vile Karma, why worriest thou me?"

Hearing this, the maiden smiled encouragement, but the poor youth, between palpitation of the heart and hesitation about what to say, was so confused that his tongue crave to his teeth. She raised her eyebrows a little. There is nothing which women despise in a man more than modesty, for mo-des-ty—

A violent shaking of the bag which hung behind Vikram's royal back broke off the end of this offensive sentence. And the warrior king did not cease that discipline till the Baital promised him to preserve more decorum in his observations.

Still the prince stood before her with downcast eyes and suffused cheeks: even the spur of contempt failed to arouse his energies. Then the maiden called to her friend, who was picking jasmine flowers so as not to witness the scene, and angrily asked why that strange man was allowed to stand and stare at her? The friend, in hot wrath, threatened to call the slave, and throw Vajramukut into the pond unless he instantly went away with his impudence. But as the prince was rooted to the spot, and really had not heard a word of what had been said to him, the two women were obliged to make the first move.

As they almost reached the tank, the beautiful maiden turned her head to see what the poor modest youth was doing.

Vajramukut was formed in every way to catch a woman's eye. The Raja's daughter therefore half forgave him his offense of mod. Again she sweetly smiled, disclosing two rows of little opals. Then descending to the water's edge, she stooped down and plucked a lotus This she worshipped; next she placed it in her hair, then she put it in her ear, then she bit it with her teeth, then she trod upon it with her foot, then she raised it up again, and lastly she stuck it in her bosom. After which she mounted her conveyance and went home to her friends; whilst the prince, having become thoroughly desponding and drowned in grief at separation from her, returned to the minister's son.

"Females!" ejaculated the minister's son, speaking to himself in a careless tone, when, his prayer finished, he left the temple, and sat down upon the tank steps to enjoy the breeze. He presently drew a roll of paper from under his waist-belt, and in a short time was engrossed with his study. The women seeing this conduct, exerted themselves in every possible way of wile to attract his attention and to distract his soul. They succeeded only so far as to make him roll his head with a smile, and to remember that such is always the custom of man's bane; after which he turned over a fresh page of manuscript. And although he presently began to wonder what had become of the prince his master, he did not look up even once from his study.

He was a philosopher, that young man. But after all, Raja Vikram, what is mortal philosophy? Nothing but another name for indifference! Who was ever philosophical about a thing truly loved or really hated?—no one! Philosophy, says Shankharacharya, is either a gift of nature or the reward of study. But I, the Baital, the devil, ask you, what is a born philosopher, save a man of cold desires? And what is a bred philosopher but a man who has survived his desires? A young philosopher? A cold-blooded youth! An elderly philosopher? A leuco-phlegmatic old man! Much nonsense, of a verity, ye hear in praise of nothing from your Rajaship's Nine Gems of Science, and from sundry other such wise fools.

Then the prince began to relate the state of his case, saying, "O friend, I have seen a damsel, but whether she be a musician from Indra's heaven, a maiden of the sea, a daughter of the serpent kings, or the child of an earthly Raja, I cannot say."

"Describe her," said the statesman in embryo.

"Her face," quoth the prince, "was that of the full moon, her hair like a swarm of bees hanging from the blossoms of the acacia, the corners of her eyes touched her ears, her lips were sweet with lunar ambrosia, her waist was that of a lion, and her walk the walk of a king goose. As a garment, she was white; as a season, the spring; as a flower, the jasmine; as a speaker, the kokila bird; as a perfume, musk; as a beauty, Kamadeva; and as a being, Love. And if she does not come into my possession I will not live; this I have certainly determined upon."

The young minister, who had heard his prince say the same thing more than once before, did not attach great importance to these awful words. He merely remarked that, unless they mounted at once, night would surprise them in the forest. Then the two young men returned to their horses, untethered them, drew on their bridles, saddled them, and catching up their weapons, rode slowly towards the Raja's palace. During the three hours of return hardly a word passed between the pair. Vajramukut not only avoided speaking; he never once replied till addressed thrice in the loudest voice.

The young minister put no more questions, "for," quoth he to himself, "when the prince wants my counsel, he will apply for it." In this point he had borrowed wisdom from his father, who held in peculiar horror the giving of unasked-for advice. So, when he saw that conversation was irksome to his master, he held his peace and meditated upon what he called his "day-thought." It was his practice to choose every morning some tough food for reflection, and to chew the cud of it in his mind at times when, without such employment, his wits would have gone wool-gathering. You may imagine, Raja Vikram, that with a few years of this head work, the minister's son became a very crafty young person.

After the second day the Prince Vajramukut, being restless from grief at separation, fretted himself into a fever. Having given up writing, reading, drinking, sleeping, the affairs entrusted to him by his father, and everything else, he sat down, as he said, to die. He used constantly to paint the portrait of the beautiful lotus gatherer, and to lie gazing upon it with tearful eyes; then he would start up and tear it to pieces and beat his forehead, and begin another picture of a yet more beautiful face.

At last, as the pradhan's son had foreseen, he was summoned by the young Raja, whom he found upon his bed, looking yellow and complaining bitterly of headache. Frequent discussions upon the subject of the tender passion had passed between the two youths, and one of them had ever spoken of it so very disrespectfully that the other felt ashamed to introduce it. But when his friend, with a view to provoke communicativeness, advised a course of boiled and bitter herbs and great attention to diet, quoting the hemistich attributed to the learned physician Charndatta.

A fever starve, but feed a cold, the unhappy Vajramukut's fortitude abandoned him; he burst into tears, and exclaimed," Whosoever enters upon the path of love cannot survive it; and if (by chance) he should live, what is life to him but a prolongation of his misery?"

"Yea," replied the minister's son, "the sage hath said—

The road of love is that which hath no beginning nor end; Take thou heed of thyself, man I ere thou place foot upon it.

And the wise, knowing that there are three things whose effect upon himself no man can foretell—namely, desire of woman, the dice-box, and the drinking of ardent spirits—find total abstinence from them the best of rules. Yet, after all, if there is no cow, we must milk the bull."

The advice was, of course, excellent, but the hapless lover could not help thinking that on this occasion it came a little too late. However, after a pause he returned to the subject and said, "I have ventured to tread that dangerous way, be its end pain or pleasure, happiness or destruction." He then hung down his head and sighed from the bottom of his heart.

"She is the person who appeared to us at the tank?" asked the pradhan's son, moved to compassion by the state of his master.

The prince assented.

"O great king," resumed the minister's son, "at the time of going away had she said anything to you? Or had you said anything to her?"

"Nothing!" replied the other laconically, when he found his friend beginning to take an interest in the affair.

"Then," said the minister's son, "it will be exceedingly difficult to get possession of her."

"Then," repeated the Raja's son, "I am doomed to death; to an early and melancholy death!"

"Humph!" ejaculated the young statesman rather impatiently, "did she make any sign, or give any hint? Let me know all that happened: half confidences are worse than none."

Upon which the prince related everything that took place by the side of the tank, bewailing the false shame which had made him dumb, and concluding with her pantomime.

The pradhan's son took thought for a while. He thereupon seized the opportunity of representing to his master all the evil effects of bashfulness when women are concerned, and advised him, as he would be a happy lover, to brazen his countenance for the next interview.

Which the young Raja faithfully promised to do.

"And, now," said the other, "be comforted, O my master! I know her name and her dwelling-place. When she suddenly plucked the lotus flower and worshipped it, she thanked the gods for having blessed her with a sight of your beauty."

Vajramukut smiled, the first time for the last month.

"When she applied it to her ear, it was as if she would have explained to thee, 'I am a daughter of the Carnatic,' and when she bit it with her teeth, she meant to say that 'My father is Raja Dantawat,' who, by the by, has been, is, and ever will be, a mortal foe to thy father."

Vajramukut shuddered.

"When she put it under her foot it meant, 'My name is Padmavati'."

Vajramukut uttered a cry of joy.

"And when she placed it in her bosom, 'You are truly dwelling in my heart' was meant to be understood."

At these words the young Raja started up full of new life, and after praising with enthusiasm the wondrous sagacity of his dear friend, begged him by some contrivance to obtain the permission of his parents, and to conduct him to her city. The minister's son easily got leave for Vajramukut to travel, under pretext that his body required change of water, and his mind change of scene. They both dressed and armed themselves for the journey, and having taken some jewels, mounted their horses and followed the road in that direction in which the princess had gone.

Arrived after some days at the capital of the Carnatic, the minister's son having disguised his master and himself in the garb of traveling traders, alighted and pitched his little tent upon a clear bit of ground in one of the suburbs. He then proceeded to inquire for a wise woman, wanting, he said, to have his fortune told. When the prince asked him what this meant, he replied that elderly dames who professionally predict the future are never above [ministering to the present, and therefore that, in such circumstances, they are the properest persons to be consulted.

"Is this a treatise upon the subject of immorality, devil?" demanded the King Vikram ferociously. The Baital declared that it was not, but that he must tell his story.

The person addressed pointed to an old woman who, seated before the door of her hut, was spinning at her wheel. Then the young men went up to her with polite salutations and said, "Mother, we are traveling traders, and our stock is coming after us; we have come on in advance for the purpose of finding a place to live in. If you will give us a house, we will remain there and pay you highly."

The old woman, who was a physiognomist as well as a fortune-teller, looked at the faces of the young men and liked them, because their brows were wide, and their mouths denoted generosity. Having listened to their words, she took pity upon them and said kindly, "This hovel is yours, my masters, remain here as long as you please." Then she led them into an inner room, again welcomed them, lamented the poorness of her abode, and begged them to lie down and rest themselves.

After some interval of time the old woman came to them once more, and sitting down began to gossip. The minister's son upon this asked her, "How is it with thy family, thy relatives, and connections; and what are thy means of subsistence?" She replied, "My son is a favorite servant in the household of our great king Dantawat, and your slave is the wet-nurse of the Princess Padmavati, his eldest child. From the coming on of old age," she added, "I dwell in this house, but the king provides for my eating and drinking. I go once a day to see the girl, who is a miracle of beauty and goodness, wit and accomplishments, and returning thence, I bear my own grief at home."

In a few days the young Vajramukut had, by his liberality, soft speech, and good looks, made such progress in nurse Lakshmi's affections that, by the advice of his companion, he ventured to broach the subject ever nearest his heart. He begged his hostess, when she went on the morrow to visit the charming Padmavati, that she would be kind enough to slip a bit of paper into the princess's hand.

"Son," she replied, delighted with the proposal—and what old woman would not be? "There is no need for putting off so urgent an affair till the morrow. Get your paper ready, and I will immediately give it."

Trembling with pleasure, the prince ran to find his friend, who was seated in the garden reading, as usual, and told him what the old nurse had engaged to do. He then began to debate about how he should write his letter, to cull sentences and to weigh phrases; whether "light of my eyes" was not too trite, and "blood of my liver" rather too forcible. At this the minister's son smiled, and bade the prince not trouble his head with composition. He then drew his inkstand from his waist shawl, nibbed a reed pen, and choosing a piece of pink and flowered paper, he wrote upon it a few lines. He then folded it, gummed it, sketched a lotus flower upon the outside, and handing it to the young prince, told him to give it to their hostess, and that all would be well.

The old woman took her staff in her hand and hobbled straight to the palace. Arrived there, she found the Raja's daughter sitting alone in her apartment. The maiden, seeing her nurse, immediately arose, and making a respectful bow, led her to a seat and began the most affectionate inquiries. After giving her blessing and sitting for some time and chatting about indifferent matters, the nurse said, "O daughter! In infancy I reared and nourished thee, now the Bhagwan (Deity) has rewarded me by giving thee stature, beauty, health, and goodness. My heart only longs to see the happiness of thy womanhood, after which I shall depart in peace. I implore thee read this paper, given to me by the handsomest and the properest young man that my eyes have ever seen."

The princess, glancing at the lotus on the outside of the note, slowly unfolded it and perused its contents, which were as follows:

She was to me the pearl that clings To sands all hid from mortal sight, Yet fit for diadems of kings, The pure and lovely light.

She was to me the gleam of sun That breaks the gloom of wintry day; One moment shone my soul upon, Then passed—how soon!—away.

She was to me the dreams of bliss That float the dying eyes before, For one short hour shed happiness, And fly to bless no more.

O light, again upon me shine; O pearl, again delight my eyes; O dreams of bliss, again be mine!—No! Earth may not be Paradise.

I must not forget to remark, parenthetically, that the minister's son, in order to make these lines generally useful, had provided them with a last stanza in triplicate. "For lovers," he said sagely," are either in the optative mood, the desperative, or the exultative." This time he had used the optative. For the desperative he would substitute:

The joys of life lie dead, lie dead, The light of day is quenched in gloom The spark of hope my heart hath fled—What now withholds me from the tomb?

And this was the termination exultative, as he called it:

O joy I the pearl is mine again, Once more the day is bright and clear, And now 'tis real, then 'twas vain, My dream of bliss—O heaven is here!

The Princess Padmavati having perused this doggrel with a contemptuous look, tore off the first word of the last line, and said to the nurse, angrily, "Get thee gone, O mother of Yama, O unfortunate creature, and take back this answer"—giving her the scrap of paper—"to the fool who writes such bad verses.

I wonder where he studied the humanities. Be gone, and never do such an action again!"

The old nurse, distressed at being so treated, rose up and returned home. Vajramukut was too agitated to await her arrival, so he went to meet her on the way. Imagine his disappointment when she gave him the fatal word and repeated to him exactly what happened, not forgetting to describe a single look! He felt tempted to plunge his sword into his bosom; but Fortune interfered, and sent him to consult his confidant.

"Be not so hasty and desperate, my prince," said the pradhan's son, seeing his wild grief, "you have not understood her meaning. Later in life you will be aware of the fact that, in nine cases out of ten, a woman's 'no' is a distinct 'yes.' This morning's work has been good; the maiden asked where you learnt the humanities, which being interpreted signifies 'Who are you?'"

On the next day the prince disclosed his rank to old Lakshmi, who naturally declared that she had always known it. The trust they reposed in her made her ready to address Padmavati once more on the forbidden subject. So she again went to the palace, and having lovingly greeted her nursling, said to her, "The Raja's son, whose heart thou didst fascinate on the brim of the tank, on the fifth day of the moon, in the light half of the month Yeth, has come to my house, and sends this message to thee, "Perform what you promised; we have now come"; and I also tell thee that this prince is worthy of thee: just as thou art beautiful, so is he endowed with all good qualities of mind and body."

When Padmavati heard this speech she showed great anger, and, rubbing sandal on her beautiful hands, she slapped the old woman's cheeks, and cried, "Wretch, Daina (witch)! get out of my house; did I not forbid thee to talk such folly in my presence?"

The lover and the nurse were equally distressed at having taken the advice of the young minister, till he explained what the crafty damsel meant. "When she smeared the sandal on her ten fingers," he explained, "and struck the old woman on the face, she signified that when the remaining ten moonlight nights shall have passed away she will meet you in the dark." At the same time he warned his master that to all appearances the lady Padmavati was far too clever to make a comfortable wife. The minister's son especially hated talented intellectual, and strong-minded women; he had been heard to describe the torments of Naglok as the compulsory companionship of a polemical divine and a learned authoress, well stricken in years and of forbidding aspect, as such persons mostly are. Amongst womankind he admired—theoretically, as became a philosopher—the small, plump, laughing, chattering, unintellectual, and material-minded. And therefore—excuse the digression, Raja Vikram—he married an old maid, tall, thin, yellow, strictly proper, cold-mannered, a conversationist, and who prided herself upon spirituality. But more wonderful still, after he did marry her, he actually loved her—what an incomprehensible being is man in these matters!

To return, however. The pradhan's son, who detected certain symptoms of strong-mindedness in the Princess Padmavati, advised his lord to be wise whilst wisdom availed him. This sage counsel was, as might be guessed, most ungraciously rejected by him for whose benefit it was intended. Then the sensible young statesman rated himself soundly for having broken his father's rule touching advice, and atoned for it by blindly forwarding the views of his master.

After the ten nights of moonlight had passed, the old nurse was again sent to the palace with the usual message. This time Padmavati put saffron on three of her fingers, and again left their marks on the nurse's cheek. The minister's son explained that this was to crave delay for three days, and that on the fourth the lover would have access to her.

When the time had passed the old woman again went and inquired after her health and well-being. The princess was as usual very wroth, and having personally taken her nurse to the western gate, she called her "Mother of the elephant's trunk," and drove her out with threats of the bastinado if she ever came back. This was reported to the young statesman, who, after a few minutes' consideration, said, "The explanation of this matter is, that she has invited you tomorrow, at nighttime, to meet her at this very gate.

"When brown shadows fell upon the face of earth, and here and there a star spangled the pale heavens, the minister's son called Vajramukut, who had been engaged in adorning himself at least half that day. He had carefully shaved his cheeks and chin; his mustachio was trimmed and curled; he had arched his eyebrows by plucking out with tweezers the fine hairs around them; he had trained his curly musk-colored love-locks to hang gracefully down his face; he had drawn broad lines of antimony along his eyelids, a most brilliant sectarian mark was affixed to his forehead, the color of his lips had been heightened by chewing betel-nut—

"One would imagine that you are talking of a silly girl, not of a prince, fiend!" interrupted Vikram, who did not wish his son to hear what he called these fopperies and frivolities.

—and whitened his neck by having it shaved (continued the Baital, speaking quickly, as if determined not to be interrupted), and reddened the tips of his ears by squeezing them, and made his teeth shine by rubbing copper powder into the roots, and set off the delicacy of his fingers by staining the tips with henna. He had not been less careful with his dress: he wore a well-arranged turban, which had taken him at least two hours to bind, and a rich suit of brown stuff chosen for the adventure he was about to attempt, and he hung about his person a number of various weapons, so as to appear a hero—which young damsels admire.

Vajramukut asked his friend how he looked, and smiled happily when the other replied "Admirable!" His happiness was so great that he feared it might not last, and he asked the minister's son how best to conduct himself?

"As a conqueror, my prince!" answered that astute young man, "if it so be that you would be one. When you wish to win a woman, always impose upon her. Tell her that you are her master, and she will forthwith believe herself to be your servant. Inform her that she loves you, and forthwith she will adore you. Show her that you care nothing for her, and she will think of nothing but you. Prove to her by your demeanor that you consider her a slave, and she will become your pariah. But above all things—excuse me if I repeat myself too often—beware of the fatal virtue which men call modesty and women sheepishness. Recollect the trouble it has given us, and the danger which we have incurred: all this might have been managed at a tank within fifteen miles of your royal father's palace. And allow me to say that you may still thank your stars: in love a lost opportunity is seldom if ever recovered. The time to woo a woman is the moment you meet her, before she has had time to think; allow her the use of reflection and she may escape the net. And after avoiding the rock of Modesty, fall not, I conjure you, into the gulf of Security. I fear the lady Padmavati, she is too clever and too prudent. When damsels of her age draw the sword of Love, they throw away the scabbard of Precaution. But you yawn— I weary you—it is time for us to move."

Two watches of the night had passed, and there was profound stillness on earth. The young men then walked quietly through the shadows, till they reached the western gate of the palace, and found the wicket ajar. The minister's son peeped in and saw the porter dozing, stately as a Brahman deep in the Vedas, and behind him stood a veiled woman seemingly waiting for somebody. He then returned on tiptoe to the place where he had left his master, and with a parting caution against modesty and security, bade him fearlessly glide through the wicket. Then having stayed a short time at the gate listening with anxious ear, he went back to the old woman's house.

Vajramukut penetrating to the staircase, felt his hand grasped by the veiled figure, who motioning him to tread lightly, led him quickly forwards. They passed under several arches, through dim passages and dark doorways, till at last running up a flight of stone steps they reached the apartments of the princess.

Vajramukut was nearly fainting as the flood of splendor broke upon him. Recovering himself he gazed around the rooms, and presently a tumult of delight invaded his soul, and his body bristled with joy. The scene was that of fairyland. Golden censers exhaled the most costly perfumes, and gemmed vases bore the most beautiful flowers; silver lamps containing fragrant oil illuminated doors whose panels were wonderfully decorated, and walls adorned with pictures in which such figures were formed that on seeing them the beholder was enchanted. On one side of the room stood a bed of flowers and a couch covered with brocade of gold, and strewed with freshly-culled jasmine flowers. On the other side, arranged in proper order, were attar holders, betel-boxes, rose-water bottles, trays, and silver cases with four partitions for essences compounded of rose leaves, sugar, and spices, prepared sandal wood, saffron, and pods of musk. Scattered about a stuccoed floor white as crystal, were colored caddies of exquisite confections, and in others sweetmeats of various kinds. Female attendants clothed in dresses of various colors were standing each according to her rank, with hands respectfully joined. Some were reading plays and beautiful poems, others danced and others performed with glittering fingers and flashing arms on various instruments—the ivory lute, the ebony pipe and the silver kettledrum. In short, all the means and appliances of pleasure and enjoyment were there; and any description of the appearance of the apartments, which were the wonder of the age, is impossible.

Then another veiled figure, the beautiful Princess Padmavati, came up and disclosed herself, and dazzled the eyes of her delighted Vajramukut. She led him into an alcove, made him sit down, rubbed sandal powder upon his body, hung a garland of jasmine flowers round his neck, sprinkled rose-water over his dress, and began to wave over his head a fan of peacock feathers with a golden handle.

Said the prince, who despite all efforts could not entirely shake off his unhappy habit of being modest, "Those very delicate hands of yours are not fit to ply the pankha. Why do you take so much trouble? I am cool and refreshed by the sight of you. Do give the fan to me and sit down."

"Nay, great king!" replied Padmavati, with the most fascinating of smiles, "you have taken so much trouble for my sake in coming here, it is right that I perform service for you."

Upon which her favorite slave, taking the pankha from the hand of the princess, exclaimed, "This is my duty. I will perform the service; do you two enjoy yourselves!"

The lovers then began to chew betel, which, by the by, they disposed of in little agate boxes which they drew from their pockets, and they were soon engaged in the tenderest conversation.

Here the Baital paused for a while, probably to take breath. Then he resumed his tale as follows:

In the meantime, it became dawn; the princess concealed him; and when night returned they again engaged in the same innocent pleasures. Thus, day after day sped rapidly by. Imagine, if you can, the youth's felicity; he was of an ardent temperament, deeply enamored, barely a score of years old, and he had been strictly brought up by serious parents. He therefore resigned himself entirely to the siren for whom he willingly forgot the world, and he wondered at his good fortune, which had thrown in his way a conquest richer than all the mines of Meru.[65] He could not sufficiently admire his Padmavati's grace, beauty, bright wit, and numberless accomplishments. Every morning, for vanity's sake, he learned from her a little useless knowledge in verse as well as prose, for instance, the saying of the poet—

Enjoy the present hour, 'tis shine; be this, O man, thy law; Who e'er resew the yester? Who the morrow e'er foresaw?

And this highly philosophical axiom:

"Eat, drink, and love—the rest's not worth a fillip."

"By means of which he hoped, Raja Vikram!" said the demon, not heeding his royal carrier's "ughs" and "poohs," "to become in course of time almost as clever as his mistress."

Padmavati, being, as you have seen, a maiden of superior mind, was naturally more smitten by her lover's dullness than by any other of his qualities; she adored it, it was such a contrast to herself. At first she did what many clever women do—she invested him with the brightness of her own imagination. Still water, she pondered, runs deep; certainly under this disguise must lurk a brilliant fancy, a penetrating but a mature and ready judgment—are they not written by nature's hand on that broad high brow? With such lovely mustachios can he be aught but generous, noble-minded, magnanimous? Can such eyes belong to any but a hero? And she fed the delusion. She would smile upon him with intense fondness, when, after wasting hours over a few lines of poetry, he would misplace all the adjectives and barbarously entreat the meter. She laughed with gratification, when, excited by the bright sayings that fell from her lips, the youth put forth some platitude, dim as the lamp in the expiring fire-fly. When he slipped in grammar she saw malice under it, when he retailed a borrowed jest she called it a good one, and when he used—as princes sometimes will—bad language, she discovered in it a charming simplicity.

At first she suspected that the stratagems which had won her heart were the results of a deep-laid plot proceeding from her lover. But clever women are apt to be rarely sharp-sighted in every matter which concerns themselves. She frequently determined that a third was in the secret. She therefore made no allusion to it. Before long the enamored Vajramukut had told her everything, beginning with the diatribe against love pronounced by the minister's son, and ending with the solemn warning that she, the pretty princess, would some day or other play her husband a foul trick.

"If I do not revenge myself upon him," thought the beautiful Padmavati, smiling like an angel as she listened to the youth's confidence, "may I become a gardener's ass in the next birth!"

Having thus registered a vow, she broke silence, and praised to the skies the young pradhan's wisdom and sagacity; professed herself ready from gratitude to become his slave, and only hoped that one day or other she might meet that true friend by whose skill her soul had been gratified in its dearest desire. "Only," she concluded, "I am convinced that now my Vajramukut knows every corner of his little Padmavati's heart, he will never expect her to do anything but love, admire, adore and kiss him!" Then suiting the action to the word, she convinced him that the young minister had for once been too crabbed and cynic in his philosophy.

But after the lapse of a month Vajramukut, who had eaten and drunk and slept a great deal too much, and who had not once hunted, became bilious in body and in mind melancholic. His face turned yellow, and so did the whites of his eyes; he yawned, as liver patients generally do, complained occasionally of sick headaches, and lost his appetite; he became restless and anxious, and once when alone at night he thus thought aloud, "I have given up country, throne, home, and everything else, but the friend by means of whom this happiness was obtained I have not seen for the long length of thirty days. What will he say to himself, and how can I know what has happened to him?"

In this state of things he was sitting, and in the meantime the beautiful princess arrived. She saw through the matter, and lost not a moment in entering upon it. She began by expressing her astonishment at her lover's fickleness and fondness for change, and when he was ready to wax wroth, and quoted the words of the sage, "A barren wife may be superseded by another in the eighth year; she whose children all die, in the tenth; she who brings forth only daughters, in the eleventh; she who scolds, without delay," thinking that she alluded to his love, she smoothed his temper by explaining that she referred to his forgetting his friend. "How is it possible, O my soul," she asked with the softest of voices, that thou canst happiness here whilst thy heart is wandering there? Why didst thou conceal this from me, O astute one? Was it for fear of distressing me? Think better of thy wife than to suppose that she would ever separate thee from one to whom we both owe so much!

"After this Padmavati advised, nay ordered, her lover to go forth that night, and not to return till his mind was quite at ease, and she begged him to take a few sweetmeats and other trifles as a little token of her admiration and regard for the clever young man of whom she had heard so much.

Vajramukut embraced her with a transport of gratitude, which so inflamed her anger, that fearing lest the cloak of concealment might fall from her countenance, she went away hurriedly to find the greatest delicacies which her comfit boxes contained. Presently she returned, carrying a bag of sweetmeats of every kind for her lover, and as he rose up to depart, she put into his hand a little parcel of sugar-plums especially intended for the friend; they were made up with her own delicate fingers, and they would please, she flattered herself, even his discriminating palate.

The young prince, after enduring a number of farewell embraces and hopings for a speedy return, and last words ever beginning again, passed safely through the palace gate, and with a relieved aspect walked briskly to the house of the old nurse. Although it was midnight his friend was still sitting on his mat.

The two young men fell upon one another's bosoms and embraced affectionately. They then began to talk of matters nearest their hearts. The Raja's son wondered at seeing the jaded and haggard looks of his companion, who did not disguise that they were caused by his anxiety as to what might have happened to his friend at the hand of so talented and so superior a princess. Upon which Vajramukut, who now thought Padmavati an angel, and his late abode a heaven, remarked with formality—and two blunders to one quotation—that abilities properly directed win for a man the happiness of both worlds.

The pradhan's son rolled his head.

"Again on your hobby-horse, nagging at talent whenever you find it in others!" cried the young prince with a pun, which would have delighted Padmavati. "Surely you are jealous of her!" he resumed, anything but pleased with the dead silence that had received his joke, "jealous of her cleverness, and of her love for me. She is the very best creature in the world. Even you, woman-hater as you are, would own it if you only knew all the kind messages she sent, and the little pleasant surprise that she has prepared for you. There! Take and eat; they are made by her own dear hands!" cried the young Raja, producing the sweetmeats. "As she herself taught me to say:

'Thank God I am a man, Not a philosopher!'"

"The kind messages she sent me! The pleasant surprise she has prepared for me!" repeated the minister's son in a hard, dry tone. "My lord will be pleased to tell me how she heard of my name?"

"I was sitting one night," replied the prince, "in anxious thought about you, when at that moment the princess coming in and seeing my condition, asked, 'Why are you thus sad? Explain the cause to me.' I then gave her an account of your cleverness, and when she heard it she gave me permission to go and see you, and sent these sweetmeats for you: eat them and I shall be pleased."

"Great king!" rejoined the young statesman, "one thing vouchsafe to hear from me. You have not done well in that you have told my name. You should never let a woman think that your left hand knows the secret which she confided to your right, much less that you have shared it to a third person. Secondly, you did evil in allowing her to see the affection with which you honor your unworthy servant—a woman ever hates her lover's or husband's friend."

"What could I do?" rejoined the young Raja, in a querulous tone of voice. "When I love a woman I like to tell her everything—to have no secrets from her—to consider her another self."

"Which habit," interrupted the pradhan's son, "you will lose when you are a little older, when you recognize the fact that love is nothing but a bout, a game of skill between two individuals of opposite sexes: the one seeking to gain as much, and the other striving to lose as little as possible; and that the sharper of the twain thus met on the chessboard must, in the long run, win. And reticence is but a habit. Practice it for a year, and you will find it harder to betray than to conceal your thoughts. It hath its joy also. Is there no pleasure, think you, when suppressing an outbreak of tender but fatal confidence in saying to yourself, 'O, if she only knew this?' 'O, if she did but suspect that?' Returning, however, to the sugar-plums, my life to a pariah's that they are poisoned!"

"Impossible!" exclaimed the prince, horror-struck at the thought, "what you say, surely no one ever could do. If a mortal fears not his fellow-mortal, at least he dreads the Deity."

"I never yet knew," rejoined the other, "what a woman in love does fear. However, prince, the trial is easy. Come here, Muti!" cried he to the old woman's dog, "and off with thee to that three-headed kinsman of shine, that attends upon his amiable-looking master."

Having said this, he threw one of the sweetmeats to the dog; the animal ate it, and presently writhing and falling down, died.

"The wretch! O the wretch!" cried Vajramukut, transported with wonder and anger. "And I loved her! But now it is all over. I dare not associate with such a calamity!"

"What has happened, my lord, has happened!" quoth the minister's son calmly. "I was prepared for something of this kind from so talented a princess. None commit such mistakes, such blunders, such follies as your clever women; they cannot even turn out a crime decently executed. O give me dullness with one idea, one aim, one desire. O thrice blessed dullness that combines with happiness, power."

This time Vajramukut did not defend talent.

"And your slave did his best to warn you against perfidy. But now my heart is at rest. I have tried her strength. She has attempted and failed; the defeat will prevent her attempting again—just yet. But let me ask you to put to yourself one question. Can you be happy without her?"

"Brother!" replied the prince, after a pause, "I cannot"; and he blushed as he made the avowal.

"Well," replied the other, "better confess than conceal that fact; we must now meet her on the battle-field, and beat her at her own weapons—cunning. I do not willingly begin treachery with women, because, in the first place, I don't like it; and secondly, I know that they will certainly commence practicing it upon me, after which I hold myself justified in deceiving them. And probably this will be a good wife; remember that she intended to poison me, not you. During the last month my fear has been lest my prince had run into the tiger's brake. Tell me, my lord, when does the princess expect you to return to her?"

"She bade me," said the young Raja, "not to return till my mind was quite at ease upon the subject of m talented friend."

"This means that she expects you back tomorrow night, as you cannot enter the palace before. And now I will retire to my cot, as it is there that I am wont to ponder over my plans. Before dawn my thought shall mature one which must place the beautiful Padmavati in your power."

"A word before parting," exclaimed the prince "you know my father has already chosen a spouse for me; what will he say if I bring home a second?"

"In my humble opinion," said the minister's son rising to retire, "woman is a monogamous, man a polygamous, creature, a fact scarcely established in physiological theory, but very observable in everyday practice for what said the poet?—Divorce, friend! Re-wed thee! The spring draweth near, and a wife's but an almanac—good for the year.

If your royal father say anything to you, refer him to what he himself does."

Reassured by these words, Vajramukut bade his friend a cordial good-night and sought his cot, where he slept soundly, despite the emotions of the last few hours. The next day passed somewhat slowly. In the evening, when accompanying his master to the palace, the minister's son gave him the following directions.

"Our object, dear my lord, is how to obtain possession of the princess. Take, then, this trident, and hide it carefully when you see her show the greatest love and affection. Conceal what has happened, and when she, wondering at your calmness, asks about me, tell her that last night I was weary and out of health, that illness prevented my eating her sweetmeats, but that I shall eat them for supper tonight. When she goes to sleep, then, taking off her jewels and striking her left leg with the trident, instantly come away to me. But should she lie awake, rub upon your thumb a little of this—do not fear, it is only a powder of grubs fed on verdigris—and apply it to her nostrils. It would make an elephant senseless, so be careful how you approach it to your own face."

Vajramukut embraced his friend, and passed safely through the palace gate. He found Padmavati awaiting him; she fell upon his bosom and looked into his eyes, and deceived herself, as clever women will do. Overpowered by her joy and satisfaction, she now felt certain that her lover was hers eternally, and that her treachery had not been discovered; so the beautiful princess fell into a deep sleep.

Then Vajramukut lost no time in doing as the minister's son had advised, and slipped out of the room, carrying off Padmavati's jewels and ornaments. His counselor having inspected them, took up a sack and made signs to his master to follow him. Leaving the horses and baggage at the nurse's house, they walked to a burning-place outside the city. The minister's son there buried his dress, together with that of the prince, and drew from the sack the costume of a religious ascetic: he assumed this himself, and gave to his companion that of a disciple. Then quoth the guru (spiritual preceptor) to his chela (pupil), "Go, youth, to the bazaar, and sell these jewels, remembering to let half the jewelers in the place see the things, and if any one lay hold of thee, bring him to me."

Upon which, as day had dawned, Vajramukut carried the princess's ornaments to the market, and entering the nearest goldsmith's shop, offered to sell them, and asked what they were worth. As your majesty well knows, gardeners, tailors, and goldsmiths are proverbially dishonest, and this man was no exception to the rule. He looked at the pupil's face and wondered, because he had brought articles whose value he did not appear to know. A thought struck him that he might make a bargain which would fill his coffers, so he offered about a thousandth part of the price. This the pupil rejected, because he wished the affair to go further. Then the goldsmith, seeing him about to depart, sprang up and stood in the door way, threatening to call the officers of justice if the young man refused to give up the valuables which he said had lately been stolen from his shop. As the pupil only laughed at this, the goldsmith thought seriously of executing his threat, hesitating only because he knew that the officers of justice would gain more than he could by that proceeding. As he was still in doubt a shadow darkened his shop, and in entered the chief jeweler of the city. The moment the ornaments were shown to him he recognized them, and said, "These jewels belong to Raja Dantawat's daughter; I know them well, as I set them only a few months ago!" Then he turned to the disciple, who still held the valuables in his hand, and cried, "Tell me truly whence you received them?"

While they were thus talking, a crowd of ten or twenty persons had collected, and at length the report reached the superintendent of the archers. He sent a soldier to bring before him the pupil, the goldsmith, and the chief jeweler, together with the ornaments. And when all were in the hall of justice, he looked at the jewels and said to the young man, "Tell me truly, whence have you obtained these?"

"My spiritual preceptor," said Vajramukut, pretending great fear, "who is now worshipping in the cemetery outside the town, gave me these white stones, with an order to sell them. How know I whence he obtained them? Dismiss me, my lord, for I am an innocent man."

"Let the ascetic be sent for," commanded the kotwal. Then, having taken both of them, along with the jewels, into the presence of King Dantawat, he related the whole circumstances.

"Master," said the king on hearing the statement, "whence have you obtained these jewels?"

The spiritual preceptor, before deigning an answer, pulled from under his arm the hide of a black antelope, which he spread out and smoothed deliberately before using it as an asan. He then began to finger a rosary of beads each as large as an egg, and after spending nearly an hour in mutterings and in rollings of the head, he looked fixedly at the Raja, and repined:

"By Shiva! Great king, they are mine own. On the fourteenth of the dark half of the moon at night, I had gone into a place where dead bodies are burned, for the purpose of accomplishing a witch's incantation. After long and toilsome labor she appeared, but her demeanor was so unruly that I was forced to chastise her. I struck her with this, my trident, on the left leg, if memory serves me. As she continued to be refractory, in order to punish her I took off all her jewels and clothes, and told her to go where she pleased. Even this had little effect upon her—never have I looked upon so perverse a witch. In this way the jewels came into my possession."

Raja Dantawat was stunned by these words. He begged the ascetic not to leave the palace for a while, and forthwith walked into the private apartments of the women. Happening first to meet the queen dowager, he said to her, "Go, without losing a minute, O my mother, and look at Padmavati's left leg, and see if there is a mark or not, and what sort of a mark!" Presently she returned, and coming to the king said, "Son, I find thy daughter lying upon her bed, and complaining that she has met with an accident; and indeed Padmavati must be in great pain. I found that some sharp instrument with three points had wounded her. The girl says that a nail hurt her, but I never yet heard of a nail making three holes. However, we must all hasten, or there will be erysipelas, tumefaction, gangrene, mortification, amputation, and perhaps death in the house," concluded the old queen, hurrying away in the pleasing anticipation of these ghastly consequences.

For a moment King Dantawat's heart was ready to break. But he was accustomed to master his feelings; he speedily applied the reins of reflection to the wild steed of passion. He thought to himself, "The affairs of one's household, the intentions of one's heart, and whatever one's losses may be, should not be disclosed to any one. Since Padmavati is a witch, she is no longer my daughter. I will verily go forth and consult the spiritual preceptor."

With these words the king went outside, where the guru was still sitting upon his black hide, making marks with his trident on the floor. Having requested that the pupil might be sent away, and having cleared the room, he said to the jogi, "O holy man! What punishment for the heinous crime of witchcraft is awarded to a woman in the Dharma-Shastra?"

"Greet king!" replied the devotee, "in the Dharma Shastra it is thus written: 'If a Brahman, a cow, a woman, a child, or any other person whatsoever who may be dependent on us, should be guilty of a perfidious act, their punishment is that they be banished the country.' However much they may deserve death, we must not spill their blood, as Lakshmi flies in horror from the deed."

Hearing these words the Raja dismissed the guru with many thanks and large presents. He waited till nightfall and then ordered a band of trusty men to seize Padmavati without alarming the household, and to carry her into a distant jungle full of fiends, tigers, and bears, and there to abandon her.

In the meantime, the ascetic and his pupil hurrying to the cemetery resumed their proper dresses; they then went to the old nurse's house, rewarded her hospitality till she wept bitterly, girt on their weapons, and mounting their horses, followed the party which issued from the gate of King Dantawat's palace. And it may easily be believed that they found little difficulty in persuading the poor girl to exchange her chance in the wild jungle for the prospect of becoming Vajramukut's wife—lawfully wedded at Benares. She did not even ask if she was to have a rival in the house—a question which women, you know, never neglect to put under usual circumstances. After some days the two pilgrims of one love arrived at the house of their fathers, and to all, both great and small, excess in joy came.

"Now, Raja Vikram!" said the Baital, "you have not spoken much; doubtless you are engrossed by the interest of a story wherein a man beats a woman at her own weapon—deceit. But I warn you that you will assuredly fall into Narak (the infernal regions) if you do not make up your mind upon and explain this matter. Who was the most to blame amongst these four? The lover the lover's friend, the girl, or the father?"

"For my part I think Padmavati was the worst, she being at the bottom of all their troubles," cried Dharma Dhwaj. The king said something about young people and the two senses of seeing and hearing, but his son's sentiment was so sympathetic that he at once pardoned the interruption. At length, determined to do justice despite himself, Vikram said, "Raja Dantawat is the person most at fault."

"In what way was he at fault?" asked the Baital curiously.

King Vikram gave him this reply, "The Prince Vajramukut being tempted of the love-god was insane, and therefore not responsible for his actions. The minister's son performed his master's business obediently, without considering causes or asking questions—a very excellent quality in a dependent who is merely required to do as he is bid. With respect to the young woman, I have only to say that she was a young woman, and thereby of necessity a possible murderess. But the Raja, a prince, a man of a certain age and experience, a father of eight! He ought never to have been deceived by so shallow a trick, nor should he, without reflection, have banished his daughter from the country."

"Gramercy to you!" cried the Vampire, bursting into a discordant shout of laughter, "I now return to my tree. By my tail! I never yet heard a Raja so readily condemn a Raja." With these words he slipped out of the cloth, leaving it to hang empty over the great king's shoulder.

Vikram stood for a moment, fixed to the spot with blank dismay. Presently, recovering himself, he retraced his steps, followed by his son, ascended the sires tree, tore down the Baital, packed him up as before, and again set out upon his way.

Soon afterwards a voice sounded behind the warrior king's back, and began to tell another true story.

MANY WISE FOOLS

Tradition Bearer: Bhavabhuti

Source: Burton, Richard. "The Vampire's Seventh Story in Showing the Folly of Many Wise Fools." *Vikram and the Vampire*, ed. Elizabeth Burton. London: Tylston and Edwards, 1893, 159–180.

Date: Unavailable

Original Source: India

National Origin: India

In the following tale, the tone and style is as revealing as the content. Inflated terms and contorted sentences delivered in the vampire's sardonic tones expose the folly of the "wise fools." In the course of answering the vampire's response, undoubtedly Vikram is led to consider his own folly.

The Baital resumed.

Of all the learned Brahmans in the learnedest university of Gaur (Bengal) none was so celebrated as Vishnu Swami. He could write verse as well as prose in dead languages, not very correctly, but still, better than all his fellows—which constituted him a distinguished writer. He had history, theosophy, and the four Vedas of Scriptures at his fingers' ends, he was skilled in the argute science of Nyasa or Disputation, his mind was a mine of Pauranic or cosmogonico-traditional lore, handed down from the ancient fathers to the modern fathers: and he had written bulky commentaries, exhausting all that tongue of man has to say, upon the obscure text of some old philosopher whose works upon ethics, poetry, and rhetoric were supposed by the sages of Gaur to contain the germs of everything knowable. His fame went over all the country; yea, from country to country. He was a sea of excellent qualities, the father and mother of Brahmans, cows, and women, and the horror of loose persons, cutthroats, courtiers, and courtesans. As a benefactor he was equal to Karna, most liberal of heroes. In regard to truth he was equal to the veracious king Yudhishtira.

True, he was sometimes at a loss to spell a common word in his mother tongue, and whilst he knew to a fingerbreadth how many palms and paces the sun, the moon, and all the stars are distant from the earth, he would have been puzzled to tell you where the region called Yavana lies. Whilst he could enumerate, in strict chronological succession, every important event that happened five or six million years before he was born, he was profoundly ignorant of those that occurred in his own day. And once he asked a friend seriously, if a cat let loose in the jungle would not in time become a tiger.

Yet did all the members of alma mater Kasi, Pandits as well as students, look with awe upon Vishnu Swami's livid cheeks, and lack-luster eyes, grimed hands and soiled cottons.

Now it so happened that this wise and pious Brahmanic peer had four sons, whom he brought up in the strictest and most serious way. They were taught to repeat their prayers long before they understood a word of them, and when they reached the age of four they had read a variety of hymns and spiritual songs. Then they were set to learn by heart precepts that inculcate sacred duties, and arguments relating to theology, abstract and concrete.

Their father, who was also their tutor, sedulously cultivated, as all the best works upon education advise, their implicit obedience, humble respect, warm attachment, and the virtues and sentiments generally. He praised them secretly and reprehended them openly, to exercise their humility. He derided their looks, and dressed them coarsely, to preserve them from vanity and conceit. Whenever they anticipated a "treat," he punctually disappointed them, to teach them self-denial. Often when he had promised them a present, he would revoke, not break his word, in order that discipline might have a name and habitat in his household. And knowing by experience how much stronger than love is fear, he frequently threatened, browbeat, and overawed them with the rod and the tongue, with the terrors of this world, and with the horrors of the next, that they might be kept in the right way by dread of falling into the bottomless pits that bound it on both sides.

At the age of six they were transferred to the Chatushpati or school. Every morning the teacher and his pupils assembled in the hut where the different classes were called up by turns. They labored till noon, and were allowed only two hours, a moiety of the usual time, for bathing, eating, sleep, and worship, which took up half the period. At 3 P.M. they resumed their labors, repeating to the tutor what they had learned by heart, and listening to the meaning of it: this lasted till twilight. They then worshipped, ate and drank for an hour: after which came a return of study, repeating the day's lessons, till 10 P.M.

In their rare days of ease—for the learned priest, mindful of the words of the wise, did not wish to dull them by everlasting work—they were enjoined to disport themselves with the gravity and the decorum that befit young Samditats, not to engage in night frolics, not to use free jests or light expressions, not to draw pictures on the walls, not to eat honey, flesh, and sweet substances turned acid, not to talk to little girls at the well-side, on no account to wear sandals, carry an umbrella, or handle a die even for love, and by no means to steal their neighbors' mangoes.

As they advanced in years their attention during work time was unremittingly directed to the Vedas. Worldly studies were almost excluded, or to speak more correctly, whenever worldly studies were brought upon the carpet, they were so evil entreated, that they well nigh lost all form and feature. History became "The Annals of India on Brahminical Principles," opposed to the Buddhistical; geography "The Lands of the Vedas," none other being deemed worthy of notice; and law, "The Institutes of Manu," then almost obsolete, despite their exceeding sanctity.

But Jatu-harini [a trickster goddess] had evidently changed these children before they were born; and Shani [the planet Saturn] must have been in the ninth mansion when they came to light.

Each youth as he attained the mature age of twelve was formally entered at the University of Kasi, where, without loss of time, the first became a gambler, the second a confirmed libertine, the third a thief, and the fourth a high Buddhist, or in other words an utter atheist.

Here King Vikram frowned at his son, a hint that he had better not behave himself as the children of highly moral and religious parents usually do. The young prince understood him, and briefly remarking that such things were common in distinguished Brahman families, asked the Baital what he meant by the word "Atheist."

Of a truth (answered the Vampire) it is most difficult to explain. The sages assign to it three or four several meanings: first, one who denies that the gods exist secondly, one who owns that the gods exist but denies that they busy themselves with human affairs; and thirdly, one who believes in the gods and in their providence, but also believes that they are easily to be set aside. Similarly some atheists derive all things from dead and unintelligent matter; others from matter living and energetic but without sense or will: others from matter with forms and qualities generable and conceptible; and others from a plastic and methodical nature. Thus the Vishnu Swamis of the world have invested the subject with some confusion. The simple, that is to say, the mass of mortality, have confounded that confusion by reproachfully applying the word atheist to those whose opinions differ materially from their own.

But I being at present, perhaps happily for myself, a Vampire, and having, just now, none of these human or inhuman ideas, meant simply to say that the pious priest's fourth son being great at second and small in the matter of first causes, adopted to their fullest extent the doctrines of the philosophical Buddhas. Nothing according to him exists but the five elements, earth, water, fire, air (or wind), and vacuum, and from the last proceeded the penultimate, and so forth. With the sage Patanjali, he held the universe to have the power of perpetual progression. He called that Matra (matter), which is an eternal and infinite principle, beginningless and endless. Organization, intelligence, and design, he opined, are inherent in matter as growth is in a tree. He did not believe in soul or spirit, because it could not be detected in the body, and because it was a departure from physiological analogy. The idea "I am," according to him, was not the identification of spirit with matter, but a product of the mutation of matter in this cloud-like, error-formed world. He believed in Substance (Sat) and scoffed at Unsubstance (Asat). He asserted the subtlety and globularity of atoms which are uncreated. He made mind and intellect a mere secretion of the brain, or rather words expressing not a thing, but a state of things. Reason was to him developed instinct, and life an element of the atmosphere affecting certain organisms. He held good and evil to be merely geographical and chronological expressions, and he opined that what is called Evil is mostly an active and transitive form of Good. Law was his great Creator of all things, but he refused a creator of law, because such a creator would require another creator, and so on in a quasi-interminable series up to absurdity. This reduced his law to a manner of haphazard. To those who, arguing against it, asked him their favorite question, How often might a man after he had jumbled a set of letters in a bag fling them out upon the ground before they would fall into an exact poem? he replied that the calculation was beyond his arithmetic, but that the man had only to jumble and fling long enough inevitably to arrive at that end. He rejected the necessity as well as the existence of revelation, and he did not credit the miracles of Krishna, because, according to him, nature never suspends her laws, and, moreover, he had never seen aught supernatural. He ridiculed the idea of Mahapralaya, or the great destruction, for as the world had no beginning, so it will have no end. He objected to absorption, facetiously observing with the sage

Jamadagni, that it was pleasant to eat sweetmeats, but that for his part he did not wish to become the sweetmeat itself. He would not believe that Vishnu had formed the universe out of the wax in his ears. He positively asserted that trees are not bodies in which the consequences of merit and demerit are received. Nor would he conclude that to men were attached rewards and punishments from all eternity. He made light of the Sanskara, or sacrament. He admitted Satwa, Raja, and Tama, but only as properties of matter. He acknowledged gross matter (Sthulasharir), and atomic matter (Shukshma-sharir), but not Linga-sharir, or the archetype of bodies. To doubt all things was the foundation of his theory, and to scoff at all who would not doubt was the cornerstone of his practice. In debate he preferred logical and mathematical grounds, requiring a categorical "because" in answer to his "why?" He was full of morality and natural religion, which some say is no religion at all. He gained the name of atheist by declaring with Gotama that there are innumerable worlds, that the earth has nothing beneath it but the circumambient air, and that the core of the globe is incandescent. And he was called a practical atheist—a worse form apparently—for supporting the following dogma, "that though creation may attest that a creator has been, it supplies no evidence to prove that a creator still exists." On which occasion, Shiromani, a nonplussed theologian, asked him, "By whom and for what purpose west thou sent on earth?" The youth scoffed at the word "sent," and replied, "Not being thy Supreme Intelligence, or Infinite Nihility, I am unable to explain the phenomenon." Upon which he quoted—

How sunk in darkness Gaur must be Whose guide is blind Shiromani!

At length it so happened that the four young men, having frequently been surprised in flagrant delict, were summoned to the dread presence of the university Gurus, who addressed them as follows:

"There are four different characters in the world: he who perfectly obeys the commands; he who practices the commands, but follows evil; he who does neither good nor evil; and he who does nothing but evil. The third character, it is observed, is also an offender, for he neglects that which he ought to observe. But ye all belong to the fourth category." Then turning to the elder they said:

"In works written upon the subject of government it is advised, 'Cut off the gambler's nose and ears, hold up his name to public contempt, and drive him out of the country, that he may thus become an example to others. For they who play must more often lose than win; and losing, they must either pay or not pay. In the latter case they forfeit caste, in the former they utterly reduce themselves. And though a gambler's wife and children are in the house, do not consider them to be so, since it is not known when they will be lost. Thus he is left in a state of perfect not-twoness (solitude), and he will be reborn in hell.' O young man! thou hast set a bad example to others, therefore shalt thou immediately exchange this university for a country life."

Then they spoke to the second offender thus:

"The wise shun woman, who can fascinate a man in the twinkling of an eye; but the foolish, conceiving an affection for her, forfeit in the pursuit of pleasure their truthfulness, reputation, and good disposition, their way of life and mode of thought, their vows and their religion. And to such the advice of their spiritual teachers comes amiss, whilst they make others as bad as themselves. For it is said, 'He who has lost all sense of shame, fears not to disgrace another; 'and there is the proverb, 'A wild cat that devours its own young is not likely to let a rat escape; ' therefore must thou too, O young man! Quit this seat of learning with all possible expedition."

The young man proceeded to justify himself by quotations from the Lila-shastra, his text-book, by citing such lines as—

"Fortune favors folly and force, and by advising the elderly professors to improve their skill in the peace and war of love."

But they drove him out with execrations.

As sagely and as solemnly did the Pandits and the Gurus reprove the thief and the atheist, but they did not dispense the words of wisdom in equal proportions. They warned the former that petty larceny is punishable with fine, theft on a larger scale with mutilation of the hand, and robbery, when detected in the act, with loss of life; that for cutting purses, or for snatching them out of a man's waistcloth 'the first penalty is chopping off the fingers, the second is the loss of the hand, and the third is death. Then they call him a dishonor to the college, and they said, "Thou art as a woman, the greatest of plunderers; other robbers purloin property which is worthless, thou stealest the best; they plunder in the night, thou in the day," and so forth. They told him that he was a fellow who had read his Chauriya Vidya to more purpose then his ritual. And they drove him from the door as he in his shamelessness began to quote texts about the four approved ways of housebreaking, namely, picking out burnt bricks, cutting through unbaked bricks, throwing water on a mud wall, and boring one of wood with a center-bit.

But they spent six mortal hours in convicting the atheist, whose abominations they refuted by every possible argumentation: by inference, by comparison, and by sounds, by Sruti and Smriti, that is, revelational and traditional, rational and evidential, physical and metaphysical, analytical and synthetical, philosophical and philological, historical, and so forth. But they found all their endeavors vain. "For," it is said, "a man who has lost all shame, who can talk without sense, and who tries to cheat his opponent, will never get tired, and will never be put down." He declared that a non-ad was far more probable than a monad (the active principle), or the duad (the passive principle or matter.) He compared their faith with a bubble in the water, of which we can never predicate that it does exist or it does not. It is, he said, unreal, as when the thirsty mistakes the meadow mist for a pool of water. He proved the eternity of sound. He impudently recounted and justified all the villanies of the Vamachari or left-handed sects. He told them that they had taken up an ass's load of religion, and had better apply to honest industry. He fell foul of the gods; accused Yama of kicking his own mother, Indra of tempting the wife of his spiritual guide, and Shiva of associating with low women. Thus, he said, no one can respect them. Do not we say when it thunders awfully, "the rascally gods are dying!" And when it is too wet, "these villain gods are sending too much rain"? Briefly, the young Brahman replied to and harangued them all so impertinently, if not pertinently, that they, waxing angry, fell upon him with their staves, and drove him out of assembly.

Then the four thriftless youths returned home to their father, who in his just indignation had urged their disgrace upon the Pandits and Gurus, otherwise these dignitaries would never have resorted to such extreme measures with so distinguished a house. He took the opportunity of turning them out upon the world, until such time as they might be able to show substantial signs of reform. "For," he said, "those who have read science in their boyhood, and who in youth, agitated by evil passions, have remained in the insolence of ignorance, feel regret in their old age, and are consumed by the fire of avarice." In order to supply them with a motive for the task proposed, he stopped their monthly allowance But he added, if they would repair to the neighboring university of Jayasthal, and there show themselves something better than a disgrace to their family, he would direct their maternal uncle to supply them with all the necessaries of food and raiment.

In vain the youths attempted, with sighs and tears and threats of suicide, to soften the paternal heart. He was inexorable, for two reasons. In the first place, after wondering away the wonder with which he regarded his own failure, he felt that a stigma now attached to the name of the pious and learned Vishnu Swami, whose lectures upon "Management during Teens," and whose "Brahman Young Man's Own Book," had become standard works. Secondly, from a sense of duty, he determined to omit nothing that might tend to reclaim the reprobates. As regards the monthly allowance being stopped, the reverend man had become every year a little fonder of his purse; he had hoped that his sons would have qualified themselves to take pupils, and thus achieve for themselves, as he phrased it, "A genteel independence"; whilst they openly derided the career, calling it "an admirable provision for the more indigent members of the middle classes." For which reason he referred them to their maternal uncle, a man of known and remarkable penuriousness.

The four ne'er-do-wells, foreseeing what awaited them at Jayasthal, deferred it as a last resource; determining first to see a little life, and to push their way in the world, before condemning themselves to the tribulations of reform.

They tried to live without a monthly allowance, and notably they failed; it was squeezing, as men say, oil from sand. The gambler, having no capital, and, worse still, no credit, lost two or three suvernas at play, and could not pay them; in consequence of which he was soundly beaten with iron-shod staves, and was nearly compelled by the keeper of the hell to sell himself into slavery. Thus he became disgusted; and telling his brethren that they would find him at Jayasthal, he departed, with the intention of studying wisdom.

A month afterwards came the libertine's turn to be disappointed. He could no longer afford fine new clothes; even a well-washed coat was beyond his means. He had reckoned upon his handsome face, and he had matured a plan for laying various elderly conquests under contribution. Judge, therefore, his disgust when all the women—high and low, rich and poor, old and young, ugly and beautiful—seeing the end of his waistcloth thrown empty over his shoulder, passed him in the streets without even deigning a look. The very shopkeepers' wives, who once had adored his mustachio and had never ceased talking of his "elegant" gait, despised him; and the wealthy old person who formerly supplied his small feet with the choicest slippers, left him to starve. Upon which he also in a state of repentance, followed his brother to acquire knowledge.

"Am I not," quoth the thief to himself, "a cat in climbing, a deer in running, a snake in twisting, a hawk in pouncing, a dog in scenting?—keen as a hare, tenacious as a wolf, strong as a lion?—a lamp in the night, a horse on a plain, a mule on a stony path, a boat in the water, a rock on land?" The reply to his own questions was of course affirmative. But despite all these fine qualities, and notwithstanding his scrupulous strictness in invoking the house-breaking tool and in devoting a due portion of his gains to the gods of plunder, he was caught in a store-room by the proprietor, who inexorably handed him over to justice. As he belonged to the priestly caste, the fine imposed upon him was heavy. He could not pay it, and therefore he was thrown into a dungeon, where he remained for some time. But at last he escaped from jail, when he made his parting bow to Kartikeya, stole a blanket from one of the guards, and set out for Jayasthal, cursing his old profession.

The atheist also found himself in a position that deprived him of all his pleasures. He delighted in after dinner controversies, and in bringing the light troops of his wit to bear upon the unwieldy masses of lore and logic opposed to him by polemical Brahmans who, out of respect for his father, did not lay an action against him for overpowering them in theological disputation. In the strange city to which he had removed no one knew the son of Vishnu Swami, and no one cared to invite him to the house. Once he attempted his usual trick upon a knot of sages who, sitting round a tank, were recreating themselves with quoting mystical Sanskrit shlokas of abominable long-windedness. The result was his being obliged to ply his heels vigorously in flight from the justly incensed literati, to whom he had said "tush" and "pish," at least a dozen times in as many minutes. He therefore also followed the example of his brethren, and started for Jayasthal with all possible expedition.

Arrived at the house of their maternal uncle, the young men, as by one assent, began to attempt the unloosening of his purse-strings. Signally failing in this and in other notable schemes, they determined to lay in that stock of facts and useful knowledge which might reconcile them with their father, and restore them to that happy life at Gaur which they then despised, and which now brought tears into their eyes.

Then they debated with one another what they should study

That branch of the preternatural, popularly called "white magic," found with them favor.

They chose a Guru or teacher strictly according to the orders of their faith, a wise man of honorable family and affable demeanor, who was not a glutton nor leprous, nor blind of one eye, nor blind of both eyes, nor very short, nor suffering from whitlows, asthma, or other disease, nor noisy and talkative, nor with any defect about the fingers and toes, nor subject to his wife.

A grand discovery had been lately made by a certain physiologico-philosophico-psychologico-materialist, a Jayasthalian. In investigating the vestiges of creation, the cause of causes, the effect of effects, and the original origin of that Matra (matter) which some regard as an entity, others as a non-entity, others self-existent, others merely specious and therefore unexistent, he became convinced that the fundamental form of organic being is a globule having another globule within itself. After inhabiting a garret and diving into the depths of his self-consciousness for a few score years, he was able to produce such complex globule in triturated and roasted flint by means of—I will not say what. Happily for creation in general, the discovery died a natural death some centuries ago. An edifying spectacle, indeed, for the world to see; a cross old man sitting amongst his gallipots and crucibles, creating animalculae, providing the corpses of birds, beasts, and fishes with what is vulgarly called life, and supplying to epigenesis all the latest improvements!

In those days the invention, being a novelty, engrossed the thoughts of the universal learned, who were in a fever of excitement about it. Some believed in it so implicitly that they saw in every experiment a hundred things which they did not see. Others were so skeptical and contradictory that they would not perceive what they did see. Those blended with each fact their own deductions, whilst these span round every reality the web of their own prejudices. Curious to say, the Jayasthalians, amongst whom the luminous science arose, hailed it with delight, whilst the Gaurians derided its claim to be considered an important addition to human knowledge.

Let me try to remember a few of their words.

"Unfortunate human nature," wrote the wise of Gaur against the wise of Jayasthal, "wanted no crowning indignity but this! You had already proved that the body is made of the basest element—earth. You had argued away the immovability, the ubiquity, the permanency, the eternity, and the divinity of the soul, for is not your favorite axiom, It is the nature of limbs which thinketh in man'? The immortal mind is, according to you, an ignoble viscous; the god-like gift of reason is the instinct of a dog somewhat highly developed. Still you left us something to hope. Still you allowed us one boast. Still life was a thread connecting us with the Giver of Life. But now, with an impious hand, in blasphemous rage ye have rent asunder that last frail tie." And so forth.

229

"Welcome! Thrice welcome! This latest and most admirable development of human wisdom," wrote the sage Jayasthalians against the sage Gaurians, "which has assigned to man his proper state and status and station in the magnificent scale of being. We have not created the facts which we have investigated, and which we now proudly publish. We have proved materialism to be nature's own system. But our philosophy of matter cannot overturn any truth, because, if erroneous, it will necessarily sink into oblivion; if real, it will tend only to instruct and to enlighten the world. Wise are ye in your generation, O ye sages of Gaur, yet withal wondrous illogical." And much of this kind.

Concerning all which, mighty king! I, as a Vampire, have only to remark that those two learned bodies, like your Rajaship's Nine Gems of Science, were in the habit of talking most about what they least understood.

The four young men applied the whole force of their talents to mastering the difficulties of the life-giving process; and in due time, their industry obtained its reward.

Then they determined to return home. As with beating hearts they approached the old city, their birthplace, and gazed with moistened eyes upon its tall spires and grim pagodas, its verdant meads and venerable groves, they saw a Kanjar, who, having tied up in a bundle the skin and bones of a tiger which he had found dead, was about to go on his way. Then said the thief to the gambler, "Take we these remains with us, and by means of them prove the truth of our science before the people of Gaur, to the offense of their noses." Being now possessed of knowledge, they resolved to apply it to its proper purpose, namely, power over the property of others. Accordingly, the wencher, the gambler, and the atheist kept the Kanjar in conversation whilst the thief vivified a shank bone; and the bone thereupon stood upright, and hopped about in so grotesque and wonderful a way that the man, being frightened, fled as if I had been close behind him.

Vishnu Swami had lately written a very learned commentary on the mystical words of Lokakshi:

"The Scriptures are at variance—the tradition is at variance. He who gives a meaning of his own, quoting the Vedas, is no philosopher.

"True philosophy, through ignorance, is concealed as in the fissures of a rock.

"But the way of the Great One—that is to be followed."

And the success of his book had quite effaced from the Brahman mind the holy man's failure in bringing up his children. He followed up this by adding to his essay on education a twentieth tome, containing recipes for the "Reformation of Prodigals."

The learned and reverend father received his sons with open arms. He had heard from his brother-in-law that the youths were qualified to support themselves, and when informed that they wished to make a public experiment of their science, he exerted himself, despite his disbelief in it, to forward their views.

The Pandits and Gurus were long before they would consent to attend what they considered dealings with Yama (the Devil). In consequence, however, of Vishnu Swami's name and importunity, at length, on a certain day, all the pious, learned, and reverend tutors, teachers, professors, prolocutors, pastors, spiritual fathers, poets, philosophers, mathematicians, schoolmasters, pedagogues, bear-leaders, institutors, gerund-grinders, preceptors, dominies, brushers, coryphaei, dry-nurses, coaches, mentors, monitors, lecturers, prelectors, fellows, and heads of houses at the university at Gaur, met together in a large garden, where they usually diverted themselves out of hours with ball-tossing, pigeon-tumbling, and kite-flying.

Presently the four young men, carrying their bundle of bones and the other requisites, stepped forward, walking slowly with eyes downcast, like shrinking cattle: for it is said, the Brahman must not run, even when it rains.

After pronouncing an impromptu speech, composed for them by their father, and so stuffed with erudition that even the writer hardly understood it, they announced their wish to prove, by ocular demonstration, the truth of a science upon which their short-sighted rivals of Jayasthal had cast cold water, but which, they remarked in the eloquent peroration of their discourse, the sages of Gaur had welcomed with that wise and catholic spirit of inquiry which had ever characterized their distinguished body.

Huge words, involved sentences, and the high-flown compliment, exceedingly undeserved, obscured, I suppose, the bright wits of the intellectual convocation, which really began to think that their liberality of opinion deserved all praise.

None objected to what was being prepared, except one of the heads of houses; his appeal was generally scouted, because his Sanskrit style was vulgarly intelligible, and he had the bad name of being a practical man. The metaphysician Rashik Lall sneered to Vaiswata the poet, who passed on the look to the theo-philosopher Vardhaman. Haridatt the antiquarian whispered the metaphysician Vasudeva, who burst into a loud laugh; whilst Narayan, Jagasharma, and Devaswami, all very learned in the Vedas, opened their eyes and stared at him with well-simulated astonishment. So he, being offended, said nothing more, but arose and walked home.

A great crowd gathered round the four young men and their father, as opening the bundle that contained the tiger's remains, they prepared for their task.

One of the operators spread the bones upon the ground and fixed each one into its proper socket, not forgetting even the teeth and tusks.

The second connected, by means of a marvelous unguent, the skeleton with the muscles and heart of an elephant, which he had procured for the purpose.

The third drew from his pouch the brain and eyes of a large tom-cat, which he carefully fitted into the animal's skull, and then covered the body with the hide of a young rhinoceros.

Then the fourth—the atheist—who had been directing the operation, produced a globule having another globule within itself. And as the crowd pressed on them, craning their necks, breathless with anxiety, he placed the Principle of Organic Life in the tiger's body with such effect that the monster immediately heaved its chest, breathed, agitated its limbs, opened its eyes, jumped to its feet, shook itself, glared around, and began to gnash its teeth and lick its chops, lashing the while its ribs with its tail.

The sages sprang back, and the beast sprang forward. With a roar like thunder during Elephanta-time, it flew at the nearest of the spectators, flung Vishnu Swami to the ground and clawed his four sons. Then, not even stopping to drink their blood, it hurried after the flying herd of wise men. Jostling and tumbling, stumbling and catching at one another's long robes, they rushed in hottest haste towards the garden gate. But the beast, having the muscles of an elephant as well as the bones of a tiger, made a few bounds of eighty or ninety feet each, easily distanced them, and took away all chance of escape. To be brief: as the monster was frightfully hungry after its long fast, and as the imprudent young men had furnished it with admirable implements of destruction, it did not cease its work till one hundred and twenty-one learned and highly distinguished Pandits and Gurus lay upon the ground chewed, clawed, sucked dry, and in most cases stone-dead. Amongst them, I need hardly say, were the sage Vishnu Swami and his four sons.

Having told this story the Vampire hung silent for a time. Presently he resumed—

"Now, heed my words, Raja Vikram! I am about to ask thee, Which of all those learned men was the most finished fool? The answer is easily found, yet it must be distasteful to thee. Therefore mortify thy vanity, as soon as possible, or I shall be talking, and thou wilt be walking through this livelong night, to scanty purpose. Remember! Science without understanding is of little use; indeed, understanding is superior to science, and those devoid of understanding perish as did the persons who revivified the tiger. Before this, I warned thee to beware of thyself, and of shine own conceit. Here, then, is an opportunity for self-discipline—which of all those learned men was the greatest fool?"

The warrior king mistook the kind of mortification imposed upon him, and pondered over the uncomfortable nature of the reply—in the presence of his son.

Again the Baital taunted him.

"The greatest fool of all," at last said Vikram, in slow and by no means willing accents, "was the father. Is it not said, 'There is no fool like an old fool'?"

"Gramercy!" cried the Vampire, bursting out into a discordant laugh, "I now return to my tree. By this head! I never before heard a father so readily condemn a father." With these words he disappeared, slipping out of the bundle.

The Raja scolded his son a little for want of obedience, and said that he had always thought more highly of his acuteness—never could have believed that he would have been taken in by so shallow a trick. Dharma Dhwaj answered not a word to this, but promised to be wiser another time.

Then they returned to the tree, and did what they had so often done before.

And, as before, the Baital held his tongue for a time. Presently he began as follows.

THE VAMPIRE PUZZLES RAJA VIKRAM

Tradition Bearer: Bhavabhuti

Source: Burton, Richard. "The Vampire's Eleventh Story Which Puzzles Raja Vikram." *Vikram and the Vampire*, ed. Elizabeth Burton. London: Tylston and Edwards, 1893, 221–243.

Date: Unavailable

Original Source: India

National Origin: India

Compare the final tale and conclusion of *Vikram and the Vampire* to the conclusion of *Twenty-Two Goblins* (page 191). The two narratives are **variants** of the same core tale plot.

There is a queer time coming, O Raja Vikram!—a queer time coming (said the Vampire), a queer time coming. Elderly people like you talk abundantly about the good old days that were, and about the degeneracy of the days that are. I wonder what you would say if you could but look forward a few hundred years.

Brahmans shall disgrace themselves by becoming soldiers and being killed, and Serviles (Shudras) shall dishonor themselves by wearing the thread of the twice-born, and by refusing to be slaves; in fact, society shall be all "mouth" and mixed castes. The courts of justice shall be disused; the great works of peace shall no longer be undertaken; wars shall last six weeks, and their causes shall be clean forgotten; the useful arts and great sciences shall die starved; there shall be no Gems of Science; there shall be a hospital for destitute kings, those, at least, who do not lose their heads, and no Vikrama—

A severe shaking [of the bag by Vikram] stayed for a moment the Vampire's tongue.

He presently resumed. Briefly, building tanks feeding Brahmans; lying when one ought to lie; suicide, the burning of widows, and the burying of live children, shall become utterly unfashionable.

The consequence of this singular degeneracy, O mighty Vikram, will be that strangers shall dwell beneath the roof tree in Bharat Khanda (India), and impure barbarians shall call the land their own. They come from a wonderful country, and I am most surprised that they bear it. The sky which ought to be gold and blue is there grey, a kind of dark white; the sun looks deadly pale, and the moon as if he were dead. The sea, when not dirty green, glistens with yellowish foam, and as you approach the shore, tall ghastly cliffs, like the skeletons of giants, stand up to receive or ready to repel. During the greater part of the sun's Dakhshanayan (southern declination) the country is covered with a sort of cold white stuff which dazzles the eyes; and at such times the air is obscured with what appears to be a shower of white feathers or flocks of cotton. At other seasons there is a pale glare produced by the mist clouds which spread themselves over the lower firmament. Even the faces of the people are white; the men are white when not painted blue; the women are whiter, and the children are whitest: these indeed often have white hair.

"Truly," exclaimed Dharma Dhwaj, "says the proverb, 'Whoso seeth the world telleth many a lie'."

At present (resumed the Vampire, not heeding the interruption), they run about naked in the woods, being merely Hindu outcastes. Presently they will change—the wonderful white Pariahs! They will eat all food indifferently, domestic fowls, onions, hogs fed in the street, donkeys, horses, hares, and (most horrible!) the flesh of the sacred cow. They will imbibe what resembles meat of colocynth, mixed with water, producing a curious frothy liquid, and a fiery stuff which burns the mouth, for their milk will be mostly chalk and pulp of brains; they will ignore the sweet juices of fruits and sugar-cane, and as for the pure element they will drink it, but only as medicine, They will shave their beards instead of their heads, and stand upright when they should sit down, and squat upon a wooden frame instead of a carpet, and appear in red and black like the children of Yama. They will never offer sacrifices to the manes of ancestors, leaving them after their death to fry in the hottest of places. Yet will they perpetually quarrel and fight about their faith; for their tempers are fierce, and they would burst if they could not harm one another. Even now the children, who amuse themselves with making puddings on the shore, that is to say, heaping up the sand, always end their little games with "punching," which means shutting the hand and striking one another's heads, and it is soon found that the children are the fathers of the men.

These wonderful white outcastes will often be ruled by female chiefs, and it is likely that the habit of prostrating themselves before a woman who has not the power of cutting off a single head, may account for their unusual degeneracy and uncleanness. They will consider no occupation so noble as running after a jackal; they will dance for themselves, holding on to strange women, and they will take a pride in playing upon instruments, like young music girls.

The women, of course, relying upon the aid of the female chieftains, will soon emancipate themselves from the rules of modesty. They will eat with their husbands and with other men, and yawn and sit carelessly before them showing the backs of their heads. They will impudently quote the words, "By confinement at home, even under affectionate and observant guardians, women are not secure, but those are really safe who are guarded by their own inclinations"; as the poet sang—

"Woman obeys one only word, her heart."

They will not allow their husbands to have more than one wife, and even the single wife will not be his slave when he needs her services, busying herself in the collection of wealth, in ceremonial purification, and feminine duty; in the preparation of daily food and in the superintendence of household utensils. What said Rama of Sita his wife? "If I chanced to be angry, she bore my impatience like the patient earth without a murmur; in the hour of necessity she cherished me as a mother does her child; in the moments of repose she was a lover to me; in times of gladness she was to me as a friend." And it is said, "A religious wife assists her husband in his worship with a spirit as devout as his own. She gives her whole mind to make him happy; she is as faithful to him as a shadow to the body, and she esteems him, whether poor or rich, good or bad, handsome or deformed. In his absence or his sickness she renounces every gratification; at his death she dies with him, and he enjoys heaven as the fruit of her virtuous deeds. Whereas if she be guilty of many wicked actions and he should die first, he must suffer much for the demerits of his wife."

But these women will talk aloud, and scold as the braying ass, and make the house a scene of variance, like the snake with the ichneumon, the owl with the crow, for they have no fear of losing their noses or parting with their ears. They will (O my mother!) converse with strange men and take their hands; they will receive presents from them, and, worst of all, they will show their white faces openly without the least sense of shame; they will ride publicly in chariots and mount horses, whose points they pride themselves upon knowing, and eat and drink in crowded places—their husbands looking on the while, and perhaps even leading them through the streets. And she will be deemed the pinnacle of the pagoda of perfection, that most excels in wit and shamelessness, and who can turn to water the livers of most men. They will dance and sing instead of minding their children, and when these grow up they will send them out of the house to shift for themselves, and care little if they never see them again. But the greatest sin of all will be this: when widowed they will ever be on the lookout for a second husband, and instances will be known of women fearlessly marrying three, four, and five times. You would think that all this license satisfies them. But no! The more they have the more their weak minds covet. The men have admitted them to an equality, they will aim at an absolute superiority, and claim respect and homage; they will eternally raise tempests about their rights, and if anyone should venture to chastise them as they deserve, they would call him a coward and run off to the judge.

The men will, I say, be as wonderful about their women as about all other matters. The sage of Bharat Khanda guards the frail sex strictly, knowing its frailty, and avoids teaching it to read and write, which it will assuredly use for a bad purpose. For women are ever subject to the god with the sugar-cane bow and string of bees, and arrows tipped with heating blossoms, and to him they will ever surrender man, dhan, tan—mind, wealth, and body. When, by exceeding cunning, all human precautions have been made vain, the wise man bows to Fate, and he forgets, or he tries to forget, the past. Whereas this race of white Pariahs will purposely lead their women into every kind of temptation, and, when an accident occurs, they will rage at and accuse them, killing ten thousand with a word, and cause an uproar, and talk scandal and be scandalized, and go before the magistrate, and make all the evil as public as possible. One would think they had in every way done their duty to their women!

And when all this change shall have come over them, they will feel restless and take flight, and fall like locusts upon the Aryavartta (land of India). Starving in their own country, they will find enough to eat here, and to carry away also. They will be mischievous as the saw with which ornament-makers trim their shells, and cut ascending as well as descending. To cultivate their friendship will be like making a gap in the water, and their partisans will ever fare worse than their foes. They will be selfish as crows, which, though they eat every kind of flesh, will not permit other birds to devour that of the crow.

In the beginning they will hire a shop near the mouth of mother Ganges, and they will sell lead and bullion, fine and coarse woolen cloths, and all the materials for intoxication. Then they will begin to send for soldiers beyond the sea, and to enlist warriors in Zambudwipa (India). They will from shopkeepers become soldiers: they will beat and be beaten; they will win and lose; but the power of their star and the enchantments of their Queen Kompani, a daina or witch who can draw the blood out of a man and slay him with a look, will turn everything to their good. Presently the noise of their armies shall be as the roaring of the sea; the dazzling of their arms shall blind the eyes like lightning; their battle-fields shall be as the dissolution of the world; and the slaughter-ground shall resemble a garden of plantain trees after a storm. At length they shall spread like the march of a host of ants over the land They will swear, "Dehar Ganga!" and they hate nothing so much as being compelled to destroy an army, to take and loot a city, or to add a rich slip of territory to their rule. And yet they will go on killing and capturing and adding region to region, till the Abode of Snow (Himalaya) confines them to the north, the Sindhu-naddi (Incus) to the west, and elsewhere the sea. Even in this, too, they will demean themselves as lords and masters, scarcely allowing poor Samudradevta to rule his own waves.

Raja Vikram was in a silent mood, otherwise he would not have allowed such ill-omened discourse to pass uninterrupted. Then the Baital, who in vain had often paused to give the royal carrier a chance of asking him a curious question, continued his recital in a dissonant and dissatisfied tone of voice.

By my feet and your head, O warrior king, it will fare badly in those days for the Rajas of Hindustan, when the red-coated men of Shaka shall come amongst them! Listen to my words.

In the Vindhya Mountain there will be a city named Dharmapur, whose king will be called Mahabul. He will be a mighty warrior, well-skilled in the dhanur-veda (art of war), and will always lead his own armies to the field. He will duly regard all the omens, such as a storm at the beginning of the march, an earthquake, the implements of war dropping from the hands of the soldiery, screaming vultures passing over or walking near the army, the clouds and the sun's rays waxing red, thunder in a clear sky, the moon appearing small as a star, the dropping of blood from the clouds, the falling of lightning bolts, darkness filling the four quarters of the heavens, a corpse or a pan of water being carried to the right of the army, the sight of a female beggar with disheveled hair, dressed in red, and preceding the vanguard, the starting of the flesh over the left ribs of the commander-in-chief, and the weeping or turning back of the horses when urged forward.

He will encourage his men to single combats, and will carefully train them to gymnastics. Many of the wrestlers and boxers will be so strong that they will often beat all the extremities of the antagonist into his body, or break his back, or rend him into two pieces. He will promise heaven to those who shall die in the front of battle and he will have them taught certain dreadful expressions of abuse to be interchanged with the enemy when commencing the contest. Honors will be conferred on those who never turn their backs in an engagement, who manifest a contempt of death, who despise fatigue, as well as the most formidable enemies, who shall be found invincible in every combat, and who display a courage which increases before danger, like the glory of the sun advancing to his meridian splendor.

But King Mahabul will be attacked by the white Pariahs, who, as usual, will employ against him gold, fire, and steel. With gold they will win over his best men, and persuade them openly to desert when the army is drawn out for battle. They will use the terrible "fire weapon," large and small tubes, which discharge flame and smoke, and bullets as big as those hurled by the bow of Bharata. And instead of using swords and shields, they will fix daggers to the end of their tubes, and thrust with them like lances.

Mahabul, distinguished by valor and military skill, will march out of his city to meet the white foe. In front will be the ensigns, bells, cows'-tails, and flags, the latter painted with the bird Garura, the bull of Shiva, the Bauhinia tree, the monkey-god Hanuman, the lion and the tiger, the fish, an alms-dish, and seven palm trees. Then will come the footmen armed with fire-tubes, swords and shields, spears and daggers, clubs, and bludgeons. They will be followed by fighting men on horses and oxen, on camels and elephants. The musicians, the water-carriers, and lastly the stores on carriages, will bring up the rear.

The white outcastes will come forward in a long thin red thread, and vomiting fire like the Jwalamukhi. King Mahabul will receive them with his troops formed in a circle; another division will be in the shape of a halfmoon; a third like a cloud, whilst others shall represent a lion, a tiger, a carriage, a lily, a giant, and a bull. But as the elephants will all turn round when they feel the fire, and trample upon their own men, and as the cavalry defiling in front of the host will openly gallop away; Mahabul, being thus without resource, will enter his palanquin, and accompanied by his queen and their only daughter, will escape at night-time into the forest.

The unfortunate three will be deserted by their small party, and live for a time on jungle food, fruits and roots; they will even be compelled to eat game. After some days they will come in sight of a village, which Mahabul will enter to obtain victuals. There the wild Bhils, famous for long years, will come up, and surrounding the party, will bid the Raja throw down his arms. Thereupon Mahabul, skillful in aiming, twanging and wielding the bow on all sides, so as to keep off the bolts of the enemy, will discharge his bolts so rapidly, that one will drive forward another, and none of the barbarians will be able to approach. But he will have failed to bring his quiver containing an inexhaustible store of arms, some of which, pointed with diamonds, shall have the faculty of returning again to their case after they have done their duty. The conflict will continue three hours, and many of the Bhils will be slain: at length a shaft will cleave the king's skull, he will fall dead, and one of the wild men will come up and cut off his head.

When the queen and the princess shall have seen that Mahabul fell dead, they will return to the forest weeping and beating their bosoms. They will thus escape the Bhils, and after journeying on for four miles, at length they will sit down wearied, and revolve many thoughts in; their minds.

They are very lovely (continued the Vampire), as I see them with the eye of clear-seeing. What beautiful hair! It hangs down like the tail of the cow of Tartary, or like the thatch of a house; it is shining as oil, dark as the clouds, black as blackness itself. What charming faces! likest to water-lilies, with eyes as the stones in unripe mangos, noses resembling the beaks of parrots, teeth like pearls set in corals, ears like those of the redthroated vulture, and mouths like the water of life. What excellent forms! Breasts like boxes containing essences, the unopened fruit of plantains or a couple of crabs; loins the width of a span, like the middle of the viol; legs like the trunk of an elephant, and feet like the yellow lotus.

And a fearful place is that jungle, a dense dark mass of thorny shrubs, and ropy creepers, and tall canes, and tangled brake, and gigantic gnarled trees, which groan wildly in the night wind's embrace. But a wilder horror urges the unhappy women on; they fear the polluting touch of the Bhils; once more they rise and plunge deeper into its gloomy depths.

The day dawns. The white Pariahs have done their usual work. They have cut off the hands of some, the feet and heads of others, whilst many they have crushed into shapeless masses, or scattered in pieces upon the ground. The field is strewed with corpses, the river runs red, so that the dogs and jackals swim in blood; the birds of prey sitting on the branches, drink man's life from the stream, and enjoy the sickening smell of burnt flesh.

Such will be the scenes acted in the fair land of Bharat.

Perchance two white outcastes, father and son, who with a party of men are scouring the forest and slaying everything, fall upon the path which the women have taken shortly before. Their attention is attracted by footprints leading towards a place full of tigers, leopards, bears, wolves, and wild dogs. And they are utterly confounded when, after inspection, they discover the sex of the wanderers.

"How is it," shall say the father, "that the footprints of mortals are seen in this part of the forest?"

The son shall reply, "Sir, these are the marks of women's feet: a man's foot would not be so small."

"It is passing strange," shall rejoin the elder white Pariah, "but thou speakest truth. Certainly such a soft and delicate foot cannot belong to anyone but a woman."

"They have only just left the track," shall continue the son, "and look, this is the step of a married woman. See how she treads on the inside of her sole, because of the bending of her ankles." And the younger white outcaste shall point to the queen's footprints.

"Come, let us search the forest for them," shall cry the father, "what an opportunity of finding wives fortune has thrown in our hands. But no thou art in error," he shall continue, after examining the track pointed out by his son, "in supposing this to be the sign of a matron. Look at the other, it is much longer; the toes have scarcely touched the ground, whereas the marks of the heels are deep. Of a truth this must be the married woman." And the elder white outcaste shall point to the footprints of the princess.

"Then," shall reply the son, who admires the shorter foot, "let us first seek them, and when we find them, give to me her who has the short feet, and take the other to wife thyself."

Having made this agreement they shall proceed on their way, and presently they shall find the women lying on the earth, half dead with fatigue and fear. Their legs and feet are scratched and torn by brambles, their ornaments have fallen off, and their garments are in strips. The two white outcastes find little difficulty, the first surprise over, in persuading the unhappy women to follow them home, and with great delight, conformably to their arrangement, each takes up his prize on his horse and rides back to the tents. The son takes the queen, and the father the princess.

In due time two marriages come to pass; the father, according to agreement, espouses the long foot, and the son takes to wife the short foot. And after the usual interval, the elder white outcaste, who had married the daughter, rejoices at the birth of a boy, and the younger white outcaste, who had married the mother, is gladdened by the sight of a girl.

Now then, by my feet and your head, O warrior king Vikram, answer me one question. What relationship will there be between the children of the two white Pariahs?

Vikram's brow waxed black as a charcoal-burner's, when he again heard the most irreverent oath ever proposed to mortal king. The question presently attracted his attention, and he turned over the Baital's words in his head, confusing the ties of filiality, brotherhood, and relationship, and connection in general.

"Hem!" said the warrior king, at last perplexed, and remembering, in his perplexity, that he had better hold his tongue, "ahem!"

"I think your majesty spoke?" asked the Vampire, in an inquisitive and insinuating tone of voice.

"Hem!" ejaculated the monarch.

The Baital held his peace for a few minutes, coughing once or twice impatiently. He suspected that the extraordinary nature of this last tale, combined with the use of the future tense, had given rise to a taciturnity so unexpected in the warrior king. He therefore asked if Vikram the Brave would not like to hear another little anecdote.

"This time the king did not even say "hem!" Having walked at an unusually rapid pace, he distinguished at a distance the fire kindled by the devotee, and he hurried towards it with an effort which left him no breath wherewith to speak, even had he been so inclined.

"Since your majesty is so completely dumbfounded by it, perhaps this acute young prince may be able to answer my question?" insinuated the Baital, after a few minutes of anxious suspense.

But Dharma Dhwaj answered not a syllable.

At Raja Vikram's silence the Baital was greatly surprised, and he praised the royal courage and resolution to the skies. Still he did not give up the contest at once.

"Allow me, great king," pursued the Demon, in a dry tone of voice, "to wish you joy. After so many failures you have at length succeeded in repressing your loquacity. I will not stop to enquire whether it was humility and self-restraint which prevented your answering my last question, or whether Rajait was mere ignorance and inability. Of course I suspect the latter, but to say the truth your condescension in at last taking a Vampire's advice, flatters me so much, that I will not look too narrowly into cause or motive."

Raja Vikram winced, but maintained a stubborn silence, squeezing his lips lest they should open involuntarily.

"Now, however, your majesty has mortified, we will suppose, a somewhat exacting vanity, I also will in my turn forego the pleasure which I had anticipated in seeing you a corpse and in entering your royal body for a short time, just to know how queer it must feel to be a king. And what is more, I will now perform my original promise, and you shall derive from me a benefit which none but myself can bestow. First, however, allow me to ask you, will you let me have a little more air?"

Dharma Dhwaj pulled his father's sleeve, but this time Raja Vikram required no reminder: wild horses or the executioner's saw, beginning at the shoulder, would not have drawn a word from him. Observing his obstinate silence, the Baital, with an ominous smile, continued:

"Now give ear, O warrior king, to what I am about to tell thee, and bear in mind the giant's saying, 'A man is justified in killing one who has a design to kill him.' The young merchant Mal Deo, who placed such magnificent presents at your royal feet, and Shanta-Shil the devotee saint, who works his spells, incantations, and magical rites in a cemetery on the banks of the Godaveri river, are, as thou knowest, one person—the terrible Jogi, whose wrath your father aroused in his folly, and whose revenge your blood alone can satisfy. With regard to myself, the oilman's son, the same Jogi, fearing lest I might interfere with his projects of universal dominion, slew me by the power of his penance, and has kept me suspended, a trap for you, head downwards from the sires tree.

"That Jogi it was, you now know, who sent you to fetch me back to him on your back. And when you cast me at his feet he will return thanks to you and praise your valor, perseverance and resolution to the skies. I warn you to beware. He will lead you to the shrine of Durga, and when he has finished his adoration he will say to you, 'O great king, salute my deity with the eight-limbed reverence'."

Here the Vampire whispered for a time and in a low tone, lest some listening goblin might carry his words if spoken out loud to the ears of the devotee Shanta-Shil.

At the end of the monologue a rustling sound was heard. It proceeded from the Baital, who was disengaging himself from the dead body in the bundle, and the burden became sensibly lighter upon the monarch's back.

The departing Baital, however, did not forget to bid farewell to the warrior king and to his son. He complimented the former for the last time, in his own way, upon the royal humility and the prodigious self-mortification which he had displayed—qualities, he remarked, which never failed to ensure the proprietor's success in all the worlds.

Raja Vikram stepped out joyfully, and soon reached the burning ground. There he found the Jogi, dressed in his usual habit, a deerskin thrown over his back, and twisted reeds instead of a garment hanging round his loins. The hair had fallen from his limbs and his skin was bleached ghastly white by exposure to the elements. A fire seemed to proceed from his mouth, and the matted locks dropping from his head to the ground were changed by the rays of the sun to the color of gold or saffron. He had the beard of a goat and the ornaments of a king; his shoulders were high and his arms long, reaching to his knees: his nails grew to such a length as to curl round the ends of his fingers, and his feet resembled those of a tiger. He was drumming upon a skull, and incessantly exclaiming, "Ho, Kali! Ho, Durga! Ho, Devi!"

As before, strange beings were holding their carnival in the Jogi's presence. Monstrous Asuras, giant goblins, stood grimly gazing upon the scene with fixed eyes and motionless features. Rakshasas and messengers of Yama, fierce and hideous, assumed at pleasure the shapes of foul and ferocious beasts. Nagas and Bhutas, partly human and partly bestial, disported themselves in throngs about the upper air, and were dimly seen in the faint light of the dawn. Mighty Dai-tyas, Bramba-daityas, and Pretas, the size of a man's thumb, or dried up like leaves, and Pisachas of terrible power guarded the place. There were enormous goats, vivified by the spirits of those who had slain Brahmans; things with the bodies of men and the faces of horses, camels and monkeys; hideous worms containing the souls of those priests who had drunk spirituous liquors; men with one leg and one ear, and mischievous blood-sucking demons, who in life had stolen church property. There were vultures, wretches that had violated the beds of their spiritual fathers, restless ghosts that had loved low-caste women, shades for whom funeral rites had not been performed, and who could not cross the dread Vaitarani stream, and vital souls fresh from the horrors of Tamisra, or utter darkness, and the Usipatra Vana, or the sword-leaved forest. Pale spirits, Alayas, Gumas, Baitals, and Yakshas, beings of a base and vulgar order, glided over the ground, amongst corpses and skeletons animated by female fiends, Dakinis, Yoginis, Hakinis, and Shankinis, which were dancing in frightful revelry. The air was filled with supernatural sights and sounds, cries of owls and jackals, cats and crows, dogs, asses, and vultures, high above which rose the clashing of the bones with which the Jogi sat drumming upon the skull before him, and tending a huge cauldron of oil whose smoke was of blue fire. But as he raised his long lank arm, silver-white with ashes, the demons fled, and a momentary silence succeeded to their uproar. The tigers ceased to roar and the elephants to scream; the bears raised their snouts from their foul banquets, and the wolves dropped from their jaws the remnants of human flesh. And when they disappeared, the hooting of the owl, and ghastly "Ha! Ha!" of the curlew, and the howling of the jackal died away in the far distance, leaving a silence still more oppressive.

As Raja Vikram entered the burning-ground, the hollow sound of solitude alone met his ear. Sadly wailed the wet autumnal blast. The tall gaunt trees groaned aloud, and bowed and trembled like slaves bending before their masters. Huge purple clouds and patches and lines of glaring white mist coursed furiously across the black expanse of firmament, discharging threads and chains and loz-enges and balls of white and blue, purple and pink lightning, followed by the deafening crash and roll of thunder, the dreadful roaring of the mighty wind, and the torrents of plashing rain. At times was heard in the distance the dull gurgling of the swollen river, interrupted by explosions, as slips of earth-bank fell headlong into the stream. But once more the Jogi raised his arm and all was still: nature lay breathless, as if awaiting the effect of his tremendous spells.

The warrior king drew near the terrible man, unstrung his bundle from his back, untwisted the portion which he held, threw open the cloth, and exposed to Shanta-Shil's glittering eyes the corpse, which had now recovered its proper form—that of a young child. Seeing it, the devotee was highly pleased, and thanked Vikram the Brave, extolling his courage and daring above any monarch that had yet lived. After which he repeated certain charms facing towards the south, awakened the dead body, and placed it in a sitting position. He then in its presence sacrificed to his goddess, the White One, all that he had ready by his side—betel leaf and flowers, sandal wood and unbroken rice, fruits, perfumes, and the flesh of man untouched by steel. Lastly, he half filled his skull with burning embers, blew upon them till they shot forth tongues of crimson light, serving as a lamp, and motioning the Raja and his son to follow him, led the way to a little fane of the Destroying Deity erected in a dark clump of wood, outside and close to the burning ground.

They passed through the quadrangular outer court of the temple whose piazza was hung with deep shade. In silence they circumambulated the small central shrine, and whenever Shanta-Shil directed, Raja Vikram entered the Sabha, or vestibule, and struck three times upon the gong, which gave forth a loud and warning sound.

They then passed over the threshold, and looked into the gloomy inner depths. There stood Smashana-Kali, the goddess, in her most horrid form. She was a naked and very black woman, with half-severed head, partly cut and partly painted, resting on her shoulder; and her tongue lolled out from her wide yawning mouth; her eyes were red like those of a drunkard; and her eyebrows were of the same color: her thick coarse hair hung like a mantle to her heels. She was robed in an elephant's hide, dried and withered, confined at the waist with a belt composed of the hands of the giants whom she had slain in war: two dead bodies formed her earrings, and her necklace was of bleached skulls. Her four arms supported a scimitar, a noose, a trident, and a ponderous mace. She stood with one leg on the breast of her husband, Shiva, and she rested the other on his thigh. Before the idol lay the utensils of worship, namely, dishes for the offerings, lamps, jugs, incense, copper cups, conches and gongs; and all of them smelt of blood.

As Raja Vikram and his son stood gazing upon the hideous spectacle, the devotee stooped down to place his skull-lamp upon the ground, and drew from out his ochre-colored cloth a sharp sword which he hid behind his back.

"Prosperity to shine and thy son's for ever and ever, O mighty Vikram!" exclaimed Shanta-Shil, after he had muttered a prayer before the image. "Verily thou hast right royally redeemed thy pledge, and by the virtue of thy presence all my wishes shall presently be accomplished. Behold! The Sun is about to drive his car over the eastern hills, and our task now ends. Do thou reverence before this my deity, worshipping the earth through thy nose, and so prostrating thyself that thy eight limbs may touch the ground. Thus shall thy glory and splendor be great; the Eight Powers and the Nine Treasures shall be thine, and prosperity shall ever remain under thy roof-tree."

Raja Vikram, hearing these words, recalled suddenly to mind all that the Vampire had whispered to him. He brought his joined hands open up to his forehead, caused his two thumbs to touch his brow several times, and replied with the greatest humility,

"O pious person! I am a king ignorant of the way to do such obeisance. Thou art a spiritual preceptor: be pleased to teach me and I will do even as thou desirest."

Then the Jogi, being a cunning man, fell into his own net. As he bent him down to salute the goddess, Vikram, drawing his sword, struck him upon the neck so violent a blow, that his head rolled from his body upon the ground. At the same moment Dharma Dhwaj, seizing his father's arm, pulled him out of the way in time to escape being crushed by the image, which fell with the sound of thunder upon the floor of the temple.

A small thin voice in the upper air was heard to cry, "A man is justified in killing one who has the desire to kill him." Then glad shouts of triumph and victory were heard in all directions. They proceeded from the celestial choristers, the heavenly dancers, the mistresses of the gods, and the nymphs of Indra's Paradise, who left their beds of gold and precious stones, their seats glorious as the meridian sun, their canals of crystal water, their perfumed groves, and their gardens where the wind ever blows in softest breezes, to applaud the valor and good fortune of the warrior king. At last the brilliant god, Indra himself, with the thousand eyes, rising from the shade of the Parigat tree, the fragrance of whose flowers fills the heavens, appeared in his car drawn by yellow steeds and cleaving the thick vapors which surround the earth—whilst his attendants sounded the heavenly drums and rained a shower of blossoms and perfumes— bade the Vikramajit the Brave ask a boon.

The Raja joined his hands and respectfully replied, "O mighty ruler of the lower firmament, let this my history become famous throughout the world!"

"It is well," rejoined the god. "As long as the sun and moon endure, and the sky looks down upon the ground, so long shall this thy adventure be remembered over all the earth. Meanwhile rule thou mankind."

Thus saying, Indra retired to the delicious Amrawati Vikram took up the corpses and threw them into the cauldron which Shanta-Shil had been tending. At once two heroes started into life, and Vikram said to them, "When I call you, come!"

With these mysterious words the king, followed by his son, returned to the palace unmolested. As the Vampire had predicted, everything was prosperous to him, and he presently obtained the remarkable titles, Sakaro, or foe of the Sakas, and Sakadhipati-Vikramaditya.

And when, after a long and happy life spent in bringing the world under the shadow of one umbrella, and in ruling it free from care, the warrior king Vikram entered the gloomy realms of Yama, from whom for mortals there is no escape, he left behind him a name that endured amongst men like the odor of the flower whose memory remains long after its form has mingled with the dust.

EIGHT BROTHERS

Tradition Bearer: Unavailable

Source: Sarma, Bagwhan Das. "A Folktale from Kumaon State." *Folklore* 8 (1897): 181–184.

Date: Unavailable

Original Source: India

National Origin: India

The following tale is a **variant** of "The Rich and the Poor Peasant" (AT 1535). A common European **trickster** tale, the Indian version pits a clever younger brother against seven abusive elder brothers. The major **motifs** of the tale, however, remain close to European versions.

Once in a town lived eight brothers. The youngest of them looked a silly sort of fellow, and his brothers thought him a fool. Their father died, and they divided the patrimony among themselves, and gave the youngest much less than his due. He bought a bull-buffalo, while they bought cow-buffaloes.

Every night he carried the buffalo on his shoulders to his brothers' field and grazed him there. In the morning, when the brothers came to the field, they found the plants eaten. But as there were no marks of an animal's feet in the field they could not detect the poacher. One day the animal drank too much water, and became so heavy that he could not carry it. He left him in the field, and allowed him to graze there at large. The brothers had watered the field that very day, and the soil was so moist that the feet of the buffalo left deep marks in the field. When they went there next morning they saw the plants eaten, and the deep marks of the buffalo's feet.

Straightway they ran to their youngest brother, and showered blows on his poor buffalo till it died. He begged his brothers to leave the carcass of his dear beast for him. He then pulled off the skin and turned it into a hide, and putting it on his shoulders started for a neighboring market-town to sell it. On his way he was caught in the rain, and the hide became dripping wet.

At length he reached a sort of cave, and, feeling tired, put the hide at the mouth of it. Inside the cave were robbers who had come there to divide their booty. The hide was wet, and when he put it at the mouth of the cave it made a noise and darkened the cave. The robbers thought they had been found out, and ran away, leaving the booty to the lucky man. Entering the cave, he found gold and silver and precious stones. At once he put them all into a bundle, and, leaving the hide there, took his way home with his newly-gained riches.

Now he was a rich man, and his brothers were very jealous of him. One day they went to him, and asked him what he had done with the hide. He told them that he had sold it at a very high price to a man who lived in the Brahmans' quarter in a neighboring town. They ran home at once and killed their buffaloes, and, carrying their hides on their shoulders, went to sell them in the Brahmans' quarter their brother had pointed out. Arriving there they called out loudly, "Buffalo-hides for sale!" Great was the surprise of the Brahmans on hearing such words, and coming out of their houses they gave them a sound beating for bringing such unclean things near their houses.

They were very angry with their brother, and hurried back as fast as they could, and going straight to his house set fire to it. The house was soon reduced to ashes, but the brother escaped with his life. He collected the ashes in a bag, and putting the bag on his head made his way to a neighboring town.

He went to the palace of the Raja, and after exchanging greetings with the porter at the gate, said to him, "I have brought jewels and other valuable presents from our Raja to your Raja; please look after the bag, I am going out to wash, and shall come back very soon. But pray, allow no one to touch the bag in my absence, or the valuables will turn into ashes." Having said this, he went away, and after strolling about for some time came back and opened the bag. He had scarcely half-opened it when he began to cry "I am ruined, I am ruined. I told you beforehand that if any body touched it in my absence it would turn into ashes, and so it has happened, Now what shall I do? I have lost thousands of rupees' worth; somebody must repay me."

A crowd soon gathered on the spot, but the man would not listen to any one; and as the crowd increased his cries became more piteous, and with sobs he told the multitude how he had been ruined. At length the affair reached the ears of the Raja, who was very kind-hearted and generous. He ordered the whole amount to be paid to the man. He quickly put the money in the bag, and throwing it on his shoulders hastened home. The brothers heard of his wealth, and came to ask him how he got it.

"I sold the bag of ashes," said he, "to a merchant who deals in flour. He stood in great need of ashes, as he adulterates his flour with ashes, and thus makes a great profit." Hardly had he uttered these words before his brothers ran home and set their houses on fire. They then gathered the ashes, put them in bags, and each one carrying a bag on his shoulders went to the neighboring market. At a grocer's shop they opened the bags and began to pour out the contents into the heaps of flour exposed for sale. When the grocer saw it he was very angry, and cried, "Why, fools! What are you doing?"

"We are mixing ashes with your flour," said they. Whereupon the grocer got up and, rushing upon them, kicked them out of his shop. They were now full of wrath against their brother, and determined to put an end to his life. Hurrying to his house, they caught hold of him and shut him up in a sack. They put the sack on their shoulders and carried it to the Ganges.

When they reached the middle of the stream they threw the sack down into the river. By the man's good luck the sack floated ashore and rested against a bridge by the public way. A banker's son mounted on a good horse was going home with a bag full of jewels and gold and silver coins. When he approached the sack he heard a voice, saying, "Oh! I enjoy the sight of the three worlds."

The banker's son advancing nearer, said, "My friend, can I enjoy the sight too?"

"Yes," said the voice.

"How?" asked the banker's son.

"If you only come here," was the reply The banker's son opened the mouth of the sack and the man came out.

"Go into the sack," said he to the banker's son, and when he had got in he closed up its mouth. He then mounted the horse and galloped home with his treasure. The brothers were amazed to see him, and asked him where he got the horse.

"Our parents," said he, "gave me the horse; they live inside the Ganges. They love you much more than me because you are their elder children, and would give you immense riches if you were to see them."

"How can we see them?" asked they.

"It is very easy," said he. "I will be your guide. Take a dog with you and let him go into the Ganges in front of you; follow the dog to the spot he leads you to and you will see our parents." They all left the house taking their dog with them. When they reached the bridge the youngest brother pointed out to them with his hand the spot where he said he met his parents. First the dog went into the stream and then the seven brothers. The youngest remained on the bank. The dog continued moving his legs all the while he was swimming, and the brothers followed him till they were drowned.

HARISARMAN

Tradition Bearer: Unavailable

Source: Jacobs, Joseph. *Indian Fairy Tales*. London: David Nutt, 1912, 85–89.

Date: ca. 1880

Original Source: India

National Origin: India

The folktale labeled "Dr. Know All" (AT 1641), the story of a sham wise man who is saved from exposure by a lucky accident, enjoys a broad international distribution. For an African American example, see "'Coon in the Box" (Volume 4, page 183).

There was a certain Brahman in a certain village, named Harisarman. He was poor and foolish and in evil case for want of employment, and he had very many children, that he might reap the fruit of his misdeeds in a former life. He wandered about begging with his family, and at last he reached a certain city, and entered the service of a rich householder called Sthuladatta. His sons became keepers of Sthuladatta's cows and other property, and his wife a servant to him, and he himself lived near his house, performing the duty of an attendant.

One day there was a feast on account of the marriage of the daughter of Sthuladatta, largely attended by many friends of the bridegroom, and merry-makers. Harisarman hoped that he would be able to fill himself up to the throat with ghee [clarified butter] and flesh and other dainties, and get the same for his family, in the house of his patron. While he was anxiously expecting to be fed, no one thought of him.

Then he was distressed at getting nothing to eat, and he said to his wife at night, "It is owing to my poverty and stupidity that I am treated with such disrespect here; so I will pretend by means of an artifice to possess a knowledge of magic, so that I may become an object of respect to this Sthuladatta; so, when you get an opportunity, tell him that I possess magical knowledge." He said this to her, and after turning the matter over in his mind, while people were asleep he took away from the house of Sthuladatta a horse on which his master's son-in-law rode. He placed it in concealment at some distance, and in the morning the friends of the bridegroom could not find the horse, though they searched in every direction.

Then, while Sthuladatta was distressed at the evil omen, and searching for the thieves who had carried off the horse, the wife of Harisarman came and said to him, "My husband is a wise man, skilled in astrology and magical sciences. He can get the horse back for you. Why do you not ask him?"

When Sthuladatta heard that, he called Harisarman, who said, "Yesterday I was forgotten, but today, now the horse is stolen, I am called to mind," and Sthuladatta then propitiated the Brahman with these words, "I forgot you, forgive me," and asked him to tell him who had taken away their horse. Then Harisarman drew all kinds of pretended diagrams, and said, "The horse has been placed by thieves on the boundary line south from this place. It is concealed there, and before it is carried off to a distance, as it will be at close of day, go quickly and bring it." When they heard that, many men ran and brought the horse quickly, praising the discernment of Harisarman. Then Harisarman was honored by all men as a sage, and dwelt there in happiness, honored by Sthuladatta.

Now, as days went on, much treasure, both of gold and jewels, had been stolen by a thief from the palace of the king. As the thief was not known, the king quickly summoned Harisarman on account of his reputation for knowledge of magic. And he, when summoned, tried to gain time, and said, "I will tell you tomorrow," and then he was placed in a chamber by the king, and carefully guarded. And he was sad because he had pretended to have knowledge. Now in that palace there was a maid named Jihva (which means tongue), who, with the assistance of her brother, had stolen that treasure from the interior of the palace. She, being alarmed at Harisarman's knowledge, went at night and applied her ear to the door of that chamber in order to find out what he was about. And Harisarman, who was alone inside, was at that very moment blaming his own tongue, that had made a vain assumption of knowledge. He said, "Oh tongue, what is this that you have done through your greediness? Wicked one, you will soon receive punishment in full."

When Jihva heard this, she thought, in her terror, that she had been discovered by this wise man, and she managed to get in where he was, and falling at his feet, she said to the supposed wizard, "Brahman, here I am, that Jihva whom you have discovered to be the thief of the treasure, and after I took it I buried it in the earth in a garden behind the palace, under a pomegranate tree. So spare me, and receive the small quantity of gold which is in my possession."

When Harisarman heard that, he said to her proudly, "Depart, I know all this; I know the past, present and future; but I will not denounce you, being a miserable creature that has implored my protection. But whatever gold is in your possession you must give back to me."

When he said this to the maid, she consented, and departed quickly. But Harisarman reflected in his astonishment, "Fate brings about, as if in sport, things impossible, for when calamity was so near, who would have thought chance would have brought us success? While I was blaming my jihva, the thief Jihva suddenly flung herself at my feet. Secret crimes manifest themselves by means of fear." Thus thinking, he passed the night happily in the chamber. And in the morning he brought the king, by some skillful parade of pretended knowledge into the garden, and led him up to the treasure, which was buried under the pomegranate tree, and said that the thief had escaped with a part of it. Then the king was pleased, and gave him the revenue of many villages.

But the minister, named Devajnanin, whispered in the king's ear, "How can a man possess such knowledge unattainable by men, without having studied the books of magic. You may be certain that this is a specimen of the way he makes a dishonest livelihood, by having a secret intelligence with thieves. It will be much better to test him by some new artifice."

Then the king of his own accord brought a covered pitcher into which he had thrown a frog, and said to Harisarman, "Brahman, if you can guess what there is in this pitcher, I will do you great honor today." When the Brahman Harisarman heard that, he thought that his last hour had come, and he called to mind the pet name of "Froggie" which his father had given him in his childhood in sport, and, impelled by luck, he called to himself by his pet name, lamenting his hard fate, and suddenly called out, "This is a fine pitcher for you, Froggie; it will soon become the swift destroyer of your helpless self."

The people there, when they heard him say that, raised a shout of applause, because his speech chimed in so well with the object presented to him, and murmured, "Ah! A great sage, he knows even about the frog!"

Then the king, thinking that this was all due to knowledge of divination, was highly delighted, and gave Harisarman the revenue of more villages, with gold, an umbrella, and state carriages of all kinds. So Harisarman prospered in the world.

THE KING AND THE FOUR GIRLS

Tradition Bearer: Unavailable

Source: Swynnerton, Charles. *Indian Nights' Entertainment: Folk-Tales from the Upper Indus*. London: Elliot Stock, 1892, 56–62.

Date: ca. 1890

Original Source: India

National Origin: India

The following folktale represents the **formulaic** patterns of traditional narrative: four girls make four answers to the same question. Each is summoned before the king and interrogated in the same manner. The first three respond verbally. The fourth and most successful, however, turns the tables on the king in a variation of the well-known tale "The King's [Emperor's] New Clothes" (AT 1620).

There was once a king who, during the day, used to sit on his throne and dispense justice, but who at night was accustomed to disguise himself and to wander about the streets of his city looking for adventures.

One evening he was passing by a certain garden when he observed four young girls sitting under a tree, and conversing together in earnest tones. Curious to overhear the subject of their discourse, he stopped to listen.

The first said, "I think of all tastes the pleasantest in the world is the taste of meat."

"I do not agree with you," said the second. "There is nothing so good as the taste of wine."

"No, no," cried the third, "you are both mistaken, for of all tastes the sweetest is the taste of love."

"Meat and wine and love are all doubtless sweet," remarked the fourth girl. "But in my opinion nothing can equal the taste of telling lies."

The girls then separated and went to their homes. And the king, who had listened to their remarks with lively interest and with much wonder, took note of the houses into which they went, and, having marked each of the doors with chalk, he returned to his palace.

The next morning he called his vizier, and said to him, "Send to the narrow street, and bring before me the owners of the four houses, the doors of which have a round mark in chalk upon them."

The vizier at once went in person, and brought to the court the four men who lived in the houses to which the king had referred. Then said the king to them, "Have not you four men four daughters?"

"We have," answered they.

"Bring the girls hither before me," said the king.

But the men objected, saying, "It would be very wrong that our daughters should approach the palace of the king."

"Nay," said the king, "if the girls are your daughters, they are mine too, besides which, you can bring them privately."

So the king sent four separate litters, curtained in the usual manner, and the four girls were thus brought to the palace and conducted into a large reception room. Then he summoned them one by one to his presence as he required them.

To the first girl he said, "O daughter, what were you talking about last night when you sat with your companions under the tree?"

"I was not telling tales against you, O king," answered she.

"I do not mean that," said the king. "But I wish to know what you were saying."

"I merely said," replied she, "that the taste of meat was the pleasantest."

"Whose daughter, then, are you?" inquired the king.

"I am the daughter of a Bhábrá," answered she.

"But," said the king, "if you are one of the Bhábrá tribe, who never touch meat, what do you know of the taste of it? So strict are they, that when they drink water they put a cloth over the mouth of the vessel, lest they should swallow even an insect."

Then said the girl, "Yes, that is quite true, but, from my own observation, I think meat must be exceedingly pleasant to the palate. Near our house there is a butcher's shop, and I often notice that when people buy meat, none of it is wasted or thrown away. Therefore it must be precious. I also notice that, when people have eaten the flesh, the very bones are greedily seized upon by the dogs, nor do they leave them until they have picked them as clean as a lance head. And even after that, the crows come and carry them off, and when the crows have done with them, the very ants assemble together and swarm over them. Those are the reasons which prove that the taste of flesh-meat must be exceedingly pleasant."

The king, hearing her argument, was pleased, and said, "Yes, daughter, meat is very pleasant as food. Everyone likes it." And he sent her away with a handsome present.

251

The second girl was then introduced, and of her the king inquired likewise, "What were you talking about last night under the tree?"

"I said nothing about you, O king," answered she.

"That is true, but what did you say?" asked the king.

"What I said," replied she, "was that there was no taste like the taste of wine."

"But whose daughter are you?" continued the king.

"I am," said she, "the daughter of a priest."

"A good joke, forsooth," said the king, smiling. "Priests hate the very name of wine. Then, what do you know of the taste of it?"

Then said the girl, "It is true I never touch wine, but I can easily understand how pleasant it is. I learn my lessons on the top of my father's house. Below are the wine shops. One day I saw two men nicely dressed, who came with their servants to buy wine at those shops, and there they sat and drank. After a time they got up and went away, but they staggered about from side to side, and I thought to myself, 'Here are these fellows rolling about, knocking themselves against the wall on this side, and falling against the wall on that. Surely they will never drink wine again!' However, I was mistaken, for the next day they came again and did the very same thing, and I considered, 'Wine must be very delicious to the taste, or else these persons would never have returned for more of it'."

Then said the king, "Yes, O daughter, you are right. The taste of wine is very pleasant." And, giving her also a handsome present, he sent her home.

When the third girl entered the room, the king asked her in like manner, "O daughter, what were you talking about last night under the tree?"

"O king," answered she, "I made no reference to you."

"Quite so," said the king, "but tell me what it was you were saying."

"I was saying," replied she, "that there is no taste in the world so sweet at the taste of love-making."

"But," said the king, "you are a very young girl. What can you know about love-making? Whose daughter are you?"

"I am the daughter of a bard," answered she. "It is true I am very young, but somehow I guess that love-making must be pleasant. My mother suffered so much when my little brother was born that she never expected to live. Yet, after a little time, she went back to her old ways and welcomed her lovers just the same as before. That is the reason I think that love-making must be so pleasant."

"What you say," observed the king, "cannot, O daughter, be justly denied." And he gave her a present equal in value to those of her friends and sent her, also, away.

When the fourth girl was introduced, the king put the same question to her, "Tell me what you and your companions talked about under the tree last night."

"It was not about the king," answered she.

"Nevertheless," asked he, "what was it you said?"

"Those who tell lies, said I, must tell them because they find the practice agreeable," replied she.

"Whose daughter are you?" inquired the king.

"I am the daughter of a farmer," answered the girl.

"And what made you think there was pleasure in telling lies?" asked the king.

The girl answered saucily, "Oh, you yourself will tell lies someday!"

"How?" said the king. "What can you mean?"

The girl answered, "If you will give me two lacs of rupees, and six months to consider, I will promise to prove my words."

So the king gave the girl the sum of money she asked for, and agreed to her conditions, sending her away with a present similar to those of the others.

After six months he called her to his presence again, and reminded her of her promise. Now, in the interval the girl had built a fine palace far away in the forest, upon which she had expended the wealth which the king had given to her. It was beautifully adorned with carvings and paintings, and furnished with silk and satin. So she now said to the king, "Come with me, and you shall see God."

Taking with him two of his ministers, the king went out, and by the evening they all arrived at the palace.

"This palace is the abode of God," said the girl. "But he will reveal himself only to one person at a time, and he will not reveal himself even to him unless he was born in lawful wedlock. Therefore, while the rest remain without, let each of you enter in order."

"Be it so," said the king. "But let my ministers precede me. I shall go in last."

So the first minister passed through the door and at once found himself in a noble room, and as he looked around he said to himself, "Who knows whether I shall be permitted to see God or not? I may be a bastard. And yet this place, so spacious and so beautiful, is a fitting dwelling place even for the deity." With all his looking and straining, however, he quite failed to see God anywhere. Then said he to himself, "If now I go out and declare that I have not seen God, the king and the other minister will throw it in my teeth that I am base-born. I have only one course open, therefore, which is to say that I have seen him."

So he went out, and when the king asked, "Have you seen God?" he answered at once, "Of course I have seen God."

"But have you really seen him?" continued the king.

"Really and truly," answered the minister.

"And what did he say to you?" inquired the king further.

"God commanded me not to divulge his words," readily answered the minister.

Then said the king to the other minister, "Now you go in."

The second minister lost no time in obeying his master's order, thinking in his heart as he crossed the threshold, "I wonder if I am base-born?" Finding himself in the midst of the magnificent chamber, he gazed about him on all sides, but failed to see God. Then said he to himself, "It is very possible I am base-born, for no God can I see. But it would be a lasting disgrace that I should admit it. I had better make out that I also have seen God."

Accordingly, he returned to the king, who said to him, "Well, have you seen God?" when the minister asserted that he had not only seen him, but that he had spoken with him too.

It was now the turn of the king, and he entered the room confident that he would be similarly favored. But he gazed around in dismay, perceiving no sign of anything which could even represent the Almighty. Then began he to think to himself, "This God, wherever he is, has been seen by both my ministers, and it cannot be denied, therefore, that their birthright is clear. Is it possible that I, the king, am a bastard, seeing that no God appears to me? The very thought is confusion, and necessity will compel me to assert that I have seen him too."

Having formed this resolution, the king stepped out and joined the rest of his party.

"And now, O king," asked the cunning girl, "have you also seen God?"

"Yes," answered he with assurance, "I have seen God."

"Really?" asked she again.

"Certainly," asserted the king.

Three times the girl asked the same question, and three times the king unblushingly lied. Then said the girl, "O king, have you never a conscience? How could you possibly see God, seeing that God is a spirit?"

Hearing this reproof, the king recalled to mind the saying of the girl that one day he would lie too, and, with a laugh, he confessed that he had not seen God at all. The two ministers, beginning to feel alarmed, confessed the truth as well.

Then said the girl, "O king, we poor people may tell lies occasionally to save our lives, but what had you to fear? Telling lies, therefore, for many has its own attractions, and to them at least the taste of lying is sweet."

Far from being offended at the stratagem which the girl had practiced on him, the king was so struck with her ingenuity and assurance that he married her forthwith, and in a short time she became his confidential adviser in all his affairs, public as well as private. Thus this simple girl came to great honor and renown, and so much did she grow in wisdom that her fame spread through many lands.

DIAMOND CUT DIAMOND

Tradition Bearer: Major Campbell Feroshepore

Source: Lang, Andrew. *The Olive Fairy Book*. London: Longmans, Green and Company, 1907, 144–151.

Date: Unavailable
Original Source: India
National Origin: India

The title "Diamond Cut Diamond" of the following tale is roughly equivalent to the English proverb: "It takes a thief to catch a thief." The tale is similar to "The Youth in the Land of Cheaters" (AT 978) by virtue of the fact that not only the villain of the narrative, Beeka Mull, but also the shop owners and even the victim's savior Kooshy Ram are rascals. The Punjab area from which the tale was collected lies on the border between Pakistan and India. The name Kooshy Ram suggests an Indian (Hindu) rather than Pakistani (Muslim) setting for the tale.

In a village in Hindustan there once lived a merchant who, although he rose early, worked hard, and rested late, remained very poor; and ill-luck so dogged him that he determined at last to go to some distant country and there to try his fortune. Twelve years passed by; his luck had turned, and now he had gathered great wealth, so that having plenty to keep him in comfort for the rest of his days, he thought once more of his native village, where he desired to spend the remainder of his life among his own people. In order to carry his riches with him in safety over the many weary miles that lay between him and his home, he bought some magnificent jewels, which he locked up in a little box and wore concealed upon his person; and, so as not to draw the attention of the thieves who infested the highways and made their living by robbing travelers, he started off in the poor clothes of a man who has nothing to lose.

Thus prepared, he traveled quickly, and within a few days' journey from his own village came to a city where he determined to buy better garments and—now that he was no longer afraid of thieves—to look more like the rich man he had become. In his new raiment he approached the city, and near the great gate he found a bazaar where, amongst many shops filled with costly silks, and carpets, and goods of all countries, was one finer than all the rest. There, amidst his goods, spread out to the best advantage, sat the owner smoking a long silver pipe, and thither the merchant bent his steps, and, saluting the owner politely, sat down also and began to make some purchases.

Now, the proprietor of the shop, Beeka Mull by name, was a very shrewd man, and as he and the merchant conversed, he soon felt sure that his customer was richer than he seemed, and was trying to conceal the fact. Certain purchases having been made, he invited the new-comer to refresh himself, and in a short time they were chatting pleasantly together. In the course of the conversation

255

Beeka Mull asked the merchant whither he was traveling, and hearing the name of the village, he observed,

"Ah, you had better be careful on that road—it's a very bad place for thieves."

The merchant turned pale at these words. It would be such a bitter thing, he thought, just at the end of his journey to be robbed of all the fortune he had heaped up with such care.

But this bland and prosperous Beeka Mull must surely know best, so presently he said, "Lala-ji, [a complimentary title equivalent to "Dear sir"] could you oblige me by locking up for me a small box for a short while? When once I get to my village I could bring back half-a-dozen sturdy men of my own kinsfolk and claim it again."

The Lala shook his head. "I could not do it," replied he. "I am sorry; but such things are not my business. I should be afraid to undertake it."

"But," pleaded the merchant, "I know no one in this city, and you must surely have some place where you keep your own precious things. Do this, I pray you, as a great favor."

Still Beeka Mull politely but firmly refused; but the merchant, feeling that he had now betrayed the fact that he was richer than he seemed, and being loath to make more people aware of it by inquiring elsewhere, continued to press him, until at last he consented. The merchant produced the little box of jewels, and Beeka Mull locked it up for him in a strong chest with other precious stones; and so, with many promises and compliments, they parted.

In a place like an Eastern bazaar, where the shops lie with wide open fronts, and with their goods displayed not only within but without on terraces and verandahs raised a few feet above the public roadway, such a long talk as that between Beeka Mull and the merchant could not but attract some attention from the other shop-keepers in the narrow street. If the merchant had but known it, nearly every shop-owner in that district was a thief, and the cleverest and biggest of all was Beeka Mull. But he did not know it, only he could not help feeling a little uneasy at having thus parted with all his wealth to a stranger. And so, as he wandered down the street, making a purchase here and there, he managed in one way and another to ask some questions about the honesty of Beeka Mull, and each rascal whom he spoke to, knowing that there was some good reason in the question, and hoping to get in return some share of the spoils, replied in praise of Beeka Mull as a model of all the virtues.

In this way the merchant's fears were stilled, and, with a comparatively light heart, he traveled on to his village; and within a week or so returned to the city with half-a-dozen sturdy young nephews and friends whom he had enlisted to help him carry home his precious box.

At the great market-place in the center of the city the merchant left his friends, saying that he would go and get the box of jewels and rejoin them, to which they consented, and away he went. Arrived at the shop of Beeka Mull, he went up and saluted him.

"Good-day, Lala-ji," said he. But the Lala pretended not to see him. So he repeated the salutation.

"What do you want?" snapped Beeka Mull, "you've said your "good-day" twice, why don't you tell me your business?"

"Don't you remember me?" asked the merchant.

"Remember you?" growled the other, "no, why should I? I have plenty to do to remember good customers without trying to remember every beggar who comes whining for charity."

When he heard this the merchant began to tremble. "Lala-ji!" he cried, "surely you remember me and the little box I gave you to take care of? And you promised—yes, indeed, you promised very kindly—that I might return to claim it, and ..."

"You scoundrel," roared Beeka Mull, "get out of my shop! Be off with you, you impudent scamp! Every one knows that I never keep treasures for anyone; I have trouble enough to do to keep my own! Come, off with you!" With that he began to push the merchant out of the shop; and, when the poor man resisted, two of the bystanders came to Beeka Mull's help, and flung the merchant out into the road, like a bale of goods dropped from a camel. Slowly he picked himself up out of the dust, bruised, battered, and bleeding, but feeling nothing of the pain in his body, nothing but a dreadful numbing sensation that, after all, he was ruined and lost! Slowly he dragged himself a little further from where the fat and furious Beeka Mull still stood amongst his disordered silks and carpets, and coming to a friendly wall he crouched and leant against it, and putting his head into his hands gave himself up to an agony of misery and despair.

There he sat motionless, like one turned to stone, whilst darkness fell around him; and when, about eleven o'clock that night, a certain gay young fellow named Kooshy Ram passed by with a friend, he saw the merchant sitting hunched against the wall, and remarked, "A thief, no doubt."

"You are wrong," returned the other, "thieves don't sit in full view of people like that, even at night." And so the two passed on, and thought no more of him. About five o'clock next morning Kooshy Ram was returning home again, when, to his astonishment, he saw the miserable merchant still sitting as he had seen him sit hours before. Surely something must be the matter with a man who sat all night in the open street, and Kooshy Ram resolved to see what it was; so he went up and shook the merchant gently by the shoulder. "Who are you?" asked he "and what are you doing here—are you ill?"

"Ill?" said the merchant in a hollow voice, "yes; ill with a sickness for which there is no medicine."

"Oh, nonsense!" cried Kooshy Ram. "Come along with me, I know a medicine that will cure you, I think." So the young man seized the merchant by the arm, and hoisting him to his feet, dragged him to his own lodging; where he first of all gave him a large glass of wine, and then, after he had refreshed him with food, bade him tell his adventures.

Meanwhile the merchant's companions in the market-place, being dull-witted persons, thought that as he did not return he must have gone home by himself; and as soon as they were tired of waiting they went back to their village and left him to look after his own affairs. He would therefore have fared badly had it not been for his rescuer, Kooshy Ram, who, whilst still a boy, had been left a great deal of money with no one to advise him how to spend it. He was high-spirited, kind-hearted, and shrewd into the bargain; but he threw away his money like water, and generally upon the nearest thing or person in his way, and that, alas! Most often was himself! Now, however, he had taken it into his head to befriend this miserable merchant, and he meant to do it; and on his side the merchant felt confidence revive, and without further ado told all that had happened.

Kooshy Ram laughed heartily at the idea of any stranger entrusting his wealth to Beeka Mull.

"Why, he is the greatest rascal in the city," he cried, "unless you believe what some of them say of me! Well, there is nothing to be done for the present, but just to stay here quietly, and I think that at the end of a short time I shall find a medicine which will heal your sickness." At this the merchant again took courage, and a little ease crept into his heart as he gratefully accepted his new friend's invitation.

A few days later Kooshy Ram sent for some friends to see him, and talked with them long, and, although the merchant did not hear the conversation, he did hear shouts of laughter as though at some good joke; but the laughter echoed dully in his own heart, for the more he considered the more he despaired of ever recovering his fortune from the grasp of Beeka Mull.

One day, soon after this, Kooshy Ram came to him and said, "You remember the wall where I found you that night, near Beeka Mull's shop?"

"Yes, indeed I do," answered the merchant.

"Well," continued Kooshy Ram, "this afternoon you must go and stand in that same spot and watch; and when someone gives you a signal, you must go up to Beeka Mull and salute him and say, "Oh, Lala-ji, will you kindly let me have back that box of mine which you have on trust?"

"What's the use of that?" asked the merchant. "He won't do it any more now than he would when I asked him before."

"Never mind!" replied Kooshy Ram, "do exactly what I tell you, and repeat exactly what I say, word for word, and I will answer for the rest."

So, that afternoon, the merchant at a certain time went and stood by the wall as he was told. He noticed that Beeka Mull saw him, but neither took any heed of the other. Presently up the bazaar came a gorgeous palanquin like those in which ladies of rank are carried about. It was borne by four bearers well dressed in rich liveries, and its curtains and trappings were truly magnificent. In attendance was a grave-looking personage whom the merchant recognized as one of the friends who visited Kooshy Ram; and behind him came a servant with a box covered with a cloth upon his head.

The palanquin was borne along at a smart pace and was set down at Beeka Mull's shop. The fat shop-keeper was on his feet at once, and bowed deeply as the gentleman in attendance advanced.

"May I inquire," he said, "who this is in the palanquin that deigns to favor my humble shop with a visit? And what may I do for her?"

The gentleman, after whispering at the curtain of the palanquin, explained that this was a relative of his who was traveling, but as her husband could go no further with her, she desired to leave with Beeka Mull a box of jewels for safe custody. Lala bowed again to the ground. "It was not," he said, "quite in his way of business; but of course, if he could please the lady, he would be most happy, and would guard the box with his life." Then the servant carrying the box was called up; the box was unlocked, and a mass of jeweler laid open to the gaze of the enraptured Lala, whose mouth watered as he turned over the rich gems.

All this the merchant had watched from the distance, and now he saw— could he be mistaken? No, he distinctly saw a hand beckoning through the curtain on that side of the palanquin away from the shop. "The signal! Was this the signal?" thought he. The hand beckoned again, impatiently it seemed to him. So forward he went, very quietly, and saluting Beeka Mull, who was sitting turning over the contents of this amazing box of jewels which fortune and some fools were putting into his care, he said:

"Oh, Lala-ji, will you kindly let me have back that box of mine which you have on trust?"

The Lala looked up as though he had been stung; but quickly the thought flashed through his mind that if this man began making a fuss again he would lose the confidence of these new and richer customers; so he controlled himself, and answered:

"Dear me, of course, yes! I had forgotten all about it." And he went off and brought the little box and put it into the merchant's trembling hands. Quickly the latter pulled out the key, which hung by a string round his neck, and opened the box; and when he saw that his treasures were all there he rushed into the road, and, with the box under his arm, began dancing like a madman, with great shouts and screams of laughter. Just then a messenger came running up and, saluting the gentleman attending the palanquin, he said, "The lady's husband has returned, and is prepared to travel with her, so that there is no necessity to deposit the jewels." Whereat the gentleman quickly closed and re-locked the box, and handed it back to the waiting servant.

Then from the palanquin came a yell of laughter, and out jumped—not a lady—but Kooshy Ram, who immediately ran and joined the merchant in the middle of the road and danced as madly as he. Beeka Mull stood and stared stupidly at them; then, with a shrill cackle of laughter, he flung off his turban, bounced out into the road with the other two, and fell to dancing and snapping his fingers until he was out of breath.

"Lala-ji," said the gentleman who had played the part of the relative attendant on the palanquin, "why do you dance? The merchant dances because he has recovered his fortune; Kooshy Ram dances because he is a madman and has tricked you; but why do you dance?"

"I dance," panted Beeka Ram, glaring at him with a bloodshot eye, "I dance because I knew thirteen different ways of deceiving people by pretending confidence in them. I didn't know there were any more, and now here's a fourteenth! That's why I dance!"

NAGA

WHY MEN AND TIGERS ARE ENEMIES

Tradition Bearer: Unavailable

Source: Hutton, H. "Folktales of the Angami Nagas of Assam." *Folklore* 25 (1914): 486–487.

Date: Unavailable

Original Source: Angami

National Origin: Nagaland (India)

The Angami are one of the major tribes of Nagaland, India. Nagaland is located in far northeastern India, on the border of Myanmar (Burma) and India. Statehood was officially to Nagaland in 1963. The Angamis are farmers raising their rice cops on irrigated terraces. The following **myth** explains the nature and origin of the relationships among human beings, the spirits that populate their cultural landscape, and tigers.

Man, the tiger, and the spirit (*terhuma*) were brothers, sons of one woman. The man used to attend on his mother and bathe her, but the tiger was always grumbling in the house and giving trouble to everyone. The man used to cook his food, the tiger ate his raw, and the spirit merely had his smoke-dried.

At last the mother was tired of these family squabbles and set up a mark made of grass in the jungle. She said, "Whoever touches the mark first shall live in villages, the loser in the jungle."

Then the spirit said to the man, "I will shoot over the mark with an arrow, and you can say that you touched it first." So when they had run a little way, the man called out, "I am touching the mark," and just then the spirit shot an arrow and made the mark move. Thus the tiger was deceived and went off to the jungle, where he lives to this day.

After this the man sent the cat to the tiger to say, "At all events you are my brother. Whenever you kill a deer put aside a leg for me."

But the cat muddled the message, and said, "Whenever you kill a deer put it aside for the man."

The tiger was angry, and since that time men and tigers are at enmity. All the same, they are brothers, and when a man happens to kill a tiger, he will say in his village, "The gods have killed a tiger in the jungle"; not "I have killed it." If he said he had killed it, all the other tigers would say, "This man has killed his brother," and would try to devour him. What makes the tiger eat men is that when he sees them lifting great stones, which he cannot do, he thinks they must be mightily strong.

Among the Angamis old men and some young men eat the flesh of tigers and leopards. But a Sema Naga will not touch it, as he looks on men and tigers as of one blood.

THE TALE OF AN OGRESS

Tradition Bearer: Unavailable

Source: Hutton, H. "Folktales of the Angami Nagas of Assam." *Folklore* 25 (1914): 492–493.

Date: Unavailable

Original Source: Angami

National Origin: Nagaland (India)

In the following tale, the boys fall into their desperate situation because they violate the norms of Angami society. They are orphans living apart from the village in the bush. In addition, rather than farming, they snare wild animal food. Only magic saves them in the end. Therefore, the narrative serves a **cautionary** function.

Once upon a time there were two orphan boys who did not know how to till the fields and lived by snaring birds. An ogress used to come and eat the birds' heads. One day they saw her and asked her why she did this.

She answered, "I had forgotten you. Come and live with me and I will treat you kindly." Now the land of these cannibals is surrounded by a deep river, but the ogress knew a charm by which she crossed it, and so they came to her home. She left the elder boy outside, but she put the younger in the room where she kept her charms.

When the boys went to sleep the husband of the ogress said, "Let us kill and eat."

But she felt the little boy and said, "He is not fat enough."

This happened on several nights, and the boy heard what she said. So one morning he said to his brother, "Her husband wants to eat us. He must be a cannibal."

But the elder brother said that the pair loved them, and would do them no harm.

The little boy said, "You tell her husband that you have such a bad stomach ache that you cannot sleep outside." So that night the elder boy slept in the house. In the night he heard the ogress discussing whether the boys were fat enough to eat. So the boys arranged to escape.

The younger took the charm of the ogress, and by this means they succeeded in crossing the river. As the ogress had lost her charm she could not pursue them and they got home safely.

THE CLEVER ORPHAN

Tradition Bearer: Unavailable

Source: Hutton, H. "Folktales of the Angami Nagas of Assam." *Folklore* 25 (1914): 496–497.

Date: Unavailable

Original Source: Angami

National Origin: Nagaland (India)

The "orphan boy" serves as a **trickster** figure in many Angami tales. His tricks often involve a play-on-words such as his calling his fireplace "grandmother." This trick is an allusion to an Angami maxim that "The sky is my father and the earth my mother." The Angami fireplace is only three rough stones that support the cooking pot. Hutton suggests that the tales of the orphan boy were adapted from Hindu sources rather than being indigenous to the Nagas (497).

Once there was an orphan boy who was very poor. He went to the Chief's village and heard that he had a daughter fit to be married.

So he said to the Chief, "How dark your house is!"

The Chief asked, "What is your house like?"

"Mine," he said, "is transparent, and I can see the sky from anywhere inside."

When the Chief was eating his dinner the boy asked, "Is that the only dish you have?"

"Yes," said the Chief, "but what about yours?"

"When I have done eating," said the boy, "I throw away the old dish and get a new one every time."

Then he asked the Chief, "Are these the only cows you have?"

"Yes," he replied, "and how many have you?"

"My house is so full of cattle that some of them have to stay outside."

Then the boy saw the Chief's grandmother riding a horse. "Why do you let your grandmother get so cold?"

"What do you do with your grandmother?" asked the Chief.

"Oh! She always sits warming herself at the fire."

The Chief was convinced that he was a great man, so he gave him his daughter, and she went home with her husband.

But when she saw his house she laughed, and said, "Why, this house is not transparent. We can't see the sky from inside!"

"Oh, yes, we can," and he pointed to the holes in the roof.

"And what about your plates?"

"I have none, but I make a new leaf platter every time I dine."

"And what about your cattle?"

"I have only one cow, and she lies half inside the house and half outside!"

"And your grandmother!"

"My grandmother is my fire-place," he answered.

Then his wife was so ashamed at the way she had been taken in, that she wrote to her father not to come to visit her for seven years. She sent her husband to her father to borrow some money. When he got the money he purchased a lot of rubbish and stored it in his house.

"What is the use of that?" asked his wife.

"You will see by and by," he replied, and went and borrowed more money, which he spent in the same way. The third time he brought gold, made a number of sling-pellets of clay and gilded them all over. These he sold to the people from whom he had bought the rubbish. After a time they found they had been cheated, and complained to the Chief. He sent for his son-in-law and asked him what he meant.

"Yes, O Chief, I did what they say, but when I borrowed money from you they sold me rubbish for it. So I in turn sold them mud-pellets covered with gold."

The Chief asked the people, "Did you really sell him rubbish for gold?"

They admitted the fact, and the Chief said, "Serve you right!" So the orphan boy prospered and became in time a wealthy man.

THE RAT PRINCESS AND THE GREEDY MAN

Tradition Bearer: Unavailable

Source: Hutton, H. "Folktales of the Angami Nagas of Assam." *Folklore* 25 (1914): 494–495.

Date: Unavailable

Original Source: Angami

National Origin: Nagaland (India)

The following narrative is an Angami **variant** of the internationally distributed "Stronger and Strongest" (AT 2031).

One day a man was going to his field, and on the way he caught a rat. He brought it home and put it in a box, and when later on he went to look at it he found the rat had turned into a beautiful girl.

When he saw her he said to himself, "If I could marry her to the richest man in the world I should become a rich man myself." So he went to find the greatest man in the world, and he came to the Chief.

He said, "You are the greatest man in the world, and you had better marry her."

But the Chief said, "I should like to marry her, but you say that she must marry the greatest man in the world. Now I am weaker than water, because if I go into a river in flood it carries me away. Hence water is stronger than I am."

The man went to Water, and spoke to it as he had spoken to the Chief. But Water said, "I am not the strongest, for when I am still Wind comes and blows me into waves. Wind is greater than I am." So the man went to Wind,

But Wind said, "Mountain is stronger than I, because, blow as hard as I can, I cannot stir it." So he went to Mountain, who said, "Yes, I am stronger than most things, but even a rat can pierce my side when he pleases. Hence the rat is greater than I." The man knew no where else to go, so he came home, and he found the girl turned into a rat as she was before.

ANIMAL TALES

Tradition Bearer: Unavailable

Source: Hutton, H. "Folktales of the Angami Nagas of Assam." *Folklore* 25 (1914): 490–529.

Date: Unavailable

Original Source: Angami

National Origin: Nagaland (India)

Commonly, **animal tales** serve as **fables**. They convey a moral, in many cases as a succinct statement at the tale's conclusion. Of the Naga examples below, "A Tale of a Snake" and "The Boiled Crab" clearly fulfill this expectation. The "Monkey and the Jackal" operates as a **trickster** tale, with the two central characters alternating the roles of trickster and dupe. "The Birds and the Snakes," however, seems neither to teach nor to allow tricksters to show their skills. The author suggests that the tale is a borrowed fragment from the anthology of Buddhist fables *The Jataka*.

A Tale of a Snake

One day a girl went to work in the field, and on her way she met a snake on the path. The snake would not let her pass until she said, "Do not bite me and I will marry you." So at last she said it, and the snake let her go and afterwards married her.

Then he bit her in the breast and ornaments grew there, and he bit her in the leg and she got leggings. Another girl saw this, and she too met a snake.

To him she said Let us marry." So she took him and put him in her basket, but he said nothing, and bit her in the arm so that she died.

The Boiled Crab

One day a little bird went to work in her field, and called all her companions to help her. Among them came the crab. At noon the little bird called her friends from the field to the field-house. She put a pot on the fire, and perching on the rim laid an egg into the pot for each of her friends to eat.

The next day they all went to work in the crab's field. He brought nothing for dinner, because he had seen what the little bird had done, and meant to imitate her. When the pot was boiling in the field-house, he perched on the rim and tried to lay an egg, but he fell in and was boiled to death.

Meanwhile his friends were hoping he would ask them to dinner. But as they got tired of waiting, one of them went into the field-house and saw the crab boiled in the pot. He went and told the others. So they all came and ate the crab.

The Birds and the Snakes

Once upon a time a lizard and a little bird went shares in a well. Whenever the lizard went to draw water he used to make the well muddy. The bird complained, but the lizard would not listen to him.

At last the lizard said, "Go and call all your birds, and I will go and call all the reptiles under yon tree." So they each called their people, and there was a great fight. The birds flew down and carried away all the snakes, save one, a big fellow, whom they feared. Now he was the priest of the snakes. The crow caught him in his beak, but he dropped him on a stone, and immediately a lot of snakes were produced.

The birds were afraid, but the little bird went to the biggest of all birds and said, "Come and kill the priest snake."

He said, "But who will feed my young?"

"I will," said the little bird. Then the big bird swooped and killed the snake.

The Monkey and the Jackal

One day a monkey and a jackal met in the jungle, and the jackal said, "I wish I were a monkey, able to climb trees and get any fruit I like."

The monkey replied, "I wish I were a jackal, and able to go into men's houses and get rice and meat and chickens and anything else I wanted."

Then the monkey said, "Let us each bring the best food we can get, and see whose is the better."

When they met the monkey said, "Please give me your food first." The jackal put it into the monkey's hand, and he ran up the tree, ate it all, and gave nothing in return to the jackal.

The jackal was very angry, and went off muttering, "I will make you pay for that." So he went and stopped at a patch of wild yams which looked very tasty.

The monkey came up and asked, "What are you doing?"

"I am only eating the Sahib's [used as a respectful term for a male European in colonial India] sugar cane, and it is very sweet."

"Please give me some," said the monkey.

"But the Sahib will be angry."

"Oh, no, he won't," said the monkey.

"Well, come and pick some for yourself." He picked a yam, peeled it, and began to eat it. But it burnt his mouth, and his lips swelled so that he could hardly speak.

Then the monkey went to a bees' nest and said to the jackal, "Don't bite that."

But the jackal would not mind, and the monkey said, "All right! But don't touch it till I get behind the hill."

When the monkey was out of sight, the jackal bit the nest, and the bees came out and stung him badly. Then the jackal went and lay down in some reeds which concealed a stream of water.

"What are you doing?" asked the monkey.

"I am watching the Sahib's clothes."

"I am coming to help you," said the monkey.

"Don't," said the jackal.

But the monkey jumped down and fell into the water under the reeds and was drowned.

PAKISTAN

RAJA RASALU

Tradition Bearer: Unavailable

Source: Jacobs, Joseph. *Indian Fairy Tales*. London: David Nutt, 1912, 136–149.

Date: 1912

Original Source: Punjabi

National Origin: Pakistan

Raja Rasalu is the chief hero of Punjabi **legend**. According to popular tradition, he was the son of Sâlivâhana (Salabhan in the following tale) who established the Saka (Scythians of east central Asia) in the first century C.E. According to the legend **cycle** that grew up around Raja Rasalu, he had a brother (Puran) who was killed by a wicked step-mother. The familiar **motifs** of the helpful dead man, the grateful animals, gambling for life, and the magical objects that appear in this narrative are internationally distributed. The sections of verse that are interspersed throughout the following account give the tale an epic tone.

Once there lived a great Raja, whose flame was Salabhan, and be had a Queen, by name Lona, who, though she wept and prayed at many a shrine, had never a child to gladden her eyes. After a long time, however, a son was promised to her.

Queen Lona returned to the palace, and when the time for the birth of the promised son drew nigh, she inquired of three Jogis [yogis] who came begging to her gate, what the child's fate would be, and the youngest of them answered and said, "Oh, Queen! The child will be a boy, and he will live to be a great man.

But for twelve years you must not look upon his face, for if either you or his father see it before the twelve years are past, you will surely die! This is what you must do; as soon as the child is born you must send him away to a cellar underneath the ground, and never let him see the light of day for twelve years. After they are over, he may come forth, bathe in the river, put on new clothes, and visit you. His name shall be Raja Rasalu, and he shall be known far and wide."

So, when a fair young Prince was in due time born into the world, his parents hid him away in an underground palace, with nurses, and servants, and everything else a King's son might desire. And with him they sent a young colt, born the same day, and sword, spear, and shield, against the day when Raja Rasalu should go forth into the world.

So there the child lived, playing with his colt, and talking to his parrot, while the nurses taught him all things needful for a King's son to know.

Young Rasalu lived on, far from the light of day, for eleven long years, growing tall and strong, yet contented to remain playing with his colt, and talking to his parrot; but when the twelfth year began, the lad's heart leapt up with desire for change, and he loved to listen to the sounds of life which came to him in his palace-prison from the outside world.

"I must go and see where the voices come from!" he said; and when his nurses told him he must not go for one year more, he only laughed aloud, saying, "Nay! I stay no longer here for any man!"

Then he saddled his Arab horse Bhaunr, put on his shining armor, and rode forth into the world; but, mindful of what his nurses had oft told him, when he came to the river, he dismounted, and, going into the water, washed himself and his clothes.

Then, clean of raiment, fair of face, and brave of heart, he rode on his way until he reached his father's city. There he sat down to rest awhile by a well, where the women were drawing water in earthen pitchers. Now, as they passed him, their full pitchers poised upon their heads, the gay young prince flung stones at the earthen vessels, and broke them all. Then the women, drenched with water, went weeping and wailing to the palace, complaining to the King that a mighty young Prince in shining armor, with a parrot on his wrist and a gallant steed beside him, sat by the well, and broke their pitchers.

Now, as soon as Raja Salabhan heard this, he guessed at once that it was Prince Rasalu come forth before the time, and, mindful of the Jogis' words that he would die if he looked on his son's face before twelve years were past, he did not dare to send his guards to seize the offender and bring him to be judged. So he bade the women be comforted, and take pitchers of iron and brass, giving new ones from the treasury to those who did not possess any of their own.

But when Prince Rasalu saw the women returning to the well with pitchers of iron and brass, he laughed to himself, and drew his mighty bow till the sharp-pointed arrows pierced the metal vessels as though they had been clay.

Yet still the King did not send for him, so he mounted his steed and set off in the pride of his youth and strength to the palace. He strode into the audience hall, where his father sat trembling, and saluted him with all reverence; but Raja Salabhan, in fear of his life, turned his back hastily and said never a word in reply.

Then Prince Rasalu called scornfully to him across the hall:

> I came to greet thee, King, and not to harm thee!
> What have I done that thou shouldst turn away?
> Scepter and empire have no power to charm me—
> I go to seek a worthier prize than they!

Then he strode away, full of bitterness and anger; but as he passed under the palace windows, he heard his mother weeping, and the sound softened his heart, so that his wrath died down, and a great loneliness fell upon him, because he was spurned by both father and mother.

So he cried sorrowfully,

> Oh heart crown'd with grief, hast thou nought
> But tears for thy son?
> Art mother of mine? Give one thought
> To my life just begun!

And Queen Lona answered through her tears:

> Yea! mother am I, though I weep,
> So hold this word sure—
> Go, reign king of all men, but keep
> Thy heart good and pure!

So Raja Rasalu was comforted, and began to make ready for fortune. He took with him his horse Bhaunr and his parrot, both of whom had lived with him since he was born. So they made a goodly company, and Queen Lona, when she saw them going, watched them from her window till she saw nothing but a cloud of dust on the horizon; then she bowed her head on her hands and wept, saying:

> Oh! son who ne'er gladdened mine eyes,
> Let the cloud of thy going arise,
> Dim the sunlight and darken the day;
> For the mother whose son is away
> Is as dust!

Rasalu had started off to play chaupur [a game essentially like pachisi] with King Sarkap. And as he journeyed there came a fierce storm of thunder and lightning, so that he sought shelter, and found none save an old graveyard, where a headless corpse lay upon the ground; So lonesome was it that even the corpse seemed company, and Rasalu, sitting down beside it, said:

> There is no one here, nor far nor near,
> Save this breathless corpse so cold and grim;
> Would God he might come to life again,
> 'Twould be less lonely to talk to him.

And immediately the headless corpse arose and sat beside Raja Rasalu. And he, nothing astonished, said to it:

> The storm beats fierce and loud,
> The clouds rise thick in the west;
> What ails thy grave and shroud,
> Oh corpse! That thou canst not rest?

Then the headless corpse replied:

> On earth I was even as thou,
> My turban awry like a king,
> My head with the highest, I trow,
> Having my fun and my fling,
> Fighting my foes like a brave,
> Living my life with a swing.
> And, now I am dead,
> Sins, heavy as lead,
> Will give me no rest in my grave!

So the night passed on, dark and dreary, while Rasalu sat in the graveyard and talked to the headless corpse. Now when morning broke and Rasalu said he must continue his journey, the headless corpse asked him whither he was going, and when he said "to play chaupur with King Sarkap," the corpse begged him to give up the idea saying, "I am King Sarkap's brother, and I know his ways. Every day, before breakfast, he cuts off the heads of two or three men, just to amuse himself. One day no one else was at hand, so he cut off mine, and he will surely cut off yours on some pretence or another. However, if you are determined to go and play chaupur with him, take some of the bones from this graveyard, and make your dice out of them, and then the enchanted dice with which my brother plays will lose their virtue. Otherwise he will always win."

So Rasalu took some of the bones lying about, and fashioned them into dice, and these he put into his pocket. Then, bidding adieu to the headless corpse, he went on his way to play chaupur with the King.

Now, as Raja Rasalu, tender-hearted and strong, journeyed along to play chaupur with the King, he came to a burning forest, and a voice rose from the fire saying, "Oh, traveler! for God's sake save me from the fire!"

Then the Prince turned towards the burning forest, and, lo! the voice was the voice of a tiny cricket. Nevertheless, Rasalu, tender-hearted and strong, snatched it from the fire and set it at liberty. Then the little creature, full of, gratitude, pulled out one of its feelers, and giving it to its preserver, said, "Keep this, and should you ever be in trouble, put it into the fire, and instantly I will come to your aid."

The Prince smiled, saying, "What help could *you* give *me?*" Nevertheless, he kept the hair and went on his way.

Now, when he reached the city of King Sarkap, seventy maidens, daughters of the King, came out to meet him—seventy fair maidens, merry and careless, full of smiles and laughter; but one, the youngest of them all, when she saw the gallant young Prince riding on Bhaunr Iraqi, going gaily to his doom, was filled with pity, and called to him saying:

> Fair Prince, on the charger so gray,
> Turn thee back! Turn thee back!
> Or lower thy lance for the fray;
> Thy head will be forfeit today!
> Dost love life? Then, stranger, I pray,
> Turn thee back! Turn thee back!

But he, smiling at the maiden, answered lightly:

> Fair maiden, I come from afar,
> Sworn conqueror in love and in war!
> King Sarkap my coming will rue,
> His head in four pieces I'll hew;
> Then forth as a bridegroom I'll ride,
> With you, little maid, as my bride!

Now when Rasalu replied so gallantly, the maiden looked in his face, and seeing how fair he was, and how brave and strong, she straightway fell in love with him, and would gladly have followed him through the world.

But the other sixty-nine maidens, being jealous, laughed scornfully at her, saying, "Not so fast, oh gallant warrior! If you would marry our sister you must first do our bidding, for you will be our younger brother."

"Fair sisters!" quoth Rasalu gaily, "give me my task and I will perform it."

So the sixty-nine maidens mixed a hundredweight of millet seed with a hundredweight of sand, and giving it to Rasalu, bade him separate the seed from the sand.

Then he bethought him of the cricket, and drawing, the feeler from his pocket, thrust it into the fire. And immediately there was a whirring noise in the air, and a great flight of crickets alighted beside him, and amongst them the cricket whose life he had saved.

Then Rasalu said, "Separate the millet seed from the sand."

"Is that all?" quoth the cricket, "had I known how small a job you wanted me to do, I would not have assembled so many of my brethren."

With that the flight of crickets set to work, and in one night they separated the seed from the sand.

Now when the sixty-nine fair maidens, daughters of the king, saw that Rasalu had performed his task, they set him another, bidding him swing them all, one by one, in their swings, until they were tired.

Whereupon he laughed, saying, "There are seventy of you, counting my little bride yonder, and I am not going to spend my life swinging girls! Why, by the time I have given each of you a swing, the first will be wanting another! No! If you want a swing, get in, all seventy of you, into one swing, and then I'll see what can be done."

So the seventy maidens climbed into one swing, and Raja Rasalu, standing in his shining armor, fastened the ropes to his mighty bow, and drew it up to its fullest bent. Then he let go, and like an arrow the swing shot into the air, with its burden of seventy fair maidens, merry and careless, full of smiles and laughter.

But as it swung back again, Rasalu, standing there in his shining armor, drew his sharp sword and severed, the ropes. Then the seventy fair maidens fell to the ground headlong; and some were bruised and some broken, but the only one who escaped unhurt was the maiden who loved Rasalu, for she fell out last, on the top of the others, and so came to no harm.

After this, Rasalu strode on fifteen paces, till he came to the seventy drums, that every one who came to play chaupur with the King had to beat in turn; and he beat them so loudly that he broke them all. Then he came to the seventy gongs, all in a row, and he hammered them so hard that they cracked to pieces.

Seeing this, the youngest Princess, who was the only one who could run, fled to her father the King in a great fright, saying:

> A mighty Prince, Sarkap! making havoc, rides along,
> He swung us, seventy maidens fair, and threw us out headlong;
> He broke the drums you placed there and the gongs too in his pride,
> Sure, he will kill thee, father mine, and take me for his bride!

But King Sarkap replied scornfully:

> Silly maiden, thy words make a lot
> Of a very small matter;

For fear of my valor, I wot,
His armor will clatter.
As soon as I've eaten my bread
I'll go forth and cut off his head!

Notwithstanding these brave and boastful words, he was in reality very much afraid, having heard of Rasalu's renown. And learning that he was stopping at the house of an old woman in the city, till the hour for playing chaupur arrived, Sarkap sent slaves to him with trays of sweetmeats and fruit, as to an honored guest. But the food was poisoned. Now when the slaves brought the trays to Raja Rasalu, he rose up haughtily, saying, "Go, tell your master I have nought to do with him in friendship. I am his sworn enemy, and I eat not of his salt!"

So saying, he threw the sweetmeats to Raja Sarkap's dog, which had followed the slave, and lo! The dog died.

Then Rasalu was very wroth, and said bitterly, "Go back to Sarkap, slaves! And tell him that Rasalu deems it no act of bravery to kill even an enemy by treachery."

Now, when evening came, Raja Rasalu went forth to play chaupur with King Sarkap, and as he passed some potters' kilns he saw a cat wandering about restlessly; so he asked what ailed her, that she never stood still, and she replied, "My kittens are in an unbaked pot in the kiln yonder. It has just been set alight, and my children will be baked alive; therefore I cannot rest!"

Her words moved the heart of Raja Rasalu, and, going to the potter, he asked him to sell the kiln as it was; but the potter replied that he could not settle a fair price till the pots were burnt, as he could not tell how many would come out whole. Nevertheless, after some bargaining, he consented at last to sell the kiln, and Rasalu, having searched all the pots, restored the kittens to their mother, and she, in gratitude for his mercy, gave him one of them, saying, "Put it in your pocket, for it will help you when you are in difficulties." So Raja Rasalu put the kitten in his pocket, and went to play chaupur with the King.

Now, before they sat down to play, Raja Sarkap fixed his stakes—on the first game, his kingdom; on the second, the wealth of the whole world; and, on the third, his own head. So, likewise, Raja Rasalu fixed his stakes—on the first game, his arms; on the second, his horse; and, on the third, his own head.

Then they began to play, and it fell to Rasalu's lot to make the first move. Now he, forgetful of the dead man's warning, played with the dice given him by Raja Sarkap, besides which, Sarkap let loose his famous rat, Dhol Raja, and it ran about the board, upsetting the chaupur pieces on the sly, so that Rasalu lost the first game, and gave up his shining armor.

Then the second game began, and once more Dhol Raja, the rat, upset the pieces; and Rasalu, losing the game, gave up his faithful steed. Then Bhaunr, the Arab steed, who stood by, found voice, and cried to his master,

Sea-born am I, bought with much gold;
Dear Prince! Trust me now as of old.
I'll carry you far from these wiles—
My flight, all unspurr'd, will be swift as a bird,
For thousands and thousands of miles!
Or if needs you must stay; ere the next game you play,
Place hand in your pocket, I pray!

Hearing this, Raja Sarkap frowned, and bade his slaves, remove Bhaunr, the Arab steed, since he gave his master advice in the game. Now, when the slaves came to lead the faithful steed away, Rasalu could not refrain from tears, thinking over the long years during which Bhaunr, the Arab steed, had been his companion. But the horse cried out again,

Weep not, dear Prince! I shall not eat my bread
Of stranger hands, nor to strange stall be led.
Take thy right hand, and place it as I said.

These words roused some recollection in Rasalu's mind, and when, just at this moment, the kitten in his pocket began to struggle, he remembered all about the warning, and the dice made from dead men's bones. Then his heart rose up once more, and he called boldly to Raja Sarkap, "Leave my horse and arms here for the present. Time enough to take them away when you have won my head!"

Now, Raja Sarkap, seeing Rasalu's confident bearing, began to be afraid, and ordered all the women of his palace to come forth in their gayest attire and stand before Rasalu, so as to distract his attention from the game. But he never even looked at them, and throwing the dice from his pocket, said to Sarkap, "We have played with your dice all this time; now we will play with mine."

Then the kitten went and sat at the window through which the rat Dhol Raja used to come, and the game began.

After a while, Sarkap, seeing Raja Rasalu was winning, called to his rat, but when Dhol Raja saw the kitten he was afraid, and would not go further. So Rasalu won, and took back his arms. Next he played for his horse, and once more Raja Sarkap called for his rat; but Dhol Raja, seeing the kitten keeping watch, was afraid. So Rasalu won the second stake, and took back Bhaunr, the Arab steed.

Then Sarkap brought all his skill to bear on the third and last game, saying,

Oh molded pieces! Favor me today!
For sooth this is a man with whom I play.
No paltry risk—but life and death at stake;
As Sarkap does, so do, for Sarkap's sake!

But Rasalu answered back,

> Oh molded pieces! Favor me today!
> For sooth it is a man with whom I play.
> No paltry risk—but life and death at stake;
> As Heaven does, so do, for Heaven's sake!

So they began to play, whilst the women stood round in a circle, and the kitten watched Dhol Raja from the window. Then Sarkap lost, first his kingdom, then the wealth of the whole world, and lastly his head.

Just then, a servant came in to announce the birth of a daughter to Raja Sarkap, and he, overcome by misfortunes, said, "Kill her at once! for she has been born in an evil moment, and has brought her father ill luck!"

But Rasalu rose up in his shining armor, tender-hearted and strong, saying, "Not so, oh king! She has done no evil. Give me this child to wife; and if you will vow, by all you hold sacred, never again to play chaupur for another's head, I will spare yours now!"

Then Sarkap vowed a solemn vow never to play for another's head; and after that he took a fresh mango branch, and the new-born babe, and placing them on a golden dish gave them to Rasalu.

Now, as he left the palace, carrying with him the new-born babe and the mango branch, he met a band of prisoners, and they called out to him,

> A royal hawk art thou, oh King, the rest
> But timid wild-fowl. Grant us our request—
> Unloose these chains, and live for ever blest!

And Raja Rasalu hearkened to them, and bade King Sarkap set them at liberty.

Then he went to the Murti Hills, and placed the new-born babe, Kokilan, in an underground palace, and planted the mango branch at the door, saying, "In twelve years the mango tree will blossom; then will I return and marry Kokilan."

And after twelve years, the mango tree began to flower, and Raja Rasalu married the Princess Kokilan, whom he won from Sarkap when he played chaupur with the King.

THE YOUNG MAN AND THE SNAKE

Tradition Bearer: Unavailable

Source: Swynnerton, Charles. *Indian Nights' Entertainment: Folk-Tales from the Upper Indus*. London: Elliot Stock, 1892, 133–138.

Date: ca. 1890

Original Source: Pakistan

National Origin: Pakistan

In this **variant** of "Ungrateful Serpent Returned to Captivity" (AT 155), the serpent is not merely placed in peril again, he is destroyed by his benefactor's clever wife. As is the case with other variants of this **tale type**, the ungrateful animal is portrayed as having ethical principles that allow a **trickster** to turn the tables. See, for example, "The Brahman, the Tiger, and the Six Judges" (page 153).

There was once a farmer who was extremely poor. It happened that when his poverty was greatest a son was born to him, and this son was such a lucky child that his father speedily became quite as rich as he was before poor, and obtained a great name over all the country.

After a certain time the farmer thought to himself, "I must get my son betrothed somewhere. I was poor once, but I am now rich, and my son is lucky. It is right that he should be betrothed to the daughter of some rich man like myself."

It was long before he found a suitable match, but at last he betrothed the boy to a girl who lived in a distant town. The ceremony came on, much money was spent, many guests were invited, and much food was given away. In short, the betrothal was splendid. The son had scarcely grown to manhood when the father died, leaving him in the world alone.

The parents of his betrothed, when they heard the sad news, felt very sorry for him, and at first they would have brought him to live at their own house. But the mother said, "He is old enough now to come and take our daughter home with him, so let us send for him that he may do so. No friend like a good wife."

A messenger was accordingly sent off, and the lad, when he received the invitation, dressed himself up in his best, and, mounting his mare, set off.

On the way he came to a lonely jungle, in which he saw a mongoose and a snake of enormous dimensions, engaged in deadly combat. He reined up his horse to look on. The mongoose soon began to wear out his adversary, and to inflict such wounds as would have put an end to its life in a short time. Seeing which, the boy considered to himself, "When two are contending, it is an act of charity to separate them." So he tried to separate the combatants, but every time he failed, as the mongoose again and again sprang upon his adversary in spite of him. Finding he could not prevail, he drew his sword and dealt the warlike little mongoose his death-blow.

After this he went on again, but he had not proceeded far when he found that the snake had rushed round and intercepted him.

Then began the boy to remonstrate. "I did you good service," said he. "Why, then, have you pursued me?"

"It is true," answered the snake, "that you saved me from my enemy. But I shall not let you go. I shall eat you."

"Surely," replied the lad, "one good turn deserves another. Will you injure me because I assisted you? In my country we do not deal with each other thus."

"In these parts," said the snake, "the custom is different. Everyone here observes the rule of returning evil for good."

The boy then began to argue with the snake, but he argued in vain, for the snake was determined to eat him. At last he said, "Very well, snake, you can eat me. But first give me eight days to go about my business, after which I shall come back."

With this request the snake complied, saying, "Be it so. In eight days you must return to me."

The snake, which had coiled himself round about the boy's body, now released his hold and suffered him to depart. So he rode on once more and completed his journey.

All his friends were very glad to see the young bridegroom, and especially his little wife, and at his father-in-law's house he remained for several days. But as he was always downcast and sad, they asked him, "Why are you so sorrowful?" For six days they asked in vain. On the seventh they spoke to their daughter, "Is he angry? What is the matter with him" But she also asked him in vain.

When the eight day came, he said, "Now let me go home." The father and mother then gave the daughter her portion [of her inheritance as a dowry], and, having placed them both in a bullock cart, they sent the young couple away.

So the two traveled until they had left the village far behind them. Then said the lad to his wife and to her servants, "Return now back again to your own home. As for me, it is decreed that I shall die on the way."

All the servants, being alarmed, at once returned, but his young wife said, "Where you fall, I shall fall. What am I to do at my house?" So she continued to accompany her husband.

When he arrived at the spot appointed, he dismounted from his horse and called forth the snake.

"I have come," said he, "in accordance with my promise. If you wish to eat me, come and eat me now!"

His wife, hearing his ominous words, descended also, and came and stood by her husband's side. By and by a dreadful hissing sound was heard, and the snake crawled out from the jungle, and was preparing to devour the unfortunate boy, when the girl exclaimed, "Why are you going to eat this poor youth?"

The snake then told her the whole story, how he was fighting with a mongoose, and how her husband interfered and killed his adversary. "And in this country," continued he, "our custom is to return evil for good!"

The young wife now tried all the arguments she could think of to divert the monster from his purpose, but he was deaf to her pleadings and refused to listen to them. Then said she, "You say that in this country people do evil in return for good. This is so strange a custom, and so very unreasonable, that I would fain know the history of it. How did it all come about?"

"Do you see those five talli trees?" answered the snake. "Go you to them and cry out to them, 'What is the reason that in this country folks do evil in return for good?' and see what they will say to you!"

The girl went and did as she was bidden, addressing her request to the middle of the five.

The tree straightway answered her, "Count us! We are now five, but once we were six—three pairs. The sixth tree was hollow, having a vast cavity in its trunk. It happened once upon a time, many years ago, that a certain thief went and robbed a house, and that the people followed him. He ran and ran and ran, and at last he came in among us. It was night, but the moon was shining, and the thief hid himself in the hollow talli tree. Hearing his pursuers close at hand, he besought the tree, saying, "O tree, tree, save me!"

When the talli tree heard his miserable cry it closed up its old sides upon him, and hid him in a safe embrace, so that the people searched for him in vain, and they had to return without him. When all pursuit was over, the tree once more opened and let him go.

Now, in this old talli tree there was sandal wood, and the thief, when he went forth, had the scent of sandal wood so permanently fixed upon him that wherever he was, and wherever he appeared, he diffused a delightful fragrance. It so happened that he visited the city of a certain king, and a man passing him on the road suddenly stopped, and asked him, "Where did you get this beautiful scent?"

"You are mistaken," answered the thief. "I have no scent."

"If you will give me this scent," said the man, "I will pay you its value."

Again the thief answered, "I have no scent—none."

Then the man, who was shrewd and intelligent, went his way to the king and told him, "There is a stranger arrived here who possesses a most wonderful scent. To your highness, perhaps, he might be induced to give it up."

The king then ordered the thief into his presence, and said to him, "Show me the scent you have."

"I have none," said he.

"If you will give it up to me quietly," said the king, "you shall be rewarded. If not, you shall be put to death."

When the thief heard this he got frightened and said, "Do not kill me, and I will tell the whole story." So he told the king how his life was preserved in the heart of the talli tree, and how the scent of sandal wood had never left him since.

Then said the king, "Come along and show me that wonderful tree of which you tell me."

Arriving at this very spot, the king instantly gave orders to his followers to cut the tree down and to carry it to his palace. But when the talli tree heard his order, and when it understood the reason of it, it cried aloud, "I have saved the life of a man, and for this I am to lose my own life. For the future, therefore, let it be decreed within this jungle that whosoever dares to do good, to him it shall be repaid in evil!"

The girl, having heard this doleful story, returned once more to her husband's side.

"Well," said the snake, "have you consulted the talli tree? And do you find that our custom here is even as I told you?"

She was compelled to admit that it was so. But as the monster advanced to his victim, she wept and said, "What will become of me? If you must eat my husband, you must begin by eating me!"

The snake objected to an arrangement so unreasonable. "You?" cried he. "But you have never done me the smallest good. You have not even done me harm. How, then, can I be expected to eat you?"

"But if you kill my husband," replied she, "what's left for me? You acknowledge yourself that I have done you no good, and yet you would inflict this injury upon me."

When the snake heard these words he stopped, and began to grow remorseful, especially as she wept more copiously than ever. That the boy must be eaten was certain, but how should he comfort the girl? Wishing to devise something, he crept back to his hole, and in a few minutes he returned with two magic globules or pills. "Here, foolish woman," said he, "take these two pills and swallow them, and you will have two sons to whom you can devote yourself, and who will take good care of you!"

The girl accepted the pills, but, with the cunning natural to a woman, said, "If I take these two pills, doubtless two sons will be born. But what about my good name?"

The snake, who knew not that she was already wed, hearing her speech, became exasperated with her. "Women are preposterous beings," cried he, and he crept back once more to his hole. This time he brought out two more pills, and when handing them to the disconsolate girl he said, "Revenge will sweeten your lot. When any of your neighbors revile you on account of your sons, take one of these pills between finger and thumb, hold it over them, rubbing it gently so that some of the powder may fall on them, and immediately you will see them consume away to ashes."

Tying the former pills in her cloth, the girl looked at the other pills incredulously, and then, with a sudden thought, she gently rubbed them over the snake, saying with an innocent air, "O snake, explain this mystery to me again! Is this the way I am to rub them?"

The moment an atom of the magic powder had touched the snake, he was set on fire, and in another instant he was merely a long wavy line of gray dust lying on the ground.

Then with a glad face the little wife turned to her husband and said, "Whosoever does good to anyone, in the end good will be done to him. And whosoever does evil to anyone, in the end evil will be done to him. You did good, and lo! You are rewarded. The snake did evil, and evil befell him. All things help each other. The Almighty brings everything to rights at last."

After this the two went on their way to their own home, where they lived in happiness and contentment for many a year.

THE DEATH AND BURIAL OF THE POOR HEN-SPARROW

Tradition Bearer: Hajjan

Source: Steel, Flora Annie. *Tales of the Punjab: Told by the People*. London: Macmillan and Company, 1894, 148–158.

Date: ca. 1880

Original Source: Punjabi

National Origin: Pakistan

The following **cumulative tale**, true to form, emphasizes ever-accumulating detail, rhythm, and rhyme in a story built on "The Death of the Little Hen" (AT 2022).

Once upon a time there lived a cock-sparrow and his wife, who were both growing old. But despite his years the cock-sparrow was a gay, festive old bird, who plumed himself upon his appearance, and was quite a ladies' man. So he cast his eyes on a lively young hen, and determined to marry her, for he was tired of his sober old wife.

The wedding was a mighty grand affair, and everybody as jolly and merry as could be, except of course the poor old wife, who crept away from all the noise and fun to sit disconsolately on a quiet branch just under a crow's nest, where she could be as melancholy as she liked without anybody poking fun at her.

Now while she sat there it began to rain, and after a while the drops, soaking through the crow's nest, came drip-dripping onto her feathers. She, however, was far too miserable to care, and sat there all huddled up and peepy till the shower was over. Now it so happened that the crow had used some scraps of dyed cloth in lining its nest, and as these became wet the colors ran, and dripping down on to the poor old hen-sparrow beneath, dyed her feathers until she was as gay as a peacock.

Fine feathers make fine birds, we all know, and she really looked quite spruce; so much so, that when she flew home, the new wife nearly burst with envy, and asked her at once where she had found such a lovely dress.

"Easily enough," replied the old wife, "I just went into the dyer's vat."

The bride instantly determined to go there also. She could not endure the notion of the old thing being better dressed than she was, so she flew off at once to the dyer's, and being in a great hurry, went pop into the middle of the vat, without waiting to see if it was hot or cold. It turned out to be just scalding. Consequently the poor thing was half boiled before she managed to scramble out.

Meanwhile, the gay old cock, not finding his bride at home, flew about distractedly in search of her, and you may imagine what bitter tears he wept when he found her, half drowned and half boiled, with her feathers all awry, lying by the dyer's vat.

"What has happened?" quoth he.

But the poor bedraggled thing could only gasp out feebly:

> The old wife was dyed—
> The nasty old cat!
> And I, the gay bride,
> Fell into the vat!

Whereupon the cock-sparrow took her up tenderly in his bill and flew away home with his precious burden. Now, just as he was crossing the big river in front of his house, the old hen-sparrow, in her gay dress, looked out of the window, and when she saw her old husband bringing home his young bride in such a sorry plight, she burst out laughing shrilly, and called aloud,

> That is right! That is right! Remember what the song says:
> Old wives must scramble through water and mud,
> But young wives are carried dry-shod o'er the flood.

This allusion so enraged her husband that he could not contain himself, but cried out, "Hold your tongue, you shameless old cat!"

Of course, when he opened his mouth to speak, the poor draggled bride fell out, and, going plump into the river, was drowned. Whereupon the cock-sparrow was so distracted with grief that he picked off all his feathers until he was as bare as a plowed field. Then, going to a pipal tree, he sat all naked and forlorn on the branches, sobbing and sighing.

"What has happened?" cried the pipal tree, aghast at the sight.

"Don't ask me!" wailed the cock-sparrow. "It isn't manners to ask questions when a body is in deep mourning."

But the pipal would not be satisfied without an answer, so at last poor bereaved cock-sparrow replied:

> The ugly hen painted.
> By jealousy tainted,
> The pretty hen dyed.

Lamenting his bride,
The cock, bald and bare,
Sobs loud in despair!

On hearing this sad tale, the pipal became overwhelmed with grief and, declaring it must mourn also, shed all its leaves on the spot.

By and by a buffalo, coming in the heat of the day to rest in the shade of the pipal tree, was astonished to find nothing but bare twigs.

"What has happened?" cried the buffalo. "You were as green as possible yesterday!"

"Don't ask me!" whimpered the pipal. "Where are your manners? Don't you know it isn't decent to ask questions when people are in mourning?"

But the buffalo insisted on having an answer, so at last, with many sobs and sighs, the pipal replied:

The ugly hen painted.
By jealousy tainted,
The pretty hen dyed.
Bewailing his bride,
The cock, bald and bare,
Sobs loud in despair;
The pipal tree grieves
By shedding its leaves!

"Oh dear me!" cried the buffalo. "How very sad! I really must mourn too!"

So she immediately cast her horns, and began to weep and wail. After a while, becoming thirsty, she went to drink at the riverside.

"Goodness gracious!" cried the river, "What is the matter? And what have you done with your horns?"

"How rude you are!" wept the buffalo. "Can't you see I am in deep mourning? And it isn't polite to ask questions."

But the river persisted until the buffalo, with many groans, replied:

The ugly hen painted.
By jealousy tainted,
The pretty hen dyed.
Lamenting his bride,
The cock, bald and bare,
Sobs loud in despair;
The pipal tree grieves
By shedding its leaves;
The buffalo mourns
By casting her horns!

"Dreadful!" cried the river, and wept so fast that its water became quite salt [salty].

By and by a cuckoo, coming to bathe in the stream, called out, "Why, river! What has happened? You are as salt as tears!"

"Don't ask me!" mourned the stream. "It is too dreadful for words!" Nevertheless, when the cuckoo would take no denial, the river replied:

> The ugly hen painted.
> By jealousy tainted,
> The pretty hen dyed.
> Lamenting his bride,
> The cock, bald and bare,
> Sobs loud in despair;
> The pipal tree grieves
> By shedding its leaves;
> The buffalo mourns
> By casting her horns;
> The stream, weeping fast,
> Grows briny at last!

"Oh dear! Oh dear me!" cried the cuckoo. "How very, very sad! I must mourn too!" So it plucked out an eye, and going to a corn [grain] merchant's shop, sat on the doorstep and wept.

"Why, little cuckoo! What's the matter?" cried Bhagtu the shopkeeper. "You are generally the pertest of birds, and today you are as dull as ditchwater!"

"Don't ask me!" sniveled the cuckoo. "It is such terrible grief! Such dreadful sorrow! Such-such horrible pain!"

However, when Bhagtu persisted, the cuckoo, wiping its one eye on its wing, replied:

> The ugly hen painted.
> By jealousy tainted,
> The pretty hen dyed.
> Lamenting his bride,
> The cock, bald and bare,
> Sobs loud in despair;
> The pipal tree grieves
> By shedding its leaves;
> The buffalo mourns
> By casting her horns;
> The stream, weeping fast,
> Grows briny at last;

> The cuckoo with sighs
> Blinds one of its eyes!

"Bless my heart!" cried Bhagtu, "But that is simply the most heartrending tale I ever heard in my life! I must really mourn likewise!" Whereupon he wept, and wailed, and beat his breast, until he went completely out of his mind. And when the queen's maidservant came to buy of him, he gave her pepper instead of turmeric, onion instead of garlic, and wheat instead of pulse.

"Dear me, friend Bhagtu!" quoth the maidservant. "Your wits are woolgathering! What's the matter?"

"Don't! Please don't!" cried Bhagtu. "I wish you wouldn't ask me, for I am trying to forget all about it. It is too dreadful—too, too terrible!"

At last, however, yielding to the maid's entreaties, he replied, with many sobs and tears:

> The ugly hen painted.
> By jealousy tainted,
> The pretty hen dyed.
> Lamenting his bride,
> The cock, bald and bare,
> Sobs loud in despair;
> The pipal tree grieves
> By shedding its leaves;
> The buffalo mourns
> By casting her horns;
> The stream, weeping fast,
> Grows briny at last;
> The cuckoo with sighs
> Blinds one of its eyes;
> Bhagtu's grief so intense is,
> He loses his senses!

"How very sad!" exclaimed the maidservant. "I don't wonder at your distress. But it is always so in this miserable world! Everything goes wrong!"

Whereupon she fell to railing at everybody and everything in the world, until the queen said to her, "What is the matter, my child? What distresses you?"

"Oh!" replied the maidservant, "The old story! Everyone is miserable, and I most of all! Such dreadful news!

> The ugly hen painted.
> By jealousy tainted,
> The pretty hen dyed.

Lamenting his bride,
The cock, bald and bare,
Sobs loud in despair;
The pipal tree grieves
By shedding its leaves;
The buffalo mourns
By casting her horns;
The stream, weeping fast,
Grows briny at last;
The cuckoo with sighs
Blinds one of its eyes;
Bhagtu's grief so intense is,
He loses his senses;
The maidservant wailing
Has taken to railing!

"Too true!" wept the queen, "Too true! The world is a vale of tears! There is nothing for it but to try and forget!" Whereupon she set to work dancing away as hard as she could.

By and by in came the prince, who, seeing her twirling about, said, "Why, mother! What is the matter?"

The queen, without stopping, gasped out:

The ugly hen painted.
By jealousy tainted,
The pretty hen dyed.
Lamenting his bride,
The cock, bald and bare,
Sobs loud in despair;
The pipal tree grieves
By shedding its leaves;
The buffalo mourns
By casting her horns;
The stream, weeping fast,
Grows briny at last;
The cuckoo with sighs
Blinds one of its eyes;
Bhagtu's grief so intense is,
He loses his senses;
The maidservant wailing
Has taken to railing;
The queen, joy enhancing,
Takes refuge in dancing!

"If that is your mourning, I'll mourn too!" cried the prince, and seizing his tambourine, he began to thump on it with a will. Hearing the noise, the king came in, and asked what was the matter.

"This is the matter!" cried the prince, drumming away with all his might:

> The ugly hen painted.
> By jealousy tainted,
> The pretty hen dyed.
> Lamenting his bride,
> The cock, bald and bare,
> Sobs loud in despair;
> The pipal tree grieves
> By shedding its leaves;
> The buffalo mourns
> By casting her horns;
> The stream, weeping fast,
> Grows briny at last;
> The cuckoo with sighs
> Blinds one of its eyes;
> Bhagtu's grief so intense is,
> He loses his senses;
> The maidservant wailing
> Has taken to railing;
> The queen, joy enhancing,
> Takes refuge in dancing;
> To aid the mirth coming,
> The prince begins drumming!

"Capital! Capital!" cried the king, "That's the way to do it!" So, seizing his zither, he began to thrum away like one possessed.

And as they danced, the queen, the king, the prince, and the maidservant sang:

> The ugly hen painted.
> By jealousy tainted,
> The pretty hen dyed.
> Bewailing his bride,
> The cock, bald and bare,
> Sobs loud in despair;
> The pipal tree grieves
> By shedding its leaves;
> The buffalo mourns
> By casting her horns;

> The stream, weeping fast,
> Grows briny at last;
> The cuckoo with sighs
> Blinds one of its eyes;
> Bhagtu's grief so intense is,
> He loses his senses;
> The maidservant wailing
> Has taken to railing;
> The queen, joy enhancing,
> Takes refuge in dancing;
> To aid the mirth coming,
> The prince begins drumming;
> To join in it with her
> The king strums the zither!

So they danced and sang till they were tired, and that was how everyone mourned poor cock-sparrow's pretty bride.

THE SEVEN WISE MEN OF BUNEYR

Tradition Bearer: Unavailable

Source: Swynnerton, Charles. *Indian Nights' Entertainment: Folk-Tales from the Upper Indus.* London: Elliot Stock, 1892, 305–307.

Date: ca. 1890

Original Source: Pakistan

National Origin: Pakistan

There is heavy irony in the title "The Seven Wise Men of Buneyr," because this is a classic **numskull** tale concerning a group of men who behave in an absurdly foolish fashion. The basic plot of the tale is provided by "Numskulls Unable to Count Their Own Number" (AT 1287), while other incidents compound the foolishness until the shepherd to whom they become indebted begs for mercy.

Seven men of Buneyr once left their native wilds for the purpose of seeking their fortunes. When evening came they all sat down under a tree to rest, when one of them said, "Let us count to see if we are all here." So he counted, "One, two, three, four, five, six," but, quite omitting to reckon himself, he exclaimed, "There's one of us missing, we are only six!"

"Nonsense!" cried the others, and the whole company of seven began counting with uplifted forefingers, but they all forgot to count themselves.

Fearing some evil, they now rose up, and at once set out to search for their missing comrade. Presently they met a shepherd, who greeted them civilly and said, "Friends, why are you in such low spirits?"

"We have lost one of our party," answered they, "we started this morning seven in number, and now we are only six. Have you seen any one of us hereabouts?"

"But," said the shepherd, "seven you are, for I have found your lost companion; behold: one, two, three, four, five, six, *seven!*"

"Ah," answered the wise men of Buneyr, "you have indeed found our missing brother. We owe you a debt of gratitude. Because you have done us this service, we insist on doing a month's free labor for you."

So the shepherd, overjoyed with his good fortune, took the men home with him.

Now, the shepherd's mother was a very old woman, in her dotage, utterly feeble and unable to help herself. When the morning came he placed her under the care of one of the Buneyris, saying to him, "You will stay here and take care of my old mother."

To another Buneyri he said, "You take out my goats, graze them on the hills by day, and watch over them by night."

To the other five he said, "As for you, I shall have work for you tomorrow."

The man who was left in charge of the old crippled mother found that his time was fully occupied in the constant endeavor to drive off the innumerable flies which in that hot season kept her in a state of continual excitement and irritation. When, however, he saw that all his efforts were fruitless, and that he flapped the wretches away in vain, he became desperate, and, lifting up a large stone, he aimed it deliberately at a certain fly which had settled on the woman's face. Hurling it with all his might, he of course missed the fly, but, alas! he knocked the woman prone on her back. When the shepherd saw this he wrung his hands in despair. "Ah," cried he, "what has your stupidity done for me? The fly has escaped, but as for my poor old mother, you have killed her dead."

Meanwhile, the second Buneyri led his flock of goats up and down among the hills, and when midday came he rested to eat his bread, while many of the assembled goats lay down beside him. As he was eating he began to observe how the goats were chewing the cud and occasionally looking at him. So, he foolishly imagined that they were mocking him, and waxed wroth. "So," cried he, "because I am taking my food, you must needs crowd round and make game of me, must you?" And, seizing his hatchet, he made a sudden rush at the poor animals, and he had already struck off the heads of several of them, when the shepherd came running to the spot, bemoaning his bad luck and crying to the fellow to desist from slaughter.

That night was a sorrowful one for the trustful shepherd, and bitterly he repented his rashness. In the morning the remaining five wise men of Buneyr came to him, and said, "It is now our turn. Give us some work to do, too!"

"No, no, my friends," answered he, "you have amply repaid me for the trifling favor I did for you in finding your missing companion; and now, for God's sake, go your way and let me see you no more."

Hearing these words, the wise men of Buneyr resumed their journey.

PUNJABI

THE GRAIN OF CORN

Tradition Bearer: Unavailable

Source: Steel, Flora Annie. *Tales of the Punjab: Told by the People*. New York: Macmillan and Company, 1894, 198–202.

Date: ca. 1890

Original Source: Punjabi

National Origin: India

In this and all other **variants** of the **cumulative tale** "Bird's Pea Gets Stuck in Socket of Mill-Handle" (AT 2034), a bird's life is in peril over a minor object (for example, a pea or a grain of corn). In the end, this minor affair has repercussions extending to the highest levels of society. Compare this tale's development to "The Death and Burial of the Poor Hen-Sparrow" (page 281) for differing uses of rhyme and rhythm. Punjab is a rich agricultural region straddling the border between India and Pakistan. Because of the necessity for reciting long chains of events quickly, these tales often pose a challenge for performers.

Once upon a time a farmer's wife was winnowing corn, when a crow, flying past, swooped off with a grain from the winnowing basket and perched on a tree close by to eat it. The farmer's wife, greatly enraged, flung a clod at the bird with so good an aim that the crow fell to the ground, dropping the grain of corn, which rolled into a crack in the tree.

The farmer's wife, seeing the crow fall, ran up to it, and seizing it by the tail, cried, "Give me back my grain of corn, or I will kill you!"

The wretched bird, in fear of death, promised to do so, but, lo and behold! When he came to search for the grain, it had rolled so far into the crack that neither by beak nor claw could he reach it.

So he flew off to a woodman, and said:

> Man! man! cut tree;
> I can't get the grain of corn
> To save my life from the farmer's wife!

But the woodman refused to cut the tree; so the crow flew on to the king 's palace, and said:

> King! king! kill man;
> Man won't cut tree;
> I can't get the grain of corn
> To save my life from the farmer's wife!

But the king refused to kill the man; so the crow flew on to the queen, and said:

> Queen! queen! coax king;
> King won't kill man;
> Man won't cut tree.
> I can't get the grain of corn
> To save my life from the farmer's wife!

But the queen refused to coax the king; so the crow flew on till he met a snake, and said:

> Snake! snake! bite queen;
> Queen won't coax king;
> King won't kill man;
> Man won't cut tree;
> I can't get the grain of corn
> To save my life from the farmer's wife!

But the snake refused to bite the queen; so the crow flew on till he met a stick, and said:

> Stick! stick! beat snake;
> Snake won't bite queen;
> Queen won't coax king;
> King won't kill man:
> Man won't cut tree;

> I can't get the grain of corn
> To save my life from the farmer's wife!

But the stick refused to beat the snake; so the crow flew on till he saw a fire, and said:

> Fire! fire! burn stick;
> Stick won't beat snake;
> Snake won't bite queen;
> Queen won't coax king;
> King won't kill man;
> Man won't cut tree;
> I can't get the grain of corn
> To save my life from the farmer's wife!

But the fire refused to burn the stick; so the crow flew on till he met some water, and said:

> Water! water! quench fire;
> Fire won't burn stick;
> Stick won't beat snake;
> Snake won't bite queen;
> Queen won't coax king;
> King won't kill man;
> Man won't cut tree;
> I can't get the grain of corn
> To save my life from the farmer's wife!

But the water refused to quench the fire; so the crow flew on till he met an ox, and said:

> Ox! ox! drink water;
> Water won't quench fire;
> Fire won't burn stick;
> Stick won't beat snake;
> Snake won't bite queen;
> Queen won't coax king;
> King won't kill man;
> Man won't cut tree;
> I can't get the grain of corn
> To save my life from the farmer's wife!

But the ox refused to drink the water; so the crow flew on till he met a rope, and said:

Rope! rope! bind ox;
Ox won't drink water;
Water won't quench fire;
Fire won't burn stick;
Stick won't beat snake;
Snake won't bite queen;
Queen won't coax king;
King won't kill man;
Man won't cut tree;
I can't get the grain of corn
To save my life from the farmer's wife!

But the rope wouldn't bind the ox; so the crow flew on till he met a mouse, and said:

Mouse! mouse! gnaw rope;
Rope won't bind ox;
Ox won't drink water;
Water won't quench fire;
Fire won't burn stick;
Stick won't beat snake;
Snake won't bite queen;
Queen won't coax king;
King won't kill man;
Man won't cut tree;
I can't get the grain of corn
To save my life from the farmer's wife!

But the mouse wouldn't gnaw the rope; so the crow flew on until he met a cat, and said:

Cat! cat! catch mouse;
Mouse won't gnaw rope;
Rope won't bind ox;
Ox won't drink water;
Water won't quench fire;
Fire won't burn stick;
Stick won't beat snake;
Snake won't bite queen;
Queen won't coax king;
King won't kill man;
Man won't cut tree;
And I can't get the grain of corn
To save my life from the farmer's wife!

The moment the cat heard the name of mouse, she was after it; for the world will come to an end before a cat will leave a mouse alone.

> So the cat began to catch the mouse,
> The mouse began to gnaw the rope,
> The rope began to bind the ox,
> The ox began to drink the water,
> The water began to quench the fire,
> The fire began to burn the stick,
> The stick began to beat the snake,
> The snake began to bite the queen,
> The queen began to coax the king,
> The king began to kill the man,
> The man began to cut the tree;
> So the crow got the grain of corn,
> And saved his life from the farmer's wife!

THE BILLY GOAT AND THE KING

Tradition Bearer: Major Campbell Feroshepore

Source: Lang, Andrew. *The Olive Fairy Book.* London: Longmans, Green and Company, 1907, 211–215.

Date: Unavailable

Original Source: Punjabi

National Origin: India

In this **variant** of "The Animal Languages" (AT 670) a gift has become a curse. Ironically, in the end, the curse leads to a solution to the protagonist's dilemma.

Once there lived a certain king who understood the language of all birds and beasts and insects. This knowledge had of course been given him by a fairy godmother; but it was rather a troublesome present, for he knew that if he were ever to reveal anything he had thus learned he would turn into a stone. How he managed to avoid doing so long before this story opens I cannot say, but he had safely grown up to manhood, and married a wife, and was as happy as monarchs generally are.

This king, I must tell you, was a Hindu; and when a Hindu eats his food he has a nice little place on the ground freshly plastered with mud, and he sits in the middle of it with very few clothes on—which is quite a different way from ours.

Well, one day the king was eating his dinner in just such a nice, clean, mud-plastered spot, and his wife was sitting opposite to wait upon him and keep him company. As he ate he dropped some grains of rice upon the ground, and a little ant, who was running about seeking a living, seized upon one of the grains and bore it off towards his hole. Just outside the king's circle this ant met another ant, and the king heard the second one say, "Oh, dear friend, do give me that grain of rice, and get another one for yourself. You see my boots are so dirty that, if I were to go upon the king's eating place, I should defile it, and I can't do that, it would be so very rude."

But the owner of the grain of rice only replied, "If you want rice go and get it. No one will notice your dirty boots; and you don't suppose that I am going to carry rice for all our kindred?"

Then the king laughed.

The queen looked at herself up and down, but she could not see or feel anything in her appearance to make the king laugh, so she said, "What are you laughing at?"

"Did I laugh?" replied the king.

"Of course you did," retorted the queen, "and if you think that I am ridiculous I wish you would say so, instead of behaving in that stupid way! What are you laughing at?"

"I'm not laughing at anything," answered the king.

"Very well, but you did laugh, and I want to know why."

"Well, I'm afraid I can't tell you," said the king.

"You must tell me," replied the queen impatiently. "If you laugh when there's nothing to laugh at you must be ill or mad. What is the matter?"

Still the king refused to say, and still the queen declared that she must and would know. For days the quarrel went on, and the queen gave her husband no rest, until at last the poor man was almost out of his wits, and thought that, as life had become for him hardly worth living while this went on, he might as well tell her the secret and take the consequences.

"But," thought he, "if I am to become a stone, I am not going to lie, if I can help it, on some dusty highway, to be kicked here and there by man and beast, flung at dogs, be used as the plaything of naughty children, and become generally restless and miserable. I will be a stone at the bottom of the cool river, and roll gently about there until I find some secure resting-place where I can stay for ever."

So he told his wife that if she would ride with him to the middle of the river he would tell her what he had laughed at. She thought he was joking, and laughingly agreed; their horses were ordered and they set out.

On the way they came to a fine well beneath the shade of some lofty, widespreading trees, and the king proposed that they should get off and rest a little, drink some of the cool water, and then pass on. To this the queen consented; so they dismounted and sat down in the shade by the well-side to rest.

It happened that an old goat and his wife were browsing in the neighborhood, and, as the king and queen sat there, the nanny goat came to the well's brink and peering over saw some lovely green leaves that sprang in tender shoots out of the side of the well.

"Oh!" cried she to her husband, "come quickly and look. Here are some leaves which make my mouth water; come and get them for me!"

Then the billy goat sauntered up and looked over, and after that he eyed his wife a little crossly.

"You expect me to get you those leaves, do you? I suppose you don't consider how in the world I am to reach them? You don't seem to think at all; if you did you would know that if I tried to reach those leaves I should fall into the well and be drowned!"

"Oh," cried the nanny goat, "why should you fall in? Do try and get them!"

"I am not going to be so silly," replied the billy goat.

But the nanny goat still wept and entreated.

"Look here," said her husband, "there are plenty of fools in the world, but I am not one of them. This silly king here, because he can't cure his wife of asking questions, is going to throw his life away. But I know how to cure you of your follies, and I'm going to."

And with that he butted the nanny goat so severely that in two minutes she was submissively feeding somewhere else, and had made up her mind that the leaves in the well were not worth having.

Then the king, who had understood every word, laughed once more.

The queen looked at him suspiciously, but the king got up and walked across to where she sat.

"Are you still determined to find out what I was laughing at the other day?" he asked.

"Quite," answered the queen angrily.

"Because," said the king, tapping his leg with his riding whip, "I've made up my mind not to tell you, and moreover, I have made up my mind to stop you mentioning the subject any more."

"What do you mean?" asked the queen nervously.

"Well," replied the king, "I notice that if that goat is displeased with his wife, he just butts her, and that seems to settle the question—"

"Do you mean to say you would beat me?" cried the queen.

"I should be extremely sorry to have to do so," replied the king, "but I have to persuade you to go home quietly, and to ask no more silly questions when I say I cannot answer them. Of course, if you will persist, why—"

And the queen went home, and so did the king; and it is said that they are both happier and wiser than ever before.

SRI LANKA

THE FROG PRINCE

Tradition Bearer: Unavailable

Source: Parker, Henry. *Village Folk Tales of Ceylon*. Vol. 1. London: Luzac and Company, 1910, 67–71.

Date: ca. 1910

Original Source: Sri Lanka

National Origin: Sri Lanka

Sri Lanka (called Ceylon before 1972) is located about 18 miles off the southern coast of India. Since ancient times it has served as a crossroads between continental South Asia, West Asia, Southeast Asia, and Europe. The early residents were the people known as Veddahs, and later the Dravidian people arrived on the island. The following **ordinary tale** is an inverted **variant** of the well-known "Frog Prince" (AT 440) plot, a plot in which ordeals lead to the transformation of a frog or other animal into a prince. Any significance between the transformation of the protagonist by the use of rice and the date palm has been lost in the cross-cultural transmission of the tale. It may be worth noting, however, that the date palm provides the raw materials for making the palm wine traditionally consumed in Sri Lanka as well as in other areas of South Asia. A major element of the plot involves the "Obstacle Flight" **motif** (D617).

A t a city there is a certain king; a widow lives at a house near his palace. She subsists by going to this royal palace and pounding rice there; having handed it over, she takes away the rice powders and lives on it.

During the time while she was getting a living in this way, she bore a frog, which she reared there. When it was grown up, the king of that city caused this proclamation to be made by beat of tom-toms, "I will give half my kingdom, and goods amounting to an elephant's load to the person who brings the Jeweled Golden Cock that is at the house of the Rakshasi (Ogress).

The frog took the bundle of rice, and hanging it from his shoulder, went to an Indi (wild date) tree, scraped the leaf off a date spike (the mid-rib of the leaf), and strung the rice on it. While going away after stringing it, the frog then became like a very good-looking royal prince, and a horse and clothing for him made their appearance there. Putting on the clothes he mounted the horse, and making it bound along he went on till he came to a city.

Hearing that he had arrived, the king of that city prepared quarters for this prince to stay at, and having given him ample food and drink, asked, "Where art thou going?"

Then the Prince said, "The King of our city has made a proclamation by beat of tom-toms, that he will give half his kingdom and an elephant's load of gold to the person who brings him the Jeweled Golden Cock that is at the Rakshasi's house. Because of it I am going to fetch the Jeweled Golden Cock."

The King, being pleased with the prince on account of it, gave him a piece of charcoal. "Should you be unable to escape from the Rakshasi while returning after taking the Jeweled Golden Cock, tell this piece of charcoal to be created a fire-fence, and cast it down," he said. Taking it, he went to another city.

The king of that city in that very manner having prepared quarters, and made ready and given him food and drink, asked, "Where art thou going?"

The prince replied in the same words, "I am going to bring the Jeweled Golden Cock that is at the house of the Rakshasi."

That king also being pleased on account of it, gave him a stone, "Should you be unable to escape from the Rakshasi, tell this stone to be created a mountain, and cast it down," he said.

Taking the charcoal and the stone which those two kings gave him, he went to yet another city. The king also in that very manner having given him quarters, and food and drink, asked, "Where art thou going?" The prince in that very way said, "I am going to bring the Jeweled Golden Cock." That King also being greatly pleased gave him a thorn. "Should you be unable to escape from the Rakshasi, tell a thorn fence to be created, and cast down this thorn," he said.

On the next day he went to the house of the Rakshasi. She was not at home; the Rakshasi's daughter was there. That girl having seen the prince coming and not knowing him, asked "Elder brother, elder brother, where are you going?"

The prince said, "Younger sister, I am not going anywhere whatever. I came to beg at your hands the Jeweled Golden Cock which you have got."

To that she replied, "Elder brother, today indeed I am unable to give it. Tomorrow I can. Should my mother come now she will eat you; for that reason come and hide yourself."

Calling him into the house, she put him in a large trunk at the bottom of seven trunks, and shut him up in it.

After a little time had passed, the Rakshasi came back. Having come and seen that the prince's horse was there, she asked her daughter, "Whose is this horse?"

Then the Rakshasi's daughter replied, "Nobody's whatever. It came out of the jungle, and I caught it to ride on."

The Rakshasi having said, "If so, it is good," came in. While lying down to sleep at night, the sweet odor of the prince having reached the Rakshasi, she said to her daughter, "What is this, Bola [a familiar and somewhat condescending term of address]? A smell of a fresh human body is coming to me."

Then the Rakshasi's daughter said, "What, mother! Do you say so? You are constantly eating fresh bodies; how can there not be an odor of them?"

After that, the Rakshasi, taking those words for the truth, went to sleep.

At dawn on the following day, as soon as she arose, the Rakshasi went to seek human flesh for food. After she had gone, the Rakshasa-daughter, taking out the prince who was shut up in the box, told that prince a device on going away with the Jeweled Golden Cock, "Elder brother, if you are going away with the cock, take some cords and fasten them round my shoulders. Having put them round me, take the cock, and having mounted the horse, go off, making him bound quickly. When you have gone, I shall cry out. Mother comes when I give three calls. After she has come, loosening me will occupy much time; then you will be able to get away."

In the way she said, the Prince tied the Rakshasa-daughter, and taking the Jeweled Golden Cock mounted the horse, and making it bound quickly came away.

As that Rakshasa-daughter said, while she was calling out, the Rakshasi came. Having come, after she looked about (she found that) the Rakshasa-daughter was tied, and the Jeweled Golden Cock had been taken away. After she had asked, "Who was it? Who took it?" the Rakshasa-daughter said, "I don't know who it was." After that, she very quickly unfastened the Rakshasa-daughter, and both of them came running to eat that Prince.

The Prince was unable to go quickly. While going, the Prince turned round, and on looking back saw that this Rakshasi and the Rakshasa-daughter were coming running to eat that Prince.

After that, he cast down the thorn which the above-mentioned king of the third city gave him, having told a thorn fence to be created. A thorn fence was created. Having jumped over it, they came on.

After that, when he had put down the piece of stone which the king of the second city gave him, and told a mountain to be created a mountain was created. They sprang over that mountain also, and came on.

After that, he cast down the charcoal which the king of the first city gave him, having told a fire fence to be created. In that very manner, a fire fence was created. Having come to it, while jumping over it, both of them were burnt and died.

From that place, the prince came along. While coming, he arrived at the Indi tree on which he had threaded the rice, and having taken off it all that dried-up rice, he began to eat it. On coming to the end of it, the person who was like that prince again became a Frog.

After he became a frog, the clothes that he was wearing, and the horse, and the Jeweled Golden Cock vanished. Out of grief on that account, that frog died at that very place.

THE KING WHO LEARNED THE SPEECH OF ANIMALS

Tradition Bearer: Unavailable

Source: Parker, Henry. *Village Folk Tales of Ceylon.* Vol. 3. London: Luzac and Company, 1910, 258–260.

Date: ca. 1910

Original Source: Sri Lanka

National Origin: Sri Lanka

The following tale is a **variant** of "The Animal Languages" (AT 670). In the course of this narrative, the jackal uses a typical **trickster** strategy of directing action by inference and analogy. In this way, he accomplishes goals without risk to himself. Compare this folktale to "The Billy Goat and the King" (page 295).

In a certain country a king was rearing wild animals. The king had learnt in a thorough manner the speech of animals.

One day at that time the fowls were saying, "Our king assists us very much; he gives us food and drink." They thanked the king very much. The king having heard their talk, the king laughed with pleasure.

The royal queen having been near, asked, "What did you laugh at?"

"I merely (*nikan*) laughed," the king said. Should he explain and give the talk to any person the king will die. Because of it he did not explain and give it. That the king knows the speech of animals he does not inform anyone.

The royal queen says, "There is no one who laughs in that way without a reason. Should you not say the reason I am going away, or having jumped into a well I shall die."

Thereupon the king, because he was unable to be released from [the importunity of] the queen, thought, "Even if I am to die I must explain and give this."

Thinking thus, he went to give food to the animals. Then it was evident to those animals that this king is going to die. Out of the party of animals first a cock says, "His majesty our king is going to be lost. We don't want the food. We shall not receive assistance. Unless his majesty the king perish thus we shall not perish. In submission to me there are many hens. When I have called them the hens come. When I have told them to eat they eat. When I have told them to go they go. The king, having become submissive in that manner to the thing that his wife has said, is going to die."

The king having heard it, laughed at it also.

Then, also, the royal queen asked, "What did you laugh at?"

Thereupon, not saying the [true] word, the king said, "Thinking of constructing a tank, I laughed."

Then the queen said, "Having caused the animals that are in this Lankawa (Ceylon) to be brought, let us build a tank."

Then the king having said, "It is good," caused the animals to be brought. The king having gone with the animals, showed them a place [in which] to build a tank; and telling them to build it came away.

The animals, at the king's command being unable to do anything, all together began to struggle on the mound of earth. Those which can take earth in the mouth take it in the mouth. All work in this manner. The jackal, not doing work, having bounded away remained looking on.

After three or four days, the king having gone [there] trickishly stayed looking on. The king saw that the other animals are all moving about as though working. The jackal, only, having bounded off is looking on.

Having seen it he asked the jackal, "The others are all working. Thou, only, art looking upward. Why?"

Thereupon the jackal said, "No, O lord, I looked into an account."

Then the king asked, "What account art thou looking at?"

The jackal says, "I looked whether in this country the females are in excess or the males are in excess."

The king asked, "By the account which thou knowest, are the females in excess or the males in excess?"

The jackal said, "So far as I can perceive, the females are in excess in this country."

Then the king said that men are in excess. Having said it the king said, "I myself having gone home and looked at the books, if males are in excess I shall give thee a good punishment."

The king having come home and looked at the books, it appeared that the males were in excess. Thereupon the king called the jackal, and said, "Bola, males are in excess."

Then the jackal says, "No, O lord, your majesty, they are not as many as the females. Having also put down to the female account the males who hearken to the things that females say, after they counted them the females would be in excess."

Then the jackal said, "Are the animals able to build tanks? How shall they carry the earth?"

Thereupon the king having considered it, and having said, "Wild animals, wild animals, you are to go to the midst of the forest," came home.

At that time, the queen asked, "Is the tank built and finished?"

Then the king, taking a cane, began to beat the queen. Thereupon the queen, having said, "Ané! O lord, your majesty, I will never again say anything, or even ask anything," began to cry aloud.

The king got to know that the jackal was a wise animal.

SOUTHEAST ASIA

BORNEO

THE BEGINNING

Tradition Bearer: Unavailable

Source: Evans, Ivor H. N. "Folk Stories of the Tempassuk and Tuaran Districts, British North Borneo." *The Journal of the Royal Anthropological Institute of Great Britain and Ireland* 43 (1913): 471–473.

Date: ca. 1910

Original Source: Borneo

National Origin: Malaysia

The Southeast Asian region of Borneo, located in the midst of the Indonesian archipelago is the third largest island in the world. In the twenty-first century, it is apportioned among Indonesia, Malaysia, and Brunei. The Dusun, Bajau, and Illanun from whom the following narratives were collected are among the three dozen ethnic groups indigenous to the island. The subsistence bases of the indigenous cultures vary from fishing to agriculture, depending on the region in which each resides. Many groups, such as the Bajau and Illanun, for example, have been profoundly influenced by Islam. Indigenous belief systems are at the core of such narratives as "The Beginning," however. Kenharingan and Munsumundok are the primary deities of the Dusuns of Borneo. In the following creation **myth**, the pair create land and living things as well as introduce death into the universe.

At first there was a great stone in the middle of the sea. At that time there was no earth only water. The rock was large and it opened its mouth and out of it came a man and a woman. The man and the woman looked around and there was only water. The woman said to the man,

"How can we walk, for there is no land?" They descended from the rock and tried to walk on the surface of the water and found that they could.

They returned to the rock and sat down to think; for a long time they stopped there; then again they walked upon the water and at length they arrived at the house of Bisagit (the spirit of small-pox), for Bisagit had made land though it was very far away. Now the man and his wife were Kenharingan and Munsumundok. They spoke to Bisagit and asked for some of his earth and he gave it to them.

So going home they pounded up the rock and mixed Bisagit's earth with it and it became land. Then Kenharingan made the Dusun and Munsumundok made the sky. Afterwards Kenharingan and Munsumundok made the sun as it was not good for men to walk about without light. "Then," said Munsumundok, "there is no light at night, let us make the moon," and they made the moon and, the seven stars, the blatek and the kukurian [constellations].

Kenharingan and Munsumundok had one son and one daughter. Now Kenharingan's people wept because there was no food. So Kenharingan and: Munsumundok killed their girl child and cut it up, and from the different portions of its body grew all things good to eat: its head gave rise to the coconut, and you can see the marks of its eyes and mouth on the coconut till this day; from its arm-bones arose sugar cane; its fingers became bananas and its blood [rice] padi. All the animals also arose from pieces of the child.

When Kenharingan had made everything he said, "Who is able to cast off his skin? If anyone can do so, he shall not die." The snake alone heard and said, "I can." And for this reason, till the present day, the snake does not die unless killed by man. (The Dusun did not hear or they would also have thrown off their skins and there would have been no death.) Kenharingan washed the Dusun in the river, placing them in a basket; one man, however, fell out of the basket and floating away down the river stopped near the coast. This man gave rise to the Bajau who still live near the sea and are skilful at using boats.

When Kenharingan had washed the Dusun in the river he menghadjied [held a ritual for] them in his house, but one man left the house before Kenharingan had menghadjied and went off into the jungle to search for something and when he came back he could not enter the house again for he had become a monkey. This man is the father of the monkeys.

THE THREE RAJAHS

Tradition Bearer: Gergoi

Source: Evans, Ivor H. N. "Folk Stories of the Tempassuk and Tuaran Districts, British North Borneo." *The Journal of the Royal Anthropological Institute of Great Britain and Ireland* 43 (1913): 463–465.

Date: ca. 1910

Original Source: Borneo
National Origin: Malaysia

Myth commonly describes a dividing and ordering process during which the present state of the universe, including ethnic and political systems, is established. In the following narrative, the Dusun of Borneo offer an explanation for the current relationships between themselves, their Islamic neighbors, and the Europeans who colonized Borneo. The custom of taking human heads was common among the Dusun in the relatively recent past. This is especially true at the beginning of the twentieth century when the myth below was performed.

Long ago there were no men in this country of the Tempassuk; men's first place was at Naragang Nonok, up country. In this village there were many Nonok trees and men lived in them. When the kampong was over full they called a council and they agreed to divide the country between them. So three men with their wives and children and followers set out at different times from the kampong.

The first man who started at length came to a place where there was a threefold fork in the road; he kept straight on and set a mark on the road by which he had traveled. The second man chose the road to the left hand, and the third took that to the right. So the companions of the first man followed him along the straight road and at last they made a village. The parties of the second and third men, who had gone to the left and right, also made kampongs.

Seven days after the first man had made his kampong a white stag came to the place. The men of the kampong agreed to try and catch the stag, but it always escaped them, although it did not go far away from the village. Now the name of the man who followed the straight road was the Rajah Kapitan and he had seven wives, and he said to them, "I cannot catch this stag; you had better make me some cakes of banana and flour" (linobok). Then the Rajah, taking with him seven cooks to carry his food and baggage, got on his horse and set out to hunt the stag. So he hunted, and at night the Rajah and the stag both stopped.

The next morning, early, as soon as the Rajah had eaten, he again started off after the stag and for three days he chased it, but at last he lost it. Then the Rajah, finding that he did not know where he was, agreed with his men to push on till they should come to some kampong, if there was one. At last they came to a kampong and the Rajah said, "Why, there are other people in this country; I thought that my village was the only one." Then he asked in the village whose it was, and he was told the Rajah Kretan's ["King Shark"] and that the Rajah had seven wives.

"Well," said the Rajah Kapitan, "if it is true that he has seven wives, he is like me, and I will ask him for betel-nut, telling him, if his wives come to me, to send those that are the most beautiful." So the Rajah's two most beautiful wives came to him, one to give him betel-nut and the other to make him rook [cigarettes]. They were lovely, one as a star and the other as the moon. The Rajah Kretan, however, slept in his house. When the two beautiful women had waited upon the Rajah Kapitan he immediately killed them both and cutting off their heads started for home. This he did because he was angry at losing the stag. Then the Rajah Kretan awoke and when he found what had happened he caught his great dog and using it as a horse pursued the Rajah Kapitan. Now the Rajah Kapitan, who was afraid of being attacked because of the heads he had taken, when he had got home made a fort three fathoms in height.

So the Rajah Kretan came to the fort, and his dog jumped the wall. When he had got inside he asked whose kampong it was, and men answered, "The Rajah Kapitan's."

"How many wives has he got?" he asked, and a man answered "Seven."

"If that is so," said the Rajah Kretan, "let them bring me roko and pinang [betel-nut]." So the two most beautiful wives of the Rajah Kapitan came out to give him roko and pinang, and when he had been served he immediately cut off their heads, and leaping on his dog called out that he was now avenged on the Rajah Kapitan. The dog took the wall at a leap and in a little time the Rajah Kretan was nearly home. Now the Rajah Kretan was the second man who had started from Naragang Nonok, but the Rajah Kapitan knew nothing of the other men who had followed behind him. When the Rajah Kapitan awoke, for he had been asleep, he asked where his two favorite wives were, and he was told how they had been killed.

So he started out alone on his horse to hunt the Rajah Kretan and overtook him just as he was going to enter his house. Then the Rajah Kretan seeing him, threw the heads on the ground and made off on his dog, and the Rajah Kapitan hunted him on his horse. After they had been going thus for a week, the Rajah Kretan running away, and the Rajah Kapitan pursuing him, they left the Rajah Kretan's country behind and came out upon a plain. So the Rajah Kretan dismounted from his dog and the Rajah Kapitan from his horse and the two fought, but neither conquered the other. Now while they were still fighting they came into a kampong but did not know it until they struck their backs against the posts of the houses. And the men of the kampong were astonished for they saw that the two men were strangers. Then the Rajah Bassi, who was the Rajah of the village, awoke, and coming out of the house, asked why they were fighting, and the Rajah Kapitan told him how he had hunted the stag and how being angry at losing it he had cut off the heads of the Rajah Kretan's wives. And the Rajah Kretan told him how he had avenged himself on the Rajah Kapitan, and how the latter had pursued him. Then said the Rajah Bassi, "Do not quarrel any more about your wives, for I have twenty-seven who are all beautiful and you can replace your dead wives from them. This only, I beg, do not fight in my country." So the Rajah Bassi's twenty-seven wives came out of the house, and the Rajah Kapitan and the Rajah Kretan each chose two wives like their former wives in appearance.

And the Rajah Bassi said, "I have given you wives and you must fight no more; for we three men all came from Naragang Nonok, but I only know the way back. You, Rajah Kapitan, have become a Dusun, you, Rajah Kretan, have become a Mohammedan, while I have become a white man; and in future time if I have any trouble you must give me your help."

Then the Rajah Kretan and the Rajah Kapitan thanked him and promised to help him. "For," said they, "you have become a great Rajah and we will help you; and you shall judge us and our children and shall help us in time of sickness." So the Rajah Bassi said that their answer was good and that they should help him and that he would judge their peoples and give them help, "And," said he, "you must pay me a yearly tax on each head (male) of your people." And so to the present day the Rajah Bassi (the white people) judge the Rajah Kapitan (the Dusun), and the Rajah Kretan (the Mohammedans) and take a tax from them for each man. Further he spoke, saying, "There shall be in this pelompong [island] many people, for that is my wish."

So we Dusun to the present day are descendants of the Rajah Kapitan and the Bajau of the Rajah Kretan, and as the white people are the descendants of the Rajah Bassi we obey the Government and clean the paths and do other work in which the Government asks our help. For the Rajah Bassi said, "Though you have made me great I am mortal and shall die, but I will tell this story to my grandchildren, and you, Rajah Kapitan, and you, Rajah Kretan, shall tell it to yours and they shall observe it."

AKI GAHUK, THE FATHER OF THE CROCODILES

Tradition Bearer: Sirinan

Source: Evans, Ivor H. N. "Folk Stories of the Tempassuk and Tuaran Districts, British North Borneo." *The Journal of the Royal Anthropological Institute of Great Britain and Ireland* 43 (1913): 454–455.

Date: ca. 1910

Original Source: Borneo

National Origin: Malaysia

According to the following narrative, the crocodile was the result of filial impiety. In this **myth**, Grandfather Gahuk's children neglected him, regretted their actions too late, and brought about the origin of a major predator in their environment.

Long ago Aki ["grandfather"] Gahuk was chief of Kampong Tengkurus. He was a very old man and he had seven sons and four daughters. His sons all wished to take wives, and his daughters, husbands, and so they married. At last Aki Gahuk became so, old that he could no longer walk, and his children did not wish to provide for him. Then Aki Gahuk said to them, "Why do you not wish to support me, for I am an old man and can no longer get my living?" But his children answered that they wished he were dead, as he was only an encumbrance to them. So Aki Gahuk wept and said, "If you wish me dead you had better put me into the river, for although you give me food, you give me no clothes and I am naked and ashamed."

Then his children put him into the river, for they did not wish to buy clothes for him; and Aki Gahuk stopped there in the water, and every night and morning they gave him food. There was a large stone in the middle of the stream and when he was cold Aki Gahuk used to climb slowly up on to this and sit there like a toad. Now after he had been in the water for three or four months, Aki Gahuk no longer climbed the big stone and his feet and legs as far as his knees became like those of a crocodile. His children who brought him food saw that his feet had become like a crocodile's and said, "Father, we thought you would die but you are becoming a crocodile." Then all the brothers and sisters came together to look at their father and said to him, "Father, if you are not going to die, let us take you home again to the house and give you clothes, for we do not wish you to become a crocodile."

But Aki Gahuk said, "How can I go home with you, for I have become a crocodile. Before, you had no pity on me and now that you have pity on me I am unable to go home." So his children wept and said that they did not wish him to turn into a crocodile and Aki Gahuk said to them, "You can tell this story to your descendants; perhaps also it is good that I should become a crocodile. On feast days you can call to me, and when there is a flood I will take you across the river on my back." After some days his whole body became like that of a crocodile and his children were afraid that he would eat men, but he could still speak and he told them that he would never eat men though perhaps his descendants might do so. Then after a year Aki Gahuk called to his children and told them that he wished to go seawards, saying that if his children went in that direction they were to call him, "For," said he, "I wish to take a wife."

Said his children, "How will you take a wife for there are no other crocodiles?"

"I will call one to me," said their father, "I will call the Pang (iguana) and she will become my wife." Then Aki Gahuk went seawards and the Pang became his wife and from their offspring arose all the crocodiles.

THE MOSQUITOS' VILLAGE

Tradition Bearer: Si Ungin

Source: Evans, Ivor H. N. "Folk Stories of the Tempassuk and Tuaran Districts, British North Borneo." *The Journal of the Royal Anthropological Institute of Great Britain and Ireland* 43 (1913): 446–447.

Date: ca. 1910

Original Source: Borneo

National Origin: Malaysia

The **motif** of the two siblings, one kind and respectful and the other rude and haughty, appears to be popular in this traditional repertoire. Compare the following tale with "Ligat Liou" (page 315).

A long time ago a man was once hunting in the jungle and when it was near nightfall he wished to return home, but having wandered from the path he was unable to find it. While he was still searching for the way he came upon a large house near a kampong. So he went into it and meeting there an old man he told him how he was lost and asked for leave to sleep there. "Yes," said the old man, "you can sleep here, for you cannot find your way home tonight, as it is already dark." After a time, other people, men, women, and children, came to the house, and the old man told them about the stranger, saying, "Let us give him a bed for the night."

Then they brought him food, but instead of water they gave him blood, and for rice they gave him maggots. "Perhaps I am among evil spirits," thought the stranger; so he ate a little of what they had given him.

"Why do you not eat?" said the old man; and the stranger replied that he was troubled about having lost his way home. "If you cannot find your way home," said his host, "tomorrow I will send one of my men with you to show you the path." Then the women of the house said that they would find him a mat to sleep on; but when they brought it, it was only a banana leaf. So the stranger and the people of the house lay down, but the former could not sleep owing to the great number of mosquitoes. Then as he heard none of the other men in the house striking at the mosquitoes, he thought, "Perhaps this is the mosquitoes' kampong," and so he also did not try to kill them but brushed them gently from his body; and when he had done this once they no longer returned to disturb him. However, he did not sleep for he was afraid.

When morning came the old man looked at the stranger's mat and seeing no dead mosquitoes there he said to him, "Well, my son, you wish to go home and you shall have someone to show you the way. This, my younger brother, shall go with you, and you shall become brothers to one another, only do not bring him to your house but let him go when you find your path; for we are all mosquitoes, and that was man's blood you drank last night. You must take this bombing [bamboo box] with you, and when you get home call your father and mother and brothers and sisters to see what it contains, but do not open it before you get to your house."

So the stranger went home, the old man's younger brother accompanying till he found the path. When he got to his house he told his relations what had happened to him and how the old man had given him the bamboo box and had ordered him to open it in the presence of his father and mother; speaking thus, he opened the box and from it he brought out gold ornaments, rings and brace-lets, and fine clothes.

Now when the stranger's elder brother saw the gold and the fine clothes he said, "I also will go to the kampong and tell the people that I am your brother." So he started and after a time he too 'lost his way in the jungle. When it was near night he came to the kampong of the mosquitoes and asked the old man to let him sleep there; and he told the old man how his brother had lost his way in the jungle before and how he had come upon a house when he was lost and that the people of the house had given him gold and fine clothing. "But," said he, "I do not know if this is the house." Then the old man ordered them to bring food for the elder brother, and for water they brought him blood, and for rice, maggots. "What sort of food is this you give me?" said the elder brother. "Blood and maggots! I cannot eat it." When the time for sleep came they brought him a banana leaf instead of a mat; and he said again, "What is this you have brought me? This is a house not the jungle. I want to sleep on a mat, not on a banana leaf." Said the old man, "These are our mats; sleep on it if you will, but if not, what can I do, only do not say I have no respect for you." So the elder brother slept, but before long he awoke and found that he was being bitten by swarms of mosquitoes. Then he started slapping away at them right and left, and in the morning when he wished to go home there was no blood left in his body.

In the morning the old man told him that he must return and gave him a bamboo, telling him not to open it till he came to his house. "But," said the elder brother, "how can I go home for I do not know the way!" The old man replied that he must find the way for himself. So setting out he at length came upon the path and reached home safely. Then he called together all his rela-tions and friends and said, "I also have got a bamboo and I think there must be gold and fine clothes in it too." But his younger brother asked him, "Did a man guide you home?" and the elder brother said "No." So the elder brother opened the box and from it came out scorpions and centipedes and other poisonous ani-mals and stung him to death, but no one else in the house was touched by them. Thus the elder brother fell down and died; and the younger said, "My brother must have offended the people of the kampong."

LIGAT LIOU

Tradition Bearer: Sirinan

Source: Evans, Ivor H. N. "Folk Stories of the Tempassuk and Tuaran Districts, British North Borneo." *The Journal of the Royal Anthropological Institute of Great Britain and Ireland* 43 (1913): 439–442.

Date: ca. 1910

Original Source: Borneo

National Origin: Malaysia

The following tale is reminiscent of the **ordinary folktale** "The Kind and the Unkind Girls" (AT 480) in which two girls set out on the same path. The first is rewarded for acts of kindness, while the second is punished for refusing to perform the same acts for a supernaturally powerful stranger. Compare this tale to the Caribbean tale "The Witch at Bosen Corner" (Volume 4, page 434).

There was once a man named Tamburan. One day he took his parang [machete] and spear and his bareit [basket] and went off to look for vegetables in the jungle, for he was poor and had no food. He searched and searched but could find nothing; at last, however, he came to an old kabun [garden] and seeing a sulap [hut] near it he went to look if there were any people in it, for he thought that the kabun was still being used as there were many gourds there. Putting down his bareit and spear he climbed up into the hut, and there he saw a woman lying down. Now she was unable to sit up because her head was very large while her neck was only as thick as my little finger. The woman, whose name was Ligat Liou ["little neck"], spoke to him and said, "Tamburan, why have you come here?"

"I have come looking for vegetables," answered Tamburan, "for I have nothing to eat and nothing with which I can buy padi."

"If you are hungry," said Ligat Liou, "there is some rice ready cooked there on the saleian [shelf above the fire], which you can eat and you will find fish there too."

"How does she manage to pound her rice," thought Tamburan, "for she cannot even sit up." Then he said, "I do not like to eat alone."

"I have eaten just now," said Ligat Liou, "do not be ashamed to eat" So Tamburan took the rice and ate and when he had finished Ligat Liou asked him to come and search for lice in her hair; so he went to search, but instead of lice he found in her hair scorpions and little snakes and centipedes and all other sorts of poisonous animals. Then he killed them all till there were none left and Ligat Liou thanked him, saying that none of the women who came there would search for lice in her hair. "But now," said she, "I shall be able to stand up, for my head is light since I am free of all these lice."

So she stood up and said to Tamburan, "Take seven gourds from this kabun." So Tamburan took the gourds and brought them into the sulap. Then said Ligat Liou, "Take this first gourd as soon as you get home and cut it in two; the second one cut open when you get into your room; the third you must open in your store room; the fourth on the padi shelf, the fifth on the verandah, the sixth below the steps, and the seventh below the house."

Then Tamburan went home and on reaching his house he did as Ligat Liou had instructed him, for his children were crying for food. When he cut open the first gourd he found rice and all other kinds of food ready cooked in it, together with plates and drinking cups. So they ate and when they had finished he cut open the second gourd in his sleeping room and in it were mats for sleeping on and all the furnishings for a bedroom. The third gourd he opened in his store room and from it came gongs of all kinds and other goods besides. The fourth gourd he opened on the padi shelf and from it came great quantities of padi. The fifth he opened on the verandah and in it were many hens. The sixth he opened below the steps and out of it came great numbers of pigs. The seventh held many kerbaws [carabaos]; this also he cut open, as he had been ordered, within the fence below the house.

Now when the gourds were cut open there was a man in the house named Sikinding, who lived in another room. This man was also poor and he carne to Tamburan and said, "Brother (Pori San), where did you get all these goods from?"

Said Tamburan, "I was astonished at getting them myself, for I dreamed I was rich and when I woke up I found it was true."

"Ah," said Sikinding, "I always dream at night but I have never become rich from it," for he did not believe Tamburan's words. "It is true," said Tamburan, "for you know well that yesterday I was as poor as you and went with the rest of the men to look for vegetables in the jungle." But Sikinding still did not believe him and said, "Perhaps you got them from someone."

"I spoke truth," said Tamburan, "and this is my dream, I dreamed that I came to an old kabun and that I went into a hut there, and that I got the goods from the person who lived in the hut."

"Well," said Sikinding, "I will try and find this kabun and the person you dreamed of."

"Just as you like," said Tamburan, "for as I told you I only dreamed of the place."

"I shall start tomorrow," said Sikinding.

"Well, I am not ordering you," replied Tamburan, "you are going to please yourself." So the next day Sikinding set out to look for the kabun, but having searched for two days and not finding it he went back and told Tamburan that he thought he was a liar, saying that he had searched for the kabun for two days and not found it. "For," said he, "I think you really went to the kabun and not that you dreamed about it" But Tamburan again replied that it had been a dream. "Ah," said Sikinding, "I don't believe you, how many times have men dreamed in this kampong and never yet got rich from it."

"Well, try once more to find the place," said Tamburan, "and perhaps you will succeed."

So on the next day Sikinding set out again and not finding it returned after he had searched for four days. Thought Sikinding, "Perhaps Tamburan is trying to kill me by sending me into the jungle, this time I will take my spear and parang when I ask him, and if he will not tell me, I will kill him." Then Sikinding went to Tamburan's door and said, "I still do not believe your story though I have hunted for the kabun for four days. If you do not tell me the truth this time I will kill you, for if my luck had been bad in the jungle I should have died there." But Tamburan still declared it was a dream, and Sikinding getting angry snatched the sheath from his spear and Tamburan ran away. Then Tamburan cried out that he would tell the truth, for he was afraid that Sikinding would kill him; so Sikinding stopped chasing him and Tamburan told him how he had gone to the kabun and how he had marked the trees with his parang, so as to know the way back. "Well," said Sikinding, "I will not kill you if you will show me the way."

"But, perhaps," said Tamburan, "you will not be brave enough to hunt for the lice in her hair."

"Oh," said Sikinding, "however brave you are, I am braver."

"Well, when you come to the kabun," said Tamburan, "if anybody asks you to search for lice, you must not be afraid, for many men have been there, but I only was brave enough."

"Oh, I shall not be afraid," said Sikinding. So the next day he set out and followed the marks which Tamburan had made on the trees, and at length he came to the kabun. When he was still some way from the hut he began calling out to know if there was anyone inside; but no answer came. So when he had come to the hut he put down his bareit, and going in saw Ligat Lion there and she said to him, "What do you come for?"

"Oh," said Sikinding. "I have no padi and I have come to look for vegetables; I am very hungry; where is your rice?"

"How should I have rice?" said Ligat Liou, "for I cannot get up to pound it."

"Oh! That's not true," said Sikinding, "for how can you live if you have no rice?"

"Well, it is true," said Ligat Liou, "for as you see yourself I cannot get up." So Sikinding went to get her rice from the shelf over the fireplace, but on taking down the plate he found nothing but earth in it.

"Ah," he said, "you people in this kampong are no good; you eat earth."

"I told you I had no rice," said Ligat Liou, "but you can take a gourd from the kabun." Then Sikinding went and took a gourd, and going up again into the but he asked Ligat Liou how he was to eat it. "You must cut it open," said she, "and eat what is inside it." So he cut it open and found a little rice and one fish in it, and from this he made his meal. When he had finished eating the rice and fish he said to Ligat Liou, "That is not enough; I'll go and take another gourd and that will be sufficient."

"You can take another," said she, "but only one." So he brought another gourd, and cutting it open found inside it only rice in the husk and uncooked fish.

"I've not had enough to eat," said he, "where can I get it from?"

"You can cook the food here," said Ligat Liou.

"No, I won't do that," said Sikinding, "I will take it home and cook it; but I want seven gourds to take home with me."

"I will give them to you," said Ligat Liou, "but first come and look for lice in my hair." So Sikinding went to look for lice but when he saw the scorpions and snakes and other poisonous things he cried out and was not brave enough to kill them and he let Ligat Liou's head fall first to one side and then to the other. "Well," said Ligat Liou, "if you are afraid to kill my lice you had better go home. But take one gourd with you; you may take a large one, but do not take more than one." Then Sikinding took the gourd and Ligat Liou said to him, "When you get home and wish to open this gourd, get into your tankob [large storage vessel] and make your wife and children get into it as well; but shut up the top of the tankob well so that nothing can get out." So Sikinding ran home and calling his wife and children, they all got into the tankob with the exception of one small child, for whom there was no room. Then Sikinding opened the gourd and from it came out snakes and scorpions, which bit Sikinding and his wife and children until they died. The only person who remained alive was the small child for whom there had been no room in the tankob.

GINAS AND THE RAJAH

Tradition Bearer: Unavailable

Source: Evans, Ivor H. N. "Folk Stories of the Tempassuk and Tuaran Districts, British North Borneo." *The Journal of the Royal Anthropological Institute of Great Britain and Ireland* 43 (1913): 468–469.

Date: ca. 1910

Original Source: Borneo

National Origin: Malaysia

The extraordinary nature of Ginas, the protagonist of the following tale, is revealed at conception, if the possible translation of his mother's name ("virgin") is correct. He is precocious physically and intellectually, but he refuses to be fettered by the rules of proper behavior or even by the rajah's dictates. Ginas demonstrates his cleverness in a contest of wits involving a series of tests imposed upon him by the ruler. He trumps the rajah's ploys in handy fashion, in one case with a task of his own ("Making a Rope of Sand," AT 1174). The narrative demonstrates the affection the Dusun of Borneo have for the **trickster**.

A long time ago there was a man and his wife whose names were Rakian and Sumundok. On the day when they married many others also had married and each couple had at least two children, but Rakian and Sumundok had none, though Sumundok was expecting a child.

Rakian fell ill, and he said to his wife, "Perhaps I shall die before I see my child, but you must bring him up well, for we are not wanting in possessions."

Then Rakian died and after a time Sumundok gave birth to a male child, and she said to it, "I will give you a name; your name is Ginas, but I will not bring you up, I will put you in a box." So Sumundok put the child into a box, and after two or three months she went to look at it and found that it had grown and could walk. When the child had come out of the box it spent its time in hunting the pigs and its mother did not forbid it, "For," thought she, "if it should kill a pig, I can replace it." But the people of the kampong became angry because Sumundok's child was always chasing their pigs.

One day Ginas went to the Rajah's house, and for two days he hunted the pigs there below the house. Then the Rajah said to one of his men, "Go to Ginas's house and tell his relations that he must not hunt pigs any more, for I have had no sleep from it for two nights. If he does not follow my orders I will make him my slave." So three men went to Ginas's house and told him that if he chased the Rajah's pigs any more he would make him a slave. But Ginas paid no heed to the Rajah's words, and going to the Rajah's house he again hunted the pigs. Then said the Rajah, "All men follow my orders, this Ginas only, who is still small, does not obey me." So the Rajah sent to Ginas saying, "For three nights I have not been able to sleep for the noise of the waves in the sea. Go and chase them and see if you can stop them." When the Rajah's men came to the house of Ginas they said to him that the Rajah wished him to stop the waves, and Ginas said, "You must stop here tonight and eat with me." The three men stopped there; and when it was night Ginas went down to the sea-shore, and, taking sand, wrapped it in his handkerchief.

Then going back to the house, he woke the Rajah's men and said to them, "Give this sand to the Rajah and tell him to have a rope made from it and when the rope is made I will use it to catch the waves with." So the men went home and the Rajah asked them what Ginas had said to his order to stop the waves. Then the Rajah's men told him that Ginas had said that he would catch the waves, only that as he was short of rope he was sending some sand to the

Rajah of which to make a cord, and that when the cord was made he would catch the waves with it. And the Rajah had to admit that he was beaten, and threw the sand away.

Then the Rajah had seven jars of Tapai made, and killed three cattle; then he sent three men to call Ginas to drink. The three men came to Ginas and he replied that he would come on the next day. On the morrow, Ginas brought out clothes all covered with gold, and, putting them on, set out. When he got to the Rajah's house the Rajah asked him to sit down on his mattress, and all kinds of food and drink were brought to them, and there was a bowl there for washing the hands, seven punkals [hand spans] in circumference. After they had eaten, the Rajah said to Ginas, "Ginas, you shall wash your hands on my mattress, and if the mattress is not wetted you shall replace me as Rajah, and shall have all my property and my daughter for your wife; but if you wet the mattress you shall become my slave."

So when Ginas was washing out his mouth he was afraid to spit the water out on to the mattress, so he sent it into the Rajah's face instead, saying, "I was afraid to put it anywhere else, but your face does not matter, since you are blind in one eye, and thus your face is damaged. Take this looking-glass and look." So the Rajah took the glass, and, seeing that one of his eyes was damaged, and that no one else had so ugly a face, was ashamed and ran away from the country, taking with him only one of his wives. As for Ginas, he took his place and became Rajah.

RAKIAN

Tradition Bearer: Sirinan

Source: Evans, Ivor H. N. "Folk Stories of the Tempassuk and Tuaran Districts, British North Borneo." *The Journal of the Royal Anthropological Institute of Great Britain and Ireland* 43 (1913): 457–459.

Date: ca. 1910

Original Source: Borneo

National Origin: Malaysia

The **motif** of the spouse who changes from animal to human and back again is widely distributed. The plot of "Rakian" is typical: discovery of the animal wife who causes her husband to prosper, followed by his violation of the oath of secrecy about her animal nature, which leads to her abandoning him.

Once there was a mangis tree in which there were large bees' nests, and when there was sufficient honey in the nests a man named Rakian went to the tree and began to drive bamboo pegs into it so that he could climb up. It was getting towards evening when he began to work. Now there were many bees' nests in the tree and Rakian, seeing that the bees of the nest right at the top of the tree were white, decided to take it, "For," thought he, "I have never yet seen white bees." Then he climbed up the steps he had made in the tree to take the bees' nest and when he was close he drew his parang to cut it down.

But the bees did not swarm out from the nest and while he was sawing away at the branch from which it hung he heard the bees say "That hurts." Then Rakian, wondering, sheathed his parang and the bees said to him, "If you wish to take the nest take it gently and do not cut it down." So he took the nest with the bees in it and putting it into his bareit [basket] he descended the tree and went home. When he came to his house he put the bareit with the bees in it into his room.

Early the next morning Rakian went to his kabun and did not return until near dark when, on coming back to his house, he found rice and fish ready cooked on his shelf above the fire. "Then," thought Rakian, "who can have cooked for me for I am the only man who lives in this house: this fish is not mine though the rice is. The rice is cold and must have been cooked for a long time. Perhaps somebody has come here and cooked and taken away my bees' nest." So he went to his bareit and found the bees' nest still there. Then Rakian sat down to eat. "Well," he thought, "if, someone is going to cook for me, so much the better."

In the morning he ate the remains of the rice from the day before, and again went to his kabun. As on the previous day he came home before nightfall and again there was food prepared for him. "Who is this," thought Rakian, "who comes to my house and cooks?" and once more he went to see if his bees' nest had been stolen; and thus it happened that there was always food ready for him when he came home. One day he determined to return early and see who was cooking his food for him.

So early in the morning he set out as if for his kabun, but when he had gone a little way he went straight home again and hid himself near the house. For a long time he waited and nothing happened, but at last the door of his house creaked and a beautiful woman came out of his room and taking his bamboo water vessel went out of the house to the river to get water. Then when she had gone down to the river Rakian entered his room without the woman seeing him and went to look at his bees. But when he opened his bareit he found that there were no bees in it, but only the nest. So he took the nest from the bareit and hid it and concealed himself in the house.

After a time the woman came back from the river and went to the bareit to look for the bees' nest. "Oh," said she, "who has taken my box (sarong)?" So she hunted for the nest and at last began to weep, saying, "Who can have taken it? It cannot be Rakian for he has gone to work at his kabun. I am afraid that he will come back and find me." When it was nearly dark Rakian came out from his hiding-place as if he had just come back from his kabun; but the woman sat there without speaking.

"Why are you here?" said Rakian, "perhaps you want to steal my bees."

"I do not know anything about your bees," said the woman. So he went to the bareit to look for his bees but of course they were not there for Rakian himself had hidden the nest. "Oh," said he, "my bees' nest is not here, perhaps you have taken it. "How should I know anything about your bees' nest," said she. "Well, it does not matter," said Rakian, "will you cook for me, for I am very hungry?"

"I do not want to cook," said the woman, "for I am vexed." So Rakian kept on telling her to cook for him, but the woman refused and at last she said, "Where is my sarong?"

"I have not taken it," said Rakian. "I believe you have hidden it," said the woman, "and all my clothes and goods are in it." At last Rakian said, "I will not give it to you for I am afraid you will get into it again."

"I will not get into it," said the woman, "if you like you can take me for your wife. My mother wished to give me to you in this way because you have no wife here and I have no husband either in my country." Then Rakian took the bees' nest and gave it to the woman.

"But," said she, "if you take me as your wife do not ever call me a bee woman, for if you do I shall be much ashamed." So they married and had a child. Now one day there was a feast at a neighboring house and Rakian went to eat there. "Where is your wife from?" said a man at the feast, "for we have never seen such a beautiful woman before."

"She is from this kampong," replied Rakian. When all the men had become drunk they still kept asking him whence he had got his wife, and saying that they had never before seen such a beautiful woman. At last Rakian, who had up to that time always replied that he had taken his wife from the kampong, became drunk also. Then he forgot his promise and said, "The truth is that my wife was at first a bee." So the men stopped questioning him and Rakian went home.

When he got to the house his wife would not speak to him. "Why will you not speak?" said Rakian. "What did I tell you long ago?" said she. "I think you have been saying things to make me ashamed."

"I have not said anything," replied Rakian. "You are lying," said his wife, "for though the house is far off I heard. When men asked whence I came, at first you would not tell them, but when you became drunk, then you told them everything." Then Rakian in his turn became silent. "I will go home," said she, "for you have made me ashamed; but the child I will leave with you. In seven days my father will pass on his way home to his country and I will go with him." So Rakian wept. At the end of seven days Rakian saw a white bee flying to his house, and his wife came down the steps from his house and saying, "There is my father," she became a bee again and flew off after the other.

Then Rakian rushed into the house and seized the child, for it was in his heart to follow his wife and her father, "For," said he, "if my wife is not here the child will die because it is still little." So he hunted for the bees until he saw them going in front of him in the jungle. At the end of seven days he had lost sight of them and still he had not come to any kampong. On the eighth day he came to a bathing-place at a river. Then both he and the child, being hungry and weary, lay down by the side of the river and slept. At last a woman came from the kampong and woke Rakian and said, "Rakian, why don't you go to your wife's house instead of sleeping here with your child, for the house is not far off?"

"When I have bathed," said Rakian, "you must show me the way," and the woman replied, "Very well." So Rakian bathed and then he followed the woman and it was not long before they came to a kampong. "That is her house," said his guide, pointing to a long-house, "but her room is right in the middle of it. There are eleven rooms in the house and if you enter it you must not be afraid, for the roof beams are full of bees, but they do not attack men." So Rakian climbed up into the house and found it full of bees, both large and small, but in the middle room there were none. Men in the house there were none, only bees. Then the child began to cry and Rakian sat down. "Otun [term of endearment]," said a voice in the middle room, "Why do you not come out? Have you no pity on your child who is weeping here?" Then after a time Rakian's wife appeared in the room and the child ran to her at once, and Rakian's heart became light; but his wife said to him, "What did I tell you at first that you were not to tell whence I came? If you had not been able to follow me here, certainly there would have been distress for you." When she had finished speaking all the bees dropped down from the roof beams to the floor and became men. As for Rakian and his child they stayed in the kampong and did not go back any more.

LANGAON

Tradition Bearer: Sirinan

Source: Evans, Ivor H. N. "Folk Stories of the Tempassuk and Tuaran Districts, British North Borneo." *The Journal of the Royal Anthropological Institute of Great Britain and Ireland* 43 (1913): 435–439.

Date: ca. 1910

Original Source: Borneo

National Origin: Malaysia

As in the tale of "Rakian" (page 320), a man acquires an animal wife, but he fails to keep her because he violates the rules that have been imposed upon him. In his initial wandering and later in his quest to recover his wife, he learns courage and integrity and at last becomes worthy of marriage to a goddess.

Langaon had made a kabun [garden] sufficient in which to sow two mandores of padi [rice] and after a time it bore fruit. When the padi harvest
came the men of the kampong went to reap in their kabuns and Langaon
went also to reap in his, but when he had finished his reaping he found the produce of it was only two mandores, just what he had sown at first. "Why is this?"
said Langaon. "Other men all have a good return from their sowing; I alone have
no padi." So he went to the old men of the kampong and told them about it.

However, he decided to make another kabun and this time to sow three
mandores. So he made his kabun, and sowed three mandores, and when his padi
came up it was better than anyone else's in the kampong; when it began to fruit
too it was finer than that in any other kabun. At length harvest time came and
Langaon this time got three mandores of padi for his harvest while every other
man had at least a full tankob [large bin].

Then he made up his mind to leave the village and search for better ground
in which to plant padi. So he set out and after he had wandered for a long time
in the jungle, at last he carne to a small river and made himself a sulap there.
Here he stopped and made borusats [fish traps] in the stream. The next morning
he went to look at his traps, and found that he had got a large catch of fish.
"Then," said he, "it would be good to stop here for there is no lack of fish; only
I have no salt and no padi, and how can I live without them?" So he set out
with his fish to look for some place where he might sell them for salt or padi.
After a time he came to a kampong and the people said to him, "Oh, Langaon,
where are you going?"

"I have run away from my kampong and am living near the river," said Langaon. "I have caught many fish but as I have neither salt nor padi, I have come
here to sell them." Then they called him to come into the house and they gave
him padi and salt and cooking pots and mats in exchange for his fish. So Langaon was much pleased and the people of the kampong asked him to come every
day and bring them fish. When he got home he had sufficient to eat and vessels
in which to cook, for hitherto he had used bamboo to cook in. So he decided to
stop at the river, and make himself a large hut.

The next morning there were again many fish in his traps and Langaon
thought, "I shall be ashamed if I go every day to the kampong, so I will dry
these fish in the sun, and tomorrow I will take them the dry fish and any fresh
fish I get from the traps." On the following day, Langaon again went to the
kampong, and the people of the kampong gave him parangs [machetes] and
spears and cloth in exchange for his fish. Then Langaon said to himself, "I had
better tell them I shall not come again at once, as the river has fallen since
there has been no rain, and until rain comes again I shall have no fish." So he
told them, but they said to him, "If you have no fish, come all the same." Langaon went home, and though he got many fish he did not go to the kampong
for another week. At last, however, he started for the kampong with his fish,
but when be got there, he said, "Today I do not wish to sell my fish; I will

divide them among you, but I will not take anything in return." So he divided the fish among them and each man got two tempurongs [half of a coconut shell used as a drinking or food vessel] full.

"Why do you not ask a price for your fish," said the people of the kampong.

"I am not without food," said Langaon, "I still have much left from what you gave me before, but if I have no food left and catch no fish, I will come and ask you for what I want." So it was agreed, and Langaon asked them, when was the time for making kabuns there, and they said, "As soon as this month is finished we begin to make them." When the month was finished, Langaon went back to the kampong, bringing with him a little fish to give to the people, and again he asked them when they would start making kabuns.

"Oh, any time we feel inclined," said they, "tomorrow or the next day," and they asked him to come and live in their kampong, but Langaon refused. So he went home and the next day he began to make a kabun, and when he had cut down all the trees, his kabun was large enough to sow two mandores of seed in. "Well," he thought, "I will rest a little till other people begin to burn" (the cut trees). After about twenty days he saw great quantities of smoke coming from near the kampong and going to his kabun, he fired it until not a single tree trunk was left. "This is, troublesome," thought he, "I have no seed to sow in my kabun."

In the morning, he took his fish with him and went to the kampong to ask for seed, and when he was still far off, they started calling to him to bring his fish. So he divided his fish among them, everybody getting a tempurong full; and the people of the kampong asked him if he had sown his padi. "Not yet," said Langaon, "I came here today, to ask you to give me some seed."

"How big is your kabun?"

"About two or three mandores large," replied Langaon. So each man in the kampong gave him a mandore of seed, until there were none left who had not given.

"Why do you give me so much?" said Langaon, "for my kabun is not a large one, only enough for two mandores. If each man were to give me one or two tempurongs full I shall not finish it, but this you have given me is much more than I shall use; besides, how shall I get it home, for I shall only be able to carry two or three mandores."

"Never –mind," said the men of the kampong, "whatever you do not want to sow you can leave here, and you can use it to eat." So when he went home he took only three mandores of seed with him, and the next day he started and sowed two mandores in his kabun. The padi sprouted and thrived, and Langaon said, "Ah, perhaps this year I shall have plenty of padi," and each day he went to his kabun, though there were no weeds in it. At last he said, "What use is it for me to go to the kabun for there are no weeds in it," and for six days he remained at home. On the seventh day he went back and found that Maragang monkeys had broken into his kabun and damaged his padi. Then Langaon wept,

"Ah," said he, "all my padi has been destroyed." So he tried to raise the stems which the monkeys had beaten down, and he resolved to move his house to the kabun, so that he might guard what remained of the crop. He stayed there at the kabun until his padi had recovered, and when it was ripe, he said to himself, "I must make my binolet [storage vessel]." Then he went into the jungle to get wood for the binolet, and slept a night there, but when he returned home he found not a single grain of padi left in his kabun, all the ears of grain had been taken and only the straw left standing, and there were tracks of many monkeys everywhere. "Ah," said Langaon, "I will run away from here, for first of all the monkeys damaged my crop, and now when it is ripe they have come again and eaten it all." So he set out again, and after he had wandered in the jungle for a long time, at last he made another sulap [hut], but this time there was no river near, and he had to live on whatever he could find in the jungle. He had brought away with him the one mandore of padi seed which he had not planted in his former kabun, and here he again made a kabun and sowed the seed in it. This time he made his kabun round his house so that he might keep a guard on his crop, and when the padi came up it was very good. There he lived until his padi was in the ear.

One day he went to fetch water from the river and on coming back he saw a great many Maragang monkeys near his kabun; though they had not yet entered it and eaten his padi. Then he dropped his water vessel and went to drive away the Maragangs, but the monkeys attacked him, and Langaon ran away, for he had first come from the river, and had neither parang nor spear with him. When he got to his sulap he snatched up his spear and wounded one of the monkeys and they all ran off, except the largest of them, which still fought with him. Then Langaon retreated from the monkey backwards, until without noticing it, he became entrapped between four large tree stumps which stood in the kabun; and there both Langaon and the monkey stopped fighting while after some time the monkey suddenly became transformed into a beautiful woman.

Langaon seeing this, came out from the tree stumps and spoke to her. "Where do you come from?" said he.

"My mother ordered me to come here," replied the woman. "When you made a kabun before, I came there also, but you did not guard your padi. The padi which you said monkeys ate was reaped and I also was among the reapers."

"Where did you put the padi?" said Langaon.

"In my house," said the woman, "and the people of my kampong reaped with me."

"Well," said Langaon, "I have no food, for this padi is not yet ripe."

"You had better come home to my house," said the woman. So Langaon followed the woman home, and found that her house was in the jungle, and not far from his kabun. "I am alone here," said she, "for my father and mother and my companions are in my kampong which is a long way off. My father has much pity for you because you have no wife, and I also. All this padi in my house is yours, for when you made the kabun in your village, it was I who stole your padi, and when you made a kabun by the river, I went there also."

So Langaon stopped there, and the woman told him how she was really a Maragang monkey, but had become a woman. Then she became his wife, and Langaon said, "I will search for some kampong near, for it is evil for us to be all alone here."

"Oh," said the woman, "if you want a kampong, there is one not far off," and she pointed out a kampong to him which he had not noticed before; but his wife besought him not to go there, and so he remained with her. At last, when they had a child, Langaon said, "I should like to go to the kampong; if I start today I shall return today also, for it is not far away."

His wife said, "Do not go, for I shall be very much frightened, while you are away there." But Langaon did not pay attention to his wife's words, and after a while she said to him, "Well, if you go do not sleep the night there, for I shall be all alone here with the child." So Langaon started off, and when he got to the kampong he found a great feast going on, and joining in it he became drunk and forgot about going home. For seven days he stopped there eating and drinking, and on the sixth night he fell in love with a woman of the kampong. However, on the seventh day he started home. and when he came to his house, his wife was very angry and would not speak to him. "Why are you angry?" said he.

"Why should I not be angry," said his wife, "for you have been unfaithful with another woman, for though you were far off, I know it, and you have a mark on you by which I can tell." But Langaon denied it. "If," said his wife, "you deny it, I will take from you the mark by which I know that you have been unfaithful."

"You may take it," said Langaon.

"Well," said she, "I will show you, for I am the God of your kampong (Kenharingan Tumanah)," and taking a looking-glass she showed him the appearance of the other woman and himself in the glass. Then said Langaon, "It is true."

"I will leave you," said his wife, "and take the child with me, for you have now a wife in the kampong." But Langaon asked for pardon, saying he would pay what was according to custom, as a recompense. But still his wife refused to stop with him; so when it was near night he bound her hands and feet to his, for he was frightened that she would run away. So they slept, but when Langaon awoke in the morning, the ropes were opened, and his wife and child had gone. Then Langaon wept, for he did not know the kampong in which his wife lived. On the second day he stopped weeping and started out to look for his wife, "For," said he, "wherever I find a kampong there will I search." So he wandered in the jungle and one day he met a herd of deer which attacked him. Then Langaon ran away and crept into a hole in the ground and hid, and the deer could not catch him.

The next morning he came out of the hole and started again, but he had not gone far before he met a herd of wild pigs and these also attacked him, and as before he ran away until, coming to the same hole, he again got into it to hide. There he slept and dreamed, and in his dream a man came to him and said, "Langaon, you are a coward to run from the deer and wild pig, for if I were looking for my wife I would fight them."

"How can I fight them," said Langaon, "for I am all alone and they are many?"

"If you journey again tomorrow and are brave," said the man, "you will get your wife back, for she will ride a rhinoceros."

"Formerly I was not afraid even of the rhinoceros," said Langaon, "but I found that I was afraid of these stags and wild pig."

"If you are afraid," said the man, "you will not get your wife back."

"How shall I know the animal she is riding," said Langaon, "for the other animals had no one riding them?"

"You will know the one," said the man, "because it will have bells on it; that is the one you must hunt, but do not let it go or you will lose your wife."

In the morning Langaon awoke, and set off early in search of his wife, and, after a time, he came upon a herd of rhinoceros and among them he saw a large one which had bells hanging round its neck. So he waited for the rhinoceros with the bells to attack him, and did not run away, and when he caught hold of it by the bells round its neck all the rest of the herd vanished. The one he had caught also tried to escape, but Langaon struggled with it for three days, until he stumbled and fell close to his own house, and in falling he let go the bells. The rhinoceros disappeared and Langaon sat down to think outside his house. After a time he heard a child begin to weep inside and he went in to see who was there, and opening his door found that his wife and child had returned.

THE MOUSE DEER AND THE GIANT

Tradition Bearer: Si Ungin

Source: Evans, Ivor H. N. "Folk Stories of the Tempassuk and Tuaran Districts, British North Borneo." *The Journal of the Royal Anthropological Institute of Great Britain and Ireland* 43 (1913): 477–478.

Date: ca. 1910

Original Source: Borneo

National Origin: Malaysia

Like hare, tortoise, and spider in Africa, spider in the Caribbean, rabbit in the African American south, and coyote in many Native American traditions, mouse deer—plandok—plays a **trickster** role in parts of Southeast Asia, especially Borneo, Java, Sumatra and the Malay Peninsula. As is the case with other trickster **cycles**, the incidents commonly are arranged as a sequence of related tales, but the sequence of incidents is subject to considerable variation. In general, however, the cycle begins with the trickster cleverly exploiting one of his fellows and incurring the victim's lasting enmity. The following collection of mouse deer trickster tales begins with an interrelated set of narratives told by a single narrator, Si Ungin. In this and the following series of five tales, it is clear that one of mouse deer's primary motivations is demonstrating the superiority of his wits over his fellow creatures' physical attributes. The gergasi in the following narrative is a giant forest demon who carries a spear over his shoulder.

Once upon a time there were seven kinds of animals, the kerbau (buffalo), the sapi (ox), the dog, the stag, the horse, the plandok (mouse-deer), and the kijang (barking-deer, *Cervulus muntjac*). These animals agreed to catch fish and when they had cast a round net into the sea they drew it to the edge and there were many fish in it. They placed their fish on the sand, and someone said, "Who will guard our fish while we go and cast the net again, for we are afraid of the gergasi." Then said the kerbau, "I will guard the fish for I am not afraid of him, if he comes here I will fight him with my horns."

When the other animals had gone away the gergasi came and said, "Ha, ha, ha, what a lot of fish you have caught! I'll eat them directly, and if you don't like it I'll eat you too."

Said the kerbau, "All right, come here and I'll horn you."

"Very well," said the gergasi, "if you won't give me your fish I will eat you." When the gergasi had got close, and the kerbau made as if to horn him, he seized hold of its horns and the kerbau could do nothing, because the gergasi was very big and strong.

Then the kerbau cried out, "Let go; if you let me go you can eat the fish." So the gergasi let him go and the kerbau swam off to his companions, who were in the sea catching fish. When he came there, he said to them, "The gergasi has eaten our fish; he caught hold of my horns and I could do nothing."

Then the other animals were angry with the kerbau and said, "If we were to go on fishing till we died the gergasi would get all our fish"; and the horse said to him, "You fish with these others this time; I'll guard the fish, and if I don't manage to bite the gergasi at any rate I'll kick him." So the animals brought the fish to the same place and leaving them there in charge of the horse went again to catch more.

When the other animals had been gone a good time, out came the gergasi again, and said "Ha, ha, ha, if you don't swim off again to your companions, I'll eat you as well as the fish."

"Well," said the horse, "come and take them if you can, but I will guard them till I die." On the gergasi's approach the horse tried to bite him; but the gergasi caught him by the head and he could do nothing. Then the horse reared up and the gergasi let go his head. When he had got free he let fly at the gergasi with his heels but the gergasi caught him by the hind legs. So the horse begged to be let go and the gergasi let him go, and while the horse was swimming away to his companions the gergasi ate the fish.

When the horse reached his companions he said, "I too have done my best, but the gergasi has got the fish. First I tried to bite him, and he caught me by the head. Then I reared and, having shaken him off, tried to kick him, but he only caught me by the legs, and I had to give in."

Then his companions said, "What is the use of our catching fish, we only get tired and the gergasi eats them; it is best that we should go home." So the sapi, the stag, the dog and the kijang said, "What is the use of our trying to fight the gergasi, for we are afraid; all the strong animals have tried but they have all been beaten. Let us go home."

The plandok only remained silent, and when all the others had had their say he said, "You go and catch fish again and I will stop on guard."

"What can you do," said the horse, "who are so small? How can you fight the gergasi?"

"Nevermind," replied the plandok, "I can't fight him or kill him but I should like to guard the fish." The other animals wanted to go home, but the plandok persuaded them and they again caught many fish and these they placed on the sand in the same spot. Then said the stag, "Who is going to guard the fish?" and the kerbau replied, "Why the plandok said just now that he would."

"Very well," said the plandok, "I will guard them but perhaps some other animal would prefer to, as my body is so small." But none of the other animals were willing, so the plandok said, "All right, I will guard them, but put them in a heap and cover them with leaves so that they cannot be seen." Then his companions heaped up the fish and covered them with leaves and having done so went back to the fishing. When the others had gone the plandok went and got some rattan and cut it into strips such as are used for binding anything.

As soon as he had finished, out came the gergasi and said, "Ha, ha, ha, is the plandok guarding here? Why, I got the fish from the kerbau and the horse, what do you think you, who are so small, can do? You had better give me the fish or I'll eat you along with them."

Then the plandok said, "I'm not guarding the fish, I'm working cutting up rattan," and the gergasi, who had come near but had not seen the fish said, "What are you doing with the rattan?"

"I'm binding it round my knees," replied the plandok. "Why are you doing that?" said the gergasi. "Don't you see the sky?" said the plandok, "it looks like falling, see how low it has got; that's why I am binding up my knees."

"Why do you bind up your knees if the sky looks like falling?" asked the gergasi.

"I'm binding up my knees so that I can get into our well here; for, if the sky falls, I shall not get hurt when I'm down there." Then the gergasi looked at the sky and saw that it was very low. "Don't bind up your legs first," said he, "bind mine."

"All right," said the plandok, "only go over to the well first." So the two went to the well, the plandok carrying the rattan. Then the gergasi said, "You bind yourself up first," but the plandok replied, "If I bind myself up first how can I bind you up afterwards."

"Very well," said the gergasi, "bind me first, but you shall be the first to go into the well."

"If I do that," said the plandok, "I shall not die from the sky falling on me but from your falling on top of me in the well." So the gergasi agreed to go first as what the plandok said seemed reasonable; and the plandok bound up the gergasi firmly, tying his hands to his knees.

"Why have you bound me so tightly?" said the gergasi, but the plandok only gave him a push and he fell into the well.

"Ah, now you can stop there till you die," said the plandok you don't know the plandok's cleverness."

"I suppose I shall die here," said the gergasi.

"Yes," said the plandok, "for you have always stolen our fish." After a little time there came the plandok's companions, bringing more fish. "Ah, see how clever I am," said the plandok, "for I have bound the gergasi! You said the gergasi was strong. How then have I managed to tie him up?"

"You lie," said the kerbau, and the horse, "How could *you* manage to bind him."

"If you don't believe me," said the plandok, "look into that well and see if he's not there." So all the animals went to the well and saw the gergasi.

Then said the horse and the kerbau, "How did you bind him?"

"What's the use of your asking," said the plandok, "you don't know the plandok's cunning. However, you'd better kill him with a spear or something because he's stolen our fish so often." So they killed the gergasi with a spear.

When the gergasi was dead they agreed to eat on the shore, and when they had cooked their fish and rice they found only one thing wanting, and that was pepper. So as they had no red pepper they did without it, though as they were accustomed to it they did not enjoy their food so much.

Then while they were eating, the plandok saw that the end of the dog's penis was showing red, "Ah," said he, "we were seeking for red pepper just now- there is some I see." And he pointed to the dog's penis. The dog did not understand and the stag and the kijang said, "Where is pepper."

"There," said the plandok, and he again pointed to the dog. Then the dog became very angry because he was ashamed and the stag and the kijang had laughed at him. Then the stag, the kijang, and the plandok became frightened and ran away and the dog pursued them. And the dog always hunts these three until the present day, because they made him ashamed.

The dog was hot on the track of the plandok when they entered the jungle. The plandok, however, managed by using its teeth and feet to climb a tree. The dog came below the tree but could neither see the plandok's tracks nor follow its scent beyond this spot. So the dog left following the plandok and went to hunt the stag and kijang. When he got to the place where the animals had fed he found that they had all gone but their fish and rice were left behind. Then he hunted the stag and the kijang but could not catch them. At last he said, "Well, if I ever see either the stag or the kijang or the plandok I will kill them, and my children and their descendants shall do the same." And so they do down to the present day.

A little time after the dog met the horse, the kerbau and the ox and these four animals shared the food, for the dog was not angry with them, because they had not laughed at him.

THE MOUSE DEER AND THE TIGER

Tradition Bearer: Si Ungin

Source: Evans, Ivor H. N. "Folk Stories of the Tempassuk and Tuaran Districts, British North Borneo." *The Journal of the Royal Anthropological Institute of Great Britain and Ireland* 43 (1913): 474.

Date: ca. 1910

Original Source: Borneo

National Origin: Malaysia

Tiger is a typical adversary of mouse deer in his traditional role of **trickster**. In this tale, the narrator states that "the plandok went in search of the tiger" with the apparent intent of tormenting him. The orut is a sash bound around the abdomen during battle to hold in intestines if the wearer is wounded.

When the dog had gone home the plandok went in search of the tiger, and on his way he came across a lot of snakes which were lying coiled up in circles near the tiger's house. The plandok waited there and the snakes did not move. Then came the tiger, and the tiger and the plandok saw each other at the same moment.

The tiger, however, did not see the snakes, and said to the plandok, "Plandok, what are you doing here?"

"Oh," said he, "I've been waiting here a long time on guard, because the Rajah has ordered me to."

"What are you guarding?" said the tiger. "I am guarding the Rajah's goods here, his oruts [sash]," said he, pointing to the snakes. Then the tiger looked at the oruts, and seeing them coiled up, he said, "What if we drag them undone, then I can tie them round my waist and see if they are good ones or not."

"I dare not let you do it," said the plandok, "as the Rajah has put me here to guard his goods, but if you like I will ask him." Now the plandok was frightened of the tiger and wanted to beat a retreat, so be said, "I will go ahead, and if I meet the Rajah I will call to you." Then the plandok started in search of the Rajah, and when he had got some little way off, he called to the tiger and said, "I have met the Rajah, and he says that you can try on the cloths." Then the tiger caught hold of the snakes and dragged at them, and they, waking, attacked him, winding themselves about his body and biting him. Thus the tiger died. As for the plandok he ran off, saying, "Ah, you tiger, you consider yourself strong, don't you? But you are no match for the cunning of the plandok."

THE MOUSE DEER AND THE BEAR

Tradition Bearer: Si Ungin

Source: Evans, Ivor H. N. "Folk Stories of the Tempassuk and Tuaran Districts, British North Borneo." *The Journal of the Royal Anthropological Institute of Great Britain and Ireland* 43 (1913): 474–475.

Date: ca. 1910

Original Source: Borneo

National Origin: Malaysia

Mouse deer reveals a "duelist's mentality" in the following narrative, in that he is said to go out in pursuit of strong animals to defeat.

When the tiger was dead the plandok began to think how he could get the best of the bear, for he had heard that the bear was also a strong animal. As he was walking along one day he came across a bees' nest in a tree, and sat down near it to wait. After he had been there for some time there came the bear. "What are you doing here?" said he.

"I am guarding the Rajah's tawag-tawag [gong]," answered the plandok, "which he has left in my charge."

"May I try its sound," said the bear, "whether it is good or not?" The plandok answered as before that he must ask the Rajah first, and when he had gone off and had got some distance away, he called out, "The Rajah says you can strike the gong." So the bear struck the nest and the bees, coming out in a fury, stung him to death.

THE MOUSE DEER AND THE HERMIT CRAB

Tradition Bearer: Si Ungin

Source: Evans, Ivor H. N. "Folk Stories of the Tempassuk and Tuaran Districts, British North Borneo." *The Journal of the Royal Anthropological Institute of Great Britain and Ireland* 43 (1913): 475–476.

Date: ca. 1910

Original Source: Borneo

National Origin: Malaysia

The following narrative is a **variant** of the widely distributed **tale type** "Race Won by Deception" (AT 1074) in which the **trickster** loses out to an adversary who is even more clever that he. The best-known variant to this type is "The Tortoise and the Hare."

When the plandok had cheated all the strong animals and had brought about their deaths, he wished to have a contest of wits with an animal who considered himself clever, so he went in search of one, and at last he met the omong [hermit crab] and the omong said to him, "Plandok, all the strong animals have been killed by your cunning, but if you like to try your wits against mine, I am ready."

"Very well," said the plandok, "that is just for what I am looking, animals who consider themselves long-headed; but how would you like to compete with me?"

"I should like to race you," said the omong, "and if you win I will acknowledge your cleverness and your power of running."

"What, *you* want to race with *me?*" said the plandok, "you can only walk sideways on the sand, and you don't race with your body only for you have to carry a shell as well." So the plandok felt ashamed to run a race with the omong, but he said, "When are we to race?"

"Tomorrow," replied the omong, "we will meet in the middle of the sands and race. You had better call your companions and I will call mine too."

"Very well," said the plandok, "I will come tomorrow."

"We will make a four-sided course for the race," said the omong, "and we will race along the sides of the square from post to post." On the morrow the plandok and his companions came, and also the omong with his, and it was decided that whoever won should be considered the champion over all the animals, for the plandok had already overcome, all the strongest of them.

When they arrived at the open sand by the sea they made a square, placing stakes at the corners. Now the plandok collected all his followers into one place as did also the omong. The omong, however, had made a plot and cho-sen three of his companions like him in appearance and size, and had told them to bury them-selves in the sand by three of the corners of the racecourse, but to leave the fourth corner, the starting-point, vacant. Then said the omong to the plandok, "When you get to the first post call out, 'Omong,' and if I don't answer you will know that I have been left behind and that you have won the race." So the plandok and the omong started to race from the first post, the omong saying, "Run." When the plandok heard the omong say "Run," he gave a jump and the omong, who of course was left behind, quickly buried himself in the sand, without anyone seeing him; for the spectators were some way off and the omong small. So the plandok ran without looking back, and when he got near the first post the second crab had come out of the sand and was waiting for him. When the plandok got to the post he called out, "Omong," and the crab answered, "Yes." So the plandok seeing what was appa-rently the same crab gave another jump and started running for the second post. The same thing happened here also, and the plandok said to himself, "How is it that the omong who walks so slowly manages to keep up with me?" At the third post the crab again answered, and the plandok, who was breathing heavily from running at top speed, set off as fast as he was able, for the original starting-post, which was also to be the finish of the race. When he got there the omong was waiting for him, and again when the plandok called out, "Omong," he was answered. Then the plandok was ashamed and wished to die, so he ran from stake to stake until his breath was exhausted, and when he reached the starting point he called out again, "Omong," and the omong answered, "Yes." Thereupon the plandok, who had no breath at all left, fell down and died, and the omongs cried out that the omong was the champion; but the plandok's followers kept silence.

THE MOUSE DEER AND THE CROCODILE

Tradition Bearer: Anggor

Source: Evans, Ivor H. N. "Folk Stories of the Tempassuk and Tuaran Districts, British North Borneo." *The Journal of the Royal Anthropological Institute of Great Britain and Ireland* 43 (1913): 475.

Date: ca. 1910

Original Source: Borneo

National Origin: Malaysia

As is the case with the tiger, numerous tales are told of the tricks played by the mouse deer on the crocodile.

The plandok was walking one day near the edge of a river and he saw some fruit on a tree on the other side. He was just going to cross when he saw the crocodile. "Who is that?" said the plandok, but the crocodile did not answer. Then said the plandok, "Ah, I know who you are, you are the crocodile. In seven days' time I will bring my whole tribe to fight you, and do you also bring your people." When the seventh day had arrived, the plandok went down to the river very early, before the crocodile had come, and walked backwards and forwards until the whole of the river margin was covered with its tracks. After a time the crocodile and his companions arrived. Then the plandok, who was awaiting them, spoke and said, "You are late in coming; my followers waited and waited for you, but at last they grew tired and have gone home. If you do not believe me, look at their tracks on the bank. I should like to count how many you and your companions are, so draw yourselves up in a row from one side of the river to the other." So the crocodiles did so, and the plandok started walking on their backs counting "One, two, three," when suddenly he gave a jump and reached the other bank. Then he called out, "Ah, I have cheated you, for how else could a plandok fight with crocodiles. I saw the fruit on the other side of the river, but I was afraid to swim across as I knew you were waiting for me."

"Very well," said the crocodile, "wait till you come down to the river to drink and I'll eat you." A few days afterwards the plandok, who had forgotten about the crocodile, came down to the river to drink, and the crocodile caught him by the leg. Then the plandok took hold of a piece of wood and pulled it towards him, and when he had done this he called out, "That is not my leg you have caught hold of; this is my leg," said he, pointing to the piece of wood. So the crocodile let go of the plandok's leg and the plandok sprang away, calling out, "Ah, I have cheated you again, how foolish is the crocodile!"

"Very well," said the crocodile, "another time I won't let go of your foot so easily."

THE MOUSE DEER IN A HOLE

Tradition Bearer: Orang Tua Ransab

Source: Evans, Ivor H. N. "Folk Stories of the Tempassuk and Tuaran Districts, British North Borneo." *The Journal of the Royal Anthropological Institute of Great Britain and Ireland* 43 (1913): 477.

Date: ca. 1910

Original Source: Borneo

National Origin: Malaysia

The following tale demonstrates the **trickster's** typical willingness to sacrifice innocent parties to serve his own ends.

The plandok when wandering in the jungle one day fell into a large hole in the ground and could not get out again. After a time the timbadou [wild cow] carne to the hole, and seeing the plandok, said, "Why, plandok, what are you doing there?"

"Oh," said the plandok, "I've come here to see my mother and father, my sisters and brothers."

"Wait a bit," said the timbadou, "and I will come down too, for I also wish to see my mother and father, sisters and brothers," but the plandok told the timbadou he was not to come down. Then the timbadou answered that if he said that again he would fall on him from above, and he, the plandok, would die. So the plandok gave the timbadou leave to get into the hole and the timbadou came down.

When he was down the timbadou said to the plandok, "Where are my father and mother?"

"Wait a little," said the plandok, "I've lost them just at present." So the timbadou waited and after a time the rhinoceros came to the hole and asked them what they were doing. Then the plandok answered as before that he was amusing himself, that he was seeing his father and mother and that there were lots of shops down there.

Whereupon the rhinoceros came down too, "For," said he, "my father and mother are dead and I would like to meet them and see how they have come to life again." Next came the stag and asked what they were doing and the plandok replied that he was seeing his father and mother and that there were many people sailing away on voyages down there. So the stag also jumped down. After that came the kijang [barking-deer], and he receiving the same answer from the plandok came down too. Then since the other animals were standing on each other's backs in the hole, the timbadou at the bottom and the kijang at the top, the plandok was able to scramble up to the top on their backs and make his escape from the place. Now when he had got out he met a man and his dog hunting, and the dog having got on his scent pursued him. Then the plandok made for the hole and running round it once or twice departed. So the dog, while following the scent of the plandok, came to the hole and seeing the timbadou and the other animals stopped there barking. Then the man came up and killed them all. As for the plandok he got off scot-free.

INDONESIA

THE FIRST VILLAGE

Tradition Bearer: Unavailable

Source: Pleyte, C. M. "An Unpublished Batak Creation Legend." *Journal of the Anthropological Institute of Great Britain and Ireland* 26 (1897): 103–109.

Date: ca. 1897

Original Source: Indonesia

National Origin: Indonesia

The Batak, for whom this **myth** offered their traditional explanation of the creation and population of the world, comprise several distinct ethnic groups who reside in the highlands of north Sumatra, an Indonesian island located north of Java and west of Malaysia. Like all mythologies, theirs accounts not only for physical features of the universe, but also for technology (the fire brought down from the other world by cow flea) and features of the supernatural universe (the benevolent mythic figure from other narratives, Rumari, an old widow who lives in a paradise called Pulo porlak pagaran, "fenced island garden"). The opening lines of the myth are an invocation that constitutes the customary opening for Batak tales.

"I Fold my hands respectfully above my head, O gods on high!"

"Seven times pardon, lord, for naming thy name, *Batara guru doli* [the major deity of the Batak] who reignest among the gods of the upper regions!"

"Lord of the seven strongholds, whose walls are so high, that the elephants stoop before them, the surrounding bamboo compels the storm to respect."

"Possessor of the bathing place *Si-mangera-era*, situated in an inaccessible region."

The ficus *Yambu bares* extends its vault over thee, when thou enjoyest thyself with thine in the fields, or pronouncest judgment in the shade of its foliage, wherein the birds of the sky hover to and fro, flapping their wings and warbling sweetly."

Si-tapi Sindar di mata ni ari ["Si-tapi who is illuminated by the sun"] daughter of *Batara guru*, sat at the gate of heaven, dressing her hair, wherein she made an extraordinarily beautiful parting. She felt a desire to look downward, but her heart was struck with sadness when she could discover nothing but a bare plain. When she came home, her father remarked the alteration of her features and asked with compassionate interest, "What is the matter, my dear daughter? You seem put out."

"Nothing is the matter with me, father, why should I be discontented? I have the happiness to be your daughter, and is it not already blithe to see the birds *Patija raja* and *Burukburuk bolajan?*"

Batara guru slept and had a bad dream. "I woke disturbed, for in my sleep I saw an unwonted agitation in the air, and the ground shook as if it were moved by an earthquake," he said to his daughter, and turning to one of his *Mandi-swallows*," he ordered it to go down.

"How shall I get there, lord?"

"Here is a jacket of my father's, put it on in order not to get too tired with flying in such a vast space," said *Si-tapi Sindar di mata ni ari*.

The swallow sailed downward, tracing wide circles in the air, but it saw nothing whatever on which it could rest. At last it espied the rock *Tanjuk tolu*, and let itself, quite exhausted, down upon it. Then it rolled up the jacket and used it as a cushion on which to take the rest it so much wanted.

Si-tapi Sindar di mtata ni ari became impatient on account of the long absence of the swallow, and sent the bird *Patija raja* to look after it. *Patija raja* was also provided with a jacket and hovered on it downward. After it had looked for a long time in all directions, it discovered at last the swallow sleeping peacefully.

"Why do not you come?"

"The Storm wind makes it impossible for me to fly upward."

"Say rather that you are not willing; why such a false pretence? Look how I shall manage."

Patija raja flew up in mid-air, but it was overmastered by the strong wind which drove him towards the east, and he was obliged to come back without delay.

"What did I tell you, it *is* impossible!"

"Now then we shall have to stay here for the present."

"What can be the reason that they stay so long?" said the princess, growing more and more impatient. She called the cowflea and said, "Please go down and see why they do not come back."

"I must, you say, go thither; but is there nothing that I have to take with me?"

"Here is a firesteel [flint and steel used to strike sparks for making fire]; take it in your armpit, and be careful that nobody here shall know that I have given it to you."

The cowflea went, and one would say that the little balls protruding from his head had been his eyes, if it were not known that his organs of sight were in his armpits. The flea despaired at first of finding the two birds, but had nevertheless had the good luck of meeting them still on the *tanjuk tolu*. "Why do not you come? The princess is so angry!"

"The strong wind has made our return impossible, and that is why we are still sitting here."

The three began to consider together what they ought to do. They resolved to go to the rock *Nanggar jati* [an immense rock reaching to the sky] and to try to make their return from its top. When they had reached the rock, *Patija raja* began to climb it. He arrived half way up and looked on all sides, but he discovered nothing that could be of use to them in their embarrassment. Only a bare plain was spread before his eyes. Therefore he climbed higher, and first, when he reached the top, he saw the roots of the *Yambu barus* dangling gently above him. He hoped now to be soon back, provided he succeeded in grasping one of the roots, but notwithstanding all his efforts, they still remained out of his reach. He began to lament loudly, for his last hope was gone.

His cries rose upward and were heard by the princess, who thought that she recognized the voice of her favorite bird. She sent one of her servants to see what had happened, and was soon after aware of the truth. She asked then for her betel-pouch, and opened it so that the scent spread far off, and *Patija raja*, who smelt it, was full of sad thoughts on account of his beloved mistress.

Si-tapi Sindar di mata ni ari went to the gate of heaven and took with her a magic ring, her betel-pouch, and seven hen's eggs. When arrived, she sat down and looked downward, upon. which, espying *Patija raja*, she said to him, "Do not cry any more but hasten to come up."

"Alas, princess, I cannot reach the roots of the *Yambu bares*, all my endeavors have been in vain."

"Since it cannot be otherwise, you must make up your mind to go down again; I shall take care that you want nothing."

She let down the magic ring and gave *Patija raja* these directions When you three have settled on the *Tanjuk tolu*, then you must open the eggs, and you will find in them all the plants and trees which you may require; but if you want to have cattle, you must call on the magic ring, and you will get not only cattle but also all kinds of animals, habitations, council-houses, and whatever more you may wish for."

When the adventurers found themselves together again on *Tanjuk tole*, they opened the eggs, scattered round about them the contents, and by this means soon saw splendid fields and gardens appear. In a short time they were, by the power of the magic ring, put in possession of houses and all they wanted.

They feasted then, eating and drinking good things, and settled also that *Patija raja* should be king, the swallow vice-king, and the cowflea commander of the warriors of the newly established village. Then they prayed to *Batara gurut* that they might have offspring in order to people the village.

When he had heard their prayer, *Batara guru* ordered his sister *Pandan rumari*, to go to the earth.

"But, brother, how shall I get there?"

"Do not be anxious about your journey, aunt; I shall make it as easy as possible for you," said *Si-tapi Sindar di mata ni ari.*

"You must choose a good spot to settle there, aunt; and when you have made your establishment, you must promise me that on the next festival Saturday [the Saturday preceding the full moon of each month] you will come on to the top of the rock."

Si-tapi Sindar di mata ni ari now twisted her hair into a basket, wherein her aunt *Pandan rumari*, after having put a magic ring on her finger, placed herself to be let down on the *Nanggar jaii.* When she arrived on the top, she looked fearfully round about, but finally went down the rock. She settled at the foot of it, and called her abode *Pulo porlak pagaran.* When the festival Saturday arrived, *Pandan rumari* went to the top of the *Nanggar jati*, where the roots of the *Yambu bares still* dangled. She tried to take hold of one, but failed, and, not knowing what to do, she began to weep loudly.

At the moment *Si-tapi Sindar mata n, ari* heard the sobbing, she said to herself, "Is not this my aunt?" And going to the gate of heaven to look down, she found at once that she was right. At the same time she remembered what had been concerted. She ordered a servant to bring her a woman's jacket, a jew's harp, a pair of ear ornaments, a mirror, and lemons, twelve different kinds grown on the same branch. She let all these things down to her aunt and then took leave of her with the following words, "Go back down the rock, dear aunt, and take with you the bird *Imbulu Man*, who can be of service to you, if you want to enter into relation with *Patija raja* and his comrades."

Pandan rumari then got the bird *Imbulu Man* to accompany her, who was no ordinary bird, since she had no feathers, and she was like a human being as regarded her skin. She was also, through the will of *Batara guru*, pregnant of a human fruit.

When she had returned to her dwelling, *Pandan rumari*, on account of the situation in which the bird found herself, gave her an appropriate couch, surrounded by mats arranged like curtains.

One day, *Pandan rumari* lighted a great fire, the smoke of which rose on high and was perceived by the inhabitants of *Tanjuk tole.*

"Go and see who makes a fire there," said *Patija raja* to the swallow.

"But when I arrive there and find somebody, I shall have to say something."

"If you do not know the person, ask him who has made him come there."

The swallow came to *Pandan rumari* and asked her who had sent her to that place. "*Batara guru* sent me here. But you come as if called for, because *Imbulu Man* must be with you at *Tanjuk tole*," answered *Pandan rumari*.

When the swallow arrived at *Tanjuk tole* with *Imbulu Man*, this last addressed *Patija raja* as follows, "The reason why I have been sent here by the princess, is that I should provide you offspring so that you do not remain without subjects." After some time, *Imbulu Man* was delivered of two daughters, of whom *Patija raja* and the swallow each took one for his wife. If *Imbulu Man* were to give birth to one more daughter later, then the cowflea was to have her for a wife. The cowflea was by no means satisfied, and thinking that he might have to wait a very long time for his wife, he secretly got *Imbulu Man* with child, in order to secure his wish. It appeared soon that she was again pregnant, and she declared that this was the cowflea's doing; but he was let off after a slight reprimand from *Patija raja*.

Imbulu Man was afterwards delivered of a son, who had the name of *Bala porang*. After that *Patija raja* had by his wife a son, to whom they gave the name of *Raja Manuksang di portibi*. As for the swallow, he had two daughters, the one of whom they called *Sada lumbar*, and the other *Boru dognu*; at the feast of the naming of his daughters, the swallow gave himself the title of *Namora Mangipa*.

As they made their children intermarry, the inhabitants of *Tanjuk tole* could soon rejoice in the possession of numerous descendants, whose swarms filled the newly founded village.

SRY NAGASARY

Tradition Bearer: Unavailable

Source: Scheltema, J. F. "Sry Nagasary." *Journal of American Folklore* 32 (1919): 324–342.

Date: Unavailable

Original Source: Indonesia

National Origin: Indonesia

From the beginning of the Common Era (first century A.D.), the Indonesian archipelago has been influenced by the Hindu religion from the Indian subcontinent. In the fourteenth century through the beginning of the sixteenth century, the powerful Hindu Majapahit Empire extended its influence from its seat of power in Java throughout a large portion of Indonesian and into the Malay Peninsula to the north. Even when Islam established dominance in around 1500 C.E., Hinduism remained influential in the traditions of Indonesia. The following tale, which seems to derive from a Javanese **variant**, reflects not only this continuing Hindu influence, but also the moral codes that grew out of the synthesis of Hindu, indigenous, and Islamic values.

Once upon a time there was a man, named Kyahy Taboos, who lived in a village near the mouth of a river that flowed from the blue mountains in the interior of one of the Sunda Islands toward the sea. He had four sons: Bagal, a wood-carver; Sompoq, a merchant; Paning, a jeweler; and Mashmool who, being the last-born and favorite, was allowed to follow his natural bent toward music and poetry instead of learning a more useful and profitable trade than that of a merry-andrew [jester] as the elder brothers contemptuously called him when discussing his gifts of entertainment. Though brought up in a very religious way and considering themselves of the elect and knowing that the teachings of Batara Guru, the great god, urged man to goodwill and kindliness in his dealings with all his fellow-creatures, and especially to love and charity in his relations with his kindred, envy had taken possession of their hearts because their father indulged Mashmool upon whom therefore they looked with eyes of hatred.

So when Kyahy Taboos had been summoned by the gods to receive the amount of his due, Bagal, speaking also for Sompoq and Paning even on the day of their father's burial, said to Mashmool with a lying tongue, "How dost thou propose to provide thy share in our means of subsistence? Our father has left us little more than this house in which we live. Thy brother Sompoq buys and sells merchandise at a profit; thy brother Paning is a worker in gold and silver, and a dealer in precious stones, and whatever passes through his hands leaves also substantial gain behind; I am thoroughly acquainted with the nature and qualities of the different kinds of wood and proficient, for the good of our common household, in turning kayu mahar into shafts for lances and spears, and into sheaths for krisses, using kayu kamuning for the upper parts where the steel touches first in sending the weapon home, improving by skilful carving the design of kayu pelèt to enhance the mysterious play of its black and red-brown spots on its luminous grain, a premonition of deeds of darkness and blood, but thou, what canst thou do to earn thy rice and salt?"

"I am a musician," answered Mashmool, dignified and self-conscious for all his modesty, "I can recite in fitting language what has been preserved in our chronicles of ancient wisdom and what they record of high mettle and tender devotion, of virtue and purity in mortals emulating the gods."

"And who cares?" asked Sompoq.

"No one sufficiently to untie his purse-string for accomplishments of the sort," remarked Paning.

"Nor is it incumbent on us to encourage idlers," continued Bagal.

These words were hard to hear and since his brothers persisted in their abusive speech, finding fault with everything he did or left undone, Mashmool resolved to part from them. When he made known his intention to travel and see the wide world and seek his fortune in distant lands, they laid their heads together, discussing how to defraud him of his portion of their father's inheritance, at least how to put him off with a most inadequate payment in cash. But the generous Mashmool, whose mind was not set on worldly considerations, never thought of a settlement; trustful because upright himself, he deemed it quite regular that his brothers should remain in undivided possession of their father's patrimony until his return, an arrangement perfectly agreeable to them. And so, at his departure, with his *suling* [bamboo flute] under his arm to try his luck as a wandering minstrel, his brothers' farewell with ostentatious wishes for his success in crossing the seven seas and roaming the seven empires, was of the most affectionate description, touching enough, in fact, to make him search his innocent heart when under way, as to whether perhaps he had done the sons of his father an injustice by doubting their brotherly love. But he walked on.

After Mashmool had gone, the trade of the wicked brothers in their respective occupations began to fall off. It seemed that with him prosperity had turned its back on them. At first they thought that Mashmool, incensed by his treatment at their hands, had sought the assistance of some wizard to obtain revenge through the agency of malevolent spirits, ever prone to mischief and rancorous tricks. To foil these demons they attached strips of white cloth to the roof-corners and other conspicuous parts of their dwelling, a potent means to draw the attention of well-disposed deities to the sinister work of the servants of Evil in the abode of godly men, for so the trio considered themselves, being scrupulously strict in the observance of the ceremonial duties prescribed by their creed, very godly indeed, provided that godliness did not interfere with their greed.

Their astonishment knew no bounds at noticing, when the pieces of white cloth had been fluttering in the wind for a while, that the host of malignant fiends who had chased off their customers, persisted in pursuing them with ill luck. The men with well-tempered lance and spear points to be mounted on strong, flexible shafts, and with beautifully damascened krisses to be further embellished with sheaths of a correct pattern and artistically carved hafts, still passed their door with averted heads to entrust the delicate work to one of Bagal's competitors. The women going to market still avoided the booths of Sompoq and Parting whatever pains they took to attract both matrons and virgins by a cunning display of silk and gold brocade, of ear-rings and bangles and necklaces, jewelry fit for princesses and queens, beyond price yet dirt-cheap if the fair ones only would venture a bid.

Putting the blame on the minor deities who neglected to protect Batara Guru's [supreme god in the Sundanese pantheon] own, Mashmool's brothers never suspected the real cause of the adverse circumstances they had to struggle against, namely, their hardness in their dealings, their rapacity which did not even stop short at cheating and turned people away from them.

One night, after having spent the evening with Sompoq and Parting in their habitual grumbling at the incomprehensible attitude of the rulers of the universe inflicting hardships on the deserving, Bagal had a dream. He fancied himself carving out of wood, and he took special note that it was *kayu nagasary*, the image of an *apsara,* one of the hand-maidens of Indra, that amuse the god by dancing before his throne on Mount Mandara; and when the image was ready, it took life and showered gold on its maker. Marveling at his vision and not being able to make out its meaning, Bagal told Sompoq and Paning, who did not understand any better than he. They resolved therefore to refer the matter to a saintly hermit with a great reputation for the interpretation of dreams. Charging his usual price for the accustomed offerings to the divine guardians of the secrets of the past, present and future, and keeping them moreover in long suspense while engaged in pressing those lords of the recondite for precise information, the saintly hermit made at last known as Batara Guru's, the upper god's manifest will, revealed by the aforesaid sapient beings after the completion of the sacrifice, that Bagal should do, consciously in his waking state, that which his soul had been made to do without the cooperation of the body. Rich reward would be the result.

So Bagal carved a life-sized image of an *apsara,* and it was a fine piece of sculpture and he called it Sry Nagasary after the name of the wood suggested by his dream. Sompoq and Parting, desirous of participating in the promised rich reward, which they construed to mean abundant wealth, clothed the puppet with silk and brocade, and adorned it with jewelry. Bagal, loath to share his good fortune, told them repeatedly that this was not in the dream but as they insisted and were two to his one, he had to acquiesce, pretending with a sour face that he conferred the solicited favor upon them out of the fullness of his brotherly affection. And this display of fraternal disinterestedness became the more fervent the less inclination Sry Nagasary evinced to realize the hopes excited by the saintly hermit's words.

Her presence, remarked the brothers to one another, brought no change in their condition, and if they did not know what to think of a world that refused to acknowledge their superior virtue, or of a heaven full of gods whom they lost no opportunity to wheedle into the belief of their obedient piety but who, nevertheless, suffered their neighbors to treat them according to their works rather than according to their professions, neither could they conceive why the saintly hermit had deluded them by a false interpretation of the dream, making them the laughing-stock of the village for the affair had become known and every one ridiculed the credulity of Kyahy Taboos's sons, who expected a wooden image, dressed and bedecked with jewels like a woman of quality, to restore the credit and standing which they had lost by their grasping dishonesty.

When they complained to the saintly hermit and sought redress, they received his assurance that his interpretation of the dream was right. "You should break yourselves of the bad habit of blaming others for your own faults," he added. "The truth of the *apsara*'s failure to gratify your wishes is a long distance beside your surmise. To exercise her functions in discharge of the task assigned to her, she needs not only a human shape, since she is now dwelling among mortals; and clothes for decency's sake, since she is earthly on earth; and garnishment of her beauty, since even a celestial female will strive with might and main to please men, but also music to guide her dancing. Oh that you had not driven away your younger brother, the musician!"

They were surprised and pained by the reproof implied in the saintly hermit's remark and replied somewhat hotly, though he was a holy man, that Mashmool had gone of his own accord. And with respect to his excellence in music, he did not possess a monopoly of the art. If it were not for their sure knowledge of its being an empty, almost sinful pastime, they could no doubt learn to play any instrument as well and better than he.

"Hearts absorbed in the contemplation of the divine will cannot be corrupted by the arts that soothe and recreate," rejoined the saintly hermit, a faint smile enlivening his emaciated countenance.

Then he dismissed the brothers who, returning home, had a serious argument, evoked by this utterance as a sequel to his fuller explanation of his interpretation of the dream. Considering and reconsidering, it now appeared entirely clear to them: the rich reward for their righteousness, at last acknowledged by Batara Guru, was to arrive through the *apsara* dancing to their music; and all their religious scruples about the propriety of that frivolous diversion vanished the moment they saw their advantage in it.

Bagal commenced practicing the *rabab* [violin], Sompoq the *gendang* [drum] and Paning the *katram* [cymbals] in order to form a complete orchestra, by far more sonorous and melodious, more adequate to accompany a celestial dancer, they flattered themselves, than Mashmool's feeble efforts with a simple bamboo flute ever could be.

After persistent and strenuous toil they noticed slight movements in the puppet. It began to quake and quiver; with their progress in the production of a concordant combination from the sounds they generated, to change its posture and position at the measure of the tune to which they strove to do justice. The achievement put an end to the scoffing of their neighbors who, compelled by curiosity, sought their company for ocular evidence of their prodigious command over a wooden image into which they had blown life, causing it to go through its paces as if it were a real dancing-girl.

The neighbors were, of course, made to pay for the privilege. Sry Nagasary's monetary value expelled from the minds of the brothers all doubts of her divine mission to recompense them for their holiness, tardily but now fitly recognized by Batara Guru. This was the rich reward foretold by the saintly hermit, which flowed more and more richly as their proficiency in handling their musical instruments increased, to wit, their mechanical proficiency, always short of the artistic touch born from an inspiration intrinsically foreign to their coarse-grained temperament. And this was the reason, but they knew it not, why Sry Nagasary, instead of budding into life, remained a marionette with lips always sealed; set, truly, in machine-like motion by their music such as it was, but stark again the instant it ceased.

Even though they prospered, thanks to the *apsara's* offices, the brothers began to mistrust her lack of animation unless specially roused to activity. Constitutionally suspicious and spiteful, they also mistrusted one another, each meditating in his mind how he could become her sole possessor, secure for himself alone the rich reward by releasing the aerial nymph from her wooden prison and marrying her. Surely, Batara Guru had decreed her transmigration into an earthly shape for the highest good. And was not the highest good attainable in this case that the rich reward should go to the most meritorious, the most godly of the three as each of them believed himself to be?

For ways and means the saintly hermit could be consulted. So once more they went up to him; not together, however, but separately and secretly, in fear of being caught at their knavish game, turning on their heels at every few steps to keep their father's spirit off their track for Kyahy Taboos, angered in the narrow valley of death at their intent to cheat one another, might contrive to cross it with calamitous result. The saintly hermit showed not the least surprise at their coming and gave each the same answer to his request for advice, again faintly smiling as Bagal, Sompoq and Paning, to conceal their base motives, feigned an ardent solicitude for the ultimate fate of the wooden *apsara*, whose incarnation they said that they wished to compass for her own weal, namely, to insure her happiness in union with Batara Guru's chosen one.

"To fulfill her destiny and yours, according to Batara Guru's will," declared the saintly hermit, "your *apsara* needs a human soul to conclude in its human stage the divine labor enjoined on her. Whoever, with a clean heart and clean hands, gives his soul to her in token of his true love, shall have hers." Having spoken these words to Bagal, Sompoq and Paning successively, the saintly hermit declined to tell them anything more.

They spent their days and nights in pondering the queer, puzzling recommendation that they should give their souls to Sry Nagasary. Uncertain how to act upon it and avoiding one another because burning with envy, they endeavored to despoil destiny of its secrets by communicating with soothsayers, whose divinations at the cost of incessant offerings on numberless altars to numberless gods, brought them not a step farther. When they met to join in their musical performances, necessary to induce the *apsara* to dance, it was no pleasure to them, rather a vexation, to observe her growing skill, which attracted to their house people from far and near, and made the treasure in their coffers swell. They got their gold and silver too dear, prospering at the expense of their tranquility of mind for each of the three was constantly scheming how to defraud the others of that source of income and finally of lasting comfort to its exclusive possessor. Since they had to share their good fortune, it made them utterly miserable.

Meanwhile the fame of the dancing image had spread to distant lands. Mashmool, the youngest brother, heard it spoken of on his travels and also somewhat homesick notwithstanding his unpleasant experience, he resolved to go and see for himself. After many new adventures and subsisting on his minstrelsy during his journey back as he had done all the time, he arrived at last, tired and footsore, in his native village. It was evening and nobody recognized him because he had become taller of stature while his features, too, had undergone a change reflecting a wider knowledge of the world, a riper insight which nevertheless abided by the guileless sincerity of his candid nature.

To reach his home he had either to cross the river in a boat or to skirt it upstream for quite a distance to pass over a bridge and return by the opposite bank. Standing near the water's edge, he looked at the rising ground on the other side, purple in the rays of the setting sun. Behind the first bend where, giving way to cultivated ground, the tangled mangroves ceased to fringe the stream, lay the house of his desire. In the growing darkness he saw many lights glimmering between the palms that masked its landing-place. Many more lights floated onward with the flood. They belonged to *sampans* and larger craft, *koleks* and *jukoongs*, all making for the luminous headland. Mashmool inquired of a man, just embarked and ready to push off, what was going on that the whole village, and strangers too, it seemed, were speeding toward the semblance of some palace of a thousand torches, transplanted from a fairy tale to reality.

"Whence comest thou?" asked the man. "Even the people that live beyond the stars know of Sry Nagasary and of her dancing every market day. Jump in if thou hast a wish to behold the marvelous lady, a runaway from Indra's paradise."

Eyeing Mashmool more closely as he did jump in, his flute in his hand and his violin under his arm, a Sumatra *rabab* he had learned to play when associating with the Rawas brethren of his guild, the man continued, voicing the misgivings naturally awakened by a strolling minstrel's appearance, "That is, supposing thou possessest the wherewithal to satisfy the craving for lucre which dishonors the sons of Kyahy Taboos who exhibit the *apsara*. Thou, companion of the road, canst pander to their infamy with cash? If not, thy going up is bootless and unavailing fatigue."

"Verily, thy words lack wisdom," retorted Mashmool, pointing to his instruments. "Shall music be barred where dancing sways the night?"

"Thou speakest truth," assented the man, beginning to paddle. "And oh for the dancing there would be with the youngest son of Kyahy Taboos leading instead of Bagal, who draws his bow across the copper strings as if he were sawing wood, while Sompoq and Paning bang the drum and clank the cymbals like irate husbandmen in their ricefields shooing off the birds. But Mashmool, where does he wander and what has happened to him since his shameless brothers turned him out?"

Mashmool had his reasons not yet to reveal his identity. His answers to the friendly but garrulous boatman's questions about the country he hailed from, his musical training, the object of his visit and so forth, were short and evasive. Aided by the tide, which was setting in, they soon rounded the point near the landing-place, beached the boat and joined the crowd that sought admittance to the spacious hall where the performance was to be given. Originally open on three sides, it had been closed by means of screens of split bamboo between the pillars to prevent impecunious or penurious curiosity procuring gratification without pecuniary sacrifice. Over the outer gate, truly, was an inscription in large characters, a motto from the sacred books of ancient lore, extending a cordial welcome to friends, acquaintances and every one else who chose to enter, but Bagal, guarding the door, assisted by Sompoq and Paning, construed that greeting in a fashion which made their guests comment with wry faces upon words soft as butter proceeding from demons of avarice lurking in their hearts.

When Mashmool entered, paying them the gate-money, the brothers never suspected their father's preferred son they had wronged, in the travel-worn stranger questing admission. They took him for a wandering musician attracted by the renown of their marvelous preeminence in his art, which forced even inanimate objects to sympathetic obedience, and saluted him with the obligatory phrase in addressing visitors from foreign parts, "Our gain is great, O bestower of favors! That thy voyage has not been impeded by the perils of the road."

"The gain is mine, O you on whom Batara Guru showers his blessings! And it is your favor I seek," answered Mashmool in a low tone not to let his voice betray him.

Thereupon Bagal ordered the servants to spread mats for the spectators to sit upon with due regard to their rank and station, lining three sides of the space, also covered with matting, which was reserved for the performing puppet. He himself with Sompoq and Paning took place on the fourth side, muttering prayers while in the middle incense was burned as an indispensable preliminary to the exhibition. Then, getting up from their crouched position, they pushed the wooden doll forward, Sry Nagasary, in the regulation dress of a dancing girl: from her hips down she was clothed in *a kahin*, a garment of brocade wound round her middle and kept securely attached by the weight of its own graceful folds; her body was wrapped in the *kemben*, a narrow strip of silk, encircling her upward to the armpits and held tight by passing the ends under its loops; a *pending*, that is, a golden girdle, fastened more firmly both *kahin* and *kemun*; a *slendang* or scarf, stuck to right and left between the *pending* and her waist, completed her costume with a string of *melaty* [variety of jasmine] hanging down from her neck, and the *kerabu* [type of earring], bracelets and finger-rings which were the special admiration of her female beholders.

These could be heard but not seen behind the slatted shutters and screens of split bamboo through the interstices of which they watched over the heads of their squatted men-folk what was bechancing the aerial nymph dispatched from heaven for their amusement. Their excited whispers subsided into a long-drawn "Ah!" as they perceived the first signs of animation in her hands and arms and visage, yellow with *boreh* [preparation of curcuma and cocoa oil, used at ceremonial functions to anoint and color the parts of the body which remain bare} when the three brothers, each coaxing his instrument into laborious discipline without minding the other two, began to attack the dancing music proper after an equally cacophonous prelude. Bagal, keeping his bow between his fingers as if manipulating a saw, to repeat the boatman's simile, worked the strings in an unsteady, painful manner of which his *rabab* complained loudly in screechy, chiding accents, like those of a testy old woman. Sompoq thwacked the drum, altogether independent of his lead, and Paning belabored the cymbals quasi-derisively of that shrill scolding, its strident sound going through interminable, monotonous, ill-executed variations of the attempted tune, wrangling with the jeering response of the *gendang*'s bing-bang and the *katram*'s click-clack, until at last by sheer reiteration of the invitation to dance, it persuaded Sry Nagasary to perform her *sembah*, the salutation expressive of her readiness to commence.

It was hailed with exclamations of unbounded, though, owing to the awe attending her astounding feats, of suppressed enthusiasm. While, with clumsy movements like those of an automaton, she took hold of her scarf, disengaging it from her girdle to raise it to her shoulders, putting it round her neck with the ends hanging down to her knees, Bagal, as leader of the orchestra, redoubled his vigor. Without prejudice on behalf of key or melody or harmony, he dispensed his fortes in an audaciously liberal style, goading Sompoq and Paning to surpass his energetic zeal with vicious fortissimos on *their* instruments, the three producing a combination of dissonants which gave an alarming foretaste of the futurist music that enraptures ultra-modern audiences in our Temples of Symphony and Philharmonic Halls.

Sry Nagasary made the best of it. Dancing slowly and mechanically, she warmed up to her divine art—that is, to a certain extent, to the extent permitted by the character of her accompaniment. Her stolid face, indeed, smeared with *boreh*, had nothing human, still less anything indicative of her heavenly extraction, yet, first the women and then the men remarked that her eyes, as she glided round, languidly lifting and twisting her arms and hands and fingers, began to move in her head. They moved sleepily, though, like the eyes of one acting under the impulse of a dream.... But lo! Her hair, it had become real hair and in it was stuck a leaf of the *waringin-tree*, just as if she were a common dancing-girl, performing in the street and desirous to attract lovers....

Encouraged by these familiar associations, the chief of the village, who attended *ex officio*, got up and took Sry Nagasary's scarf from her clumsily fumbling hands. Thereupon, followed by the tottering doll, he approached with the mincing steps prescribed by native etiquette his superior, the *demang* or chief of the district, also present, to squat down opposite the latter and to offer it as an invitation to the first dance *a deux*, an honor pertaining to the guest highest in rank. Again according to native etiquette there was a protracted contest of courtesy between the two officials, the one insisting with due deference, the other politely refusing to accept the scarf until at last he yielded and, begging to be excused on account of his age while handing it back to the wooden lady, produced a silver coin, tendering the money to her as the price of his exemption from a precedence incompatible with his hoary dignity.

"The proper thing to do," muttered the bystanders who watched Sry Nagasary clutching the coin with an awkward gesture and sliding by fits and starts, unconscious of her actions, toward a copper vessel in front of Bagal, into which she let it fall.

The chinking sound of its striking the rim and bottom displeased the women behind the shutters and screens. "An unmannerly dancing girl," they whispered to one another, commenting upon this trick which, like the ostentatious display of a waringin-leaf, is a common one among the artists of the streets, who take good care to make the tangible evidence of approval, extracted from a male admirer, ring in its receptacle to stimulate the generosity of his rivals.

Moving away from the collection-bowl, Sry Nagasary halted before the village chief, whose turn had now come either to dance with her or to open his purse. He chose the former course, seconded by two of his elders, one to his right, the other to his left. Squirming about, contorting their limbs, encircling the unsightly image of a celestial virgin at the measureless measure of a wildly unharmonious orchestra, they presented a sight extravagantly weird and lugubrious in their *chasse-croise* with the grotesque *apsara*, descended from Indra's court for the delectation of mortals. Although some of the onlookers enlivened the scene by clapping their thighs in time with the drum and cymbals, genially and affably to show the appreciation obligatory on well-bred neighbors, the pause, announced by an unearthly yelp of Bagal's *rabab*, was welcomed as a relief even by the most curious.

Sry Nagasary relapsed at once into her original state of superlative woodenness. Never before, however, had she done so well, danced in such a life-like style as that night. The three brothers took, of course, all the credit of her progress in pose and attitude and elegant carriage to themselves. But those of the company who had not been wholly absorbed in the spectacle because distracted by their close observation of the stranger in their midst, the wandering minstrel half hid in a corner with his eyes riveted on the dancing doll that seemed to gain in vitality under his gaze, were of a different opinion.

"He has the air of a *gandharva* [a heavenly musician] in search of his *apsara*: no wonder that she responds," said the women and girls, favorably impressed by the looks and deportment of the handsome youth.

"Is not this Mashmool, come back to claim his portion among the sons of Kyahy Taboos?" A selectman asked of the village scribe.

The accosted authority, whose wife had nursed Mashmool after the death of his mother in childbed, scrutinized him closely and cried. "Indeed it is and my hearty greeting to him!"

The exclamation and the crowding forward of the villagers to salute the wanderer happily restored to his friends, awakened his brothers to a sense of something unusual going on, an event not on the evening's program. Joining the circle which had formed around Mashmool, they now recognized him too, their preoccupation as owners, managers and orchestra of the show having so far prevented their taking much notice of him. His arrival did not suit them at all but they went up to him with sugary words and a grand display of joy at his return, and they entreated him to consider himself at home in their father's house, forgetting that it was his as well as theirs.

In their vexation at Mashmool's unexpected reappearance, they solaced themselves with the thought that their generous but vague assurances of hospitable intent could easily be modified after they had had time to consider the case at their leisure, basing their line of conduct on mature reflection. For the present Sry Nagasary's resuscitation claimed their undivided attention. So they took up again their instruments to resume their arduous functions in the eagerly awaited second part of the performance. But, while they preluded with more than ordinary absence of concord and consonance, owing to their perturbed state of mind, the *demang,* after a whispered consultation with the village chief, interrupted their play and proposed an arrangement the idea of which had already occurred to several others: since Mashmool was known to be an excellent musician, could not Bagal leave the musical direction to him the better to discharge the duties of the general management?

Bagal argued that Sry Nagasary, being a personal gift from Batara Guru to himself and, he added under the stress of their presence, to his brothers Sompoq and Paning, would most certainly decline to dance to any music but his own. One might try, answered the *demang. His* proposition in favor of the change being carried by acclamation, Bagal was obliged to give in and resign the leadership of the orchestra to Mashmool who, rejecting his elder brother's fiddle, commenced tuning the Sumatra *rabab* which he had learned to play during his peregrinations in Jamby and the Rawas. Besides other differences in construction, it had three strings of twisted silk instead of the two copper ones which Bagal never succeeded in stretching properly to sound the right notes of the *salendro-octave.* Mashmool's prelude revealed at once his indisputable superiority as an apt pupil of the eminent virtuoso that made Batang Asay, where this maestro had established a school, a name famous among the connoisseurs from Majapahit to Manang Kabau.

The coarse, raw noises, suggestive of an abusive hag, a shrieking virago, which Bagal had inflicted upon his audience, gave way to soft tones like those of a love-sick maiden whose hopes and desires are bursting into song. Mashmool's masterly execution of the opening strains profoundly touched the cloistered women and girls who, for all his having been recognized as Kyahy Taboos's youngest son, could not get rid of the fanciful belief that the wandering minstrel was an incarnation of the primal and essential Gandharva, the patron of their sex, the deity of courtship and marriage. His tender call to come forth and dance, a gentle but irresistible summons to the completion of high events, had a still more wonderful effect upon the *apsara*, manifestly so anxious to do his bidding that it almost petrified Bagal, who sat motionless with mingled feelings of amazement and exasperation while Sompoq and Paning, no less confounded, fortunately forgot to follow their younger brother's lead with their drum and cymbals.

In fact, every one doubted the evidence of his senses when Sry Nagasary stepped airily to the middle of the space assigned for the exhibition of her art, subject to a transformation unlike and much greater than that which had enabled the lumbering doll, fashioned by Bagal and dressed and bedecked with jewels by Sompoq and Paning, to go through its twitching paces. Her features took a living hue; the layer of *boreh* disappeared from her face and arms and hands, leaving them tinted like the dusky-yellow rind of the succulent *langsah*. The life-blood, vital principle of human existence, rushed up from its source beneath the lotus and tinged her cheeks; her bosom heaved; her brow expanded; her lustreless eyes began to sparkle; the *waringin* leaf in her hair-knot blossomed into a red-glowing rose.

Nimble, yet stately, she danced to the measure of Mashmool's accords, swaying her lithe body on her haunches, extending and bending upward her fingers, spreading and waving her scarf with winding, graceful movements. Timidly advancing, shyly receding, she seemed to hold converse with the all-spirit, wooing its creative essence and being wooed, trembling under unseen caresses, mellowed to conceive and bear like a flower-bud in the warmth of the sun. How beautiful she was! And her dancing in agitation of ecstasy an elation of the soul, a solution of the riddle of man and woman, of the noble and the base, of heaven and earth!

The hearts of those who beheld her throbbed with rapture. They were now perfectly convinced that she was one of Indra's hand-maidens, her home the abode of the gods. And, miracle upon miracle, when she finished her dance with Mashmool's last note quavering sky-ward, she did not subside into the rigid inanity from which he had quickened her, but, after craving with *a sembah* and obtaining his permission to withdraw, disappeared into the women's apartments, bestowing on him a parting glance which made the young folks turn white, then scarlet under their brown skins as their tumultuous blood ceased its flow, immediately to dash on again through their veins in fiery waves.

And one of the elders said, "The *ghandarva* fully deserves his reward."

"Nay, call him Kama, the god of the flowery bow, smiled upon by Raty, his fond spouse," replied the village scribe, who was something of a prig.

The *demang*, rising to depart after thanking Bagal for the rare entertainment provided and Mashmool for its exceptional success, gave the sign for the assembly to break up. The village chief followed suit, escorting him home at the head of a numerous retinue. Thereupon the rest of the guests dispersed in due sequence, taking a perfunctory leave of their host and his two brothers next in age, but very cordially commending themselves to the youngest and complimenting him upon the new proof of his surpassing talent they had just enjoyed. Mashmool accepted their praise with a modesty which endeared him still more, especially to the fair among his admirers. Yet, however unassuming his behavior, this homage to his musical proficiency, not to mention Sry Nagasary's evident preference for his person and accompaniment, was not at all to his seniors' liking. On the other hand, they saw their advantage in retaining him until they had mastered the trick, for so they considered it, which wrought the magical transition of a wooden image into an embodiment of the transports of paradise, far beyond their own past achievements unaided by occult artifice.

So they, too, complimented him, feigning to be overjoyed at his return, cajoling him, beseeching him to stay and live with them forever but resolved in their minds to get rid of him the instant they had wheedled him out of his secret. They ordered the servants to spread a sleeping-mat for him in the verandah over the stream that laved the basement of the house, his favorite place to pass the night in as they affectionately remembered. Without doubt he was tired and they needed also a good rest after the fatigue of the night's performance, wherefore they begged him to excuse them for the nonce from expatiating upon their contentment caused by his hale and hearty presence, from exchanging the news of the village for an account of his travels and adventures: the morrow would bring time for that together with the festive celebration of his restitution to the parental roof.

Meanwhile they were consumed with a desire to see Sry Nagasary in the flesh as she withdrew from the dance, to speak to her privately, to establish their claims on the promised reward, each for himself to the exclusion of the other two. But at the women's quarters they were told in reply to their sly inquiries, that the lady had gone to the river for a bath, as might have been expected from an *apsara*, a water-nymph reincarnate; that she had imperiously commanded when retiring for repose after the refreshing expedition, on no pretext to suffer any one to annoy her with requests for an interview, least of all Bagal, Sompoq or Paning.

Mashmool, believing in his brothers' fond protestations, had laid himself down upon his sleeping-mat, thinking of the strange events of the day, of the ungainly wooden doll transfigured by the effective energy of his music into a celestial princess, of the fervid glance that lovely, peerless being had shot at him, grateful for her delivery, promising worlds of joy. It made him inexpressibly happy, gave him a feeling of beatitude that mingled in the surrounding darkness with the blissful smell of the juicy herbs of the pasture grounds and the sappy buds of the sprouting trees in the jungle, carried from far inland on the wings of the cooling mountain breeze. The growing stillness disposed him to slumber but his rest was not untroubled.

Tossing about, Mashmool was dreaming of the *apsara*, whom he fancied at his side, leaning over him and looking at him with eyes that plucked his heart out of his body, when a stronger scent, a scent of flowers, delicious and exciting, woke him up. The scent came from *melaty* and *champaca* [variety of magnolia] strung profusely in the thick coils of her hair from which now the rose had vanished as, earlier in the evening, the waringin-leaf. Sitting up, fully awakened by the emotion produced by her close proximity, Mashmool saw however nothing, though he heard a faint rustle of flowing robes, soon lost in the gurgle of the water that swirled past beneath his feet. Had she come to him, the spirit of divine delight, Sry Nagasary? Or had it been one of the comely shaped witches that prowl by night to tear open the breasts of men in search of the clotted drop of blood?

Whoever or whatever it might have been, Mashmool resolved to watch for a new manifestation, surveying the black, eddying current, trying to pierce the murky wall of river and cloud blurred together, that closed him in. Wrapped in his *sarong*, he sat quite still, noting every suspicious ticking and creaking of rafters and flooring, every shuffle of unshod feet he discerned moving in the house between the whir of fluttering bats and the yelping bark of the wild dogs that were snapping at one another over the carrion thrown up by the tide. Nervously vigilant he sat until the first glimmer of the rising moon, blinking through the thin, flying filaments of vapor that detached them-selves from the heavy mist which rested on land and sea, began to disperse the gloom. Then he took his flute and played a piece in laud of the soft, silvery light, so melodious that the occupants of the women's quarters, from mistress to lowest serving wench, spoke the next morning of heavenly lutes they had heard.

And his heart being full, Mashmool laid aside his flute to address himself to the moon in verses of the kind whose meter, in the guise of an eagle, once mounted to the realm of sublime felicity and stole the celestial liquor *soma*, lulling its guardian to neglectful sleep. And having done his duty by the benign luminary, Mashmool gave vent to the love he felt in him for Sry Nagasary and he sang:

> My lady is like the yolk of the egg of the world
> She is the cause and the aim of all that exists;
> Of her true lover's anguish and bliss for ever and ever,
> Of the pain he exultantly bears for her sake.

No more time elapsed than necessary to sheathe a kris, when a voice responded, a voice sweet as honey and distinct as the tones of Vishnu's conch that stirs creation from its crest to its navel at his passing astride on the bird Garuda:

> Through trials and suff'ring prepare to enter thy kingdom.
> Man's strength's steel'd by patience and man's love by delay.
> Is not the air cleared and cleansed by thunder and lightning?
> Steadily chase thy desire by night and by day.

Mashmool had wooed and won the *apsara* without the assistance of the saintly hermit, and deep silence, the mysterious silence of the hours before dawn ushers the work and battle of mortal existence, confirmed the announcement of her conditional surrender.

The incident did not escape the attention of the brothers who, stung by the *apsara's* refusal to see them, were spying on her to keep track of further developments. Though the more jealous of one another the more beautiful she had become and the more accomplished in her profitable art without collapsing the moment she lost the spur of musical incitement, they dropped their rivalry to unite in their common envy of Mashmool. Their backs hunched up and their livers burst of hatred at her response to his declaration, the first articulate utterance that proceeded from her lips in their hearing, and such an utterance!

"We have labored," said Bagal, "and his is the gain!"

"We have admitted him to our home, him who came as driftwood," added Sompoq, "and extended our hospitality to him and this is how he repays our kindness, licking up the mead poured out for us by the gods."

"He has brought with him a spirit of evil, his master," continued Paning, "the one that taught him those tricks, and benefactions to the wicked are always punished by the gods, adverse as they must needs be to dealings with devils and the children of their wrath."

So they talked, wicked words leaving their mouths, sinful words suggested by the spirits of evil that lived in themselves who could not apprehend the fact of Mashmool's superior power over the heavenly nymph originating simply in his superior musical skill backed by his superior cast of mind. Acting on the prognostics of Bagal's dream, as interpreted by the saintly hermit, and competing for the promised reward, they had prepared for everything except that which now had happened. To obviate its consequences, they resolved upon the sacrifice of a human life, (and whose life could it be but Mashmool's?), first to frighten his demonic master into revealing to them the coveted secret; secondly to serve the gods, notably Batara Guru, whose evident will it was that the *apsara's* mission should redound to their advantage, not his. Dreadful deeds are sometimes planned and done in the professed service of the gods!

Mashmool was asleep after his amorous vigil. Having ascertained this, the conspirators armed themselves and stealthily entered the verandah over whose balustrade they hoped to cast him, when finished, into the river which, as they knew by experience, never gave back what had sunk, properly weighted, beneath its whirling surface to its slimy bottom. Mashmool's regular breathing augured well for their undertaking. But suddenly, already near his sleeping mat and reaching for their krisses, their fratricidal hands were arrested by an apparition, luminous in the moon glow. Startled, they drew back. Sry Nagasary, premonished by her divine perception, had come to warn them off and they went, turning tail like beaten dogs, yet self-righteous enough, even in the hour of their discomfiture and repudiation, to make one another believe that it was they who renounced her since they detected their danger: do not the gods when the holy practices of sanctified men threaten damage to their pre-eminence, employ *apsaras* to lure those saints from the blessed road? Enlightened by the happenings of the night, they would abstain.

When the mean, by far too crafty fools had gone, withering under her contemptuous stare, Sry Nagasary stooped and touched Mashmool's forehead. He woke up a second time and, looking around, unquiet as a budding plant stirred by the longings of spring, he saw now plainly before him the earthly form of her who had become a dweller in his heart. Bending toward him her dainty figure that seemed wrought of the sheen of the waning moon, she carried her clean beauty proudly as a regal garment. Perplexed and afraid to speak to one descended from the highest sphere to expose herself to contact with mortals, ordained for a purpose he could not divine, to disport among them as she was wont to do among the gods, he gazed at her in silence, intoxicated by the blithesome influence of her personality, the very marrow of love.

"Thy singing has moved me strangely," she said. "Hast thou the strength to be mine?"

"Forgive me," he answered. "I forgot myself: thou belongest to my brothers and my manifest duty is to go."

"Thy brothers are a rottenness at the core of the sanctity they pretend. They sham devotion, disturbing its limpid course, stirring up its dregs and besmirching themselves. Indra's thunderbolt will destroy them: Rudra, the blueblack demon, is already tracing their path. But, by the light of the moon! I have a more important matter in hand than to discuss thy brothers' share in my assuming this shape, which will confound them through their rascal stupidity. Therefore again: Hast thou the strength to be mine; mine in my master's palace of Amaravati, in the fragrant gardens of Randana?"

Though his courage never turned away from a legitimate object, Mashmool repeated that he would resume his wanderings rather than contend with his brothers for a treasure he prized above all but considered theirs. Thereupon Sry Nagasary, unfolding their machinations and disclosing their intention to kill him, as a king's messenger unwraps a royal dispatch from its yellow silken cover and discloses its contents, told him of their frustrated attempt on his life, adding that their fate, whatever he might wish or do, was in the hands of Varuna, the god of justice and punishment. This having dissipated his scruples, he gladly confessed his love and declared his readiness to prove it by performing any task she might be pleased to appoint.

Her answer fed the lurking suspicion always associated with the unexpected fulfillment of a strong desire:

"My home is in heaven and, though the celestial beverage of delight I dispense, can be drunk by gods or by men at Batara Guru's discretion, the privileged mortal has to select between earthly marriage, which is a short, counterfeit happiness, and lasting felicity in *svarloka,* the palace and gardens of eternal bliss, which to gain requires fortitude and continence and high endeavor while traversing the valley of sorrow. It is in thy choice to abase me, *an apsara*, to thy own uncleansed condition, or to raise thyself to mine as *a gandharva*, my consort before the throne, a servant of Agni, the effulgent, and of Varuna, the exalted judge. Choose thy destiny for me to follow!"

Flurried by the alternative and impelled by the rash impatience that marks the hot lover, Mashmool had it on the tip of his tongue to beg her consent for immediate espousal, but the knowledge of its brief, incomplete satisfaction marred the tempting picture of undeferred possession as the shadow of a cloud darkens a sun-lit landscape. He stood motionless: gratification of the sin-ridden flesh for a fleeting hour or the soul's reward in undecaying beatitude, the real treasure in Sry Nagasary's gift?

Dawn had now arrived, Ushas, the shimmer of newborn day, sweethearting with the streaks of vapor in the sky, turning their complexion from palest pink to deepest carmine, and the celestial virgin took her bridegroom by the hand, leading him out of the house to the riverside.

There she held back and spoke, "Look, the moon, the lady of fecundity under whose influence Indra created the universe and fixed the orbits of the planets, Soma, restored to her dominion, is drunk up by the gods; she waneth and will not be filled ere I return to my place on high. What is thy choice? Which way shall we travel, either together for a little while, constantly menaced by irrevocable separation as between a mortal and a child of the stars; or apart for a little while, thou undoing thy desire of its low, lustful wrappings to let me precede where, after trial and purification in the accomplishment of thy task, thou shalt become my other self among the diamonds that stud the roof of the world?"

Loaded with the perfumes of bourgeoning woods, the land wind rippled the water whose playful wavelets rocked the coconut shells which the girls of the village, praying to Soma, had filled with sweet-meats and sent floating down the stream to dispose to favor the deity in charge of the matrimonial market.

The passing fisher-folk as they steered their boats seaward before the auspicious breeze, and the husbandmen as they made up to plough their ricefields and saw them standing, Mashmool and Sry Nagasary, silhouetted against the amber and garnet welkin, in earnest, affectionate communion, said, "Lo! The *apsara* has found her *gandharva*."

From afar they were watched by the saintly hermit, who had been drawn from his holy meditations by the rapidly spreading news of Sry Nagasary's release from bondage by the charm of Mashmool's enchanting melodies, and was curious to know whether the youngest of the sons of Kyahy Taboos, conquering himself, would reap the rich reward Batara Guru had empowered the *apsara* to bestow on the most deserving.

"Oh she," he muttered, "she, the cloud-spirit, groping in her deliverance for the liberation of her lover from the thralldom of carnal appetite, will she attain her wish and elevate him to glory?"

Mashmool seemed to hesitate. Anxious for a token, he scanned the horizon to the North where Kubera, the god of worldly indulgence, keeps his court, and to the North-East where Chandra illuminates the joys of paradise.

"Thou, Surya, direct his decision!" pleaded Sry Nagasary, invoking the sun, which began to climb the firmament in his golden chariot behind his milk-white, lucent horses.

At his advent Mashmool obtained the inspiration he had sought. And Surya soon reigning supreme, Mashmool loudly published his choice, erect on the ridge at the river's edge, gorgeously clothed in the lord of fruition's reflected radiance as in shining armor, clenching shining weapons, put in his hands by the resplendent god: a flaming sword to strike at error and deceit, a lance with flashing head to drive back falsehood into slanderous throats, the minstrel having enlisted as a warrior in Batara Guru's army of the upright.

And Sry Nagasary contemplated him contentedly, fain to ascend whence she had come, going before with a cheery word of trust in a speedy consummation of their union; with a prayer in her heart for its perfection in purity, such a prayer as no god can resist: May my soul be his soul as his soul is my soul, one forever in whole, undying truth!

SUNRISE

Tradition Bearer: Unavailable

Source: Dixon, Roland. *Oceanic Mythology*. Boston: Marshall Jones Company, 1916, 224–227.

Date: Unavailable

Original Source: Indonesia

National Origin: Indonesia

The following tale contains the common elements of questing for a lost sibling, animal helpers, and mistaken identification of a reflection in the water. These and other **motifs** in "Sunrise" are worldwide. The inclusion of the garuda, a monstrous mythic bird recognized both by Hindus and Buddhists, points to a more direct influence from South Asia. In contrast, the motif of an animal or object answering for an escaping fugitive is characteristically Indonesian.

Two sisters, whose parents had been killed and eaten by a tiger and a *garuda* bird, saved themselves from their parents' fate by hiding in a drum; but one day a man went out hunting, and his arrow falling on the roof of the house where the two were hidden, he found the girls and took the older, whose name was Sunrise, as his wife.

After a time the man said to his sister-in-law, "Bring me a piece of bamboo, that I may knock out the partition (at the nodes) and make a water-vessel for you to get water in," but when he fixed it, he secretly made holes through the bottom also. He then gave her the water-vessel, and she went to the stream to bring water, but the bamboo would not hold it; and after she had tried for a long time, she discovered the holes in the bottom. Accordingly she returned to the house, but found that Sunrise and her husband had gone, for he had pierced the bottom of the water-vessel so that he and his wife might have time to run away.

Before going off, however, Sunrise had left two lice behind her and had instructed them to answer for her when her sister should return and thus delay pursuit, her orders being, "If she calls me from the landside, do you answer from the seaside; if she calls me from the seaside, do you answer from the land-side; if she asks you the way, show it to her." When the deserted sister returned to the house, she called to Sunrise and thought she heard an answer, but when she went thither, the reply came from the opposite direction. Thus deceived by the false calls, she was long delayed; but finally she discovered the trick, asked the way which Sunrise had taken, and set off in pursuit.

By and by she came upon an old woman, to whom she called, "Oh, granny! Oh, granny! look here!"

The old woman said to herself, "Well, ever since the world was made, I have lived alone, so I won't look," but, nevertheless, she did look, and then asked, "Well, Granddaughter, where do you come from?"

"Granny, I am seeking my older sister," said the other sister, whose name was Kokamomako; and then hearing the sound of a drum, she inquired, "Granny, why are they having a feast over there?"

The old woman answered, "Just now they went by with your sister," and so Kokamomako, continued on her way.

When she came to the house, she called out, "Show me the hair of my sister in the window," but the people inside held up the hair of a cat, whereupon Kokamomako said, "My sister is indeed ugly, but that is the hair of a cat. You must show me her foot."

Then the people took the foot of a cat and thrust it out of the window, saying, "If you want us to produce your sister, you must pick up a basket of rice that we will throw out," whereupon they threw it out and scattered it. Then Kokamomako wept, for this was a task which she could not accomplish; but a rice-bird came up to her and asked, "What is your trouble, and what do you want, that you are picking that up?"

She replied, "I have no trouble, and I don't want anything, but they have hidden my elder sister."

Then the rice-bird helped her, and it was not long before the rice was all gathered; but still the people would not bring out her sister, Sunrise; whereupon Kokamomako said, "If you don't produce my sister, I will go home and set fire to my house," adding, "when you see blue smoke, that will be the furniture;

when you see white smoke, that will be money; when you see red smoke, that will be I." Then she went away, and soon they saw that she had set fire to her house, perceiving that the smoke was first blue, then white, and then red. Knowing that her sister was now dead, Sunrise went and bathed, and when she came back to the house, she took a knife and stabbed herself and died. By and by her husband went to carry her food, and found her dead, whereupon he also took a knife and tried to kill himself, but did not succeed.

Now there was a slave in the house who went to get water at the river, and when she looked in the stream, seeing the reflection of Sunrise, she thought it was her own and called out, "Oh, sirs, you said that I was ugly, but really I am beautiful." Proud of her supposed good looks and thinking herself too good to be a slave, she threw away her water-vessel and broke it; but when she went back to the house, they sent her back again for water and once more she saw the reflection of Sunrise, for the latter and her younger sister (their ghosts) were hidden in the top of a tree that leaned over the stream. This, however, the slave did not know, and again she said, "Oh, sirs, you said that I was ugly, but I am really beautiful," and again she threw away the water-vessel and broke it, doing this seven times before she told the people in the house that she had seen the reflection of Sunrise.

In the house was another slave who suffered from wounds on his legs, and the husband of Sunrise ordered him to dive into the stream in order to seize her, but he refused. So all set upon him, and he was forced to do as he was bid; but though he dove and dove, and broke open his wounds, and colored the stream with his blood, he could not find Sunrise.

Accordingly he came ashore and said, "I told you just now that I could not do it, and now you have forced me to try, and I have broken my wounds open again."

Thereupon, as they sat by the stream, the husband happened to look up, and seeing his wife in the top of the tree, he called out, "Let down a rope, so that I may climb up."

So she lowered a copper wire, saying, "When you get half way up, don't hold on so tight," but when he climbed up and reached the halfway point, she cut the wire, and he fell and was dashed to pieces.

THE LIZARD HUSBAND

Tradition Bearer: Unavailable

Source: Dixon, Roland. *Oceanic Mythology.* Boston: Marshall Jones Company, 1916, 210–213.

Date: Unavailable

Original Source: Indonesia

National Origin: Indonesia

Many Indonesian folktales tell the story of an animal spouse. These frequently take the form of "Beauty and the Beast" (AT 425C). As in the following narrative, the animal husband is misjudged, but by means of enchantment, he triumphs over those who maltreat him.

Once there was an old woman who lived alone in the jungle and had a lizard which she brought up as her child. When he was full grown, he said to her, "Grandmother, go to the house of Lise, where there are seven sisters; and ask for the eldest of these for me as a wife." The old woman did as the lizard requested, and taking the bridal gifts with her, went off; but when she came near the house, Lise saw her and said, "Look, there comes Lizard's grandmother with a bridal present. Who would want to marry a lizard! Not I."

The old woman arrived at the foot of the ladder, ascended it, and sat down in Lise's house, whereupon the eldest sister gave her betel, and when her mouth was red from chewing it, asked, "What have you come for, Grandmother? Why do you come to us?"

"Well, Granddaughter, I have come for this: to present a bridal gift; perhaps it will be accepted, perhaps not. That is what I have come to see." As soon as she had spoken, the eldest indicated her refusal by getting up and giving the old woman a blow that knocked her across to the door, following this with another that rolled her down the ladder.

The old woman picked herself up and went home; and when she had reached her house, the lizard inquired, "How did your visit succeed?"

She replied, "O! Alas! I was afraid and almost killed. The gift was not accepted, the eldest would not accept it; it seems she has no use for you because you are only a lizard."

"Do not be disturbed," said he, "go tomorrow and ask for the second sister," and the old woman did not refuse, but went the following morning, only to be denied as before. Each day she went again to another of the sisters until the turn of the youngest came. This time the girl did not listen to what Lise said and did not strike the old woman or drive her away, but agreed to become Lizard's wife, at which the old woman was delighted and said that after seven nights she and her son would come.

When this time had passed, the grandmother arrived, carrying the lizard in a basket. Kapapitoe (the youngest sister) laid down a mat for the old woman to sit on while she spread out the wedding gifts, whereupon the young bride gave her food, and after she had eaten and gone home, the lizard remained as Kapapitoe's husband. The other sisters took pains to show their disgust. When they returned home at night, they would wipe the mud off their feet on Lizard's back and would say, "Pitoe can't prepare any garden; she must stay and take care of her lizard," but Kapapitoe would say, "Keep quiet. I shall take him down to the river and wash off the mud."

After a while the older sisters got ready to make a clearing for a garden, and one day, when they had gone to work, the lizard said to his wife, "We have too much to bear. Your sisters tease us too much. Come, let us go and make a garden. Carry me in a basket on your back, wife, and gather also seven empty coconut-shells." His wife agreed, put her husband in a basket, and after collecting the seven shells, went to the place which they were to make ready for their garden. Then the lizard said, "Put me down on the ground, wife, so that I can run about," and thus he scurried around, lashing the grass and trees with his tail and covering a whole mountain-side in the course of the day; with one blow he felled a tree, cut it up by means of the sharp points on his skin, set the pieces afire, and burned the whole area, making the clearing smooth and good.

Then he said to Kapapitoe, "Make a little seat for me, so that I can go and sit on it," and when this was done, he ordered the seven coconut shells to build a house for him, after which he was carried home by his wife. The older sisters returning at evening, saw the new clearing and wondered at it, perceiving that it was ready for planting. When they got home they said to their sister, "You can't go thus to the planting feast of Ta Datoe. Your husband is only a lizard," and again they wiped their feet on him.

The next day Lizard and his wife went once more to their clearing and saw that the house had already been built for them by the coconut shells, which had turned into slaves; whereupon the lizard said, "Good, tomorrow evening we will hold the preliminary planting festival, and the next day a planting feast." Ordering his seven slaves to prepare much food for the occasion, he said to his wife, "Let us go to the river and get ready," but on arriving at the stream, they bathed far apart, and the lizard, taking off his animal disguise, became a very handsome man dressed in magnificent garments. When he came for his wife, she at first did not recognize him, but at last was convinced; and after she had been given costly new clothes and ornaments, they returned toward Lise's house. As they came back, the preliminary planting festival had begun, and many people were gathered, including Kapapitoe's elder sisters, Lise, and the old woman.

The six sisters said, "Tell us, Grandmother, who is that coming? She looks so handsome, and her sarong rustles as if rain were falling. The hem of her sarong goes up and down every moment as it touches her ankles."

The old woman replied, "That is your youngest sister, and there comes her husband also," whereupon, overcome with jealousy, the six sisters ran to meet their handsome brother-in-law and vied with each other for the privilege of carrying his betel-sack, saying, "I want to hold the *sirih*-sack of my brother-in-law." He, however, went and sat down, and the six went to sit beside him to take him away from their youngest sister, but the lizard would have none of them.

Next day was the planting, and his sisters-in-law would not let the lizard go in company with his wife, but took possession of him and made him angry. Accordingly, when Lise and the sisters were asleep, the lizard got up, waked Kapapitoe, and taking a stone, laid four pieces of bark upon it and repeated a charm, "If there is power in the wish of the six sisters who wipe their feet on me, then I shall, when I open my eyes, be sitting on the ground just as I am now. But if my wish has power, when I open my eyes, I shall be sitting in my house and looking down on all other houses."

When he opened his eyes, he was seated in his house high up on the mountain, for the stone had grown into a great rock, and his house was on top of it. His sisters-in-law tried to climb the cliff, but in vain, and so had to give up, while he and his wife, Kapapitoe, lived happily ever after.

KANTJIL THE MOUSE DEER

As noted in the discussion of the Plandok (mouse deer) **cycle** in Borneo, this **trickster** figure is popular in Southeast Asia. In Indonesia, the mouse deer is commonly teamed with or pitted against three other figures: ape, crocodile, and tiger. See the Dusun "Mouse Deer the Trickster" cycle (page 328) for additional information and comparative data from Borneo.

Mouse Deer and Tiger

Tradition Bearer: Unavailable

Source: Dixon, Roland. *Oceanic Mythology*. Boston: Marshall Jones Company, 1916, 186–188.

Date: Unavailable

Original Source: Indonesia

National Origin: Indonesia

One day the kantjil was resting quietly when he heard a tiger approaching and feared for his life, wherefore, quickly taking a large leaf, he began to fan a pile of dung which happened to lie near. When the tiger came up, and overcome by curiosity asked what he was doing, the mouse-deer said, "This is food belonging to the king. I am guarding it."

The tiger, being very hungry, at once wished to be allowed to eat the royal food, but the kantjil refused for a long time, advising him not to touch it and saying that it would be wrong to betray his trust; but at last he agreed to let the tiger have his way if he would promise to wait before eating it until he, the kantjil, had gone; for thus the blame might be escaped.

No sooner said than done; so when the kantjil had reached a safe distance, he called back to the tiger, "You may begin now," whereupon the tiger hungrily seized what he thought was a delicious morsel, only to be cruelly deceived. Furious at the trick played upon him by the little kantjil, he hurried after the fugitive to get his revenge.

His intended victim, had meanwhile found a very venomous snake, which lay coiled up asleep. Sitting by this, he awaited the tiger's arrival, and when the latter came up raging in pursuit, he told him that he had only himself to blame, since he had been warned not to eat the food. "But," said the kantjil, "you must keep quiet, for I am guarding the girdle of the king. You must not come near it, because it is full of magic power." The tiger's curiosity and desire being, of course, only stimulated by all this, he insisted that he be allowed to try on the precious girdle, to which the kantjil yielded with apparent reluctance, again warning him to be very careful and, as before, saying that the tiger must first let him get safely away, in order that no guilt might attach to him. When the kantjil had run off, the tiger seized the supposed magic girdle, only to be bitten by the snake, which he did not succeed in killing until after a severe struggle.

Thirsting for vengeance, the tiger again took up the pursuit of his clever little adversary, who, meanwhile, had stopped to rest, so that when the tiger caught up with him, he found him sitting near a clump of tall bamboo. The kantjil greeted the tiger warmly and said, without giving the latter time to express his anger, that he had been appointed keeper of the king's trumpet. The tiger, immediately desiring to try this wonderful instrument, was induced to put his tongue between two of the bamboos, being told that, as soon as the wind blew, they would give fine music. The trickster ran off, and presently a strong gust arose, swayed the bamboos, and thus pinched the tiger's tongue entirely off.

Again the tiger gave chase, and this time found the kantjil standing beside a great wasp's nest. As before, the trickster warned the tiger not to disturb him, for he was guarding the king's drum which gave out a very wonderful tone when struck; but the tiger, of course, was most anxious to have the opportunity of sounding it. With feigned reluctance, the kantjil at last agreed, stipulating, as before, that he be allowed to get out of the way. As soon as he had put a safe distance between himself and the tiger, he gave the signal, and the tiger struck the nest, only to be beset the next instant by a swarm of angry wasps.

Mouse Deer, Tiger, and Ape

Tradition Bearer: Unavailable

Source: Dixon, Roland. *Oceanic Mythology*. Boston: Marshall Jones Company, 1916, 191–192.

Date: Unavailable

Original Source: Indonesia

National Origin: Indonesia

The tiger was seeking the kantjil to cat him, when the latter hastened to find a *djati*-plant, whose leaves he chewed making his mouth blood-red; after which he went and sat down beside a well. By and by the tiger came along, and the trickster, assuming a fierce aspect and driveling blood-red saliva from his mouth, said that the tiger had better look out, as he, the mouse-deer, was accustomed to cat tigers, and if the latter did not believe it, let him look in the well, in which he would see the head of the last one that he had finished. The tiger was much alarmed, though not wholly convinced, so he went to look in the well, where he saw, of course, the reflection of his own head. Thinking that this was really the head of the tiger which the mouse-deer had just eaten, and convinced of the trickster's might, the tiger ran away as fast as he could.

The ape, however, encouraged the tiger not to be afraid of the trickster, who was not so terrible a person after all, and to prove this, he said that he would go with the tiger to seek the kantjil once more; while to demonstrate his good faith he proposed that they should tie their tails together so that they might thus make a common attack, the ape riding on the tiger's back.

The latter agreed and in this way again approached the clever little rascal; but as soon as the latter saw them coming, he called out, "Ha! That is strange! There comes the ape who usually brings me two tigers every day as tribute, and now he is bringing only one." Terrified at this, the tiger ran away as fast as his legs would carry him; and the ape, being tied to his tail, was dashed against the rocks and trees and was killed.

Mouse Deer and Crocodile

Tradition Bearer: Unavailable

Source: Dixon, Roland. *Oceanic Mythology*. Boston: Marshall Jones Company, 1916, 190.

Date: Unavailable

Original Source: Indonesia

National Origin: Indonesia

Once kantjil wished to cross a river which he was unable to wade or swim because it was in flood, so, standing upon the bank, he called for the crocodiles, saying that the king had given command that they should be counted. Accordingly, they came in great numbers and by the trickster's directions arranged themselves in a row extending from bank to bank, whereupon the mouse-deer pretended to count them, jumping from one to the other and calling out, "one," "two" "three," etc., until he reached the opposite bank, when he derided them for their stupidity.

Resolving to be avenged, the crocodile bided his time, and when the trickster came later to the river to drink, he seized one of the mouse-deer's legs in his mouth. Nothing dismayed, the captive picked up a branch and called out, "That is not my leg; that is a stick of wood. My foot is here." The crocodile accordingly let go and snapped at the branch, thinking that it was really the trickster's leg; but this gave the needed opportunity, and the clever mouse-deer bounded away to safety, leaving the stupid crocodile with the stick in his mouth.

The crocodile, however, determined not to go without his revenge, lay in wait, floating like a water-soaked log until the mouse-deer should visit the river again. When, after a while, he did come to the stream and saw the crocodile motionless, he stood on the bank and said, as if he were in doubt whether or not it was a log, "If that is the crocodile, it will float downstream." The crocodile, resolving not to give himself away, remained motionless; and then the trickster added, But if it is a log, it will float upstream." At once the crocodile began to swim slowly against the current, and the mouse-deer, having discovered what he wished, called out in derision, "Ha! Ha! I have fooled you once more."

ROOSTAM THE GAME-COCK

Tradition Bearer: Unavailable

Source: Scheltema, J. F. "Roostam the Game-cock." *Journal of American Folklore* 32 (1919): 306–323.

Date: Unavailable

Original Source: Indonesia (Sumatra)

National Origin: Indonesia

"Roostam the Game-cock" is set during the later period of Dutch influence over Indonesia, a territory in the Dutch East Indies. From 1602 until 1945, with the exception of Japanese conquest in World War II, the Netherlands, first through private enterprise and later via colonialism, exerted dominance in the area. Continuing enmity between the local population and "the Company" as well as rivalries between coastal and highlands regions pervades the **legend** as adapted by J. F. Scheltema. The symbolic importance of cock-fighting in Indonesia and Southeast Asia, in general, is obvious in the narrative. Success of one's bird brings not only financial gain, but prestige and power. The title clearly demonstrates the close identification between bird and owner.

The Malays of the Padang Highlands in Sumatra are born cock-fighters. But for a main of game-fowls, arranged to take place near the beautiful lake of Maninju, sweet, pretty Raissa would be at home instead of on the road between Matoor and Pasar Lawang.

It is early, between eight and ten, the hour specified in native speech as most propitious for spreading out the rice in the hull to dry. The people of the Lowlands, truly, would call it late, seeing that they observe much earlier hours for going to market and the transaction of business because the sun makes them. In the cool Highlands, however, there is no such fear of the burning Eye of Day.

The road leads through coffee-gardens and here and there a primitive sugar-plantation with the old-fashioned mill, worked by hand or by a yoke of oxen. Farther away the watered rice-fields are watched over by giant mountains in the hazy distance. Everywhere, in the valleys and on the hills, mother earth lifts up her opulence to the favoring light of heaven, which descends in the glory of a newborn tropical day.

It is not considered proper for young girls to attend market-places, where conversation is held of such meaning, where people are encountered of such an adventurous disposition as ought to be met only by men and old women who know something of the world and its ugly snares. But Raissa, though the child of a well-to-do mother, yea, living in a house with gables pointed upward like horns, the exclusive privilege of the free-born Malay, Raissa is all for new ideas. She has been a pupil of the native school at Matoor, where six *gurus*, appointed by the Dutch Government, instruct some two hundred children, among whom are already fifteen girls. Female emancipation is beginning to spread around the lake of Maninju And Raissa has still another excuse, quite sufficient in her opinion if maidenly coyness may come to the rescue of old-time institutions: Raissa is in love.

Behold her, then, brown but comely, her dark red scarf, embroidered with gold, folded over her head after the manner of the daughters of the land; her eyes, black and bright, brighter yet by the effect of a blue powder rubbed into the lower lids, haughtily looking down upon the other women, who trot to the market loaded with baskets of merchandise. Raissa is proud; proud of her mother's standing in her village; proud of her fine clothes, of the gold bracelets on her wrists, of the gold rings in her ears, while everybody knows that at home she keeps even more golden treasure, to be admired at every feast, gold pins to keep her hair smooth and a gold diadem, the envy of all her friends. Raissa is a girl of consequence and proud of it indeed, very proud, but most proud in the affection of Roostam, surnamed the Game-Cock.

Roostam, a daredevil sort of a young fellow, did not get that nickname for nothing. Apart from his natural proclivity to cock-fighting as a Sumatran Malay and, more particularly, as a scion of the family which has held the record for the raising of game-fowl in the whole country from time immemorial, his maternal uncle, Haji [honorific title given to a Muslim who has taken a pilgrimage to Mecca] Yusoof, being the greatest authority on everything connected with the sport, far and near in the Highlands and in the Lowlands too, Roostam himself is the veriest game-cock among men. Though generous and kind-hearted, his friends and acquaintances know him to be quick at taking offense. He does not suffer any one to slight his interests or, worse still, his pretensions. He is a free-born man, a stickler for the Malay code of etiquette; his young, hot blood rebels against even the thought of compromise; his kris [dagger] lives next door to his ire.

When the old women of the village found out that a match between Roostam and Raissa was a foregone conclusion, they warned their daughters and granddaughters against him with all their might, calling him a scapegrace, a dangerous wild bull in the herd, who sooner or later would get himself and all his kin into trouble, and the girls assented with faces suggestive of sour grapes for secretly they admired Roostam as the flower of chivalry and manly excellence, and they hated Raissa, whose success with him exasperated them. The old men, too, thinking of their own youth or what they made themselves believe that their own youth had been, cherished Roostam's exploits in their hearts and yarned about the vigor of past ages revived in his person.

Especially Haji Yusoof, who had traveled, improving his knowledge by the pilgrimage to Mecca, and through that feat, together with his unequaled experience in the matter of game-fowl, had become a personage of influence, extended his protection to Roostam, as indeed he should, being the lad's maternal uncle. The fundamental principle of all social institutions on the West Coast of Sumatra is the succession by inheritance according to the rules of a strict matrilineal descent. The Malay family, in the narrower sense of the word, consists there of the mother with her offspring. The father does not belong to it; his relationship to his brothers and sisters is of far more consequence than his relationship to his wife and children. And since he is not a member of the social group they constitute, he cannot be its head. The duties and privileges attached to that position devolve upon the eldest brother of his wife, the eldest maternal uncle of his children, called their *mammak*.

On her way to Pasar Lawang, Raissa passes a trail which leads her through a coffee-plantation to the place where she knows that a cock-fight is on. True, the Government has prohibited that kind of sport, but then Sumatra is, like the rest of the Dutch East Indies, a country of ordinances not enforced and regulations not attended to. Wherever the police raise a cry about cock-fighting, something more lies behind it than the cock-fighting itself, a native vendetta or a native quarrel of some sort, or simply a native desire to worry the Dutch officials. Since, however, the written law must be respected, at any rate by the minions of the law, if not in fact at least in outward appearance, the cock-fights are removed from the market-places to more secluded nooks and corners, an arrangement quite satisfactory to the said minions, who indulge in the national pastime without further re-serve, as every one else does, and engage their game-fowls to be pitted either by their own hands or by proxy. So it happened in the case of a native police officer, by common consent called *murei*, which is the name of a bird with an unmelodious, unpleasant squeak. The nickname was aptly bestowed as Malay nicknames always are. A stranger in the land, a man from Bencoolen, thrown upon the country by the influence of an official who put him on the police force in consideration of personal services, Murei had established his reputation as a sneak, not to be trusted on any account and a braggart withal. He found pleasure in lifting his voice against the breed of game-fowls that were the glory of Roostam and Roostam's *mammak*, Haji Yusoof. The battle now in progress was planned to cure him of his pluming himself as the possessor of a cock, brought all the way from Padang, which, he boasted, could kill in single combat all the game-cocks between the lake of Maninju and the lake of Singkarah. This morning that valorous bird was to step forward against Roostam's favorite.

Feeling much interested, Raissa has eagerly watched the preparation for the odd fights that are to follow the main as far as game-fowls from Matoor may take part. She has witnessed the infinite care bestowed on the separation of the fat cocks from the middling and the middling from the lean before their being cooped and, after the necessary purging of the fat ones, before their being put to their diet. She has followed the sparring exercises, the providing of the spears with muffs, the minute, periodical examination of the feathers, the beak, the eyes, to see if the fowls are in good health. And then, three days before the battle, at the auspicious hour set for the removal of the fighters to the scene of their future great deeds, she attended the last probing of their temper and listened to the animated debates, the endless discussions as to whether they were game or not and which one was most game and how the chances stood, and so forth, and so forth.

Meanwhile Roostam had trained his cock with the utmost assiduity under the guidance of his *mammak*, Haji Yusoof. All that time of anxious care he hardly allowed Raissa to come near him; but as it concerned a matter of so much moment, she bore him no ill will for being neglected. Sharing his enthusiasm she resigned herself and her unescorted walk to Pasar Lawang, inconsistent with the habitual reserve of a maiden of her rank and station, has no other purpose than to learn the issue of the battle immediately after its having been fought for, surely, the very first thing its promoters will do is to send word to the market-place where the itinerant tradesmen are awaiting the news to spread it through the whole district as far as Bukit Tinggi. It would be a calamity indeed if a game-cock of Haji Yusoof's breed, in Roostam's hands, lost against a Padang cock in the hands of a man from Bencoolen, and Murei at that. Raissa's excitement running higher and higher, her expectations are, however, of the very best.

Hearing steps behind her and some one calling her by her name, she turns round to see Roostam's *mammak* coming up, extremely venerable in his regulation dress of a *haji*, with a tuft of sparse white hair under his chin. He reads the question in her eyes and tells her that, at the time he left the pit, they were still at the preliminaries. Raissa thinks it strange that Roostam's *mammak* has not waited for the end; yet she ventures no direct inquiry. But soon she understands that something is amiss, when informed of Murei's determination to stay away himself and be represented by one of his underlings. Haji Yusoof does not say so but Raissa feels that he suspects foul play and, being of the elect, declines to get mixed up in the affray which is likely to follow. Haji Yusoof holds an office of responsibility as the chief of the kampong Lawang and, therefore, though of all cock-fights his heart goes out to this special one, he deems it desirable, with a view to possible consequences of possible happenings, that he be able to say: I was not in it.

Solicitous to please Roostam's *mammak* as women, brown or white, are always eager to please whenever it can further some ultimate purpose, Raissa lets Haji Yusoof pass before her and walks behind him to Pasar Lawang.

The venerable looking Haji Yusoof is a great talker as indeed all Sumatra Malays are, but now he keeps silent and, having reached his dwelling, where he bids Raissa enter with him for a chat with his womenfolk, he goes straight up to where his *ketitiran* hangs in its cage, suspended from a roof-beam, and takes it down, putting it beside him. The natives are very fond of pigeons, in particular of some kinds that live wild in the woods, as the *ketitiran* and the *punei,* which are caught and tamed and then become the constant companions of their owners. Haji Yusoof's *ketitiran is* a famous one, reputed to bring extraordinary luck. As a matter of fact, Haji Yusoof prospers exceedingly in a worldly sense, harvesting from many rice fields.

Very soon quite a number of callers drop in, anxious to hear about the cock-fight which, for some reason or other, they are not able to attend; anxious also to let their own fowl profit by Haji Yusoof's advice. They have made it a habit on Monday, the market day at Kampong Lawang, to consult Haji Yusoof in that way when visiting the *pasar* for their weekly purchases. People travel even from Bukit Tinggi and Padang Panjang, yea, from Bua and Solok, to avail themselves of his skill in dealing with the maladies and disorders that fowl, especially game-fowl, are heir to.

On the main battle, now raging between the cocks of Roostam and his opponent, Haji Yusoof has not much to say, and his visitors perceive very soon that the subject is better dismissed in his presence. But he readily imparts his superior wisdom in the treatment of such ailments among poultry as indigestion, costiveness, diarrhea, fever, asthma, gout, consumption, inflammation of the eye, obstruction of the nostrils, melancholy or moping, rheumatism or lifts, with useful hints about molting, loss of feathers, vermin, etc., thrown in. A man from Bua has brought with him an old rheumatic rooster and the younger females of Haji Yusoof's household derive great amusement from the spectacle of this bird, once a game-cock of some renown, strutting round, lifting its legs high and putting them down with care, stiff in limbs and joints, as if it were marching to the sound of the solemn march sometimes heard at Bukit Tinggi when the soldiers, in garrison at Fort de Kock, turn out for a military funeral.

After treating this patient, Haji Yusoof examines the sick-looking eyes, nostrils and mouth of a hen with ruffled feathers, that is suffering from croup, breathing laboriously, and he advises to give her plenty of fresh air, to grease her swollen head every morning before sunrise, to hide her from the moon. Thereupon a bad case of pip claims his attention and he warns against unclean food and muddy water, and prescribes a dose of pepper, administered with coconut-oil or, if that proves insufficient, the cutting off, as a last resort, of the tip of the tongue. Almost forgetting the cock-fight in his endeavors to sustain his reputation as a breeder and physician of poultry, he expatiates upon a remedy against the gapes, somewhat heroic but recommended by long experience …

Raissa, impatient to learn the result of the battle, slips out to the *pasar* proper (that is, the place where the *pakan or* market is held), cunningly calculating that, as soon as anything positive becomes known, it will be proclaimed there first of all. Picking her way to the enclosure of peace, a spot marked off by flat stones standing on end, where formerly the elders used to meet in council and to preside over the bull-fights, cock-fights and other such amusements before the Government stepped in to forbid them, picking her way between the little booths whose owners deal in the produce of the land and articles of daily use in Malay households, she meets many acquaintances, mostly old women for the reason already referred to. If anything, the marriageable girls of the Padang Highlands are even more shy about showing themselves in public than those of other Malay lands. Little girls, however, run about in plenty and several of them, children of poor mothers who squat at the roadside with the fruit of their gardens for sale, offer *kopi daoen* to the thirsty, a concoction of the leaves of the coffee-shrub. Too poor to drink real coffee while tending the richest of coffee-plantations, they have to leave the berries and beans alone after picking them for export oversea.

Raissa does not worry about such things when she finds herself in the *pasar*, which is no less a delight to the native fair ones than are the pretentious shops of Rijswijk and Noordwijk at Batavia to their sisters of the ruling race. Raissa worries about Roostam, the Game-Cock, though, for all that, she cannot help admiring the printed cotton goods temptingly displayed by merchants from Padang, trashy stuff, imported from Europe as a cheap substitute for the fine but expensive *bajus* and *sarongs* and *slendangs* of silk and gold lace, the pride of the Highland damsels in days of yore, finery altogether out of the financial reach of the present generation, save of a few who carry them as heirlooms.

A few strangers stroll about, their respective habitats being indicated by their raiment in a country where, if not the material, at least the cut, with purely local variations, has remained stationary from the time when Parapatih Sabateng of Body Chiniago and Kiahy Tumanggangan of Kota Pilihan, in the picturesque valley of Priangan Padang Panjang, laid the foundation of the Malay institutions as they continue up to this day, notwithstanding sharp conflicts between western innovations and the *hadat*, the ancient, unwritten law. The men of Agam, who frown at the naked legs of their brethren that hail from the XIII Kotas, can be recognized by their long inexpressibles, and Raissa notices even one or two visitors in Acheh-trousers, very wide and loose from the hips down. They make her think of a fellow who lately has courted Roostam's company, at night for he avoids the light of day, gossip marking him as a deserter from the Dutch army in close touch with the malcontents that are opposing the regular troops in Korinchy, and sent in quest of able men for reinforcement of the marauding bands in the North. As to the women who throng the market at Lawang, the strangers among them are still more easily distinguishable, and those of the XIII Kotas, accustomed to arrange their hair in braids, heartily despise the *kondeh*, the more or less elaborate knot adopted by all the rest. The children, most of them with noses in sad need of wiping, wear their hair—boys (under the age of the head-covering) as well as girls—in most comical little plaits, five for the free-born and four for the common raff.

As noon approaches with the sun high up in the sky, Raissa can hardly master her agitation. Where she passes, the old women eye her maliciously and whisper of Roostam's girl possessing *a pusar*, a birthmark—they know it for certain—which will make him who marries her or even aspires to her hand, unlucky in all his dealings. Signs and marks on women, horses and pigeons, portending good luck or bad luck to husbands or owners, are an ever welcome theme for discussion.

"Look at her," says one of the hags, "look at her as she goes there, proud of her finery. I am sorry for Roostam!"

"And the old man, Roostam's *mammak*," says another, "who ought to know and yet encourages his passion for this ill-omened daughter of calamity!"

"What is the will of Haji Yusoof against the will of the young game-cock?"

"And why then does he carry his head so high, wise in forebodings and *pusars* and *krimans*, if he cannot stay the evil that comes to his own?"

"Hide thy envy as closely as the wrinkles of age hide thy good looks," some one chimes in, making all the bystanders laugh.

The gossips look up. It is the *dubalang,* one of the elders of the village, who continues, "It is coming to a fine pass indeed when the *orang banyak* (the plebs) give the *orang patoob* (the upper ten) a free ride on their tongues."

"Next thing," remarks a waggish youth, "they will find fault with all the good things the Company [Dutch East Indies Company] promises and does not do."

This speech meets with applause from the lad's friends among those who are gathering round, but the more advised look grave and the *dubalang* answers, "Thou, wait till thy turn of speaking arrives with thy tooth of discernment!"

Meanwhile at the cockpit, in a sheltered nook off the road, excitement began to run high. For the main battle, in which the game-cock of Roostam was to be pitted against the game-cock of Murei, the latter had failed to appear. The crowd waited with murmuring and growing discontent until at last a messenger from Murei arrived with his bird and the information that he withdrew his patronage. He had bethought himself of the Government prohibition against cock-fighting and, suddenly mindful of his duty as a police officer, declined to countenance the game. Not to disappoint the many then and there assembled to witness the battle, he had nevertheless condescended to send his rooster, permitting them to let it take part as previously arranged, with only this proviso that it was to fight not under his name but under the name of his *wakil* (substitute), accompanied by quite a number of followers, most of them no free-born Malays, strangers to the country, adventurers of evil repute, a sorry pack.

At this stage of the proceedings, Haji Yusoof, suspecting foul play, left the battleground, not however before giving a piece of advice to Roostam, with a parting glance at Roostam's game-cock, which looked somewhat depressed as if it had been tampered with. The wings and the tail, to be sure, were not cut shorter than they ought to have been and the joints appeared all right, but the animal's general weariness suggested the idea of poison. Knowing the youngster's temper, Haji Yusoof did not speak of it but the thought had occurred to Roostam himself and did not dispose him to calm reasoning when Murei's *wakil*, after Haji Yusoof's departure, proposed with the utmost impudence that the handling of his fowl be left to the contending party.

Meeting, of course, the strongest opposition, this absurd proposal gave rise to a lengthy discussion and the bystanders, later on, in the light of subsequent events, freely expressed their opinion that such an intermezzo was the real purpose of the claim put forward because it would be helpful in giving the drug, administered to Roostam's bird, the necessary time to operate. It soon became evident to everyone that something was wrong with the Highland favorite. Roostam's friends declared openly that his fowl had been doctored, and tried to persuade him to retire from the main, while others goaded him to the extremity of his pride in their reluctance to lose the chance of a contest between the distasteful Murei and the young hero of the district, for the fight between the roosters was essentially a fight between their owners and the interests they represented.

Roostam was worked up to a dangerous pitch of excitement and this dark young fellow with his fierce eyes, supple and strong, quick and nimble in his movements, fully deserved the nickname that had been given to him, among men no less keen on proving his mettle in any combat offered to him, than a game-cock in condition among poultry.

But his bird, alas! The pride of all the countryside, was clearly *not* in condition and when, at length, after wearisome exceptions, Murei's *wakil* consented to the birds being weighed, preparatory to the great encounter, no coaxing or urging, no spurring prevailed upon the animal to show fight. Then it was also discovered that Murei's game-cock had been gaffed [fitted with sharp extensions to his natural spurs] in a fashion strictly prohibited by the regulations as highly unfair to the opposite party, which engendered a new dispute between the backers of Roostam and the backers of Murei, the latter pretending that Roostam had lost because his cock refused battle, the former insisting upon the fact that Murei's cock would have been debarred anyway. The umpire, a man from Matoor, decided in favor of Roostam, whereupon Murei's men withdrew, every one of them declining to stay for the games which were to follow the main, after having demanded in vain that the case be referred to another umpire, chosen on the spot from those present.

The withdrawal of the Murei crew caused no sorrow and, while Roostam nursed his cock without saying a word but white with rage under his brown skin, the owners of the other birds that were to compete, prepared them for the odd fights. Taking turns, each cocker, fowl in hand, went to his station to set his bird, sharply eyeing his adversary for no one is allowed to assist in the fight after it has been declared on, either to encourage or to discourage, save to avail himself of the privilege to relieve a rooster which has landed on its back.

The stirring sensations of the game made those who experienced them almost forget what had happened to the champion, defender of the country's honor against all comers. Closely pressing round, squatting after the manner of the land, they grew highly agitated over the gallant behavior of two cocks that proved very evenly matched and took a long time to decide between victory and defeat. The birds renewed the attack vigorously after every separation, viciously slashing round with their armed spurs, flying up with ruffled feathers, struggling to get behind each other for a final assault in the rear. Some of the most admiring ascribed their endurance to the fact of their having been breasted according to the highest requirements of the art; others, critically inclined, considered it an effect of bad heeling. Anyhow, the victory was hotly contested; no more odds were accepted; the timorous hedged their bets—everybody had money on, this way or that, in the majority of cases more than he could afford to lose and the gamblers hung in suspense.

Roostam himself, with a scowl on his face and his sick pet in his lap, was being carried away by the general emotion when, raising his eyes at the sound of nearing footsteps, he suddenly jumped to his feet. Murei, his enemy, stood before him, surrounded by the men who a few moments before were so disagreeably noisy as the backers of that despised trickster's Lowland cock. The boys set to watch the approaches to the pit, had left their posts to gratify their curiosity and thus it happened that Murei with his gang found the road open and safe. The crowd hardly took notice of him in the growing agitation of the fight. Murei was a policeman but what of that? Had he not pitted a cock himself, even for the main battle, the very same morning?

Roostam, however, felt that Murei meant business, that he intended either to profit by the law being transgressed so as to gain an advantage in their personal feud, or simply to avenge himself for the barring out of his bird, the victory having been adjudged to the Highlands, notwithstanding his treacherous ruse. But if Roostam's feathered champion refused battle, Roostam did not and growled in defiance:

"You in uniform? In the uniform of the Company? Don't you know that the Company does not countenance cock-fighting?"

"I know it and that is why I am here: to stop this game and to arrest you, my fine game-cock."

The incriminated sports thought first that he jested but he proved to be in dead earnest and, while some began stealing away, the others jeered him:

"Come! Come now! And how about that bird of yours, pitted by your *wakil?*"

"A liar who says so! Where is my bird? Where is my *wakil?*"

"Do you pretend to deny that the fellows you are this moment hiding behind, came here this morning, sent by you to pit your Padang crower against my Highland beauty?" asked Roostam with glittering eyes.

"These men are the men I sent this morning to report all about your cock-fight to *me* and they will be used as witnesses against *you.*"

"Lying witnesses and you a lying son of a Bencoolen [town in southwest Sumatra]...." Roostam advanced,

"Step out from behind your spies, you cur, and take me if you want me!"

An old man, seeing that all the trouble was only between Roostam and Murei, and desirous to compromise, took the young fellow by the sleeve of his jacket and whispered to him,

"We will settle with Murei. You skip!"

Roostam shook him off, "I will settle for myself. Let him come and take me!"

Murei still delayed executing his threat though he repeated that, being *in* the Company's service, he had to stop the cock-fight.

A voice replied by quoting an old Malay adage, playing upon Murei's name to signify that his reference to the Company's orders was counted by those present as an empty tale, not worth any consideration.

And another spoke up, "Well, you have stopped the fight, what do you want more?"

"I want my prisoner, the principal of the fight."

"Come and take me!" said Roostam again. "Come and take me if you dare!"

They all taunted Murei, who urged his men to arrest Roostam:

"Come, Murei, bird of the delectable voice, come and take him!" Nobody stirred.

"Skip!" repeated the old man.

"Well" continued Roostam, "if you won't come to me, I'll go to you, you scurvy dog, and spit in your face!"

Quick as lightning, Roostam, the Game-Cock, unsheathed his kris and leaped upon his enemy, spitting in the hateful face, while he sent the cold, blue steel right to the man's heart. Then he turned round to Murei's underlings, who had jumped back, beginning to cry *amok*, and he said, disappearing in the jungle, "Now take me!"

Raissa, waiting in the market-place of Lawang, is getting nervous under the strain of the cock-fight lasting so provokingly long. The sun has already sunk half way down the sky and still no tidings. Surely there must be something amiss and she remembers the Government injunctions against the sport, but then is not Murei, the police officer, one of the principals?

She has sought the shade of a booth kept by a dealer in woman's apparel, who stands haggling with an old dame, a sharp customer. He reminds her of days long past, when his stock in trade consisted of hand-woven goods, of silk and gold brocade, while now there is no money even to buy the cheap, poor, imitation fabrics from over the sea at prices he lays under the obligation to cut down to the ridiculous:

"My grandfather," he says, "amassed wealth in this trade, and my father was able to keep it, but I shall be bankrupt ere long, selling below cost, and yet to live I have to sell."

"So it is with all of us," groans the crone. "What we had, is far behind us and what we have, is less than nothing. I offer thee what I said for this piece of goods."

"Plague on the Company that takes and talks fine and never makes any return! If thou must have this piece of goods for thy granddaughter, who is going to be married as thou sayest, I cannot deny thee, but thou art working my ruin."

"I think that I might have the same stuff even for less, of certain dealers I know at Bukit Tinggi and Payacombo."

"I take the Prophet for a witness that thou laborest under a misapprehension! Though the white merchants of Padang have their agents everywhere in the land to undersell us, whose business it has been to supply this commodity from father to son, for innumerable generations, yet none of them is able to beat my prices. And let it not be rumored about that I agreed to the sum thou hast named, for everybody would come and solicit the same kindness and rob me of my goods! Indeed, it is robbery to exact such dealings! Nevertheless, most venerable mother, this being intended for thy granddaughter, who is to marry."

The philanthropist's eloquence is checked by the passing of a boy, who cries something which creates great consternation all over the market. The merchants leave their merchandise and gather in groups with their customers. In the confusion of voices Raissa distinguishes that the cock-fighters have been surprised and that Roostam, refusing to be taken prisoner, has killed Murei. She hurries to the house of Haji Yusoof. He, if any one, will know whether Roostam has made good his escape.

Haji Yusoof's house is closed. The curious, who rightly suppose with Raissa that Roostam's *mammak* will have the first and best information as to his course and plans after the scrape at the cockpit, are refused admission. Haji Yusoof, so an attendant tells them, cannot be disturbed in his mid-day nap; he has been sleeping since noon; the report, current in the market-place, has not yet reached him; Haji Yusoof knows nothing.

The curious understand. Roostam's *mammak*, to be sure, will see his nephew out of this trouble without openly showing his hand. And they approve. Roostam, the Game-Cock, doing ten times better than winning the main in the cockpit, has rid them of Murei, the odious, punishing him for going so far in his boastful pretensions as to set a vile Padang rooster against the game-fowl of the Highlands. Roostam rises high in their esteem and no one entertains for a moment the idea of his being apprehended for the deed. They agree that Haji Yusoof lies under an obligation to keep him concealed in the *rimbu gedang* (the great jungle as distinguished from the *rimbu ketek,* the little jungle), until the affair is forgotten or he can be spirited away.

Raissa, being on terms of intimacy with the women of Haji Yusoof's household, has slipped in and found Roostam's *mammak* wide awake, considering ways and means. She asks him, with a failing heart, what he intends to do in this most serious affair, and he answers, "Nothing but deliver Roostam to the *commandoor* [local civil servant] as soon as he is caught."

Raissa, greatly agitated, stands aghast at this answer of Roostam's *mammak.*

"But so far he is not caught," adds the *haji.*

"And will he be caught?"

Haji Yusoof looks her straight in the eyes and then, affecting the speech he has heard at Mecca, as he is accustomed to do on grave occasions, waives further questions with pious commonplace, "The secrets of the future are with the Most High, the Most Merciful and Compassionate."

Raissa's short interview with Haji Yusoof has made it clear to her that Roostam will not be handed over to the retribution of the rigorous and withal strangely complicated law of the white men. On that score she is satisfied. His safety, however, requires also that he be shielded from the vengeance of Murei's clique and if he has to leave for a while, she wants to see him before he goes and say good-bye. Therefore she resolves not to return to Matoor for the time being, but to stay at Haji Yusoof's house where doubtless ere long his hiding-place will be known.

Keenly watchful on the steps that lead to the door of Haji Yusoof's dwelling, which is built on piles, according to the custom of the land; on the alert to intercept the expected messenger from the fugitive to his *mammak*, Raissa hears some one whispering her name. The voice comes from behind a rice-shed and there she perceives a boy, ten or eleven years old, who bids her follow the path from the village to the little market-place near the lake and wait at the pillar set by the triangulation service. There he will meet her again, by Roostam's command, and he urges her to set out at once, warning her not to ask or answer any questions concerning the Game-Cock's whereabouts. He himself has been charged to inform Haji Yusoof.

The boy is known to Raissa as one of the first disciples of *a faqir* recently arrived in the neighborhood to open a school and teach religion. Obeying him, she observes punctiliously the directions given her in the name of Roostam and reaches the triangulation pillar to the left of the road where it slopes down to the beach in sharp descent. To avoid the risk of meeting curious acquaintances in the little market-place on the right, she sits down among the high ferns that cover the hilltop overlooking the sheet of water deep down, the lovely lake of Maninju.

It is now late in the afternoon but somehow or other the clouds that roll on from the South with the heat of day to veil its loveliness after the sun has smiled upon it and taken possession in passionate embrace, somehow or other the clouds are tardy in gathering on the hills. Silent and tranquil the lake lies as it lay when the ardent lover withdrew, its surface shining like a polished shield of bronze engraved in strange design, long strips and whirls of water-weeds framing the reflections of the blue sky and the steep, wooded banks. The islands of Moko Moko, near the mouth of the Batang Antokan, the eastern ridges that run out to Tanjong Padang, rest dreamily in the last splendor of glorious light and when at last the clouds do come, throwing a belt of white round waving green, invading the plain to the North, they leave a gleamy dimness trailing over the trees, over the houses of Baju and Anam Kota half hidden among the *klapah* plantations. And still they come, airy flakes before a curtain of mist. Where the lake has been, in the depth below, nothing but hazy waves of vapor, rising higher and higher, hiding even the fire-mountains far away, the giants that lift their heads to guard the broad valleys from sea to sea.

The view of Lake Maninju from this spot, from the triangulation pillar, is perhaps still more striking than from the little pavilion, built expressly for a belvedere on the top of one of the steep hills that close it in, but Raissa is not in a mood to enjoy the beauty of her surroundings. She waits and waits and does not notice how the people to the right of the road, between their buying and selling, point their fingers at her: the girl of Roostam, the girl of the Game-Cock who has killed Murei; they know the whole story.

A kindly old woman, who is selling salt, takes pity on her and invites her to the bamboo shed she occupies, saying that for somebody's sake she ought not to expose herself too much, "The greater the danger, the greater must be the caution and where they find the loving bird, there they will look for its mate."

Then the old woman begins to complain of the stress of the times, a general complaint. Is she not compelled, at her age, to gain her living by fetching salt from Bukit Tinggi and carry it all the way to the lake of Maninju? And still she has occasion to call herself lucky because she is able to keep body and soul together by saving others the trouble of journeying many miles to the Government salt-store for a week's provision or sometimes less.

Raissa turns but an inattentive ear to the mournful tale of the mumbling crone who, when darkness falls, gathers her baskets together and leaves for home. The little market-place lies deserted now. Beneath, the enshrouded lake; overhead, the glimmering of the stars. Fear and weariness oppress the lonely girl as the night creeps on. At last she hears a stealthy step approaching. It is the boy, Roostam's messenger to Haji Yusoof, who instructed her to bide further developments at the triangulation pillar.

Raissa arises and follows him in the gloom along a trail that leads them through wood and underbrush to *a teratak*, a clearing with an enclosure for corralling the cattle of the village near by. Two or three other boys are lying around a large fire, lighted to keep the tigers off; seemingly fast asleep, they take no notice of the newcomers. Her guide precedes her to a rudely constructed hut, the door and windows of which are wide open, and there, having entered, she finds four persons together, three men and a woman. In the glare of the fire outside, she recognizes one of the men as Roostam. Nobody greets her and she, too, says not a word as she squats down beside the woman, Roostam's mother, who sits muttering incantations. Roostam's mother, the sister of Haji Yusoof, prides herself no less than he does upon their descent from a fighting family, true to the *hadat*, a family very conspicuous in the Padri War, the last effort of the Malays of the Padang Highlands to regain their independence; and Roostam's mother possesses many a secret descended through centuries from eldest daughter to eldest daughter, many a charm of the highest value on trying occasions. She is a fierce sort of a woman. Fierceness runs in the blood of her clan and Roostam's spirit shows plainly the truth of the saying that, in breeding, it is the hen as much as the cock which determines the temper of the chick.

At arm's length before her on the ground stands a cage with a pigeon in it. Raissa knows it by the embroidered covering; it is Haji Yusoof's and she infers that the old man must be near, the *mammak* watching over his charge.

The incantations give way to prayer, several *ayats* of the Quran being recited in succession by an unfamiliar voice, while the others respond in a drone, "Amin! Amin!"

Raissa surmises the leader to be the *faqir*, the new religious teacher, which explains how one of the youths of the school just opened came to act as her guide. And when the second stranger, after prayer has ceased, speaks to Roostam of the joys of the holy war against the infidels, she recognizes him as the deserter from the Dutch army who, though donning Acheh-trousers, affects the Batavia [modern Jakarta on the island of Java] lock over the ear and a pronounced Batavia accent, ae-ing his a's.

It becomes evident to Raissa that they are inciting Roostam, the Game-Cock, to battle. The deserter, who arrived from Korinchy, she remembers, is on his way to Acheh, propagating the good cause, and Roostam, being in trouble, seems perfectly willing to extricate himself by a course altogether in his line: war to the knife against the white men that send fellows like Murei to harass and annoy the real lords of the soil—plague on the cur and his employers!

And the *faqir* promises success: the Moslemin are destined to rule in this life the nations of the earth as in the life to come they are destined for everlasting bliss.

And Roostam's mother dwells upon the traditions of the family, upon the exploits of its members at Bonjol, where the *mammak* of his *mammak* was killed on the side of the Padri under Tuanku Imam, valorous warriors who sacrificed their lives for their country and whose death has not been avenged.

Shall her son, with such blood in his veins, be afraid because the white men have guns, big guns, and repeating-rifles and dynamite bombs, fighting from afar? Why not lure them to the mountains and tackle them hand to hand, the unbelievers?

"The killers of the weak and unprotected," continues the deserter, eyewitness of the horrors at Kampong Pulau Tengah in Korinchy. "Shall strong and able youths sit still and hush their voices and play girls' games when such things are going on?"

Roostam's eyes sparkle while they goad him, "I am not afraid of blood," he says slowly.

"And blood is thirsting for blood," says his mother.

"And the blood of the infidel opens the gates of Paradise to the faithful," says the *faqir*.

Raissa lifts her head, trembling, wishing to speak in her turn, but Roostam's mother sees the movement and shrieks in her face, "What art thou doing here, thou with the mark that brought bad luck to my son? Art thou not content with his bird, our bird, refusing to fight a Padang bird? Is it to deliver him now to Murei's evil-eyed gang that thou hast come hither, thou daughter of ill-repute? Out with thee!"

She threatens to strike the girl, but Roostam jumps to his feet. "None of this!" he cries.

"If thou stayest or goest where I can go with thee, I will give thee something that undoes the spell of all marks and signs," begs Raissa, pulling a ring from her finger.

Roostam looks at her and the deserter says tauntingly, "Another game-cock that shows the white feather!"

Roostam feels the sting and sits down again.

"Don't gibe him," entreats Raissa in despair. "It is my grandmother's ring, a ring of virtue."

"Can it confound the bloodhounds of the white men now on his track? Can it make him invisible?" asks the deserter, whose mysterious strength lies in the last named accomplishment. "If not, what is the good of his staying here?"

"It undoes all spells," Raissa rejoins doggedly.

"Keep thy ring!" yells the old woman. "Has he not enough sorrow by virtue of thy mark? Go! Go!"

Roostam does not move and by this token Raissa knows that all is over. She arises and goes, but returns and addresses him once more,, "Thou wilt leave us and do dangerous things. I, the girl with the mark, shall wait for thee here, trusting in the power of this ring on my finger, and pray that, if unhappily the spell comes to nought and thou fallest, male blood-relations may be near to wash thy corpse, and female blood-relations to strew flowers on thy grave."

Then she steps out into the night, while the *faqir* again falls to praying, "On the hearts of His followers that are slain in the holy war, the most Exalted sits extended as on His throne."

"Amin! Amin!"

Raissa, full of anguish, has not gone far in the utter darkness which precedes dawn, when she is terrified by an apparition. Phantom-like, it stands upright near a projecting rock beside the road, shrouded in white, awe-inspiring, an image of the angel of death. She holds her breath in terror, but soon recognizes in that specter Roostam's *mammak*, Haji Yusoof. Having left his house to pass the night in watching the trail which leads to the place where his nephew lies in hiding, he has donned for this occasion the white dress used by him and other fervent Muslims in praying, the dress come down to them from the "white time" so called, the time of the Padri, whose uprising was an outcome of the doings of the Wahhabites, the purifiers of the faith. It seems but proper that Haji Yusoof should have chosen those garments for his watch has been a continuous communion with the Invisible Great Watcher in the Night. At the approach of day, between the dawn of the elephants and the dawn of man, he has composed himself to the regulation early morning prayer with its necessary gestures. So it is that Raissa sees him standing, ghost-like, in her path. Drawing near, she hears him, raising his voice to curse the infidels, the strivers against the behests of the Most Gracious, whom he invokes, for Roostam's sake, the true believer being nearest to God when he treads down God's enemies. And, confusing the articles of Muslim faith with the traditions of Menangkabau, he prays on, imploring assistance and mercy for those who seek shelter with the Lord and refuge in the *hadat*, calling down destruction on the heads of the usurpers, who darken the luster of the purified through consecration, of the elect of earth and heaven, set apart for highest honor by anointment and the sprinkling of water, all the fragrance of all flowers not equaling the fragrance of King Adityawarnan....

From the holy Quran he has wandered to the holy inscriptions on the stones of the holy graves at Batu Beragoong and Pagar Ruyong where the old Hindu rulers of the land lie buried.

Raissa listens, glad to have a friend near her in the jungle, which is peopled at night with shetans, jinn and all kinds of evil sprites. It is almost an hour now, the space of time required for the cooking of three allowances of rice, since she has left Roostam in the company of his mother and his wicked counselors; and the dawn of man, the dawn proper, has already streaked the eastern sky with its delicate hues when Haji Yusoof notices her.

He makes a movement which gives her courage to address him, "Roostam wants to fight the Company," she says.

"Young men should do what old men think."

"But ..."

"Now leave me, for prayer is better than idle talk."

Behind her, in a cattle-pen, Raissa hears the little bells of the oxen that are getting up to their work and, alone with her grief, she turns away and takes the path to Matoor, to her mother's house.

MALAYSIA

RAJA DONAN

Tradition Bearer: Mir Hassan

Source: Maxwell, W. E. "Raja Donan: A Malay Fairy Tale." *The Folk-Lore Journal* 6 (1888): 134–139.

Date: Unavailable

Original Source: Malay

National Origin: Malaysia

The following Malay tale has the complexity and episodic nature of the **ordinary folktale**. The miracles surrounding the birth of Raja Donan, his early abandonment "Exposure in a Boat" (*Motif* S141), and prodigious feats in battle and magic are reminiscent of heroes cross-culturally. The Semang tribes, whose appearance the protagonist borrowed for his disguise, are a "Negrito" minority who lived in the mountains of peninsular Malaysia.

Once upon a time, in the kingdom of Mandi Angin, there reigned a certain King Raja Besar, whose wife was the Princess Lindongan Bulan. He was blessed in every way that the gods bless mortals, except in one respect, which was that he had no son and heir. By constant prayers and the giving of alms, at length when the king had reigned nearly eight years, there was a prospect of Raja Besar's happiness being completed. All the astrologers were summoned to tell whether the child would be male or female, and what was the lot in store for it. The astrologers, having for a long time continued their incantations, at length perceived that the expected child would be a prince, and that he would be gifted with extraordinary qualities. But the astrologers hated the king, and so they did not tell him the truth, but told him that his child would be a prince who was fated to be a curse to all who would come in contact with him.

Next day the king summoned an old astrologer who was both blind and deaf and infirm to tell the destinies of the child. The old man having pursued his divinations from sunset to sunrise, announced to the king that his son would be a highly gifted prince, and that under him the kingdom would attain an unheard-of prosperity. "This is altogether different," said the king, "from the prognostication of the former soothsayers."

"I am blind and deaf and of failing memory," said the old man, "but in all things that concern the prince your highness may rely on what I say."

At last, a terrible storm then raging, the princess gave birth to a son. The infant disappeared into the earth; then he was vomited out again, seated on a cushion, and with him a sword, a hen's egg, a swivel-gun, a flute, a piece of scented wood for burning, and some incense. The king, influenced by the opinion of the seven lying astrologers, directed that the child should at once be put into a rickety old boat and set adrift on the river. The princess wept on hearing what was to be the fate of her child, and directed her maids to put into the boat a basket full of clothes and another full of provisions for the child. This done, the boat was cast off amid the roaring of cannons which the king had ordered to be fired off for joy that evil had been averted from his kingdom.

The king's elder brother, Bandahara Tua, was living some distance away, at the mouth of the river, and, hearing the cannons, he said, "Surely a prince has been born, and the king has believed the lying astrologers and cast his son away." He prayed that God would send his newborn nephew to him, and, after waiting a day and a night on the bank of the river, at last the little boat was wafted up to his very steps.

The Bandahara went into the cabin to seek his nephew, and having found him he brought him on deck to take him to his house, but found that while he was below the boat had floated into mid-stream, and was being rapidly carried out to sea. Day and night for a year the boat went on, and at the end of that time the little castaway, now able to talk, gave himself the name of Raja Donan.

One day the Bandahara, at the request of his nephew, who said he felt a presentiment of approaching evil, climbed into the look-out place and carefully scanned the horizon, and at length sighted a great fleet of 99 ships approaching them, whose masts were like a grove of cotton trees. Raja Donan now prepared for the worst, and put on the magic garments which his mother had given him, and girded on the sword which was supernaturally produced at the time of his birth.

The fleet approached; it was that of Raja Chamar Lant, of Mundam Batu, who was on board the "Biduri," the largest of all. On sighting the little boat, Raja Chamar Lant ordered one of his galleys to be manned to see who was on board the stranger. This huge boat, carrying 44 rowers, came alongside, and those on board it saw no one but a pretty child, who said that he came from the country of Mandi Angin, from the rice-fields where there are no embankments, from the waters where no fish are ever seen, a lonely place where the ape howls nightly, inhabited only by people who live on fern-shoots." The officers of the galley said that tribute must be paid to his master, or the little boat would be seized as a prize. Raja Donan said he did not refuse to pay, but he should first ask the port-fire of his cannon and the blade of his sword, and if they answered that he should pay there was an end of the matter. With this answer the officer returned to his master, who at once ordered his men to fire and blow the little craft to pieces.

For seven days and nights did the fleet keep up a terrible shower of ball from cannon and musket, and at the end of that time the order to cease firing was given. When the smoke cleared away, there stood the little boat, brighter than ever, and quite unharmed. Raja Chamar Lant was furious. He would show his men how to shoot, and so he fired at Raja Donan's boat. But he did not harm it. Raja Donan now fired his little brass swivel-gun which was thrown out of the earth when he was born, and with the one shot he sunk the whole 99 ships, leaving only the "Biduri" afloat. His trusty craft bore him alongside the survivor. With a terrible shout he boarded it. For three days and nights, single-handed, he kept up the battle with the warriors on board, and finally killed them all, the last being Raja Chamar Lant.

The prince found in the cabin of the "Biduri" the younger sister of Raja Chamar Lant, who prayed him that he would kill her. He, however, soothed her with an account of his woes, and she agreed to go into his boat and remain with him. Raja Donan brought his prahu [Malayan sailboat with a triangular sail and single outrigger] alongside with a wave of his turban, and, having got the princess into it, he then stepped in and sank the "Biduri."

Che Amborg, as the princess was called, told Raja Donan that the reason she had left her beautiful home was that Petukal, a powerful raja, had asked for her in marriage, but her brother had taken her to sea to save her from Petukal, who was even now pursuing them. Raja Donan now prayed for a breeze that would bring them up to Petukal, a breeze "so strong as to be visible in a form resembling human shape, which would lay prostrate the cattle feeding in the fields, and sweep away the young cocoa nuts growing in the courtyard."

For seven days and seven nights they ran before the wind that sprang up, and on the eighth day, about noon, the fleet of Petukal, 99 ships in all, was seen right ahead. Raja Petukal, observing the new comer, sent off his eighty-oared galley to make inquiries. Raja Donan answered them as he had the officers of Raja Chamar Lant, and met their demand for tribute in the same way. In the same way Raja Petukal opened fire, and continued it for seven days and nights, at the end of which time he ordered the firing to cease. So dense was the smoke that it took three days to clear away, and then the little home of Raja Donan was seen to be quite untouched. Raja Petukal, having, like Raja Chamar Lant, fired some of his guns with his own hand, had no better luck. Then Raja Donan with a single shot from his gun sent the whole fleet, excepting the raja's vessel, to the bottom. Raja Donan boarded this, and slew all his enemies except their chief: with him he had a dreadful struggle. Once Raja Donan's sword shivered in his hand when he made a thrust at Raja Petukal, and before he could recover himself his opponent threw him overboard. His prayer to be put back again on deck was answered; and in the next struggle Raja Petukal was hurled into the sea, where he perished.

Che Muda, a sister of Raja Petukal, was found in the cabin, and went with Raja Donan aboard his boat. Guided by the princesses, he sought the shores of the country in which resided the beautiful Princess Ganda Iran. He played his magic flute, and, though he was many miles away, his prayer was heard that the Princess Ganda Iran should be able to hear his music.

She was enraptured, and dispatched a kite to bear to the youth a cap made of beautiful flowers. The kite carried his message, and placed the cap in the hands of Rajah Donan, who in return sent three rings, one as a sign of betrothal, one to bind the promise, and one as a sign that whatever was undertaken would be successfully carried out, and a shawl as a sign of intimacy. When the kite had safely delivered the prince's message, the beautiful princess again dispatched the bird with all kinds of sweetmeats, and in return the prince sent some other presents, telling the kite that they were setting out at once for the princess's palace.

By the prayer of Raja Donan all the troops of Raja Chamar Lant and Raja Petukal were restored to life, and his little bolt was turned into a magnificent palace. He called all the restored warriors together, and, putting chiefs over them, he set out on his journey on foot, taking with him his sword and his magic flute. When on his way, a certain princess, named Linggam Chahya, who resided in heaven, but came down often to the earth to amuse herself, met and fell in love with him, and sent her favorite bird to ask him to come to see her. He pleaded another appointment, but promised to come within three years, three months, and ten days.

Disguised as a Semang, or wild hill-man, with all the skin diseases and sores which disfigure those people, he gained admittance to the Princess Ganda Iran. The raja, her father, forced him to play his magic flute, which when the princess heard she fell down, and was thought to be dead. Preparations were made for her funeral, and the Semang was promised her hand in marriage, and the sovereignty of the country if he restored her to life. He played his magic flute, and when he saw her coming back to life disappeared from the palace.

The Semang could not be found, but in their search the officers of the raja met a pretty child by the roadside. They brought him to the palace, where the princess took a great fancy to him. The child suddenly changed one day into Raja Donan, a handsome young man, and the princess, having heard who he was, was exceedingly happy.

Raja Piakas, who had been affianced to the princess, being exceedingly jealous, on losing her, went to his home and begged his sister that she would help him to take revenge on the country of the Princess Ganda Iran. Now the sister of Raja Piakas had power over all dragons, crocodiles, and all beasts of the earth. These she summoned from all parts of the world, and ordered them to invade the country of the princess who had injured her brother. The reptiles and animals advanced, doing immense mischief; but at the prayer of Raja Donan the sea rushed over the whole land and drowned all these creatures.

Raja Piakas then fitted out an expedition against his former friends, but he was slain in single combat by Raja Donan. The magnanimous conqueror, however, brought him back to life, and married him to the princess Che Amborg.

Raja Donan now set off with his uncle and a large fleet to find his old home in Mandi Angin. After a long voyage they arrived at the well known river, but found everything desolate, the palace gone, the cottages burnt. An old man told them that the king had been dethroned years ago by seven lying astrologers, who were living like rajas far up the river.

Raja Donan found his parents occupying a poor but in a wood; but, having slain the lying astrologers, he put his parents on the throne again, and made Mandi Angin as prosperous and peaceful as it had ever been. Having done this, Raja Donan sailed away to his kingdom, where he ever after dwelt in peace and happiness. He was absent for a short time, however, when he kept his word and visited the Princess Linggan Chahya in the heavens.

PHILIPPINES

ADVENTURES OF THE TUGLAY

Tradition Bearer: Unavailable

Source: Benedict, Laura Watson. "Bagobo Myths." *The Journal of American Folklore* 26 (1913): 27–35.

Date: Unavailable

Original Source: Mindanao

National Origin: Philippines

Tuglay ("old man") and Tuglibung ("old woman") were the Mona, the beings who lived on the earth before time began. The Mona were very poor and possessed only the rudiments of technology. The names Tuglay and Tuglibung do not refer to specific mythic personages, rather they are generic terms for all the "old people" who are characters in Bagobo **myth**. The Buso are evil entities, in both human and animal form. The Bagobo universe is infested with them. The Malaki are a large group of semidivine beings. Many, but by no means all, are associated with features and forces of nature. Salamia'wan and Panguli'li are high gods of heaven. The former resides in the second heaven, and the latter in, the ninth. Eight, a sacred number that appears repeatedly, is sacred and therefore found throughout indigenous Bagobo ceremony, myth, and theology.

It was eight [number of ritual importance to the Moros] million (*kati*) years ago, in the days of the Mona, that the following events took place.

The Tuglay lived in a fine house the walls of which were all mirrored glass, and the roof was hung with brass chains. One day he went out into the woods to snare jungle-fowl, and he slept in the woods all night. The next day, when he turned to go home, he found himself puzzled as to which trail to take. He tried one path after another, but none seemed to lead to his house. At last he said to himself, "I have lost my way: I shall never be able to get home."

Then he walked on at random until he came to a vast field of rice, where great numbers of men were cutting the *palay*. But the rice-field belonged to Buso, and the harvesters were all buso-men. When they saw Tuglay at the edge of their field, they were glad, and said to one another, "There's a man! We will carry him home."

Then the *buso* caught Tuglay, and hastened home with him. Now, the great Buso's mansion stretched across the tops of eight million mountains, and very many smaller houses were on the sides of the mountains, all around the great Buso's house; for this was the city of the *buso* where they had taken Tuglay. As he was carried through the groves of coconut-palms on Buso's place, all the Coconuts called out, "Tuglay, Tuglay, in a little while the Buso will eat you!"

Into the presence of the great chief of all the *buso*, they dragged Tuglay. The Datto Buso was fearful to look at. From his head grew one great horn of pure ivory, and flames of fire were blazing from the horn. The Datto Buso questioned the man.

"First of all, I will ask you where you come from, Tuglay."

"I am come from my house in T'oluk Waig," replied the man.

And the great Buso shouted, "I will cut off your head with my sharp *kris* [Malay sword]!"

"But if I choose, I can kill you with your own sword," boldly answered Tuglay.

Then he lay down, and let the Buso try to cut his neck. The Buso swung his sharp sword; but the steel would not cut Tuglay's neck. The Buso did not know that no knife could wound the neck of Tuglay, unless fire were laid upon his throat at the same time. This was eight million years ago that the Buso tried to cut off the head of Tuglay.

Then another day the Tuglay spoke to all the *buso*, "It is now my turn: let me try whether I can cut your necks."

After this speech, Tuglay stood up and took from his mouth the chewed betel-nut that is called *isse*, and made a motion as if he would rub the *isse* on the great Buso's throat. When the Buso saw the *isse*, he thought it was a sharp knife, and he was frightened. All the lesser *buso* began to weep, fearing that their chief would be killed; for the *isse* appeared to all of them as a keen-bladed knife. The tears of all the *buso* ran down like blood; they wept streams and streams of tears that all flowed together, forming a deep lake, red in color.

Then Tuglay rubbed the chewed betel on the great Buso's throat. One pass only he made with the *isse*, and the Buso's head was severed from his body. Both head and body of the mighty Buso rolled down into the great lake of tears, and were devoured by the crocodiles.

Now, the Tuglay was dressed like a poor man, in dark garments. But as soon as he had slain the Buso, he struck a blow at his own legs, and the bark trousers fell off. Then he stamped on the ground, and struck his body, and immediately his jacket and kerchief of bark fell off from him. There he stood, no longer the poor Tuglay, but a Malaki T'oluk Waig, with a gleaming *kampilan* [broad sword] in his hand.

Then he was ready to fight all the other *buso*. First he held the *kampilan* in his left hand, and eight million *buso* fell down dead. Then he held the *kampilan* in his right hand, and eight million more *buso* fell down dead. After that, the Malaki went over to the house of Buso's daughter, who had but one eye, and that in the middle of her forehead. She shrieked with fear when she saw the Malaki coming; and he struck her with his *kampilan,* so that she too, the woman-buso, fell down dead.

After these exploits, the Malaki T'oluk Waig went on his way. He climbed over the mountains of benati, whose trees men go far to seek, and then he reached the mountains of barayung and balati wood. From these peaks, exultant over his foes, he gave a good war-cry that re-echoed through the mountains, and went up to the ears of the gods. Panguli'li and Salamia'wan heard it from their home in the Shrine of the Sky (*Tambara ka Langit*), and they said, "Who chants the song of war (*ig-sungal*)? Without doubt, it is the Malak T'oluk Waig, for none of all the other *malaki* could shout just like that."

His duty performed, the Malaki left the ranges of balati and barayung, walked down toward the sea, and wandered along the coast until he neared a great gathering of people who had met for barter. It was market-day, and all sorts of things were brought for trade. Then the Malaki T'oluk Waig struck his legs and his chest, before the people caught sight of him; and immediately he was clothed in his old bark trousers and jacket and kerchief, just like a poor man. Then he approached the crowd, and saw the people sitting on the ground in little groups, talking, and offering their things for sale.

The Malaki Lindig Ramut ka Langit and all the other *malaki* from the surrounding country were there. They called out to him, "Where are you going?"

The Tuglay told them that he had got lost, and had been traveling a long distance. As he spoke, he noticed, sitting among a group of young men, the beautiful woman called Moglung.

She motioned to him, and said, "Come, sit down beside me."

And the Tuglay sat down on the ground, near the Moglung. Then the woman gave presents of textiles to the Malaki Lindig Ramut ka Langit and the other *malaki* in her crowd. But to the Tuglay she gave betel-nut that she had prepared for him.

After that, the Moglung said to all the *malaki*, "This time I am going to leave you, because I want to go home."

And off went the Moglung with the Tuglay, riding on the wind.

After many days, the Moglung and the Tuglay rested on the mountains of barayung, and, later, on the mountains of balakuna trees. From these heights, they looked out over a vast stretch of open country, where the deep, wavy meadow-grass glistened like gold; and pastured there were herds of cows and carabao and many horses. And beyond rose another range of mountains, on the highest of which stood the Moglung's house. To reach it they had to cross whole forests of coconut and betel-nut trees that covered eight million mountains. Around the house were all kinds of useful plants and trees. When they walked under the floor of the house [typical Malay houses are pile-dwellings, the floor being raised several feet above the ground], the Moglung said, "My grandmother is looking at me because I have found another grandchild for her."

Then the grandmother (Tuglibung) called to them, saying, "Come up, come up, my grandchildren!"

As soon as they entered the house, the Tuglay sat down in a corner of the kitchen, until the grandmother offered him a better place, saying, "Do not stay in the kitchen. Come and sleep on my bed."

The Tuglay rested eight nights in the grandmother's bed. At the end of the eight nights the Moglung said to him, "Please take this betel-nut that I have prepared for you."

At first Tuglay did not want to take it; but the next day, when the Moglung again offered the betel, he accepted it from her and began to chew. After that, the Tuglay took off his trousers of bark and his jacket of bark, and became a Malaki T'oluk Waig. But the Moglung wondered where the Tuglay had gone, and she cried to her grandmother, "Where is the Tuglay?"

But the Malaki stood there, and answered her, "I am the Tuglay." At first the Moglung was grieved, because the Malaki seemed such a grand man, and she wanted Tuglay back.

But before long the Malaki said to her, "I want you to marry me."

So they were married. Then the Moglung opened her gold box, and took out a fine pair of trousers and a man's jacket, and gave them to the Malaki as a wedding gift.

When they had been living together for a while, there came a day when the Malaki wanted to go and visit a man who was a great worker in brass, the Malaki Tuangun; and the Moglung gave him directions for the journey, saying, "You will come to a place where a hundred roads meet. Take the road that is marked with the prints of many horses and carabao. Do not stop at the place of the cross-roads, for if you stop, the Bia ["Lady" used as an honorific term] who makes men giddy will hurt you."

Then the Malaki went away, and reached the place where a hundred roads crossed, as Moglung had said. But he stopped there to rest and chew betel-nut. Soon he began to feel queer and dizzy, and he fell asleep, not knowing anything. When he woke up, he wandered along up the mountain until he reached a house at the border of a big meadow, and thought he would stop and ask his way. From under the house he called up, "Which is the road to the Malaki Tuangun?"

It was the Bia's voice that answered, "First come up here, and then I'll tell you the road."

So the Malaki jumped up on the steps and went in. But when he was inside of her house, the Bia confessed that she did not know the way to the Malaki Tuangun's house.

"I am the woman," she said, "who made you dizzy, because I wanted to have you for my own."

"Oh! That's the game," said the Malaki. "But the Moglung is my wife, and she is the best woman in the world."

"Never mind that," smiled the Bia. "Just let me comb your hair."

Then the Bia gave him some betel-nut, and combed his hair until he grew sleepy. But as he was dropping off, he remembered a certain promise he had made his wife, and he said to the Bia, "If the Moglung comes and finds me here, you be sure to waken me."

After eight days had passed from the time her husband left home, the Moglung started out to find him, for he had said, "Eight days from now I will return."

By and by the Moglung came to the Bia's house, and found the Malaki there fast asleep; but the Bia did not waken him. Then the Moglung took from the Malaki's toes his toe-rings, and went away, leaving a message with the Bia:

"Tell the Malaki that I am going back home to find some other, *malaki*: tell him that I'll have no more to do with him."

But the Moglung did not go to her own home; she at once started for her brother's house that was up in the sky-country.

Presently the Malaki woke up, and when he looked at his toes, he found that his brass toe rings were gone.

"The Moglung has been here!" he cried in a frenzy. "Why didn't you waken me, as I told you?" Then he seized his sharp-bladed *kampilan*, and slew the Bia. Maddened by grief and rage, he dashed to the door and made one leap to the ground, screaming, "All the people in the world shall fall by my sword!"

On his war-shield he rode, and flew with the wind until he came to the horizon. Here lived the Malaki Lindig Ramut ka Langit. And when the two *malaki* met, they began to fight; and the seven brothers of the Malaki Lindig that live at the edge of the sky, likewise came out to fight. But when the battle had gone on but a little time, all the eight *malaki* of the horizon fell down dead. Then the angry Malaki who had slain the Bia and the eight young men went looking for more people to kill; and when he had shed the blood of many, he became a *buso* with only one eye in his forehead, for the *buso* with one eye are the worst *buso* of all. Everybody that he met he slew.

After some time, he reached the house of the great priest called "Pandita," and the Pandita checked him, saying, "Stop a minute, and let me ask you first what has happened to make you like this."

Then the Buso-man replied sadly, "I used to have a wife named Moglung, who was the best of all the *bia*; but when I went looking for the Malaki Tuan-gun, that other Bia made me dizzy, and gave me betel, and combed my hair. Then she was my wife for a little while. But I have killed her, and become a *buso*, and I want to kill all the people in the world."

"You had better lie down on my mat here, and go to sleep," advised the Pandita. While the Buso slept, the Pandita rubbed his joints with betel-nut; and when he woke up, he was a *malaki* again.

Then the Pandita talked to him, and said, "Only a few days ago, the Moglung passed here on her way to her brother's home in heaven. She went by a bad road, for she would have to mount the steep rock-terraces. If you follow, you will come first to the Terraces of the Wind (Tarasu'ban ka Kara'mag'), then you reach the Terraces of Eight-fold Darkness (Walu Lapit Dukilum), and then the Terraces of the Rain (Tarasuban k'Udan).

Eagerly the Malaki set out on his journey, with his *kabir* [woven carrying bag] on his back, and his betel-nut and buyo-leaf in the *kabir*. He had not traveled far, before he came to a steep ascent of rock-terraces, the Terraces of the Wind, that had eight million steps. The Malaki knew not how to climb up the rocky structure that rose sheer before him, and so he sat down at the foot of the ascent, and took his *kabir* off his back to get out some betel-nut. After he had begun to chew his betel, he began to think, and he pondered for eight days how he could accomplish his hard journey. On the ninth day he began to jump up the steps of the terraces, one by one. On each step he chewed betel, and then jumped again; and at the close of the ninth day he had reached the top of the eight million steps, and was off, riding on his shield.

Next he reached the sharp-edged rocks called the "Terraces of Needles" (Tarasuban ka Simat), that had also eight million steps. Again he considered for eight days how he could mount them. Then on the ninth day he sprang from terrace to terrace, as before, chewing betel-nut on each terrace, and left the Tarasuban ka Simat, riding on his shield.

Then he arrived at the Terraces of Sheet-Lightning (Tarasuban ka'Dilam-dilam); and he took his *kabir* off his back, and prepared a betel-nut, chewed it, and meditated for eight days. On the ninth day he jumped from step to step of the eight million terraces, and went riding off on his war-shield. When he reached the Terraces of Forked-Lightning (Tarasuban ka Kirum), he surmounted them on the ninth day, like the others.

But now he came to a series of *cuestas* [rock ledges] named "Dulama Bolo Kampilan," because one side of each was an abrupt cliff with the sharp edge of *a kampilan*; and the other side sloped gradually downward, like a blunt-working bolo. How to cross these rocks, of which there were eight million, the Malaki did not know; so he stopped and took off his *kabir*, cut up his betel-nut, and thought for eight days. Then on the ninth day he began to leap over the rocks, and he kept on leaping for eight days, each day jumping over one million of the *cuestas*. On the sixteenth day he was off, riding on his shield.

Then he reached the Terraces of the Thunder (Tarasuban ka Kilat), which he mounted, springing from one terrace to the next, as before, after he had meditated for eight days. Leaving these behind him on the ninth day, he traveled on to the Mountains of Bamboo (Pabungan Kawayanan), covered with bamboo whose leaves were all sharp steel. These mountains he could cross without the eight days' thought, because their sides sloped gently. From the uplands he could see a broad sweep of meadow beyond, where the grass glistened like gold. And when he had descended, and walked across the meadow, he had to pass through eight million groves of coconut trees, where the fruit grew at the height of a man's waist, and every coconut had the shape of a bell (*korung-korung*). Then he reached a forest of betel-nut, where again the nuts could be plucked without the trouble of climbing, for the clusters grew at the height of a man's waist. Beyond, came the meadows with white grass, and plants whose leaves were all of the rare old embroidered cloth called *tambayang*. He then found himself at the foot-hills of a range of eight million mountains, rising from the heart of the meadows, and, when he had climbed to their summit, he stood before a fine big house.

From the ground he called out, "If anybody lives in this house, let him come look at me, for I want to find the way to the Shrine in the Sky, or to the Little Heaven, where my Moglung lives."

But nobody answered.

Then the Malaki sprang up the bamboo ladder and looked in at the door, but he saw no one in the house. He was weary, after his journey, and sat down to rest in a chair made of gold that stood there. Soon there came to his ears the sound of men's voices, calling out, "There is the Malaki T'oluk Waig in the house."

The Malaki looked around the room, but there was no man there, only a little baby swinging in its cradle. Outside the house were many *malaki* from the great town of Lunsud, and they came rushing in the door, each holding a keen blade without handle (*sobung*). They all surrounded the Malaki in the gold chair, ready to fight him. But the Malaki gave them all some betel-nut from his *kabir*, and made the men friendly toward him. Then all pressed around the Malaki to look at his *kabir*, which shone like gold. They had never before seen a man's bag like this one. "It is the *kabir* of the Malaki T'oluk Waig," they said. The Malaki slept that night with the other *malaki* in the house.

When morning came, the day was dark, like night, for the sun did not shine. Then the Malaki took his *kampilan* and stuck it into his belt, and sat down on his shield. There was no light on the next day, nor on the next. For eight days the pitchy darkness lasted; but on the ninth day it lifted. Quick from its cradle jumped the baby, now grown as tall as the bariri-plant; that is, almost knee-high.

"Cowards, all of you!" cried the child to the Malaki Lunsud. "You are no *malaki* at all, since you cannot fight the Malaki T'oluk Waig." Then, turning to the Malaki T'oluk Waig, the little fellow said, "Please teach me how to hold the spear."

When the Malaki had taught the boy how to make the strokes, the two began to fight; for the boy, who was called the Pangalinan, was eager to use his spear against the Malaki. But the Malaki had magical power (*matulu*), so that when the Pangalinan attacked him with sword or spear, the blades of his weapons dissolved into water. For eight million days the futile battle went on. At last the Pangalinan gave it up, complaining to the Malaki T'oluk Waig, "How can I keep on fighting you, when every time I hit you my knives turn to water?"

Disheartened, the Pangalinan threw away his spear and his sword. But the Malaki would not hurt the Pangalinan when they were fighting; and as soon as the boy had flung his weapons outside the house, the Malaki put his arm around him and drew him close. After that, the two were friends.

One day the Pangalinan thought he would look inside the big gold box that stood in the house. It was his mother's box. The boy went and raised the lid, but as soon as the cover was lifted, his mother came out from the box.

After this had happened, the Pangalinan got ready to go and find the Moglung whom the Malaki had been seeking. The boy knew where she lived, for he was the Moglung's little brother. He took the bamboo ladder that formed the steps to the house, and placed it so that it would reach the Shrine in the Sky, whither the Moglung had gone. Up the bamboo rounds he climbed, until he reached the sky and found his sister. He ran to her crying, "Quick! Come with me! The great Malaki T'oluk Waig is down there."

Then the Moglung came down from heaven with her little brother to their house where the Malaki was waiting for her. The Moglung and the Malaki were very happy to meet again, and they slept together that night.

Next day the Moglung had a talk with the Malaki, and said, "Now I want to live with you; but you remember that other woman, Maguay Bulol, that you used to sleep with. You will want her too, and you had better send for her."

So the Malaki summoned Maguay Bulol, and in a few minutes Maguay Bulol was there. Then the Malaki had two wives, and they all lived in the same house forever.

STORY OF LUMABAT AND WARI

Tradition Bearer: Unavailable

Source: Benedict, Laura Watson. "Bagobo Myths." *The Journal of American Folklore* 26 (1913): 21–23.

Date: Unavailable

Original Source: Mindinao

National Origin: Philippines

The following narrative is another **myth** concerning the earliest times. The tale chronicles the creation of physical features and animal species of the world, and the creation of a god from the son of the "Old Man" and the "Old Woman" (see "Adventures of the Tuglay," page 388, for background on Tuglay and Tuglibung). The myth also serves moral goals in noting Bagobo disapproval of incest.

Tuglay and Tuglibung had many children. One of them was called Lumabat. There came a time when Lumabat quarreled with his sister and was very angry with her. He said, "I will go to the sky, and never come back again."

So Lumabat started for the sky-country, and many of his brothers and sisters went with him. A part of their journey lay over the sea, and when they had passed the sea, a rock spoke to them and said, "Where are you going?"

In the beginning, all the rocks and plants and the animals could talk with the people.

Then one boy answered the rock, "We are going to the sky-country." As soon as he had spoken, the boy turned into a rock. But, his brothers and sisters went on, leaving the rock behind.

Presently a tree said, "Where are you going?"

"We are going to the sky," replied one of the girls.

Immediately the girl became a tree. Thus, all the way along the journey, if any one answered, he became a tree, or stone, or rock, according to the nature of the object that put the question.

By and by the remainder of the party reached the border of the sky. They had gone to the very end of the earth, as far as the horizon. But here they had to stop, because the horizon kept moving up and down (*supa-supa*). The sky and the earth would part, and then close together again, just like the jaws of an animal in eating. This movement of the horizon began as soon as the people reached there.

There were many young men and women, and they all tried to jump through the place where the sky and the earth parted. But the edges of the horizon are very sharp, like *a kampilan* [sword], and they came together with a snap whenever anybody tried to jump through; and they cut him into two pieces. Then the parts of his body became stones, or grains of sand. One after another of the party tried to jump through, for nobody knew the fate of the one who went before him.

Last of all, Lumabat jumped quick, quicker than the rest; and before the sharp edges snapped shut, he was safe in heaven. As he walked along, he saw many wonderful things. He saw many *kampilans* standing alone, and fighting, and that without any man to hold them. Lumabat passed on by them all. Then he came to the town where the bad dead live. The town is called "Kilut" [City of the Dead]. There, in the flames, he saw many spirits with heavy sins on them. The spirits with little sins were not in the flames; but they lay, their bodies covered with sores, in an acid that cuts like the juice of a lemon. Lumabat went on, past them all.

Finally he reached the house of Diwata, and went up into the house. There he saw many *diwata*, and they were chewing betel-nut [nut of the areca palm]. And one *diwata* spit from his mouth the *isse* [the cud, the solid part of the betel-nut that remains after the juice has been extracted] that he had finished chewing. When Lumabat saw the *isse* coming from the mouth of the god, it looked to him like a sharp knife. Then Diwata laid hold of Lumabat, and Lumabat thought the god held a sharp knife in his hand. But it was no knife: it was just the *isse*. And Diwata rubbed the *isse* on Lumabat's belly, and with one downward stroke he opened the belly, and took out Lumabat's intestines (*betuka*).

Then Lumabat himself became a god. He was not hungry any more, for now his intestines were gone. Yet if he wanted to eat, he had only to say, "Food, come now!" and at once all the fish were there, ready to be caught. In the sky-country, fish do not have to be caught. And Lumabat became the greatest of all the *diwata*.

Now, when Lumabat left home with his brothers and sisters, one sister and three brothers remained behind. The brother named Wari felt sad because Lumabat had gone away. At last he decided to follow him. He crossed the sea, and reached the border of the sky, which immediately began to make the opening and shutting motions. But Wari was agile, like his brother Lumabat; and he jumped quick, just like Lumabat, and got safe into heaven. Following the same path that his brother had taken, he reached the same house. And again Diwata took the *isse*, and attempted to open Wari's belly; but Wari protested, for he did not like to have his intestines pulled out. Therefore the god was angry at Wari.

Yet Wari staid on in the house for three days. Then he went out on the *atad* that joined the front and back part of the gods' house, whence he could look down on the earth. He saw his home town, and it made him happy to look at his fields of sugarcane and bananas, his groves of betel and coconuts. There were his bananas ripe, and all his fruits ready to be plucked. Wari gazed, and then he wanted to get back to earth again, and he began to cry; for he did not like to stay in heaven and have his intestines taken out, and he was homesick for his own town.

Now, the god was angry at Wari because he would not let him open his belly. And the god told Wari to go home, and take his dogs with him. First the god fixed some food for Wari to eat on his journey. Then he took meadow-grass (*karan*), and tied the long blades together, making a line long enough to reach down to earth. He tied Wari and the dogs to one end of the line; but before he lowered the rope, he said to Wari, "Do not eat while you are up in the air, for if you eat, it will set your dogs to quarreling. If I hear the sound of dogs fighting, I shall let go the rope."

But while Wari hung in the air, he got very hungry, and, although he had been let down only about a third of the distance from heaven to earth, he took some of his food and ate it. Immediately the dogs began to fight. Then Diwata in the sky heard the noise, and he dropped the rope of meadow-grass. Then Wari fell down, down; but he did not strike the ground, for he was caught in the branches of the tree called *lanipo*. It was a tall tree, and Wari could not get down. He began to utter cries; and all night he kept crying, "Aro-o-o-o-i!" Then he turned into a kulago-bird? At night, when you hear the call of the kulago-bird, you know that it is the voice of Wari.

The kulago-bird has various sorts of feathers, feathers of all kinds of birds and chickens; it has the hair of all animals and the hair of man. This bird lives in very high trees at night, and you cannot see it. You cannot catch it. Yet the old men know a story about a kulago-bird once having been caught while it was building its nest. But this was after there came to be many people on the earth.

The three dogs went right along back to Wari's house. They found Wari's sister and two brothers at home, and staid there with them. After a while, the woman and her two brothers had many children.

"In the beginning," say the old men, "brother and sister would marry each other, just like pigs. This was a very bad custom."

THE STORY OF BANTUGAN

Tradition Bearer: Unavailable

Source: Porter, Ralph S. "The Story of Bantugan," *Journal of American Folklore* 15 (1902): 143–161.

Date: 1900

Original Source: Philippines (Mindinao)

National Origin: Philippines

Mindanao is the second largest and easternmost of the more than 7,000 Philippine Islands. The island maintained a strong Muslim presence in the area from around the fourteenth century, the date of the founding of the Sultanate of Sulu. The **legend** below recounts the exploits of the Moro (Muslim) hero Bantugan. Present within the narrative, however, are elements of indigenous religion that predate Filipino contact with either Islam or Christianity. Thus, characters are able to become invisible, bladed weapons are magical, and spirits animate the environment. The following elements of Moro culture are useful for an understanding of the tale. Mbama is a package of bongo nut, bulla leaf, lime, and tobacco, considered a delicious combination for a chew by the Moros. If a Moro woman presents a roll of this to a man, it signifies that she is willing to be courted by him. The Tiruray tribe is regarded as the most primitive culture of Mindanao. They live up in the mountains and sometimes in trees. The concept of "juramentado" refers to a Moro who makes a vow before the priest to die taking the blood of a Christian, and believes that in so doing he will go at once to heaven. So he starts out with his sword and attacks every Christian he can find until he is himself killed. The kinship ties among the various characters of this legend are complex, as a guide for the reader, collector Ralph S. Porter offers this genealogy. "Bantugan and his relatives were: Palamata Bantugan, son of Tinumanan sa Lugun Minulucsa Dalendeg (brother of the earthquake and thunder). The brothers of Bantugan were: 1, Mapalala Macog; 2, Madali Macaban-cas; 3, Dalumimbang Dalanda; 4, Damadag la Lupa; 5, Maladia Langig; 6, Marandang Datto Sulug; 7, Malinday Asabarat; 8, Mudsay sa Subu Subu; 9, Pasandalan na Murud; 10, Bendera Mudaya; 11, Pamanay Mac-alayan; 12, Pandi Macalele. The sisters of Bantugan were: 1, Alcat Ulauanan; 2, Mandanda Uray; 3, Dalinding u Subangan. The sons of Bantugan were: 1, Balatama Lumana; Pandumagan Dayuran; 2, Alungan Pidsiana Lumalang sa Dalisay; 3, Malinday Abunbara Lumanti Dowa Dowa; 4, Tankula Bulantakan Bulu Bulu sa Lagat; 5, Tagatag sa Laya-gum sa Pigculat; 6, Lumbay sa Pegcaualau Daliday Malindu; 7, Lumbay Magapindu" (Porter 143).

Once upon a time there came a terrific hurricane which carried the house of the sister of Bantugan from the village of Bombalan to the seacoast.

While there it was seen by a Spanish general who was lying off the coast in his warship. The Spanish general's name was Mindalunu sa Tunu-Miducau sa da Uata.

The general put the house with the sister of Bantugan on his warship and carried her away to his town of Sugurungan a Lagat.

The king of this town was Dumakulay Amalana Dumombang Mapamatu. For capturing this maiden the general was given high rank and honor and was ordered to build a house for the sister close to the house of the king.

Now when the king asked Alcat (which was the name of Bantugan's sister) to give him some mbama to chew, she refused, saying, "Do not talk to me, for I have been taken from my brothers and am heavy at heart; if you wish to marry me, go to my brothers and ask them for me."

When the brothers of Alcat knew that she had been stolen away from them, they were heavy at heart also. Then said Bantugan, "Prepare all of our war boats and launch my great warship Linumuntan Mapalo Mabuculud Linayum. Put out all our battle-flags and let all my brothers gather with me to search for our sister."

When they were all aboard the captain of Bantugan's warboat called out to it, "Sail like the wind, Linumuntan, so that we may overtake the wicked Spanish general who has carried away the sister of our datto" (chief).

But the ship did not obey his command, and Malinday Asabarat, the seventh brother of Bantugan, said, "It must be that we have a bad soldier on board; let us find out who he is and kill him, that we may proceed on our journey." Then Malinday pointed out a soldier whose name was Masualo Savani Masunu Sakasumba, whose great fault was that he made love to the wives of the dattos and other married women.

When this man knew he was to die, he said, "Tell my friends when you return that I died in battle and not that I was executed."

Then Malinday took him to the bow of the ship and with one stroke of his campilan (Moro broadsword) cut off his head. When the soldier was dead the ship at once began to speed through the water with tremendous velocity, so that all the great fish of the sea were much afraid.

Before long they came to a small island and there anchored, and four men carried the body of the soldier ashore and buried it.

Mapalala Macog now suggested that they rest here a while and sleep. While they were sleeping there came to anchor on the other side of the island a warship of Datto Baningan, who was the accepted lover of Bantugan's sister, Alcat Ulauanan, who had been carried away by the Spaniard, and whom Bantugan had started to search for.

Baningan had ordered the colintangan (large Moro xylophone) to be played in his warship, which was called the Katipapabayan Lumbayan Dakadua, meaning the two-tailed crocodile of the sea.

Now Bendera Mudaya, the tenth brother of Bantugan, heard the loud playing of Baningan's colintangan and he became very wroth, for he thought it would disturb his brother Bantugan's rest, so he called a thousand soldiers and had the lantakas (cannon) fired at the ship of Baningan, and the shot carried away all the principal masts of Baningan's ship and killed many of his soldiers.

Now Baningan's brother, whose name was Mapandala sa Dalen Matankin sa Gavi (he that bites like the pepper of the deep forest), called the master of the ship, whose name was Salindala Kabunga Salgangka sa Bukau, and ordered him to return the fire; but said the master, "Let us first ask permission of Datto Baningan," who just now awakened and inquired what had happened. Mapandala replied that Bantugan's ship had fired on them and begged to be allowed to fire back.

"No," said Baningan, "if we fire on Bantugan I can then never marry his sister."

"But," said the brother, "look at the ruin of the ship and the loss of men. Let this woman go and let us revenge ourselves."

"No," said Baningan, "seeing that you my brother still live not even the loss of ships or men will compel me to attack the great and honorable Bantugan."

So Baningan gave orders for his anchors to be raised and his ship to be sailed straight for Bantugan's ship, that they might converse. Baningan sat in the bow (ulunan) with two gold embroidered umbrellas held over him.

Now when Bendera Mudaya recognized that it was Baningan he had fired at, he broke into tears and cried out, "Ama ku" (my father), "do not scold me. I thought your ship was the ship of our enemies. It is all my fault; do with me as you will."

"No," said Baningan, "we are equally sad, let us say no more of it. I but beg of Bantugan to allow me to lash my ship to his." This was soon done and the dattos greeted each other.

Then Baningan asked, "What brings you out in your warship with so many soldiers and lantakas?" When Baningan had been told that his sweetheart had been carried away by the Spaniards his grief was very great, and with a common enemy these two dattos sealed their friendship.

After a council it was decided that Bantugan should continue the search by sea and that Baningan should go by land, as his ship was no longer seaworthy.

After the council Baningan returned to his own ship and cast loose from Bantugan, who sailed away. All the panditas (priests) were now called together by Baningan and were asked for their advice as to how to proceed to find the lost maiden. They told him, when he started out, not to go as a datto with fine raiment and many followers, but to go alone in the disguise of a tiruray, and that if he went this way he would surely meet with success.

So Baningan sent his brother Mapandala back with the ship to their village of Cudarangen, there to be ruler in his stead. But the brother's heart was heavy, for he wanted to go also on the trip, and he begged unavailingly of Baningan to let him go, but he would not consent. So Baningan went ashore and Mapandala put his ship about to return home, but when Baningan was well out of sight Mapandala turned again and started to follow Bantugan as best he could, making many repairs to his ship.

In a day or two he passed by a large town called Pamamaluy a ig Alamay a Lagat, and there encountered a great Spanish warship whose captain inquired where he was from. Mapandala answered, "From Cudarangen." Then the Spaniard asked him where he was going. Mapandala answered, "To search for the sister of Datto Bantugan." Whereupon the Spanish fired upon him; the general on the ship was the same one who had carried away Bantugan's sister, and he ordered Mapandala to return to Cudarangen, saying that not far away there was a fleet of a thousand Spanish ships waiting for Bantugan and his followers.

"Nevertheless," said Mapandala, "I shall not return." And the battle began at once, between Mapandala and the Spaniard. The latter soon won, and Mapandala was badly injured so that his entrails fell out. Both boats were badly injured and many were killed on both sides, but the Spaniards were able to float and navigate, and they looted Mapandala's boat and then returned to their village.

Mapandala's boat was finally cast upon the beach, where it was seen by Baningan who came by there on foot at that very moment. He at once boarded her, and when Mapandala saw someone coming he cried out for water which Baningan brought him. When they recognized each other Baningan embraced his brother and wept to see him so sorely wounded. Mapandala said, "I am surely dying." But Banignan called for a fairy from Cudarangen to take his brother back and cure him there of his wounds with a great medicine which he had at home in his chest. When the fairy had taken Mapandala, Baningan went on his way.

The warship of Bantugan finally reached the village of the Spaniards, Sudurungan a Lagat, and there found a thousand Spanish war-ships, who at once fired upon them, but the only effect of their firing was to push Bantugan farther away, not a single cannon-ball penetrating his ship.

Baningan continued on his road, and after many days reached a high hill from which he could see the great city of the Spaniards, with many ships in the harbor and many more on guard at its entrance. This great display frightened Baningan very much, for he thought to himself, "At the very door of the city I will die." So he decided to go back to the brother of Bantugan, who was named Pasandalan na Murud, and who was the sultan of I Labumbalan Tankulabulantakan, and ask him what he should do in the face of such dreadful obstacles.

He had not gone far until two little golden birds alighted on his shield (klung) and told him not to go back, for he would be laughed at, and all would say that he was not worthy of his sweetheart. Baningan then smote his breast and decided to return to the search even though he died ten times. He then hid his shield and campilan (broadsword) in a hollow rock and carried only a bow and arrows.

As he was passing along the coast he saw the ships of the Spanish general sailing by who had destroyed his own boat. The Spanish general also saw him and called to him to come on board his ship, for he did not think that he had the walk or carriage of a poor tiruray. So Baningan went aboard the Spanish ships, and the soldiers were so thick on the deck that he could not help stepping on them as he passed. This made the soldiers mad, but the general said, "Never mind; he is only a poor tiruray, and does not know good manners." The tiruray walked right up and sat down close by the side of the general, which made the general mad on the inside, but he did not show it. Then the general asked him, "Where are you from?"

He answered, "From Lalansayan Lalanun." Now the general knew that the king's brother lived with this family and so the tirurary, who was Baningan in disguise, said that he had been sent by the king's brother to inquire if it was true that the king had captured the sister of Bantugan, and for the king to beware, for Bantugan was a powerful and dangerous enemy. Then the general told a great lie, saying that they had had a big war with Bantugan and that Alcat had been given as a peace offering.

This great lie maddened the tiruray, so that for a minute he wanted to go "idzavil" (run amuck or juramentado). The general noticed that the tiruray was getting mad, and asked, "Why are you red in the face? I believe that you are Baningan, and if you are you will go no farther. But the tiruray answered and said, "Show me Baningan, and I myself will slay him." Then the general said, "Tell me truly from where you come?"

The tiruray answered and said, "From Lansayan Aluna Lundingan Apamalui Deliday Linauig Lumbay Lungan a Lagat, whose datto is Daliday Linauig Lumbay Alungan a Lagat, who is a brother to your king."

Then the general and the tiruray shook hands, and the general asked, "What is your errand here?"

The tiruray answered, "1 come by order of the brother of the king to see if it was true that the king had the sister of Datto Bantugan in his city and if she was beautiful or not."

The general said, "She is as beautiful as the moon."

The tiruray now asked the general to take him to see the sister of Bantugan, for he alone would not be allowed to pass the gates. So the general and Baningan went ashore and walked towards the city of the king, and when they reached the gates the guard would only allow the general to pass and would not admit the tiruray.

But the general said, "This tiruray is a good man and comes from the town of the king's brother."

Then the captain of the guard said, "No, he cannot pass, for I know that in the city of the king's brother there are no tirurays."

"Yes," said Baningan, "that is true, but I do not claim to live in the town of the king's brother, but in a village near it named Malasan sa Ulay Uluban sa Bulauan."

"Well," said the captain of the guard, "You may go in; you look innocent at any rate."

So in they went, and soon they came to the second guard, whose captain asked the general, "What is your business with the king?"

The general said, "To beg permission of the king to return to my family."

"Who is the tiruray with you," asked the captain of the guard.

"Oh, he is all right, I will vouch for him," said the general.

Then the captain of the guard said, "Well, you may both pass, but the law is that all who pass this gate must pass through dancing." So they both danced their way through the gate.

By and by they reached the house of the king, where there were many guards, who did not care to have the tiruray pass, but the king, when he heard that there was a tiruray below, ordered the guard to admit him and bring the man up to him, and when the tiruray had entered the palace he found the floor covered with soldiers sitting and lying down. He clumsily stepped on several, who immediately wanted to kill him, but the king said, "No, he is only a tiruray and knows no manners; do not hurt him." Then the tiruray walked straight up to the throne and sat right down beside the king, to the great fear of the general, who told him not to, for the king would surely scold him or kill him. When the courtiers saw this poor beggar take his seat by the king's side, they begged permission to kill him for his presumption. But the king said, "No, I will question him first."

While Baningan was seated beside the king he saw the armor of his brother lying on the floor and covered with blood. His face became red and the tears fell from his eyes, and he again wanted to be an "idzavil," but on second thought decided not to, for if he did he could not succeed in seeing his sweetheart.

The king asked him why his face was so red and why he was crying. Baningan answered, "I cry, for I cannot see the sister of Bantugan."

Then asks the king, "What do you know of the sister of Bantugan, and where do you come from?"

Baningan answered, "From your brother's town."

Then the king at once asked him, "Is my brother well and happy?"

"Yes," said the tiruray, who then asked, "Is the sister of Bantugan as beautiful as she is reported to be?"

"Yes," said the king, "she is as beautiful as the moon." Then Baningan asked the king's permission to see her so that he could tell the king's brother of her beauty. So the king told the tiruray to go and ask Alcat for bulla for the king to chew, and to tell her that if she would not give it he would have her head cut off.

When the tiruray reached the house in which the sister of Bantugan was kept, a wife of the king (whose name was Salagambal Kla Undiganan) came forward and asked him what he wanted. When he told her, she asked him to come in and sit down, but Baningan said, "I wait for the order of the sister of Bantugan." But the sister of Bantugan did not care to order the tiruray to come in, for he was of low blood. But on the solicitation of the other wives of the king, she told him to come in and sit down.

When the tiruray came in the house he sat down close to Alcat, who scolded him for it, and ordered him away, but the wives of the king said, "No, he is only a poor tiruray and knows no better; let him stay and we will have some sport with him."

Then Bantugan's sister asked him from whence he came.

He answered, "From Mapulud Salin Kikan Palau sa Linun Kayo."

Then Alcat at once asked him if he knew Datto Bantugan. The tiruray answered and said, "Yes, I know him, but I have heard that he was killed not long ago in a fight with the Spaniards. Also his brother Mapalala Macog, who was killed by a crocodile, and all the other brothers are dead in the warship of Dalumimbang Dalanda."

When hearing this the sister of Bantugan fell in a faint (the name of the warship was Timbalangay a Uatu Timbidayala Sunga).

When Alcat had recovered from her faint, she asked the tiruray if he knew Baningan. At this the tiruray laughed and showed his teeth, which the sister of Bantugan recognized at once, but she gave no sign of recognition. Then the tiruray said, "Baningan fell in a cave a week ago and has not come out yet." Then he took a ma-lung (a Moro dress) and put it on in Moro style and seized the sister of Bantugan and put her on his lap.

She did not scold him, but asked, "Can you win in a fight with the Spaniards and take me home to my family?"

Baningan answered and said, "Win or lose, I will not leave you. The king has sent me to bring him bulla from you and if you don't give it he will kill you."

"Well," said Bantugan's sister, let him kill me; I will not give him the bulla."

Baningan now called the fairies to bring his campilan and rodella and prepared himself for a fight.

Alcat cried and said, "If you leave me now even for a minute, you will never come back."

"Yes," said Baningan, "I will come back." He then made himself invisible by a spell and went out to the harbor mouth where he could get a stone to sharpen his campilan.

While all this was going on, the king became very impatient at the non-return of the tiruray and sent for him. The women told the messenger that the tiruray had gone some time before, and when the king heard this he said, "The tiruray does not return, for he is ashamed to return without the bulla which Bantugan's sister has refused."

The king then ordered a well dug and had the sister of Bantugan brought to it, that she might be drowned in it. But the courtiers begged that she be spared, for, they said, "If you kill the sister of Bantugan, we will surely have a war with Bantugan and his brothers, and they are very brave men and have many followers." But the king became more and more angry and took his saber to kill the sister of Bantugan.

At that moment Baningan returned in his invisible state and stood by her side. Alcat now said to Baningan, "What are you going to do now?"

He answered, "I will take you up to the top of the highest coconut tree," which he did, and when he returned, became visible to all the court clad in armor and with his campilan and klung. He was at once surrounded by the general and the soldiers of the court, who attacked him, but Baningan defended himself so well that every stroke of his campilan cut off ten heads.

In the mean time, Bantugan arrived at the harbor mouth and heard a great commotion in the city, which was caused by the fight that was going on between Baningan and the king's soldiers. On learning this Bantugan ordered his ship to pass under the water instead of on top, until he reached the point not far from the Spanish fleet. His ship then ascended to the surface, causing great commotion and excitement among the Spaniards. Madali Macabancas now suggested that the ship be anchored bow and stern. This was scarcely done before the Spaniards opened fire on them, and for seven days the fire continued, so that the smoke was so thick that it made the day the same as night.

At the end of the seventh day the smoke rose a little and the Spaniards saw that Bantugan's boat was still uninjured, while they were badly cut up. Their bullets had simply *pushed* Bantugan's ship farther away.

Marandang Datto Sulug now said, "Let us go ashore with campilan (sword) and klung" (shield). This was done, and the course of fighting was done at once. At the same time Baningan was still fighting within the walls.

Just at this time Datto Sulune Cudungingan sa Colingtongan, of the town of Sungiline a Dinal Hayrana Amiara, arrived in his great warship, Galawongat Tinumcup Ukil a Keranda. This datto, whose sister Bantugan was in love with, came to see if he could not act as a peacemaker and have the quarrel cease, so that all should be friends.

He first spoke to Bantugan and told him to quit fighting, so that he could arrange matters with the king, and that anyway Bantugan could not win, for the Spaniards were too many for him. Bantugan answered, and said, "If they give back my sister, I will fight no more, but if not, we will fight to the death."

"Well," said the datto, "wait till I have spoken to the king before you fight any more."

So the datto went in and reached the place where Baningan was fighting and also prevailed upon him to wait and fight no more till he had spoken to the king.

When the datto reached the palace, the king agreed to quit fighting if Bantugan would give Alcat to him in marriage.

But the datto said, "If you insist on that condition, the war will last for many years, for Bantugan surely will not give his sister to you, for he has contracted to give her to Baningan."

"Well," said the king, "Alcat can go, but her companions must stay, for I prefer Moros to Spaniards."

Then the datto said, "No, this is not good, the fighting will surely continue if you insist on this."

"Well," said the king, "let them all go, but I do not want to see Bantugan at all."

So the datto carried the house and all the women and Alcat down to the ship of Bantugan and put them on board, and Bantugan then returned to his country with Baningan (the country of Bantugan was named Ilian a Bumbalan Tankalabulantakan), and when they reached there the house was replanted in its former place, and all were happy.

Now the older brother (Mapalala Macog) said, "Now let Bantugan marry." And it was decided that Bantugan should marry Minilig Urugung Managam a Dalendeg, who was the daughter of the sultan Minialungan Simban of Minifigi a Lungung Minaga na Dalendeg.

Pasandalan na Murud now called Dalumimbang Dalanda and Damagag da Lupa, and ordered them to make a journey to the country of the sultan and ask his daughter's hand in marriage for Bantugan.

"Well," they said, "if the sultan refuses we will not return until we have punished them well."

"No," said Pasandalan, "that will not do. I will get another messenger"; and he called Mapalala Macog, who answered the same as did all the other brothers.

"Well," said Pasandalan, "I will go myself"; but Pandi Macalayan objected and said, "No, let us send Bantugan's son, Balatama Lumana Alcat, Pandumagan Dayuran." (This boy was the son of Bantugan's sister whom Bantugan had married innocently, because when Bantugan was born he was sent away on a ship and did not return until he was grown up, and not knowing his sister Alcat, fell in love with her and married her, and this boy was born before they knew of their relationship.)

When the son was found, he was brought before Pasandalan and said, "Why am I, a child, to be sent on this errand. Why do not some of my uncles go?"

"Well," said Pasandalan, "I will go."

"No," said the son, "let me go as the rest wish." But now Bantugan interrupted and objected to this small boy being sent on so important and dangerous an errand. But the brothers all insisted, and so he was sent away to prepare himself and to return to be instructed. When he came back properly dressed, his mother also came crying, not wanting him to go so far away. But the boy said, "I go because my uncles cannot."

Now Pasandalan said to him, "Have patience and speak good word with the sultan, and even if they speak ill to you have patience as long as you can, but when you cannot stand it any longer, of course you must fight."

So the arms of Bantugan were given him, and when he started away he told them that if he did not return in three months it would surely be that he was dead. So he bade good-bye to all and started on his journey.

After he had been gone some hours Dalumimbang Dalanda disguised himself and went out to try the boy's courage, and appeared before Balatama as an old man and asked him where he was going. Balatama answered and told his errand.

Then Dalumimbang said, "You cannot go any farther; you must return."

But the boy said, "No, I will continue on my errand."

"Well, then," said the old one, "if you don't go back I will kill you."

At this the boy took his campilan and struck at the old one, who disappeared in the air.

Then he kept on his journey, and on reaching a high stone he was able to look back and see the village from which he had come. The sight made him cry and he wanted to return, but the recollection of the order of his uncles made him keep on his way.

By and by a little bird came by and perched upon his shoulder, and asked him where he was going, and on being told said, "Do not go any farther because

Mimdalanu sa Tunu Midsicau di Uato is waiting for you to kill you." But the boy went on just the same, and that night slept on the beach in a bed made of magical snake-belt. In the morning his heart called to him to awake, and when he arose it was with such a bound that it made the beach tremble.

So he continued on his journey, and by and by came to a stone in the form of a man. It was named Mamilbang a Uato and was surrounded by a fence made out of wood called Kayo Naniarugun Kayo Rani Dalandeg, and the land which this fence enclosed belonged to the wife of Satan. It lay across the road and obstructed his way, so he took his campilan and cut down the fence, which made the wife of Satan very mad, so she made the air to be as dark as night; and the boy began to cry, for he could not see his way to continue the journey. Then the wife of Satan made it rain stones as large as houses, but the boy protected himself by holding his shield over him and prayed and called for the winds from the home land to come and help him, which they did, and the air became clear again and the rain ceased, and then Balatama saw the wife of Satan in a window of her house and took her to be his mother, for she resembled her so much. The woman called to him to come up into the house, which he did, and then she asked him what his errand was, and on being told said to him, "Do not go any farther, for the Spaniards are waiting for you to kill you." But the boy said he would go on his way nevertheless.

Then the woman asked him if he had a charm of gold in the shape of a man. The boy answered, and said that he had one. Then he bade good-bye to Satan's wife and started on his journey again.

Soon on the road he met a big man-monster with horns who asked him where he was going. The boy told him, and then the monster said to him, "You cannot go any farther; go back to your country where you come from." But Balatama took his campilan and made a stroke at the monster, who disappeared in the air.

A little farther on he came across a great snake on the road, who also asked his errand, and on being told, the snake said, "No, you cannot pass, for I am the guard on the road, and none can pass here." So the snake made a motion to seize him, but the boy with his campilan cut the snake into two pieces and threw one half into the sea and one half into the mountains and then went on his way.

After many days he came to a stone set in the middle of the road. It glowed and glistened as if it were made of pure gold, and from this point he could see the city to which he was going. It was a fine large town with ten harbors. He saw one house which seemed to be made of crystal and which he supposed was the house of the sultan. When he came nearer the city, he saw a house made of pure gold.

It took him a long time to reach the harbor mouth, although from the golden stone it appeared to be but a short distance.

When he entered the city gates, he was very careful not to mix with the crowds, for he did not know what kind of people he would meet. When he did meet some of the people they asked him where he was going, but he did not answer them, for they were only workingmen and he, a datto's son, would not converse with them. As he passed the streets all the people stared at him, but he was very beautiful and was admired by all; as he went along he passed a number of datto's sons playing "sefa." They asked him to play, but he said he did not know how. Then one of them said, "Who are you and from where, that you cannot play sefa?" but the son of Bantugan said, "You needn't ask of me; are you the sultan of this town?"

The young man who had questioned him (Batalasalapay an Datto sa Ginaeunan) said, "I am of high blood," and was very wroth.

"Well," said the son of Bantugan, "if you want to fight, I guess you can do so now."

So they fought until an old man came and made them stop. In the mean time some one had carried word to the sultan that there were two people fighting, so the sultan ordered them both brought before him. When they were brought, the son of Bantugan went up and sat down next to the sultan, which made all the other Moros furious, and then the courtiers begged that he might be killed, but the sultan said, "No, let us question him first." Bantugan's son said that before he told his errand to the sultan he wanted all the dattos' sons and dattos present to hear, but they told him it would take too long to gather them. Then Balatama said that before he spoke he wanted all persons to take off their helmets. But they thought this was too much and were very wroth, and wanted to kill him at once. The son of Bantugan then said, "Pshaw, what are you all to me? You are nothing."

Then the sultan said, "Tut, tut, let all take off their helmets so that we can hear this young man's story, for if we kill him we will know nothing of his errand, or from where he comes." So all the helmets were taken off and Balatama arose and told him his name and where he was from. And then all became of a good heart again and the sultan then asked Balatama to tell them his errand.

"I am sent by Pasandalan na Murud Bandelo Madayo to ask for the daughter of the sultan for Datto Bantugan."

The sultan then said to his courtiers, "You, my friends, answer the request."

One courtier then said (Bambay sa Pananian), "I don't see how Bantugan can marry the sultan's daughter, because the first gift (sungut) must be a figure of a man or a woman in pure gold."

"Well," said Bantugan's son, "I am here to hear what you want and to say whether it could be given or not."

"Well," said another datto, "you must also give a great yard with the floor of gold, three feet thick" (this datto's name was Midtumula Buisan Ninbantas Balabagan).

"Well," said Bantugan's son, "all this can be given."

"Then the sister of the princess spoke up and said, "The gifts must be as many as the blades of grass in this city."

"It can be given," said Balatama.

A datto named Daliday sa Lugungan said, "You must also give a bridge (talitay) built of stone, to cross the Pulangui (Rio Grande de Mindanao)."

"It can be given," said Balatama.

Batatalatayan now said, "You must change this city from a city of wooden buildings to a city of stone buildings."

And Dalendegen Sangilan said, "You must give a ship of stone."

Daliday su Milen demanded that all the coconuts in the sultan's grove be turned into gold and also the leaves.

"All this would be done," said the son of Bantugan. "Mapalala Macog will give the yard of gold; Malinday Assabarat the bridge of stone; Dalumimbang Dalanda the boat of stone; Matabalau Man. Guda will give the many gifts; Siagambalanua the golden cocoas. The golden statue I will give. Very well," said Balatama, "but I will have to go back my to father's town (Bombalan) to get it."

At this one of the dattos scolded and said, "You are surely a liar and do not intend to get the statue at all. Let us cut his head off."

And the sultan said, "Yes, let us have the golden statue now or we will kill you."

"No," said Balatama, "if I give you the statue now there will be dreadful storms, rain, and darkness." But they only laughed at him and demanded the statue. So he reached into the helmet and drew forth the statue of gold, and immediately there was a great storm and earthquakes and it rained stones as big as houses. And the sultan called to Balatama to put back the statue, for they would surely be all killed if he did not.

"Well," said Balatama, "you would not believe me when I told you, and now I am going to let the storm continue." But the sultan begged him to put back the statue, and said that if he would put it back Bantugan might come and marry his daughter and give no other presents at all but the golden statue. So Balatama put back the statue, and the air became calm again, to the great relief of the sultan and the dattos.

"Now," said Balatama, "I will return. But first let me see the future wife." This was granted, and they asked him when Bantugan would come to the wedding. He told them in three months. So Balatama went to the palace and at the door was stopped by a female guard (Siagambal Anunan Kelam Anandinganan). She told him to sit down and have some bulla to chew. But he answered and said that he was but a child, and did not chew it.

When the princess saw the boy she asked him what he came for. He told her that he had come to see her and then go back and tell his father of her beauty. The princess gave him a ring and a handkerchief for a present and then he bade her good-bye.

On the road home he again met the wife of Satan, who compelled him to stay with her for four months.

There was a sailor of the sea from Kindalungan Minaga Delandeg and another from Ibat a Kadalan, a Spanish town. They met on the high seas, and after greeting each other the second one asked the first one, "Is it true that Bantugan is going to marry the daughter of the sultan?"

"Yes," said the first one, "great preparations are being made for it."

Then the second one said, "Why, does he not know that the great General Linumimbang Sandaw Minabi Salungan is going to marry the same princess?"

"No," said the first, "and I suppose it would not make any difference if he did know." So the sailors separated, and the Spanish sailor went straight up to the general and told him that Bantugan was preparing to marry the sultan's daughter.

The general at once ordered a great expedition to be prepared, and called the chief pandita (Batataswalian) and asked him if he thought it was a good hour for it.

"No," said the chief, "if you go now they will surely have a big fight and you will lose." Nevertheless the general embarked in his great warship, the Minanaga su Macag Maluba Kuman sa Tau, also with him were all of his brothers and following after him were ten thousand other ships. They went to the sultan's city, and their number was so great that they filled the harbor, greatly frightening the people of the city.

And the general's brother disembarked and went to the house of the sultan, where he demanded the princess for his brother, saying that if she was not given the fleet would destroy the city and all the people. This frightened the sultan and his courtiers very much, so they decided to give the daughter to the general and asked him to fix the date for the wedding. He told him that it would be the first full moon. Then the general's brother left, saying that the general would soon come to see them.

Bantugan prepared everything for the wedding, which he expected would take place at the appointed time. But the days went by and Bantugan and his brothers were very much afraid, for the boy had not returned and they feared that he was dead. So after the three months had passed, Bantugan prepared a big expedition to go in search of *his* son. The great warship was decorated with flags of gold and all the mosquito bar was made of silk.

When they came in sight of the sultan's city one of Bantugan's brothers saw the Spanish fleet in the harbor, and advised Bantugan not to enter until the Spaniards had left. So they brought their ship to anchor, and all felt very sad because they could go no farther. Pidsayana Alungan, a son of Bantugan, came and asked his uncles why they were so sad, but they would not answer him, so he went back, and another son, Bulubulu sa Lagat, came and asked the same of his uncles, but they would not answer him.

Another son now came. Lumbay sa Layagum Pegcaualau Daliday Malindu came and asked the same of his uncles, but none would answer him. Lumbay Magapindu came and asked the same question, but they would give him no answer.

Now came Datto Baningan, who asked the same question of the brothers of Bantugan, saying, "Fear not." But they would give him no answer.

Pandi Macalele came and asked of his brothers, "Why didn't you answer? Why don't we go on? Even if the grass turns into Spaniards we need not fear."

Then Mapalala Macog came and asked the same, saying, "Why do you fear? Even if the cannon balls come like rain and lightning, we can fight always." But still no answer.

Then Marandung Datto Sulung came and spoke to Bantugan. "Why do all our brothers not answer when questioned? Do they fear the Spaniards? Anyway, we are here only to find the son who has not returned, so let us return to Bombalan."

"No," said Bantugan, "let us seek my son, and even if we enter the harbor where the Spaniards are, let us continue the search." So at Bantugan's command the anchors were raised and they sailed into the harbor where lay the Spanish fleet.

The general and his brother were about to go and call to see the princess, and when they reached the palace the daughter called them in and was very nice to them, offering the bulla to the gentlemen.

The general's brother admired one of the sisters of the princess very much, and asked her for bulla, but she laughed at him and would not give it, called him names, and made much fun with him, saying, he was not the general's brother, etc., etc., but only a bilan, manobo, or tiruray, and could not marry her, for he must marry a tiruray. This made the brother of the general very mad and he drew his kris to strike her, but his companion stopped him.

Then the sister of the princess said to him, "Why don't you kill me? I am not afraid of you" and then she went to the window to cool off, for she was very mad at the general and his brother. And the sight of the Spanish fleet in the harbor increased her rage, but just then a parrot with golden plumage hopped into the window and told her to look out into the harbor mouth and there she saw Bantugan's ships entering the harbor, so she called her sister to see them, who came, but could not tell whose flags they were.

Then the general's brother came and looked and said, "We must go and see at once whether it is the fleet of Bantugan, and if it is we must go and kill him and all his people."

So the brother returned to the sultan and asked him if he knew whose ships were coming into the harbor.

The sultan said, "No, I do not know, but will send for my father and see if he knows." So he sent one of his brothers to go and call the father, who, as he was very old, was kept in a little dark room by himself, so he could not get hurt.

The sultan said, "If he is so bent with age that he cannot see, talk, or walk, tickle him in the ribs, and that will make him young again, and you, my brother, carry him here yourself. Do not trust him to the slaves, for if he should fall he would break himself and die."

So the old man was brought, and when he looked at the flags on the ship he said that they were the flags of Bapa ni Bantugan (father of Bantugan), who was a great friend of his in his younger days; and then he told the sultan that he and Bantugan's father had made a contract years ago that their children and children's children should intermarry, and now the sultan had promised his daughter to two people and that great trouble would come on the land.

So the sultan said to the general, "Here are two claimers to my daughter's hand. Go aboard your ships and you and Bantugan go and fight it out, and he who wins will have my daughter."

So the Spaniards opened fire upon Bantugan, and for three days the earth was covered with smoke from the battle, so that neither could see his enemy. The Spanish general said, "I cannot see Bantugan or the fleet anywhere, so let us go and claim the princess."

And when they reached the sultan they demanded his daughter, but the sultan said, "No, let us wait until the smoke rises to make sure that Bantugan is gone."

Pamanay Macalayan called to Maladia Langig and they two went to Bantugan and decided to engage the Spanish fleet. They took down the flags of gold and put up the battle-flags, and when they came within range of the Spanish fleet they opened fire, and their cannon balls carried away great pieces of the mountains, and many of the Spanish fleet were sunk and great darkness and smoke came over the earth.

When the smoke arose the ships of Bantugan were seen to be all unharmed, so the sultan said, "Bantugan has surely won, for his fleet is uninjured and yours is badly damaged and you have lost."

"No," said the general, "we will fight it out on land." So he landed all of his troops and cannon and made ready to meet Bantugan on the land, and when all were landed and ready the Spaniard sent his challenge against Bantugan. Bantugan landed his troops and cannon, but before he commenced fighting he paid his respects to the princess and sultan in case he should be killed. After the fight had begun the Spaniards saw that they could never win with guns and cannon, so they set upon Bantugan with campilans (or "kampilan," long sword used by the Moros of the Philippines) and spears, and soon the general's brother (Masuala Subangam) was killed by Bantugan. Before long the ground was covered with corpses and the rivers were dammed up with their numbers. So the sultan sent word for them not to fight any more, for the air and water were so polluted with the dead bodies.

But the Spaniard answered and said, "If you give your daughter to Bantugan we will fight forever or until we are dead."

The sultan sent a messenger to Bantugan saying, "Let us deceive the Spaniard in order to get him to go away. Let us tell him that you will not marry my daughter, and then we are sure he will leave, and then after he is gone, we can have the wedding."

Bantugan agreed to this, and word was sent to the Spaniards that Bantugan would not marry the sultan's daughter, and that the fighting should cease, because the cannon balls were killing many of the women and children in the city. The Spaniard and Bantugan agreed that neither of them should marry the Princess and that they should be friends. So both the Spaniard and Bantugan sailed away to their home. But Bantugan soon returned and married the princess and continued on his search for his son. He soon found him in the house of the wife of Satan, and took him home with him.

The Spanish general sailed away for about a week, for his home, and then turned about to return to take the princess away by force, for his heart was deceitful, and when he arrived at the city of the sultan, and found that the princess had been carried away by Bantugan, his wrath knew no bounds, so that he destroyed the sultan, his city, and all of its people, and then sailed away to his own city to prepare a great expedition with which he should utterly annihilate Bantugan and his country.

When he arrived off the mouth of the Pulangui with his enormous fleet, their numbers were so great that the horizon could not be seen in any direction.

When Bantugan saw this display of force, his heart sank within him, for he saw that he and his country were doomed to destruction, as he could not hope to gain in a fight with so formidable an antagonist, and such great superiority in numbers. They called a meeting of all the dattos and none could offer any advice, so Bantugan arose and said, "My brothers, the Christian dogs have come to destroy the land, and we cannot successfully oppose them, yet we can die in defense of the fatherland."

So the great warship of Bantugan was again prepared and all the soldiers of Islam embarked thereon, and all their dattos, and with Bantugan standing at the bow they sailed forth to meet their fate. As they approached the Spanish fleet, Bantugan shouted forth his war-song.

"With my campilan which kills many, with my bloody campilan, shining with its gold ornaments, its bombol (a tassel of red hair attached to the handle of the campilan) made from the hair of a beautiful widow, which flashes like the ray of the sun at sunrise. With the beauty of its golden grip coming from the heaven heavenly. Its edge sharp as lightning and reaching even to the heavens. Flashing of its own accord and thirsting for the blood of the Christian dogs, I take it in my hands with such force that the gems in my rings burst from their settings, and fly away like birds. I take my shield painted by my sister, inlaid with flashing pearl. Its grip made of pure gold. Its button a great brilliant. My belt of golden snake. My amulets of pearl, the buttons on my armor taken from the stars. My turban of silver cloth and my helmet of gold. I go to my death, but with me shall die many of ye, Christian dogs."

The fighting soon became fast and furious, but in less than a day it was plainly seen that the Spaniards were winning, and the great warship of Bantugan was filling with water until at last it sank, drawing with it hundreds of the Spaniard's ships, and then a strange thing happened. At the very point where Bantugan's warship sank there arose from the sea a great island covered with bongo palms.

The wife of Bantugan, when she saw that her husband was no more and that his warship was destroyed, gathered together the remaining warriors and set forth herself to avenge him. In a few hours her ship was also sunk and in the place where it sank there arose the mountain of Timaco.

This is the Moro version of the Spanish occupation of Mindanao. Bongos Island is situated about three miles off the mouth of the Rio Grande de Mindanao and is the island said by the Moros to have arisen where Bantugan's ship had sunk. They say that deep within its mountains lives Bantugan and his warriors, and that whenever a Moro's vinta or sailing boat passes by Bongos Island, Bantugan has watchers out to see whether or not there are women *in* the vinta, and if there are any that suit his fancy, they are snatched from their seats and carried deep into the interior of the mountain. For this reason the Moro women are very reluctant to go to the island of Bongos or even to sail by it.

Timaco is an island marking the south side of the entrance to the north branch of the Rio Grande de Mindanao. It consists of one tall hill thickly covered with trees, and on it are found the only specimens of the "white monkey." These are said by the Moros to be the servants of Bantugan's wife, who lives in the center of the mountain. A Moro would not hurt one of them, but feeds them regularly. It is said that on a still day if one goes high up the mountain and listens carefully, he can hear the chanting and singing of the waiting girls of the wife of Bantugan and also hear the colingtangan (Moro musical instrument like a xylophone).

THE MONKEY AND THE TORTOISE

Tradition Bearer: Unavailable

Source: Benedict, Laura Watson. "Bagobo Myths." *The Journal of American Folklore* 26 (1913): 58–62.

Date: Unavailable

Original Source: Mindinao

National Origin: Philippines

This tale casts a series of characters in the **trickster** role. The scatology is typical of tricksters cross-culturally. The widely known ploy that is at the heart of "The Briar Patch Punishment for Rabbit" (AT 1310) is used by the tortoise to escape the monkey's revenge.

One day, when a Tortoise was crawling slowly along by a stream, he saw a baby-monkey drinking water. Presently the Monkey ran up to the Tortoise, and said, "Let's go and find something to eat."

Not far from the stream there was a large field full of banana trees. They looked up, and saw clusters of ripe fruit.

"That's fine!" said the Monkey, "for I'm hungry and you're hungry too. You climb first, Tortoise."

Then the Tortoise crawled slowly up the trunk; but he had got up only a little distance when the Monkey chattered these words, "*Roro s'punno, roro s' punnol*" ("Slide down, slide down, Tortoise!").

At once the Tortoise slipped and fell down. Then he started again to climb the tree; and again the Monkey said, "*Roro s'punno!*" and again the Tortoise slipped and fell down. He tried over and over again; but every time he failed, for the Monkey always said, "*Roro s'pilnno!*" and made him fall. At last he got tired and gave it up, saying to the Monkey, "Now you try it."

"It's too bad!" said the Monkey, "when we're both so hungry." Then the Monkey made just three jumps, and reached the ripe fruit. "Wait till I taste and see if they're sweet," he cried to the Tortoise, while he began to eat bananas as fast as he could.

"Give me some," begged the Tortoise.

"All right!" shouted the Monkey, "but I forgot to notice whether it was sweet." And he kept on eating, until more than half of the fruit was gone.

"Drop down just one to me!" pleaded the Tortoise.

"Yes, in a minute," mumbled the Monkey.

At last, when but three bananas were left on the tree, the Monkey called, "Look up! Shut your eyes."

The Tortoise did so. The Monkey then told him to open his mouth, and he obeyed. Then the Monkey said, "I'll peel this one piece of banana for you."

Now, the Monkey was sitting on a banana leaf, directly over the Tortoise; but, instead of banana, he dropped his excrement into the Tortoise's mouth. The Tortoise screamed with rage; but the Monkey jumped up and down, laughing at him. Then he went on eating the remainder of the bananas.

The Tortoise then set himself to work at making a little hut of bamboo posts, with a roof and walls of leaves. The upper ends of the bamboo he sharpened, and let them project through the roof; but the sharp points were concealed by the leaves. It was like a trap for pigs (*sankil*).

When the Monkey came down from the banana tree, the Tortoise said, "You climb this other tall tree, and look around at the sky. If the sky is dark, you must call to me; for the rain will soon come. Then you jump down on the roof of our little house here. Never mind if it breaks in, for we can soon build a stronger one."

The Monkey accordingly climbed the tree, and looked at the sky. "It is all very dark!" he exclaimed.

"Jump quick, then!" cried the Tortoise.

So the Monkey jumped; but he got killed from the sharp bamboo points on which he landed.

Then the Tortoise made a fire, and roasted the Monkey. He cut off the Monkey's ears, and they turned into buyo-leaves. He cut out the heart, and it turned into betel-nut. He took out the brain, and it became lime (*apog*). He made that all into *pungaman*. The stomach he made into a basket. He put into the basket the betel and the lime and the pungaman and the buyo, and crawled away.

Soon he heard the noise of many animals gathered together. He found the monkeys and the deer and the pigs and the wild birds having a big rice-planting. All the animals were rejoiced to see the Tortoise coming with a basket, for they all wanted to chew betel. The monkeys ran up, chattering, and tried to snatch the betel-nuts; but the Tortoise held them back, saying, "Wait a minute! By and by I will give you some."

Then the monkeys sat around, waiting, while the Tortoise prepared the betel-nut. He cut the nuts and the pungaman into many small pieces, and the buyo-leaf too, and gave them to the monkeys and the other animals. Everybody began to chew; and the Tortoise went away to a distance about the length of one field (*sebad kinamat*), where he could get out of sight, under shelter of some trees. Then he called to the monkeys, "All of you are eating monkey, just like your own body: you are chewing up one of your own family."

At that, all the monkeys were angry, and ran screaming to catch the Tortoise. But the Tortoise had hid under the felled trunk of an old *palma brava* tree. As each monkey passed close by the trunk where the Tortoise lay concealed, the Tortoise said, "Drag your member [that is, penis]! Here's a felled tree."

Thus every monkey passed by clear of the trunk, until the last one came by; and he was both blind and deaf. When he followed the rest, he could not hear the Tortoise call out, "*Scapa tapol basic*"; and his member struck against the fallen trunk. He stopped, and became aware of the Tortoise underneath. Then he screamed to the rest; and all the monkeys came running back, and surrounded the Tortoise, threatening him.

"What do you want?" inquired the Tortoise.

"You shall die," cried the monkeys. "Tell us what will kill you. We will chop you to pieces with the axe."

"Oh, no! That won't hurt me in the least," replied the Tortoise. "You can see the marks on my shell, where my father used to cut my body: but that didn't kill me."

"We will put you in the fire, then, and burn you to death," chorused the monkeys. "Will that do?"

"Fire does not hurt me," returned the Tortoise. "Look at my body! See how brown it is where my father used to stick me into the fire."

"What, then, is best to kill you?" urged the monkeys.

"The way to kill me," replied the Tortoise, "is to take the punch used for brass, and run it into my rectum. Then throw me into the big pond, and drown me."

Then the monkeys did as they were told, and threw him into the pond. But the Tortoise began to swim about in the water.

Exultantly he called to the monkeys, "This is my own home: you see I don't drown." And the lake was so deep that the monkeys could not get him.

Then the monkeys hurried to and fro, summoning all the animals in the world to drink the water in the lake. They all came—deer, pigs, jungle-fowl, monkeys, and all the rest—and began to drink. They covered their *pagindis* [ure-thras] with leaves, so that the water could not run out of their bodies. After a time, they had drunk so much that the lake became shallow, and one could see the Tortoise's back.

But the red-billed bakaka-bird that lived in a tree by the water was watching; and as quick as the back of the Tortoise came into sight, the bird flew down and picked off the leaves from the *pagindis* of the deer. Then the water ran out from their bodies until the lake rose again, and covered the Tortoise. Satisfied, the bird flew back into the tree. But the deer got fresh leaves to cover their *pagindis*, and began to drink again. Then the bird flew to the monkeys, and began to take the leaves from their *pagindis*; but one monkey saw him doing it, and slapped him. This made the bird fall down, and then all the monkeys left the Tortoise in the lake, and ran to revenge themselves on the bird.

They snatched him up, pulled out every one of his feathers with their fingers, and laid him naked upon the stump of a tree. All the animals went home, leaving the bird on the stump.

Two days later, one Monkey came to look at the Bakaka. Little feathers were beginning to grow out; but the Monkey thought the bird was dead.

"Maggots are breeding in it," said the Monkey.

Three more days passed, and then the Monkey came again. The Bakaka's feathers had grown out long by that time; and the Monkey said, "It was all rotten, and the pigs ate it."

But the bird had flown away. He flew to the north until he reached a meadow with a big tual tree in the middle. The tree was loaded with ripe fruit.' Perched on one of the branches, the bird ate all he wanted, and when done he took six of the fruit of the *tual*, and made a necklace for himself. With this hung round his neck, he flew to the house where the old Monkey lived, and sat on the roof. He dropped one *tual* through the roof, and it fell down on the floor, where all the little monkey-children ran for it, dancing and screaming.

"Don't make such a noise!" chided the old Monkey, "and do not take the *tual*, for the Bakaka will be angry, and he is a great bird."

But the bird flew down into the house, and gave one *tual* to the old Monkey.

"That is good," said the old Monkey, tasting it. "Tell me where you got it." But the bird would not tell. Then the old monkey stood up, and kissed him, and begged to be taken to the tual tree.

At last the Bakaka said to all the monkeys, "Three days from now you may all go to the tual tree. I want you *all* to go, the blind monkey too. Go to the meadow where the grass grows high, and there, in the center of the meadow, is the tual tree. If you see the sky and the air black, do not speak a word; for if you speak, you will get sick."

At the set time, all the monkeys started for the meadow, except one female monkey that was expecting a baby. The deer and all the other animals went along, except a few of the females who could not go. They all reached the meadow-grass; and the monkeys climbed up the tual tree that stood in the center of the field, until all the branches were full of monkeys. The birds and the jungle-fowl flew up in the tree; but the deer and the other animals waited down on the ground.

Then the sky grew black, for the Bakaka and the Tortoise were going around the meadow with lighted sticks of *balekayo*, and setting fire to the grass. The air was full of smoke, and the little monkeys were crying; but the old Monkey bit them, and said, "Keep still, for the Bakaka told us not to speak."

But the meadow-grass was all ablaze, and the flames crept nearer and nearer to the tual tree. Then all the monkeys saw the fire, and cried, "Oh! What will become of us?"

Some of the birds and most of the chickens flew away; but some died in the flames. A few of the pigs ran away, but most of them died. The other animals were burned to death. Not a single monkey escaped, save only the female monkey who staid at home. When her baby was born, it was a boy-monkey. The mother made it her husband, and from this pair came many monkeys.

It was the same with the deer. All were burned, except one doe who stayed at home. When her little fawn was born, it was a male. She made it her husband, and from this one pair came many deer.

POOR LITTLE MARIA

Tradition Bearer: Cornelio

Source: Gardner, Fletcher, and W. W. Newell. "Filipino (Tagalog) Versions of Cinderella." *Journal of American Folklore* 19 (1906): 265–270.

Date: 1903

Original Source: Tagalog

National Origin: Philippines

"Poor Little Maria" consists of two folktales that merge at the conclusion of the narrative. The first tale, is a Filipino adaptation of "Cinderella" (AT 510A). After the marriage of Maria to the king, the tale plot is extended with a **variant** of "The Three Golden Sons" (AT 707). The combination of these two tales is uncommon.

Once there were a man and his wife who had a daughter named Maria. Maria was a very pretty child and very happy, but unfortunately her father fell in love with a woman who was not his wife, and one day taking his wife out to fish with him he murdered her and threw her body into the water.

Poor little Maria cried a great deal after her mother's death, but her lot was worse after her father married the other woman, for the stepmother set her all kinds of cruel tasks and threatened her with awful penalties if she failed.

Maria had a pet pig, with which she played a great deal, and her stepmother ordered her to kill and clean it. Poor little Maria cried and begged, but the woman forced her to kill the pig. When the pig was cleaned, the stepmother gave Maria ten of the refuse pieces and told her to clean them in the river, and if one piece was missing when she returned, she would be beaten to death. Maria cleaned the pieces in the river, but one slipped away and went down stream.

The child cried and lamented over her fate so that an old crocodile going by asked her what was amiss. "That is nothing," said the crocodile, and he straightway swam after the piece and brought it back. As he turned to swim away, he splashed with his tail and a drop of water fell on her forehead where it became a most beautiful jewel, flashing like the sun and fastened so tightly that it could not be removed.

The little girl went home with the jewel on her fore-head shining so brightly that it made every one cross-eyed to look at it, so that it had to be covered with a handkerchief.

The cruel stepmother asked many questions about Maria's good fortune, and when she found out all about it she sent her own daughter to kill a pig and do in all respects as the stepsister had done.

She did so and threw a piece of the refuse meat into the river and cried as it floated off.

The crocodile inquired of this girl also the cause of the trouble, and again brought the meat, but this time when he splashed with his tail, instead of a jewel on the girl's forehead, there was a little bell that tinkled incessantly. All the people knelt and crossed them-selves because they thought the "Viaticum" passed, but when they saw the bell on the girl's forehead they laughed and pointed at her. So the daughter had to tie up her forehead for shame, for the bell could not be gotten off.

The stepmother was more cruel than ever to Maria now that she had met with good fortune and her daughter with ill. She set the girl to every kind of dirty work till her whole body was filthy and then sent her to the river to bathe, telling her that if she did not wash her back clean she would beat her to death.

Maria struggled and scrubbed, but she could not reach her back either to see whether it was clean or to wash it, and she began to cry. Out of the river came a great she-crab, that asked the girl her trouble.

"Oh," said Maria, "if I do not wash my back clean my stepmother will beat me to death."

"Very well," said the crab, "that is easily remedied," and jumping on to Maria's back scrubbed and scrubbed till her back was perfectly clean. "Now," said the crab, "you must eat me and take my shell home and bury it in the yard. Something will grow up that will be valuable to you." Maria did as she was told, and from the place grew a fine lukban (grape fruit) tree which in time bore fruit.

One day the stepmother and her daughter wished to go to church and left Maria to get the dinner. The stepmother told her that dinner must be ready when she returned and must be neither cold nor hot. Maria wept again over the impossibility of the task and was about to despair when an old woman came in, to whom she told her troubles.

The old woman was a stranger but was apparently very wise, for she told Maria to go to church and that she would prepare the dinner. The girl said she had no clothes, but the old woman told her to look in the fruit of the lukban tree, and from the fruit Maria took out all the garments of a princess, a beautiful chariot and eight horses.

Quickly she bathed and arrayed herself and drove by the king's palace to the church, the jewel on her forehead shining so that it nearly blinded all who looked. The king, seeing such a magnificently dressed princess, sent his soldiers to find out about her, but they could learn nothing and had nothing to show when they returned but one of her little slippers which fell off as she left the church.

Maria went home and hastily put the dress and equipage back into the lukban fruit, and the old woman was there waiting with the dinner, which was neither cold nor hot. When the stepmother came from church, she saw only her stepdaughter there in rags, and everything ready according to her order.

Now the king wished to know who this princess was and ordered a "bando" sent around to every woman and girl in the kingdom, saying he would marry whomever the shoe would fit. The stepmother and her daughter went to the palace, but tied Maria in a sack and set her in the fireplace, telling her that she would be beaten to death if she stirred. The shoe fitted nobody at the palace; whether their feet were long, short, broad, narrow, big, little, or otherwise, it fitted no one.

So the soldiers were sent out again to bring in every one who had not obeyed the "bando" and they looked into the house where Maria lived, but they did not see her. Just then a cock crowed and said, "Kikiriki, that's the girl." Kikiriki, there in the fireplace; the shoe fits her foot." So the soldiers made Maria dress in her finery with the mate to her little slipper on her foot, and with her little chariot and the eight ponies she went to the king's palace, and the other little slipper fitted exactly.

The stepmother and her daughter were envious, but could do nothing against the king's wishes, and the king married Maria with great pomp, but none of the jewels were so beautiful as the one that blazed on Maria's forehead.

In due time it came to be known that an heir would be born, but the king was called away to war. He arranged that a signal should be set, however, a white flag if all went well and a black flag if anything went wrong.

He left the princess in the care of her stepmother and two wise women, and warned them not to let anything bad happen to the queen. The stepmother had not forgotten her hate for Maria, and when the little princes were born, for there were seven, she and the other women took them away and substituted seven little blind puppies.

When the king returned he saw the black flag flying over the tower and hurried to the queen's rooms to find her in tears over the puppies. He ordered the puppies drowned and his wife put into a corner under the staircase, until a place could be built for her. Then he had a hut built outside the palace and placed the queen there in chains.

The seven little princes, stolen from their mother, were put into a box which was cast into the sea and which drifted far away to a shore near an enchanter's cave. This enchanter had an oracle which spoke to him and said, "Go by the mountains and you will be sad, go by the shore and you will be glad," as he was setting out for his daily walk. Obedient to the oracle, he went to the shore and there heard the crying of the babies. He secured the box and carried it and the babies to his cave, and there they lived for several years untroubled.

One day a hunter, chasing deer with dogs, went by that way and saw the children. He returned to town and told what he had seen, and it came to the ears of the old women. They, being afraid that the king would learn of the children's being there, made "maruya," which is a kind of sweetmeat, and mixed poison with it. Then they went out to where the children were and gave them the poisoned sweets, so that they all died. When night came the enchanter was greatly troubled because the children did not come, and taking a torch he set out to look for them. He found the little bodies lying at the foot of a tree, and wept long and bitterly. At last he took them to his cave and laid them in a row on the floor and wept again.

As he lamented he heard the voice of the oracle, which was like a beautiful woman's voice, accompanied by a harp, singing most sweetly, and bidding him beg a medicine of the mother of the Sun, who lives in the house of the Sun across seven mountains to the west. This, she promised, would restore them to life.

So he set out on his long journey, and when he had crossed three mountains he came to a tree on which the birds never lit, and the tree was lamenting the fact. The enchanter inquired the way to the Sun's house, and the tree told him thus and so, but begged him to ask the mother of the Sun why the birds never lit on it. The enchanter went on, and on the next mountain he saw two men sitting in a pair of balances, which pitched up and down like a barca (boat) in a storm. From them he asked again the way to the Sun's house, and they told him and asked him to speak to the mother of the Sun as to why they were condemned to ride the limb of a tree like a boat in a storm.

He went on to the next mountain and there he saw two poor, lean cattle feeding on rich grass. From them also he inquired the direction of the Sun's house, and they told him and requested that he ask the mother of the Sun why they were always lean and fed on rich herbage. He promised and passed on to the next mountain, and there he saw a black ox eating nothing but earth and still fat and sleek. This animal told him how to find the Sun's house and wished to know of the mother of the Sun why he was always fat though he ate only dust.

The enchanter gave his word and went on. At last, late in the afternoon, he arrived at the Sun's house and went boldly upstairs. The mother of the Sun met him and inquired his business, which he told her, and then she told him that he was in great danger, for if her son, the Sun, came home and found him there he would eat him. The enchanter told her that he would not go away without the medicine, and at last the mother of the Sun agreed to hide him; so she wrapped him up so that the Sun could not smell him when he came in and carried him up to the seventh story of the house. There he was to remain until the next morning after the Sun had started off on his journey across the Heavens.

Soon the Sun came in and asked his mother where the man was, but his mother told him there was none and gave him such a fine supper that he forgot about the man, though he remarked once or twice that he certainly thought he smelled man. At last morning came, and when the Sun was far enough away to leave no danger, the mother of the Sun gave the enchanter the medicine that he wanted and started him off on his long journey. She told him, too, the answer to the questions asked by the cattle, the men, and the tree.

When he came to the black ox which lived on the dust, he told it that it was always fat because it was going to Heaven, and it was glad.

To the two oxen which fed on rich pasture and yet were poor, he said that they were so because they were condemned to Hell, and they were sorrowful.

To the men sitting in the pair of balances, he said that they were there because of their sins, and they became sad.

To the tree on which the birds never lit, he said that it was because it was made out of silver and gold, and the tree rustled its leaves in pride.

Finally he came to his cave, and there instead of the bodies of seven young children he saw the bodies of seven handsome young men, for they had grown greatly while he was away. He gave them the medicine, and they at once stood up. Then he told them all of his adventures.

When the boys heard the story, the youngest, who was a dare-devil, set out to find the gold and silver tree and from its branches he shook down a great quantity of gold and silver leaves, which he carried back to the enchanter. The enchanter was proud of the boy and yet angry with him for his rashness, but no one could be angry with him for long, for he was a gentle lad.

The enchanter then took the gold and silver and made clothes for them of cloth of gold, silver sabers, golden belts, and a golden trumpet for the youngest, and sent them away on a Sunday morning to church in the city where the king lived. As they came up close to the city wall, the trumpeter lad blew a merry blast on his horn, and the king sent out to inquire who they might be and to invite them to dinner after church. So they went to the palace after church and sat down to the king's table, and the dishes were brought on. The enchanter had warned them to eat nothing until they had fed a little to a dog, and one of the boys gave some meat to a dog that was with them. The dog was dead in a moment.

The king, ashamed, ordered everything to be changed and new cooks put into the kitchen, for of course he knew nothing of the wickedness against his sons, whom he did not recognize as yet. The boys now very respectfully requested that the woman chained in the hut be brought to the table with them, though they did not know why they should ask such a thing. So the king took his sword and with his own hands, from shame, set his wife free, and had her dressed as a queen and brought to the table. The jewel still glowed on her forehead. As they sat at the table, a stream of milk miraculously coming from the breast of the mother passed to the mouth of the youngest son. Then the king understood, and when he had heard the story of the sons he put the queen again into her rightful place and caused the wicked stepmother and her two accomplices to be pulled to pieces by wild horses.

The king, the queen, and the seven princes, having made an end of their rivals, lived long and happily together.

THE FIFTY-ONE THIEVES

Tradition Bearer: Unavailable

Source: Gardner, Fletcher. "Tagalog Folk-Tales I." *Journal of American Folklore* 20 (1907): 114–115.

Date: Unavailable

Original Source: Tagalog

National Origin: Philippines

"The Fifty-One Thieves" is a Tagalog version of "The Forty Thieves" ["Robbers Smuggled Into House in Food Containers"] (AT 954). This folktale enjoys broad distribution cross-culturally, but perhaps the best-known **variant** is "Ali Baba and the Forty Thieves" drawn from the Middle Eastern classic *One Thousand and One Nights*. Both Spanish Catholic and Muslim cultures had a profound influence of the culture of the Philippines from the European Renaissance to the present day. Therefore, the Tagalog variant could have been derived from either European or Middle Eastern (Southwest Asian) sources.

There were once two brothers, Juan and Pedro. Pedro was rich and was the elder, but Juan was very poor and gained his living by cutting wood. Juan became so poor at last that he was forced to ask alms from his brother, or what was only the same thing, a loan. After much pleading, Pedro gave his brother enough rice for a single meal, but repenting of such generosity, went and took it off the fire, as his brother's wife was cooking it, and carried it home again.

Juan then set out for the woods, thinking he might be able to find a few sticks that he could exchange for something to eat, and went much farther than he was accustomed to go. He came to a road he did not know and followed it for some distance to where it led to a great rocky bluff and there came to an end.

Juan did not know exactly what to think of such an abrupt ending to the roadway, and sat down behind a large rock to meditate. As he sat there a voice within the cliff said, "Open the door," and a door in the cliff opened itself. A man richly dressed came out, followed by several others, whom he told that they were going to a town at a considerable distance. He then said, "Shut the door," and the door closed itself again.

Juan was not sure whether any one else was inside, but he was no coward and besides he thought he might as well be murdered as starved to death, so when the robbers had ridden away to a safe distance without seeing him, he went boldly up to the cliff and said, "Open the door."

The door opened as obediently to him as to the robber, and he went in. He found himself inside a great cavern filled with money, jewels, and rich stuffs of every kind.

Hastily gathering more than enough gold and jewels to make him rich, he went outside, not forgetting to say, "Close the door," and went back to his house.

Having hidden all but a little of his new wealth, he wished to change one or two of his gold pieces for silver so that he could buy something to eat. He went to his brother's house to ask him for the favor, but Pedro was not at home, and his wife, who was at least as mean as Pedro, would not change the money. After a while Pedro came home, and his wife told him that Juan had some money; and Pedro, hoping in turn to gain some advantage, went to Juan's house and asked many questions about the money. Juan told him that he had sold some wood in town and had been paid in gold, but Pedro did not believe him and hid himself under the house to listen. At night he heard Juan talking to his wife, and found out the place and the password. Immediately taking three horses to carry his spoils, he set out for the robbers' cave.

Once arrived, he went straight to the cliff and said, "Open the door," and the door opened immediately. He went inside and said, "Close the door," and the door closed tight. He gathered together fifteen great bags of money, each all he could lift, and carried them to the door ready to put on the horses. He found all the rich food and wine of the robbers in the cave, and could not resist the temptation to make merry at their expense; so he ate their food and drank their fine wines till he was foolishly drunk. When he had reached this state, he began to think of returning home. Beating on the door with both hands, he cried out, "Open, beast. Open, fool. May lightning blast you if you do not open!" and a hundred other foolish things, but never once saying, "Open the door."

While he was thus engaged, the robbers returned, and hearing them coming he hid under a great pile of money with only his nose sticking out. The robbers saw that some one had visited the cave in their absence and hunted for the intruder till one of them discovered him trembling under a heap of coin. With a shout they hauled him forth and beat him until his flesh hung in ribbons. Then they split him into halves and threw the body into the river, and cut his horses into bits, which they threw after him.

When Pedro did not return, his wife became anxious and told Juan where he had gone. Juan stole quietly to the place by night, and recovered the body, carried it home, and had the pieces sewn together by the tailor.

Now the robbers knew that they had been robbed by some one else, and so, when Pedro's body was taken away, the captain went to town to see who had buried the body, and by inquiring, found that Juan had become suddenly rich, and also that it was his brother who had been buried.

So the captain of the robbers went to Juan's house, where he found a ball going on. Juan knew the captain again and that he was asking many questions, so he made the captain welcome and gave him a great deal to eat and drink. One of the servants came in and pretended to admire the captain's sword till he got it into his own hands; and then he began to give an exhibition of fencing, making the sword whirl hither and thither and ending with a wonderful stroke that made the captain's head roll on the floor.

A day or two later, the lieutenant also came to town, and began to make inquiries concerning the captain. He soon found out that the captain had been killed in Juan's house, but Juan now had soldiers on guard at his door, so that it was necessary to use strategy. He went to Juan and asked if he could start a "tienda," or wine-shop, and Juan, who recognized the lieutenant, said, "Yes." Then the lieutenant went away, soon returning with seven great casks, in each of which he had seven men.

These he stored under Juan's house until such time as Juan, being asleep, could be killed with certainty and little danger. When this was done, he went into the house, intending to make Juan drunk and then kill him as Juan had the captain. Juan, however, got the lieutenant drunk first, and soon his head, like the captain's, rolled on the floor.

The soldiers below, like all soldiers, wished to have a drink from the great casks, and so one of them took a borer and bored into one of the casks. As he did so, a voice whispered, "Is Juan asleep yet?"

The soldier replied, "Not yet," and went and told Juan. The casks by his order were all put into a boat, loaded with stones and chains, and thrown into the sea. So perished the last of the robbers.

Juan, being no longer in fear of the robbers, often went to their cave, and helped himself to everything that he wanted. He finally became a very great and wealthy man.

JUAN THE FOOL

Tradition Bearer: Unavailable

Source: Gardner, Fletcher. "Tagalog Folk-Tales I." *Journal of American Folklore* 20 (1907): 106–107.

Date: Unavailable

Original Source: Tagalog

National Origin: Philippines

In the folklore of the Philippines, the figure of "Juan" (or often "Juan Puson" in Tagalog folktales) is the archetypal **trickster**, **numskull**, and ne'er-do-well rolled into one conventional character. In the following tale modeled on "The Table, the Ass and the Stick" (AT 563), Juan succeeds in spite of himself.

Juan was lazy, Juan was a fool, and his mother never tired of scolding him and emphasizing her words by a beating. When Juan went to school he made more noise at his study than anybody else, but his reading was only gibberish.

His mother sent him to town to buy meat to eat with the boiled rice, and he bought a live crab which he set down in the road and told to go to his mother and be cooked for dinner. The crab promised, but as soon as Juan's back was turned ran in the other direction.

Juan went home after a while and asked for the crab, but there was none, and they ate their rice without *ulam* [relish to be eaten with rice, meat especially]. His mother then went herself and left Juan to care for the baby. The baby cried and Juan examined it to find the cause, and found the soft spot on its head. "Aha! It has a boil. No wonder it cries!" And he stuck a knife into the soft spot, and the baby stopped crying. When his mother came back, Juan told her about the boil and that the baby was now asleep, but the mother said it was dead, and she beat Juan again.

Then she told Juan that if he could do nothing else he could at least cut firewood, so she gave him a bolo [machete] and sent him to the woods.

He found what looked to him like a good tree and prepared to cut it, but the tree was a magic tree and said to Juan, "Do not cut me and I will give you a goat that shakes silver money from its whiskers." Juan agreed, and the bark of the tree opened and the goat came out, and when Juan told him to shake his whiskers, money dropped out. Juan was very glad, for at last he had something he would not be beaten for. On his way home he met a friend, and told him of his good fortune. The man made him dead drunk and substituted another goat which had not the ability to shake money from its whiskers, and when the new goat was tried at home poor Juan was beaten and scolded.

Back he went to the tree, which he threatened to cut down for lying to him, but the tree said, "No, do not kill me and I will give you a magic net which you may cast even on dry ground or into a treetop and it will return full of fish," and the tree did even so.

Again he met the friend, again he drank tuba [fermented juice of cocoa, buri, or nipa palms] until he was dead drunk, and again a worthless thing was substituted, and on reaching home he was beaten and scolded.

Once more Juan went to the magic tree, and this time he received a magic pot, always full of rice; and spoons always full of whatever ulam might be wished, and these went the way of the other gifts, to the false friend.

The fourth time he asked of the tree he was given a magic stick that would without hands beat and kill anything that the owner wished. "Only say to it 'Boombye, boomba,' and it will obey your word," said the tree.

When Juan met the false friend again, the false friend asked him what gift he had this time. "It is only a stick that if I say, 'Boombye, boomba,' will beat you to death," said Juan, and with that the stick leaped from his hand and began to belabor the wicked man. "Stop it and I will give you everything I stole from you." Juan ordered the stick to stop, but made the man, bruised and sore, carry the net, the pot, and the spoons, and lead the goat to Juan's home. There the goat shook silver from his beard till Juan's three brothers and his mother had all they could carry, and they dined from the pot and the magic spoons until they were full to their mouths.

"Now," said Juan, "you have beaten me and called me a fool all my life, but you are not ashamed to take good things when I get them. I will show you something else. Boombye, boomba!" and the stick began to beat them all. Quickly they agreed that Juan was head of the house, and he ordered the beating to stop.

Juan now became rich and respected, but he never trusted himself far from his stick day or night. One night a hundred robbers came to break into the house, to take all his goods, and kill him, but he said to the stick, "Boombye, boomba!" and with the swiftness of lightning the stick flew around, and all those struck fell dead till there was not one left. Juan was never troubled again by robbers, and in the end married a princess and lived happily ever after.

THE STORY OF JUAN AND THE MONKEY

Tradition Bearer: Unavailable

Source: Gardner, Fletcher. "Tagalog Folk-Tales I." *Journal of American Folklore* 20 (1907): 108–109.

Date: Unavailable

Original Source: Tagalog

National Origin: Philippines

In this Filipino **variant** of "Puss in Boots" (AT 545B), the protagonist is localized to a poor farmer rather than an orphaned youngest sibling. Rather than inheriting an animal helper as in the classic versions of this **tale type**, Juan spares a monkey who has been raiding his crops, thus introducing the "Animal Grateful for Rescue from Peril of Death" **motif** (B360). The asuang whose wealth the monkey cleverly appropriates after killing him is a creature from Filipino folklore. The asuang is a human who has acquired supernatural powers by eating human flesh. It is a shape-shifter and possesses the power to cause harm and even death by the use of its spells.

J uan was a farmer, a farmer so poor that he had only one shirt and one pair of trousers. Juan was much annoyed by monkeys, who stole his corn. So he set a trap and caught several of them. These he killed with a club until he came to the last, which said to him, "Juan, don't kill me and I will be your servant all your life."

"But I will," said Juan. "You are a thief and do not deserve to live."

"Juan, let me live, and I will bring you good fortune, and if you kill me you will be poor all your life." The monkey talked so eloquently that Juan let himself be persuaded, and took the monkey home with him. The monkey was true to his word, and served Juan faithfully, cooking, washing, and hunting food for him, and at night going to distant fields and stealing maize and palay [rice] which he added to Juan's little store.

One day the monkey said to Juan, "Juan, why do you not marry?"

Said Juan, "How can I marry? I have nothing to keep a wife."

"Take my advice," said the monkey, "and you can marry the king's daughter." Juan took the monkey's advice and they set out for the king's palace. Juan remained behind while the monkey went up to the palace alone.

Outside he called, as the custom is, "Honorable people!" and the king said, "Come in."

The king said, "Monkey, where do you walk?" and the monkey said, "Mr. King, I wish to borrow your *salop*. My master wishes to measure his money."

The king lent him the *salop* (a measure of about two quarts), and the monkey returned to Juan. After a few hours he returned it with a large copper piece cunningly stuck to the bottom with paste. The king saw it and called the monkey's attention to it, but the monkey haughtily waved his hand, and told the king that a single coin was of no consequence to his master.

The next day he borrowed the *salop* again and the coin stuck in the bottom was half a peso, and the third day the coin was a peso, but these he assured the king were of no more consequence to his master than the copper. Then the king told the monkey to bring his master to call, and the monkey promised that after a few days he would.

They went home, and as Juan's clothes must be washed, Juan went to bed while the monkey washed and starched them, pulling, pressing, and smoothing them with his hands because he had no iron.

Then they went to call on the king, and the king told Juan that he should marry the princess as soon as he could show the king a large house, with a hundred head of cattle, carabao [domesticated water buffalo], horses, sheep, and goats. Juan was very despondent at this, though he was too brave to let the king know his thoughts. He told his troubles to the monkey, who assured him that the matter was very easy.

The next day they took a drum and a shovel and went into the mountains, where there was a great enchanter who was a very wealthy man and also an *asuang*. They dug a great hole and then Juan hid in the woods and began to beat his drum, and the monkey rushed up to the enchanter's house and told him the soldiers were coming, and that he would hide him. So the enchanter went with the monkey to the hole and the monkey pushed him in and began with hands and feet to cover him up. Juan helped, and soon the enchanter was dead and buried. Then they went to the house and at the first door they opened they liberated fifty people who were being fattened for the enchanter's table. These people were glad to help Juan convey all the money, cattle, and all the enchanter's wealth to the town. Juan built a house on the plaza, married the princess, and lived happily ever after, but his friend the monkey, having so well earned his liberty, he sent back to the woods, and their friendship still continued.

JUAN PUSONG

Tradition Bearer: Unavailable

Source: Maxfield, Berton L., and W. H. Millington. "Visayan Folk-Tales I." *Journal of American Folklore* 19 (1902): 107–112.

Date: 1904

Original Source: Panay, Visayan

National Origin: Philippines

Juan Pusong ("Tricky John") is the prototypical **trickster** among the people of the Visayas, the central cluster of the Philippine Islands located between Luzon to the north and Mindanao to the south. As is the case with tricksters cross-culturally, Juan Pusong is cunning, dishonest, and willing to sacrifice friends and family to his own ends. In this tradition, as in many others in Southeast Asia, the trickster often comes to a bad end.

As the name implies, he is represented as being deceitful and dishonest, sometimes very cunning, and, in some of the stories told of him, endowed with miraculous power. The stories are very simple and of not very great excellence. The few which follow will serve as samples of the narratives told of this popular hero.

Juan Pusong was a lazy boy. Neither punishment nor the offer of a reward could induce him to go to school, but in school-time he was always to be found on the plaza, playing with the other boys.

His mother, however, believed him to be in school, and each day prepared some dainty for him to eat upon his return home. Juan was not satisfied with deceiving his mother in this way, but used to play tricks on her.

"Mother," he said, one day, "I have already learned to be a seer and to discover what is hidden. This afternoon when I come home from school I will foretell what you have prepared for me."

"Will you?" said his mother joyfully, for she believed all he said, I will try to prepare something new and you will not be able to guess it."

"I shall, mother, I shall, let it be whatever it may," answered Juan.

When it was time to go to school, Juan pretended to set out, but instead he climbed a tree which stood near the kitchen, and hiding himself among the leaves, watched through the window all that his mother did.

His mother baked a bibingca, or cake made of rice and sweet potato, and hid it in a jar. "I will bet anything," she said, "that my son will not guess what it is." Juan laughed at his mother's self-conceit.

When it was time for school to close he got down, and with a book in his hand, as though he had really come from school, appeared before his mother and said Mother, I know what you are keeping for me."

"What is it?" asked his mother.

The prophecy that I have just learned at school says that there is a bibingca hidden in the olla [jar]."

The mother became motionless with surprise. "Is it possible?" she asked herself, "my son is indeed a seer. I am going to spread it abroad. My son is a seer."

The news was spread far and wide and many people came to make trial of Pusong's powers. In these he was always successful, thanks to his ability to cheat.

One day a ship was anchored in the harbor. She had come from a distant island. Her captain had heard of Pusong's power and wished to try him. The trial consisted in foretelling how many seeds the oranges with which his vessel was loaded contained. He promised to give Juan a great quantity of money if he could do this.

Pusong asked for a day's time. That night he swam out to the vessel, and, hidden in the water under the ship's stern, listened to the conversation of the crew. Luckily they were talking about this very matter of the oranges, and one of them inquired of the captain what kind of oranges he had.

"My friend," said the captain, "these oranges are different from any in this country, for each contains but one seed."

Pusong had learned all that he needed to know, so he swam back to the shore, and the next morning announced that he was ready for the trial.

Many people had assembled to hear the great seer. Pusong continued to read in his book, as though it was the source of his information. The hour agreed upon struck, and the captain of the vessel handed an orange to Juan and said, "Mr. Pusong, you may tell us how many seeds this orange contains."

Pusong took the orange and smelled it. Then he opened his book and after a while said, "This orange you have presented me with contains but one seed."

The orange was cut and but the one seed found in it, so Pusong was paid the money. Of course he obtained a great reputation throughout the country, and became very rich.

Juan Pusong's father drove his cows out one day to pasture. Juan slipped secretly from the house, and going to the pasture, took the cows into the forest and tied them there. When his father was going for the cows he met Juan and asked, "Where did you come from?"

The boy replied, "I have just come from school. What are you looking for?"

"I am looking for our cows," said his father.

"Why, didn't you tell me that before," asked Juan. "Wait a minute," and he took his little book from his pocket and, looking into it, said, "Our cows are in such a place in the forest, tied together. Go and get them." So his father went to the place where Juan said the cows were and found them.

Afterwards it was discovered that Juan could not read even his own name, so his father beat him for the trick he had played.

Pusong had transgressed the law, and was for this reason put into a cage to be in a short time submerged with it into the sea.

Tabloc-laui, a friend of Pusong's, passed by and saw him in the cage. What are you there for?" Tabloc-laui asked.

"Oh!" answered Pusong, "I am a prisoner here, as you see, because the chief wants me to marry his daughter and I don't want to do it. I am to stay here until I consent."

"What a fool you are!" said Tabloc-laui. "The chief's daughter is pretty, and I am surprised that you are not willing to marry her."

"Hear me, Tabloc-laui!" said the prisoner. "If you want to marry the chief's daughter, let me out and get in here in my place; for tomorrow they will come and ask you if you will consent. Then you will be married at once."

"I am willing!" exclaimed Tabloc-laui. "Get out and I will take your place!"

Next morning the chief ordered his soldiers to take the cage with the prisoner to the sea and submerge it in the water.

Tabloc-laui, on seeing the soldiers coming toward him, thought they would make inquiries of him as Pusong had said. "I am ready now," he said, "I am ready to be the princess's husband."

"Is this crazy fellow raving?" asked the soldiers. "We are ordered to take you and submerge you in the sea."

"But," objected Tabloc-laui, "I am ready now to marry the chief's daughter."

He was carried to the sea and plunged into the water, in spite of his crying, "I am not Pusong! I am Tabloc-laui!"

The next week the chief was in his boat, going from one fish-trap to another, to inspect them. Pusong swam out to the boat.

The chief, on seeing him, wondered, for he believed that Pusong was dead. "How is this?" he asked. "Did you not drown last week?"

"By no means. I sank to the bottom, but I found that there was no water there. There is another world where the dead live again. I saw your father and he charged me to bid you go to him, and afterwards you will be able to come back here, if you wish to do so."

"Is that really true, Pusong?" asked the chief.

"Yes, it is really true," was the reply.

"Well, I will go there. I will have a cage made and go through the way you did."

So the next morning the chief was submerged in the water, with the hope of coming back. When a considerable time had elapsed without seeing his return, his servants searched for Pusong, in order to punish him, but he had escaped to the mountains.

There was once a king who had three young and beautiful daughters named Isabel, Catalina, and Maria.

In the capital city of the kingdom lived a young man known by the name of Juan Pusong. He had as friends an ape, named Amo-Mongo, and a wildcat, whose name was Singalong. The three friends were passing one day in front of the palace, and, seeing the three young ladies, were greatly charmed by their beauty.

Pusong, who posed as a young aristocrat of considerable learning, determined to go before the king and declare his love for the Princess Isabel. The king received him favorably, and offered him a seat; but Juan refused to sit down until he should know the result of his request.

The king was astonished at his manner, and asked him what he wanted. Juan replied that he had presumptuously allowed himself to be charmed by the beauty of the Princess Isabel, and humbly requested the king's consent to their marriage. The king had the princess summoned before him, and in the presence of Pusong asked her if she would accept this man as her husband. She dutifully expressed her willingness to do whatever her father wished, so the king granted the request of Pusong, who was immediately married to Isabel.

When Amo-Mongo saw how successful Pusong had been, he presented himself before the king, as his friend had done, and requested the hand of the Princess Catalina. The king, somewhat unwillingly, gave his consent, and these two were also married.

When Singalong saw to what high positions his friends had attained, he became desirous of like fortune, so he went to the king and obtained his consent to his marriage with the Princess Maria.

All three of the king's sons-in-law lived with their wives at the palace, at the king's expense. The latter seeing that his daughters' husbands were lazy fellows, determined to make them useful, so he sent Pusong and Amo-Mongo out to take charge of his estates in the country, while to Singalong he gave the oversight of the servants who worked in the kitchen of the palace.

Pusong and Amo-Mongo went out to the hacienda with the intention of doing something, but when they arrived there, they found so much to do that they concluded that it would be impossible to attend to everything and so decided to do nothing.

The latter, after merely looking over the estate, entered the forest, in order to visit his relatives there. His fellow monkeys, who knew of his marriage with the princess, believed him to be of some importance, and begged him to save them from the famine which was devastating the forest. This Amo-Mongo, with much boasting of his wealth, promised to do, declaring that at the time of harvest he would give them plenty of rice.

When Pusong and his companion returned to the palace they were asked by the king how many acres they had cleared. They replied that they had cleared and planted about one thousand acres. The king was satisfied with their answer, and, at Amo-Mongo's request, gave orders for a large quantity of rice to be carried from the store-house to the spot in the forest where his son-in-law had promised the monkeys that they should find it.

On the other hand, Singalong during the day did nothing, and as the king never saw him at work he disliked his third son-in-law very much. Yet every morning there were great piles of fish and vegetables in the palace kitchen. Amo-Mongo, knowing that his brother-in-law usually went out at night in order to bring something home, contrived to get up early and see what there was in the kitchen, so as to present it to the king as the result of his own labors. In this way, Amo-Mongo became each day dearer and dearer to the king, while Singalong became more and more disliked.

Maria knew that her husband procured their food in some way, for every morning he said to her, "All that you see here I have brought." However, the king knew nothing of all this.

When the early harvest time came, the king commanded Amo-Mongo to bring rice to make pilipig. (Rice pounded into flakes and toasted, a dish of which Filipinos are very fond.)

Amo-Mongo did not know where he could find it, but set out in the direction from which he had seen Singalong coming each morning, and soon came to an extensive rice field bearing an abundant crop. He took a goodly portion of it and, returning to the palace, had the pilipig prepared and set before the king and his household. Every one ate of it, except Singalong, who was the real owner, and his wife, who had been secretly notified by him of the truth of the matter.

Maria was greatly perplexed by what her husband had told her, so she determined one night to watch him. She discovered that, as soon as the other people were asleep, her husband became transformed into a handsome prince and left the palace, leaving behind him his cat's dress. As soon as he had gone, Maria took the cast-off clothing of her husband and cast it into the fire. Singalong smelt it burning and returned to the palace, where he found his wife and begged her to return to him his cat's dress. This she was unable to do, since it was entirely consumed. As a result, Singalong was obliged to retain the form of a prince, but he was afraid to appear before the king in this guise, and so hid himself.

In the morning, Maria went to the king and told him the truth about her husband. Her father, however, thought that she was crazy, and when she insisted, invited her to accompany him to Amo-Mongo's farm, in order to convince her of her error. Many people went with them, and Amo-Mongo led them to the farm, which was really Singalong's, but told them that it belonged to himself. Besides other things, Singalong had planted many fruits, among them atimon [melon] and candol.

Amo-Mongo, seeing the diversity of fruits, began to eat all he could, until he became unable to move a step. Whenever his wife urged him to come away, he would take an atimon under his arm and a candol or so in his hands, until at last his wife, angry at his greediness, gave him a push which caused him to fall headlong, striking his head against a stone and being instantly killed.

Then Singalong, who had secretly followed the crowd from the palace, showed himself to the king in his proper form. After making suitable explanations, he led them to a fine palace in the middle of the hacienda. There they all lived together, but Pusong and his wife, who in former times had treated Singalong very harshly, giving him only the bones and scraps from the table, were now obliged to act as servants in the kitchen of the king's new palace.

TRUTH AND FALSEHOOD

Tradition Bearer: Unavailable

Source: Maxfield, Berton L., and W. H. Millington. "Visayan Folk-Tales I." *Journal of American Folklore* 19 (1902): 100–102.

Date: 1904

Original Source: Panay, Visayan

National Origin: Philippines

The **fable** "Truth and Falsehood" utilizes personified abstractions (that is, truth and falsehood) to make its moral point. The familiar **motifs** "Dead Man as Helper" (E341.1) and "Grateful Animals" (B350) are used in the plot to permit the triumph of "truth" over his resentful companion "falsehood."

One day Truth started for the city to find some work. On his way he overtook Falsehood, who was going to the city for the same purpose. Falsehood asked permission to ride on the horse with Truth, and his request was granted.

On the way they questioned each other as to the sort of work they wanted. Truth stated that he intended to be a secretary, so that he might always be clean and white. Falsehood declared that he would be a cook, because then he would always have plenty of fine things to eat.

As they were riding along, they met a man carrying a corpse to the cemetery. He had no one to help him, and Truth, in his great pity for the man, jumped off his horse and helped him. After the corpse was buried, Truth asked, "Did you pray for the repose of the soul of the dead?"

"No," was the reply, "I do not know how to pray, and I have no money to pay the priest for candles."

Then Truth gave the man all the money he had, that he might have prayers said for the dead man, and went back to his companion.

When dinner time came, Falsehood was very angry at finding out that Truth had given all his money away, but finally proposed that they should go to the river and catch some fish for dinner. When they arrived at the river, they found some fish which had been caught in a shallow pool near the bank, and caught all they wanted. But Truth was very sorry for the fish, and threw his half back into the river. Falsehood murmured at him and said, "It would have been better for you to give them to me. If I had known that you would throw them into the river, I would not have given you any of them."

Then they rode on. As they were going through a thick wood in the heart of the mountain they heard a noise as of crying, far away. Truth went forward to find what it was, but Falsehood, trembling with fear, hid himself close behind his comrade. At last they saw seven little eagles in a nest high in a tree. They were crying with hunger, and their mother was nowhere to be seen. Truth was sorry for them, and killed his horse, giving some of the meat to the young eagles, and spreading the rest on the ground beneath the tree, so that the mother-bird might find it.

Falsehood hated his comrade for having killed the horse, because now they were obliged to travel on foot. They went down the mountain, and entering the city, presented themselves before the king, desiring to be taken into his service, the one as secretary and the other as cook. The king granted both requests.

When Falsehood saw that his former companion sat at the table with the king and was always clean and dressed in good clothes, while he himself was dirty and had to eat in the kitchen, he was *very* angry and determined to do something to ruin the one whom now he hated so bitterly.

One day the king and queen went to sail on the sea. As they were far from land, the queen dropped her ring overboard. When False-hood heard of the accident, he went to the king and said, "My Lord, the King, my friend—your secretary—has told me that he was endowed with magic powers and is able to find the queen's ring. He says if he does not find it he is willing for you to hang him."

The king immediately sent for Truth, and said to him, "Find the queen's ring without delay, or I will have you hanged early tomorrow morning."

Truth went down to the shore, but seeing how impossible it would be to find the ring, began to weep. A fish came near, and floating on top of the water, asked, "Why are you weeping?"

"I weep," Truth replied, "because the king will hang me early tomorrow morning unless I find the queen's ring, which has fallen into the sea."

The fish swam out and got the ring and gave it to Truth. Then he said, "I am one of the fishes which you found on the bank of the river and threw back into the water. As you helped me when I was in trouble, I am very glad that I have been able to help you now."

On another day, Falsehood went to the king and said, "My Lord King, do you remember what I told you the other day?"

"Yes," replied the king, "and I believe you told me the truth, as the ring has been found."

"Well," replied Falsehood, "my friend told me last night that he is a great magician and that he is willing for you to hang him in the sight of all the people, since it will not hurt him."

The king sent for Truth and told him, "I know what you have said to your friend. Tomorrow I will have you hanged in the sight of all the people, and we will see whether you are the great magician you claim to be."

That night Truth could not sleep. About midnight, as he was in great distress, a spirit suddenly appeared to him and asked what was the cause of his grief. Truth related his trouble, and the spirit said, "Do not weep. Tomorrow morning I will take your form and wear your clothes, and let them hang me."

The next morning, just at dawn, the spirit put on Truth's clothes and went out to be hanged. Many people came to see the hanging, and after it was over, returned to their homes. What was the astonishment of the king and those with him when, upon their return to the palace, they found Truth there before them, alive and well!

That night the spirit appeared to Truth and said, "I am the spirit of the dead man for whom you gave your money that prayers might be said for the repose of his soul." Then it disappeared.

On another day Falsehood appeared before the king, and said, "My Lord the King, my friend the secretary told me last night that if you would let him marry your daughter, in one night his wife should bring forth three children." The king sent for Truth and said, "I will give you my daughter to be your wife and if tonight she does not bear three children, I will have you buried alive tomorrow morning."

So they were married. But at midnight, as Truth lay awake thinking of the fate that was in store for him in the morning, an eagle flew through the window, and asked the cause of his sorrow. Truth related his tale, and the eagle said, "Do not worry; I will take care of that." Then he flew away, but just before the break of day three eagles came, each bearing a new-born babe.

Truth awakened the princess and said to her, "My dear wife, these are our children. We must love them and take good care of them."

Then the king, who had been awakened by the noise of children crying, sent to ask what it was all about. When he heard the news he came into the tower where the princess was, and when he saw the children he was overcome with joy; for he had no sons, and greatly desired to have an heir to his throne. So the king made a great feast and gave over his crown and scepter to his son-in-law, to be king in his stead.

Thus we see that those who help others when in trouble shall themselves be aided when they are in difficulty.

Glossary

anecdote: Originally, a short, humorous tale. Now, the term commonly refers to single-episode narratives, regarded as true and commonly concentrating on an individual.

animal tales: Narratives told as conscious fictions in which the characters, though they speak and behave like human beings, are animals. These animal characters are commonly stock types. For example, in many Native American traditions, coyote is regarded as an exploitive, impulsive manipulator. In African American tales, rabbit is type cast in the same role. The tales are most often moralistic ("don't be greedy") or etiological (why the frog has no tail) in intent.

belief tales: Legends or personal experience narratives that are told with the purpose of validating a particular folk belief.

cautionary tales: Narratives whose plots embody a message cautioning against the consequences of particular kinds of behavior.

culture hero: Character in myth who finishes the work that brings technology (usually symbolized as fire), laws, religion, and other elements of culture to humans. Culture heroes may take over the business of creating order out of chaos where a Supreme Creator left off. The culture hero serves as a secondary creator or transformer of the universe. He/she transforms the universe by means of his gifts into a universe in which humans can live. In some myths, the culture hero cleanses the universe of things that threaten human existence: monsters, cannibals, or meteorological phenomena.

cumulative tale: A tale that begins with an incident, action, or phrase and adds a succession of elements to create a lengthy chain of events.

cycle: A group of tales that focuses on a central character, plot, or theme.

fable: Fictional narrative ending with a didactic message that is often couched in the form of a "moral" or proverb.

fairy tale: See **ordinary folktale**.

family saga: Chronologically and often thematically linked collection of legends constituting the folk history of a particular family, usually over several generations. The term was coined by folklorist Mody C. Boatright.

folk history: Accounts based on perceptions of historical events rather than on written documentation or similar media.

formula/formulaic element: Conventional elements that recur in folk narrative. For example, clichés, structural patterns, stock characters, or situations.

framing: The act of setting apart a traditional performance from other types of activity by words, occasions of performance or other distinguishing features.

genre: Type, category.

legend: Narrative told as truth, set in the historical past, and that does not depart from the present reality of the members of the group.

local legend: Legends derived from and closely associated with specific places and events believed to have occurred in those locales.

märchen: See **ordinary folktale.**

motif: Small element of traditional narrative content, such as an event, object, concept, or pattern.

myth: Narratives that explain the will (the intent) and the workings (the orderly principles) of a group's major supernatural figures. Myth is set in a world that predates the present reality.

natural context: Setting, in all its elements, in which a performance would ordinarily take place.

novelle: Romantic tale.

numskull: Character who behaves in an absurdly ignorant fashion, also called "noodle."

ordinary folktale: Highly formulaic and structured fictional narrative that is popularly referred to as "fairytale" and designated by folklorists as *märchen* or "wonder tale." Term coined by folklorist Stith Thompson.

personal experience narrative: Narrative intended as truth performed in the first person by the individual to whom the described events happened.

personal legend: Narrative intended as truth told about a specific (usually well-known) individual.

resource person: The bearer of a particular tradition, such as the performer of a folktale.

stock character: Recurrent narrative character who invariably plays a stereotyped role such as trickster or fool.

tale type: Standard, recurrent folk narrative plot.

tall tale: Fictional narrative often told as a firsthand experience, which gradually introduces hyperbole until the audience realizes by the conclusion that the tale is a lie.

trickster: Character who defies the limits of propriety and often gender and species. Trickster lives on the margins of his world by his wits and is often regarded as possessing supernatural power. Often a mythic figure such as a coyote or hare will function as both culture hero and trickster.

validating device: Any element occurring within a traditional narrative that is intended to convince listeners that the tale is true.

variant: Version of a standard tale type.

Bibliography to Volume 2

Batchelor, John. "Specimens of Ainu Folk-Lore." *Transactions of the Asiatic Society of Japan* 18 (1890): 25–85.

Bayliss, Clara Kern. "Philippine Folktales." *Journal of American Folklore* 21 (1908): 46–53.

Benedict, Laura Watson. "Bagobo Myths." *The Journal of American Folklore* 26 (1913): 13–63.

Bogoras, Waldemar. "Chukchee Mythology." *The Jessup North Pacific Expedition*, ed. Franz Boas. *Memoir of the American Museum of Natural History New York*. Vol. VIII. New York: The American Museum of Natural History New York, 1910.

Bogoras, Waldemar. "The Folklore of Northeastern Asia as Compared with that of Northwest America." *American Anthropologist* 4 (1902): 577–683.

Bogoras, Waldemar. *Koryak Texts, Publications of the American Ethnological Society V.* Leyden: E. J. Brill, Ltd., 1917.

Brauns, David. *Japanische Märchen und Sagen.* Leipzig: Verlag von Wilhelm Friedrich, 1885.

Burton, Richard. *Vikram and the Vampire*, ed. Elizabeth Burton. London: Tylston and Edwards, 1893.

Colum, Padric. *Orpheus: Myths of the World.* New York: The Macmillan Company, 1930.

Dixon, Roland. *Oceanic Mythology.* Boston: Marshall Jones Company, 1916.

Evans, Ivor H. N. "Folk Stories of the Tempassuk and Tuaran Districts, British North Borneo." *The Journal of the Royal Anthropological Institute of Great Britain and Ireland* 43 (913): 422–479.

Frere, Mary. *Old Deccan Days.* London: J. Murray, 1868.

Gardner, Fletcher, and W. W. Newell. "Filipino (Tagalog) Versions of Cinderella." *Journal of American Folklore* 19 (1906): 265–280.

Gardner, Fletcher, and W. W. Newell. "Tagalog Folk-Tales I." *Journal of American Folklore* 20 (1907): 104–116.

Hearn, Lafcadio. *In Ghostly Japan.* Boston: Little, Brown, and Co., 1899.

Hearn, Lafcadio. *Kwaidan: Stories and Studies of Strange Things.* Boston: Houghton, Mifflin and Co., 1904.

Hutton, H. "Folktales of the Angami Nagas of Assam." *Folklore* 25 (1914): 476–498.

Jacobs, Joseph. *Indian Fairy Tales.* London: David Nutt, 1912.

Lang, Andrew. *The Crimson Fairy Book.* London: Longmans, Green and Company, 1903.

Lang, Andrew. *The Green Fairy Book.* London: Longmans, Green and Company, 1892.

Lang, Andrew. *The Olive Fairy Book.* London: Longmans, Green and Company, 1907.

Lang, Andrew. *The Pink Fairy Book.* London: Longmans, Green and Company, 1897.

Lang, Andrew. *The Violet Fairy Book.* London: Longmans, Green and Company, 1901.

Mackenzie, Donald A. *Indian Myth and Legend.* London: The Gresham Publishing Company, Ltd., 1913.

Maxfield, Berton L., and W. H. Millington. "Visayan Folk-Tales I" *Journal of American Folklore* 19 (1902): 97–112.

Maxwell, W. E. "Raja Donan: A Malay Fairy Tale." *The Folk-Lore Journal* 6 (1888): 134–139.

Miura, Kiyoko. "Two Songs That Were Sung and Danced by Owl God." *Yakura Epos of the Ainus: Study and Translation of Kamuy-Yukara.* http://www.harvest-fields.ca/ebook/etexts1/01/38/00.htm (July 2, 2007).

O'Connor, W. F. *Folk Tales from Tibet.* London: Hurst and Blackett, Ltd., 1906.

Parker, Henry. *Village Folk Tales of Ceylon.* London: Luzac and Company, 1910.

Pilsudski, Bronislas [Bronislaw]. "Ainu Folklore." *Journal of American Folklore* 25 (1912): 72– 86.

Pleyte, C. M. "An Unpublished Batak Creation Legend." *Journal of the Anthropological Institute of Great Britain and Ireland* 26 (1897): 103–109.

Porter, Ralph S. "The Story of Bantugan." *Journal of American Folklore* 15 (1902): 143–161.

Ryder, Arthur W., trans. [author unknown, Sanskrit title *Vetalapañchavimsati*]. *Twenty-Two Goblins.* London: J.M. Dent, 1917.

Sarma, Bagwhan Das. "A Folktale from Kumaon State." *Folklore* 8 (1897): 181–184.

Scheltema, J. F. "Roostam the Game-cock." *Journal of American Folklore* 32 (1919): 306–323.

Scheltema, J. F. "Sry Nagasary." *Journal of American Folklore* 32 (1919): 324–342.

Shelton, A. L. *Tibetan Folktales.* St. Louis, MO: United Christian Missionary Society, 1925.

Smith, Richard Gordon. *Ancient Tales and Folklore of Japan.* London: A. and C. Black, 1908.

Steel, Flora Annie. *Tales of the Punjab: Told by the People.* New York: Macmillan and Company, 1894.

Swynnerton, Charles. *Indian Nights' Entertainment: Folk-Tales from the Upper Indus.* London: Elliot Stock, 1892.

Cumulative Index

Boldface numbers refer to volume numbers.

4:309; Snow White, 3:261; unseen, 4:98–101

"The Animal Languages," 2:295, 2:301, 3:109

Animals: clan totems, 4:89; dwarves, 3:81; folk tale characters, 1:64; grateful, 1:242; guise for spirit helpers, 4:327; hero transformation, 3:139; possessing spirits, 4:447; taming of wild, 3:313; tricksters, 2:328, 2:333; weak and larger, 2:121; witches as, 4:284; world vs. humans, 3:352

"Animals Grateful for Rescue from Peril of Death," 2:176

Animal skin, 3:212

Animal spouse: husband, 3:86; justice, 4:255; lizard husband, 2:362; transformation, 2:320, 2:323; wife, 1:265, 4:431

Animal tales, 1:35, 4:329; African American and Caribbean sources, 1:130–34; Bantu, 1:31; cat and mouse, 2:128; Creek and African American, 4:63; danger descriptions, 1:149; fable function, 1:66, 2:126; fable trickster/culture hero, 4:161; fox nature in, 3:334; konehu cycle, 4:343; moral lesson, 4:110; moral precepts, 1:116; myth combination, 1:303, 1:306; Naga, 2:265–67; narrative functions, 3:313; origins explanation, 1:306; plot features, 1:57; question-and-answer pattern, 2:152; self-serving characters, 1:35. See also Trickster

Animism, 2:3; environmental elements, 2:14; shape-shifting, 2:17; Tibetan, 2:113

"Annancy and the Yam Hill," 1:61, 4:424–25

Ann Nancy, 4:163–64

"The Antelope Boy," 4:102–5

Anthropomorphic animals, 4:415; bears, 4:89; spider, 4:324

Anthropomorphic beings, 1:67, 1:353, 3:316

Antigua, 4:405–13

Anti-Semitism, 3:379

Anxieties, 3:360, 4:76

Apache, 4:25–32, 4:273

Ape, 2:365–66

Appalachian folktales, 4:225–43

Arabian Peninsula, 1:179

Arabic folk tradition, 1:220, 2:83

Arab influence, 1:12, 1:49

Arabs, 1:260

Arahat (people), 2:156

Arawak (people), 4:297–98, 4:443–52

Archetype tales, 3:67

Arctic, 4:72, 4:74

Arctic peoples. See Circumpolar cultures; Eskimo

Aristocracy, 1:98

Arizona (Native Americans), 4:285, 4:291

Arjuna, 2:142

Armenia, 1:169–79

Ascetics, 2:92

Ashanti, 1:61

Ashkenazim, 3:141–48, 3:147

Asia: East, 2:1–130; Malabasy influence, 1:33; South, 2:131–303; Southeast, 2:305–438

Assassination, 2:64

Assimilation, 1:201

Asuang, 2:429

Ataro, 1:333, 1:341

Athabascans, 4:72

Athletic competition, 4:95

Audience, 1:126, 1:176

Aurohuac, 4:297–98

Australia, 1:297–327

Autobiography, 4:258

Avenger, 1:240, 4:19

"Awa-Wanga Animal Fables," 1:30

Axaiacatzin, 4:400

Aymara (people), 4:299–305

Aztec, 4:393

Babalawo, 1:129

"Baboon Disguises Himself and Becomes a Farmer," 1:56–57

"The Babracote and the Camundi," 4:448–49

Baca, Elfego, 4:275–79

Badger, 2:97

Baghdad, 1:10

Bagobo (people), 2:388

Bahamas, 4:414–22

Bajau, 2:307

"The Baker of Beauly," 3:54–58

Ball games, 4:364

Bands of families, 4:74

Bantu, 1:29, 1:30–31, 1:49, 1:58, 1:64, 1:68

Banyan, 1:52

Bards, 2:74

Basque, 3:339–59

Batak (people), 2:338

Bats, 4:341

Battles, 2:74, 2:383, 3:54, 3:339

Baule (people), 1:61

Bear, 3:81, 4:40, 4:89; Brer, 4:161–62; fox and, 1:133–34; John the, 4:376; as maiden, 4:136–39; Mouse Deer and, 2:333; origin, 4:39–42; women lover, 4:118–20

"The Bear and the Fox," 1:133–34

Beards, 3:81

"Bear Maiden," 4:136–39

"The Beautiful and the Ugly Twin," 3:373

"Beauty and the Beast," 2:362

Beckwith, Martha Warren, 1:380, 4:420, 4:425, 4:426, 4:430

Bedouin, 1:179–80

Bee, 3:174

"The Beginning," 2:307–8

Beliefs: animistic, 2:3; Bön, 2:113; indigenous, 2:307; shape-shifting, 2:17

Belief tale: hag legend, 4:199; spirit possession, 4:203; white deer, 4:228; witch identity, 4:284

Bell, Robert, 4:57

Bella Bella, 4:72

Benevolence, 1:216–17; ancestral ghosts, 1:333; fallen angles, 1:264; ironic, 4:89; naiveté,

England, 3:3–38
English influence, 4:229, 4:440
"Enmity of Fowl and Cockroach," 4:430
Environment: animistic beliefs, 2:14; arctic, 4:72, 4:74; Australian Aborigines, 1:297; cleansing by culture hero, 1:324, 3:231, 4:84, 4:148, 4:359; culture heroes, 1:398; explanation, 1:393, 3:351, 3:352; plot modification, 4:410
Epics, 2:142, 2:268
Er tin tin, 4:324
Eskimo, 4:70–78
Ethics, 2:277, 4:3–4
Ethnic groups: Appalachian region, 4:229; Aztec sacred history, 4:393; Borneo, 2:307; conflict, 4:450; Congo, 1:78; Jewish communities, 3:141. *See also names of specific groups*
Euripides, 3:245
Europe, 3:1–398
European influence: Brer Rabbit trick, 4:188; Central American folklore, 4:367; Cheyenne, 4:54; Creek tale, 4:65; Efik, 1:80; Natchez, 4:121; tale elements, 4:136–37; West African trade, 1:64
Evil, 1:264, 4:389
Evil eye, 3:174
Evil one, 4:193–98
Evil spirits, 2:105
Exaggeration, 4:285, 4:291
Exchanges of eyes, 1:80
Excommunication rites, 3:28
"An Exile's Revenge," 1:345–47
Explanation, 2:80, 2:261, 4:423; animal nature, 1:80; animal tale mythic, 1:303; animal tales, 1:31, 1:35; emergence from underworld, 4:302; fable moralization, 1:112; historical enmity, 4:450; justice, 4:409; local features, 3:28; Muslim prohibitions, 1:12; origins, 1:306; prayer wand, 2:14; rational in legend, 4:301; relationships with other peoples, 2:309; sacred objects,

1:308; taboo adherence, 1:67; tattooing, 1:425
"The Exploits of Koneho," 4:342–48
Explorer accounts, 4:291
"Exposure in a Boat," 2:383
Expulsion, 1:260
Eyamba, 1:87
Eyes: animal, 1:80–82; closing, 2:128; evil, 3:174; exchanges of, 1:80

"The Fable of the Leopard and Hyena," 1:31
Fables, 1:112; admonition, 1:121; animal tale, 1:66, 2:126, 2:265, 3:313, 4:161; animal tricksters, 1:76; Bulu, 1:64; envy, 2:102; moralizing, 1:33, 1:112; personified morals, 2:436; trickster/culture hero, 4:161
Fábrega, H. Pittier de, 4:353
The Facetious Nights (Straparola), 3:275
Facts, 2:67
Fairies, 4:247
Fair tales, 3:360, 3:364
Fairy queen, 3:21
"Faithful John," 2:159
Fallen angels, 1:264
Fall from grace, 1:196, 4:453
Falling fruit, 1:169, 1:176
"The Fall of Man and the Punishment of the Serpent," 1:196–200
False bride, 1:87
Falsehood, 2:435–38
Family: animal helpers, 3:59; bands, 4:74; divine lineage, 2:59; escape of abusive, 3:59; ghosts as guardian, 1:333; human and divine, 1:417; property reclamation, 4:189; relationships, 4:448
Family sagas, 4:159
Family trees, 1:353
"Famine," 4:67–69
"The Famine and the Spider," 1:132–33
Fang (people), 1:64
"Fangono," 1:419–25
Fantastic animals, 1:36
Fante, 1:61, 1:96–97

Far away land, 2:13
Farmers, 2:262; Angami, 2:261; good, 3:285–88; origin myth, 4:3; Pueblo practices, 4:102; rain-bringing, 4:83
Fate of warrior, 3:304
"The Father and Son Who Married Mother and Daughter," 2:184, 2:191–95, 3:275
Fathers: jealousy of sons, 4:426; marriage, 2:191–95; sibling rivalry, 1:106; unkind sister partiality, 3:18
Fathers-in-law, 1:322
Fattening houses, 1:82–83
Faust legends, 3:160
"Fear," 1:257–60
Fear of night hag, 4:225
Fellahin, 1:3–4
Female beauty, 1:82
Female creator, 4:332
Female figures, 2:40
Female jinn, 1:24
Female protagonists, 3:34, 4:255
Females, 4:3–4, 4:83
Female spirits, 2:40, 4:74
"Ferdinand the True and Ferinand the False," 3:364
Feudal lords, 2:70
Fez, 1:16
"The Fifty-One Thieves," 2:424–27
Figonas, 1:335–41, 1:339
Fin-back whale, 4:79
Fire, 1:319; acquisition, 1:398; gift of, 1:29; making motif, 4:13; theft, 4:27, 4:64
Fire Dragaman, 4:16, 4:236–40
"The First People," 2:62–63
First person myths, 2:13, 2:16
"The First Village," 2:338–42
Fish, 4:420
"The Fisher and His Wife," 2:102
"The Fisherman and the Boyard's Daughter," 3:182–84
"The Fisherman and the Jinn," 1:220–23, 2:184, 3:275
"The Fish Lover," 4:420
"The Fish Peri," 1:176, 1:264–67, 1:268
"The Flight," 4:436

Mina, **1**:297

Mindanao, **2**:398–99

Minotaur, **3**:231

Miracle worker, **1**:240

"A Miraculous Sword," **2**:59, 2:64–66

"Miti' and Magpie Man," **2**:110–12

Mizrahim, **1**:238

Modernization of folktales, **4**:189

Moldavia, **3**:178

Mole, **4**:86

Money, **3**:54

Monkey, **2**:267, **2**:428–30, **4**:405

"The Monkey and the Jackal," **2**:267

"The Monkey and the Jellyfish," **2**:80–83

"The Monkey and the Tortoise," **2**:415–19

"The Monkey's Fiddle," **1**:147–48

"Monkey Who Left His Heart at Home," **2**:80

Monks, **2**:184–85

Monsters, **1**:282; cleansing environment of, **1**:324, **4**:124; garuda, **2**:359; griffin, **3**:185; man-eagle, **4**:85; slaying of, **4**:34; stupid, **3**:316–17, **3**:351; trickster skills over, **4**:53; twins cleansing from, **4**:84, **4**:148; wit over, **1**:282

Monster-slayer: tricksters, **4**:16–17; twins, **4**:84, **4**:148; youthful, **1**:120

Moon, **2**:97, **4**:385

Mooney, James, **4**:47

Moon gods, **4**:359

Moralistic tales, **4**:380

Morality: comic misunderstanding, **1**:223; Pueblo view, **4**:110

Moral lessons, **2**:203

Morals: code synthesis, **2**:343; fable personifications, **2**:436; fables, **1**:112; goals, **2**:396; origin explanations, **1**:306; precepts, **1**:33, **1**:116

"More Cunning than Father," **4**:425–28

Morocco, **1**:12–25

"The Mosquito's Village," **2**:313–14

Mother, **1**:106, **1**:158; boasting, **3**:120; eating of fruit, **3**:253; marriage, **2**:191–95. *See also* Stepmother

"Mother Goose," **3**:360

"Mother Holle," **3**:89–92, **4**:253

Mothers-in-law, **1**:322

Motif, **2**:359; animal gratitude, **2**:176, **2**:268, **2**:277, **2**:429, **2**:436, **3**:113, **3**:364, **4**:329–30; black ship sails, **3**:253; cleansing of world, **1**:324, **3**:231, **4**:84, **4**:124, **4**:148, **4**:359; combinations, **4**:385; concealing murder, **4**:343; creation myth, **2**:62; cross-cultural, **1**:45; cruel stepmother, **1**:119, **1**:260, **2**:167, **3**:18; "Dead Man as Helper," **2**:436; defiance by young women, **4**:76; devil's questions test, **4**:194; disguise and trickery, **1**:57; disguised deities, **4**:315; divided villages, **4**:148; eating fruit, **3**:253; "Enmity of Fowl and Cockroach," **4**:430; exchanges, **4**:121–22; "Exposure in a Boat," **2**:383; expulsion by stepmother, **1**:45; fire making, **4**:13; folly turned to fortune, **4**:215; forgotten fiancée, **3**:12; ghost obligation fulfillment, **2**:86; "The Girl as Helper in the Hero's Flight," **3**:12, **3**:125, **3**:152, **3**:171, **4**:248, **4**:435–36; human/animal spouse transformation, **2**:320; Indo-European central, **2**:167; legend international, **2**:268; lost islands, **2**:66; magic power of song, **4**:431; magic sword, **3**:96; obstacle flight, **2**:62, **2**:298, **4**:118, **4**:194, **4**:385; ocean migration, **4**:13; rescue from supernatural abduction, **2**:24; tale classification, **1**:87; theft of food, **4**:409; tragic event signs, **4**:448; transformation into stones, **4**:319; treacherous husband, **4**:450; trickster cousins,

3:49; trickster shape-shifting, **4**:170; twin, **1**:347, **4**:456; two siblings, **2**:313; underworld symbolism, **3**:152; unnatural suitor, **1**:85; weak animal deceives larger, **2**:121; "What Is in the Dish: Poor Crab," **4**:184; witch, **3**:216; younger brothers, **2**:245

Motivations: Anansi, **4**:429; stupidity, **4**:218; tricksters, **2**:329, **4**:175, **4**:214

Mountain lion, **4**:31

"Mountain of the Bell," **1**:179–80

Mountain spirits, **4**:247

Mount Yoshino, **2**:70

Mouse, **2**:128

Mouse deer, **2**:328–37, **2**:364–67

"The Mouse Deer and Crocodile," **2**:366–67

"The Mouse Deer and the Bear," **2**:333

"The Mouse Deer and the Crocodile," **2**:335–36

"The Mouse Deer and the Giant," **2**:328–32

"The Mouse Deer and the Hermit Crab," **2**:334–35

"The Mouse Deer and the Tiger," **2**:332–33, **2**:364–65

"The Mouse Deer in a Hole," **2**:336–37

"The Mouse Deer, Tiger, and Ape," **2**:365–66

Mozambique: Swahili people, **1**:49

"Mr. Deer's My Riding Horse," **4**:173–75, **4**:214

"Mr. Hard Time," **4**:411–12

Much Ado About Nothing (Shakespeare), **3**:34

Mules, **4**:212–14

Mullah, **1**:42

Mullah Nasrudin, **1**:6–9

Münchhausen, Karl Friedrich Hieronymus von, **4**:291

Munsumundok, **2**:307

Mura-mura, **1**:300, **1**:301, **1**:319

"The Mura-Mura Darana," **1**:308–9

Murder: avengers and justice, **4**:19; bone accusation, **4**:412–13; curse for, **3**:304; justice, **2**:181; trickster concealment, **4**:343

by Playing Godfather," **4**:164;
ungrateful animals, **2**:277

Tall tales, **4**:240, **4**:285, **4**:291

Tangaroa, **1**:431

Tanuki, **2**:95–96, **2**:97–100

Tanzania, **1**:49

Taoism, **2**:28

"Taraematawa," **1**:341–43

Taranga, **1**:398

Tar baby, **1**:78, **2**:156, **4**:121–23,
4:209–12, **4**:367, **4**:414

"The Tar Baby," **4**:121–23, **4**:414

"The Tarbaby and the Rabbit,"
2:156, **4**:367

Tartaro, **3**:350–51

Tasks to win spouse, **2**:195, **4**:137

"Tattoo," **1**:425–30

Technology: creation myth, **2**:338;
fire, **4**:64; gift of Africa, **1**:29

Temptation, **1**:36

Tengu, **2**:92–94

Tensions, **2**:123

Territorial rights, **3**:351

Tests: bride, **1**:47, **3**:289; child
trickster, **2**:319; by devil, **4**:194;
drawing of sword, **3**:96; sincerity,
3:148; wife, **1**:66

Tetragrammaton, **1**:238

Texas, **4**:258

Texas A&M University students,
4:220

Texas Revolution of 1836, **4**:13

Theft: of fire, **4**:27, **4**:64; of food,
3:334, **4**:409; of sword, **3**:304

"Theft of Butter (Honey) by Playing Godfather," **4**:164, **4**:409

"The Theft of Fish," **3**:334

"Them Petrified Buzzards," **4**:285,
4:290–94

Theseus, **3**:231

Thomas, Mary, **4**:159

Thompson, Stith, **1**:420, **4**:110

"Thor in Peril," **3**:298–303

"The Thrall's Curse," **3**:304–7

"Three Animals as Brothers-in-
law," **1**:274

"The Three Golden Sons," **2**:419

"The Three Lemons," **3**:130–38,
3:163, **3**:185

"Three Little Pigs and the Big Bad
Wolf," **4**:186

"Three Men of Galway," **3**:49–53

"The Three Precepts," **3**:54

"The Three Rajahs," **2**:308–11

Three (sacred number), **3**:201

"The Three Stolen Princesses,"
3:253

Tibet, **2**:113–30

Tiger, **2**:152–56, **2**:332, **2**:364–65

"The Tiger and the Frog," **2**:121–22

"The Tiger Changed into a
Woman," **4**:446–48

"Tiger Softens His Voice," **4**:431–34

Ti Jean, **4**:219

"Ti Jean Cannot Tell a Lie," **4**:219

Time: mythic events, **1**:324; story
classification, **4**:89

Tiruray tribe, **2**:399

Titans: myth of, **2**:28

Tiyo, **4**:85–88

Tlingit (people), **4**:140–45,
4:140–47

Tobacco, **4**:338, **4**:397

Togo: Yoruba culture, **1**:124

Tolba, **1**:24

Toltecs, **4**:393

"Tom Thumb," **3**:3, **3**:21

Tone: revealing content, **2**:221

Tools: culture hero, **1**:398

Tortoise, **1**:68–77, **1**:80, **1**:82–85,
1:152, **2**:415–19

"The Tortoise and the Elephant,"
1:68–70

"The Tortoise and the Hare,"
2:334

"The Tortoise with a Beautiful
Daughter," **1**:82–85

Totem animals, **4**:89

Totemic clans: culture heroes,
1:301

Toyotomi Hidetsugu, **2**:67

Toyotomi Hideyoshi, **2**:67

Trade: Efik-European, **1**:80; West
African, **1**:116

Trade routes: morality on, **1**:223

Traders, **2**:152

Tradition: immigrant community
preservation, **1**:251

Traditional arts, **4**:253

Traditional healers: roles and
methods, **1**:92

Tradition bearers, **4**:253

Trances, **4**:338

Transformation, **1**:310; act inversion, **3**:174; animal spouse,
2:320, **2**:323; anthropomorphic
to wild, **4**:415; external, **2**:107;
heroes into stars, **4**:148–55; plot
inversion, **2**:298; somersaults,
3:185; song power of, **4**:431;
spouse, **2**:167; into stones,
4:319; twins in stars, **4**:456. *See
also* Shape-shifting

Transformation tales: hero identity,
3:139

Transvestites: Native Americans,
4:13

Transylvania, **3**:104, **3**:178

Trapping, **4**:57

"Trapping a Hag," **4**:198–99

Traps: magical, **1**:78

Travel between worlds, **2**:43

"The Treacherous Jackal," **1**:57–58

Treasure: dwarves, **3**:81; lost, **4**:268

Trees, **3**:299

Trials: siblings in arctic communities, **4**:72

"Tricking of Gylfi," **3**:292

Trickster: Abu'n-Nuwâ's, **1**:251;
African animal tales, **1**:68;
Algonquin cultures, **4**:124; amor-
ality and guile, **1**:70; Anansi,
1:61, **1**:96, **4**:163, **4**:324, **4**:326,
4:329–30, **4**:425–30; animal
fables, **1**:76; animal myth, **1**:303;
animal tales, **1**:57, **1**:80, **2**:328,
4:161–62; Ann Nancy, **4**:163;
Bantu tales, **1**:68–77; being
tricked, **4**:410; Big Raven,
2:105; blame shifting, **1**:72,
4:165; Boudreaux, **4**:220; Brer
Rabbit, **4**:45, **4**:166–89, **4**:170;
buzzard, **4**:182; cat, **2**:128; cockroach, **4**:430; community interest, **4**:172; community service,
1:80; cousins bested, **3**:49;

About the Editor

THOMAS A. GREEN is Associate Professor of Anthropology at Texas A&M University. His many books include *The Greenwood Library of American Folktales* (Greenwood, 2006), and *Martial Arts in the Modern World* (Praeger, 2003).